Introduction to Hospitality Management

SECOND EDITION

Introduction to Hospitality Management

John R. Walker

McKibbon Professor of Hotel and Restaurant Management
University of South Florida
Sarasota–Manatee

PEARSON

Prentice
Hall

Upper Saddle River, New Jersey 07458

Library of Congress Cataloging-in-Publication Data

Walker, John R.
  Introduction to hospitality management / John R. Walker.—2nd ed.
    p. cm.
  ISBN 0-13-236920-6
    1. Hospitality industry—Management. I. Title.

TX911.3.M27W3515 2006
647.94068—dc22   2006007209

Editor-in-Chief: Vernon R. Anthony
Senior Editor: William Lawrensen
Associate Editor: Marion Gottlieb
Director of Manufacturing and Production: Bruce Johnson
Managing Editor: Mary Carnis
Production Liaison: Jane Bonnell
Production Editor: Emily Bush, Carlisle Publishing Services
Manufacturing Manager: Ilene Sanford
Manufacturing Buyer: Cathleen Petersen
Executive Marketing Manager: Ryan DeGrote
Senior Marketing Coordinator: Elizabeth Farrell
Marketing Assistant: Les Roberts
Senior Design Coordinator: Miguel Ortiz
Interior Design: Carlisle Publishing Services/Miguel Ortiz
Cover Designer: Wanda España
Cover Image: Vince Streano, Getty Images—Stone Allstock
Composition: Carlisle Publishing Services
Manager of Media Production: Amy Peltier
Media Production Project Manager: Lisa Rinaldi
Printer/Binder: R. R. Donnelley & Sons Company
Cover Printer: Phoenix Color

Text photo credits begin on page 657, which constitutes a continuation of the copyright page.

To Judy Genshaft, Renu Khator, Laurey Stryker,

Peter French, Robert Sullins, and Jay Schrock

in recognition of your outstanding academic leadership

and especially to John McKibbon in appreciation

of your generosity

Brief Contents

Part 5   Managerial Areas of the Hospitality Industry   477

Contents

CHAPTER 2

Careers in Hospitality 31

CHAPTER 3

Tourism   81

CHAPTER 5

Rooms Division Operations   159

CHAPTER 6
Food and Beverage Operations 207

PART 3 Restaurants and Managed Services 239
CHAPTER 7
The Restaurant Business 241

CHAPTER 8
Restaurant Operations   269

CHAPTER 9
Managed Services   307

CHAPTER 10

Beverages   337

PART 4 Recreation, Gaming Entertainment, and Assembly Management   379

CHAPTER 11
Recreation, Theme Parks, and Clubs   381

CHAPTER 17

Communication and Decision Making   553

To the Student

Dear Future Hospitality Professional:

This textbook is written to empower you and help you on your way to becoming a future leader of this great industry. It will give you an in-depth overview of the world's largest and fastest-growing business. There is a chapter on **Careers in Hospitality** to help you learn more about the many different career opportunities and career paths to senior management. Each chapter has a **careers advice** section as well as **profiles of industry practitioners and leaders**. Additionally, industry experts speak on their area of specialization in **focus boxes**.

Read the Book

Read and study the text, including the profiles, focus boxes, applications, and case studies. Answer the Check Your Knowledge questions and review questions. By using the many tools throughout this textbook—including boldface key words and concepts—you will be amazed at how much more you get out of class by preparing ahead of time.

Use the Resources Accompanying This Book

Make use of the excellent **Companion Web Site** (**www.prenhall.com/walker**) for this book with its sample test questions and links to hospitality Web sites. You will improve your chances of achieving success in this class and will find that you enjoy learning.

Success in the Classroom

Faculty constantly says that the best students are the ones who come to class prepared. I know that, as a hospitality student, you have many demands on your time: work, a heavy course load, family commitments, and, yes, fun—plus a lot of reading and studying for your other courses. With these thoughts in mind, I tried to make this book visually appealing, easy and engaging to read, and enjoyable.

I wish you success in your studies and career.

Sincerely,
John R. Walker

Take some time to turn the page and review descriptions of all the features and tools in this book, and find out how they will facilitate your reading and understanding of the concepts. **Discover** the exciting opportunities in the numerous and varied segments of the hospitality industry.

Tastes of the Industry

As you begin to read the book, you'll recognize this hallmark "tastes of the industry" theme that characterizes the text. Because the book was written by an author with years of industry operations experience, there are numerous industry examples that illustrate the key topics. This not only makes for a more engaging read, but it also helps you understand the materials presented.

Text Organization

The book is organized into five distinct parts, with each part offering a comprehensive overview of a specific segment of the industry.

Part 1: The Hospitality Industry and Careers in Hospitality—Welcomes you to explore this fascinating industry.

Part 2: Lodging—Three chapters reveal and differentiate the diverse aspects of the lodging industry.

Part 3: Restaurants and Managed Services—Four chapters help you uncover the latest trends and characteristics of the different foodservice segments.

Part 4: Recreation, Gaming Entertainment, and Assembly Management—Three exciting chapters spotlight these specialized services.

Part 5: Managerial Areas of the Hospitality Industry—This part focuses on what hospitality managers actually do and the most important challenges facing industry leaders today and tomorrow. The topics include leadership and management, planning, organizing, communication and decision making, human resources and motivation, and control.

Careers in Hospitality

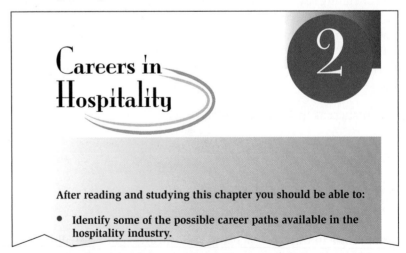

Careers in Hospitality

2

After reading and studying this chapter you should be able to:

● Identify some of the possible career paths available in the hospitality industry.

This introductory chapter describes career opportunities in all facets of the hospitality industry. *Is the hospitality industry for you?* By exploring your career goals based on your interests, skills, and self-assessment activities, you can uncover potential career paths. You'll also find guidance on the important topics of résumé writing and interviewing skills.

Boxed Features Connect You to the Real World

These boxed segments introduce you to *real people* and *real jobs* with *engaging true-to-life scenarios*.

Day in the Life of . . .

A Day in the Life of Ryan Adams
Guest Services Manager, Hotel del Coronado, San Diego, California

From what I gather there is supposed to be some sort of magical formula for how everything works out. You should have some plan with some kind of divine guidance; if you are spiritual, then you are on your way. However, I cannot rightly say that this has become known to me. I was lucky enough to develop a plan and have made some rather good decisions to get where I am.

I have been in the industry now for 11 years and I am always amazed at the magnetic draw this industry has on you. I always tell people, "It's not the job that is so hard, that is rudimentary; it is people that really make the challenge worth undertaking." I wake up at 5:30 A.M. every morning and prepare myself mentally before I go to work on how I am going to tackle the day.

My automatic coffee maker wakes me up and I establish my bearings as I proceed to take my shower and then turn on ESPN to catch sport

Outlook to see what meetings I have dedicated my time to. I then make a list of what I need to respond to and work on the pile of papers on my desk. I usually have a pile of papers from the night before as I get a lot of mail. I look at my 14-day forecast to see what events or groups we have in house and touch base with my bell phone receptionist who usually has good insight into the day's events.

My responsibilities are to oversee the functions of the bellman, elevator operators, doorman, valet runners, kiosk cashiers, mass transportation, parking control, and the concierge. I have two assistant guest services managers that come in at 11 A.M. and 2:30 P.M. to cover the other shifts. I also have a parking operations supervisor and a cashier supervisor. We hold a weekly meeting so I can share the vision of the company and my own. After all, I am not just a manager; I am a leader who has to take people somewhere where they would not have gone other

---

This feature highlights selected key hospitality individuals with accounts of their real-life activities. These day-in-the-life-of boxes give a "from-the-heart" up-close and personal view of their work.

Personal Profiles

Personal Profile: Regynald G. Washington

Vice-President and General Manager for Disney Regional Entertainment and Vice-President of New Business Initiatives for Walt Disney Parks and Resorts

For a student majoring in hotel and restaurant management, being a general manager, president, or even chief executive officer in the food industry is a goal to be achieved. For Regynald G. Washington, not only has it been a goal reached, but a dream realized. His bright smile spells success. As a child growing up in a middle-income family in the town of Marathon in the Florida Keys, working was mandatory. At the early age of 13, he was introduced to the food industry. His first job consisted of waiting on and busing tables and doing other chores in the Indies Inn Resort and Yacht Club. He took this on as an exciting and new challenge.

For Regynald, attitude is everything. His positive attitude toward being the best that he can be was derived from a phrase his parents used to repeat to him: "A chip on your shoulder earns a lack of respect from colleagues, friends, and family." His great

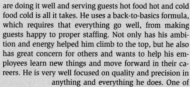

are doing it well and serving guests hot food hot and cold food cold is all it takes. He uses a back-to-basics formula, which requires that everything go well, from making guests happy to proper staffing. Not only has his ambition and energy helped him climb to the top, but he also has great concern for others and wants to help his employees learn new things and move forward in their careers. He is very well focused on quality and precision in anything and everything he does. One of his number one concerns is food safety.

To make sure everything is intact and going well, Regynald and his support team perform unannounced inspections every quarter. A specific food and beverage facility is concentrated on and fully evaluated for its table turns, guest service, food quality, and training programs. Specialists act as the guests and observe and report anything that seems less than perfect.

You're introduced to industry practitioners' careers, the issues and challenges they encounter, and their achievements and contributions. From dreams to reality . . . follow the career path to success for industry leaders and learn from their experiences.

Corporate Profiles

Corporate Profile: Hyatt Hotels

When Nicholas Pritzker emigrated with his family from the Ukraine to the United States, he began his career by opening a small law firm. His outstanding management skills led to the expansion of the law firm, turning it into a management company. The Pritzkers gained considerable financial support, which allowed them to pursue their goals of expansion and development. These dreams came into reality with the opening of the first Hyatt Hotel, inaugurated on September 27, 1957.

Today, Hyatt Hotel Corporation is a multibillion-dollar hotel management and development company; together with Hyatt International, they are among the leading chains in the hotel industry, with close to 8 percent of the market share.[1] Hyatt has earned worldwide fame as the leader in providing luxury accommodations and high-quality service, targeting especially the business traveler, but strategically differentiating its properties and services to identify and market to a very diverse clientele. This differentiation has resulted in the following types of hotels:

1. The *Hyatt Regency Hotels* represent the company's core product. They are usually located in business city centers and are re_____ _ __ star hotels.

Hyatt Hotels Corporation has been recognized by the *Wall Street Journal* as one of the 66 firms around the world poised to make a difference in the industries and markets. The effective management that characterized the company in its early years with the Pritzker family has continued through time. Hyatt Hotels Corporation is characterized by a decentralized management approach, which gives the individual general manager a great deal of decision-making power, as well as the opportunity to stimulate personal creativity and, therefore, differentiation and innovation. The development of novel concepts and products is perhaps the key to Hyatt's outstanding success. For example, the opening of the Hyatt Regency Atlanta, Georgia, gave the company instant recognition throughout the world. Customers were likely to stare in awe at the 21-story atrium lobby, the glass elevators, and the revolving rooftop restaurant. The property's innovative architecture, designed by John Portman, revolutionized the common standards of design and spacing, thus changing the course of the lodging industry. The atrium concept introduced there represented a universal challenge to hotel architects to face the new trend of grand,

Learn about the practices, growth, and scope of leading corporations and organizations. For example, Marriott International did not start out as a multibillion-dollar company; the company began as a nine-seat root beer stand in 1927.

Career Information

CAREER INFORMATION

Hotel and Rooms Division Operation

Hotel management is probably the most popular career choice among hospitality educational program graduating seniors. The reason for hotel management's popularity is tied to the elegant image of hotels and the prestige associated with being a general manager or vice-president of a major lodging chain. Managing a hotel is a complex balancing act that involves keeping employees, customers, and owners satisfied while overseeing a myriad of departments, including reservations, front desk, housekeeping, maintenance, accounting, food and beverage, security, concierge, and sales.

their interrelationship makes up the lodging environment. The first step down this career path is getting a job in a hotel while you are in college. Once you become proficient in one area, volunteer to work in another. A solid foundation of broad-based experience in the hotel will be priceless when you start your lodging career. Some excellent areas to consider are the front desk, night audit, food and beverage, and maintenance. Another challenging but very important place to gain experience is in housekeeping. It has been said that if you can manage the housekeeping department, the rest of lodging management is easy. An internship with a large hotel chain property can also be a powerful learn-

These boxes give you more information and descriptions of career opportunities, along with a listing of related Web sites. Learn about skills, challenges, and realities of careers in each segment of the hospitality industry.

Focus on . . .

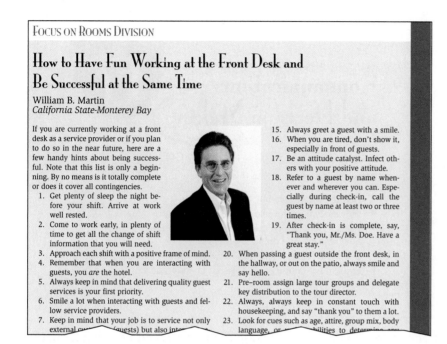

Written by contributing expert authors, these boxes offer unique personal perspectives on chapter topics.

Timeliness

Trends

A list of trends appears in each chapter to give you an up-to-date and realistic picture of factors shaping the future of that segment of the industry.

Management Focus

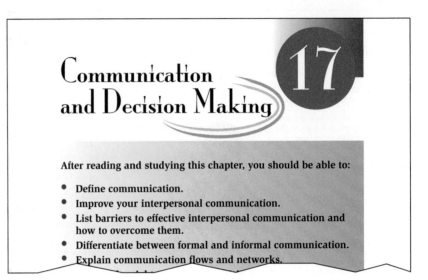

Communication and Decision Making 17

After reading and studying this chapter, you should be able to:

- Define communication.
- Improve your interpersonal communication.
- List barriers to effective interpersonal communication and how to overcome them.
- Differentiate between formal and informal communication.
- Explain communication flows and networks.

Communication and decision making are integral and challenging parts of all the management functions. They are ongoing processes that are vital to management's success in any hospitality enterprise.

Hone Your Critical Thinking Skills

Mini Case Studies

CASE STUDY

Short Staffed in the Kitchen

Sally is the general manager of one of the best restaurants in town, known as The Pub. As usual, at 6:00 P.M. on a Friday night, there is a 45-minute wait. The kitchen is overloaded, and they are running behind in check times, the time that elapses between the kitchen getting the order and the guest receiving his or her meal. This is critical, especially if a complaint is received because a guest has waited too long for a meal to be served.

Mini case studies in each chapter challenge you to test your skills and knowledge as you address real-world situations and recommend appropriate actions.

Internet Exercises

WEB RESOURCES	
Pannell Kerr Forster Consulting Firm http://www.pkf.com/	**Four Seasons** www.fourseasons.com
Bellagio Las Vegas http://www.bellagio.com/	**Marriott** marriott.com
Hilton www.hilton.com	

Surf the net to uncover answers to specific hospitality questions. The Internet Exercises challenge you to learn more and prepare you for a career in this fascinating industry.

Apply Your Knowledge

APPLY YOUR KNOWLEDGE	
In a casual Italian restaurant, sales for the week of September 15 are as follows: Food sales $10,000 Beverage sales 2,500 Total $12,500 1. If the food cost is 30 percent, how much did the food actually cost?	2. If the beverage cost is 25 percent of beverage sales, how much did the beverages cost? 3. If the labor cost is 28 percent, how much money does that represent and how much is left over for other costs and profit?

Apply the knowledge and skills learned in each chapter to real-life industry topics.

Important Memory Tools

Learning Objectives

> **After reading and studying this chapter you should be able to:**
>
> - Identify some of the possible career paths available in the hospitality industry.
> - Establish career goals.
> - Assess your own strengths and weaknesses.
> - Describe some of the potential careers in the hospitality and tourism industry.
> - Discuss aspects of professionalism.
> - Write a résumé.
> - Prepare for an interview.

At the start of each chapter, this list gives you a "heads up" to what will be discussed and how to organize your thoughts. The learning objectives summarize what you need to know after studying the chapter and doing the exercises, cases, questions, and Apply Your Knowledge.

Check Your Knowledge

> ### Check Your Knowledge
> 1. What departments does the food and beverage director oversee?
> 2. What are the responsibilities of a food and beverage director on a day-to-day basis?
> 3. Explain how the pour/cost percentage is used in a bar to measure efficiency.

Every few pages, the Check Your Knowledge section will help you to review and to reinforce material that has just been covered.

Chapter Summary

The chapter summary highlights the most important points in the chapter. This summary is a brief review of the chapter that reinforces the main terms, concepts, and topics.

Key Words and Concepts

Highlighted in bold with easy-to-understand definitions in the glossary, the key words and concepts help you to recall the importance of and meaning of these important terms. Master the key words and concepts of the text and improve your test scores.

Review Questions

By answering these review questions, you will reinforce your mastery of the materials presented in the text and most likely will improve your test scores.

Visuals

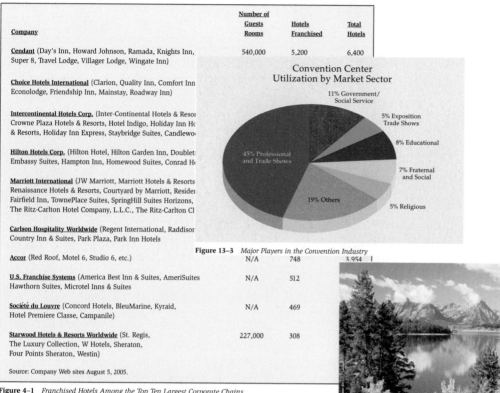

Company	Number of Guests Rooms	Hotels Franchised	Total Hotels
Cendant (Day's Inn, Howard Johnson, Ramada, Knights Inn, Super 8, Travel Lodge, Villager Lodge, Wingate Inn)	540,000	5,200	6,400
Choice Hotels International (Clarion, Quality Inn, Comfort Inn, Econolodge, Friendship Inn, Mainstay, Roadway Inn)			
Intercontinental Hotels Corp. (Inter-Continental Hotels & Resor Crowne Plaza Hotels & Resorts, Hotel Indigo, Holiday Inn Ho & Resorts, Holiday Inn Express, Staybridge Suites, Candlewo			
Hilton Hotels Corp. (Hilton Hotel, Hilton Garden Inn, Doublet Embassy Suites, Hampton Inn, Homewood Suites, Conrad Ho			
Marriott International (JW Marriott, Marriott Hotels & Resorts Renaissance Hotels & Resorts, Courtyard by Marriott, Resider Fairfield Inn, TownePlace Suites, SpringHill Suites Horizons, The Ritz-Carlton Hotel Company, L.L.C., The Ritz-Carlton Cl			
Carlson Hospitality Worldwide (Regent International, Raddisor Country Inn & Suites, Park Plaza, Park Inn Hotels			
Accor (Red Roof, Motel 6, Studio 6, etc.)	N/A	748	3,954
U.S. Franchise Systems (America Best Inn & Suites, AmeriSuites Hawthorn Suites, Microtel Inns & Suites	N/A	512	
Société du Louvre (Concord Hotels, BleuMarine, Kyraid, Hotel Premiere Classe, Campanile)	N/A	469	
Starwood Hotels & Resorts Worldwide (St. Regis, The Luxury Collection, W Hotels, Sheraton, Four Points Sheraton, Westin)	227,000	308	

Source: Company Web sites August 5, 2005.

Figure 4–1 *Franchised Hotels Among the Top Ten Largest Corporate Chains*

Figure 13–3 *Major Players in the Convention Industry*

One of the most beautiful places in America is Jackson Lake, Grand Teton National Park, Wyoming.

Color format with lively photographs, drawings, and tables will maintain your interest and provide visual aids to learning.

Additional Student Resources

Companion Web Site www.prenhall.com/walker

This online student study guide has been designed specifically to help you review, reinforce, and apply the concepts presented in the book. This interactive site features chapter-specific modules—practice exams with immediate answer assessment, help in the "Hints" section, and relevant Internet links.

Student Study Guide

A paperback student Study Guide is available for purchase. The Study Guide offers you additional review activities to further supplement your understanding of each chapter's material.

We now invite you to join us and share the enthusiasm for hospitality!

Preface

Hospitality management is an exciting professional discipline offering numerous career opportunities. *Introduction to Hospitality Management, Second Edition,* is a comprehensive tour of the fascinating and challenging fields of the hospitality industry: travel and tourism, lodging, foodservice, meetings, conventions and expositions, leisure and recreation.

The hospitality management chapters (Chapters 14 through 19) focus on what hospitality managers actually do and the most important challenges facing industry leaders today and tomorrow. The topics include leadership and management, planning, organizing, communication and decision making, human resources and motivation, and control. Security focus boxes, written by experts in this field, present the most up-to-date information pertinent to security in the hospitality industry.

This text is designed for the hospitality management professionals of tomorrow. By involving readers in each step of this exciting journey, *Introduction to Hospitality Management* invites students to share the unique enthusiasm surrounding the hospitality industry. Each chapter has been vetted by industry professionals and includes several hands-on examples, which help students understand the how-to aspects of the hospitality industry.

The primary goals and objectives of this text are to:

- Prepare students to advance in their hospitality career by offering a foundation of knowledge about the hospitality industry presented in a lively, interesting manner with an extensive array of features to facilitate the learning process.
- Assist students in learning the details of the hospitality industry by offering chapters on the managerial aspects of the hospitality industry.
- Facilitate learning by offering a student-friendly text to students and an outstanding instructional package to professors.

The new and continuing features of *Introduction to Hospitality Management, Second Edition,* include:

- **Text organization**—The book is organized into five parts, with each offering a comprehensive overview of a specific segment of the industry.
  - Part 1: The Hospitality Industry and Careers in Hospitality
  - Part 2: Lodging
  - Part 3: Restaurants and Managed Services
  - Part 4: Recreation, Gaming Entertainment, and Assembly Management
  - Part 5: Managerial Areas of the Hospitality Industry
- **New chapter** entirely devoted to Careers in the Hospitality Industry
- **Chapter objectives** that help the reader focus on the main points discussed in the chapter
- **Bold key words and concepts** that help the reader internalize the various topics presented in the chapter

- **Contributing authors** who bring their expertise to each chapter
- **Personal Profiles** of industry practitioners that describe the careers of a number of hospitality industry leaders, including Valerie Ferguson, past chair of the American Hotel & Motel Association and regional vice president of Loews Hotels; Caesar Ritz; Rich Melman; Ruth Fertel; Reg Washington; Robert Mondavi; and Steve Wynn
- **Day in the Life of** features that describe the daily activities of several hospitality professionals, from chefs to cruise directors to guest services managers and convention center sales managers. Each explains the key functions of their job
- **Corporate Profiles** that give an overview of leading corporations of excellence including Hyatt Hotels, Marriott International, Outback Steakhouse, T.G.I. Friday's, Las Vegas Convention & Visitors Authority, ARAMARK, Starbucks Coffee Company, Four Seasons Regent Hotels, Club Med, and Cendant Corporation
- **Career Information** boxes that give a description of career opportunities along with a listing of related Web sites
- **Check Your Knowledge** in-text features that encourage students to ask questions relevant to the material covered every few pages
- **"Focus on"** sidebars written by industry experts offer personal views of key hospitality topics
- Thorough identification and analysis of trends, issues, and challenges that will have a significant impact on hospitality in the future
- Scope of coverage and the international perspective on present and future industry issues
- **Summaries** that correspond to the chapter learning objectives
- **Competency-based and SCANS** (Secretary's Commission on Achieving Necessary Skills) related critical thinking review questions that review important aspects of the text. They differ from the Check Your Knowledge and Apply Your Knowledge questions
- **Case studies** that challenge students to address real-world situations and recommend appropriate action
- **Internet exercises** that invite students to "surf the Net" to answer specific, relevant hospitality questions
- **Apply Your Knowledge** questions that offer students the chance to apply their knowledge of hospitality industry topics
- A **glossary** that explains the meaning of special words throughout the text.

Supplement Package

Prentice Hall prides itself on offering to faculty the most extensive supplement package, which includes the following:

1. A Companion Website with Web-based activities and resources for each chapter reinforces the material and offers self-tests and links to numerous hospitality Websites; available at www.prenhall.com/walker
2. An Instructor Resource CD-ROM contains a professional PowerPoint presentation, Instructor's Manual, and Test Bank
3. Print Instructor's Manual
4. Video segments
5. A new student study guide

Acknowledgments

Thanks to the many students and professors, especially those who have made valuable contributions to this edition—and to the industry professionals who contributed to this text.

I am particularly grateful to Hank Christen and Paul Maniscalco for the security sidebars. Their contribution focuses on the all-important topic of disaster management.

Hank Christen, MPA, EMT, is Director of Emergency Response Operations for Unconventional Concepts Inc. He is responsible for consulting services in the fields of emergency response and counter-terrorism for Department of Defense agencies, federal agencies, and local government public safety agencies.

Paul M. Maniscalco is Senior Research Scientist and Assistant Professor at The George Washington University, Homeland Security Policy Institute.

Thanks go to all my CHRIE colleagues, many of whom encouraged me to undertake this project and made valuable suggestions. I would also like to thank the following contributing authors, who graciously allowed their material and expertise to be included in this and previous editions: Charlie Adams, Bart Bartlett, Lynne Christen, Fred DeMicco, Kathleen Doeller, William Fisher, Claudia Green, Kathryn Hashimoto, Linda Hoops, Christine Jaszay, Robert Kok, Peter LaMacchia, William B. Martin, Brian Miller, Catherine Rabb, James Reid, Jay Schrock, Andrea Sigler, Karen Smith, Dave Tucker, and Mike Zema.

The following reviewers made valuable suggestions regarding the organization and content: Edward Addo, St. Cloud State University; Diana S. Barber, Georgia State University; Robert Bennett, Delaware County Community College; Jane Boyland, Johnson & Wales University, Providence, RI; John M. Courtney, Johnson County Community College; Ken Jarvis, Anne Arundel Community College; Tammie J. Kaufman, University of Central Florida; Chris Roberts, University of Massachusetts; Eva Smith, Spartanburg Technical College; Muzzo Uysal, Virginia Polytechnic Institute and State University; Gary Ward, Scottsdale Community College; William H. Weber, Johnson & Wales University, Charleston, SC; and Jim Whitlock, Brenau University.

Eva Smith, thank you for the great job you did on the PowerPoints and Study Guide. Gary Ward, your work on the Companion Website is greatly appreciated. Michael Petrillose, thank you for your work on the Instructor's Manual. And gratitude to James Bennett for your authorship of the Test Bank. It was a pleasure working with all of you.

This book would not have been possible without the extraordinary help of Yasmeen Hossain; Simone Trafford; Yolanda Rucker; Bart Bartlett, Ph.D., Pennsylvania State University; Karl Titz, Ph.D., Conrad N. Hilton College, University of Houston; Denny Bhatka; Alfred Lewis, D.B.A. Alliant International University; Jay Schrock, Ph.D., University of South Florida; Ken Crocker, Ph.D., Bowling Green State University; Ed Rothenberg; Esther Lee, Evans Hotels; Tim Mulligan; Roger Huldi; Jody Nicholas; Mark Testa, Ph.D., San Diego University; MICROS Systems, Inc.; and Sodexho.

About the Author

Dr. John R. Walker, D.B.A., FMP, CHA, is the McKibbon Professor of Hotel and Restaurant Management at the University of South Florida, Sarasota-Manatee. John's years of industry experience include management training at the Savoy Hotel London. This was followed by terms as food and beverage manager, assistant rooms division manager, catering manager, and general manager with Grand Metropolitan Hotels, Selsdon Park Hotel, Rank Hotels, Inter-Continental Hotels, and the Coral Reef Resort, Barbados, West Indies.

He has taught at two- and four-year schools in Canada and the United States. In addition to being a hospitality management consultant and text author, he has been published in *The Cornell Hotel Restaurant Administration Quarterly* and *The Hospitality Educators Journal.* He is a ten-time recipient of the President's Award for teaching, scholarship, and service; and he has received the Patnubay Award for exemplary professional performance through teaching and authorship of tourism and hospitality publications.

John is an editorial advisory board member for *Progress in Tourism and Hospitality Research.* John is a past president of the Pacific Chapter of the Council on Hotel, Restaurant, and Institutional Education (CHRIE). He is a certified hotel administrator (CHA) and a certified Foodservice Management Professional (FMP). He is married to Josielyn T. Walker and they have twins, Christopher and Selina. The Walkers live in Sarasota, Florida.

Introduction to Hospitality Management

Welcome to the Hospitality Industry

1

After reading and studying this chapter, you should be able to:

- Describe the characteristics of the hospitality industry.
- Explain corporate philosophy.
- Discuss why service has become such an important facet of the hospitality industry.
- Suggest ways to improve service.

The Pineapple Tradition

The pineapple has enjoyed a rich and romantic heritage as a symbol of welcome, friendship, and hospitality. Pineapples were brought back from the West Indies by early European explorers during the seventeenth century. From that time on, the pineapple was cultivated in Europe and became the favored fruit to serve to royalty and the elite. The pineapple was later introduced into North America and became a part of North American hospitality as well. Pineapples were displayed at doors or on gateposts, announcing to friends and acquaintances: "The ship is in! Come join us. Food and drink for all!"

Since its introduction, the pineapple has been internationally recognized as a symbol of hospitality and a sign of friendliness, warmth, cheer, graciousness, and conviviality.

Welcome, future industry leaders to the world of **hospitality.** As Mike Hurst, former president of the National Restaurant Association, said, "We're glad you're here!"

This text gives you the benefit of several years of industry and teaching experience. Several colleagues, who are both great professors and industry experts, give you the benefit of their experience in the form of contributions to various sections of the chapters. Their insightful career suggestions are based on years of experience and knowledge. To each of them I am especially grateful. So, as Joyce Evans, a former student said, let's "enjoy the journey as much as the destination."

The **National Restaurant Association (NRA)** forecasts a need for thousands of supervisors and managers for the hospitality and tourism industry. Are you wondering if there's room in this dynamic industry for you? You bet! There's room for everyone. The best advice is to consider what you love to do most and get some experience in that area—to see if you really like it—because our industry has some distinct characteristics. For starters, we are in the business of giving service. When Kurt Wachtveilt, 30-year veteran general manager of the Oriental Hotel in Bangkok, Thailand—considered by many to be one of the best hotels in the world—was asked, "What is the secret of being the best?," he replied, "Service, service, service!" That doesn't mean that we are servants. Ask any Ritz-Carlton employee—they are ladies and gentlemen whose job is to serve ladies and gentlemen.

A pineapple is the symbol for hospitality.

Hospitality and Tourism

The hospitality and **tourism** industry is the largest and fastest-growing industry in the world. One of the most exciting aspects of this industry is that it is made up of so many different professions. James Reid, a professor at New York City Technical College, contributed his thoughts to this section.

As diverse as the hospitality industry is, there are some powerful and common dynamics, which include the delivery of services and products and the guests' impressions of them. Whether an employee is in direct contact with a guest (**front of the house**) or performing duties behind the scenes (**back of the house**), the profound and most challenging reality of working in this industry is that hospitality employees have the ability to affect the human experience by creating powerful impressions—even brief moments of truth—that may last a lifetime.

For the hospitality and tourism industries, imagine all the reasons why people leave their homes temporarily (whether alone or with others) to go to other places near and far. Think of the many people who provide services to travelers and have the responsibility of representing their communities and creating experiences that, when delivered successfully, are pleasurable and memorable. These people welcome, inform, comfort, and care for tourists and are collectively a part of a process that can positively affect human lives and well-being.

People travel for many reasons. A trip away from home might be for vacation, work, to attend a conference, or maybe even to visit a college campus, just to name a few. Regardless of the reason, under the umbrella of travel and tourism, many professions are necessary to meet the needs and wants of people away from home. Figure 1–1 shows the interrelated nature of the hospitality and tourism industries.

The hotel business provides career opportunities to many associates who help make reservations, greet, assist, and serve guests in hospitality operations of varied sizes and in locations all over the world. Examples include a husband and wife who operate their own bed and breakfast (B&B) in upstate Vermont. This couple provides the ideal weekend retreat for avid skiers during a frosty February, making their guests want to return year after year. Another example is the hundreds of employees necessary to keep the 5,505-room MGM Grand in full swing 365 days a year! Room attendants, engineers, front-desk agents, food servers, and managers are just a few of the positions that are vital to creating experiences for visitors who come to Las Vegas from around the globe.

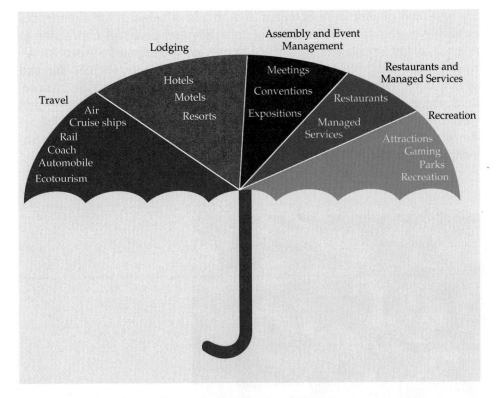

Figure 1–1 *Scope of the Hospitality and Tourism Industry*

The Venezia Tower rises from the glowing grounds of the Venetian Resort Hotel Casino on the Las Vegas Strip. The Mirage Hotel can be seen in the background.

The restaurant business is also a vital piece of the travel and tourism umbrella. People go to restaurants to fulfill diverse needs and wants. Eating is a biological need that restaurants accommodate, but restaurants and the people who work in them fulfill numerous other human desires, such as the need for socialization and to be entertained.

Gramercy Tavern restaurant in New York may be the perfect location for a certain group of friends to celebrate a twenty-first birthday. The individual guest who turned 21 may remember this fête for a lifetime because the service and food quality were excellent and an added value to the experiences for all the celebrants. For this kind of collective and powerful impression to be made, many key players are needed to operate and support the service delivery system. The several front-of-the-house staff members, such as the food servers, bartenders, greeters, managers, and bus attendants, and the back-of-the-house employees, such as the chefs, dishwashers, food purchaser, and stewards (to name a few), had to coordinate a diversity of activities and responsibilities to create this dynamic, successful, and, for the restaurant ownership, profitable event.

Guests enjoying Gramercy Tavern.

In managed services, foodservices are provided for airlines, military facilities, schools, colleges and universities, health care operations, and business and industry. These foodservice operations have the dual challenge of meeting the needs and wants of both the guests and the client (i.e., the institution itself). The employees who are part of these enterprises have responsibilities very much like those of other restaurant operations. The quality of food products delivered in an airline, for example, may be the key to winning customers back in the future and creating positive word of mouth advertising that attracts new customers.

Since recorded history, beverages have provided a biological need that has expanded the beverage menu far beyond water alone! Whether it is the cool iced tea garnished with lemon and mint served poolside at a Riviera resort or the champagne toast offered at a fiftieth wedding anniversary party in Boston, beverages have played a major role in satisfying people and adding to the many celebrations of life.

As with food products, the creation and delivery systems for beverage products are vital components of the hospitality industry. These operations involve many people that consumers rarely see: the farmer in Napa Valley who tends to his vineyard every day of the year, the coffee bean harvester in Colombia, the sake server in Tokyo, or the orchard owner crating oranges in Florida. These individuals behind the scenes have diverse and crucial responsibilities so that guests, whether in a resort, office, hospital, college, or roadside snack bar, can have the quality of products they want.

Check Your Knowledge

1. What is the contribution of hospitality, travel, and tourism to the global economy?

Characteristics of the Hospitality Industry

Hospitality businesses are open 365 days a year and 24 hours a day. No, we don't have to work all of them, but we do tend to work longer hours than some other industries. Those on their way to senior positions in the hospitality industry and many others for that matter, often work 10 hours per day. However, due to managerial burn out, there is a trend of "working" managers 50 hours a week to attract and retain generation Xers. Evenings and weekends are included in the workweek—so we have to accept that we may be working when others are enjoying leisure time. The hospitality industry depends heavily on shift work. Early in your career, depending on the department, you will likely work one of four shifts. Supervisors and managers often begin at 8 A.M. and work until 6 or 8 P.M. Basically, there are four shifts, beginning with the morning shift, so you may be getting up as early as 5 A.M. to get to the shift that starts at 7 A.M. The midshift is normally from 10 A.M. to 7 P.M.; the evening shift starts at 3 P.M. and goes on until 11:30 P.M.; and finally there is the graveyard shift that begins at 11 P.M. and lasts until 7:30 A.M. Well, success does not come easily.

One essential difference between the hospitality business and other business sectors is that we produce **guest satisfaction**—an ephemeral product or, as they say in the services literature, an **intangible.** The guest cannot "test drive" a night's stay, "kick the tires" prior to boarding a shuttle, or "taste the steak" before dining. Our product is for the guest's use only, not for possession. Even more unique, for us to produce this product we must get the guest's input. Imagine GE building a refrigerator with the customer in the factory, participating in the actual construction of the product! Yet we do it every single day, numerous times per day, and in a uniquely different way each time. The literature refers to this as the **inseparability** of production and consumption of the service product and the inherent heterogeneity of the product due to each guest's unique demands.

The other unique dimension of our industry is the **perishability** of our product. For example, we have 1,400 rooms in inventory—that is, available to sell—but we sell only 1,200 rooms. What do we do with the 200 unsold rooms? Nothing—we have permanently lost 200 room nights and their revenue.

Check Your Knowledge

1. List and describe the four shifts in the hospitality industry.
2. Identify and explain the two differences between the hospitality business and the other business sectors.

Each year the NRA invites the best and brightest students from universities and colleges to participate in the annual restaurant show in Chicago. The highlight of the show is the "Salute to Excellence" day when students and faculty attend forums, workshops, and a gala award banquet with industry leaders. The event is sponsored by Coca-Cola and several other corporations involved in the industry.

During the day students are invited to write their dreams on a large panel, which is later displayed for all to enjoy reading. Here are a few of the previous year's hopes and dreams:

- To help all people learn and grow. (Jason P.)
- To be the best I can. (NMC)
- To establish a chain of jazz cafés in six years and go public in ten years. (Richard)
- To successfully please my customers. (J. Calicendo)
- To be happy and to make others happy, too.
- To put smiles on all faces.
- To be one of the most creative chefs—I would like to be happy with everything I create.
- To make a difference in the lives of people through food! (Mitz Dardony)
- To be successful professionally, socially, and financially. (Marcy W.)

Where are you going? Take a moment and think about your future career prospects. Where do you want to be in 5, 10, or 20 years?

- To preserve our natural resources by operating a restaurant called Green. (Kimberley Mauren)
- Anything I do I like to do it in such a way that I can always be meaningful to people. (Christian Ellis-Schmidt)
- To reach the top because I know there is a lot of space up there. (P. W., Lexington College)
- To use the knowledge that I've gained throughout my career and pass it on to others in hopes of touching their lives in a positive way! To smile and to make smiles. (Armey P. DaCalo)
- I want to be prosperous in my desire to achieve more than $. Happiness and peace are the keys to life. (D. McKinney)
- To teach and be as good as those who have taught me. (Thomas)

So what are your dreams and goals? Take a moment to think about your personal dreams and goals. Keep them in mind and look back on them often. Be prepared to amend them as you develop your career.

_____

_____

_____

_____

_____

_____

Commit Yourself to Excellence

As you begin your career in the hospitality industry, it is important to *commit yourself to excellence.* You can become whatever you aspire to become—remember, it's your attitude that determines your altitude. You can become whatever you aspire to become—somebody has to be the president of the company.

Corporate Philosophy

Current **corporate philosophy** has changed from one of managers' planning, organizing, implementing, and measuring to that of managers' counseling associates, giving them resources, and helping them to think for themselves. The outcome is a more participative management style, which results in associate **empowerment,** increased productivity, and guest and employee satisfaction. Corporate philosophy has strong links to quality leadership and the **total quality management (TQM)** process. (TQM is discussed in a later section.)

Corporate philosophy embraces the values of the organization, including ethics, morals, fairness, and equality. The new paradigm in corporate American hospitality is the shift in emphasis from the production aspect of our business to the focus on guest-related services. The philosophy of "Whatever it takes" is winning over "It's not my job." Innovation and creativity are winning over "That's the way we've always done it." Successful organizations are those that are able to impart corporate philosophies to employees and guests alike. Disney Corporation, as discussed later, is a good example of a corporation that has a permeating corporate philosophy.

Service Philosophy Is a Way of Life

J. W. (Bill) Marriott, Jr. is chairman of the board of directors of Marriott International. Marriott's Web site defines the "Marriott Way" as "about serving the associates, the customer, and the community." These ideals serve as the cornerstone for all Marriott associates who strive to fulfill the "Spirit to Serve."[1] The values originate from deep inside the people themselves—authentic, bone deep, passionately held. Marriott's core values include the belief that people are number one ("Take care of Marriott people and they'll take good care of Marriott guests"), a commitment to continuous improvement and overcoming adversity, and a good old-fashioned dedication to hard work and having fun while doing it.

Marriott's core values drive the culture. Our culture influences the way we treat associates, customers, and the community that impacts all our successes. In the words of J. W. Marriott, Jr., "Culture is the life-thread and glue that links our past, present, and future."[2]

Corporate Culture

Corporate culture is the overall style or feel of a company. A company's culture governs how people relate to one another and their jobs. It can be summed up with the phrase "This is how we do things around here." The casual image of the Chart House restaurant chain is a definite part of their corporate culture. However, don't be fooled—their managers may appear casual, but they are very professional. Each major corporation has a culture, some more pronounced than others. It is a good idea to align yourself with a corporation that blends with your own personal culture, values, and style.

J. W. (Bill) Marriott, Jr., Chairman of the Board of Directors of Marriott International

Mission Statement

A **mission statement** is a short statement of the central purposes, strategies, and values of a company. Essentially, a corporation's mission statement should answer the question "What business are we in?" A good mission statement will go beyond the obvious and include the corporation's purpose, values, and strategies.

Another hotel's mission statement is very simple: "To WOW the guests."

Check Your Knowledge

1. What is the purpose of a mission statement?

Goals

A **goal** is a broad statement of what a company or department wishes to accomplish. For example, a hotel may have the goal of being the industry leader in the **average daily rate (ADR).**

A goal is a quantification of the mission in measurable terms. In a hotel, for instance, one of the goals might be to increase occupancy from 80 to 85 percent. Another might be to achieve an ADR of $128 by December 2007. Goals can be written for each department on a variety of topics from alcohol awareness training to reduction of employee turnover. Today, most corporations involve their employees in goal setting. This not only ties in with total quality management, but also encourages employees to "buy into" the process and increases the likelihood that goals may even be exceeded.

Strategies

Strategies are the actions (game plan) that are needed to accomplish the goal. Using the hotel occupancy example, the strategy will state how the goal will be met. The strategy identifies the specific actions

Mission Statement

The Ritz-Carlton, Laguna Niguel, will be recognized internationally as the leading five-star, five-diamond resort in North America. We will be unique in combining the genuine warmth and vitality of southern California with the traditional setting found in the finest hotels in Europe.

Every guest will feel that he or she is our most important guest. They will find us easy to do business with, and will be impressed by our uncompromising, consistent service and our ability to anticipate and fulfill even their unexpressed wishes. They will appreciate our creative, sophisticated, world-class cuisine and services. Our versatile entertainment will enhance our elegant, relaxing atmosphere. In addition, our guests will enjoy the unparalleled beauty of our location along with the museum-quality art collection.

Our employees will be proud of their association with the hotel and will be an integral part of our success. They will see the Ritz-Carlton as the best hotel to work in, a place where they can grow personally and professionally. Our staff will remain committed to continuously improving and refining our facilities and service.

The owners and the corporate office will be proud of the hotel, and will have confidence in us. They will see us as a source of qualified managers for new hotels. The owners and corporate office will be committed to helping us refine the facility's quality and improve its profitability, in partnership with the executive committee.

The community will also be proud of the hotel, and will see it as a cooperative, involved business resident of the county.

necessary to produce the desired result. For the hotel to increase the occupancy from 80 to 85 percent, specific actions to be taken might include the following:

Conduct a sales blitz in key feeder cities.
Host ten key travel agent familiarization (FAM) tours.
Send direct mail to a number of American Express, Visa, MasterCard, and
    Discover card holders, and so on.

Once the corporate philosophy, culture, mission, goals, objectives, and strategies are finalized, the management functions will have guidance and direction to help steer the organization to success.

The Focus on Service

With so much focus on service, why is it so inconsistent today? Giving good service is a very difficult task; our educational system does not seem to teach service. Few businesses give enough priority to education and training in service. We suffer from an overreliance on technology. Service providers are often not motivated to give good service. For example, when checking a guest into the hotel, the front-desk associate may greet the guest but then look down at the computer for the remainder of the service encounter, even when asking for the guest's name. Or consider the reservations associate who says nothing when asked for a specific type of guest room because he is waiting for the computer to indicate availability.

In his best-selling book *At America's Service*, Karl Albrecht lists the "Seven Deadly Sins of Service":

1. Apathy
2. Brush-off
3. Coldness
4. Condescension
5. Robotics
6. Rule book
7. Runaround

Money magazine published a list of "The Six Rudest Restaurants in America."[3] It detailed a number of characteristically negative experiences guests had with restaurants noted more for their high ideals than their hors d'oeuvres. These included some of the swankiest of the swank. The author, Michael Williams, identified the most common insults to guests:

1. Grossly overbooked reservations
2. Holding better tables for favorite guests
3. Maître d's who could suddenly conjure up a table for a heavy tip
4. Treating guests with attitudes bordering on arrogance

Success in Service

What needs to happen to achieve success in service? Given that approximately 70 percent of the American and Canadian economies and an increasing percentage of other countries are engaged in service industries, it is critical to offer guests exceptional service, but what is exceptional service? *Service* is defined in *Webster's New World Dictionary* as "the act or means of serving." To *serve* is to "provide goods and services for" and "be of assistance to."

Personal Profile: Luis Barrios

General Manager, Wyndham Hotel, San Diego
Chairman of California Hotel/Motel Associations, Education Committee

Luis Barrios has come a long way in his career. He graduated from the hotel school at Miami-Dade Community College, from the Marketing and the General Managers program at Cornell University, and later from the Leadership and Guest Services program at the University of Disney. He was also at the Universidad Javeriana, Bogota, Colombia, in the economics program. His career began as a food and beverage controller, and then he was in sales with the Hilton Corporation at the Waldorf Astoria in New York in 1969. He became a director of sales for Hilton International Hotels in St. Thomas, Virgin Islands. He later went back to being a food and beverage controller at the Statler Hilton.

In 1974, Luis became food and beverage controller and assistant director of food and beverage at the New York Sheraton. Two years later, he became director of food and beverage at the Omni Shoreham in Washington, D.C.

Between 1976 and 1994, he served at the Omni Hotels. He was first a food and beverage director and then assistant general manager at Ambassador East in Chicago and at Omni Biltmore Plaza in Providence. Then he became general manager at the Massachusetts and Virginia Omni properties as well as the Mission Inn in Riverside, Omni San Diego, in San Diego and the Omni Northstar Hotel in Minneapolis.

While he was the general manager of the Catamaran Resort Hotel in San Diego, he was also general manager for the Lodge at Torrey Pines in La Jolla for two years.

For his great work in California, Luis was awarded the 1993 San Diego Hotel Person of the Year Gold Key Award. He is also president of the San Diego Hotel/Motel Association. He is a member of the board of directors for the California Hotel/Motel Association, chair of the Education Committee for the California Hotel/Motel Association, and a member of the Marketing Committee, San Diego Convention & Visitors Bureau.

Mr. Barrios had this to say to potential hospitality industry professionals:

Welcome to the exciting world of hospitality! Ours is a business that is fun, exciting, and creative. It is a field that embraces many professions in order to achieve our objective. Our business is a well-organized discipline, one that offers you the unique opportunity to exercise your professional expertise. Whether your expertise is in accounting, marketing, human resources, or engineering, you will enjoy the experience of dealing with people from all over the world, people with different backgrounds, customs, and expectations.

Working in the hotel industry is to experience the same operational challenges and opportunities as shared by individuals that manage a community: water and energy conservation, understanding transportation, communications and garbage disposal, all the while being required to be graceful hosts, wine connoisseurs, and psychologists.

On the other hand, we must approach our daily tasks with the determination to create unique experiences for both those who work with us and our guests who are the essence of our industry. It is then imperative to understand the needs of all our customers (internal and external). We must then respond to them with a positive attitude, efficient service, and a quality product if we are to succeed in creating wonderful memories.

With thousands of guest encounters or moments of truth each day, it is critical to incorporate service excellence through each hospitality organization. Some corporations adopt the expression "If you're not serving the guest, you had better be serving someone who is." This is the essence of teamwork, someone in the back of the house is serving someone in the front of the house, who is serving the guest.

A guest is anyone who receives or benefits from the output of someone's work. The external guest is the customer that most people think of in the traditional

FOCUS ON SERVICE

Hospitality Is Offering a Cup of Kindness

William B. Martin
Cal Tech—Monterey Bay

Customer service is a central focus of hospitality. It is what hospitality is all about—what we do. If you are interested in a hospitality career, it is important to understand and learn as much as possible about customer service and particularly how to be successful at it. Your success will come from a complete understanding of hospitality.

Let's begin by exploring why we provide hospitality. Why are hospitality businesses in business? What is the primary purpose of a foodservice operation? A lodging establishment? A travel- or tourism-related business? Is it just for the money? Many of you might answer an easy yes to this question. But, as you will see, hospitality is much more than just about money. Money is important, but it is important as a means and as a necessary ingredient to help us get to where we want to go. Money is not the primary reason for hospitality. Then, what is the primary purpose of hospitality?

Our job, first and foremost, is to enhance the lives of those people (guests, customers, passengers, etc.) to whom we are dedicated to serve. Yes, it is that simple (and complex at the same time). Our job is to make the lives of others better in a small way or big way; it makes no difference. Whatever it is, we are out to make people's lives on this planet a little bit better, or maybe even a lot better. This is our purpose. It is where we find meaning. We in the hospitality industry are about enhancing the lives of others—period. Ultimately, that is what makes it all worthwhile.

With that said, where does customer service fit in? Good question. If you are a sharp student, you've already got it. You can readily see that if the purpose of hospitality is to enhance the lives of others, the way we do that is through service. And what is service? It is how we go about treating our guests—how we make (or fail to make) their lives better by how we treat them. And we can go a long way toward treating them well by simply offering them a cup of kindness.

What does this mean? What does it take to be kind? What do we have to do? How do we enhance the lives of others through kindness? We begin by understanding what it is that they need. The problem is that all of our guests come to us with many needs. Some we can meet, some we can't. But of all the needs they come with, four of them are specifically hospitality related. If you can work toward helping them satisfy these needs, you can go a long way toward making their lives better through kindness. Let me offer a few examples.

Have you ever been in a customer service situation where the people providing service (the service providers) just didn't get it? They failed to understand what you wanted. Maybe they didn't care. Maybe they misread you or the situation. Regardless, the service providers failed to understand what it was that you needed or wanted or failed to connect to you in a meaningful way. If you can relate to any of these situations as a guest, you will see that an important hospitality need was not being met: the *need to be understood*. You, like all guests, have a basic need to be understood, not only in what you say, but also by how you say it. Quality customer service demands that service providers understand what it is that you want. Kindness, after all, comes through understanding.

Here is another example. Have you ever been somewhere (perhaps in a hospitality setting) where, for some reason, you felt out of place? You did not feel welcome. Maybe it was the way you were dressed, your age, or your unfamiliarity with the place. For whatever reason, you felt unwelcome. If this situation sounds familiar, your basic hospitality *need to feel welcome* went unmet. What a shame. If we are to enhance the lives of others, we need to make all people feel welcome. Kindness is demonstrated by making everyone feel welcome.

Have you ever been in a service situation where you were made to work for what you got? You had to jump through a few hoops, maybe. In other words, the service provider failed to take care of you. You had to take care of yourself. You were on your own, for better or worse, to survive or not. No help. No directions. Lots of stress. If you have experienced this situation, your basic hospitality *need for comfort* was not met. Quality customer service requires that we make all guests feel comfortable—that we provide the assurance, and follow through, that they will be taken care of. They don't need to worry; they are in good hands. In short, when we can do this we are filling their cups with more kindness.

Have you ever been in a service situation where you were humiliated, made to look stupid or silly or in some way less than desirable? All humans have the need to feel important, particularly in social settings such as hospitality situations, when you are with your friends and/or relatives. To be demeaned, belittled, or embarrassed in any way is totally unacceptable. Quality service demands that all guests, whether they deserve it or not, be made to feel important. Why? Because, we all have a *need to feel important*. This is a part of our job. Moreover, it is another important way we can show kindness to our guests.

With these examples, you should readily see how customer service is and must remain the central focus of hospitality. We need to stay focused on the primary purposes of hospitality. We need to understand the power of kindness and the importance of satisfying the four basic customer service needs of our guests. In the final analysis, hospitality and customer service success are found in our ability to enhance the lives of others through how we treat them—with a little cup of kindness.

sense. The satisfaction of external customers ultimately measures a company's success, since they are the people who are willing to pay for its services. The internal guests are the people inside any company who receive or benefit from the output of work done by others in the company.

For success in service we need to:

1. Focus on the guest.
2. Understand the role of the guest-contact employee.
3. Weave a service culture into education and training systems.
4. Emphasize high-touch instead of just high-tech.
5. Thrive on change.

As hospitality professionals, we need to recognize situations and act to relieve them or avoid them. Imagine how an associate can win points by showing empathy—that is, putting herself in someone else's shoes—in the following situation: A party of eight people arrives at a restaurant: Mom, Dad, and the kids, who are running all over the place. Mom and Dad just had a huge fight in the minivan. Obviously, the associate would want to welcome the party to the restaurant, seat them as quickly as possible, and then give the kids something to play with or munch on until the food comes. Also, it would be a good idea to offer Mom and Dad a margarita, a glass of wine, or some other cocktail.

Another key objective in the service equation is to create guest loyalty. We not only need to keep guests happy during their stay, but also to keep them returning—with their friends, we hope! It costs several times more to attract new guests than to retain existing ones. Imagine how much more profit a hospitality business would make if it could retain just 10 percent more of its guests as loyal guests. Losing a guest equates to losing much more than one sale—the potential can be loss of a lifetime guest. Consider a $20 restaurant lunch for two people. If the guests return twice a month over several years—say, ten—the amount quickly becomes huge ($4,800). If they bring their friends, this amount will be even higher.

OK, so now please write down your worst service experience.

_____

_____

_____

_____

_____

And now your most positive service experience.

_____

_____

_____

_____

We know that service is a complex yet critical component of the hospitality industry. In their book *Service America!*, Albrecht and Zemke suggest two basic kinds of service: "Help me!" and "Fix it."[4] "Help me!" refers to guests' regular and special needs, such as "Help me find the function room" or "Help me to get a reservation at the best restaurant in town." "Fix it" refers to services such as "Please fix my toilet, it won't flush" or "Please fix the TV so we can watch the World Series."

Moments of Truth

"Moments of truth" is a term coined by Jan Carlson. When Carlson became president of Scandinavian Airline System (SAS), it was ranked at the bottom of the European airline market. He quickly realized that he had to spend a lot of time on the front line coaching SAS associates in how to handle guest encounters or, as he called them, "moments of truth." As a result of his efforts, SAS was soon ranked at the top of the European airlines for service. Service commitment is a total organizational approach that makes the quality of service, as perceived by the customer, the number one driving force for the operation of the business.[5]

Every hospitality organization has thousands of moments of truth every day. This leads to tremendous challenges in maintaining the expected levels of service. Let's look at just some of the moments of truth in a restaurant dining experience:[6]

1. Guest calls the restaurant for a table reservation.
2. Guest tries to find the restaurant.
3. Guest parks.
4. Guest is welcomed.
5. Guest is informed that the table is not ready.
6. Guest either waits or goes to the lounge for a cocktail.

7. Guest tries to attract the bartender's attention for a cocktail because there are no seats available.
8. Guest is called over a loudspeaker or paged.
9. Guest is seated at the table.
10. Server takes order.
11. Server brings beverages or food.
12. Server clears food or beverages.
13. Server brings check.
14. Guest pays for meal.
15. Guest departs restaurant.

From your own experiences, you can imagine just how many moments of truth there are in a restaurant dining experience.

Check Your Knowledge

1. Why is service so important?
2. What is a moment of truth?

Ways to Improve Service

To help improve service in the hospitality industry, the Educational Foundation of the National Restaurant Association, one of the hospitality industry's leading associations, developed a number of great programs that will enhance your professional development. Further information may be obtained from the NRA's Web site (**www.restaurant.org**).

Among the various programs and courses is one on Foodservice Leadership. Effective leaders are those who make things happen because they have developed the knowledge, skills, and attitude required to get the most out of the people in their operation.

Leadership involves change; in fact, change is the one thing we can be sure of in the coming years. Our guests are constantly changing; so is technology, product availability, and, of course, our competition. To cope with this constant change, the NRA's group suggests that (1) all change is likely to meet with some resistance, and (2) when implementing change, do the following:

1. State the purpose of the change.
2. Involve all employees in the process.
3. Monitor, update, and follow up.

One way in which leaders involve employees in the process is through total quality management (TQM) and empowerment.

Service and Total Quality Management

The increasingly open and fiercely competitive marketplace is exerting enormous pressure on service industries to deliver superior service. Inspired by rising guest expectations and competitive necessity, many hospitality companies have jumped on the service-quality bandwagon.

The Employee Promise

At the Ritz-Carlton, our Ladies and Gentlemen are the most important resource in our service commitment to our guests.

By applying the principles of trust, honesty, respect, integrity, and commitment, we nurture and maximize talent to the benefit of each individual and the company.

The Ritz-Carlton fosters a work environment where diversity is valued, quality of life is enhanced, individual aspirations are fulfilled, and the Ritz-Carlton mystique is strengthened.

© The Ritz-Carlton Hotel Company, L.L.C. All rights reserved. Reprinted with the permission of The Ritz-Carlton Hotel Company, L.L.C.

The Malcolm Baldrige National Quality Award is the highest level of national recognition for quality that a U.S. company can receive. The award promotes an understanding of quality excellence, greater awareness of quality as a critical competitive element, and the sharing of quality information and strategies.

The Ritz-Carlton Hotel Company, winner of the 1992 and 1999 Malcolm Baldrige National Quality Award, was founded on principles of groundbreaking levels of customer service. The essence of this philosophy was refined into a set of core values collectively called the Gold Standards. The credo is printed on a small laminated card that all employees must memorize or carry on their person at all times when on duty. The card lists the three steps of service:

1. A warm and sincere greeting; use the guest name, if and when possible.
2. Anticipation and compliance with guests' needs.
3. Fond farewell; give them a warm good-bye and use their names if and when possible.

The quality movement began at the turn of the century as a means of ensuring consistency among the parts produced in the different plants of a single company so that they could be used interchangeably. In the area of service, TQM is a participatory process that empowers all levels of employees to work in groups to establish guest service expectations and determine the best way to meet or exceed these expectations. Notice that the term *guest* is preferred over the term *customer*. The inference here is that if we treat customers like guests, we are more likely to exceed their expectations. One successful hotelier has insisted for a long time that all employees treat guests as they would like to be treated themselves.

TQM is a continuous process that works best when managers are also good leaders. A successful company will employ leader–managers who create a stimulating work environment in which guests and employees (sometimes called internal guests; one employee serves another employee, who in turn serves a guest) become an integral part of the mission by participating in goal and objective setting.

Installing TQM is exciting, because once everyone becomes involved, there is no stopping the creative ways employees will find to solve guest-related problems and improve service. Other benefits include cost reductions and increased guest and employee satisfaction, leading ultimately to increased profits.

Top executives and line managers are responsible for the success of the TQM process; when they commit to ownership of the process, it will be successful. Focused commitment is the foundation of a quality service initiative, and leadership is the critical component in promoting commitment. Achieving TQM is a top-down, bottom-up process that must have the active commitment and participation of all employees from the top executives down to the bottom of the corporate ladder. The expression "If you are not serving the guest, then you had better be serving someone who is" still holds true today.

A Commitment to Excellence and Quality Service Worldwide

The Ritz-Carlton Hotel Company, L.L.C. was officially organized in the summer of 1983, although The Ritz-Carlton history and tradition long precede that date. Indeed, this tradition has entered our language: to be "ritzy" or "putting on the ritz" denotes doing something with class. With the purchase of The Ritz-Carlton, Boston and the acquisition of the exclusive rights to use the name came a rich heritage.

The legacy of The Ritz-Carlton begins with the celebrated hotelier Cesar Ritz, the "king of hoteliers and hotelier to kings." His philosophy of service and innovations redefined the luxury hotel experience in Europe through his management of The Ritz Paris and The Carlton in London. The Ritz-Carlton, Boston revolutionized hospitality in America by creating luxury in a hotel setting.

Cesar Ritz died in 1918, but his wife Marie continued the expansion of hotels bearing his name. In the United States, The Ritz-Carlton Investing Company was established by Albert Keller, who bought and franchised the name. In 1927, The Ritz-Carlton, Boston was opened by Edward N. Wyner, a Boston real estate developer, with room rates at $15 per night. Because of the reputation of Ritz in Europe and the cosmopolitan society in Boston, Wyner knew The Ritz-Carlton name would secure immediate success.

Fast-forward to 1983 when William B. Johnson acquired the rights to establish The Ritz-Carlton Hotel Company. The company now operates 57 hotels worldwide (35 city hotels and 23 resorts). Further expansion plans are included for Europe, Africa, Asia, the Middle East, and the Americas.

The Ritz-Carlton Hotel Company was named the winner of the prestigious Malcolm Baldrige National Quality Award in 1992 and again in 1999. The Ritz-Carlton is the only hospitality organization ever to have won this coveted honor for quality management, given by the U.S. Department of Commerce. Seven categories make up the award criteria: leadership, strategic planning, customer and market focus, information and analysis, human resources focus, process management, and business results. At The Ritz-Carlton, a focus on these criteria has resulted in higher employee and customer satisfaction, and increased productivity and market share. Perhaps most significant is increased profitability.

Simon F. Cooper was named president and chief operating officer of The Ritz-Carlton in February 2001. He took over from Horst Schultze, founding president and CEO, whose vision and leadership was the driving force behind the success in obtaining the Malcolm Baldrige Awards. Since joining the company, Cooper has been responsible for the successful opening of 23 hotels. This expansion continues with over a dozen hotels and resorts slated for opening over the next decade. The Residences at The Ritz-Carlton Residences and The Ritz-Carlton Club have also been successfully developed and launched under Cooper's tenure.

Committed employees rank as the most essential element. All employees are schooled and carry a pocket-sized card stating the company's Gold Standards, which include a credo, motto, three steps of service, and 20 Ritz-Carlton basics. Each employee is expected to understand and adhere to these standards, which describe processes for solving problems that guests may have as well as detailed grooming, housekeeping, and safety and efficiency standards. "We are Ladies and Gentlemen serving Ladies and Gentlemen" is the motto of The Ritz-Carlton, exemplifying anticipatory service provided by all staff members. "Every employee has the business plan of The Ritz-Carlton—constantly reinforcing that guest satisfaction is our highest mission," says Cooper.

The company has quickly grown a collection of the finest hotels around the world. Several of these hotels are historic landmarks, following a commitment of the company to preserving architecturally important buildings. Some examples are The Ritz-Carlton, Central Park; The Ritz-Carlton, San Francisco; The Ritz-Carlton, Philadelphia; The Ritz-Carlton, New Orleans; and The Ritz-Carlton, Huntington Hotel & Spa. Each property is designed to be a comfortable haven for travelers and a social center for the community. The architecture and artwork are carefully selected to complement the hotel's environment. "We go to great lengths to capture the spirit of a hotel and its locale," says Cooper. "This creates a subtle balance and celebrates a gracious, relaxed lifestyle. The Ritz-Carlton is warm, relaxed yet refined; a most comfortable home away from home." The Ritz Carlton Hotel Company is now owned and operated by Marriott International.

- Consider themselves a network of professionals.
- Have the authority to make their own decisions when serving guests.

To empower employees, managers must do the following:

1. Take risks.
2. Delegate.
3. Foster a learning environment.
4. Share information and encourage self-expression.
5. Involve employees in defining their own vision.
6. Be thorough and patient with employees.

Check Your Knowledge

1. List five attributes, traits, and characteristics of a leader.
2. What is a Malcolm Baldrige National Quality Award?

The Disney Approach to Guest Service

The Disney mission statement is simple: "We create Happiness." Disney is regarded as one of the excellent corporations throughout the text. The following discussion, adapted from a presentation given by Susan Wilkie to the Pacific-CHRIE conference outlines their approach to guest service.

When conceiving the idea to build Disneyland, Walt Disney established a simple philosophical approach to his theme park business, based on the tenents of quality, service, and show. The design, layout, characters, and magic of Disneyland grew out of Walt's successful experience in the film industry. With Disneyland he saw an opportunity to create a whole new form of entertainment: a three-dimensional live show. He wanted Disneyland to be a dynamic, ever-changing experience.

To reinforce the service concept, Disney has guests, not customers, and cast members, not employees. These terms set the expectations for how guests will be served and cared for while at the park or resort. This commitment to service means:

- Disney clearly understands their product and the meaning of their brand.
- They look at the business from the guests' perspective.
- They consider it their personal responsibility to create an exceptional experience for every individual who enters their gates.

Disney executives say that "our inventory goes home at night." Disney's ability to create a special brand of magic requires the talents of thousands of people fulfilling many different roles. But the heart of it is the frontline cast members. So what is it that makes the service at Disney so great? The key elements of Disneyland guest services include:

- Hiring, developing, and retaining the right people
- Understanding their product and the meaning of the brand
- Communicating the traditions and standards of service to all cast members
- Training leaders to be service coaches
- Measuring guest satisfaction
- Recognizing and rewarding performance

Disney has used profile modeling but says it all comes down to a few simple things:

- Interpersonal–relationship building skills
- Communication
- Friendliness

Disney uses a 45-minute team approach to interviewing called *peer interviews.* In one interview there may be four candidates and one interviewer. The candidates may include a housewife returning to the work force, a teacher looking for summer work, a retiree looking for a little extra income, or a teenager looking for a first job. All four candidates are interviewed in the same session. The interviewer is looking for how they individually answer questions but also how well they interact with each other—a good indicator of their future onstage treatment of guests.

The most successful technique used during the 45 minutes is to *smile.* The interviewer smiles at the people being interviewed to see if they *return the smiles.* If they don't, it doesn't matter how well they interview—they won't get the job.

On the first day at work, every new Disney cast member participates in a one-day orientation program at the Disney University, "Welcome to Show Business." The main goal of this experience is to learn the Disney approach to helpful, caring, and friendly guest service.

How does this translate into action? When a guest stops a street sweeper to ask where to pick up a parade schedule and the sweeper not only answers the question but recites the parade times from memory, suggests the best viewing spots on the parade route, offers advice on where to get a quick meal before parade time, *and* ends the interaction with a pleasant smile and warm send-off, people can't help but be impressed. It also makes the sweepers feel their jobs are interesting and important—which they are!

The Show is why people go to Disneyland. Each land tells a unique story through its theme and attention to detail, and the cast members each play a role in the Show. The most integral component of the training is the traditions and standards of guest service. The first of these is called the *Personal Touch.* The cast members are encouraged to use their own unique style and personality to provide a personal interaction with each guest. One of the primary ways Disney accomplishes this is through name tags. Everyone, regardless of position, goes by his or her first name. This tradition was started by Walt and continues today. It allows cast members to interact on a more personal level with guests. It also assists internally, by creating an informal environment that facilitates the flow

I Am Your Guest

We can all find inspiration from these anonymous words about people who make our business possible:

- *I am your guest*—Satisfy my needs, add personal attention and a friendly touch, and I will become a "walking advertisement" for your products and services. Ignore my needs, show carelessness, inattention, and poor manners, and I will cease to exist as far as you are concerned.

- *I am sophisticated*—Much more so than I was a few years ago. My needs are more complex. It is more important to me that you appreciate my business; when I buy your products and services I'm saying you are the best.

- *I am a perfectionist*—When I am dissatisfied, "take heed." The source of my discontent lies in something you or your products have failed to do. Find that source and eliminate it or you will lose my business and that of my friends as well. For when I criticize your products or services, I will talk to anyone who will listen.

- *I have other choices*—Other businesses continually offer "more for my money." You must prove to me again and again that I have made a wise choice in selecting you and your company above all others.

Opening Disneyland

Disneyland opened on July 17, 1955, to the predictions that it would be a failure. And, in truth, everything that could go wrong did:

- Plumbers went on strike.
- Tickets were duplicated.
- Attractions broke down.
- There was a gas leak in Fantasyland.
- The asphalt on Main Street didn't harden in time, so in the heat of July, horses' hooves and women's high heels stuck in the street.

As Walt once said, "You may not realize it when it happens, but a kick in the teeth might be good for you." Walt had his fair share of challenges, one of which was obtaining financing to develop Disneyland—he had to deal with more than 300 banks.

of open communication and breaks down some of the traditional barriers.

So what is the Disney service model?

It begins with a smile. This is the universal language of hospitality and service. Guests recognize and appreciate the cast members' warmth and sincerity.

Make eye contact and use body language. This means stance, approach, and gestures. For instance, cast members are trained to use *open* gestures for directions, not pointed fingers, because open palms are friendlier and less directive.

Respect and welcome all guests. This means being friendly, helpful, and going out of the way to *exceed* guests' expectations.

Value the magic. This means that when they're onstage cast members are totally focused on creating the magic of Disneyland. They don't talk about personal problems or world affairs, and they don't mention that you can find Mickey in more than one place.

Initiate guest contact. Cast members are reminded to actively initiate guest contact. Disney calls this being aggressively friendly. It's not enough to be responsive when approached. Cast members are encouraged to take the first step with guests. They have lots of little tricks for doing this, such as noticing a guest's name on a hat and then using the name in conversation or kneeling to ask a child a question.

Creative service solutions. For example, one Disneyland Hotel cast member recently became aware of a little boy who had come from the Mid-

Cinderella's castle soaring above tourists at Walt Disney World, Orlando.

west with his parents to enjoy the park and then left early because he was ill. The cast member approached the supervisor with an idea to send the child chicken soup, a character plush toy, and a get-well card from Mickey. The supervisor loved the idea, and all cast members are now allowed to set up these arrangements in similar situations without a supervisor's approval.

End with a "thank you." The phrases cast members use are important in creating a service environment. They do not have a book of accepted phrases; rather, through training and coaching, cast members are encouraged to use their own personality and style to welcome and approach guests, answer questions, anticipate their needs, thank them, and express with sincerity their desire to make the guest's experience exceptional.

Taken individually, these might sound pretty basic. But, taken together, they help define and reinforce the Disney culture. Once initial cast member training is completed, these concepts must be applied and continually reinforced by leaders who possess strong coaching skills. Disney uses a model called the *Five Steps of Leadership* to lead the cast member performance.

Each step in the leadership model is equally important in meeting service and business goals. Each leader must:

1. Provide clear expectations and standards.
2. Communicate these expectations through demonstration, information, and examples.
3. Hold cast members accountable for their feedback.
4. Coach through honest and direct feedback.
5. Recognize, reward, and celebrate success.

To supplement and reward the leadership team, Disney provides technical training to every new manager and assistant manager. In addition, the management team also participates in an acculturation process at the Disney University to learn the culture, values, and the leadership philosophy necessary to be successful in the Disney environment.

Disney measures the systems and reward process by distributing 1,000 surveys to guests as they leave Disneyland and 100 surveys to guests who stayed at each of the Disney hotels. The guests are asked to take the surveys home and mail them back to Disney. In return, their names are entered for a drawing for a family weekend package at the park and hotel.

Feedback from the surveys has been helpful in improving the guest experience. For example, as a result of the surveys, the entertainment division realized that the opportunity to interact with a character was a key driver to guest satisfaction. So the entertainment team designed a brochure, The Characters Today, which is distributed at the main entrance daily. This brochure allows guests to maximize their opportunity to see the characters. This initiative has already raised guest satisfaction by ten percentage points.

Cast members are also empowered to make changes to improve service. These measures are supplemented by financial controls and "mystery shops" that allow Disney to focus resources on increasing guest satisfaction.

The reward system does not consist of just the hard reward system we commonly think of, such as bonuses and incentive plans, important though they are. Recognition is not a one size fits all system. Disney has found that noncash recognition is as powerful if not more powerful a recognition tool in many situations. Some examples are:

- Disney recognizes milestones of years of service. They use pins and statues and have a formal dinner for cast members and guests to reinforce and celebrate the value of their experience and expertise at serving Disney's guests.
- Throughout the year, Disney hosts special social and recreational events that involve the cast members and their families in the product.
- Disney invites cast members and their families to family film festivals featuring new Disney releases to ensure that they are knowledgeable about the latest Disney products.
- The Disneyland management team hosts the Family Christmas Party after hours in the park. This allows cast members to enjoy shopping, dining, and riding the attractions. Management dresses in costumes and runs the facilities.

Trends

There is a healthy increase in hospitality and tourism not only in North America but around the world.

We can identify a number of trends that are having and will continue to have an impact on the hospitality industry. Some, like diversity, are already here and are sure to increase in the future. Here, in no particular order, are some of the major trends that hospitality professionals indicate as having an influence on the industry. You will find these and others discussed in the chapters of this text.

- *Globalization.* We have become the global village that was described, a few years ago. We may have the opportunity to work or vacation in other countries, and more people than ever travel freely around the world.
- *Safety and security.* Since September 11, 2001, we have all become more conscious of our personal safety and have experienced increased scrutiny at airports and federal and other buildings. But it goes beyond that; terrorists kidnap tourists from their resorts and hold them for ransom, thugs mug them, and others assault them. Two security experts have made valuable contributions to each chapter that follows by giving us the benefit of their experience and expertise.
- *Diversity.* The hospitality industry is the most diverse of all industries; not only do we have a diverse employee population, but we also have a diverse group of guests. Diversity is increasing as more people with more diverse cultures join the hospitality work force.

- *Service.* It is no secret that service is at the top of guest's expectations, yet few companies offer exceptional service. World-class service does not just happen; training is important in delivering the service that guests have come to expect.
- *Technology.* Technology is a driving force of change that presents opportunities for greater efficiencies and integration for improved guest service. However, the industry faces great challenges in training employees to use the new technology and in standardization of software and hardware design. Some hotels have several systems that do not talk to each other, and some reservation systems bounce between 7 and 10 percent of sales nationally.
- *Legal issues.* Lawsuits are not only more frequent, but they cost more if you lose and more to defend. One company spent several million dollars just to defend one case. Government regulations and the complexities of employee relations create increased challenges for hospitality operators.
- *Changing demographics.* The U.S. population is gradually increasing and the baby boomers are retiring. Many retirees have the time and money to travel and utilize hospitality services.
- *Price–value.* Price and value are important to today's more discerning guests.
- *Sanitation.* Sanitation is critical to the success of any restaurant and food-service operation. Guests expect to eat healthy foods that have been prepared in a sanitary environment.
- *Security.* Security of all types of hospitality and tourism operations is critical and disaster plans should be made for each kind of threat. Personal safety of guests must be the first priority.

SUMMARY

1. The hospitality and tourism industry is the largest and fastest-growing industry in the world.
2. Now is a great time to be considering a career in the hospitality and tourism field because thousands of supervising managers are needed for this dynamic industry.
3. Common dynamics include delivery of services and guest impressions of them.
4. Hospitality businesses are open 365 days a year and 24 hours a day and are likely to require shift work.
5. One essential difference between the hospitality business and other businesses is that in hospitality we are selling an intangible and perishable product.
6. Corporate philosophy is changing from managers planning, organizing, implementing, and so on, to that of managers counseling associates, giving them resources, and helping them to think for themselves.
7. Corporate philosophy embraces the values of the organization, including ethics, morals, fairness, and equality. The philosophy of "do whatever it takes" is critical for success.
8. Corporate culture refers to the overall style or feel of the company or how people relate to one another and their jobs.
9. A mission statement is a statement of central purposes, strategies, and values of the company. It should answer "What business are we in?"
10. A goal is a specific target to be met; objectives or tactics are the actions needed to accomplish the goal.
11. Total quality management has helped improve service to guests by empowering employees to give service that exceeds guest expectations.

KEY WORDS AND CONCEPTS

Average daily rate (ADR)
Back of the house
Corporate culture
Corporate philosophy
Empowerment

Front of the house
Goal
Guest satisfaction
Hospitality
Inseparability

Intangible
Mission statement
National Restaurant
    Association (NRA)
Perishability

Strategy
Total quality management
    (TQM)
Tourism

REVIEW QUESTIONS

1. Why is service so critical in the hospitality and tourism industry?
2. Describe and give an example of the following:
Mission statement
Goal

Strategy
Moment of truth
3. What is the Disney service model?
4. Explain why Ritz-Carlton won the Malcolm Baldrige award.

INTERNET EXERCISES

1. Organization: **World Travel and Tourism Council**
Web site: **www.wttc.org**
Summary: The World Travel and Tourism Council (WTTC) is the global business leaders' forum for travel and tourism. It includes all sectors of industry, including accommodation, catering, entertainment, recreation, transportation, and other travel-related services. Its central goal is to work with governments so that they can realize the full potential economic impact of the world's largest generator of wealth and jobs: travel and tourism.
(a) Find the latest statistics or figures for the global hospitality and tourism economy.

2. Organization: **Ritz-Carlton Hotels**
Web site **www.ritzcarlton.com**
Summary: The Ritz-Carlton is renowned for its elegance, sumptuous surroundings, and legendary service. With 58 hotels worldwide, a majority of them award winning, The Ritz-Carlton reflects 100 years of tradition.
(a) What is it about Ritz-Carlton that makes it such a great hotel chain?

3. Organization: **Disneyland and Walt Disney World**
Web site: **disney.go.com** and **www.disney.com**
(a) Compare and contrast Disneyland's and Walt Disney World's Web sites.

APPLY YOUR KNOWLEDGE

1. Write your personal mission statement.

2. Suggest ways to improve service in a hospitality business.

SUGGESTED ACTIVITY

Prepare some general hospitality and career-related questions, and interview two supervisors or managers in the hospitality industry. Share and compare the answers with your class next session.

ENDNOTES

1. **http://marriott.com.**
2. **http://marriott.com/corporateinfo/culture/ coreCulture.mi. July 6, 2005.**
3. You can see the list at **http://static.highbeam.com/ m/money/october011987/thesixrudestrestaurantsi namericaincludesrelatedart/index.html.**
4. Karl Albrecht and Ron Zemke, *Service America!* Homewood, IL: Dow Jones-Irwin, 1985, pp. 2–18.
5. Karl Albrecht, *At America's Service.* New York: Warner Books, 1992, p. 13.
6. Ibid., p. 27.

WEB RESOURCES

The National Restaurant Association
www.restaurant.org

Marriott International
www.marriott.com

Wyndham Hotels
www.wyndham.com

Ritz-Carlton Hotels
www.ritzcarlton.com

Disney
www.disney.com

World Travel and Tourism Council
www.wttc.org

Careers in Hospitality

After reading and studying this chapter you should be able to:

- Identify some of the possible career paths available in the hospitality industry.
- Establish career goals.
- Assess your own strengths and weaknesses.
- Describe some of the potential careers in the hospitality and tourism industry.
- Discuss aspects of professionalism.
- Write a résumé.
- Prepare for an interview.

Career Paths

Now we know that the hospitality industry is the largest and fastest-growing industry in the world, so let's explore some of the many **career paths** available to graduates of hospitality schools.

The concept of career paths describes the career progression available in each segment of the hospitality industry. A career path does not always go in a straight line, as sometimes described in a career ladder. You could liken it to jumping into a swimming pool; you get wet and then you swim over to the other side—not always in a straight line. It's like that in the hospitality industry, too. We may begin in one area and later find another more attractive. Opportunities come our way, and we need to be prepared to take advantage of these. That's fine, because there are plenty of choices available. To illustrate, a few years ago Barbara was a hospitality management major and decided that, because she was not as outgoing as some of the other students, she should become a hotel accountant, and she did. A few years later we visited the hotel where she was working only to be welcomed, from behind the front desk, by a beaming Barbara. She had moved from accounting to become front-office manager. Later, after three years in the sales and marketing department, she went on to become general manager.

Progression means that we can advance from one position to another. In the hospitality industry we don't use straight-line career ladders because we need experience in several areas before becoming, say, a general manager, director of human resources, catering manager, meeting planner, or director of marketing. The career path to general manager may go through food and beverage, rooms division, marketing, human resources, or finance and accounting or, more likely, a combination of these, because it is better to have experience in several areas (cross-training). The same is true with restaurants. A graduate with service experience will need to spend a few years in the kitchen learning each station, then bartend for a few months, before becoming an opening or closing assistant manager, or a general manager, regional manager, vice-president, or president.

Sometimes we want to run before we can walk; we want to progress quickly. But remember to enjoy the journey as much as the destination. If you advance

A professional appearance is important in this industry.

too quickly, you may not be ready for the additional responsibility, and you may not have all the skills necessary for the promotion. Be prepared and be ready because you never know when an opportunity will present itself. For instance, you cannot expect to become a director of food and beverage in a hotel until you really know "food and beverage," and this means spending a few years in the kitchen. Otherwise, how can you expect to relate to an executive chef? You have to know how the food should be prepared and served. You have to set the standards—not have them set for you.

Career Goals

You may already know that you want to be a director of accounting, an event manager, a director of food and beverage, or a restaurant manager. If you are not sure of which career path you want to pursue, that's OK. Now is the time to explore the various segments of the industry to gain the information you need to make a decision about which career path to follow. A great way to do this is through internships and work experience. Try a variety, rather than sticking with the same job.[1]

If we follow the umbrella scope of hospitality and tourism, we first examine careers in travel; followed by lodging; assembly and event management; restaurants and managed services; and recreation: theme parks and attractions, clubs, gaming, parks and recreation. Allied industries include suppliers, consultants, party rentals, and related services.

Check Your Knowledge

1. What is a career path?
2. What is a career goal?

Is the Hospitality Industry for You?

In Chapter 1 we described some characteristics of the hospitality industry. Due to the size and scope of the hospitality industry, career prospects are excellent. We also know that it is an exciting and dynamic industry with growth potential, especially when the economy is strong. In the hospitality industry we are often working when others are at leisure—think of the evening or weekend shift; however, in some positions and careers, evenings and weekends can be yours to enjoy as you wish.

The hospitality industry is a service industry; this means that we take pride in caring about others as well as ourselves. Ensuring that guests receive outstanding service is a goal of hospitality corporations. This is a business that gets in your blood! It is fun, exciting, and seldom dull, and almost everyone can succeed in the hospitality industry. So what are the characteristics for success in the hospitality industry? The personal characteristics, qualities, skills, and abilities that are beneficial for a career in the hospitality industry are honesty, hard work, being a team player, being prepared to work long hours spread over various shifts, the ability to cope with stress, good decision-making skills, good communication skills, being dedicated to exceptional service, and having a desire to exceed guest expectations. Leadership, ambition, and the will to succeed are also important and necessary for career success.

Recruiters look for **service-oriented** people who can "walk their talk," meaning they can do what they say they're going to do; good work experience, involvement in on-campus and professional organizations, a positive person, a good grade point average—it shows a commitment to your studies. Career-minded individuals who have initiative and are prepared to work hard and make a contribution to the company, which has to make a profit, is what companies look for in their recruits.

Self-Assessment and Personal Philosophy

The purpose of doing a self-assessment is to assess our current strengths and weaknesses and determine what we need to improve on if we are going to reach our goals. Self-assessment helps by establishing where we are now and the links to where we want to go—the goals. In a self-assessment we make a list of those things that are positive attributes about ourselves. For example, we may have experience in a guest service position; this will be helpful in preparing for a goal of becoming a hospitality industry general manager. Other positive attributes include our character and all the other things that recruiters look for, as listed previously. A good place to start is by reading *Now, Discover Your Strengths*.[2]

We also make a list of areas where we might want to make improvements. For example, we may have reached a certain level of culinary expertise, but would need more experience and a course in this specialty. Or you may want to improve your Spanish language skills because you intend to work with Spanish-speaking people. Your **philosophy** is your beliefs and the way you treat others and your work. It will determine who you are and what you stand for. You may state that you enjoy giving excellent service by treating others as you would like to be treated and that you believe in honesty and respect.

A great Web resource for self-assessment is **www. queendom.com**; this site provides several self-assessment quizzes.

Professionalism and Etiquette

Every profession has its norms. In our case, being on time is critical because guests do not want to wait for services. Several companies, including Marriott International, have a policy of requiring associates to clock in ten minutes before or clock out ten minutes after their shift. Failure to do this once results in a verbal warning; the second time it's a written warning. The third time and you're out! So you'd better opt for the evening shift if you're not a morning person.

Always be prepared for the next career move.

We need to be professional in our appearance—that is, our clothes and accessories. You may have noticed that several hospitality and tourism associates wear a uniform; this is a part of their profession. Female managers wear a business suit (pants or skirt) with a blouse and polished dress shoes. Male managers wear a business suit with a shirt and tie and polished dress shoes. When going for an interview, you should dress in a business suit. Men should wear ties in "powerful" colors—red or blue is best—never yellow. Be discrete; limit rings, no body piercing, and no heavy perfume. Women must not wear too much makeup or jewelry.

Etiquette is about how we behave in a given setting—for example, like children we are taught to say "please" and "thank you." In a hospitality business setting we are expected to abide by certain norms. For example, it is important to send a personal, handwritten note of thanks to the person who interviewed us. Not only does it make a good impression; it says that we are courteous. How we behave among others at a business lunch or dinner says a lot about our preparedness for a successful career. Do we have good table manners? Or do we behave inappropriately? Do we treat others with dignity and respect?

Check Your Knowledge

1. Name three qualities beneficial for a career in hospitality.
2. Define etiquette and explain how it relates to the hospitality industry.

Now Is the Time to Get Involved

For your own enjoyment and personal growth and development, it is important to get involved with on-campus and professional hospitality and tourism organizations. You don't have to take a leadership role at first; you can just learn how the organization works and participate in the organization of events. Recruiters notice the difference between students who have become involved with the various organizations, and they take that into consideration when assessing candidates for positions within their companies.

Becoming involved will show your commitment to your chosen career and lead you to meet interesting peers and industry professionals who can potentially help you along the career path you have decided to take. You will develop leadership and organizational skills that will help you in your career.

Professional Organizations and Associations

Professional organizations include becoming a student member of the International Council on Hospitality Education (CHRIE), whose Web site is **www.chrie.org**. You can also access an excellent Webzine called Hosteur that is published especially for students. CHRIE offers its members free access. The National Restaurant Association (NRA) (**www.restaurant.org**) is another organization to join. You will likely find several magazines and publications produced by the NRA very helpful. Both the NRA and your State Restaurant Association are affiliated and have trade shows that are worth attending. Each year at the NRA's annual convention, students are invited to attend not only the convention and trade show, but also the Salute to Excellence, a day of activities for students that culminates with a gala dinner. Only two students from each school are invited to this special event. Try to be one of them.

The American Hotel and Lodging Association (**www.ahla.com**) would be a good organization to belong to if you are interested in a career in the lodging segment of the industry. Some benefits of joining are access to the AH&LA's Career Center powered by Hcareers.com, the largest online database of career opportunities in the lodging industry; a subscription to *Lodging Magazine,* a leading industry publication with news, product information, and current articles on industry-related topics; subscriptions to *Lodging News, Lodging Law,* and *Lodging H/R* e-newsletters; and use of the AH&LA's information center—helpful for those pesky term papers! There is even scholarship information!

The International Special Events Society (ISES) has as members over 3,000 professionals representing special event producers, from festivals to trade shows. Membership brings together professionals from a variety of special events disciplines. The mission of the ISES is to educate, advance, and promote the special events industry and its network of professionals, along with related issues. For more information, visit the ISES Web site at **www.ises.org**.

The Professional Convention Management Association (PCMA) is a great resource for convention management educational offerings and networking opportunities. More information is available on their Web site at **www.pcma.org**.

The National Society of Minorities in Hospitality (NSMH) has a membership of several hundred minority hospitality majors who address diversity and multiculturalism, as well as career development via events and programs. For more information, visit their Web site at **www.nsmh.org**.

FOCUS ON CAREERS

Your Career in the Hospitality Industry

William Fisher
University of Central Florida

A short while ago, after giving a talk to a hospitality management class, I was approached by a student who asked, "What advice do you have for students who want to progress in a career in the hospitality industry?" It's a thoughtful question and deserves a thoughtful answer. Here is what I said.

1. *Know Yourself.* Come to terms with yourself through an unvarnished assessment of your values, strengths, and areas that need development. Decide that you will always be a person of integrity, exhibit total honesty, live up to your word, and do the right thing for the organization(s) you serve. Live by these values and emblazon them on your total being!

2. *Know Your Immediate Objectives.* You have decades of working years ahead of you, and it is important to have a dream of where you want to be in the future. Today comes before tomorrow, however, and you need to focus on and manage the present if you are ever going to realize your dream for the future. Have a clear view, a firm conviction, and a realistic expectation with respect to the positions you accept. Each position should be one element in a progressive pattern. Recognize that linkages exist. Throughout your career, bring with you the maturity, set of principles, and techniques that you gained from all your prior positions. Build for your future!

3. *Establish a Time Frame.* Set a realistic time period, given the level and complexity of the position. Many young people are impatient and believe they are ready to move on before they really are. A rule of thumb is to multiply the time it took to learn the position—not just the mechanics, but the nuances, relationships, and issues—by two or three. For example, if it takes you a year to be in full command of a position, an appropriate time frame for that position would be two to three years. The timing may be shortened or lengthened depending on circumstances, but there is no magic elixir that will accelerate your management maturity other than hard work and devotion to your assignment!

4. *Remember Names.* Use people's names when addressing them. This applies to everyone—customers, employees, suppliers, and visitors. If name recollection is not one of your strengths, work to improve it. Nothing is so personal to an individual as his or her name. By recognizing and using people's names, you confirm their existence and dignity!

5. *Be an Inside Volunteer.* Your organization will have a number of events, projects, and perhaps crises when employees will be asked to volunteer. Stepping forward demonstrates a good attitude, a cooperative demeanor, and a desire for participation, which can be professionally and developmentally rewarding for you. If appropriate, seek a leadership role, realizing you can be a leader without having a high position!

6. *Be an Outside Volunteer.* Join and participate in at least two outside organizations. One should be related to your industry and/or profession for professional development and networking purposes. The other should contribute to your community in some way, such as a charitable or children's organization.

7. *Follow Up.* Get back to people when you say you will, send thank you notes, send congratulatory messages, compliment good performance, and call people to emphasize appreciation.

8. *Develop a Reputation for Getting Results.* Make good things happen, exceed the expectations of others, demonstrate achievement, and keep a positive future orientation. Read regularly and stay on the cutting edge of your industry and profession!

9. *Maintain a Sense of Humor.* Always be invigorated by life. Never allow yourself to be defeated. You will experience difficult times, but they will pass. You will experience good times, but don't allow them to absorb you. Develop a quick wit, look at the bright side of things, smile frequently, and laugh heartily. It will do wonders for others—and for you!

Overall, be a "can do" person, but also be a *"candid"* person!

Ethics

Ethics is a set of moral principles and values that people use to answer questions about right and wrong. Because ethics is also about our personal value system, you will understand that there are people with value systems different from ours. Where did the value system originate? What happens if one value system is different from another? Fortunately, certain universal guiding principles are agreed on by virtually all religions, cultures, and societies. The foundation of all principles is that all people's rights are important and should not be violated. This belief is central to civilized societies; without it, chaos would reign.

Today, people have few moral absolutes; they decide situationally whether it is acceptable to steal, lie, or drink and drive. They seem to think that whatever is right is what works best for the individual. In a country blessed with so many diverse cultures, you might think it is impossible to identify common standards of ethical behavior. However, among sources from many different times and places, such as the Bible, Aristotle's *Ethics*, William Shakespeare's *King Lear*, the Koran, and the *Analects* of Confucius, you'll find the following basic moral values: integrity, respect for human life, self-control, honesty, and courage. Cruelty is wrong. All the world's major religions support a version of the Golden Rule: Do unto others as you would have them do to you.[3]

In the foreword to *Ethics in Hospitality Management*, edited by Stephen S. J. Hall,[4] Dean Emeritus of Cornell University, Robert A. Beck poses this question: "Is overbooking hotel rooms and airline seats ethical? How does one compare the legal responsibilities of the innkeeper and the airline manager to the moral obligation?"(p. 75). He also asks, What is a fair or reasonable wage? A fair or reasonable return on investment? Is it fair or ethical to underpay employees for the benefit of investors?

English Common Law, on which American law is based, left such decisions to the "reasonable man." A judge would ask the jury, "was this the act of a reasonable man?" Interestingly, what is considered ethical in one country may not be in another. For instance, in some countries it is considered normal to bargain for room rates; in others, bargaining would be considered bad form.

Ethics and morals have become an integral part of hospitality decisions, from employment (equal opportunity and affirmative action) to truth in menus. Many corporations and businesses have developed a code of ethics that all employees use to make decisions. This became necessary because too many managers were making decisions without regard to the impact of such decisions on others. Stephen Hall is one of the pioneers of ethics in hospitality; he has developed a code of ethics for the hospitality and tourism industry:[5]

Don't listen to the devil; maintain your moral values and behavior.

1. We acknowledge ethics and morality as inseparable elements of doing business and will test every decision against the highest standards of honesty, legality, fairness, impunity, and conscience.
2. We will conduct ourselves personally and collectively at all times so as to bring credit to the hospitality and tourism industry.

3. We will concentrate our time, energy, and resources on the improvement of our own products and services and we will not denigrate our competition in the pursuit of our success.
4. We will treat all guests equally regardless of race, religion, nationality, creed, or sex.
5. We will deliver all standards of service and product with total consistency to every guest.
6. We will provide a totally safe and sanitary environment at all times for every guest and employee.
7. We will strive constantly, in words, actions, and deeds, to develop and maintain the highest level of trust, honesty, and understanding among guests, clients, employees, employers, and the public at large.
8. We will provide every employee at every level all the knowledge, training, equipment, and motivation required to perform his or her tasks according to our published standards.
9. We will guarantee that every employee at every level will have the same opportunity to perform, advance, and be evaluated against the same standard as all employees engaged in the same or similar tasks.
10. We will actively and consciously work to protect and preserve our natural environment and natural resources in all that we do.
11. We will seek a fair and honest profit, no more, no less.

As you can see, it is vitally important for future hospitality and tourism professionals to abide by this code. Here are some ethical dilemmas in hospitality. What do you think about them?

Ethical Dilemmas in Hospitality

Previously, certain actions may not have been considered ethical, but management often looked the other way. A few scenarios follow that are not seen as ethical today and are against most companies' ethical policies.

1. As catering manager of a large banquet operation, the flowers for the hotel are booked through your office. The account is worth $15,000 per month. The florist offers you a 10 percent kickback. Given that your colleague at a sister hotel in the same company receives a good bonus and you do not, despite having a better financial result, do you accept the kickback? If so, whom do you share it with?
2. As purchasing agent for a major hospitality organization, you are responsible for purchasing $5 million worth of perishable and nonperishable items. To get your business, a supplier, whose quality and price are similar to others, offers you a new automobile. Do you accept?
3. An order has come from the corporate office that guests from a certain part of the world may only be accepted if the reservation is taken from the embassy of the countries. One Sunday afternoon, you are duty manager and several limos with people from "that part of the world"

FOCUS ON ETHICS

Ethics and Career Planning

Christine Jaszay, PhD
Director of Isbell Hospitality Ethics, School of Hotel and Restaurant Management, Northern Arizona University

One of our primary responsibilities, as hospitality managers, is to assure that we have adequate numbers of carefully selected employees who are capable of and willing to do the specific tasks each position requires. Not every person is a good match for every hospitality position. Some positions require high energy and excellent people skills; others call for people who can work quietly alone with great concentration and attention to details. If we do not make good selection choices, we may hire people who do not have the personal characteristics or skill sets necessary to successfully fill the positions. And we will be stuck with them and the problems created by poor hires.

To be in the position of making good employee selections, we first have to find management positions for ourselves. It is the responsibility of our interviewer to determine whether we have the characteristics and skill sets necessary for the position we are being interviewed for. If he or she makes a poor choice, he or she will be stuck with us and all the problems that are created by not hiring the right person for the job. If we are not a good match for the position, we will, most likely, not be very happy and may change jobs sooner than we might have liked.

The job interview process is a time when we also must discern whether the particular position and company are a good match for who we are. After four or five years of college poverty, we may find any well-paid management position appealing. Once we get used to having adequate money, though, the mismatches become more and more apparent until we find ourselves less than satisfied with the position or company.

So what does this have to do with ethics? Ethics are about honesty, doing our very best work, modeling good behavior for our employees, being trustworthy, being loyal, being positive leaders, being fair, having integrity, and caring about our employees and customers. If we work for a company or are in a position that is not a good match for us, it will be more difficult to be ethical managers. We must be able to embrace, model, and enforce the company policies and proce-

dures. If we do not agree with them, will we be able to do this? And if we do, when we do not really believe in them, are we being honest? Are we exhibiting integrity? Hardly.

All companies are not the same. They have individual cultures and philosophies. It is important that we identify the culture and philosophy that is compatible with our own beliefs and personal characteristics. If we are people who like structure and direction and take a position in a laid-back environment where we will be expected to self-direct, we may not be comfortable and able to do our best work. We may chafe under close supervision if we are people who need lots of autonomy. If we are somewhat formal and shy, we may not like a "touchy-feely" atmosphere, and may not fit in well. Others of us might prefer a more impersonal environment where the focus is on the task at hand.

To be able to make this good match, we have to be able and willing to honestly look at ourselves and figure out who we really are and what we really like. Have we ever thoughtfully considered what is truly important to us and what we want our future lives to look like and be about? We can be so busy and distracted that we assume we know what we really want. We can take opportunities that come along—some good, some not so good—and perhaps find ourselves in places or situations that might not have been our preference had we thought about it in advance.

So, you're in college. This *is* advance. This is the time to start thinking about what is important to you, what you like, what you want, and where you want to be in the future. Start thinking about the kind of person you are, based on your past experience, and the kind of person you want to be. Start making changes and/or adjustments that will begin shaping you into the vision you have of yourself. We have little control over anything other than ourselves in this life. It is within our control to be the kind of people we want to be.

Once we are in hospitality management, our task now is to determine what type of company and what type of position we should be seeking in order to excel. This means we can begin exploring the various hospitality companies: checking their Web sites, attending job fairs, going to information sessions with recruiters, and talking to students who have worked for the various hospitality companies. As we become familiar with some of the companies, we become more aware of how they differ and which companies we are more comfortable with.

By figuring out who we are, what is important to us, and where we want to be in the future, we can look for companies and positions where these personal characteristics are desired and honored and our personal needs can be met. If we do not honestly look at our-selves, we may not be able to make the right career moves that will take us on the journey to a pleasurable, fulfilling, and successful future.

Ethics are about living our lives with honesty and integrity. Starting with personal knowledge of ourselves, integrity is then developed over time by the decisions and choices we make, which should be in line with our fundamental beliefs. We cannot do this unless we know what our fundamental beliefs are. This takes reflection and honesty. Career planning is personal and requires self-knowledge. Planning implies action. We can look at ourselves, look at the various companies, and make a good match.

request rooms for several weeks. You decline, even though there are available rooms. They even offer you a personal envelope, which they say contains $1,000. How do you feel about declining their request?

These and other ethical dilemmas are not always simply right or wrong. Three key categories of questions need to be answered when making decisions:

1. Is it legal? Will I be violating civil law or company policy? Also, will I get fired if I accept it, allow it, or do it?
2. Is it balanced? Is it fair to all concerned in both the short term and the long term? Does it promote win–win relationships?
3. How will it make me feel about myself? Will it make me proud? Would I feel good if my family knew about it?

Check Your Knowledge

1. If you were interested in a career in lodging, what would be a good organization to belong to?
2. What are the questions one should ask when making an ethical decision?

Social Responsibilities in Business

Ethics is broadly concerned with how persons or organizations act, or should act, in relation to others. The breakdown of socially acceptable behavior appears to be a universal problem. Whatever the cause, this has affected business, government, and society.

Several issues are related to social responsibility in business. They range from truth in menu, nutrition, and obesity to the Atkins diet, recycling, and Ronald McDonald House.

In recent years, society's interest in, and awareness of, **social responsibility** has increased enormously. For example, the "greening" of America and other countries around the world has led to a decrease in the use of hazardous chemicals, including some pesticides. The protection and preservation of the environment have become major issues.

Social responsibility, however, goes beyond doing away with nonbiodegradable fast-food containers to becoming involved in the community in which a company or one of its hospitality or tourism operations is located. This is known as giving something back to the community.

Careers in Travel and Tourism

Travel includes air, sea, rail, and automobile, and tourism includes the attractions and places that people visit. The airline industry has a number of career opportunities for college graduates. From the flight deck to operations, from marketing to accounting and finance to flight attendant, there are plenty of career opportunities. Graduates looking for a career path in aviation as a pilot will enroll in flight school and gain first a single- and then a multiengine and night rating and license. It is necessary to log hundreds of hours to gain the experience required by the major airlines. Once employed by an airline, you will be trained on a particular type of aircraft and, when ready, become a copilot or navigator. As with all careers, there are pluses and minuses. For example, pilots have to check the aircraft before departure, so if there is a 6:30 A.M. departure, you can guess what time the pilot has to get up. The same goes for the crew of flight attendants; they need also to be on board to check aircraft readiness before passengers come on board.

Before you give up on the idea of becoming a pilot, remember they only fly from about 60 to 100 hours a month and can earn over $200,000 a year. Ticket agents range from $18,000 to $31,200 annually. Operations managers receive a salary of about $65,000. Station managers range from $50,000 to $75,000 annually, and airport managers range from $50,000 to $130,000 annually.

An American Airlines departure manager assists a passenger on departure.

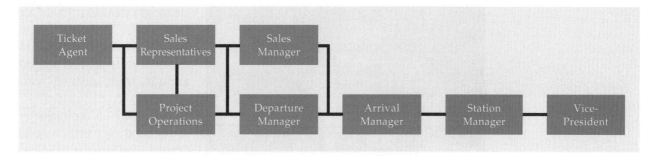

Figure 2–1 *Example of a Career Path in Travel and Tourism*

The cruise industry has a limited number of onboard positions, such as cruise director and hotel manager. Most ships have foreign crews because they can avoid American laws on things like overtime. Americans would not tolerate the conditions, the long hours, and the length of time away. There are numerous on-shore careers in marketing and sales, human resources, accounting, and finance.

Cruise directors arrange all the onboard activities and entertainment. This sounds exciting, and it is as long as you're organized and can work under pressure. (There is a profile of Jeff Martin, a cruise director for Royal Caribbean International, in Chapter 3.) The career path to a cruise director begins with a position as an activities staff member or a sports and fitness specialist. Then, after a year or more at each of these positions, promotion to a supervisor in one department and then other departments occurs, leading to becoming an assistant cruise director.

Chapter 3 has more on the many other careers in the diverse tourism industry, including travel manager, destination management, tour operators, and convention and visitors bureaus. Figure 2–1 shows a travel and tourism career path.

Careers in Restaurants and Managed Services

Restaurants

The restaurant industry employs over 12 million people in 878,000 locations and continues to grow. It is projected that in the year 2010 the industry will have one million locations and employ 13 million people.[6] Due to the number of restaurants, careers are readily available. The key is determining which aspect of the restaurant is most favorable to you. The typical restaurant career leads to kitchen manager, bar manager, restaurant manager, general manager, vice-president, president, and owner.

During the college years, it is best to gain experience in as many areas of the restaurant as possible. Because most food and beverage service jobs are part time, it is easy to fit them around your school schedule. One may start out as a food runner, primarily delivering meals to guests, or a busser, clearing tables of used dishes; sticking with the job can result in advancement to a food server. A food server's primary job is to be sure that the guest has a pleasurable dining experience. Servers greet guests, take orders, refill drinks, serve guests, and

A Busy Scene at an Outback Steakhouse

clean up tables to prepare for new guests. The job of a food server is often fast paced and requires patience and a good attitude when dealing with guests.

Tips make up the majority of a food server's wages. Competition among employees often arises at fine dining restaurants where potential earnings from tips are greatest. It is usually not the server with the most seniority who is given the best tables but instead the server with the best people skills and guest turnover is given priority. Once a food server is fully competent in his or her area, advancements can be made to shift leader. A shift leader has the same responsibilities as a food server but is also often responsible for training new staff, opening and closing the restaurant, and scheduling sections for the day. After being a shift leader, you will need to gain experience as a bar-back (the person who stocks and preps the bar prior to service), then bartender. Being bartender can be challenging, but is mostly great fun and is well paid.

Because servers work primarily for tips, it is difficult to determine an average salary. The average hourly earnings of food servers, not including tips, is $6.42. For most servers, higher earnings are primarily the result of receiving more in tips rather than higher hourly wages. Tips usually average between 10 and 20 percent of guests' checks, so servers working in busy, expensive restaurants earn the most.[7]

Another aspect of the restaurant industry that appeals to many is the career of kitchen manager or chef. Since the food served in a restaurant is the primary reason guests continue to patronize the restaurant, it is up to the chef to be sure that the guests receive a meal that meets or exceeds their expectations. In chain-operated restaurants, menus are prepared at the corporate office; in independent restaurants, chefs prepare menus, measure and mix ingredients, and use a variety of pots, blenders, and the like to prepare meals. The kitchen usually consists of a kitchen manager or chef and at least one prep cook who performs preliminary tasks, such as gathering ingredients and preparing them for use. Large operations employ several chefs that specialize in one area of cooking. For example, a pastry cook may be hired to make desserts, a pantry cook may prepare cold dishes for lunch and dinner, and a grill cook will take care of that station.

Most chefs start out as prep cooks to gain experience. Cooking not only requires education; it is also about experience. After acquiring basic skills and a college degree in culinary arts, it is not hard to advance to higher positions.

However, to achieve the level of skill required of an executive chef or cook in a fine restaurant, several years of training and experience are necessary. More and more chefs are choosing to obtain formal training through vocational programs, colleges and universities, or at culinary institutes.

The salary of a chef greatly depends on the location and type of restaurant he or she works in. Chefs in high-end restaurants can make as much as $58,000, with executive chefs in very famous restaurants earning much more—up to and over $100,000 if they are in the top group of superstars. Some chefs go on to own their own restaurants.

Restaurant managers have a variety of tasks to perform. Not only do they oversee the daily activities in the restaurant, but they must also be proficient in all areas of the establishment, from the kitchen to the host stand to visiting tables. They select menu items, predict daily food and beverage consumption totals, and place orders based on these predictions. Managers also act as the human resources department, recruiting, hiring, firing, and keeping peace among the employees. One of a manager's toughest tasks is employee retention, as turnover in the industry is incredibly high.

Because peak restaurant times are nights and weekends, managers often work long shifts at these times. It is not uncommon for a manager to log more than 50 hours of work in a week, work six or seven days a week, and sometimes work 12 to 15 hours per day. However, most restaurant companies have adjusted to a five-day week.

Some restaurants recruit managers from two- or four-year college hospitality programs. Although others hire those with a degree of any sort, the hospitality degree with work experience in the industry is preferred. Advancement in management will come with experience over time. Willingness to relocate is also a big factor in advancement because opportunities often arise in regional management positions within restaurant chains.

Restaurant managers and general managers can earn from about $55,000 to $150,000, depending on the size, volume, and amount of bonus. In addition to typical benefits, managers also receive free meals and continued education and training, depending on the length of their employment. Restaurant general managers can advance to regional manager or director with salaries of about $60,000 to $175,000. Vice-presidents and presidents can make from $75,000 to over $300,000.

Figure 2–2 provides a restaurant industry career path.

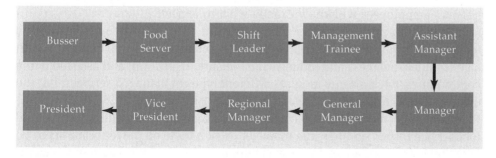

Figure 2–2   *A Career Path in the Restaurant Industry*

A Day in the Life of Josh Shear
Assistant Kitchen Manager, Old Salty Dog Restaurant, Sarasota, Florida

On a typical day I arrive at the restaurant between 8:30 and 9:00 A.M. I start off with booting up the computer and organizing all reports that were printed overnight. I then read any notes from the night before and begin my work in the kitchen. First thing that is done is the cleaning of the fryers, which usually takes about 20 minutes. I then turn on the grille and fryers to start my prep work for the day. The prep cooks usually show up about this time and check their prep lists and begin their work. Deliveries usually start to show up about this time also, and most of my morning is consumed by checking in orders and writing checks. My prep work for the day consists of grilling onions and mushrooms, making bacon, and stocking the line with fish, burgers, and all other items.

Our hours of operation are from 11:00 A.M. to 10:00 P.M., and between those times my main duties are to see that everything is done properly. If that means cook, prep, expo, or anything else that needs to be done to make the restaurant run smoothly and efficiently, that is what I do. Upon closing, it is my job to check out all kitchen employees' work stations and to make sure things are cleaned and stored properly.

Managed Services

Managed services are a $25 billion industry that serves more than 19,500 sites nationwide. Managed services focus not only on pleasing a guest, but, because they are usually housed in a facility where the main business is not foodservice, it is also important to please the owner of the establishment, known as the client.

Managed services are also unique in that they prepare very large batches of food to be consumed in a fixed period of time. Three batches of the same meal may be prepared in shifts each day to be sure that the last guest served receives a meal as fresh as the one the first guest of the day received.

It is much easier to predict the amount of food needed each day in a managed service operation. The volume of guests served on a daily basis is relatively consistent, therefore making the task easier of deciding how many servings of each meal and how many portions of certain products are necessary. Because of this advantage, managed services are often looked at as being a better employment opportunity than commercial foodservices. Hours are typically consistent so employees will know exactly what to expect.

Managed services consist of many different arenas. They include airlines; military, elementary, and secondary schools; colleges and universities; health care facilities; business and industry; and leisure, recreation, and assisted living communities. Each avenue requires different types of managed services, but the overall service provided is similar.

Managers in foodservices have many responsibilities. In addition to actual foodservice responsibilities, the manager must handle employee relations to be sure that employees are working well with one another and that they are working in a positive environment that is conducive to learning and advancement.

*A Sodexho manager
checks the production
sheet with a chef.*

Managers must also keep up with the human resources management department with regards to hiring and firing of employees, wages and benefits, and disciplinary actions. Special care must also be taken to be sure that all activities are in compliance with Occupational Safety and Health Administration (OSHA) requirements and federal and state laws.

Monitoring the company's budget and keeping records of all costly activities are also part of the manager's responsibilities. Preparing budgets, billing and collecting, monitoring accounts payable and receivable, and auditing are all in the job description.

The manager must also be sure that the working environment is a safe one. Monthly inspections must take place, and employees must be informed of all possible hazards in the workplace. Employees must be trained to handle dangerous equipment if such is to be used. Menu planning is part of management as well, although menus are developed at the corporate headquarters. The preparation of menus and the presentation of the food are very important steps to ensure that the companies will come out ahead of the competition. Food waste and production must also be recorded to be sure that resources are being used efficiently.

Sanitation is another very important area in which managers must take extra care. A productive cleaning regimen must be developed to prevent food-borne illnesses. Activity must be monitored daily to be sure that employees are handling all foods and possible contaminants correctly. The manager is also in charge of making sure all employees are trained properly in all areas of foodservice. This step can be made much easier if good employees are recruited to begin with and are given training opportunities.

Someone who is interested in becoming a district manager in managed food services must take several steps (see Figure 2–3). The typical entry-level position is that of an assistant foodservice director. This type of position can be gained upon completing college and once a solid résumé of experience has been built up. The typical salary of an assistant foodservice director is between $30,000 and $37,000 plus benefits.

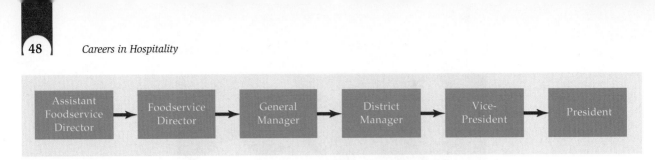

Figure 2–3   *A Career Path in the Managed Service Sector of the Hospitality Industry*

After some time spent as an assistant, one can move up to foodservice director. Directors make from $40,000 to $60,000 a year. Usually one would gain experience as a director at several establishments before moving up to general manager.

A general manager makes from $60,000 to $75,000 a year plus benefits. Progression as a general manager typically takes place in several establishments. One would likely move from a small arena to a larger one, and so on.

After several years as a general manager, one can be a district manager. District managers can make from $75,000 to $85,000 plus benefits. District managers have many responsibilities, which often include being in charge of multiple establishments at one time. Proposals to gain new accounts and negotiations with current clients are also the duty of the district manager.

Two of the biggest companies in the managed service industry are Sodexho and ARAMARK. Currently, Sodexho is the largest managed services company in North America and the world. Over 110,000 Sodexho employees serve customers every day all over the United States and in Canada. Sodexho provides service to the corporate, military, health care, and education markets, which includes food and beverage services, housekeeping, groundskeeping, plant operations and maintenance, and integrated facilities management. To learn more about Sodexho and its mission, go to **www.sodexhousa.com**.

ARAMARK's goal is not to simply be the favorite in the United States, but to be the worldwide leader in managed services. It works with clients around the world and provides a broad range of customized services. ARAMARK strongly emphasizes its commitment to understanding cultural differences and works to meet a diverse variety of needs.

ARAMARK has facilities in eighteen countries, including the United States, and caters to business and industry, colleges and universities, conference and convention centers, correctional and health care institutions, parks and resorts, public safety professionals, school districts, sports (including the Olympics) and entertainment. More information on ARAMARK can be found at **www.aramark.com**.

Check Your Knowledge

1. What are two onboard cruise positions?
2. How are managed services unique from other types of foodservices?

Careers in Lodging

There are about 3.5 million hotel rooms in thousands of hotels in North America, and more abroad, so you can imagine that there are several career paths in the lodging sector of the hospitality and tourism industry. If you are smart and gain valuable line or hourly paid experience in a variety of hotel departments during college, you will be better able to join a **management-training program** with a major hotel company. If you prefer a smaller hotel, a limited service hotel, or a bed and breakfast inn, it would be better to gain experience with a type of property similar to the one that you want to work in or own.

Graduates who join the major hotel companies normally spend a few months in several departments to gain all-round experience in operations. There may be an emphasis on rooms or food and beverage management if the individual wants a career path toward a director of rooms, a director of operations, or a director of food and beverage. If we select a career path toward a director of food and beverage, we should first learn what a director of food and beverage does (Figure 2–4).

The first department you will likely join is one of the restaurants, the lounge, or catering, stewarding, beverage service, F&B controller, or the kitchen; it is advisable to spend three or four years in the kitchen, covering each station so that you know food preparation. Otherwise, how can you relate to the chef when you become food and beverage manager? Others are room service or, if you are really unlucky, stewarding. It's considered unlucky because this department is responsible for cleaning and storing all the plates, glasses, cutlery, and related food and beverage equipment, including silver items. Remember to treat these associates like gods because you don't want someone to stick a fork in the cogs of the dishwasher and bring it to a grinding halt at 11 P.M. on a busy function night! These departments are all described in more detail in later chapters.

Now that we have spent several years working in all the food and beverage departments, we are ready for promotion to an assistant manager's position, usually at another hotel within the group. The corporate human resources Web site posts details of all positions available, and you can apply for them. It's competitive, so you had better have an exemplary record and start networking from day one! If you're a "high flyer," you may land a position as, for example, an assistant department manager for restaurants or room service. If you are successful in this position, you will be ready for additional challenges in a year or two. The next position would likely be in another department at the same or another hotel in the group, perhaps a larger hotel and a larger department. Again, after about a year or two, you will be ready for the next move, to department manager and/or a food and beverage manager, responsible for a part of the F&B operation and duty manager.

The salary levels for the trainee management program are from about $34,000, assistant department managers make about $38,000 and department manager's range between $38,000 and $54,000, food and beverage managers range from $44,000 to $55,000, and food and beverage directors range from $65,000 to $90,000, depending on the size of the hotel.

As with the food and beverage division, it is better to gain experience in the rooms division during the college years so that you can accelerate you career

POSITION TITLE: *Director of Food and Beverage:*
                         Food and Beverage
REPORTS TO: *General Manager*

PURPOSE

Directs and organizes the activities of the food and beverage department to maintain high standards of food and beverage quality, service, and merchandising to maximize profits

EXAMPLES OF DUTIES

Average %
of time

10%   Plan and direct planning and administration of the food and beverage department to meet the daily needs of the operation

10%   Clearly describe, assign, and delegate responsibility and authority for the operation of the various food and beverage subdepartments, for example, room service, restaurants, banquets, kitchens, steward, and so on

10%   Develop, implement, and monitor schedules for the operation of all restaurants and bars to achieve a profitable result

10%   Participate with the chef and restaurant managers in the creation of attractive menus designed to attract a predetermined customer market

10%   Implement effective control of food, beverage, and labor costs among all subdepartments

10%   Assist area managers in establishing and achieving predetermined profit objectives and desired standards of quality for food, service, cleanliness, merchandising, and promotion

10%   Regularly review and evaluate the degree of customer acceptance of the restaurant and banquet service to recommend to management new operating and marketing policies whenever declining or constant sales imply (1) dissatisfaction by the customers, (2) material change in the make-up of the customer market, or (3) change in the competitive environment

10%   Develop (with the aid of subdepartment heads) the operating tools necessary and incidental to modern management principles, for example, budgeting, forecasting, purchase specifications, recipes, portion specifications, menu abstracts, food production control, job descriptions, and so on

10%   Continually evaluate the performance and encourage improvement of personnel in the food and beverage department. Planning and administering a training and development program within the department will provide well-trained employees at all levels and permit advancement for those persons qualified and interested in that career development.

Other

Regular attendance in conformance with standards established by management. Employees with irregular attendance will be subject to disciplinary action, up to and including termination of employment.

Due to the cyclical nature of the hospitality industry, employees may be required to work varying schedules to accommodate business needs.

On employment, all employees are required to fully comply with rules and regulations for the safe and efficient operation of facilities. Employees who violate rules and regulations will be subject to disciplinary action, up to and including termination of employment.

Supportive Functions

In addition to performance of the essential functions, employees may be required to perform a combination of the following supportive functions, with the percentage of time performance of each function to be determined solely by the supervisor:

Participate in manager-on-duty coverage program, requiring weekend stayover, constant monitoring, and trouble-shooting problems

Operate word processing program in computer

Perform any general cleaning tasks using standard cleaning products to adhere to health standards

SPECIFIC JOB KNOWLEDGE, SKILLS, AND ABILITIES

The employee must possess the following knowledge, skills, and abilities and be able to explain and demonstrate that he or she can perform the essential functions of the job, with or without reasonable accommodation, using some other combination of skills and abilities:

Considerable skill in complex mathematical calculations without error

Ability to effectively deal with internal and external customers, some of whom will require high levels of patience, information, and the ability to resolve conflicts

Ability to move throughout all food and beverage areas and hospitality suites and continually perform essential job functions

Ability to read, listen, and communicate effectively in English, both verbally and in writing

Ability to access and accurately input information using a moderately complex computer system

Hearing, smelling, tasting, and visual ability to observe and distinguish product quality and detect signs of emergency situations

QUALIFICATION STANDARDS

Education: College degree in related field required. Culinary skills and service background required

Experience: Extensive experience in restaurant, bar, banquet, stewarding, kitchen, sales, catering, and management required

License or certification: No special licenses required

Grooming: All employees must maintain a neat, clean, and well-groomed appearance (specific standards available)

Other: Additional language ability preferred

Courtesy Hilton Hospitality, Inc.

Figure 2–4   *Job Description for a Director of Food and Beverage in a Large Hotel*

A Management Trainee at
an Embassy Suites
Property Front Desk

and not have to spend too long in some departments due to lack of previous experience. A management-training program in the rooms division normally lasts about 18 months. In the rooms division we could begin as a communications associate, answering the telephone and being the communications center for the hotel. Remember that the communications center is often the first impression gained by guests; it is also a good place to absorb all that is going on around you in the front office and reservations. A few weeks or months in the communications center would be followed by a few months as a front desk associate—and then on to reservations, guest services, and housekeeping. These departments, plus concierge and security, form the basis of the rooms division.

Once the management-training program is successfully completed, you will likely be offered a position as an assistant department head. Again, this will probably be in another hotel within the group. After a year or two you will be offered either another assistant manager's or a department head's position. You may go from a medium-sized to a larger hotel within the group. This exposure allows you to learn more about the company and gives you greater flexibility when the next promotion comes. Front-office and housekeeping manager are the two most challenging departments in the rooms division, so it is a good idea to gain plenty of experience in these departments before becoming a director of rooms division.

The salary levels for the rooms division have a wide range: A reservations manager makes about $35,000 to $40,000, a front-office manager $40,000 to $55,000, an executive housekeeper $45,000 to $70,000, and a director of rooms division $70,000 to $90,000, depending on the size and location of the hotel.

There are other positions in the hotel, such as director of marketing or sales and marketing (the terms are used interchangeably), director of human resources, and controller or director of finance. For each of these positions you would do the management-training program and then specialize in the department, doing all the positions in them. For instance, in the marketing and sales department there is a cocoordinator and several sales managers, each with a territory or specialty such as associations, local market, incentive market, and corporate accounts. Sales managers receive a salary of about $44,000 to

Corporate Profile: Hyatt Corporate Management Training Program[8]

The Hyatt Corporation is continuously seeking to enhance its reputation by ensuring that the best possible candidates join their management-training program. Whether you are interested in accounting, catering, culinary arts, engineering, human resources, operations, or sales, the Hyatt has a program for you.

Hyatt's management training process consists of programs that vary from 6 to 18 months in length, depending on the program concentration. Participants will be placed in the area that best suits their interests. First they will be on a rotating schedule in which they will experience all aspects of the hotel. After a given number of weeks on the rotation, they will switch and will then spend the remainder of their time in the program focused on one aspect of the hotel.

Upon completion of the program the participant will be ready to join the Hyatt work force at an assistant manager or manager-level position in the division of the training concentration. For example, operations trainees coming off the program may be placed as an assistant manager or floor manager in housekeeping, front-office shift leader, or supervisor, reservations supervisor, assistant restaurant manager, or banquets as a few possibilities. Culinary trainees may be placed as a station chef, and accounting trainees as credit manager, accounts receivable, or payable supervisor.

Applicants must meet the following requisites to qualify for the management-training program:

- Bachelor's degree in hospitality management or a related field
- Minimum GPA of 2.8
- Nine months of relative industry work experience
- Leadership and involvement in extracurricular activities and on-campus organizations
- Positive references from two previous employers (no character references)
- Continuous authorization to work in the United States

Hyatt offers a competitive salary for corporate management trainees based on the trainee's geographic placement. Compensation for the corporate management training program is determined by the current average cost of living in the geographic region of the hotel. The trainee salary is based on a five-day, 50-hour workweek, with additional compensation for hours worked in excess of 50 hours per week.

Graduates of the program will most likely begin their management careers in familiar surroundings, because the hotel where the training takes place has the first opportunity to place the trainees. If appropriate positions are not available at the hotel where training is completed, the trainee may be transferred to another Hyatt property for management placement.

To find out more about Hyatt and the corporate management training program go to **www.hyatt.com**. Look for careers under Hyatt and access the Hyatt on the Campus page. For further employment opportunities, see the listing of current management openings nationwide at **www.careers.hyatt.com**.

Source: Hyatt Hotels and Resorts.

$55,000 and directors of marketing $75,000 to $100,000 plus. Directors of human resources receive salaries of about $55,000 to $75,000 and directors of accounting or finance $65,000 to $85,000.

All these senior positions can lead to general manager and beyond to regional and corporate executive positions with even greater responsibilities and, yes, salaries. Figure 2–5 shows a career path in lodging management.

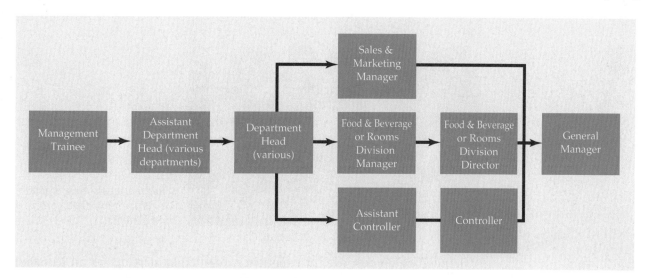

Figure 2–5 *A Career Path in Lodging Management*

Club managers share many of the same responsibilities as hotel managers. They are in charge of preparing budgets and forecasting future sales, as well as monitoring restaurants on the property and the various internal departments such as human resources and making sure maintenance work is done properly. They are responsible for the overall well-being of the club. The Club Managers Association of America (**www.cmaa**) is the professional association that grants club managers certification and other membership benefits, such as professional development and networking. Their Web site is worth a visit.

Club management is different from hotel management in that the guests at a club are members and typically pay for their memberships. Because of this, many feel a much stronger tie to the club and therefore expect a higher level of service.

Of the many types of clubs within the club management industry, the most predominant are golf, country, city, athletic, and yacht clubs. Country clubs are the most common. They are typically based around outdoor activities. Golf is the main draw, but other sports such as tennis and swimming are also common. Some country clubs also offer a variety of classes and social activities to their members. They typically have a lounge and/or restaurant on the property as well. Country clubs can be private or semiprivate. If a club is private, its facilities are only available to members; a semiprivate club offers some services to nonmembers.

There is no one definite career path when it comes to club management. However, most people make the transition to club manager from positions in kitchen or bar management (see Figure 2–6). It is rare that employees move from areas such as accounting to become club managers.

Club managers have a great career with excellent salary and benefits.

Depending on the level of experience, one might start out as an assistant banquet or dining room manager and then progress to a position as catering manager or assistant clubhouse manager. The next step takes place according to the amount of time spent in these positions, as well as to the quality of the experience. For example, four to six years in a club that has a gross income of $1.5 million in food and beverages would most likely lead to a club management position.[9]

One aspect of being a club manager is the fact that regular hours are not kept. When the club is busy, long hours are worked. In contrast, when the club is slow, hours worked are much less. Club managers usually create their own schedules according to fluctuations in activity. On average, managers typically work five or six days a week, ten hours a day.

Most entry-level club management positions have set salaries that range from $27,000 to $33,000. **Entry-level positions** are usually not subject to negotiation. Midlevel position salaries, however, can often be negotiated until an agreeable sum is met. The actual salary depends on the amount of experience the employee has and the strength of his or her references. The best aspect of working as a club manager is that the environment and facilities are usually top notch. Managers typically have access to the club's facilities and receive meals. Excel-

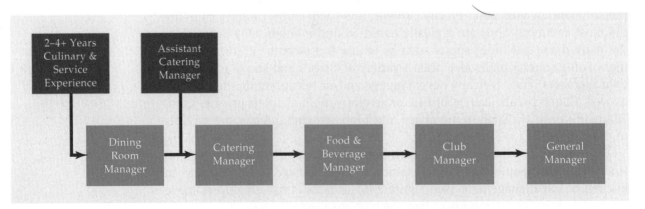

Figure 2–6 *A Career Path to Club General Manager*

lent opportunities for advancement come frequently. Club managers also often receive bonuses based on performance. These bonuses range from 5 to 15 percent of the manager's base salary of more than $100,000 annually, and the highest-paid country club general manager makes $350,000 annually. (Yes, that's $350,000!)

Careers in Conventions and Expositions

Convention planners coordinate meetings, conventions, and special events for very large groups of people. They are similar to event planners in the types of organization and skill they require; yet the activities are on a much larger scale.

Convention managers are in constant communication with all aspects of the event. From the catering staff to the speaker's bureau to the trade staff, such as the electricians and laborers who set up and take down equipment, convention managers must be keenly aware of everything happening around them. They are also usually responsible for hiring outside sources to come in and do various tasks, such as sound, lighting, and equipment setup where necessary, as well as catering if needed.

Convention managers are typically given a budget and are expected to stay within the budget. This can sometimes be difficult, as conventions and expositions can be huge and require spending large sums of money. Consideration must be made for possible mishaps that could require extra time and money. Contracts must also be established with all outside help and fees must be negotiated.

The legal aspects of such events are also the responsibility of the convention manager. When an event is going to take place in a certain area, the manager must

Perhaps you will be the one to manage this computer convention at the Moscone Center in San Francisco.

Personal Profile: Beth Lukens

I first became interested in the hospitality industry as an employee at Big Olaf Creamery, a charming ice cream shop on Siesta Key in Sarasota, Florida. After spending my high school years as a Big Olaf employee, I enrolled at Florida State University as an art major. I continued to work at Big Olaf on my breaks from school and developed strong relationships with the management, the locals, and the vacationers who returned year after year.

While on breaks from Florida State, I also worked at several other restaurants in Florida. I worked as a hostess and waitress at First Watch, a popular breakfast and lunch establishment in Sarasota. The fast pace of such a busy restaurant gave me valuable work experience and taught me how to work well under pressure. I also worked as a waitress at Garfield's, a chain restaurant in Tallahassee.

As time progressed, I realized more and more that my part-time jobs were becoming much more than ways to earn some extra money; they were becoming something I was truly passionate about. After three years at Florida State, I decided to make a life change. I transferred to the University of South Florida's Sarasota campus. Coincidentally, USF was just opening its School of Hotel and Restaurant Management.

I immediately enrolled in classes and began my new endeavor. Upon returning to Sarasota, I applied for and obtained a job as a waitress at Sam Snead's Tavern. Sam Snead's has a reputation across the country as an upscale establishment, and I felt it was important to gain experience in a variety of hospitality arenas.

After several months, I returned to work at Big Olaf and was promoted to manager. With the change in role came an increase of responsibility. I was now relied on to keep everything at Big Olaf running smoothly. Because I truly loved working at Big Olaf, the task of maintaining it was never a chore. Having spent portions of the previous six years at Big Olaf, I was familiar with every aspect of the business and adjusted to the new position comfortably.

As a hospitality student at USF, I learned a great deal about the inner workings of the hospitality industry. I feel that the combination of actual work experience and education has prepared me well for the future. I have gained the necessary confidence and skills needed to handle whatever situations may arise on the job. Having taken classes with an emphasis on very specific areas, I realize that there is always more to learn about the hospitality industry. This is perhaps the best part of this industry; it is ever changing, which keeps it exciting.

Now I am just two semesters shy of becoming one of the first graduates from the university's School of Hotel and Restaurant Management. While at USF I have maintained a grade-point average of 3.7, while continuing to build on my experiences in the hospitality industry. Within the coming months I hope to obtain an internship at the Hyatt in Sarasota and, upon graduating, plan to join in the management-training program of Hyatt Hotels Corporation.

In the future I hope to progress through various aspects of the hotel industry. I enjoy working with people, and it is my goal to become a director of human resources with a major hotel corporation. While working with my mentor and through hard work and diligence, I hope to achieve my goals. I realize that there are many steps to take in this process and I look forward to the challenges ahead.

be aware of all fire code regulations, floor plans, and space limitations. Without proper knowledge of these aspects, it is possible that lawsuits could result.

Convention managers must be very organized individuals. A good convention manager keeps careful written records of each transaction and decision that is made throughout the planning process. Communication skills are also key, as everyone involved in the event must be aware of important happenings.

The convention manager does not act alone. Typically, he or she has a staff to handle sales, registration, marketing, and other specific areas of the event. It is the manager's responsibility to see that each member of the employment team does his or her part to ensure that the event will go smoothly from start to finish.

Figure 2–7 *A Career Path to Becoming a Convention Manager*

Follow-up evaluations are also usually done after the event so the next time proper provisions can be made to ensure that problems are fixed and all goes well.

Convention managers can be employed by a specific convention, convention bureaus, the tourism industry, and convention halls and exhibitions. A four-year degree is preferred, and a background in public relations, sales, marketing, or travel is encouraged. Many convention managers even have graduate degrees.

Advancement as a convention manager, like most careers, comes with experience. With increased experience come positions with increased responsibility (see Figure 2–7). Eventually, one may move up to a position in senior management or go into business for oneself. Managers with a good reputation in the community may also receive bigger and better offers from other firms and can advance their careers in this manner.

Opportunities for convention managers are growing every day. More and more events are being planned in the United States, which means expanding opportunities for work exist. The average annual salary for a convention planner is between $35,000 and $59,999. Several make $90,000 or more, and a few are in the $150,000 or more category. To learn more about convention management, go to the Professional Convention Management Association at **www.PCMA.org**.

Careers in Meeting Planning, Event Management, and Catering

Meeting Planning

The job title of meeting planner can go under many headings, including event planner, meeting manager, conference coordinator, and convention planner. The meeting planner's duties may include establishing a site for an event; making travel, hotel, and food arrangements; and planning the program and overseeing registration. Events can range from the negotiation and coordinating of a worldwide event to a small, in-house meeting in which few people are involved. While some professional companies have employees on staff that serve as meeting planners, many organizations hire from outside the company and call on firms that specialize in meeting planning.

The meeting planning profession was recognized as a career only a few years ago. As companies began to expand, the need for meeting planning became evident. Putting together an event that involves people and equipment from all over the world requires much advanced planning to be sure that a site can be chosen, travel and hotel arrangements can be made, and guest speakers can be booked.

The way meetings are conducted has changed as well. With the increase of technological advances in the past decade, meetings can now be held through videoconferencing, over the Internet, and with cyber meetings, in addition to conference calls. Thus, the meeting planner needs to have a good knowledge of technology and projection equipment.

A meeting planner's duties depend on the type of firm he or she works for. Typically, planners organize and plan events such as meeting, conventions, and special celebrations. Gathering times are usually booked according to key executive's schedules, and everything else is filled in accordingly. Rooms where the event will take place must be chosen. It is the planner's job to evaluate possible sites and research outside sources to find the best location. Registration procedures must be established and food, room layouts, equipment needs, and instructors lined up.

An in-house meeting planner often handles small events, whereas both the in-house planner and an outside source working on contract sometimes coordinate larger events. In the case of a very large event, travel arrangements must be made for everyone in attendance. Often hotel and airline tickets are booked well in advance if the number of people expected is great. Additional staff may also be necessary to accommodate large numbers of people.

Practically all meeting planners must have a four-year college degree to work for a company, corporation, convention, or travel center. While some colleges and universities offer specific degrees in meeting planning or hospitality management, degrees in English, communication, business, marketing, public relations, sales, or travel are also acceptable in many workplaces. Typically, employees planning to become company heads have earned graduate degrees as well. As with most careers, advancement opportunities are more readily available to those with additional education.

People interested in a career as a meeting planner should be creative individuals who possess optimal organizational skills and the ability to plan projects effectively. They must be able to work well with their peers and to anticipate their needs and wants in advance. Even if a task is not in their job description,

Meeting planners coordinate a client event.

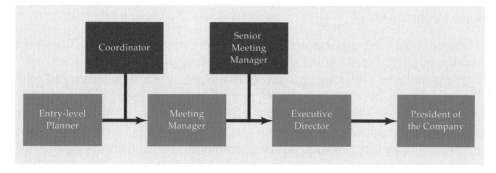

Figure 2–8 *A Career Path to a Meeting Planner*

they should be willing to put forth the extra effort to see that all duties are done correctly. They should be able to act quickly and professionally should an unforeseen situation arise, and they should always be fair and take all aspects of the circumstance into account. They need to be familiar with the business industry and the way meetings are planned and conducted, as well as being familiar with trade shows and conventions. Overall, meeting planners should be good negotiators who can push for what they want, yet still remain tactful.

Students interested in becoming meeting planners should first obtain an internship at a convention bureau, exhibit center, travel agency, or meeting planning company. Internships are excellent ways to develop people skills and to learn about the industry. They are also wonderful ways to gain contacts for possible future job placement. Some colleges and universities offer internship placement. Classified ads and trade magazines are a good resource for finding open positions as well.

Advancement opportunities are good for those in the meeting planning field. Increased responsibility can come easily with increased experience (see Figure 2–8). After putting in a fair amount of time in an entry-level position, one can advance to a position as a senior manager or executive director in a variety of situations, from private businesses and hotels to travel corporations and museums. Meeting planners who have established a good reputation among their community and peers are often recruited by other firms and can choose to advance their careers in this manner.

Job opportunities for meeting planners are continuously growing. New technology and broader business practices are creating a greater need for planners than ever before. In fact, conventions, trade shows, and meetings support more than 1.5 million American jobs. Depending on the level of responsibility and the years of experience, the salaries for these jobs can range from $34,000 starting out to over $100,000 for executive directors. These events account for more than $80 billion in annual spending. It should also be noted that the majority of meeting planners are women, so this career field offers great opportunities for women.[10]

Check Your Knowledge

1. Name three of the five most predominant types of clubs.
2. What has changed the way meetings are conducted in the past decade?

Event Management

Many different careers fall under the category of event management. Two of the most popular and well known are wedding planning and party planning.

More and more brides are choosing to hire wedding planners, also called wedding consultants or bridal consultants, to help them plan their big day. With the average wedding costing about $20,000, it is no wonder that many brides wish to have a little assistance to assure them that the big event is worth the time and money and provides them with the lasting memories they have always dreamed of.

Wedding planners provide brides with assistance in all aspects of planning the wedding. They give cost estimates, make ceremony arrangements, choose reception sites, pick out invitations and flowers, and offer advice on wedding etiquette and tradition. Most wedding planners are on call throughout the reception and ceremony, and some are ever present at the event to be sure that every last detail is taken care of.

The most important quality a wedding planner can have is the ability to remain calm and organized in stressful situations. Wedding plans can often change at the spur of the moment, and a good planner is always prepared for such changes. He or she must also be personable and a good negotiator. It is the planner's responsibility to be sure that the best services are found for the lowest prices.

Networking is a large aspect of wedding planning. Since most wedding planners are home based, it is important to develop a good reputation and establish good connections to ensure good business in the future.

On average, wedding planners charge 10 to 15 percent of the cost of the wedding. Based on the average wedding cost of $20,000, the planner's earning per wedding would be between $2,000 and $3,000. However, the cost of a wedding varies by region, meaning earnings will vary according to where the wedding takes place.

Wedding planners need most of the business skills acquired by students in colleges and universities. However, a degree is not a necessity when becoming a wedding planner. In recent years, many operations have developed certification and training programs. An example of one such program is the Association of Bridal Consultants, or ABC. The program consists of a variety of courses that can be taken individually or all at one time. The courses lead to professional designations

Event managers get to plan and organize different events such as weddings and sports events.

such as Professional Bridal Consultant, Accredited Bridal Consultant, and Master Bridal Consultant. It takes at least six years to reach the senior level. To learn more about ABC, go to **www.trainingforum.com**.

Another aspect of event management is party planning. Party planners are often self-employed or work out of small firms and are hired by individuals, families, and small companies to plan small parties for special occasions. Party planners help to plan and organize events from birthdays, christenings, bar and bat mitzvahs, themed parties, and celebrations. Planners can be responsible for the entire event, from invitations to catering to cleanup, or they may work on one aspect of the party, such as planning a menu or serving guests.

Party planners must be very well organized and pay close attention to detail. It is best to keep long to-do lists to be sure that every aspect of the event is taken care of and no minute detail is forgotten. Party planners must also be creative, as clients often have very specific ideas in mind. Patience is of utmost importance, too, as planning can often mean spending hours on the phone working out every last detail.

If planning to start your own party planning business, several items are necessary. A computer, printer, fax, and cell phone, and car, van, or SUV to carry decorations and props to party locations are a must. Successful party planners also typically keep a portfolio containing party photos, sample invitations, and menus to show potential clients. It is also a good idea to have subscriptions to several lifestyle magazines to keep up to date with current trends.

There are several costs associated with starting a business as a party planner. If not already owned, computer and hardware must be purchased. In addition, $500 to $1,000 will be needed to cover the expense of a business license, marketing materials, and basic party supplies. A vehicle may also need to be purchased. If this is the case, a good used van can be bought for about $10,000.

For big corporate events, weddings, bar and bat mitzvahs, large family reunions, fund-raisers, and the like, most party planners charge 10 percent of the total cost of the party. For small birthday or anniversary parties, it is typical to charge per person attending, ranging from $10 to $40 a head and depending on how much planning is required. Some planners work out hourly fee arrangements with clients, starting at $20 an hour and up.

The best way to get started as a party planner is through word of mouth and by starting small. Party kits can be bought online as a start, and business cards can be handed out manually. Place ads in local papers and flyers, or offer services for trade to showcase what is available. After developing contacts, it is fairly easy to branch out over time into larger groups and parties.

Figure 2–9 shows a possible career path for an event manager.

Figure 2–9   *A Career Path for an Event Manager*

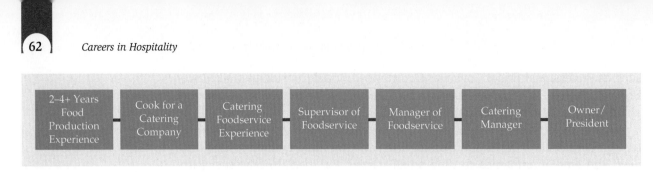

2–4+ Years Food Production Experience	Cook for a Catering Company	Catering Foodservice Experience	Supervisor of Foodservice	Manager of Foodservice	Catering Manager	Owner/ President

Figure 2–10   *A Career Path to a Catering Manager*

Catering

Catering offers a career choice for the entrepreneur. Catering is like restaurants; they are relatively easy to get into, but it is not easy to make a profit. Students should work for catering companies during college to gain as much experience as possible in setting up the functions and serving or prepping cooking. Graduates can gain additional experience in the preparation and execution of functions and as a coordinator planning and assisting in the organization of the function. Some catering functions are complex and require experience to ensure success. Functions are often held on location, meaning not in a hall or hotel. Catering professionals need to remember everything—including the corkscrew!

Promotion to catering manager often comes quickly as business grows and companies expand (see Figure 2–10). Catering managers are in charge of each function—remember that many catering organizations handle more than one function a day. You are responsible to ensure that everything goes well and that guest's expectations are exceeded. This can be a challenge, because you are working with several different people, from chefs to decorator's set-up people and servers. It's like conducting an orchestra; your job is to make sure that the music is harmonious! Owners or company executives are exciting positions, especially if you can attract and book the business to make good money. Catering professionals need a good knowledge of food and sanitation, including what causes food-borne illnesses and how to prevent them. Catering salaries are from $25,000 for coordinators and $30,000 to $50,000 and up to over $100,000 for owners of medium-sized catering companies.

A catering manager and chef check the finished setup of a catered event.

Careers in Recreation and Leisure, Amusement and Theme Parks, and Gaming

Recreation and Leisure

About 230,000 recreation workers are employed in the United States. In comparison to other jobs, the field of recreation has a very high number of part-time, seasonal, and volunteer jobs. However, excellent careers can be developed through hard work and dedication. Figure 2–11 illustrates a career path in recreation, leisure, and amusement and theme parks.

Recreation workers plan, organize, and direct various recreational activities, such as aerobics, arts and crafts, Little League baseball, tennis, camping, and softball. These activities take place in a variety of locations, such as local parks and recreation centers, health clubs, churches, and theme parks.

Recreation workers can be employed in a variety of positions, depending on the amount of responsibility they want and are capable of handling. Recreation leaders are in charge of daily operations within recreation programs. They can lead classes, schedule facility and equipment use, and ensure proper equipment use. They are also in charge of bringing in activity specialists who instruct or coach participants in specific activities, such as art, music, swimming, or tennis.

Recreation supervisors oversee recreation leaders and plan, organize, and manage activities such that they appeal to a variety of people. Supervisors also serve as go-betweens for the director of the parks and the recreation leaders. Recreation supervisors with more knowledge and skills may also oversee specific programs or events and develop programs for people with special needs. Supervisors can create programs for one specific center or for an entire region, depending on the level of responsibility given to the employee.

Directors of recreation and parks create and manage large, comprehensive programs in parks, playgrounds, and a variety of other settings. They are typically advisors to the state and local recreation departments and are often responsible for park and recreation budgets.

Camp counselors supervise and instruct children and adults in a variety of nature-based activities at parks, resorts, and recreation centers. Counselors set

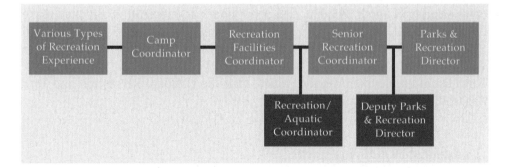

Figure 2–11 *A Career Path in Recreation, Leisure, and Amusement and Theme Parks.* (Source: The National Park Service)

For those who like the great outdoors, managing this kind of recreation would be fun.

up activities, such as hiking, camping, horseback riding, and canoeing. They also may give group classes on subjects such as ceramics, woodworking, and basket weaving.

Recreation workers typically work about 44 hours a week. Many employees in this field, especially camp counselors, often work odd hours, including some nights and weekends. Most of the work is done outdoors; however, recreation directors and supervisors tend to spend more time in an office setting because they are more like managers than activity leaders.

Most full-time recreation worker positions require a bachelor's degree and some even require a graduate degree. As with most positions, experience is preferred. Employers are most favorable toward applicants with a degree in recreation and a strong background in business administration. Many areas of recreation also require specialized training, such as gaining knowledge about allergies and dietetic requirements.

Starting out, full-time recreation workers earn between $24,000 and $28,000 per year. However, with experience and added responsibility, up to $34,500 can be earned yearly by recreation coordinators. Senior recreation coordinators receive salaries of about $45,000, and deputy park and recreation directors make between $75,000 and $112,000. Parks and recreation managers make between $95,000 and more than $175,000. Most employers provide full-time employees with typical benefits, although part-time employees receive few if any benefits. For a list of employment opportunities, visit the National Recreation and Park Association at **www.nrpa.org**.

Amusement and Theme Parks

The theme park industry provides a wide variety of jobs to employees with varying skill levels. Regardless of your position, it is important to remember that patrons to a theme park are at the establishment to have a good time, and they expect friendly, fun-loving workers to be on staff.

There are over 350,000 workers in the theme park industry. These employees come to work every day because they enjoy being surrounded by people who are enjoying a fun and exciting experience. There are many areas of work in theme parks. Just a few of these are designer and artists, inspectors and repairers, scientists, and another area called other professionals.

Designers and artists do everything from coming up with new ride concepts to developing technical plans for the ride to painting and decorating the finished product. They also may create costumes for shows and backdrops for stage setups. They are usually creative individuals who enjoy working with a team to get a project done correctly.

It is helpful for designers in the industry to have some knowledge of computer programs, such as Computer Aided Drafting (CAD), Adobe Illustrator, or Photoshop. Those wanting to aid in the design of new rides should have a background in structural, mechanical, or electrical engineering.

There are many job opportunities for inspectors and repairers in the theme park industry. These employees are very important because they are the people who ensure the safety of everyone at the park. Safety inspectors and specialists are responsible for checking rides for comfort, safety, and durability. Safety inspectors must be certified through the National Association of Amusement Ride Safety Officials and should have at least one year of experience before advancing.

After proper experience and education in the inspection area, one can advance to a senior or lead inspector. These people have a very strong background in any type of engineering and use special equipment and test dummies to evaluate the ride. They conduct experiments that calculate the effect of physical forces on a passenger and do other calculations or experiments to discover whether a rider will get a headache or neck strain from the ride and the restraints.

Ride mechanics and maintenance managers are also integral to the operation of rides. They are responsible for identifying specific problems and fixing them. These jobs also require a background in structural or mechanical engineering.

Scientists of different types are also important to theme park operation. Horticulturists and landscape architects are needed to landscape the park. They maintain the landscaping and often oversee large groups of people to be sure that all plants are healthy and cared for. They typically have associate's or bachelor's degrees in their field.

Biologists and zoologists play a huge role in many theme park operations. Often parks have wildlife attractions, and some even consider animals to be the main draw for crowds. These employees take care of the animals, oversee their habitats, and sometimes even participate in shows with the animals. The educational requirements for this field range from an associates degree to a doctorate.

Countless other occupations are involved in the operation of a theme park. Most parks employ human resources and public relations specialists. These people are in charge of communicating with other employees and the public. A strong background in communications or human resources is recommended for these positions.

Theme parks offer several career paths in retail, operations, food and beverage, and rides.

Sales and marketing specialists also work at theme parks. They are responsible for promoting the amusement park and bringing in guests. They promote the park on a large scale, offering vacation packages to travel agents and large groups. They also analyze park data to determine the best marketing strategies. Backgrounds in sales and marketing are necessary for these jobs.

Theme park managers work in all areas and at all levels of the amusement park industry. General managers or upper-level managers oversee many different departments. They usually need bachelor's or master's degrees in business or management, as well as years of experience.

Beneath park managers are department managers, such as food and beverage service managers or ride operation managers. More managers may work within these departments. For example, a manager for a particular restaurant works under the food and beverage service department manager.

One of the best ways to get involved in the theme park industry is to obtain an internship. Internships provide valuable work experience and are great ways to learn more about various areas of the industry. Having had an internship also is very appealing to potential employers. The Walt Disney Company offers a great college program, which is a good place to spend a summer working for one of America's premier companies. The Disney World Web site is **www.wdwcollegeprogram.com**.

Salaries for theme park front-line managers range from $20,000 to $50,000 per year. Middle managers earn up to $75,000, and general managers earn up to $100,000 annually. One of the biggest perks of being a theme park employee is that all employees, regardless of position, typically receive free admission to the park, complimentary and discount tickets, as well as discounts on food, beverages, merchandise and college scholarship programs.[11]

The Gaming Industry

In the past 25 years, the gaming industry in the United States has seen huge growth. Gambling, once considered illegal in almost every state, is now accessible throughout the country. Eleven states have commercial casino gaming, and 29 states authorize Native American casino-style gaming. Gaming is now also available worldwide, even further expanding the opportunities for employment in the industry.

The gaming industry employs over 700,000 people. The vast expansion of the gaming industry has resulted in a variety of new job openings. People choose to work in the industry because it is known to place people first, whether it be employees or customers. The industry also has many opportunities for employees to learn new skills, which lead to growth and advancement in their careers.

Many tangible benefits may be obtained as an employee in the gaming industry. Most careers include impressive benefits packages and offer many career advancement opportunities. Casinos are known to hire from within, which gives current employees a greater chance to move into better positions over time. Because the gaming industry's positions are so varied, many educational and experiential backgrounds can be adapted to a specific casino's policies.

A variety of careers are specific to the gaming industry (see Figure 2–12). Just a few of these jobs are dealer, slot attendant, marketing director, and casino surveillance. More and more opportunities are becoming available every day as new technology creates more openings. For example, systems such as MindPlay's Table Management System, IGT's EZpay technology, and the introduction of advanced guest service technology will surely create new and exciting technical employment opportunities within the industry.

Although it may appear as if many gaming jobs have very specific qualifications, it is important not to focus too narrowly on one sector. Knowledge of all areas of the industry is integral for advancement. For example, today's casinos now rely on entertainment as well as gaming to bring in patrons. Therefore, an employee at such a casino also needs to have knowledge of the entertainment industry and how casinos operate such events.

A key component to obtaining a job in the gaming industry is that one must have very thorough knowledge of the legal, regulatory, and compliance issues related to daily operations in the casino. Violation of laws can result in lawsuits and cost the company large sums of money. This can be avoided if all employees have the proper background knowledge.

While observing daily activity in a casino provides invaluable work experience, it is also crucial to obtain a college or graduate degree. Even though much

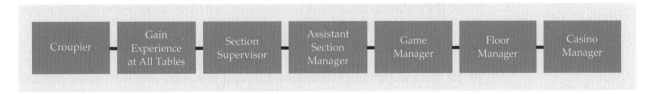

Figure 2–12 *A Career Path in Gaming Entertainment*

A career in gaming entertainment could begin as a croupier.

of the necessary education can take place on the job, applicants who have received an outside education, as well as attended gaming certification programs, have a much better chance of standing out from the competition.

General managers in the gaming industry earn a starting average of $72,800 annually. Casino operators begin at about $36,000, and marketing and sales employees start out at $50,000. Positions typically include full health benefits and yearly bonuses and other compensation, depending on the casino.[12]

Careers in Allied Areas

Several interesting career paths are available in the areas **allied** to the hospitality industry (see Figure 2–13 for an example). Many companies are supplying the hospitality organizations. Imagine, someone has to supply all the food, beverage, furniture, furnishings, and equipment for new hotels, restaurants, resorts, stadiums, clubs, cruise ships, airlines, and so on.

After graduating, it is necessary to obtain a detailed knowledge of the companies' products and services; working in the various departments does this. After gaining an overall knowledge of the company, you can decide if you want to be in sales or one of the other departments, like obtaining supplies from farmers or manufacturers. Some smaller suppliers specialize in a limited number of products, such as menus or uniforms, and have become very successful by offering the industry the products necessary for them to give the standard and level of service expected by their guests.

One advantage of a career in the allied sector of the hospitality industry is that your evenings and weekends are mostly yours to enjoy as you wish. Some people work in the hospitality industry for a few years and then move into the allied area because of the more normal working hours. Salaries in allied areas vary from starting salaries of about $25,000 to over $100,000 per year.

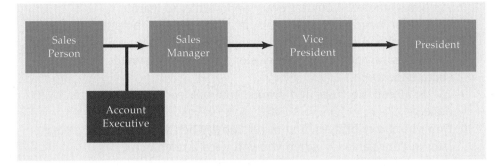

Figure 2–13 *A Career Path for an Allied Area Manager or President*

Internships, Mentorships, and Job Shadowing

Internships and co-ops, either paid or unpaid, offer an opportunity to learn about a particular company and to show the employer that you would make a great permanent employee. Many two- and four-year programs have an internship requirement of supervised practical training that might begin at the front desk, in reservations or communications, or as housekeeping or bell staff in the rooms division. In the food and beverage division the likely beginning positions are server or banquet associate in a house person's position or in the stewarding department, the kitchen, or stores. (These positions will be explained in more detail throughout the text.) An internship will also help you to better relate to the concepts and materials presented in the classroom. Here are some tips for interns:

1. Don't be afraid to talk to people. Don't be intimidated because you are a student. People are sometimes too busy to roll out the red carpet, so you have to make the first move to talk to coworkers and supervisors.
2. Ask for things to do. Don't wait to be told what to do. Solving problems and taking initiative are the best ways to stand out from the crowd.
3. Learn all you can about the industry. Talk to people in different departments as well as clients and vendors.
4. Read everything you can get your hands on. You won't find everything you need to know in the training manual. Reading contracts, letters, memos, press releases, and trade publications helps you become informed on all elements of the business.
5. Don't gripe about the grunt work. There is always something more to learn. How long you do grunt work depends on what you make of it. Everything has a purpose, so learn how the small tasks fit into the big picture.

Internships

An internship gives you a chance to try out the company and the position. It is a good idea to do at least one internship as an hourly paid employee and then continue on as a regular part-time employee during the school year. You can then work full time during the summer, preferably going through the various departments for a couple of years and then doing a management internship. The management internship will give you the chance to experience aspects of supervision that are essential for future success.

6. Act like a student! Look for every opportunity to learn!
7. Hitch your wagon to a star. Learn from the people who are the superstar performers and most respected individuals in the department.
8. Get in the information loop. Decisions aren't always made in a conference room.
9. Ask to attend meetings and events. You will learn how things really get done.
10. Don't burn any bridges. You never know when you will see someone later in your career or when you will need a reference.

A **mentor** is a guide through life, someone who can show you the ropes along the way. A mentor can help you avoid some basic career mistakes by offering advice or by simply listening to you talk through a problem to its solution.

Remember to thank your mentor with a personal handwritten note from time to time. If you do not have a mentor, now is a good time to get one. Ask someone you respect to be your mentor, or ask more than one person. For instance, some people have one mentor for school and one for industry.

Job shadowing is often the first experience related to work or a career that many of us experience. The purpose of job shadowing is to gain familiarity with a particular job or jobs. Today, several high schools and colleges arrange with industry to organize Groundhog Day in February when thousands of students look toward the hospitality industry for a day's experience of job shadowing. Suggestions for a successful job shadow:

1. Learn about the company before you arrive.
2. Set a goal for what you want to accomplish.
3. Dress professionally.
4. Show true interest in the environment.
5. Ask questions.
6. Make the most of limited time.
7. Network.
8. Be an active participant.
9. Follow safety and security procedures.
10. Follow up with a handwritten "thank you" note to your host.

Don't forget to have fun! And remember while you're interning or job shadowing that somebody has to be general manager, department head, supervisor, and so on.

Career Paths and Résumé Writing

Creating your own career path can be both an exciting and a daunting task. Often, we do not know exactly where we want to be in five or ten years. The best advice is to follow your interests. Do what you love to do and success will soon come. Often we assess our own character and personality to determine a suitable path. Some opt for the accounting and financial and control side of the business; others, perhaps with more outgoing personalities, vie for sales and marketing; others prefer operations, which could be either in back or in front of the house.

Résumés

It is a good idea to build your résumé with work experience. The experience will also help you relate your academic course work to the real world. Most colleges have a system of faculty advisors, many of whom have industry contacts that may be helpful in taking the first step along a career path.

Corporate recruiters have to distinguish your résumé from among hundreds they receive each year. Here are some tips from a selection of recruiters that should help you to succeed in your career.[13]

Are you hardworking and conscientious? What will you do for the Company? Does your résumé match the job specifications? Make sure your résumé is letter perfect. Have your résumé proofread by several industry practitioners as well as professors and friends.

A good résumé includes the following information:

- Heading with your name, address, and telephone number
- Career objective
- Career experience
- Other accomplishments such as scholarships, awards, honors, teams, volunteer work, and so on
- Education
- References, including telephone numbers, on a separate page

A suggested format for a résumé is shown in Figure 2–14.

Perfecting a résumé requires careful thought. It is a good idea to show it to several people who know you and some who are used to reviewing résumés. It is natural to be slightly unsure of the right words to use. One suggestion is to consider your accomplishments. You may have worked on the school prom committee or as a volunteer for a worthy organization. Everyone has done something that can embellish the résumé—remember that you have to stand out from your peers or competition.

Consider a young woman who was a star on the track team in high school. She was not going to put that on her résumé because she did not think it was important. But, when asked what she did to become an accomplished athlete, she replied that she had to train (long hours of practice require dedication); when asked what it took to win, she replied, "Determination." These same qualities are the same as what it takes to be successful in business.

Cover Letters

Every time you mail a résumé, you should also send a cover letter to introduce yourself and explain why you are sending your résumé. Because this is your first contact with the company you are approaching, you need to make a good

Your Name
Address
Telephone Number

Career Objective

Work Experience

Awards/Honors

Skills

Education

References

Figure 2–14   *Sample Résumé Format*

impression. A businesslike letter has your name, address, and telephone number at the top right-hand corner of the page. The letter should begin with "Dear Ms. or Mr. _____:" and might continue "I am pleased to apply for the position of _____ at the XYZ company. I will be available for summer work experience on May 28, 2008. Your company was recommended to me by _____, who worked with you last year. Enclosed is a copy of my résumé in which you will notice (here is where you mention some skills or relevant experience that qualifies you for the position)."

The final paragraph should restate your keen interest in the position and end by requesting an interview. The appropriate closing is "Yours sincerely," followed by your name, leaving room for your signature.

Are you qualified? Recruiters typically look at three things to judge a student's job qualifications: academic record, work experience, and extracurricular activities.

Academic Record

A recruiter can easily discard résumés of students with a cumulative GPA below 3.00. Jeff Speck suggests that omitting a mediocre GPA from your résumé is not the best solution, simply because most students willingly include their averages.[14] If you have a low overall GPA, one solution might be to list your GPA in the major if that is significantly higher.

If you have good grades, were on the dean's list, graduated with honors, and so on, put this on your résumé. Academic distinction is one sure way of gaining the attention of a recruiter.

Work Experience

Your record should prove that you have accomplished something every summer and possibly while going to school. Obviously, experience in the same or a similar capacity is desirable. An internship or co-op work experience is an additional asset. Include other work experiences that you have had because they all add up—even jobs such as hostessing can suggest that you have obtained some good interpersonal experience. Being a busperson or a quick service food employee may not sound very exciting, but it is where most of us began. Each of the beginning level positions gives us exposure to a workplace environment and allows us to gain experience.

Extracurricular Activities

Achieving recognition as an Eagle Scout or in activities like student leadership always improves your chances for employment. If you excelled in sports or club activities, use this information on your résumé to show commitment and dedication. Volunteer work is an excellent way to look good on a résumé, especially if you organize an event that contributes to an organization. A résumé, in itself, will not secure you employment, but it can open the doors to an interview.

Check Your Knowledge

1. What are the reasons for Disney's service success?
2. Which do you think are the most important tips on internships, mentors, and job shadowing?
3. What path will your career follow?

Job Interviews

No matter how many interviews we do, most people still get butterflies in the stomach when faced with another one. These feelings are natural because we are on edge about a face-to-face meeting that could have a major impact on our career and lives. An interview is like sitting next to someone on an airplane flight—it takes us about 20 seconds to determine if we really want to talk to the person sitting next to us or read a magazine instead.

How to Interview

Mona Melanson, a staffing consultant with Bank of America, has wisely suggested a ten-step approach to polish your interviewing skills.[15]

1. Ask yourself how well you fit the jobs for which you're interviewing. You are going to be grilled about your skills, education, motivation, accomplishments, strengths, and weaknesses. The interviewer is asking himself or herself, "Why should I hire you for this job?"
2. A good way to begin is to match your skills and qualifications to those required for that position. You could gather data from a variety of sources, in categories such as education and training, extracurricular activities, summer and part-time jobs, and volunteer and community service. In these categories, jot down feedback from your professors, employers, and other people with whom you have interacted. Remember that in management training interviews, recruiters want to see leadership and initiative capabilities.
3. Once you have completed your list, you will probably be surprised at how many items there are. Next, highlight five or six items that correspond to some of the job qualifications specified. Then prepare a brief talk about those so you can use them during an interview.
4. Do your homework on the company. Do research on the Internet, in the library, call the company's public relations office, and ask your career office for the names of former students now working for the corporation in which you are interested. Find out about the corporation's philosophy, mission, goals, objectives, and culture. Become knowledgeable about the size, organization structure, and future plans of the corporation.
5. Be ready to ask questions of the interviewer. Ideally, these should be work-related questions; wait until later to discuss salary (have patience; nothing disturbs an interviewer more than someone who wants to discuss money up front). The appropriate time to inquire about the compensation and benefit package is generally toward the end of the interview—if the interviewer has not already mentioned it.
6. Stage a number of dress rehearsals with someone else—a roommate, a friend, a career counselor, or a professor. Give your interviewer a list of questions that you think you might be asked. Record or, even better, video your interviews. Remember, some taboos include the following:
   * Shaking hands like a wet fish
   * Mumbling, fidgeting
   * Going off on tangents
   * Appearing unnecessarily tense

- Using slang or malapropisms
- Speaking too softly or too loudly
- Avoiding eye contact

Body language is important during interviews. Some experts suggest adopting a posture similar to that of the interviewer. Remain composed, relaxed, and confident, and demonstrate visible interest.

7. Dress in a businesslike manner. A man should wear a business suit, dress shoes, a pressed white shirt, or a reasonably conservative shirt—and no earrings. A woman should wear a business suit, blouse, hose, and shoes, with conservative jewelry and makeup. For both men and women, the first impression is extremely important. Image is everything!

8. Arrive early; if possible, go to the location once before the interview to be certain you know where it is. Remember that a smile and a firm handshake make a good impression. Once the interview has begun, listen to the questions carefully, because interviewers often complain that students do not answer questions correctly. One tip is to rephrase part of each question you are asked at the beginning of your answer. This technique also gives you more time to formulate your responses. Remember to stress your strengths. For example, offer statements such as "I have been told by one of my professors that I express myself well both in writing and orally" or "I work well under pressure" or "I have a positive attitude."

9. At the close of the interview, thank the interviewer for the opportunity to discuss your qualifications. Before shaking hands, it is fully acceptable to ask the interviewer about when you might expect to hear about a decision.

10. Write a thank you note to the interviewer, reinforcing the reasons why you feel you could perform well on that job.

Here are some suggestions for questions to ask the interviewer:
- What are the duties and responsibilities of this position?
- Please describe the training program.
- How would you characterize the management philosophy at your company?
- If I join your company, what will my career path likely be?
- Given my education and background, how would you estimate my chances for advancement?
- Does your company offer promotional opportunities by region, nationally, or internationally?

Do not ask how much salary the position offers until either you have been offered a position or until you are well into the final stages of the interview.

Here are some questions an interviewer might ask:
- What are your future career plans?
- When are you available and what are your available hours?
- What is your (hotel, restaurant, or tourism) work experience?
- What are/were your duties and responsibilities?

- How well do you think you succeeded in meeting your duties and responsibilities?
- What are your goals and ambitions?
- Where do you see yourself three to five years from now?
- What did you like most and least about your job?
- Describe how you would prepare an item of the menu.
- Why should I hire you?
- What qualifications do you have that make you think you will be successful in the hospitality industry?

Overall, remember that good judgment comes from experience, and experience comes from bad judgment, and success is not what you are but what you have overcome to be what you are.

Trends

- Several companies do on-campus recruiting; the number goes up in a strong economy and down in a weak economy.
- Due to cost-cutting measures, some companies do not have the extensive formal management training program they used to; instead they offer graduates regular employment and promote depending on performance, as positions become available.
- Companies are realizing that they cannot burn out managers by working them too many hours. Many now require their managers to work a 50-hour week and have two days off.
- Professionalism and ethics are increasingly important as a foundation for success in the hospitality industry.

CASE STUDY

Don't Call Us ...

Erick was wondering why he had not heard from the company he had interviewed with two weeks ago. He thought the interview had gone well, but as he reflected on it, he began to have doubts. Maybe his normal assertive behavior was not considered as being knowledgeable or authoritative. He tried to make an impact, but perhaps it was not appropriate. He remembered how the interviewer had looked at him as they shook hands. Erick wore "baggies" and had forgotten to remove the ring from his tongue; his shirt was not properly ironed and his hair coloring may have been too much.

Expecting a management position right from the get-go seemed to surprise the interviewer. Erick's experience was limited to having been a buser at a local restaurant, but he had a college degree and that, he figured, should put him in the management ranks.

Question

1. What did Erick do wrong, or what should he have done in relation to the interview?

CAREER INFORMATION

The hospitality industry offers careers that are often fast-paced, exciting, and very rewarding. Many different and stimulating types of work fall into this category, requiring varying skill levels and amounts of responsibility. It is a field that offers rapid advancement to those individuals with commitment and dedication.

The hospitality field is not for people seeking a regular five-day 40-hour workweek with weekends off. Hospitality professionals get paid to work when other people are enjoying themselves. Restaurants are often open seven days a week and hotels operate 24 hours a day 365 days a year. As a manager you can expect to work varying hours ranging from 50 to 65 hours per week. The days and times you will be expected to work will vary, along with your days off.

If you choose to become a hospitality manager, it is important that you work in the field of hospitality while attending college! A part-time job and/or internship can help you find out what you want to do. By the time you are a junior you should be working at least 20 to 30 hours per week while going to school. It is also important to develop the foundation skills needed to be a hospitality manager. Learning the basic skills associated with your area of hospitality are invaluable when you become a manager. Effective restaurant managers possess a working knowledge of the various job functions, which include cooking, scheduling, purchasing, waiting tables, expediting, washing dishes, and in many cases bartending.

An important tool for tracking your progress in developing basic skills is a résumé. Writing a résumé and keeping it current forces you to examine your strengths and weaknesses in your chosen area of hospitality. It also will cause you to ask hard questions about what you really want to do with your career. Having a current résumé also allows you to take advantage of opportunities that may present themselves unexpectedly, such as scholarships, internships, or a better employment offer.

Upon graduation from college, experience needs to reflect desire! Selling yourself in an interview is difficult if not impossible unless you have relevant experience. Recruiters' ultimate fear is employee turnover. Hiring an individual and then having that person quit in a few months is an expensive proposition for companies. Employers are extremely reluctant to hire a person who does not have relevant experience.

America has become a service-oriented economy and people are traveling and dining out more than ever. The demand for hospitality managers has never been greater. Careers offer entry-level salaries of $30,000 to $40,000 per year for college graduates. Companies are also realizing that to keep their managers they have to address quality-of-life issues. Many companies now limit the number of hours managers work and give them two days off per week. The old stories about managers working endless hours and never having time off are gone. If you ever find yourself in such a situation, it is probably time to look for another employer. Such an environment will ruin your personal relationships and eventually cause you to "burn out" and leave the industry.

A successful career doesn't just happen. It requires planning, effort, ability, and education. If you take the time to find out which hospitality career is for you and develop your foundation skills while going to college, you will find that you are entering a field that has no substitutes.

Related Web Sites

www.hcareers.com—resource for hospitality careers
www.chrie.org—Council of Hotel, Restaurant & Institutional Educators Web site
www.internshipsprograms.com—internship site
www.prenhall.com/walker—companion Web site for this book

Courtesy of Charlie Adams

SUMMARY

1. The concept of a career path shows the career progression available in each segment of the hospitality industry. It differs from a career ladder in that it is not always a straightforward progression.
2. The umbrella scope of hospitality and tourism encompasses a variety of jobs in tourism and travel, lodging, event management, restaurant and managed services, recreation, and allied industries.
3. The hospitality industry is a service industry, one in which employees take pride in caring about others.
4. The qualities and characteristics beneficial for a career in the hospitality industry are honesty, dedication, being a team player, preparedness to work long hours over various shifts, communication skills, leadership, and ambition, just to name a few.
5. To be sure that your strengths and weaknesses work well with your chosen career, it is necessary to do a self-assessment before choosing a specific career path.
6. Involvement with on-campus and professional hospitality and tourism organizations gives you a head start into the future. It is never too early to start; involvement shows potential employers that you have made a commitment to your chosen career.

KEY WORDS AND CONCEPTS

Allied areas
Career path
Entry-level position
Ethics

Etiquette
Internship
Job shadowing

Management-training
program
Mentor

Philosophy
Service oriented
Social responsibility

REVIEW QUESTIONS

1. What is the difference between a career path and a career ladder? Why does the term *career path* best describe progression in the hospitality industry?
2. What is the purpose of conducting a self-assessment?
3. Define the Golden Rule and how it applies to the hospitality industry.
4. What are the primary differences between commercial and noncommercial foodservices?
5. What kind of education is necessary to become a recreation worker?

INTERNET EXERCISES

1. Go to ARAMARK's Web site at **www.aramark.com** and compare it to Sodexho at **www.sodexhousa.com**. What is similar about these two companies? How do they differ?
2. Go to the Web site that is a companion to this book: **prenhall.com/pineapple**. It offers a comprehensive list of hospitality-related Internet resources. Select two of the major hospitality Web sites that interest you as a possible career choice and see what they have to offer. Share your results with your class.

APPLY YOUR KNOWLEDGE

1. State your career goal and write a career path for yourself, listing the positions along the way to your career goal.

SUGGESTED ACTIVITY

Write up your résumé and a cover letter for a position that you would like to apply for.

ENDNOTES

1. Personal correspondence with Duncan Dixon, January 21, 2004.
2. Marcus Buckingham and Donald O. Clifton, *Now, Discover Your Strengths,* Northampton, MA: Free Press, 2001.
3. **http://www.religioustolerance.org**. May 6, 2005.
4. Stephen S. Hall (ed.), *Ethics in Hospitality Management: A Book of Readings.* East Lansing, MI: Educational Institute, American Hotel and Lodging Association, 1992, p. 75.
5. Ibid., p. 108.
6. **http://www.restaurant.org/research/ind-glance.cfm.**
7. **www.bls.gov**. August 16, 2005. U.S. Department of Labor Stastics.
8. This profile draws on Hyatt corporation's Web site.
9. *Restaurant Voice,* December 18, 2003, p. 4.
10. Adapted from Holli R. Cosgrove, *Encyclopedia of Careers and Vocational Guidance,* vol. 2. Chicago: Ferguson, 2000–2004.

11. **www.sixflags.com.** July 19, 2005.
12. *Career Opportunities in the Casino Industry.* The Detroit New Michigan Casino Guide. November 12, 2003.
13. Personal Convesation with Holly Carvalho. August 16, 2005.
14. Ibid.
15. The section draws on Mona Melanson, "Beat the Butterflies: A Ten-Step Approach to Polish Your Interview Skills," *National Employment Weekly (College Edition),* vol. 6, no. 3, Fall 1989, p. 31.

WEB RESOURCES

Careers
www.hmscareers.com

Hotel Sales and Marketing International
www.hsmai.org

Hotel and Restaurant Jobs
www.hotelrestaurantjobs.com

American Airlines
www.aa.com

ARAMARK
www.aramark.com

Sodexho
www.sodexhousa.com

American Hotel & Lodging Association
www.al&ha.com

Hyatt Hotels
www.hyatt.com

Club Managers Association
www.cmaa.org

Club Corp
www.clubcorp.com

American Society of Association Executives
www.asaenet.org

International Society of Meeting Planners
www.iami.org

Professional Convention Management Association
www.pcma.org

Tourism

After reading and studying this chapter, you should be able to:

- Define tourism.
- Outline the important international and domestic tourism organizations.
- Describe the economic impact of tourism.
- Identify promoters of tourism.
- List reasons why people travel.
- Describe the sociocultural impact of tourism.
- Describe ecotourism.

What Is Tourism?

Tourism is a dynamic, evolving, consumer-driven force and is the world's largest industry if all its interrelated components are placed under one umbrella: travel; lodging; conventions, expositions, meetings, events; restaurants, managed services; and recreation. Tourism plays a foundational role in framing the various services that hospitality companies perform.

The leading international organization in the field of travel and tourism, the World Tourism Organization (WTO), is vested by the United Nations with a central and decisive role in promoting the development of responsible, sustainable, and universally accessible tourism, with the aim of contributing to economic development, international understanding, peace, prosperity, and universal respect for, and observance of, human rights and fundamental freedoms. In pursuing this aim, the organization pays particular attention to the interests of the developing countries in the field of tourism.

Acting as an umbrella organization for world tourism, WTO plays a catalytic role in promoting technology transfers and international cooperation, stimulating and developing public–private sector partnerships, and encouraging the implementation of the Global Code of Ethics for Tourism. The WTO is dedicated to ensuring that member countries, tourist destinations, and businesses maximize the positive economic, social, and cultural effects of tourism and fully reap its benefits, while minimizing its negative social and environmental impacts.

Through tourism, the WTO aims at stimulating economic growth and job creation, providing incentives for protecting the environment and cultural heritage, and promoting peace, prosperity, and respect for human rights. Membership includes 143 countries, 7 territories, and some 350 affiliate members representing the private sector, educational institutions, tourism associations, and local tourism authorities. Unfortunately, the United States is not a member, but it may soon be.

The WTO and the World Travel and Tourism Council declare the travel and tourism industry to have the following characteristics:[1]

- A 24-hour-a-day, 7-day-week, 52-week a year economic driver
- Accounts for 10.2 percent of world GDP
- Employer of 214 million people or 7.8 percent of the global work force
- Creation of more than 5.5 million travel and tourism jobs per year during the 2000s
- U.S. tourism spending of $72.3 billion
- Leading producer of tax revenues
- Forecasted 4.6 percent growth between 2006 and 2015 (despite the tsunami, SARS, bird flu, and terrorism)

Given the declining manufacturing and agricultural industries, and in many countries the consequent rise in unemployment, world leaders should turn to the service industries for real strategic employment gains.

Waikiki Beach is a popular tourist destination.

Tourism for Prosperity and Peace

At the start of the new millennium, tourism is firmly established as the number one industry in many countries and the fastest-growing economic sector in terms of foreign exchange earnings and job creation. International tourism is the world's largest export earner and an important factor in the balance of payments of most nations.

Tourism has become one of the world's most important sources of employment. It stimulates enormous investment in infrastructure, most of which helps to improve the living conditions of residents as well as tourists. It provides governments with substantial tax revenues. Most new tourism jobs and business are created in the developing countries, helping to equalize economic opportunities and keep rural residents from moving to overcrowded cities. Intercultural awareness and personal friendships fostered through tourism are a powerful force for improving international understanding and contributing to peace among all the nations of the world.

The World Tourism Organization encourages governments, in partnership with the private sector, local authorities and nongovernmental organizations, to play a vital role in tourism. The WTO helps countries throughout the world to maximize the positive impacts of tourism, while minimizing its possible negative consequences on the environment and societies.[2] Tourism, the world's largest industry, offers the greatest global employment prospects. This trend is caused by the following factors:

1. The opening of borders; despite security concerns, we can travel to more countries now than ten years ago. The United States has a visa waiver program with 28 European countries.
2. An increase in disposable income and vacations
3. Reasonably priced airfares
4. An increase in the number of people with more time and money
5. More people with the urge to travel

According to the World Travel and Tourism Council—the industry's business leaders' forum—tourism and travel generate, directly and indirectly, 10.2 percent of global gross domestic product (GDP), investment, and employment. The industry is forecast to grow strongly in real terms during the next ten years. This means a growth of jobs in the United States and abroad.

Long-Term Prospects: Tourism 2020 Vision

Despite the terrorism attacks and a weak economic recovery, the long-term prospects for tourism appear to be good. *Tourism 2020 Vision* is the World Tourism Organization's long-term forecast and assessment of the development of tourism for the first 20 years of the new millennium. An essential outcome of the Tourism 2020 Vision is quantitative forecasts covering a 25-year period, with 1995 as the base year and forecasts for 2000, 2010, and 2020 (Figure 3–1).

Although the evolution of tourism in the last few years has been irregular, WTO maintains its long-term forecast for the moment. The underlying structural trends of the forecast are believed not to have significantly changed. Experience shows that in the short term, periods of faster growth (1995, 1996, 2000) alternate with periods of slow growth (2001 and 2002). While the pace of growth until 2000 actually exceeded the Tourism 2020 Vision forecast, it is generally expected that the current slowdown will be compensated for in the mid-to long term.

WTO's Tourism 2020 Vision forecasts that international arrivals are expected to reach over 1.56 billion by the year 2020. Of these, 1.2 billion will be intraregional and 0.4 billion will be long-haul travelers.

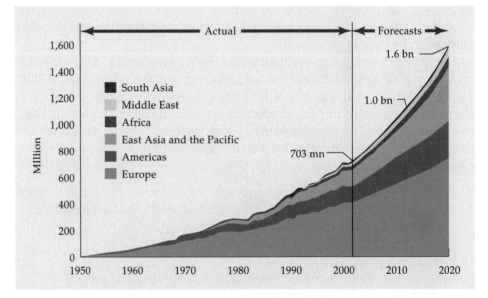

Figure 3–1 *Actual and Forecast Tourism Arrivals 1950–2020*
(Source: World Tourism Organization)

The total tourist arrivals by region show that by 2020 the top three receiving regions will be Europe (717 million tourists), East Asia and the Pacific (397 million), and the Americas (282 million), followed by Africa, the Middle East, and South Asia.

The fact that tourism is expected to grow rapidly presents both tremendous opportunities and challenges. The good news is the variety of exciting career prospects for today's hospitality and tourism graduates. Tourism, although a mature industry, is a young profession. Careful management of tourism and travel will be necessary to avoid repercussions and negativism toward the "pesky" tourist, which is already happening to some extent in Europe, where the sheer number of tourists overwhelms attractions and facilities.

There is an **interdependency** between the various segments of tourism, travel, lodging, foodservice, and recreation. Hotel guests need to travel to reach the hotel. They eat in nearby restaurants and visit attractions. Each segment is, to an extent, dependent on another for business.

Definition of Tourism

The World Tourism Organization's definition of tourism is "Tourism comprises the activities of persons traveling to and staying in places outside their usual environment for not more than one consecutive year for leisure, business, and other purposes."[3]

For many developing nations, tourism represents a relatively large percentage of gross national product and an easy way of gaining a balance of trade with other nations.

Tourism means different things to different people. To simplify tourism, it is sometimes categorized in terms of the following factors:

Geography: International, regional, national, state, provincial, country, city

Ownership: Government, quasi-government, private

Function: Regulators, suppliers, marketers, developers, consultants, researchers, educators, publishers, professional associations, trade organizations, consumer organizations

Industry: Transportation (air, bus, rail, auto, cruise), travel agents, tour wholesalers, lodging, attractions, recreation

Motive: Profit or nonprofit[4]

Grenelle Foster

Ask Mr. Foster, the oldest U.S. travel agency, began in 1888 when Ward Grenelle Foster opened a "travel information office" in St. Augustine, Florida. When the town's residents or travelers had queries concerning directions or visitors' information, they were directed not to the local Seven Eleven, but instead to W. G. Foster's gift shop, where they could "ask Mr. Foster." Foster later adopted this phrase as the name for his small business.

In the 1890s, "Ask Mr. Foster" expanded to all three coasts of the Sunshine State and later to New York and other metropolitan centers. The offices were usually conspicuously located in large buildings, such as hotels and department stores, with heavy foot traffic. The company provided free information and reservations. Their brochure promised to "plan your trip, secure your ticket, make your reservations for hotels, steamers, autos, schools, and railroads—anywhere in the world."

Despite its immense success, Foster decided to sell the business in 1928. It then changed hands several times before it was bought in 1979 by the Carlson Companies, the hospitality conglomerate based in Minneapolis, Minnesota. In 1988, the company had more than 750 offices in 46 states, and its total sales exceeded that of American Express travel agency sales.

There are now 876 Carlson Wagonlit offices that serve travelers in 140 countries. (carlson.com)

Donald E. Lundberg, *Tourist Business*, New York: Van Nostrand Reinhold, 1990, p. 9.

Airlines

Over the past few years—with the exception of Southwest, AirTran, and Jet Blue—major U.S. airlines have lost billions of dollars. One reason is competition from low-cost domestic and international airlines.

Since September 11, 2001, business travelers continue to spend less, and airlines' pension, fuel, and security costs have risen. The major airlines are laying off employees, delaying delivery of new jets, and closing some hubs, reservations, and maintenance centers in efforts to reduce costs. United Airlines is emerging from Chapter 11 bankruptcy protection and is levying an additional fuel surcharge on tickets just to stay in the air.

The major U.S. airlines have formed strategic alliances with partner airlines to provide passengers with easier ticket purchases and transportation to destinations in countries not served by U.S. airlines. Some examples are Tampa, Florida, to Hong Kong; American Airlines to Los Angeles; and Cathay Pacific to Hong Kong.

Alliances of this nature will allow airlines access to each other's feeder markets and to resources that will enable them to flourish in what will ultimately be a worldwide deregulation. A feeder market is a market that provides the source—in this case, passengers for the particular destination. Ultimately, any major European airline without a strategic alliance in the United States will only limit its own horizons and lose market share.

Southwest operates more efficiently than the competition despite the fact that its work force is unionized. Southwest gets more flight time from its pilots than American—672 hours a year versus 371—and racks up 60 percent more passenger miles per flight attendant. These efficiencies have resulted in annual profits for 30 consecutive years as a result of Southwest's dedication to a low-cost, high-customer-satisfaction strategy.

Carriers such as Southwest, AirTran, Ted (short for United), Song (Delta), and Jet Blue have lower operating costs because they use only one type of aircraft, fly point-to-point, and offer a "no frills" service. Their lower fares have forced many larger airlines to retreat.

Passenger talks with JetBlue agent.

The giant double-decker Airbus A380 aircraft can carry up to 550 passengers for a distance of up to 8,000 miles.

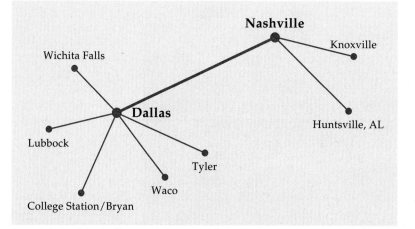

Figure 3–2 *The Hub-and-Spoke System*

To reduce losses brought about by deregulation and higher fuel costs, major carriers eliminated unprofitable routes, often those serving smaller cities. New airlines began operating shuttle services between the smaller cities and the nearest larger or hub city. This created the hub-and-spoke system (see Figure 3–2).

The Hub-and-Spoke System

To remain efficient and cost effective, major U.S. airlines have adopted a **hub-and-spoke system,** which enables passengers to travel from one smaller city to another smaller city via a hub or even two hubs. Similarly, passengers may originate their travel from a small city and use the hub to reach connecting flights to destinations throughout the world.

The hub-and-spoke system has two main benefits: (1) Airlines can service more cities at a lower cost, and (2) airlines can maximize passenger loads from small cities, thereby saving fuel.

Cruise Ships

More than 200 cruise lines offer a variety of wonderful vacations, from a Carnival cruise to freighters that carry only a few passengers. Travelers associate a certain romance with cruising to exotic locations and being pampered all day.

Being on a cruise ship is like being on a floating resort. Accommodations range from luxurious suites to cabins that are even smaller than most hotel rooms. Attractions and distractions range from early-morning workouts to fabulous meals, with nightlife consisting of dancing, cabarets, and sometimes casinos. Day life might involve relaxation, visits to the hair salon or spa, organized games, or simply reclining in a deck chair by the pool. Nonstop entertainment includes language lessons, charm classes, port-of-call briefings, cooking, dances, bridge, table tennis, shuffleboard, and more.

*Take a Princess cruise
for a dream vacation.*

For example, the *Diamond Princess* is a "super Love Boat" weighing in at 113,000 tons and costing $400 million. This ship is longer than two football fields and capable of carrying up to 3,000 passengers.

The cruise market has increased dramatically in recent years. About 9.0 million Americans cruise each year. Rates vary from a starting point of $85 per person per day on Carnival Cruise Lines to $700 on the *Radisson Diamond.* Rates typically are quoted per diem (per day) and are cruise-only figures, based on double occupancy.

Some 215 ships are providing lake and river, but mostly oceangoing cruises. The spectacular new ships with multideck atriums and razzle-dazzle entertainment cater to the market with a median income of $50,000 a year.

Carnival Cruise Lines is the most successful financially, netting about 20 percent of sales. It targets adults between the ages of 25 and 54, and expects to attract close to 3 million passengers with its spectacular atriums and round-the-clock activities. Its largest income, other than the fare itself, is from beverage service. Casino income is also high, and its casinos are the largest afloat. Carnival hopes that passengers will enjoy buying drinks and putting quarters, or preferably dollars, into the shipboard slot machines. They also hope their passengers will not mind their small cabins, since the activities on the ship occupy all their waking hours and much of the night.

No two ships are alike. Each has its own personality and character. The nationality of the ship's officers and staff contributes greatly to the ship's ambiance. For example, the ships under the Holland America flag have Dutch officers and Indonesian/Filipino crew, and those belonging to the Epirotiki flag have Greek officers and crew.

Casual ships cater to young couples, singles, and families with children. At the other end of the spectrum, ships that appeal to the upscale crowd draw a mature clientele that prefers a more sedate atmosphere, low-key entertainment, and dressing for dinner.

In 2005 alone, about 8.4 million passengers vacationed on a ship. Many passengers are remarkably loyal to their particular vessel; as many as half of the

A Day in the Life of Richard Spacey
Cruise Director, Royal Caribbean International

Voyager of the Seas, one of the largest and most innovative cruise ships ever built, has a total guest capacity of 3,700 with 1,200 crew members. *Voyager of the Seas* is truly a revolution in the cruising industry. A virtual city in itself, she features the world's first floating ice skating rink, a rock climbing wall, an inline skating track, and the largest and most technically advanced theater afloat. There is a four-story Royal Promenade shopping and entertainment boulevard spanning the length of the ship that acts as a hub for the ship's vast array of activities and entertainment. Cruise director Richard Spacey was instrumental in implementing the unique entertainment and activities program aboard with a support staff of 130 people. What follows is an account of a day in the life of the cruise director of one of the largest ships in the world.

Monday—First Day at Sea

7:30–8:30 A.M. Yesterday we embarked 3,650 guests in Miami and headed for our first port of call, Labadee, our own private island on the coast of Hispaniola. Before most of the guests are up for the day, I plan and submit our daily activities schedule for the rest of the voyage to our hotel director for his approval. All of the cruise director's staff management team have submitted their reports after our staff meeting at embarkation yesterday. Scheduling of the twelve activities staff for the week is handled by the assistant cruise director, who also submits the payroll and overtime hours for my approval. Our cruise programs administrator says that three couples were married in the wedding chapel yesterday, and they are included in the 108 couples that have chosen to spend their honeymoon with us. A special party will be held later on in the week to celebrate this happy occasion. The youth activities manager reports that there are over 600 children aboard, ranging in age from 3 to 17. The youth activities manager and her team of 13 are responsible for providing age-appropriate activities for our junior cruisers. We offer a special deck and pool area/arcade for children in addition to our extensive youth facilities, which include a teen disco.

Fourteen hundred international guests are aboard and they consist of 60 different nationalities. The international ambassador (who speaks five languages) provides translations of our daily program and acts as the cruise director's liaison for all of our international guests.

A large part of our business is group and incentive business. The group coordinator appropriates lounges and facilities for these special group events under the auspices of the cruise director. There will be seminars, group meetings, presentations, and cocktail parties. We have a state-of-the-art conference center/executive boardroom/screening room in addition to a large convention facility named "Studio B," which doubles as the ice rink. A retractable floor over the ice rink makes this a great space for large conventions. The shore excursion manager reports that tour sales are good for this voyage among the fifty land-based excursions that we offer. All of this information is consolidated into a report to the hotel director that is submitted on a daily basis.

8:45–9:30 A.M. Hotel director's meeting. All of the division heads in the Hotel Department meet to discuss the daily operation of this floating hotel. Today's agenda includes a monthly safety meeting. Each division head presents his or her monthly report on safety and environmental protection. Hospitality and the safety of our guests and crew are our top priorities.

9:45 A.M. The start of my public duties. I give a daily announcement and rundown of all the activities and entertainment happenings around the ship.

10:00 A.M. Morning walkaround. Time to kick off the first session of Jackpot Bingo for the week. On my way through the promenade, I encounter our interactive performers hamming it up with our guests. This is a troupe of two highly skilled performers. (Some of them are former Ringling Brothers' clowns.) They play different characters throughout the voyage and add quite a lot to the guest experience. I also stop by the Royal Caribbean Online Internet center, which is quite busy. We also offer an in-stateroom hook-up of personal computers for unlimited Internet access (for a fee).

10:30 A.M. The Studio B ice rink is busy with guests skating at our first All Skate session. There are several sessions throughout the day. The ice skating cast (ten individuals) are responsible for running the sessions as well as skating in our Ice Show.

11:00 A.M. Time to change out of my day uniform into a business suit and put on stage makeup for the taping of

continued

our onboard talk and information show, "Voyager Live." I produce this segment from the Royal Promenade. We have three video programmers and an interactive television technician. Interactive TV allows our guests to order room service, excursions, and movies with the click of a button in the privacy of their staterooms.

I am one of the main sources for revenue promotion on board. The television programming is a great asset in a small floating city of this size. Thirty-seven channels offer safety information, music, shopping tips, CNBC, CNN, ESPN, and free movies in several languages.

Noon Lunch with the staff in the Officers and Staff Dining Room.

1:00 P.M. Change out of the business suit into shorts and a Polo shirt to emcee the Belly Flop Competition at 1:30 poolside. Always a "big" event among our guests. Quite a few laughs. This is followed by horse racing, cruising style. We pick six jockeys who move six wooden horses by a roll of the dice. The betting is fierce as the guests cheer their favorite horses on. I become the track announcer for three races and horse auctioneer. Today we auction off the six horses for our Voyager Derby later in the week. The horses go to the highest bidder and then the "owners" run them in a race later on in the week for all the money. The six horses go for $2,100. A nice pot for one lucky winner.

2:30 P.M. I stop by the Sports Court to check out the action. The sports court is full of families enjoying our Family Hour activities with the youth staff. We offer a nine-hole miniature golf course, golf driving simulator, full-court basketball/volleyball, inline skating, Ping Pong, and a rock climbing wall that rises up the smoke-stack 200 feet above sea level—the best view in the Caribbean. By the end of the day, 125 people will have climbed the wall.

3:00–4:30 P.M. POWER NAP TIME. The day will not end until about 12:30 A.M. Being "on stage" and available practically twenty-four hours a day can take its toll. This nap will carry me through until the end of the evening.

6:00 P.M. Back to the office to catch up on e-mail and general administrative business. It is also time to work on budget and revenue forecasting for the upcoming year.

7:30 P.M. Off to the Royal Promenade deck to mingle with the guests at the Welcome Aboard reception. The captain gives his welcome speech and then we send them off to their dinner or the show at 8:30.

8:30 P.M. Meet in the Champagne Bar with the hotel director before dinner. Tonight we will entertain guests who are on their fiftieth cruise and also a representative from an insurance company who is thinking of booking 700 guests on a future cruise with us.

9:00 P.M. On my way to the dining room, I introduce our production show in the La Scala Theater for the main seating guests.

10:45 P.M. After dessert, I introduce the show for second seating guests and watch the show for quality control.

11:45 P.M. After the show finishes, I do a final walk around the lounges on the ship with my assistant. Karaoke has just finished in one of the secondary lounges and we have music playing everywhere. We have thirty-five musicians comprising several bands featuring all varieties of music (string quartet, jazz ensemble, piano bar, Calypso, Latin, Top 40). The disco is lively with singles' night tonight and there are a few couples enjoying light jazz in the Jazz Club.

12:30 A.M. A full day. Definitely a far cry from Julie on the *Love Boat*! Time for bed as I have to be on the gangway at 8:00 A.M. to welcome our guests to Labadee.

passengers on a cruise may be repeat guests. Most cruise ships sail under foreign flags because they were built abroad for the following reasons.[5]

1. U.S. labor costs for ships, officers, and crew, in addition to maritime unions, are too high to compete in the world market.
2. U.S. ships are not permitted to operate casino-type gambling.
3. Many foreign shipyards are government subsidized to keep workers employed, thereby lowering construction costs.

In addition, cruise ships sail under foreign flags (called flags of convenience) because registering these ships in countries such as Panama, the Bahamas, and Liberia means fewer and more lax regulations and little or no taxation.

The Radisson Diamond gives passengers greater stability and is known for its luxury service.

Employment opportunities for Americans are mainly confined to sales, marketing, and other U.S. shore-based activities, such as reservations and supplies. On board, certain positions such as cruise director and purser, are sometimes occupied by Americans.

The reasons that few Americans work onboard cruise ships are that the ships are at sea for months at a time with just a few hours in port. The hours are long (see the anecdote) and the conditions for crew are not likely to be acceptable to most Americans. No, you don't get your own cabin! Still interested? Try crewunlimited.com.

Segmenting the Cruise Market

There are marked differences between the segments of the cruise industry.

Mass Market: Generally people with incomes in the $30,000 to $60,000 range, interested in an average cost per person of between $85 and $175 per day, depending on the location and size of the cabin.

Middle Market: Generally people with incomes in the $60,000 to $80,000 range, interested in an average cost per person of $175 to $350 per day. These ships are capable of accommodating 750 to 1,000 passengers. The middle-market ships are stylish and comfortable, with each vessel having its own personality that caters to a variety of different guests. Among the cruise lines in the middle market are Princess Cruises, Norwegian Cruise Lines, Royal Caribbean, Holland America Lines, Windstar Cruises, Cunard Lines, and Celebrity Cruises.

Luxury Market: Generally people with incomes higher than $80,000, interested in an average cost per person of more than $350 per day. In this market, the ships tend to be smaller, averaging about 700 passengers, with superior appointments and service. What constitutes a luxury cruise is partly a matter of individual judgment, partly a matter of advertising and public relations. The ships that received the top accolades from travel industry writers and others who assign such ranks cater only to the top 2 percent

Anecdote

The maître d' on the Love Boat was explaining the dining room staff's duties, beginning with breakfast at 6 A.M. and followed by lunch and dinner. A student asked, "When does the second shift come on?" The maître d' laughed and said, "There is no second shift." Needless to say, that student's interest declined, especially when he realized the crew would be at sea for months at a time.

Figure 3–3 shows the number of passengers taking a cruise lasting more than two days, according to the Cruise Lines Association (CLA).

Carnival Triumph *Lido Deck*

Year	Passengers
1970	500,000
1980	1.4 million
1990	3.6 million
2005	9.5 million
2010	12 million

Source: Personal communication, The Cruise Line Industry Association, January 2005.

Figure 3–3   *Passengers Taking a Cruise Longer Than Two Days*

of North American income groups. Currently, the ships considered to be in the very top category are *Seabourn Spirit, Seabourn Legend, Seabourn Pride, Crystal Cruises Crystal Harmony, Radisson Diamond,* and *Silversea* Silver Wind These six-star vessels have sophisticated cuisine, excellent service, far-reaching and imaginative itineraries, and highly satisfying overall cruise experiences.

The rising demand for new cruise operators and recent mergers have sparked the travel industry. Larger ships with resort-like design, numerous activities, and amenities such as "virtual golf," pizzerias, and caviar bars have changed with time. Significant growth opportunities still exist for the industry. With only about 10 percent of the cruise market tapped and with an estimated market potential of billions, the cruise industry is assured of a bright future.

Check Your Knowledge

1. In your own words, define the term *tourism.*
2. *Research:* Which city in the United States is the biggest hub city for air travel? Approximately how many flights does this city have a day?
3. Explain the significance of the Airline Deregulation Act of 1978.

Tourism Organizations

Governments are involved in tourism decisions because tourism involves travel across international boundaries. Governments regulate the entrance and exit of foreign nationals. They become involved in the decisions surrounding national parks, heritage, preservation, and environmental protection, as well as the cultural and social aspects of tourism. Tourism is to some extent an international ambassador, fostering goodwill and closer intercultural understanding among the peoples of the world.

International Organizations

Looking first at the macro picture, the **World Tourism Organization (WTO)** is the most widely recognized organization in tourism today. The WTO is the only organization that represents all national and official tourism interests among its allied members. The WTO was described earlier in this chapter.

The International Air Transportation Association (IATA) is the global organization that regulates almost all international airlines. The purpose of IATA is to facilitate the movement of people and goods via a network of routes. In addition to tickets, IATA regulations standardize waybills and baggage checks and coordinate and unify handling and accounting procedures to permit rapid interline bookings and connections. The IATA also maintains stability of fares and rates.

The International Civil Aviation Organization (ICAO) is comprised of more than 80 governments. ICAO coordinates the development of all aspects of civil aviation, specifically with regard to the formulation of international standards and practices.

Several international development organizations share a common purpose that includes tourism development. The better-known organizations include the following:

> The World Bank (WB), which lends substantial sums of money for tourism development. Most of this money is awarded in the form of low-interest loans to developing countries.
>
> The International Bank for Reconstruction and Development, which is similar to the World Bank.
>
> United Nations Development Program (UNDP), which assists countries with a variety of development projects, including tourism.
>
> Organization for Economic Cooperation and Development (OECD), which was established by an international convention signed in Paris in 1960. The purpose of the OECD is to do the following:
>
> 1. Achieve the highest sustainable economic growth and employment and a rising standard of living in member countries, while maintaining financial stability—thus contributing to the development of the world economy
> 2. Contribute to sound economic expansion in member as well as nonmember countries through economic development
> 3. Contribute to the expansion of world trade on a multilateral, nondiscriminating basis, in accordance with international obligations
>
> The OECD's tourism committee studies various aspects of tourism, including tourism problems, and makes recommendations to governments. The committee also works on standard definitions and methods of data collection, which are published in an annual report entitled *Tourism Policy and International Tourism in OECD Member Countries.*

Other banks and organizations with similar interests include the Asian Development Bank, Overseas Private Investment Corporation, Inter-American Development Bank, and Agency for International Development.

The **Pacific Area Travel Association (PATA)** represents 34 countries in the Pacific and Asia that have united behind a common goal: excellence in travel and tourism growth. PATA's accomplishments include shaping the future of travel in the Asia/Pacific region; it has had a remarkable record of success with research, development, education, and marketing.

Domestic Organizations

Many countries have a minister of tourism, which is a cabinet-level position that can advocate tourism development, marketing, and management through the National Tourism Organization (NTO). Unfortunately, the United States does not have even a senior-level government official for tourism. Instead, an organization known as the Travel Industry of America (TIA) is the main body for the promotion and development of tourism in the United States. It speaks for the common interests and concerns of all components of the U.S. travel industry. Its mission is to benefit the whole U.S. travel industry by unifying its goals, coordinating private sector efforts to encourage and promote travel to and within the United States, monitoring government policies that affect travel and tourism, and supporting research and analysis in areas vital to the industry. Established in 1941, TIA's membership represents more than 2,000 travel-related businesses, associations, and local, regional, and state travel promotion agencies of the nation's travel industry.

State Offices of Tourism

The next level of organizations concerned with tourism is the state office of tourism. These offices are charged by their legislative bodies with the orderly

State offices of tourism promote places of interest, such as Fanuel Hall, Quincy Market, Boston, Massachusetts.

growth and development of tourism within the state. They promote information programs, advertising, publicity, and research in terms of their relationship to the recreation and tourism attractions in the state.

City-Level Offices of Tourism and Convention Centers

Cities have also realized the importance of the "new money" that tourism brings. Many cities have established **convention and visitors bureaus (CVBs),** whose main function is to attract and retain visitors to the city. The convention and visitors bureaus are staffed by representatives of the city's attractions, restaurants, hotels and motels, and transportation. These bureaus are largely funded by the transient occupancy tax (TOT) that is charged to hotel guests. In most cities, the TOT ranges from 8 to 18 percent. The balance of funding comes from membership dues and promotional activities. In recent years convention centers have sprung up in a number of large and several smaller cities. Spurred on by expectations of economic and social gain, cities operate both convention and visitors bureaus and convention centers. Both convention and visitors bureaus and convention centers are discussed in detail in Chapter 13.

The Economic Impact of Tourism

The World Travel and Tourism Council, a Brussels-based organization, commissioned a study[6] from the Wharton Economic Forecasting Association. Their report suggested that the total demand for travel and tourism will be $2,571 billion by 2010, or more than 10 percent of the world's gross national product (GNP). Tourism, says the study, grows about twice as fast as world GNP. Of the industry's total world spending, about 31 percent takes place in the European Community and 30 percent on the North American continent.

International arrivals, according to the WTO, will reach 1 billion in 2010 and 1.6 billion by 2020, more than triple the 475 million people who traveled abroad in 1992. In 2004, an estimated 46.1 million overseas residents visited the United States and spent $74.5 billion.

Nearly every state publishes its own tourism economic impact study. New York, for example, estimates its tourism revenue to be $38.5 billion; Florida, about $51.7 billion; Texas, $33 billion; and California, just over $53 billion. Tourism is Hawaii's biggest industry, with revenues of $23 billion.

The National Travel and Tourism Awareness Council's annual "The Tourism Work for America Report"[7] indicates that travel and tourism are one of the nation's leading sectors. Statistics include the following:

- International travelers spend about $94 billion on travel-related expenses (e.g., lodging, food, and entertainment) in the United States annually.
- 20.8 million people are directly employed in the industry, making travel and tourism the nation's second largest employer, after health services.
- Travel generates about $100 billion a year in tax receipts. If it were not for tourism, each U.S. household would have to pay $898 more per year in taxes.

Rank		International Tourism Receipts (US $ billion)		Change(%)	
		2003	2004*	03/02	04*/03
1	United States	64.3	74.5	-3.6	15.7
2	Spain	39.6	45.2	24.9	14.1
3	France	36.6	40.8	13.2	11.6
4	Italy	31.2	35.7	17.1	14.1
5	Germany	23.1	27.7	20.1	19.7
6	United Kingdom	22.7	27.3	11.2	20.5
7	China	17.4	25.7	-14.6	47.9
8	Turkey	13.2	15.9	10.9	20.3
9	Austria	14.0	15.4	24.2	10.4
10	Australia	10.3	13.0	20.3	25.5

*Data as collected by WTO June 2005.

Source: World Tourism Organization (WTO)©.

Figure 3–4   *World's Top Ten Tourism Earners*

- Spending by international visitors within the United States is about $21 billion more than travel-related spending by Americans outside the United States.
- Approximately 46 million international travelers visit the United States each year.
- Just a 1 percent increase in the world market would mean 7.6 million more visitors, which would create 150,000 jobs and contribute $2 billion in new tax revenue.

By employing approximately one out of every ten workers, travel and tourism is the world's largest employer and is the largest industry. The estimates are that in the year 2012 there will be 249 million jobs, accounting for 8.6 percent of total employment, which is 1 in every 11.7 jobs.

The Multiplier Effect

Tourists bring new money into the economy of the place they are visiting, and this impacts beyond their original expenditures. When a tourist spends money to travel, to stay in a hotel, or to eat in a restaurant, that money is recycled by those businesses to purchase more goods, thereby generating further use of the money. In addition, employees of businesses who serve tourists spend a higher proportion of their money locally on various goods and services. This chain reaction, called the **multiplier effect,** continues until there is a leakage, meaning that money is used to purchase something from outside the area. Figure 3–5 illustrates the multiplier effect.

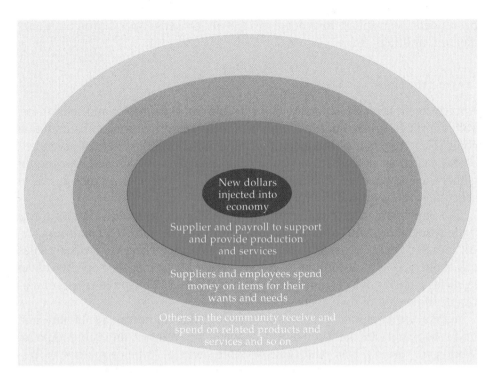

Figure 3–5 *The Multiplier Effect*

"Most developed economies have a multiplier effect between 1.5 and 2.0."[8] This means that the original money spent is used again in the community between 1.5 and 2.0 times. If tourism-related businesses spend more money on locally produced goods and services, it will benefit the local economy.

Promoters of Tourism

Tour Operators

Tour operators promote tours and trips that they plan and organize. A *tour* is a trip taken by a group of people who travel together with a professional tour manager/escort and follow a preplanned itinerary. Most tours include travel, accommodations, meals, land transportation, and sightseeing. The tour operator negotiates discounted travel, accommodation, and meals and sightseeing, and then adds a markup before advertising the package. Tour operators also offer **vacation packages** to people traveling alone. Vacation packages include a combination of two or more travel services—hotel, car rental, and air transportation—that are offered at a "package price." Most vacation packages offer a choice of components and options, allowing the client to customize his or her package to personal interests and budget.

The National Tour Association estimates that nearly 500,000 tours are conducted annually by 1,636 U.S. tour operators. These tours carry 21.2 million passengers, who spend an average of $168 per passenger per day on both one-day and multiday tours.

Travel Agencies

A travel agent is a middleperson who acts as a travel counselor and sells on behalf of airlines, cruise lines, rail and bus transportation, hotels, and auto rental companies. Agents may sell individual parts of the overall system or several elements, such as air and cruise tickets. The agent acts as a broker, bringing together the client (buyer) and the supplier (seller). An agent has quick access to schedules, fares, and advice for clients about various destinations.

The American Society of Travel Agents (ASTA) is the world's largest travel trade association, with over 20,000 members in more than 165 countries. The Airlines Reporting Corporation (ARC) reports that a travel agency's weekly sales are about $38,989. According to *Travel Weekly Magazine*, the top fifty travel agencies in terms of sales generated (approximately $25 billion in revenue) represent 30 percent of total agency sales.

Agents use computer reservation systems (CRS) to access availability and make bookings. In the United States, the main vendors are Sabre, Apollo, Worldspan, System One, and Galileo. Sabre owns a 70 percent share of Travelocity, the online site. And Cendant Corporation owns Galileo, which forms the hub of Cendant's travel-related business of hotels, car rental, and vacation ownership. Worldspan is jointly owned by Delta, Northwest, and American airlines. Worldspan manages 50 percent of all online bookings worldwide.[9]

According to the ASTA, a travel agent is more than a ticket seller. Agents serve their clients in the following ways:

- Arranging transportation by air, sea, rail, bus, car rental, and so on
- Preparing individual itineraries, personally escorted tours, group tours, and prepared package tours
- Arranging for hotel, motel, and resort accommodations; meals; sightseeing tours; transfers of passengers and luggage between terminals and hotels; and special features such as tickets for music festivals, the theater, and so forth
- Handling and advising on many details involved with travel, such as insurance, traveler's checks, foreign currency exchange, documentary requirements, and immunizations and other inoculations
- Using professional know-how and experience (e.g., schedules of air, train, and bus connections, rates of hotels, quality of accommodations, etc.)
- Arranging reservations for special-interest activities, such as group tours, conventions, business travel, gourmet tours, sporting trips, etc.[10]

Approximately 30,000 travel agencies are currently operating in the United States. The average agency has between four and seven full-time employees. The average starting salaries are $24,000. The average salary for an agent with three to five years of service is $36,000. Agents with ten-plus years average $40,000. Managers make an average of $50,000.

There is less of a need for the traditional travel agent in the age of the Internet. As you know, it is quicker and easier to go online and select travel dates,

Travel agents have a knowledge of destinations and can make air, ground, and hotel reservations making it more convenient for clients to visit popular destinations like Venice, Italy.

times, and fares. The conclusion is that the travel business has changed, resulting in a sharp decline in the number of travel agents.

Commission Caps

Travel agents once gained most of their income from airline and cruise line commissions. However, travel agencies have seen air travel commissions, their primary source of income, decline since commission caps were first imposed. The airlines have now eliminated commissions, so agencies are charging a fee for their services to offset the costs involved in providing those services.

Out of necessity, travel agents have become more specialized to make up for the loss of commission revenue from the airlines. Some have specialized in the booking of cruises because they still are paying between 10 and 15 percent of the price of the cabin booked. Others have expanded their product offerings by including meeting and event planning and management. Another way of gaining more commission is simply to charge clients an extra amount for their tickets. There are still business and leisure travelers who do not have the time or inclination to book their trips online. For them, the travel agent can provide a hassle-free service and be there for their clients. However, due to the increasing number of Internet bookings for all types of travel and tourism, the volume of travel agents' bookings has substantially decreased.[11]

Travel Corporations

There are a number of large and successful travel corporations—the largest being American Express Travel Services. American Express (AMEX) is a corporation that has a travel services division with locations worldwide. Each location is licensed and bonded with the International Air Transportation Association (IATA), which provides travel services and tickets through the corporation. The travel services division provides other services, including foreign currencies, AMEX traveler's checks in different currencies, and gift checks. Currently, the travel services division is trying to promote foreign currencies to increase revenues.

The majority of American Express Travel Services' revenues is generated in business travel through corporate accounts. The airlines give the travel agency an override to portion with the corporate client. The business contract is individually set up, based on annual travel expenses. For example, if IBM's annual travel expenses are $1 million, the airline will give AMEX a 1.4 percent override commission to split with IBM. AMEX chooses their airline vendors according to who gives the largest override percentage and whose negotiated rates are most appealing. The same policy applies to other vendors in the industry, such as cruise lines.

Travel managers for AMEX function as national account managers. Their pay is based on their grade level, region, and market. Their salary also depends on whom they service. A small, local clientele generates a lower salary, and a broader service center provides a higher salary. Depending on whether they are on- or off-site, a travel manager's salary for AMEX is between $60,000 and $95,000 for corporate clients. The salary range for general public leisure travel is between $40,000 and $65,000. Each travel manager is hired internally, and pay is based mostly on seniority.[12]

American Express Travel on the Internet searches for the best ticket price or the most convenient flights in the same reservations systems used by thousands of travel agents. In a snap, users can check out the price or search for other options and then book their own reservations online. Users can view descriptions of packages to sunny, snow-filled, cultural, or just plain fun destinations, along with full-color photos and a list of amenities. Visitors to the site currently have three options: They can book airline tickets, they can view vacation offers, and they can look up the most convenient American Express Travel office. In addition, card members may take advantage of special travel, retail, restaurant, and entertainment offers and shop for a variety of merchandise on another Internet site called ExpressNet.

Corporate Travel Manager

A corporate travel manager is a type of entrepreneur working within the framework of a large corporation. For example, Mitsubishi Electronics, in Cypress, California, was spending about $4 million for travel and entertainment. In addition, twenty-nine field offices operated independently across the United States, Canada, and Mexico. The total expenditure for travel and entertainment was $11 million. Enter John Fazio, recruited by Mitsubishi to improve efficiency and reduce costs. Fazio invited interested agencies to submit proposals based on Mitsubishi's travel needs. The fifteen initial proposals were narrowed to eight; finally, two were asked to submit their best and last offers. These offers were evaluated based on Mitsubishi's criteria: technological capabilities, locations, and ability to give personal service.

An interesting trend in corporate travel is agentless booking via electronic mail (e-mail). Travel is initiated at the keyboard, not at the switchboard. Increasingly, technologically savvy corporations are making travel bookings via e-mail.

Travel and Tour Wholesalers

Tour wholesalers consolidate the services of airline, cruise line, and bus line with ground service suppliers into a tour that is sold through a sales channel to the public.[13] Tour wholesaling came into prominence in the 1960s because airlines had vacant seats, which, like hotel rooms, are perishable. Airlines naturally wanted to sell as many seats as possible and found that they could sell blocks of seats to wholesalers close to departure dates. These tickets were for specific destinations around which tour wholesalers built a tour. Wholesalers then sold their tours directly through retail agents.

The tour wholesale business is concentrated with about 100 independent tour wholesalers; however, ten major companies account for about 30 percent of the industry's business. Tour wholesalers offer a wide range of tours at various prices to many destinations. This segment of the industry is characterized by three key types of wholesalers:

1. An independent tour wholesaler
2. An airline working in close cooperation with a tour wholesaler
3. A retail travel agent who packages tours for his or her clients

In addition, incentive travel houses and various travel clubs round out the tour wholesale business.[14]

Certified Travel Counselor (CTC)

Leading experts in the travel industry worked together to form an Institute of Certified Travel Agents (ICTA). The ICTA offers specialized professional studies for those seeking higher proficiency in the travel industry. The professional designation of CTC is awarded to individuals who have successfully passed examinations and who have five years of full-time experience in a travel agency or in the marketing and promotion of travel.[15]

National Offices of Tourism (NOT)

National offices of tourism seek to improve the economy of the country they represent by increasing the number of visitors and consequently their spending in the country. Connected to this function is the responsibility to oversee and ensure that hotels, transport systems, tour operators, and tour guides maintain high standards in the care and consideration of the tourist.[16] The main activities of NOT are as follows:

- Publicizing the country
- Assisting and advising certain types of travelers
- Creating demand for certain destinations
- Supplying information
- Ensuring that the destination is up to expectations
- Advertising[17]

Personal Profile: Patti Roscoe

Chairperson, Patti Roscoe and Associates (PRA) and Roscoe/Coltrell Inc. (RCI)

Patricia L. Roscoe landed in California in 1966, charmed by the beautiful San Diego sun compared to the cold winters in Buffalo, New York, her hometown. She was a young, brilliant middle manager who was to face the challenges of a time period when women were expected to become either nurses or teachers. She became involved with the hotel industry, working for a large private resort hotel, the Vacation Village. Those were the years to be remembered. She gained a very thorough knowledge of Southern California tourism, as well as of the inherent mechanisms of the industry. With the unforgettable help and guidance of her manager, she began to lay the foundations of her future career as a very successful leader in the field. The outstanding skills that she learned are, in fact, the very basis of her many accomplishments.

The list of her awards and honors is astounding: the prestigious CITE distinction (Certified Incentive Travel Executive), San Diego Woman of Accomplishment, and San Diego's Allied Member of the Year. The U.S. Small Business Administration gave her the Wonder Woman Award for her outstanding achievements in the field, and the San Diego Convention and Visitors Bureau has conferred on her the prestigious RCA Lubach Award for her contributions to the industry.

She is also extremely involved in civic and tourism organizations, including the Rotary Club, the American Lung Association of San Diego and Imperial Counties, and the San Diego Convention and Visitors Bureau.

The key to her success perhaps lies in her remarkable skills of interacting with people. It is the human resources, in fact, that represent the major strength of PRA. Its employees are experienced, dedicated, and service oriented. But what makes them so efficient is their dedication to working together as a team. Patti Roscoe guides, inspires, and motivates these teams. She is a self-admitted "softy," a creative and emotional leader who enjoys training her employees and following their growth step by step, to eventually give them the power of initiative they deserve, as a tool to encourage their creativity and originality. She constantly seeks to balance the concept of teamwork with the individual goals and private lives of her employees. It is through the achievement of such a balance that a profitable, healthy community is preserved. PRA is a bit more than a community, however: It is a family, and just like a mother, Patti's formula is discipline and love. At the same time, Patti's leading efforts are aimed at training her employees to "think outside of the box," and "keep one's view as broad as possible," which is the only way to rise above the commonplace, the rhetorical, and the trivial, to escape provincialism, and thus become unique individuals.

That's how the magic is done. PRA excels in creating "something that becomes exclusively yours—that has never been done before." PRA is decentralized into service teams to foster an entrepreneurial environment in which initiative and creativity can be boosted to the fullest. Therefore, PRA staff design personalized, unique events to give their customers an unforgettable time.

Since its opening in 1981, PRA has become one of the most successful destination management companies in the country, providing personal, caring service characterized by flexibility and creativity.

Destination Management Companies (DMCs)

A destination management company is a service organization within the visitor industry that offers a host of programs and services to meet clients' needs. Initially, a destination management sales manager concentrates on selling the destination to meeting planners and performance improvement companies (incentive houses).

The needs of such groups may be as simple as an airport pickup or as involved as an international sales convention with theme parties. DMCs work closely with hotels; sometimes DMCs book rooms, and other times hotels request the DMC's know-how on organizing theme parties.

Patricia Roscoe, chairperson of Patti Roscoe and Associates (PRA), says that meeting planners often have a choice of several destinations and might ask, "Why should I pick your destination?" The answer is that a DMC does everything, including airport greetings, transportation to the hotel, VIP check-in, theme parties, sponsoring programs, organizing competitive sports events, and so on, depending on budget.

Sales managers associated with DMCs obtain leads, which are potential clients, from the following sources:

- Hotels
- Trade shows
- Convention and visitors bureaus
- Cold calls
- Incentive houses
- Meeting planners

Each sales manager has a staff or team that would include the following:

- Special events manager, who will have expertise in sound, lighting, staging, and so on
- Accounts manager, who is an assistant to the sales manager
- Operations manager, who coordinates everything, especially on-site arrangements, to ensure that what is sold actually happens

For example, Patti Roscoe's destination management company organized meetings, accommodations, meals, beverages, and theme parties for 2,000 Ford Motor Company dealers in nine groups over three days for each group.

Roscoe also works closely with incentive houses, such as Carlson Marketing or Maritz Travel. These incentive houses approach a company and offer to evaluate and set up incentive plans for the sales team, including whatever it takes to motivate them. Once approved, Carlson contacts a destination management company and asks for a program.

People travel to visit quaint places like Key West, Florida.

In conclusion, thousands of companies and associations hold meetings and conventions all over the country. Many of these organizations use the services of professional meeting planners, who in turn seek out suitable destinations for the meetings and conventions. Some larger hotels and resorts now have a destination management department to handle all the arrangements for groups and conventions.

Why People Travel

There are many reasons why people travel, but the two main reasons are for pleasure and for business. Research indicates that when consumers are asked what they associate most with success and accomplishment, the number one response is travel for pleasure.

Among the reasons people travel for pleasure are the following:

- Visiting friends and relatives
- Health
- Enlightenment, education
- Beauty, nature, and national parks
- Religion
- Indulgence
- Sports
- Festivals
- Shopping
- Fun of the trip
- Gaming
- Adventure
- Heritage
- Ecotourism
- Attractions

Pleasure Travel

Eighty-two percent of domestic travel is **pleasure travel** (leisure, recreation, holidays, and visiting friends and relatives—VFR). Approximately 670 million person-trips are taken for pleasure, according to the United States Travel Data Center's (USTDC) national travel survey. Nearly half of all the pleasure travelers visited friends and relatives.

When surveyed, people tend to list the following reasons for travel:

- To experience new and different surroundings
- To experience other cultures
- To rest and relax
- To visit friends and family
- To view, or participate in, sporting/recreational activities

Travel is likely to increase in the coming years, which will have a significant impact on tourism. Some reasons for the anticipated increases are as follows:

- *Longer life span.* The average person in the United States now has a life expectancy of about 75 years. In fact, in just a few years, many baby boomers will retire.
- *Flexible working hours.* Today, many people work four 10-hour days and have longer weekends. Of course, many others, especially in the hospitality and tourism industries, work on weekends and have leisure time during the week.

- *Early retirement.* Increasingly, people are being given the opportunity to retire at age 55. This early retirement is generally granted to employees with 30 years of service to their company or government agency.
- *Greater ease of travel.* Today, it is easier to travel on holidays and weekends, for both business and leisure purposes. Each mode of travel affords increasing opportunities to take advantage of the additional leisure time.
- *Tendency to take shorter, more frequent trips.* People now tend to take shorter, but more frequent, minivacations, rather than taking all their vacation time at once. Europeans generally take much longer vacations than North Americans. For them, four weeks is the normal vacation benefit of new employees, and six weeks is typical after a few years.
- *Increase in the standard of living.* More people in many developing countries have increased their income and wish to travel. China, with its new-found enterprise zones, is producing hundreds of thousands of entrepreneurs who will soon be traveling to foreign countries. Millions of East European residents of the former Soviet Bloc countries now have the capability and the right to travel. And finally, an additional 300 million people from China and India will soon have passports.

Different Places for Different People

Obviously, travelers select destinations for different reasons—climate, history or culture, sports, entertainment, shopping facilities, and so forth. The major appeal of England for Americans seems to be history and culture. American Express surveyed people going to several destinations—Florida, California, Mexico, Hawaii, the Bahamas, Jamaica, Puerto Rico, the Virgin Islands, and Barbados. Almost half of the respondents were professionals, generally middle-aged, and well educated. Many were wealthy travelers who took frequent vacations outside the United States. These respondents ranked the appeals of travel in descending order of importance:

- Scenic beauty
- Pleasant attitudes of local people
- Suitable accommodations
- Rest and relaxation
- Airfare cost
- Historical and cultural interests
- Cuisine
- Water sports
- Entertainment (e.g., nightlife)
- Shopping facilities
- Sports (golfing and tennis)

Four basic considerations emerged as factors influencing travel: entertainment, purchase opportunities, climate for comfort, and cost. Even within a group, of course, different factors apply. One individual may select a destination primarily because of opportunities for challenging golf and tennis, another because of the friendly local people, and another because the place offers rest and relaxation. Most of the group would, however, be influenced by airfare costs.

Expectation and Reality

Karen Smith and Claudia Green of New York and Pace Universities comment: With the growth in international tourism, challenges have emerged for the traveler as well as the destination location.[18] Travelers often have culturally-based expectations for the travel experience that may or may not be met by international travel. Current research is focusing on the impact of the traveler's culture on expectations for service, as well as ways to assess customer expectations and evaluate customer satisfaction. Service providers in destination locations are making efforts to meet the needs of diverse populations of travelers.

Satisfaction, or dissatisfaction, with the travel experience, of course, depends on how it is viewed by the traveler. A glorious sunset and majestic mountain may be seen as a great bore if an individual is highly gregarious and alone on the trip. The best service in a restaurant with the finest food and decor is meaningless if the person is dyspeptic at the moment. One traveler loves the rain, another despises it. Mountains are one person's delight, heights make another person dizzy. The anthropologist revels in the remote village, the city dweller finds the same place dull. So much depends on what the person expects of the experience and how he or she actually experiences it.

Travel is an experience, not a tangible object. It results in psychic reward or punishment. It creates pleasant anticipation or aversion, excitement and challenge, or fatigue and disappointment. The anticipation, the experience, and the memory occur in the mind, leaving no tangible evidence as to why travel was undertaken and why the same trip is experienced in so many different ways by different people. Travel literature and films often falsify reality or are shot so selectively that the actual environment is not recognizable by the visitor. The phony shot that makes the pool look longer than it is, the colors that never exist in nature, the lavish buffet that was rigged especially for the photograph, the glorious sunset that occurs once a year—all of this creates expectations that cannot be realized and leads to disappointment.

One of the most beautiful places in America is Jackson Lake, Grand Teton National Park, Wyoming.

Business Travel

In recent years, business travel has declined to 18 percent of all U.S. travel, 6 percent of which is a combination of business and leisure travel.[19] The general economic climate, terrorism, SARS, and businesses reducing their travel budgets have negatively affected business travel.

Yet, a high percentage of the guests who check into upscale hotels around the world are traveling for business reasons. Much **business travel** is hard work, whether it is travel in one's own automobile or in the luxury of a first-class seat aboard an airline. A good portion of business travel is, however, mixed with pleasure.

Counted as business travelers are those who travel for business purposes, such as meetings; all kinds of sales, including corporate, regional, product, and others; conventions; trade shows and expositions; and combinations of more than one. In the United States, meetings and conventions alone attract millions of people annually. Sometimes the distinction between business and leisure travel becomes blurred. If a convention attendee in Atlanta decides to stay on for a few days after the conference, are they to be considered a business or leisure traveler? Business travelers, when compared to leisure travelers, tend to be younger, spend more money, travel farther, and travel in smaller groups, but they do not stay as long.

Business travel, long the mainstay of airlines and hotels, will likely gradually decline as a percentage of all travel, which includes leisure travel. Leisure travel is forecast to increase due to a favorable economic climate, which in turn produces increased discretionary income. Many people now have more leisure time and higher levels of education, and the cost of travel has remained constant, or even dropped, compared to inflation and other costs combined. These factors indicate a bright future for the travel industry.

An increasing number of business travelers are able to make their own travel arrangements online. For example, in the middle of a client meeting Suzie Aust, a meeting consultant, realizes that she has forgotten to book the next day's flight. She pulls out her laptop, gets online, and books the flight. Corporate America is worried about travelers like Suzie because they are often able to skirt corporate policies when making their own reservations. Some companies use a product from Microsoft and American Express. Code-named Rome, the product will allow companies to control their own travelers by insisting that employees buy their own tickets through American Express. American and United Airlines are each rolling out similar products. Ed Gilligan, president of corporate services for American Express, estimates that American companies lose $15 billion a year due to deviations from corporate policy. And the portion of that sum lost to online reservation systems is "ramping up quickly," he says. About 1.8 million business travelers are wired, according to Addison Schonland, director of aviation, travel, and marketing for CIC Research, in San Diego. The Eastman Group, a Newport Beach, California, management consulting and travel software group, predicts that by 2006, 99 percent of all airline travel will be ticketless.

FOCUS ON SECURITY

Tourism Safety

Lynne Christen

Before September 11, 2001, travelers rarely gave much thought to safety. Tourism marketers directed their market positioning to tangibles such as beautiful beaches, lavish spas, spacious and well-decorated rooms, and more amenities than the competition. Since the terrorist attacks, travel safety has become an integral part of travel planning. Tourists are saying, "I don't think it's safe to go there" and "I'm not ready to start flying again." Concerns are reinforced by frequent upgrades and downgrades of the national threat level. This is the new reality of travel and a challenge for the entire tourism industry.

The bad news is that this fear of travel has a negative impact on virtually every segment of the travel industry. The good news is that, according to studies by the Travel Industry Association of America (TIA), in spite of the concerns, both business and leisure travel are again beginning to show steady growth.

Travel agents, hospitality managers, air and cruise lines, and tour operators must take proactive steps to monitor and manage the safety and security segments of their operations. They must shift from previous approaches of downplaying potential safety problems. Successful tourism providers will prominently position safety, making it an integral and visible part of marketing strategies. Educating customers and helping them to become more confident makes them safer travelers.

It is important to note that the odds of a tourist being killed or injured by terrorism are extremely low. The biggest threat to tourist safety is everyday street crime, theft, and medical emergencies. Granted, hotel fires and cruise ship disasters occur (usually with major publicity), but they are rare. Statistics show that a sprinklered hotel or cruise ship is safer than the average home.

Based on the increased odds, one way to begin educating the tourism consumer is in basic crime prevention. Crime safety and security brochures are excellent educational tools and can easily be made available in airports, hotels, cruise ships, and tour buses. Tourists should be provided Internet Web sites, books, magazines, and media safety resources and encouraged to research their safety concerns.

It is equally important for all tourism professionals to be aware of resources available to travelers. International travelers should begin their trip planning by researching their destination countries and checking U.S. State Department travel warnings (**www.state.gov**). Travel warnings are issued when a country becomes unsafe, usually due to war, terrorism, or potential unrest.

The Central Intelligence Agency (CIA) also publishes an excellent document called *The CIA World Factbook* (**www.cia.gov**). This book has detailed information on demographics, climate, geography, economy, politics and more for every country in the world.

Researching a country's medical facilities is often overlooked as a key safety element. This is especially important for travelers who have special or chronic medical needs. Hospitals and clinics, taken for granted in the United States and western Europe, may not be available in other parts of the world. Other medical issues to consider include the availability of prescription medications, air evacuation, and insurance coverage. Many tourists are not aware that Medicare coverage and many private insurance policies do not apply outside the United States. The Centers for Disease Control (**www.cdc.gov**) provides up-to-date, accurate medical travel information, including disease warnings and vaccination recommendations.

Filing a travel plan is an overlooked component of travel safety. Tourists should print several detailed copies of their travel schedule and various accommodation addresses and telephone numbers and provide them to friends and family. Tourists in foreign countries should notify the appropriate U.S. embassy or consulate when they are staying in the country for two weeks or more. This notification includes contact information in the event of a travel warning or the need for evacuation.

Execustay by Marriott Corporate Apartment provides a "home away from home" for traveling businesspeople.

Check Your Knowledge

1. What is TOT? What is the TOT in your city of residency?
2. Brainstorm on the services offered by AMEX.

Social and Cultural Impact of Tourism

From a social and cultural perspective, tourism can leave both positive and negative impacts on communities. Undoubtedly, tourism has made significant contributions to international understanding. World tourism organizations recognize that tourism is a means of enhancing international understanding, peace, prosperity, and universal respect for, and observance of, human rights and fundamental freedom for all without distinction as to race, sex, language, or religion. Tourism can be a very interesting sociocultural phenomenon. Seeing how others live is an interest of many tourists, and the exchange of sociocultural values and activities is rewarding.

Provided that the number of tourists is manageable and that they respect the host community's sociocultural norms and values, tourism provides an opportunity for a number of social interactions. A London pub or a New York café are examples of good places for social interaction. Similarly, depending on the reason for the tourist visit, myriad opportunities are available to interact both socially and culturally. Even a visit to another part of the United States would be both socially and culturally stimulating. For example, New Orleans has a very diverse social and cultural heritage. Over the years, the city has been occupied by Spanish, French, British, and Americans. The food, music, dance, and social norms are unique to the area.

Corporate Profile: Club Med

In 1950, a Belgian diamond cutter and water polo champion conceived the first Club Med village, funded with army surplus tax money, on the little Spanish island of Majorca. The goal of that first resort was to unite people from diverse backgrounds, encourage them to share a good time, and offer them a unique escape from the stress and the tension of the everyday events of post-World War II Europe. The first adventurous vacationers to experience that new environment were mostly young couples or singles, living together in a beautiful natural setting, enjoying the atmosphere of camaraderie and no worries, playing sports, or just simply relaxing on a warm, soft beach.

The following decade was a particularly profitable one, because of the overall social climate that characterized the 1960s. The young generation, generally speaking, was wrapped up in a whirl of ideals, such as peace, communion, and the sharing of feelings and experiences, all in the framework of a return to nature. The so-called flowerchild phenomenon saw the young long for a return to primitive purity, innocence, and freedom of expression. It is not surprising, then, that Club Med's clientele rose by 500 percent in that decade. In fact, the features that characterized the resorts

A Club Med Resort

made them just the right environment to meet the needs of this target market. Club Med began its expansion throughout the Mediterranean coastlines and islands, including Greece and Italy. Centers began to spring up on the coasts of Africa and the Middle East. Today Club Med—short for Mediterranean—has more than 120 resorts and vacation villages around the world, hosted by twenty-eight countries in the Mediterranean as well as in the Caribbean, Africa, Mexico, the Bahamas, South Pacific, South America, Asia, and the United States. The little village in Majorca blossomed into a colorful, joyful, sunny, colossal empire: Club Med is the world's largest vacation village organization and the ninth largest hotel chain, with 93,000 beds and 20,000 employees. More than 9 million guests have come to the villages since 1950.

Today's philosophy doesn't differ much from the original one. Club Med intends to provide a spectacular natural setting in which its guests can enjoy life and its amenities, away from the troubles and the worries of the everyday frantic rat race. The theme on the printed advertisements points straight to this: "Club Med: Life as it should be." Sports, various entertaining activities, good food, real concern for guests' needs, and a carefree lifestyle worked wonders. Imagine all of these amenities in the context of white sand beaches and a clear blue sea that seems to stretch out indefinitely to meet a virtually cloudless sky at the horizon.

Club Med's original formula was copied by several other organizations in the travel and tourism industry. The increased competition caused Club Med to revise its management strategies and develop a different product in order to gain and hold market share. Changes in the industry were accompanied by social changes. As the years went by, the baby boomers of the 1960s and 1970s grew up, got married, and began to travel with their families. The target market thus changed again, and the necessity to change along with the market was promptly acknowledged.

The policy Club Med's managers embraced was one of differentiation and flexibility. Through assiduous market research, studies, and surveys, Club Med identified the continuously changing needs and characteristics of both the market and the clientele. On the basis of their results, they were able to take effective action to keep up with such evolution. Marketing strategies therefore were reevaluated, and the product Club Med offers was repackaged according to the demands of the guests, while still remaining faithful to the original philosophy. The image of Club Med was also reconsidered in order to determine the most appropriate one at all times.

Other significant changes included an entrance into the cruise business—Club Med I is a luxurious cruise ship that offers the excitement of yachting (thanks to a retractable platform that allows activities such as waterskiing, diving, etc.) together with the comforts of the cruise. Activities within the village were also improved and upgraded, following the guests' requests for more in-depth sports teaching, more amenities in the rooms, specialized restaurants, more security, and communication tools.

The clientele target was also widened: Club Med now attempts to attract guests other than the original youth/couples. As a consequence, the individual villages were updated by specializing in a particular area. Although all clubs offer the same basic services, some focus mainly on sports, some on tours and excursions, some on convention and meeting facilities, some on entertainment, and so on. Guests now range from sports enthusiasts to families (miniclubs and baby-clubs were recently established), honeymooners, and corporate clients. The new trend at the moment is that of finding ways to attract the older clientele.

Club Med also has had another innovative idea: Wild Card, which offers a bargain rate to vacationers who don't mind gambling on which village they visit. Wild Card confirms participants on a one-week vacation at one of Club Med's villages in the Bahamas, Caribbean, or Mexico for $999 per person, double occupancy; this is a savings of up to $500 over the weekly standard rate.

Included is the price of the airfare from specified gateway cities.

Wild Card presents a win-win situation. Club Med wins because it can utilize vacant space on air charters and accommodations; guests win because they get a great vacation at a bargain price.

To cope with the changes and implementations in the global structure of the villages, human resources staff (GOs—gentle organizers, etc.) also have been selected and trained more thoroughly. GOs come from all over the world; they must be fluent in a foreign language (to keep up with an extremely cosmopolitan clientele), skilled in sports or entertainment, and, most of all, extremely enthusiastic and people oriented. In fact, the spirit of the village depends almost entirely on the creative ideas and contact generated by the staff.

Overall, Club Med has shown a very remarkable ability to reinvent itself according to the continuous evolution of the market and society. The genuine commitment to excellence that has been demonstrated should help Club Med retain its status as the ultimate destination resort organization.

The competitiveness of international destinations is based on such attributes as service quality, as well as on value for the price, safety, security, entertainment, weather, infrastructure, and natural environment.[20] Political stability is also important in determining the desirability of a destination for international tourism. Imagine the feelings of an employee in a developing country who earns perhaps $5 per day when he or she sees wealthy tourists flaunting money, jewelry, and a lifestyle not obtainable.

Just imagine what will happen when another 300 million people become tourists by virtue of increasing standards of living and more people obtaining passports. Currently, only 21.7 percent of the U.S. population has passports. The population of

This tourist is purchasing handicrafts from a Masai tribesman in Kenya.

Côte d'Azur. Some European beaches become overcrowded in summer.

Eastern Europe and the nouveau riche of the Pacific Rim countries will substantially add to the potential number of tourists. So its no surprise that travel tourism is expected to double by 2015.

Sustainable Tourism and Ecotourism

The increasing number of tourists visiting destinations has heightened concern for the environment, physical recourses, and sociocultural degradation. The response of tourism officials has been to propose that all tourism be sustainable. The concept of **sustainable tourism** places a broadbased obligation on society—especially those involved with tourism policy; planning and development; federal, state, and local governments to harmonize tourism and tourism development by improving the quality of its environment and resources—physical and sociocultural.

Ecotourism is focused more on individual values; it is tourism with a conscience, sharing many of the same aspirations of sustainable tourism. The International Ecotourism Society (TIES) defines *Ecotourism* as "responsible travel to natural areas that conserves the environment and improves the well-being of local people." This means that those who implement and participate in ecotourism activities should follow the following principles:[21]

- Minimize impact.
- Build environmental and cultural awareness and respect.
- Provide positive experiences for both visitors and hosts.
- Provide direct financial benefits for conservation.
- Provide financial benefits and empowerment for local people.
- Raise sensitivity to host countries' political, environmental, and social climate.
- Support international human rights and labor agreements.

Most ecotourism destinations can be found in developing countries with natural surroundings and plentiful flora and fauna. Places like deserts, tropical rain forests, coral reefs, and ice glaciers are prime locations. Also important in ecotourism is the presence of a culture that is unique to the visitor. The focus of ecotourism is to provide tourists with new knowledge about a certain natural

Tourists visit Kenya to view giraffes such as these, one example of ecotourism.

area and the culture that is found within, along with a little bit of adventure. As for the natives, ecotourism is to help improve the local economy and conservation efforts. All parties are to gain a new appreciation for nature and people.

Thus far, ecotourism projects tend to be developed on a small scale. It is much easier to control such sites, particularly because of limits that are normally set on the community, the local tourism business, and the tourists. Limitations may include strict control of the amount of water and electricity being used, tougher recycling measures, regulating park and market hours, and, more importantly, limiting the number of visitors to a certain location at one time and limiting the size of the business. Another reason ecotourism projects are kept small is to allow more in-depth tours and educational opportunities.

Generally, most of the more popular ecotourism destinations are located in underdeveloped and developing countries. As vacationers are becoming more adventurous and are visiting remote, exotic places, they are participating in activities that should affect nature, host communities, and themselves in a positive manner. And because of the growing interests of travelers, many developed countries are following the trend. It is apparent from Yellowstone National Park in the United States to the Mayan Ruins of Tikal in Guatemala; from the Amazon River in Brazil to the vast safari lands of Kenya; from the snow-capped Himalayas in Nepal to the sultry jungles of Thailand; and from the Great Barrier Reef in Australia to the massive ice glaciers in Antarctica. There is no doubt that this is an attractive trend in many parts of the world.

Sustainable tourism, especially ecotourism, can be a main source of worldwide promotion of sustainable development geared toward tourists and communities in all countries.

Cultural, Heritage, and Nature Tourism

Tourism has developed to the point that there are now several special-interest areas. Culture and heritage are our legacies from the past, what we live with today, and what we pass on to future generations. Our cultures and natural heritages are irreplaceable sources of life and inspiration. Places as unique and diverse as the wilds of East Africa's Serengeti, the pyramids of Egypt, the Great Barrier Reef in Australia, and the Baroque cathedrals of Latin America make up our world's heritage. What makes the concept of world heritage exceptional is its universal application. World heritage sites belong to all the peoples of the world, no matter where they call home.[22]

Cultural Tourism: These trips are motivated by interest in cultural events like feasts or festivals or activities like theater, history, arts and sciences, museums, architecture, and religion. An example of cultural tourism would be a visit to the Polynesian Center in Hawaii where you will find the lifestyles, songs, dance, costumes and architecture of seven Pacific islands: Fiji, New Zealand, Marquesas, Samoa, Thaiti, Tonga, and Hawaii.

Heritage Tourism: This tourism is motivated by historic preservation—a combination of the natural, cultural, and architectural environment. An example of heritage tourism would be a visit to the Alamo in Texas—a battlefield that attracts 3 million visitors a year.

Both cultural and heritage tourism benefit from the **United Nations Educational, Scientific and Cultural Organization (UNESCO),** which has designated a number of World Heritage Sites worthy of protection and preservation due to the outstanding value to humanity of the natural and cultural heritage. There are 19 U.S. sites on the World Heritage List, among them the Statue of Liberty and the Grand Canyon.

Nature Tourism: These trips are motivated by nature, such as a visit to a national park. In recent years, aging baby boomers have increasingly become interested in nature tourism and include nature attractions as a part of, or reason for, their trip. (Notice that there are some similarities among these tourism areas of special interest.)

Check Your Knowledge

1. *Mini project:* Put together what you would consider your perfect vacation. You should include, but not be limited to, information about location, air travel (arrival and departure city), ground transportation, tourist attractions, weather, expense report, and currency exchange.

Trends in Tourism and Travel

- Ecotourism, sustainable tourism, and heritage tourism will continue to grow in importance.
- Globally, the number of tourist arrivals will continue to increase by about 4 percent per year, topping 1 billion by 2010.

- Governments will increasingly recognize the importance of tourism not only as an economic force, but also as a social–cultural force of increasing significance.
- More bilateral treaties are being signed, which will make it easier for tourists to obtain visas to visit other countries.
- The promotion and development of tourism is moving from the public sector (government) to the private sector (involved industry segments).
- Internet bookings will increase.
- Franchising of travel agencies and home-based travel agents will increase.
- Technology will continue to advance, allowing even more information to be available more quickly to more places around the world.
- Marketing partnerships and corporate alliances will continue to increase.
- Employment prospects will continue to improve.
- Ticketless air travel will continue to increase.
- Travel and tourism bookings via the Internet are increasing rapidly.
- As an ever increasing number of tourists visit destinations, managing these destinations is becoming a challenge.
- There will be an increase in the number of "boutique" airlines.
- Low-cost, no-frills airlines, such as Jet Blue, ATA, Ted (as in United), and, of course, Southwest, are gaining an increased market share at the expense of the six main U.S. airlines. They are attracting both business and leisure travelers.
- Airlines will try to entice travelers to book their trips via their Web sites rather than via Expedia and similar sites.
- Automatic airport check-ins will become more popular.
- The cruise industry will see continued expansion.
- There will be more alternative cruises.
- There will be increased concern for the health and safety of travel and tourism.
- Nature tourism will increase.

CASE STUDY

Congratulations! You have just been appointed to your city's council. You discover that a hot topic soon to be presented to the council is the construction of a convention center. Your initial research shows that several midsized cities are considering the convention center a way to increase economic activity, including job creation. The challenge these cities face is how to finance the convention center; projected costs are $100 million. Voters may resist a ballot to increase local taxes (either property or sales), but there is still the transient occupancy tax (TOT)—that is, taxes paid by people staying in local hotels. However, that tax is already earmarked for various local charities, and as we all know, good politicians want to get reelected, so voting against several worthy causes would not be popular. How can the center be financed and built? The city could float a bond on the market or could raise the TOT, but that might dissuade some groups from coming to your city because other cities have lower TOTs.

What would you do? What information do you need to decide whether to support or oppose the convention center?

CAREER INFORMATION

Tourism

Travel and tourism offer careers that provide information, transportation, accommodations, goods, and other services to travelers. Tourism is established almost everywhere in the world and is the world's largest employer. If restaurant- or hotel management-specific career options do not appeal to you, then you may want to consider a career in travel and tourism.

The best advice about the tourism career path is to be proactive during your college years. More than likely you will have to open your own doors to your first career position in tourism. It is important to start early in your college experience and learn as much about the industry as possible through trade publications, magazines, travel, seminars, course work, volunteer work at convention and visitors bureaus, shadowing at travel agencies, going on tours, and membership in professional organizations. It is beneficial to work in the travel and tourism industry while you are going to school. An internship can provide you with opportunities you may not be able to find on your own.

The travel and tourism business is changing because of the Internet. Many people can now access information that they once had to rely on travel agents and tour guides to provide. However, there will always be a market of individuals who are willing to pay someone else to provide these services.

Travel can serve as an important step toward global understanding, cultural appreciation, and tolerance. "To travel is to live" according to the Danish writer Hans Christian Anderson. Clearly, the travel industry can provide the opportunity for personal travel, professional accomplishment, and a rewarding career.

Related Web Sites

www.lee-county.com/leeisland/tcap/careerlist—employment possibilities associated with tourism
www.traveljobs.com/—travel jobs
www.prit.bc.ca/—advice and jobs in tourism
www.travelcareernetwork.com/—careers in the travel industry
www.vonl.com/chips/sltt.htm—books on tourism
www.crewunlimited.com/—cruise line placement
www.traveling.com/—industry information and employment
www.priceline.com/—service that lets people make their own travel arrangements

Courtesy of Charlie Adams.

SUMMARY

1. Tourism can be defined as the idea of attracting, accommodating, and pleasing groups or individuals traveling for pleasure or business. It is categorized by geography, ownership, function, industry, and travel motive.
2. Tourism involves international interaction and, therefore, government regulation. Several organizations, such as the World Tourism Organization, are responsible for environmental protection, tourism development, immigration, and cultural and social aspects of tourism.
3. Tourism is the world's largest industry and employer. It affects other industry sectors, such as public transportation, foodservice, lodging, entertainment, and recreation. In addition, tourism produces secondary impacts on businesses that are affected indirectly, which is known as the multiplier effect.
4. Travel agencies, tour operators, travel managers, wholesalers, national offices of tourism, and destination management companies serve as middlepersons between a country and its visitors.
5. Physical needs, the desire to experience other cultures, and an interest in meeting new people are some of the motives people have when they travel. Because of flexible work hours, early retirement, and the easy accessibility of traveling, tourism is constantly growing.
6. From a social and cultural perspective, tourism can further international understanding and economically improve a poor country. However, it can also disturb a culture by confronting it with mass tourism, causing the destruction of natural sites. A trend in avoiding tourism pollution is ecotourism.
7. Business travel has increased in recent years due to the growth of convention centers in several cities. As a result, business travelers have given a boost to hotels, restaurants, and auto rental companies. The number of female business travelers is rising as well.

KEY WORDS AND CONCEPTS

Business travel
Convention and visitors
    bureaus
Ecotourism
Hub-and-spoke system

Interdependency
Multiplier effect
Pacific Area Travel
    Association (PATA)
Pleasure travel

Sustainable tourism
Tourism
United Nations Educational
    Scientific and Cultural
    Organization (UNESCO)

Vacation package
World Tourism
    Organization (WTO)

REVIEW QUESTIONS

1. Give a broad definition of tourism and explain why people are motivated to travel.
2. Give a brief explanation of the economic impact of tourism. Name two organizations that influence or further the economic impact of tourism.

3. Choose a career in the tourism business and give a brief overview of what your responsibilities would be.
4. Discuss the positive and negative impacts that tourism can have on a country in consideration of tourism pollution and ecotourism.

INTERNET EXERCISES

1. Organization: **World Tourism Organization**
   Web site: **world-tourism.org/**
   Summary: The WTO is the only intergovernmental organization that serves in the field of travel and tourism and is a global forum for tourism policy and issues. It has about 138 member countries and territories. Its mission is to promote and develop tourism as a significant means of fostering international peace and understanding, economic development, and international trade.
   (a) How much was spent on international tourism in 1999?
   (b) What does the *Tourism: 2020 Vision* predict?

2. Organization: **Air Transport Association**
   Web site: **www.air-transport.org/**
   Summary: The ATA is the first and only trade organization for the principal U.S. airlines. Its purpose is to support and assist its members by promoting the air transport industry and its operations, safety, cost effectiveness, and technological advancement. It has promoted the interest of the commercial airline industry for more than 60 years and now is a key player in the global transportation market.
   (a) What were effects of the Airline Deregulation Act of 1978?
   (b) What indirect benefits does the airline industry offer the public?

APPLY YOUR KNOWLEDGE

1. Analyze your family and friends' recent or upcoming travel plans and compare them to the examples in the text for reasons why people travel.

2. Suggest some ecotourism activities for your community.
3. How would you promote or improve tourism in your community?

SUGGESTED ACTIVITY

Go online and get prices for an airline round trip between two cities for a flight
a. More than 60 days out
b. 30–59 days out for the same two cities

c. 15–29 days out
d. 7–14 days out
e. for tomorrow
Compare the prices and share the results with your class.

ENDNOTES

1. **www.wttc.org/2005sa/pd//word.pdf.p16.** July 9, 2005.
2. **www.word-tourism.org/aboutwto/eng/menu.html.**
3. Rosa Songel, "Statistics and Economic Measurement of Tourism," World Tourism Organization. **www.world-tourism.org/omt/wtich.htm.**
4. **www.wttc.org/economic_research/kystats.htm.**
5. Ibid.
6. **www.world-tourism.org/market_research/facts@figures/menus.htm.**
7. **tia.org.** August 4, 2005.
8. **www.worldspan.com/home.asp?fpageID=5.**
9. Courtesy of the American Society of Travel Agents.
10. **www.astanet.com/news/releasearchive03/12_23_03.asl.**
11. Phone interview with Mark Edwards, American Express Travel Services. July 6, 2005.
12. Personal conversation with Jay R. Schrock. January, 14, 2004.
13. This section draws on Robert McIntosh and Charles R. Goeldner, *Tourism Principles, Practices, Philosophies*, 6th ed. New York: John Wiley and Sons, 1990, pp. 100–103.
14. **www.icta.com/aboutict.htm.**
15. John R. Walker, *Tourism.* Sarasota, FL: Tourism Publications, 2006, p. 87.
16. Ibid., p. 64.
17. Personal correspondence with Karen Smith and Claudia Green. June 28, 2005.
18. Ibid.
19. Travel Industry Association of America. **www.tia.org/travel/trt.asp.** June 25, 2005.
20. **www.ecotourism.org.**
21. Ibid.
22. **http://whc.unesco.org/en/about/.** August 20, 2005.

WEB RESOURCES

World Tourism Organization
www.world-tourism.org

World Travel and Tourism Council
www.wttc.org

International Air Transport Association
www.iata.org

International Civil Aviation Organization
www.icao.int

Pacific Area Travel Association
www.pata.org

Tourism Works for America Council
www.tia.org

International Ecotourism Society
www.ecotourismsociety.org

American Society of Travel Agents
www.astanet.com

Carnival Cruise Lines
www.carnival.com

part 2

Lodging

The Hotel Business

4

After reading and studying this chapter, you should be able to:

- Describe hotel ownership and development via *hotel franchising* and *management contracts*.
- Classify hotels by type, location, and price.
- Discuss the concept and growth of vacation ownership.
- Name some prestigious and unusual hotels.

Hotel Development and Ownership

Franchising and management contracts are the two main driving forces in the development and operation of the hotel business. Once the potential of franchising caught on, there was no stopping American ingenuity; in about a half century, the hotel business was changed forever, and here is how it happened.

Franchising

Franchising in the hospitality industry is a concept that allows a company to expand more rapidly by using other people's money than if it had to acquire its own financing. The company or franchisor grants certain rights, for example, to use its trademark, signs, proven operating systems, operating procedures and possibly reservations system, marketing know-how, purchasing discounts, and so on, for a fee. In return, the franchisee agrees by signing the franchise contract to operate the restaurant, hotel, and so on, in accordance with the guidelines set by the franchisor. Franchising is a way of doing business that benefits both the franchisor—who wants to expand the business rapidly—and the franchisee—who has financial backing but lacks specific expertise and recognition. Some corporations franchise by individual outlets and others franchise by territory.

Franchising hotels in the United States began in 1907, when the Ritz Development Company franchised the Ritz-Carlton name in New York City.[1] Howard Johnson began franchising his hotels in 1927. This allowed for rapid expansion, first on the East Coast and later in the Midwest and finally in the mid-1960s into California. Today, there are more than 900 restaurants in the chain.

Holiday Inns (now a part of Intercontinental hotel corporation), one of the largest lodging enterprises in the world) also grew by the strategy of franchising. In 1952, Kemmons Wilson, a developer, had a disappointing experience while on a family vacation when he had to pay for an extra room for his children. Therefore, Wilson decided to build a moderately priced family-style hotel. Each room was comfortably sized and had two double beds; this enabled children to stay for free in their parents' rooms. In the 1950s and early 1960s, as the economy grew, Holiday Inns grew in size and popularity. Holiday Inns added restaurants, meeting rooms, and recreational facilities. They upgraded the furnishings and fixtures in the bedrooms and almost completely abandoned the original concept of being a moderately priced lodging operation.

One of the key factors in the successful development of Holiday Corporation was that they were one of the first companies to enter the midprice range of the market. These inns or motor hotels were often located away from the expensive downtown sites,

Franchised Hotels

North America is host to more than 180 hotel brand extensions and franchised hotel brands. Franchising remains a mostly North American activity, with limited opportunities in international markets. This is because what was once plentiful—the capital needed to drive hotel franchising—is now less accessible. Brand strategies for franchisers in the new millennium seem to be influenced mostly by mergers and a peaking market. Despite the constant progress, one area remains tense, and that is the relationship between hotel companies and franchisees. Tensions exist for varying reasons, including fees, services, reservations inspections, and maintenance of standards.

Interior of a Days Inn Budget Accommodation

near important freeway intersections and the more reasonably priced suburbs. Another reason for their success was the value they offered: comfort at a reasonable price, avoiding the expensive trimmings of luxury hotels.

About this time, a new group of budget motels emerged. Motel 6 (so named because the original cost of a room was $6 a night) in California slowly spread across the country, as did Days Inn and others. Cecil B. Day was in the construction business and found Holiday Inns too expensive when traveling on vacation with his family. He bought cheap land and constructed buildings of no more than two stories to keep the costs down. These hotels and motels were primarily for commercial travelers and vacationing families, were located close to major highways, and were built to provide low-cost lodging without frills. Some of these buildings were modular constructions. Entire rooms were built elsewhere, transported to the site, and placed side by side.

It was not until the 1960s that Hilton and Sheraton began to franchise their names. Franchising was the primary growth and development strategy of hotels and motels during the 1960s, 1970s, and 1980s. However, franchising presents two major challenges for the franchisor: maintenance of quality standards and avoidance of financial failure on the part of the franchisee.

It is difficult for the franchise company to state in writing all the contingencies that will ensure that quality standards are met. Recent franchise agreements are more specific in terms of the exterior maintenance and guest service levels. Franchise fees vary according to the agreements worked out between the franchisor and the franchisee; however, an average agreement is based on 3 or 4 percent of room revenue.

The world's largest franchisor of hotels, with 5,200 hotels, is Cendant of Parsippany, New Jersey. Choice Hotels International, ranked second with 4,545 franchised hotels, is a subsidiary of the Blackstone Group,

Franchising Trends

Factors propelling franchise growth include these:

- Fresh looks (curb appeal)
- Location—near highways, airports, and suburbs
- Expansion in smaller cities throughout the United States
- New markets—located in proximity to golf courses and other attractions
- Foreign expansion—a move to increase brand awareness

Company	Number of Guests Rooms	Hotels Franchised	Total Hotels
Cendant (Day's Inn, Howard Johnson, Ramada, Knights Inn, Super 8, Travel Lodge, Villager Lodge, Wingate Inn)	540,000	5,200	6,400
Choice Hotels International (Clarion, Quality Inn, Comfort Inn, Econolodge, Friendship Inn, Mainstay, Roadway Inn)	410,877	4,545	4,678
Intercontinental Hotels Corp. (Inter-Continental Hotels & Resorts, Crowne Plaza Hotels & Resorts, Hotel Indigo, Holiday Inn Hotels & Resorts, Holiday Inn Express, Staybridge Suites, Candlewood Suites)	515,000	3,200	3,330
Hilton Hotels Corp. (Hilton Hotel, Hilton Garden Inn, Doubletree, Embassy Suites, Hampton Inn, Homewood Suites, Conrad Hotels)	147,667	1,482	2,080
Marriott International (JW Marriott, Marriott Hotels & Resorts, Renaissance Hotels & Resorts, Courtyard by Marriott, Residence Inn, Fairfield Inn, TownePlace Suites, SpringHill Suites Horizons, The Ritz-Carlton Hotel Company, L.L.C., The Ritz-Carlton Club)	N/A	1,521	2,663
Carlson Hospitality Worldwide (Regent International, Raddison, Country Inn & Suites, Park Plaza, Park Inn Hotels	132,467	826	895
Accor (Red Roof, Motel 6, Studio 6, etc.)	N/A	748	3,954
U.S. Franchise Systems (America Best Inn & Suites, AmeriSuites Hawthorn Suites, Microtel Inns & Suites	N/A	512	512
Société du Louvre (Concord Hotels, BleuMarine, Kyraid, Hotel Premiere Classe, Campanile)	N/A	469	980
Starwood Hotels & Resorts Worldwide (St. Regis, The Luxury Collection, W Hotels, Sheraton, Four Points Sheraton, Westin)	227,000	308	748

Source: Company Web sites August 5, 2005.

Figure 4–1   *Franchised Hotels Among the Top Ten Largest Corporate Chains*

New York. Intercontinental Hotels and Resorts is now the third largest franchisor with 3,200 hotels. Figure 4–1 shows franchised hotels among the top ten corporate chains.

Franchising provides both benefits and drawbacks to the franchisee and franchisor. The benefits to the franchisee are as follows:

- A set of plans and specifications from which to build
- National advertising

- Centralized reservation system
- Participation in volume discounts for purchasing furnishings, fixtures, and equipment
- Listing in the franchisor's directory
- Low fee percentage charged by credit card companies

The drawbacks to the franchisee are as follows:
- High fees, both to join and ongoing
- Central reservations generally producing between 17 and 26 percent of reservations
- Franchisees must conform to the franchisor's agreement
- Franchisees must maintain all standards set by the franchisor

The benefits to the franchise company are as follows:
- Increased market share and recognition
- Up-front fees

The drawbacks to the franchise company are as follows:
- The need to be very careful in the selection of franchisees
- Difficulty in maintaining control of standards

Franchising continues to be a popular form of expansion both in North America and the rest of the world. There are always a few properties that lose their right to franchise by not maintaining standards.

Is There a Franchise in Your Future?

Courtesy of Robert Kok

Many of you may not realize the pervasiveness of franchised operations in the United States. Predictions are that more than 50 percent of all retail sales in the United States (including restaurants) will soon be transacted through franchised units. Further, franchises are available not only in the hotel, restaurant, travel, and recreation industries, but also in a large variety of other businesses that might interest you. These businesses include automotive tires and parts, retailing of all kinds, mail and copy services, janitorial and decorating services, personnel agencies, and so on. Today, many franchises can be operated from home by those interested in lifestyle changes.

If you end up working for a hospitality-related organization after graduation, chances are that your career will be influenced by franchising. You may work directly for a franchisor (the company that sells a franchised concept to an entrepreneur), whether on the corporate staff (e.g., training, franchise consulting) or in an operations position in a franchisor-owned unit. Many franchisors own their own units in order to test new operational or marketing ideas and to demonstrate the viability of the business to potential franchisees (the entrepreneurs who buy the franchised unit).

Alternatively, you may work for a franchisee (the entrepreneurs who buy a franchised unit). Some franchisees are small businesses, owning only one or a few units. Other franchisees are large corporations themselves, owning hundreds of units doing hundreds of millions of dollars in sales every year. For instance, RTM, Inc., owns and operates over 600 Arby's restaurants. Additionally,

Corporate Profile: Cendant Corporation

Cendant is an empire consisting of a loose confederation of businesses and brands. Included under Cendant's management are Days Inn, Howard Johnson, Ramada, Knights Inn, Super 8, Travelodge, Villager Lodge, Wingate Inn, Century 21, ERA (Electronic Realty Associates), Coldwell Banker, Avis Rent-a-Car, and PHH Corp. Combined, these businesses account for approximately half a million hotel rooms in the United States, Canada, Latin America, and Europe, and more than 11,500 franchised real estate offices with more than 190,000 brokers in the United States, Mexico, Canada, Puerto Rico, Europe, Africa, and the Asia-Pacific region.

Although clearly in the consumer services industry, its clients include other businesses and corporations—not individual consumers. As a franchisor, the company licenses the owners and operators of independent businesses to use Cendant's brand names, without taking on big business risks and expenses. Cendant does not operate hotels or real estate brokerage offices, but instead, provides coordination and services that allow franchisees to retain local control of their activities. At the same time, they benefit from the economies of scale of widely promoted brand names and well-established standards of service, national and regional direct marketing, co-marketing programs, and volume purchasing discounts. All Cendant brands share "extensive market research, use well-developed technology, such as proprietary reservation systems and, in the case of lodging, a room inventory tracking system, which is extremely technology intensive and eliminates waste."[1] By monitoring quality control and extensively promoting the brand names, Cendant offers its independent franchise owners franchise fees that are relatively low compared to the increased profitability they gain.

Through franchising, Cendant limits its own risks and is able to keep overhead costs low. Chief Financial Officer

Michael P. Monaco says Cendant "limits the volatility in the business as best as we can because fees come from revenue, not the franchisee's profitability.[2] A further advantage of being a franchiser of such dimension is that the company is even more protected from the cyclical nature of the economy than are other franchise ventures.

The critical mass created by all the businesses working together makes Cendant more valuable as a whole than as the sum of its parts, gives it outstanding purchasing power and market control, and makes it extremely effective in selling to a wide audience.

The wave of baby boomers consists of 76 million people who are soon to retire, and this trend will continue for a few more years. This clientele consumes primarily two things: travel and residential real estate. In light of this trend, Cendant's diversification from the hotel market turned to real estate, mortgage companies, and timeshare operators.

The synergy of Cendant is realized by providing travel, accommodation, and related services.[3] Services like Cheap Tickets, Lodging.com, Rates To Go, HotelClub.com, Cendant Travel and Galileo, a travel distribution service, are used by 44,000 travel agencies. WizCom supplies its customers with electronic distribution and e-commerce solutions for Internet Global distribution Services (GDS) and other travel reservations systems, offering the industry's first switching service. WizCom enables global distribution systems and Internet connectivity, as well as central reservations (CRS) and information services to the hotels, car rental, and tour industries.[4]

---

[1]Todd Pitock, "The Artful Acquirer," *Journal of Business Strategy*, 18, 2, March/April 1997, p. 19.
[2]Ibid.
[3]Personal conversation with Kenneth Crocker, March 14, 2004.
[4]www.cendant.com/about-cendant/travel_distribution.services/supplier-seminars.html. June 13, 2004.

---

it owns and franchises two midsized chicken restaurants, Lee's Famous Recipe Chicken and Mrs. Winner's Chicken & Biscuits. Working for a company as large as RTM would be similar to working for a large franchisor.

A third way that franchising may involve you is through ownership. Rather than starting your own independent business after college, many of you may want to consider buying a franchise. Several advantages can result. First, by

Sleep Inn, a Brand of Choice Hotels International, One of the Major Franchising Hotel Chains

working with a larger company you get the benefits of its experience in running the business that you have chosen to enter. Many of the mistakes that a new entrepreneur may make have already been overcome by your franchisor. The company might provide cash flow. The company might also provide other support services at little or no cost, such as marketing and advertising, site selection, construction plans, assistance with financing, and so on. All this assistance leads to a second key reason for buying a franchise—reducing your risk of failure. Franchising is probably less risky than starting your own business from scratch.

A key question to be answered before you buy a franchise is whether you are better suited to being a franchisee or an independent entrepreneur. Consider the following factors that many franchisors seek. Are you strongly motivated to succeed and do you have a past history of business success, even if it is in a different business? Do you have a significant sum of money as well as access to credit? Are you willing to accept the franchisor's values, philosophy, and ways of doing business, as well as its technical assistance? Do you have the full support of your immediate family as you develop your business? Are you willing to devote substantially all of your working time to the business?

Franchising does have some disadvantages, as noted by many former franchisees. Your expectations of success may not be met. Perhaps the business did not have the potential that you expected, or perhaps you were not willing to invest the time needed. In a few cases, an overzealous or dishonest franchisor representative has misled franchisees.

As a franchisee, your freedom is somewhat restricted. You must operate within the constraints set out by your franchise agreement and the operational standards manual. Although there may be some room for you to express your creativity and innovation, it is generally limited. This may mean that, over time, the work might become monotonous and unchallenging, yet you have a long-term commitment to the company due to the franchise agreement that you signed. Your failure to consistently follow the franchisor's methods for running the business could result in the termination of your contract and your forced removal from the business.

Finally, the franchisor itself may not be performing well, thereby hurting your local business. Also, they may allow other franchisees to open units so near to your operation that your business is adversely affected.

Buying a franchise can be a very rewarding business experience in many ways. But like any other business venture, it requires research and a full discussion with family, friends, and business advisors, such as your accountant and attorney. You should carefully weigh whether or not you are psychologically suited to be a franchisee. Perhaps you perform more effectively in a corporate structure as an employee. Perhaps you are better suited to starting your own business from scratch. A careful analysis can help you make an informed decision. Buying a franchise like Subway, Cold Stone Creamery, or Sea Master cruises is a lot cheaper—as in a few thousand dollars—compared to one million-plus for a hotel or even a McDonald's.

Referral Associations

Referral associations offer similar benefits to properties as franchises, albeit at a lower cost. Hotels and motels with a referral association share a centralized reservation system and a common image, logo or advertising slogan. In addition, referrals may offer group buying discounts to members, as well as management training and continuing education programs. Each independent hotel refers guests to each of the other member hotels. Hotels and motels pay an initial fee to join a referral association. Size and appearance standards are less stringent than a franchise agreement; hence guests may find more variation between the facilities than with a franchise member.

Preferred Hotels and Resorts Worldwide is a consortium of 105 independent, luxury hotels and resorts united to compete with the marketing power of chain operations. It promotes the individuality, high standards, hospitality, and luxury of member hotels. It also provides marketing support services and a reservation center.

With the decrease in airline commissions, referral organizations, especially those at the luxury end of the market, are well placed to offer incentives to agents to book their clients with the referral group's hotels. An example would be awarding trips to the property for every ten rooms booked. Another would be for the referral hotels to offer, for instance, a 20 percent commission during slow periods. Three luxury Boston-area preferred properties—the Boston Harbor Hotel, the Bostonian Hotel, and the Charles Hotel in Cambridge, Massachusetts—joined in promoting a St. Patrick's Day weekend package. Preferred Hotels in Texas—the Mansion on Turtle Creek and Hotel Crescent Court in Dallas, La Mansion Del Rio South in San Antonio, and the Washington Hotel in Fort Worth—launched a major, year-long promotion, which includes a tie-in with major retail, credit card, and airline partners.

In addition to regional marketing programs, the referral associations that handle reservations for members have joined Galileo International's Inside Availability Service. This gives agents access to actual rates and room availability that is not always available on the standard CRS databases.

Leading Hotels of the World (LHW) was set up in 1928 as Luxury Hotels of Europe and Egypt by 38 hotels, including the London Savoy; the Hotel Royal in Evian, France; and the Hotel Negresco in Nice, France, who were interested in improving their marketing. The organization worked by having hotels advise their guests to use the establishments of fellow members. It then opened a New York office to make direct contact with wealthy American and Canadian travelers wishing to visit Europe or Egypt.

LHW, which is controlled by its European members, acts as an important marketing machine for its members, especially now, with offices around the world providing reservations, sales, and promotional services. All the hotels and offices are connected by a central computer reservation system called ResStar. The number of reservations members receive from Leading Hotel members varies from place to place, but with more than 100 hotels waiting to join, it must be beneficial.

Like LHW, Small Luxury Hotels of the World (SLH) is another marketing consortium in which seventy-nine independently owned and managed hotels and resorts are members. For more than 35 years, it has sought to market and sell its membership to the travel industry and to provide an interhotel networking system for all members. Each hotel is assessed and regularly checked to ensure that it maintains the very highest standards.

Management Contracts

Management contracts have been responsible for the hotel industry's rapid boom since the 1970s. They became popular among hotel corporations because little or no up-front financing or equity was involved. Even if the hotel corporation was involved in the construction of the hotel, ownership generally reverted to a large insurance company. This was the case with the La Jolla, California, Marriott Hotel. Marriott Corporation built the hotel for about $34 million, then sold it to Paine Webber, a major investment banking firm, for about $52 million on completion. Not a bad return on investment!

The management contract usually allows for the hotel company to manage the property for a period of 5, 10, or 20 years. For this, the company receives

Hyatt hotels operates some of its hotels by management contract, rather than owning them all. Source: William Waterfall/PacificStock.com

as a management fee, often a percentage of gross and/or net operating profit, usually about 2 to 4.5 percent of gross revenues. Lower fees in the 2 percent range are more prevalent today, with an increase in the incentive fee based on profitability. Some contracts begin at 2 percent for the first year, 2.5 the second, and 3.5 the third and for the remainder of the contract.[2] Today, many contracts are for a percentage of sales and a percentage of operating profit. This is normally 2 + 2 percent. Increased competition among management companies has decreased the management contract fees in the past few years. In recent years, hotel companies increasingly have opted for management contracts because considerably less capital is tied up in managing as compared with owning properties. This has allowed for a more rapid expansion of both the U.S. and international markets.

Hotel management companies often form a partnership of convenience with developers and owners who generally do not have the desire or ability to operate the hotel. The management company provides operational expertise, marketing, and sales clout, often in the form of a centralized reservation system (CRS). Some companies manage a portfolio of properties on a cluster, regional, or national basis. The ten largest management companies are listed in Figure 4–2.

Recent management contracts have called for an increase in the equity commitment on the part of the management company. In addition, owners have increased their operational decision-making options to allow them more control over the property. General managers have increased responsibility to owners who also want their share of profit.

With international expansion, a hotel company entering the market might actively seek a local partner or owner to work within a form of joint venture.

Today, hotel management companies exist in an extremely competitive environment. They have discovered that the hotel business, like most others, has changed and they are adapting accordingly. Today's hotel owners are demanding better bottom-line results and reduced fees. Management companies are seeking sustainability and a bigger share of the business.

Company
Marriott International
Accor
Extended Stay America
Tharaldson Enterprises
Société du Louvre
InterContinental Hotels & Resorts
Westmont Hospitality Group Inc.
Starwood Hotels & Resorts/
Starwood Hotels & Resorts WW
Hilton Hotels Corp.
Prime Hospitality Group

Figure 4–2 *Ten Largest Management Companies*

Personal Profile: Conrad Hilton and Hilton Hotels Corporation

Conrad Hilton "King of Innkeepers" and Master of Hotel Finance

Hilton's success was attributed to two main strategies: (1) hiring the best managers and letting them have total autonomy, and (2) being a cautious bargainer who, in later years, was careful not to overfinance. Conrad Hilton had begun a successful career in the banking business before he embarked on what was to become one of the most successful hotel careers ever.

In 1919, while on bank business in Cisco, Texas, he bought the Mobley Hotel with an investment of $5,000. Hilton rented rooms to oil industry prospectors and construction workers. Because of high demand for accommodations and very little supply, Hilton rented rooms in eight-hour shifts, for 300 percent occupancy. On some occasions, he even rented out his own room and slept in a lobby chair.

Because Hilton knew the banking business well and had maintained contacts who would lend him money for down payments on properties, he quickly expanded to seven Texas hotels. Hilton's strategy was to borrow as much money as possible in order to expand as rapidly as possible. This worked well until the Great Depression of the early 1930s. Hilton was unable to meet the payments on his properties and lost several but did not declare bankruptcy.[1]

Hilton, like many great leaders, even during the Depression years had the determination to bounce back. To reduce

Lobby of the Waldorf Hotel, New York. Hilton bought the hotel for only $7.4 million in 1949.

costs, he borrowed money against his life insurance and even formed an alliance with the National Hotels Corporation.

Hilton's business and financial acumen is legendary. The *New York Times* described Conrad Hilton as "a master of finance and a cautious bargainer who was careful not to overfinance" and had "a flawless sense of timing."[2]

Hilton was the first person to notice vast lobbies with people sitting in comfortable chairs but not spending any money. So he added the lobby bar as a convenient meeting place and leased out space for gift shops and newsstands. Most of the additional revenue from these operations went directly to the bottom line. Today, Hilton Hotels Corporation includes Conrad Hotels, Doubletree, Embassy Suites hotels, Hampton Inn and Hampton Inns & Suites, Hilton Hotels, Hilton Garden Inn, Hilton Grand Vacation, and Homewood Suites by Hilton. These brands total thousands of hotels in cities all over the world, and "Be my guest" is still the gracious and warm way guests are received.

[1]Paul R. Dittmer and Gerald G. Griffen, *The Dimensions of the Hospitality Industry: An Introduction.* New York: Van Nostrand Reinhold, 1993, pp. 91–92; and Conrad Hilton, *Be My Guest,* pp. 184–199.
[2]Joan Cook, "Conrad Hilton, Founder of Hotel Chain, Dies at 92," *New York Times,* January 5, 1979, sec. 11, p. 5.

Check Your Knowledge

1. What main factor changed the nature of the hotel industry? What impact does it have today?
2. In your own words, define *franchising* and *management contracts.*

Real Estate Investment Trust (REIT)

Real estate investment trusts (REITs) have existed since the 1960s. In those early days, they were mostly mortgage holders. But in the 1980s, they began to own property outright, often focusing on specific sectors like hotels, office buildings, apartments, malls, and nursing homes. Today, about 300 REITs, with a combined market value of $70 billion, are publicly traded. Investors like them because they do not pay corporate income tax and instead are required to distribute at least 95 percent of net income to shareholders. In addition, because they trade as stocks, they are much easier to get into or out of than limited partnerships or the direct ownership of properties. In the hotel industry, REITs are clearly where the action is.

The leading REIT corporations are Patriot American Hospitality and Starwood Lodging Trust Patriot. American Hospitality has acquired Wyndham Hotels, which has become its operating company and given it a well-regarded brand name. Starwood Lodging Trust acquired Westin Hotels and Resorts for $1.4 billion and outbid Hilton for ITT Sheraton. Patriot and Starwood are the only REITs allowed to both manage and own properties.

Check Your Knowledge

1. Give reasons why you would like to build, manage, and own your own hotel. According to this text, what are the reasons people build, manage, and own hotel properties?

Classification of Hotels

According to the American Hotel & Lodging Association (AH&LA), the U.S. lodging industry consists of 46,000 hotels and motels, with a total of 3.3 million rooms. The gross volume of business generated from these rooms is $93.1 billion.

Unlike many other countries, the United States has no formal government classification of hotels. However, the American Automobile Association (AAA) classifies hotels by diamond award, and the Mobile Travel Guide offers a five-star award.

The AAA has been inspecting and rating the nation's hotels since 1977. Less than 2 percent of the 41,000 properties inspected annually throughout the United States, Canada, and Mexico earned the five-diamond award, which is the association's highest award for excellence. In 2000, the five-diamond award was bestowed on 58 lodgings in the United States, Canada, and Mexico. Twelve of the properties received both the five-diamond and the five-star awards.

AAA uses descriptive criteria to evaluate the hotels that they rate annually in the United States, Canada, Mexico, and the Caribbean (see Figure 4–3).

- One-diamond properties have simple roadside appeal and the basic lodging needs.
- Two-diamond properties have average roadside appeal, with some landscaping and a noticeable enhancement in interior decor.
- Three diamonds carry a degree of sophistication through higher service and comfort.

	◇	◇◇	◇◇◇	◇◇◇◇	◇◇◇◇◇
General	Simple roadside appeal Limited landscaping	Average roadside appeal Some landscaping	Very good roadside appeal Attractive landscaping	Excellent roadside appeal Professionally planned landscaping	Outstanding roadside appeal Professional landscaping with a variety of foliage and stunning architecture
Lobby	Adequate size with registration, front desk, limited seating, and budget art, if any	Medium size with registration, front desk, limited seating, carpeted floors, budget art, and some plants	Spacious with front desk, carpeted seating area arranged in conversation groupings, good-quality framed art, live plants, luggage carts, and bellstation	Spacious or consistent with historical attributes; registration and front desk above average with solid wood or marble; ample seating area with conversation groupings and upscale appointments including tile, carpet, or wood floors; impressive lighting fixtures; upscale framed art and art objects; abundant live plants; background music; separate check-in/-out; bellstation	Comfortably spacious or consistent with historical attributes; registration and front desk above average; ample seating with conversation groupings and upscale appointments; impressive lighting fixtures; variety of fine art; abundant plants and fresh floral arrangements; background music; separate check-in/-out; bellstation that may be part of concierge area; concierge desk
Guestrooms	May not reflect current industry standards	Generally reflect current industry standards	Reflect current industry standards	Reflect current industry standards and provide upscale appearance	Reflect current standards and provide luxury appearance
Service	Basic attentive service	More attentive service	Upgraded service levels	High service levels and hospitality	Guests are pampered by flawless service executed by professional staff

Figure 4–3 *Summary of AAA Diamond-Rating Guidelines* (Courtesy of Hotel and Lodging Management)

- Four diamonds have excellent roadside appeal and service levels that give guests what they need before they even ask for it.
- Five-diamond properties have the highest service levels, sophistication, and offerings.

Hotels may be classified according to location, price, and type of services offered. This allows guests to make a selection on these as well as personal criteria. A list of hotel classifications follows:

City center—luxury, first-class, midscale, economy, suites
Resort—luxury, midscale, economy suites, condominium, time-share, convention
Airport—luxury, midscale, economy, suites
Freeway—midscale, economy suites
Casino—luxury, midscale, economy
Full service

Budget $35–$49	*Economy* $49–$69	*Midprice* $69–$125	*Up Scale* $125–$225	*Luxury* $150–$450	*All-Suites* $125–$225
	Holiday Inn Express	Holiday Inn	Holiday Inn	Crown Plaza	
	Fairfield Inn	Courtyard Inn Residence Inn	Marriott	Marriott Marquis Ritz-Carlton	Marriott Suites
		Days Inn	Omni	Renaissance	
		Radisson Inn	Radisson		Radisson Suites
	Ramada Limited	Ramada Inn	Ramada		Ramada Suites
	Sheraton Inn	Sheraton Inn Four Points	Sheraton	Sheraton Grande	Sheraton Suites
			Hyatt	Hyatt Regency Hyatt Park	Hyatt Suites
Sleep Inns	Comfort Inn	Quality Inn	Clarion Hotels		Quality Suites Comfort Suites
		Hilton Inn	Hilton	Hilton Towers	Hilton Suites
		Doubletree Club	Doubletree		Doubletree Suites
Thrift Lodge	Travelodge Hotels	Travelodge Hotels	Forte Hotels	Forte Hotels	
			Westin	Westin	
Sixpence Inn	La Quinta				
E-Z-8	Red Roof Inn				
	Best Western				
	Hampton Inn				Embassy Suites

Figure 4–4 *Hotels by Price Segment*

Convention
Economy
Extended stay
Bed & breakfast

Alternatively, the hotel industry may be segmented according to price. Figure 4–4 gives an example of a national or major regional brand-name hotel chain in each segment.

City Center Hotels

City center hotels, by virtue of their location, meet the needs of the traveling public for business or leisure reasons. These hotels could be luxury, midscale, business, suites, economy, or residential. They offer a range of accommodations and services. Luxury hotels offer the ultimate in decor, butler service, concierge and special concierge floors, secretarial services, the latest WiFi or in-room technology, computers, fax machines, beauty salons, health spas, 24-hour room service, swimming pools, tennis courts, valet service, ticket office, airline office, car rental, and doctor/nurse on duty or on call. Generally, they offer a signature restaurant, coffee shop, or an equivalent name restaurant; a lounge; a name bar; meeting and convention rooms; a ballroom; and possibly a fancy night spot.

Resort Hotels

Resort hotels came of age with the advent of rail travel. Increasingly, city dwellers and others had the urge to vacation in locations they found appealing. Traveling to these often more exotic locations became a part of the pleasure experience. In the late 1800s, luxury resort hotels were developed to accommodate the clientele that the railways brought.

The leisure and pleasure travelers of those days were drawn by resorts, beaches, or spectacular mountain scenery. At first, many of these grand resorts were seasonal. However, as automobile and air travel made even the remote resorts more accessible and an increasing number of people could afford to visit, many resorts became year-round properties.

The Elegant Drake Hotel in Chicago

The Royal Hawaiian Hotel on the famous Waikiki Beach, Oahu, Hawaii, is a popular resort.

Resort communities sprang up in the sunshine belt from Palm Springs to Palm Beach. Some resorts focused on major sporting activities such as skiing, golf, or fishing; others offered family vacations. Further improvements in both air and automobile travel brought exotic locations within the reach of the population. Europe, the Caribbean, and Mexico became more accessible. As the years passed, some of the resorts suffered because the public's vacation plans changed.

The traditional family month-long resort vacation gave way to shorter, more frequent getaways of four to seven days. The regular resort visitors became older; in general, the younger guests preferred the mobility of the automobile and the more informal atmosphere provided by the newer and more informal resorts.

Hyatt hotels have organized a program consisting of a variety of activities for children, thereby giving the parents an opportunity to either enjoy some free time on their own or join their children in some fun activities. Many resort hotels began to attract conventions, conferences, and meetings. This enabled them to maintain or increase occupancy, particularly during the low and shoulder seasons.

Guests go to resorts for leisure and recreation. They want a good climate—summer or winter—in which they can relax or engage in recreational activities. Due to the remoteness of many resorts, guests are a kind of "captured clientele," who may be on the property for days at a time. This presents resort managers with some unique operating challenges. Another operating challenge concerns seasonality—some resorts either do not operate year-round or have periods of very low occupancy. Both present challenges in attracting, training, and retaining competent staff.

Many guests travel considerable distances to resorts. Consequently, they tend to stay longer than at transient hotels. This presents a challenge to the food and beverage manager to provide quality menus that are varied and are presented and served in an attractive, attentive manner. To achieve this, resorts often use a cyclical menu that repeats itself every fourteen to twenty-one days. Also, they provide a wide variety and number of dishes to stimulate interest. Menus are now more health conscious—lighter and low in saturated fats, cholesterol, salt, and calories.

The food needs to be presented in a variety of different ways. Buffets are popular because they give guests the opportunity to make choices from a display of foods. Barbecues, display cooking, poolside, specialty restaurants, and reciprocal dining arrangements with nearby hotels give guests more options.

FOCUS ON SECURITY

Hotel Security

Hank Christen

In today's world, hotel guests consider safety a prime concern. Travelers expect and demand a secure facility. Perceived threats or fears are not limited to terrorism; hotels must have an all-hazard safety and security plan that addresses crime, natural disasters, accidents, and medical emergencies.

Use these top ten aspects of hospitality safety and security as a cornerstone for an effective program.

1. An effective program has to be visible. The visibility deters threats and creates a sense of safety for guests.
2. Create and maintain a proactive, all-hazard emergency plan. Start by conducting a thorough facility security inspection and potential threat assessment. Examine past records for natural disasters at your locale. For example, hurricanes are an issue in Florida and earthquakes are a California consideration. In any location, hospitality guests may be vulnerable to theft, assault, and rape. Local emergency agencies offer invaluable planning expertise and resources at little or no cost.
3. Security must be everyone's job, not just the responsibility of management.
4. Look inside your organization for potential security problems. A thorough background check of all new employees is an essential component of security programs.
5. Recognize the risks of workplace violence. Hotels often have large staffs from culturally diverse backgrounds. Working under stress in close proximity, internal disputes can easily erupt into workplace violence. Supervisors should be trained to recognize the early precursors to these disputes and react proactively to prevent them from escalating into safety and security problems.
6. Develop a crisis response team. A major crisis is rare, but when one occurs, a crisis response team plays a significant role in minimizing consequences and repairing damage. During disasters, the team is the liaison element between the hotel and emergency first-responder agencies.
7. Every staff member must be trained and prepared for medical emergencies. Employees should be trained to recognize, report, and respond to medical incidents. Emergency plans should address responsibilities for summoning EMS and other emergency agencies.
8. Include guest education in your security plan. Provide safety and security information. Distribute security tips on brochures. Encourage guests to share their concerns with safety surveys or questionnaires. Guest education prevents many potential safety and security problems.
9. Make safety and security programs an ongoing priority. Conduct security exercises. Don't limit training to a once-a-year safety video and expect the staff to make it their personal priority. Constant emphasis reinforces the importance of staying alert and aware of security at all times.
10. Recognition and rewards create buy-in from team members. Studies show that as much as 80 percent of all behavior is determined by reward systems. Set safety and security goals and reward results for all employees.

With increased global competition, not only from other resorts but also from cruise lines, resort managers are challenged to both attract guests and to turn those guests into repeat business, which traditionally has been the foundation of the resorts viability.

To increase occupancies, resorts have diversified their marketing mix to include conventions, business meetings, sales meetings, incentive groups, sporting events, additional sporting and recreational facilities, spas, adventure tourism, ecotourism, and so on.

Because guests are cocooned in the resort, they expect to be pampered. This requires an attentive, well-trained staff and that is a challenge in some remote areas and in developing countries.

There are a number of benefits to operating resorts. The guests are much more relaxed in comparison to those at transient hotels, and the resorts are located in scenically beautiful areas. This frequently enables staff to enjoy a better quality of life than do their transient hotel counterparts. Returning guests tend to treat associates like friends. This adds to the overall party-like atmosphere, which is prevalent at many of the established resorts.

Vacation Ownership

The Growth of an Industry

From its beginnings in the French Alps in the late 1960s, vacation ownership has become the fastest growing segment of the U.S. travel and tourism industry, increasing in popularity at the rate of about 15 percent each year.

Vacation ownership is the politically correct term for time-share. Essentially, vacation ownership means a person purchases the use of a unit similar to a condominium for blocks of times, usually in weeks. Henry Silverman of Cendant, which owns the Indianapolis, Indiana-based Resort Condominiums International (RCI), says that a time-share is really a two-bedroom suite that is owned, rather than a hotel room that is rented for a transient night. A vacation club, on the other hand, is a "travel-and-use" product. Consumers do not buy a fixed-week, unit-size, season, resort, or number of days to vacation each year. Instead, they purchase points that represent currency, which is used to access the club's vacation benefits. An important advantage to this is the product's flexibility, especially when tied to a point system. Disney Vacation Club is one major company that uses a point system. General manager Mark Pacala states, "The flexibility of choosing among several different vacation experiences is what sets the Disney Vacation Club apart from many similar plans. The vacation points system allows members to select the type of vacation best suited to their needs, particularly as those needs change from year to year." Each year, members choose how to use their vacation points, either for one long vacation or a series of short getaways.[3]

The World Tourism Organization has called time-shares one of the fastest-growing sectors of the travel and tourism industry. Hospitality companies are adding brand power to the concept with corporations like Marriott Vacation Club International, the Walt Disney Company, Hilton Hotels, Hyatt Hotels, Promus' Embassy Suites, Inter-Continental, and even the Ritz-Carlton and Four Seasons are participating in an industry that has grown rapidly in recent years. Still, only about 3 percent of all U.S. households own vacation ownership. RCI estimates that the figure could rise to 10 percent within the next decade for households with incomes of more than $50,000. It is not surprising that hotel companies have found this to be a lucrative business.

Personal Profile: Valerie Ferguson

Past Chair of the American Hotel & Lodging Association and Regional Vice-President of Loews Hotels

To most "making it big" seems like a regular statement and a task easily achieved. To Valerie Ferguson, well, it comes with a lot of work, dedication, and heart. She speaks often about seizing opportunities and adding self-interest into what you do for your career.

For this African-American female, life wasn't always easy. As the managing director of Loews Philadelphia Hotel and regional vice-president of Loews Hotels, she has a lot to say about what got her where she is now.

One of her most important role models was her father, Sam Ferguson. She says, "My father and I had a great relationship in which he supported me, but in which he never put any images in front of me about what I should shoot for."

For college, Valerie applied to the University of San Francisco, where she earned a degree in government. Eventually realizing that law wasn't where her heart was, she decided to move out to Atlanta where she got a job as a nighttime desk clerk at the Hyatt Regency. She fell in love with the hotel industry and saw it as a challenge. Soon enough though, she realized that the challenges she was really facing were issues of race and gender. She explains, "I was raw in my approach to the business world, but I soon came to realize that it takes more than working hard. To succeed, a person must be able to proclaim his or her goals."

Her success comes from being out there and connecting with people and society. Valerie is past chair of the American Hotel & Lodging Association (AH&LA) board and still serves on the Diversity Committee. She is also past associate director of the National Restaurant Association. She is a director on the boards of the Pennsylvania Travel Council, Philadelphia Workforce Investment, Communities in Schools, and the Educational Institute.

Valerie was nominated general manager of the year for the Hyatt Hotels Corporation. Through the years, she has managed several hotels for the Hyatt and Ritz-Carlton. Her outstanding work and devotion to the hospitality and lodging industry has not gone unrewarded. She was named one of the Top 100 Black Women in Corporate America by *Ebony* magazine. She was named one of the Top 100 Black Women of Influence by the Atlanta Business League Pioneer. She was also named one of the 100 Most Influential Women in Travel by *Travel Agent* magazine. Her most recent honorary awards for her work in the lodging industry were the 1998 NAACP Southeast Region Trailblazer Award for Business, the Martin Luther King, Jr. Drum Major for Justice Award from Coretta Scott King and the Women of the Southern Christian Leadership Conference (SCLC). Ed Rabin, executive vice president of Hyatt and an early Ferguson mentor says, "From the get-go she demonstrated an ability and willingness to understand and learn the business and win over guests, colleagues, and peers in the process."

When Loews was just being opened, Valerie was thrilled by the excitement that came with the adventure of being with a company yet still to grow. President and CEO of Loews Jonathan Tisch became a close friend of Valerie's as they served together on the board of the AH&MA. In 1994, Valerie ran for a seat on AH&MA's executive committee and eventually succeeded Tisch as chair. She was the first African-American and second woman to serve as AH&MA chair.

She comments on the hospitality industry, "The hospitality industry is one of the last vestiges of the American dream, where you can enter from very humble beginnings and end up a success."

The great relationship she has with people has been a great contribution to her well-deserved success.

Ferguson has come a long way in her career. She is proud of what she is doing and doesn't believe that she has stopped climbing the ladder of success. She is fighting to make other women and minority members realize that there is a whole world of opportunities out there and they should set their goals high. She believes that equality of opportunity "should not come as the result of a mandate for the federal government or as the result of pressure from groups outside this industry. The impetus for change must come from within the hearts and souls of each of us."

Sources: Lodging, 23, 5, January 1998; www.loewshotels.com; www.ahma.com/about/officers/ferguson.htm; www.findarticles.co/cf_0_/mv0VOU/1998_July_30/50216477/pl/article.jhtml; www.hotel-online.com/Neo/ SpecialReports1998/Nov98_Ferguson.html.

RCI, the largest vacation ownership exchange (that allows members to exchange vacations with other locations), has more than 2.8 million member families living in 200 countries. Three thousand seven-hundred participating resorts and members can exchange vacation intervals for vacations at any participating resort, and, to date, RCI has arranged exchange vacation for more than 54 million people.[4] Vacation ownership is popular at U.S. resorts from Key West in Florida to Kona in Hawaii and from New York City and Las Vegas to Colorado ski resorts.

Interval World is a vacation exchange network made up of more than 2,000 resorts and over 1.6 million member families worldwide. Interval does not own or manage any of the resorts, but rather they provide members—vacation owners from around the world—with a variety of exchange services to enhance their vacation experiences. Members can exchange a stay at their home resort for a stay at one of the time-shares supported by Interval World.

By locking in the purchase price of accommodations, vacation ownership helps ensure future vacations at today's prices at luxurious resorts with amenities, service, and ambiance that rival any of the world's top-rated vacation destinations. Through vacation exchange programs, time-share owners can travel to other popular destinations around the world. With unparalleled flexibility and fully equipped condominiums that offer the best in holiday luxury, vacation ownership puts consumers in the driver's seat, allowing them to plan and enjoy vacations that suit their lifestyle.

Time-share resort developers today include many of the world's leading hoteliers, publicly held corporations, and independent companies. Properties that combine vacation ownership resorts with hotels, adventure resorts, and gaming resorts are among the emerging time-share trends. The reasons for purchasing most frequently cited by current time-share owners are the high standards of quality accommodations and service at the resorts where they own and exchange, the flexibility offered through the vacation exchange opportunities, and the cost effectiveness of vacation ownership. Nearly one-third of vacation owners purchase additional intervals after experiencing ownership. This trend is even stronger among long-time owners: More than 40 percent of those who have owned for eight years or longer have purchased additional intervals within the time-share.

Divi Carina Bay Resort

What Is Vacation Ownership?

Vacation ownership offers consumers the opportunity to purchase fully furnished vacation accommodations in a variety of forms, such as weekly intervals or points in points-based systems, for a percentage of the cost of full ownership. For a one-time purchase price and payment of a yearly maintenance fee, purchasers own their vacation either in perpetuity or for a predetermined number of years. Owners share both the use and the costs of upkeep of their unit and the common grounds of the resort property. Vacation ownership purchases are typically financed through consumer loans of five to ten years' duration, with terms dependent on the purchase price and the amount of the buyer's down payment. The average cost of a vacation ownership is about $12,500. Yearly maintenance fees are paid each year to a HOA for the maintenance of the resort. Just like taking care of a home, resort maintenance fees help maintain the quality and future value of the resort property.

Vacation ownership is expected to grow due to the number of retiring baby boomers who want to enjoy the good life! Vacation clubs, or point-based programs, provide the flexible use of accommodations in multiple resort locations. With these products, club members purchase points that represent either a travel and use membership or a deeded real estate product. These points are then used like currency to purchase the various size accommodations, during a certain season, for a set number of days at a participating resort. The number of points needed to access the resort accommodations will vary by the members' demand for unit size, season, resort location, and amenities. A vacation club may have a specific term of ownership or be deeded in perpetuity.

The Advantages of Vacation Ownership

Unlike a hotel room or rental cottage that requires payment for each use of rates that usually increase each year, ownership at a time-share property enables vacationers to enjoy a resort, year after year, for the duration of their ownership for only a one-time purchase price and the payment of yearly maintenance fees. Time-share ownership offers vacationers an opportunity to save on the escalating costs of vacation accommodations over the long term, while enjoying all the comforts of home in a resort setting.

Truly a home away from home, vacation ownership provides the space and flexibility to meet the needs of any size family or group. While most vacation ownership condominiums have two bedrooms and two baths, unit sizes range from studios to three, or more, bedrooms. Unlike hotel rooms, there are no charges for additional guests. Also unlike hotels, most units include a fully equipped kitchen with dining area, washer and dryer, stereo, VCRs, and more.

Early "Hotels"

Increased travel and trade made some form of overnight accommodations an absolute necessity. Because travel was slow and journeys long and arduous, many travelers depended solely on the hospitality of private citizens.

In the Greek and Roman empires, inns and taverns sprang up everywhere. The Romans constructed elaborate and well-appointed inns on all the main roads. Marco Polo later proclaimed these inns as "fit for a king." They were located about 25 miles apart to provide fresh houses for officials and couriers of the Roman government and could only be used with special government documents granting permission. These documents became revered status symbols and were subject to numerous thefts and forgeries. By the time Marco Polo traveled to the Far East, there were 10,000 inns.

Time-share resort amenities rival those of other top-rated resort properties and may include swimming pools, tennis, Jacuzzi, golf, bicycles, and exercise facilities. Others feature boating, ski lifts, restaurants, and equestrian facilities. Most time-share resorts offer a full schedule of on-site or nearby sporting, recreational, and social activities for adults and children. The resorts are staffed with well-trained hospitality professionals, with many resorts offering concierge services for assistance in visiting area attractions.

Travel the World Through Exchange Vacations

Vacation ownership offers unparalleled flexibility and the opportunity for affordable worldwide travel through vacation ownership exchange. Through the international vacation exchange networks, owners can trade their timeshare intervals for vacation time at comparable resorts around the world. Most resorts are affiliated with an exchange company that administers the exchange service for its members. Typically, the exchange company will directly solicit annual membership. Owners individually elect to become members of the affiliated exchange company. To exchange, the owner places his or her interval into the exchange company's pool of resorts and weeks available for exchange and, in turn, chooses an available resort and week from that pool. The exchange company charges an exchange fee, in addition to an annual membership fee, to complete an exchange. Exchange companies and resorts frequently offer their members the additional benefit of saving or banking vacation time in a reserve program for use in a different year.

The Los Angeles Airport Marriott Hotel offers guests the convienience of free airport shuttle service.

Airport Hotels

Many airport hotels enjoy a high occupancy because of the large number of travelers arriving and departing from major airports. The guest mix in airport hotels consists of business, group, and leisure travelers. Passengers with early or late flights may stay over at the airport hotel, while others rest while waiting for connecting flights.

Airport hotels are generally in the 200- to 600-room size and are full service. To care for the needs of guests who may still feel as if they are in different time zones, room service and restaurant hours may be extended, even offered around the clock. More moderately priced hotels have vending machines.

As competition at airport hotels intensified, some added meeting space to cater to businesspeople who want to fly in, meet, and fly out. Here, the airport hotel has the advantage of saving the guests from having to go downtown. Almost all airport hotels provide courtesy van transportation to and from the airport.

Convenient locations, economical prices, and easy and less costly transportation costs to and from the airport are some reasons why airport hotels are becoming intelligent choices for business travelers. Airport hotels can mean a bargain for groups, especially considering that the transportation to the hotel and back from the airport is usually free or is very inexpensive, says Brian Booth, director of sales and marketing at the Dallas Hyatt Regency Airport Hotel. One of the most conveniently located hotels in the country is the Miami International Airport Hotel, which is located within the airport itself.

Freeway Hotels and Motels

Freeway hotels and motels came into prominence, with the help of the Interstate Highway Act, in the 1950s and 1960s. They are smaller than most hotels—usually fewer than 50 rooms—and are frequently mom-and-pop owned and operated or franchised (like Motel 6). As Americans took to the open road, they needed a convenient place to stay that was reasonably priced with few frills. Guests could simply drive up, park outside the office, register, rent a room, and park outside the room. Over the years, more facilities were added: lounges, restaurants, pools, soft drink machines, game rooms, and satellite TV.

Motels are often clustered near freeway off-ramps on the outskirts of towns and cities. Today, some are made of modular construction and have as few as eleven employees per hundred rooms. These savings in land, construction, and operating costs are passed on to the guest in the form of lower rates.

Casino Hotels

The casino hotel industry is now coming into the financial mainstream, to the point that, as a significant segment of the entertainment industry, it is reshaping the U.S. economy. The entertainment and recreation sector has become a very important engine for U.S. economic growth, providing a boost to consumer spending, thus creating tremendous prosperity for the industry. The fastest growing sector of the entertainment field is gaming, which is discussed in Chapter 12.

Casino hotels are leaning toward making their hotels into "family friendly" hotels. The gaming business is strictly for adults; however, these hotels realize that making their hotels family friendly will attract more families to spend a day or two in their hotels. Circus Circus in Las Vegas pioneered the concept more than a decade ago. Various other casino hotels are following suit. They have baby-sitters available at any time of the day, children's attractions ranging from parks to circuses and museums, and kids menus in restaurants. For adults, in addition to gaming, a multinational cuisine for dining, health spas for relaxation, dance clubs, and dazzling shows are available.

New York Casino on the Strip in Las Vegas

Casino hotels are now marketing themselves as business hotels. They include in their rooms work space, a fax, a copier, and computer data ports. Other amenities include a full-service business center, travel bureau, and room service. Larger casino hotels also attract conventions, which represent a lucrative business. There are now more than 150 hotels in Native American tribal land. They cater to an increasing number of guests who want to stay and be entertained as well as gamble.

Convention Hotels

Convention hotels provide facilities and meet the needs of groups attending and holding conventions. Apart from this segment of the market, convention hotels also attract seasonal leisure travelers. Typically these hotels exceed 500 guest rooms with larger public areas to accommodate hundreds of people at any given time. Convention hotels have many banquet areas within and around the hotel

The Dolphin Hotel in Walt Disney World

complex. These hotels have a high percentage of double occupancies and rooms have double queen-sized beds. Convention hotels may also offer a concierge floor to cater to individual guest needs. Round-the-clock room service, an in-house laundry, a business center, a travel desk, and an airport shuttle service are other amenities found in convention hotels.

Full-Service Hotels

Another way to classify hotels is by the degree of service offered: full-service, economy, extended-stay, and all-suite hotels. Full-service hotels offer a wide range of facilities, services, and amenities, including many that were mentioned under the luxury hotel category: multiple food and beverage outlets including bars, lounges, and restaurants; both formal and casual dining; and meeting, convention, and catering services. Business features might include a business center, secretarial services, fax, in-room computer hook-ups, and so on.

Most of the major North American cities have hotel chain representation, such as Doubletree, Four Seasons, Hilton, Holiday Inn, Hyatt, Marriott, Omni, Ramada, Radisson, Ritz-Carlton, Loew's, Le Meridian, Sheraton, and Westin. Some of these chains are positioning themselves as basic full-service properties. An example of this strategy is Marriott's Courtyard hotels, which have small lobbies and very limited food and beverage offerings. The resulting savings are passed on to the guests in the form of more competitive rates. Thus, the full-service market may also be subdivided into upscale and midpriced hotels.

Economy/Budget Hotels

An economy or budget hotel offers clean, reasonably sized and furnished rooms without the frills of full-service hotels. Chains like Travelodge, Motel 6, Microtel, Days Inn, and La Quinta became popular by focusing on selling beds, but not meals or meetings. This enabled them to offer rates at about 30 percent lower than the midpriced hotels. Economy properties, which represent about 15 percent of total hotel rooms, have experienced tremendous growth.

More recent entrants to this market sector are Promus' Hampton Inns, Marriott's Fairfield, and Choice's Comfort Inns. These properties do not have restaurants or offer substantial food and beverages, but they do offer guests a continental breakfast in the lobby.

Boutique Hotels

Boutique hotels offer a different lodging experience compared to mid- to large chain hotels. Boutique hotels have a unique architecture, style, decor, and size. They are smaller than their chain competitors, with about 25 to 125 rooms and a high level of personal service. Some examples of boutique hotels are the trendy South Beach retro types and the avant-garde hotel George in Washington D.C. The George is not only style conscious but politically correct as well, with left wing design and right wing comfort.

Fairfield Inn by Marriott offers clean, reasonably sized and furnished rooms at great value.

After enjoying a wave of growth for most of the last twenty years, the economy hotel segment may be close to the saturation point. There are about 25,000 properties in this segment with many markets. The economic law of supply and demand rules; if an area has too many similar properties, then price wars usually break out as they try to attract guests. Some will attempt to differentiate themselves and stress value rather than discounting. This adds to the fascination of the business.

Extended-Stay Hotels

Other hotels cater to guests who stay for an extended period. They will, of course, take guests for a shorter time when space is available. However, the majority of guests are long term. Guests take advantage of a reduction in the rates based on the length of their stay. The mix of guests is mainly business and professional/technical, or relocating families.

Residence Inns and Homewood Suites are market leaders in this segment of the lodging industry. These properties offer full kitchen facilities and shopping services or a convenience store on the premises. Complimentary continental breakfast and evening cocktails are served in the lobby. Some properties offer a business center and recreational facilities.

Residence Inn is a Market Leader in the Extended-Stay Segment of the Lodging Industry.

All-Suite Extended-Stay Hotels

All-suite extended-stay hotels typically offer approximately 25 percent more space for the same amount of money as the regular hotel in the same price range. The additional space is usually in the form of a lounge and possibly a kitchenette area.

Embassy Suites, owned and operated by the Promus Corporation; Residence Inns, Fairfield Suites, and Town-Place Suites, all by Marriott; Extended Stay America; Homewood Suites; and Guest Quarters are the market leaders in the all-suites, extended-stay segment of the lodging industry. Several of the major hotel chains have all-suite extended-stay subsidiaries, including Radisson, Choice Hotels (which dominate the economy all-suite segment with Comfort and Quality Suites), ITT Sheraton Suites, Hilton Suites, Homegate Studios, and Suites by Wyndham Hotels. These properties provide a closer-to-home feeling for guests who may be relocating or attending seminars or are on work-related projects that necessitate a stay of greater than about five days.

There are now almost 1,500 extended-stay properties. Many of these properties have business centers and offer services like grocery shopping and laundry/dry cleaning. The designers of extended-stay properties realize that guests prefer a homelike atmosphere. Accordingly, many properties are built to encourage a community feeling, which allows guests to informally interact.

Bed and Breakfast Inns

Bed and breakfast inns, or B&Bs as they are familiarly known, offer an alternative lodging experience to the normal hotel or motel. According to *Travel Assist Magazine,* B&B is a concept that began in Europe and started as overnight lodging in a private home. A true B&B is an accommodation with the owner, who lives on the premises or nearby, providing a clean, attractive accommodation and breakfast, usually a memorable one. The host also offers to help the guest with directions, restaurants, and suggestions for local entertainment or sightseeing.

There are many different styles of B&Bs with prices ranging from about $30 to $300 or more per night. B&Bs may be quaint cottages with white picket fences leading to gingerbread houses, tiny and homey, with two or three rooms available. On the other hand, some are sprawling, ranch-style homes in the Rockies; multistoried town homes in large cities; farms; adobe villas; log cabins; lighthouses; and many stately mansions. The variety is part of the thrill, romance, and charm of the B&B experience.[5]

There are an estimated 25,000 bed and breakfast places in the United States alone. Bed and breakfast inns have flourished for many reasons. Business travelers are growing weary of the complexities of the check-in/checkout processes at some commercial hotels. With the escalation of transient rates at hotels, an opportunity has been created to serve a more price-sensitive segment of travelers. Also, many leisure travelers are looking for accommodation somewhere between a large, formal hotel and staying with friends. The B&Bs offer a homelike atmosphere. They are aptly called "a home away from home." Community breakfasts with other lodgers and hosts enhance this feeling. Each B&B is as unique as its owner. Décor varies according to the region of location and the

*A Rocky Mountain Bed
and Breakfast Inn*

unique taste of its owner. The owner of the bed and breakfast often provides all the necessary labor, but some employ full- or part-time labor.

Hotel Integration

Vertical Integration

Vertical integration is a trend that began a few years ago. Lodging companies realized that guests' accommodation needs were not just at one level; rather, they seemed to vary by price and facilities/amenities. Almost all major lodging companies now have properties in each segment of the market. Examples to illustrate this point are given in Figure 4–5.

Luxury—Clarion
Midscale—Quality Inn, Quality Suites
Budget—Comfort Inn, Friendship Inns, Rodeway Inn
Economy—Sleep Inn

Figure 4–5 *Vertical
Integration of Choice Hotels*

Check Your Knowledge

1. What characteristics do the following hotel segments encompass?
   a. City center hotels
   b. Resort hotels
   c. Airport hotels
   d. Freeway hotels and motels
   e. Full-service hotels
   f. Economy/budget hotels
   g. Extended-stay hotels
   h. Bed and breakfast inns

A Day in the Life of Sylvie Balenger

Executive Housekeeper, Four Seasons Hotels and Resorts

Once I punch in at 7:45 A.M. I find out what our occupancy was the previous night. We dropped in the count by ten rooms but two people called in sick. We are short one room attendant. The office coordinator tries to call in someone who is off, but no luck. We call in our afternoon room attendants a few hours early—great, they can do it. We're covered for the day.

I hold our daily morning briefing with the 30 room attendants in the housekeeping office. We need to be aware of a group request to remove our doorknob breakfast menus from our guest rooms since the meeting planners want to ensure that all of their attendees go to breakfast at the scheduled planned event in the ballroom. We cover other events in the hotel and go over the focus of the day in the cleaning of our guest rooms. Today it's dusting our lampshades. We finish up with stretching exercises for five minutes.

A room attendant gets an emergency phone call and has to go home. She has to drop seven rooms. We pull the lobby attendant, who has been cross-trained to clean rooms, to do the seven rooms. We ask the male lobby attendant to cover the lobby attendant's section in the lobby.

Time to attend the morning operations meeting at 8:30 A.M. with all the other operational managers. We go over the VIPs, occupancy figures for the night before and the rest of the week, any glitches with guests the previous day, and assign the follow-up. The managers bring up any operational challenges they expect for that day. The guest services manager expects a valet crunch with 200 cars arriving at the same time for a luncheon. All managers with a pager will be notified when to show up and help park cars. The banquet manager expects a tight turn in the ballroom midafternoon with only 30 minutes to convert it into a meeting space. Again, anticipate another crunch.

Hold another morning briefing with the supervisors and house attendants at 8:45 A.M. and go over the same notes on our grease board as we had with room attendants. One of the house attendants is complaining of a sore back. He says he did it here a couple of days ago and failed to re-

port it. I fill out a supervisor's injury report and send the house attendant to security. He is sent from there to the clinic.

I review the daily payroll for the department, which takes about 30 minutes. I received a call from a guest wanting to know who did their room last night because she forgot to turn down the sofa bed. I apologized to the guest and sent someone to the room to service it right away and we put a notation in the computer about their sofa bed request. I follow up with the turndown attendant and the P.M. shift manager to determine why this mistake occurred.

It's 10:00 A.M. and time for the department head meeting, then lunch for 15 minutes. I get paged to rush a suite for a VIP arrival. The president of our company is checking in and I need to inspect that suite before he arrives. The valet crunch has been called and I help park cars for 20 minutes.

It's early afternoon and we get a crunch at the uniform counter because all of the banquet staff for that turn in the ballroom are here to get ready for the event. I help out for 20 minutes.

The crunch for the ballroom turn has been called. Help set up chairs for the afternoon meeting. We are also planning on how to have a smooth turn on Sunday. We have the whole house checking out and we'll be full that night.

The morning staff is on its way down and I bid them goodnight and thank them for a great day. I'm available for anyone who has questions and concerns about schedules, vacation requests, pay in advance requests, concerns about their supervisor that day, problems with rooms such as maintenance requests, missing supplies, and so on.

The house attendants and supervisors come down at 5:00 P.M. There was an argument between a house attendant and a supervisor. I need to be the mediator in my office and this takes about 30 minutes to resolve.

I do one more final check of my e-mails and go home around 6:00 P.M.

Best, Biggest, and Most Unusual Hotels and Chains

So which is the best hotel in the world? The answer may depend on whether you watch the "Travel Channel" or read polls taken by a business investment or travel magazine. The Oriental Hotel in Bangkok, Thailand, has been rated number one in the world; so too has the Regent of Hong Kong, the Mandarin Oriental of Hong Kong, and the Connaught of London. Each "list" has other hotels. The largest hotel in the world was the 5,505-room MGM Grand in Las Vegas. This, however, has been surpassed by the new Venetian Hotel, also in Las Vegas, with 6,172 rooms.

The Best Hotel Chains

The Ritz-Carlton and the Canadian-owned and operated Four Seasons are generally rated the highest quality chain hotels. The Ritz-Carlton Hotel Company has received all the major awards the hospitality industry and leading consumer organizations can bestow. It has received the Malcolm Baldrige National Quality Award, the United States Department of Commerce—the first and only hotel company to win the award; the first and only service company to win the award two times: 1999 and 1992. Ritz-Carlton has long been recognized as the best luxury hotel chain in the industry. The Ritz-Carlton approach to quality centers on a number of basic but complex principles, many drawn from traditional TQM theory.

The Most Unusual Hotels

Among the world's most unusual hotels are ones like The Treetops Hotel in one of Kenya's wild animal parks—literally in the treetops. The uniqueness of the hotel is that it is built on the tops of trees overlooking a wild animal watering hole in the park.

Another magnificent spectacle is the Ice Hotel, situated on the shores of the Torne River in the old village of Jukkasjäsvi in Swedish Lapland. The Ice Hotel is built from scratch on an annual basis with a completely new design, new

A Bedroom of a Luxury Hotel

A guest arrives at an "ice hotel."

suites, new departments, even the "Absolute Ice Bar," a bar carved in ice with ice glasses and ice plates. The Ice Hotel can accommodate over 100 guests with each room having its own distinct style. The hotel also has an Ice Chapel, an ice art exhibition hall, and, believe it or not, a cinema.

Australia boasts an underwater hotel at the Great Barrier Reef, where guests have wonderful subterranean views from their rooms.

Japan has several unusual hotels. One is a cocoonlike hotel, called Capsule Hotel, in which guests do not have a room as such. Instead, they have a space of about 4 feet by 7 feet. In this space is a bed and a television—which you almost have to operate with your toes! Such hotels are popular with people who get caught up in the obligatory late night drinking with the boss and with visiting professors who find them the only affordable place to stay in expensive Tokyo.

Capsule Hotel. Imagine missing the last train home—people actually sleep in these 4 by 7 foot capsules.

The highest hotel in the world, in terms of altitude, is nestled in the Himalayan mountain range at an altitude of 13,000 feet. Weather permitting, there is a marvelous view of Mount Everest. As many as 80 percent of the guests suffer from nausea, headaches, or sleeplessness caused by the altitude. No wonder the hottest-selling item on the room-service menu is oxygen—at $1 a minute.[6]

International Perspective

We are all part of a huge global economy that is splintered into massive trading blocks, such as the European Union and the North American Free Trade Agreement (NAFTA) among Canada, the United States, and Mexico, with a total population of 350 million consumers.

The EU, with a population of over 400 million people in 25 nations, is an economic union that has removed national restrictions not only on trade but also on the movement of capital and labor. The synergy developed between these 15 member nations is beneficial to all and is a form of self-perpetuating development. As travel, tourism, commerce, and industry have increased within the EEC, which is soon to expand by another ten nations, and beyond, so has the need for hotel accommodations.

NAFTA will likely be a similar catalyst for hotel development in response to increased trade and tourism among the three countries involved. But Argentina, Brazil, Chile, and Venezuela may also join an expanded NAFTA, which would become known as the Americas Trading Block.

It is easy to understand the international development of hotels given the increase in international tourism trade and commerce. The growth in tourism in Pacific Rim countries is expected to continue at the same rate as in recent years. Several resorts are planned in Indonesia, Malaysia, Thailand, Mexico, and Vietnam. Further international hotel development opportunities exist in Eastern Europe, Russia, and the other republics of the former Soviet Union, where some companies have changed their growth strategy from building new hotels to acquiring existing properties.

In Asia, Hong Kong's growth has been encouraged by booming economies throughout Asia and the kind of tax system for which supply-siders hunger. Before sovereignty over Hong Kong reverted back to China, the Hong Kong government levied a flat 16.5 percent corporate tax, a 15 percent individual income tax, and no tax on capital gains or dividends. Several hotel corporations have their headquarters in Hong Kong. Among them are Mandarin Oriental, Peninsula, and Shangri-La, all world-renowned for their five-star status. They are based in Hong Kong because of low corporate taxation and the ability to bring in senior expatriate executives with minimum bureaucratic difficulty.[7]

In developing countries, once political stability has been sustained, hotel development quickly follows as part of an overall economic and social progression. An example of this would be the former Eastern European countries and former Soviet republics, who for the past few years have offered development opportunities for hotel corporations.

Trends in Hotel Development

- *Capacity control:* Refers to who will control the sale of inventories of hotel rooms, airline seats, auto rentals, and tickets to attractions. Presently, owners of these assets are in control of their sale and distribution, but increasingly control is falling into the hands of those who own and manage global reservation systems and/or negotiate for large buying groups. Factors involved in the outcome will be telecommunications, software, available satellite capacity, governmental regulations, limited capital, and the travel distribution network.
- *Safety and security:* Important aspects of safety and security are terrorism, the growing disparity between the "haves" and "have nots" in the world, diminishing financial resources, infrastructure problems, health issues, the stability of governments, and personal security.
- *Assets and capital:* The issues concerning assets and capital are rationing of private capital and rationing of funds deployed by governments.
- *Technology:* An example of the growing use of *expert systems* (a basic form of artificial intelligence) would be making standard operating procedures available online, 24 hours a day, and establishing yield management systems designed to make pricing decisions. Other examples include the smart hotel room and communications ports to make virtual office environments for business travelers; and the impact of technology on the structure of corporate offices and individual hotels.
- *New management:* The complex forces of capacity control, safety and security, capital movement, and technology issues will require a future management cadre that is able to adapt to rapid-paced change across all the traditional functions of management.
- *Globalization:* A number of U.S. and Canadian chains have developed and are continuing to develop hotels around the world. International companies are also investing in the North American hotel industry.
- *Consolidation:* As the industry matures, corporations are either acquiring or merging with each other.
- *Diversification within segments of the lodging industry:* The economy segment now has low-, medium-, and high-end properties. The extended-stay market has a similar spread of properties as do all the other hotel classifications.
- *Rapid growth in vacation ownership:* Vacation ownership is the fastest growing segment of the lodging industry and is likely to continue growing as the baby boomers enter their fifties and sixties.
- *An increase in the number of spas and the treatments offered:* Wellness and the road to nirvana are in increasing demand as guests seek release from the stresses of a fast-paced lifestyle.
- *Gaming:* An increasing number of hotels are coming online that are related to the gaming industry.
- An increasing number of hotels are being developed as multiuse, meaning hotels with residences (condominiums), spas, and recreational facilities.

CASE STUDY

To Flag or Not to Flag—and If So, Which Flag?

Joy and Bob Brown retired from the military in 1995. They bought a motel near a picturesque New England town. The Cozy Motel is clearly visible and easily accessible from the turnpike. It has 75 rooms that are in good shape, having just been refurbished, and the curbside appeal of fresh paint and attractive landscaping adds to the motel's presentation.

The motel's year-round occupancy is 58 percent, which is about 10 percentage points below the national average. The average daily rate is $38. The Cozy Motel's guests are a mix of business travelers, who are mostly from companies at the nearby business park; a few retirees traveling for pleasure; an occasional bus tour; and some sports teams.

The Browns have asked several major franchise corporations to submit their best offers. The best one indicates that the cost of a franchise application fee is $20,000, and that there is a 2 percent revenue marketing fee and a reservation fee of $4 per room booked by the Central Reservation System (CRS).

Discussion Questions

1. What would you do in the Brown's situation? Should they sign a franchise agreement or not? Make assumptions, if needed.
2. What terms and conditions of a franchise agreement would be acceptable to you, or to the Browns?
3. What additional information would you, or the Browns, need to know?

CASE STUDY

In recent years, several new lodging brands have been introduced by leading hotel chains to the market. Among the names of these brands are: DoubleTree, Candlewood Suites, Homewood Suites, Mainstay, Spring Hill Suites, and so on. In addition, there is Hyatt, which recently purchased AmeriSuites, which they have renovated and now call Hyatt Place.

A hot trend in lodging development is condo hotels. With condo hotels a developer can more quickly raise the funds necessary from investors than from other traditional sources like banks and finance houses. As a result, it makes sense for developers to encourage investors by offering an arrangement for owners to have exclusive use of the unit for a fixed number of days a year (normally 30–60 days) and for the hotel company to rent out the units/rooms for the remainder of the year. The cost of development is high and ranges from an average of $800–$900 per square foot up to $1,400. Projects like the Residences at MGM Grand Las Vegas, which sold more than $1 billion or the Hard Rock Hotel and Casino, also in Las Vegas, which launched 1,300 units in less than 10 weeks are amazing. Other areas of the U.S. are good existing or potential markets for condo hotel development.

Despite the rave reviews on Wall Street for Condo hotels, there are some unresolved issues. With time, who will develop and pay for the replacement of furniture fixtures and equipment (FF&E)? What are the association dues and what form will the relationship be between owners, the developer and the hotel company? There are the additional complexities for the hotel operator—such as space for meetings, restaurants, and recreation—and how many rooms will be available on any given night? Yet, the pay-offs for both individual investor-owners and hotel operating companies are good to great. With 78 million baby boomers ready to retire, the prospects look very good to all concerned.

Discussion Questions

1. So what is in a name? Is Hyatt right to use the name Hyatt Place?
2. Is Intercontinental or Hilton wrong not to include their name? What is your opinion?
3. Which other areas of the U.S. are good potential locations for condo hotels and why?
4. Will condo hotels split into various segments like other lodging properties?

CAREER INFORMATION

A variety of career opportunities are directly and indirectly related to hotel development and classification. *Working in the corporate offices to develop hotels* involves a knowledge of operations, plus expertise in marketing, feasibility studies (to find out if the planned hotel will be profitable), finance, and planning. *Consulting firms,* like Pannel Kew Foster (PKF), have interesting positions as consultants who provide specialized services in feasibility studies, marketing expertise, human resources, accounting, and finance due diligence—a check to ensure that what is being paid for a property is reasonable (it is a check to ensure that the building is structurally sound and that heating and cooling systems are in working order). Working for a consulting firm usually requires a master's degree plus operational experience and an area of specialty.

AAA and Mobile both have inspectors who check hotel standards. Inspectors are required to travel and write detailed reports on the properties they stay at.

Suppliers to the industry manufacture or distribute and sell all the furnishings, furniture, and equipment (FF&E). A visit to a trade show may be an eye-opener as to the number of suppliers to the hospitality industry.

It is a good idea to explores as many career paths as possible. Ask questions about lifestyle, career challenges and, yes, salaries. Map out your path to see where you want to be in 5, 10, 15, and even 20 years from now.

SUMMARY

1. Improved transportation has changed the nature of the hotel industry from small, independently owned inns to big hotel and lodging chains, operated by using concepts such as franchising, and management contracts.

2. Hotels can be classified according to location (city center, resort, airport, freeway), to types of services offered (casino, convention), and to price (luxury, midscale, budget, and economy). Hotels are rated by Mobil and AAA Awards (five-star or the five-diamond rankings).

3. Vacation ownership offers consumers the opportunity to purchase fully furnished vacation accommodations, similar to condominiums, sold in a variety of forms, such as weekly intervals or point-based systems, for only a percentage of the cost of full ownership. According to the WTO, time-shares are one of the fastest growing sectors of the travel and tourism industry.

4. Every part of the world offers leisure and business travelers a choice of unusual or conservative accommodations that cater to the personal ideas of vacation or business trips.

5. The future of tourism involves international expansion and foreign investment, often in combination with airlines and with the goal of improving economic conditions in developing countries. It is further influenced by increased globalization, as evidenced by such agreements as NAFTA.

KEY WORDS AND CONCEPTS

Franchising

Management contracts

Real estate investment trust (REIT)

Referral associations

Vacation ownership

Vertical integration

REVIEW QUESTIONS

1. What are the advantages of (a) management contracts and (b) franchising? Discuss their impacts on the development of the hotel industry.

2. Explain how hotels cater to the needs of business and leisure travelers in reference to the following concepts: (a) resorts, (b) airport hotels, and (c) vertical integration.

3. Explain what vacation ownership is. What are the different types of time-share programs available for purchase?

INTERNET EXERCISES

1. Organization: **Hilton Hotels**
   Web site: **www.hilton.com**
   Summary: Hilton Hotels Corporation and Hilton International, a subsidiary of Hilton Group plc, have a worldwide alliance to market Hilton. Hilton is recognized as one of the world's best-known hotel brands. Collectively Hilton offers more than 2,500 hotels in more than fifty countries, truly a major player in the hospitality industry.
   (a) What are the different hotel brands that can be franchised through Hilton Hotels Corporation?
   (b) What are your views on Hilton's portfolio and franchising options?
   Click on the "Franchise Development" icon. Now click on "All HHC Franchise Brands."

2. Organization: **HOTELS Magazine**
   Web site: **www.hotelsmag.com**
   Summary: Hotels magazine is a publication that offers vast amounts of information on the hospitality industry with up-to-date industry news, corporate trends, and nationwide developments..
   (a) What are some of the top headlines currently being reported in the industry?
   (b) Click on the "Hotels Giants" icon. Browse through The site of Corporate Rankings and Industry Leaders. List the top five hotel corporations and note how many rooms each one has.

APPLY YOUR KNOWLEDGE

1. From a career perspective, what are the advantages and disadvantages of each type of hotel?

2. If you were going into the lodging sector, which type of property would you prefer to work at and why?

SUGGESTED ACTIVITY

Identify which kind of hotel you would like to work at and give reasons why.

ENDNOTES

1. **http://www.nyc-architecture.com/MID/MID056.htm.** July 10, 2005.
2. Personal Conversation with Bruce Goodwin. May 4, 2004.
3. Lynn Sheldon, Timeshare Concept. Adopted by Hotel Industry **http://riroads.com/archive/timesharehotels.htm**. July 10, 2005.
4. **RCI.com**. January 11, 2004.
5. **www.travelassist.com/mag/a88.html**. July 10, 2005.
6. Jeannie Realston, "Inn of Thin Air," *American Way*, October 15, 1992.
7. Personal conversation with Lim Chen. September 4, 2002.

WEB RESOURCES

Hilton Hotels
   www.hilton.com

Starwood Hotels
   www.starwood.com

Cendant Corporation
   www.cendant.com

Choice Hotels
   www.choice.com

Patriot American
   www.patriotamerican.com

Host Marriott
   www.hostmarriott.com

American Hotel & Lodging Association
   www.ah&la.com

American Automobile Association
   www.aaa.com

Mobile Travel Guide
   www.mobiletravelguide.com

Loews Hotels
   www.loews.com

Resort Condominiums International
   www.rci.com

Interval World
   www.intervalworld.com

Preferred Hotels
   www.preferredhotels.com

Four Seasons
   www.fourseasons.com

Rooms Division Operations

5

After reading and studying this chapter, you should be able to:

- Outline the duties and responsibilities of key executives and department heads.
- Draw an organizational chart of the rooms division of a hotel and identify the executive committee members.
- Describe the main functions of the rooms division departments.
- Describe property management systems and discuss yield management.
- Calculate occupancy percentages, average daily rates, and actual percentage of potential rooms revenue.
- Outline the importance of the reservations and guest services functions.
- List the complexities and challenges of the concierge, housekeeping, and security/loss prevention departments.

This chapter examines the function of a hotel and the many departments that constitute a hotel. It also helps to explain why and how the departments are interdependent in successfully running a hotel.

The Functions and Departments of a Hotel

The primary function of a hotel is to provide lodging accommodation. A large hotel is run by a general manager and an executive committee that consists of the key executives who head major departments: rooms division director, food and beverage director, marketing and sales director, human resources director, chief accountant or controller, and chief engineer or facility manager. These executives generally have a regional or corporate counterpart with whom they have a reporting relationship, although the general manager is their immediate superior.

A hotel is made up of several businesses or revenue centers and cost centers. A few thousand products and services are sold every day. Each area of specialty requires dedication and a quality commitment for each department to get little things right all the time. Furthermore, hotels need the cooperation of a large and diverse group of people to perform well. Godfrey Bler, the general manager (GM) of the elegant 800-room General Eisenhower Hotel, calls it "a business of details."

Hotels are places of glamour that may be awe inspiring. Even the experienced hotel person is impressed by the refined dignity of a beautiful hotel like a Ritz-Carlton or the artistic splendor of a Hyatt. The atmosphere of a hotel is stimulating to a hospitality student. Let us step into an imaginary hotel to feel the excitement and become a part of the rush that is similar to show business, for a hotel is live theater and the GM is the director of the cast of players.

Hotels, whether they are chain affiliated or independent properties, all exist to serve and enrich society and at the same time make a profit for the owners. Frequently, hotels are just like pieces of property on a Monopoly board. They often make or lose more money with equity appreciation or depreciation than via operations. Hotels have been described as "people palaces." Some are certainly palatial, and others are more functional. Hotels are meant to provide all the comforts of home to those away from home.

The Grand Hall in the Willard InterContinental, Washington, DC. It was at this hotel that the term lobbyist was coined when then President Grant would retire after dinner to an armchair in the lobby. People would approach him and try to gain his support for their causes.

Role of the Hotel General Manager

Hotel general managers have a lot of responsibilities. They must provide owners with a reasonable return on investment, keep guests satisfied and returning, and keep employees happy. This may seem easy, but because there are so many interpersonal transactions and because hotels are open every day, all day, the complexities of operating become challenges that the general manager must face and overcome. The GM not only focuses on leading and operating the hotel departments but also on aspects of the infrastructure from room atmosphere to security.

Larger hotels can be more impersonal. Here, the general manager may only meet and greet a few VIPs. In the smaller property, it is easier—though no less important—for the GM to become acquainted with guests, to ensure their stay is memorable, and to secure their return. One way that experienced GMs can meet guests, even in large hotels, is to be visible in the lobby and F&B (food and beverage) outlets at peak times (checkout, lunch, check-in, and dinner time). Guests like to feel that the GM takes a personal interest in their well-being. Max Blouet, who was general manager of the famous George V Hotel in Paris for more than 30 years, was a master of this art. He was always present at the right moment to meet and greet guests during the lunch hour and at the evening check-in. Hoteliers always remember they are hosts.

The GM is ultimately responsible for the performance of the hotel and the employees. The GM is the leader of the hotel. As such, she or he is held accountable for the hotel's level of profitability by the corporation or owners.

General managers with a democratic, situational, and participating leadership style are more likely to be successful. There are, however, times when it is necessary to be somewhat autocratic—when crisis situations arise.

To be successful, GMs need to have a broad range of personal qualities. Among those most often quoted by GMs are the following:

- Leadership
- Attention to detail
- Follow-through—getting the job done

A General Manager Discussing the "Forecast" with a Rooms Division Director

Personal Profile: Cesar Ritz

Cesar Ritz was a legend in his own time; yet, like so many of the early industry leaders, he began at the bottom and worked his way up through the ranks. In his case it did not take long to reach the top because he quickly learned the secrets of success in the hotel business. His career began as an apprenticed hotel keeper at the age of 15. At 19 he was managing a Parisian restaurant. Suddenly, he quit that position to become an assistant waiter at the famous Voisin restaurant. There he learned how to pander to the rich and famous. In fact, he became so adept at taking care of the guests—remembering their likes and dislikes, even their idiosyncrasies—that a guest would ask for him and would only be served by him.

At 22, he became manager of the Grand National Hotel in Lucerne, Switzerland, one of the most luxurious hotels in the world. It was not very successful at the time Ritz became manager, but with his ingenuity and panache, he was able to attract the "in" crowd to complete a turnaround. After 11 seasons, he accepted a bigger challenge: the Savoy Hotel in London, which had only been open a few months and was not doing well. Cesar Ritz became manager of one of the most famous and luxurious hotels in the world at the age of 38.

Cesar Ritz

Once again, his flair and ability to influence society quickly made a positive impression on the hotel. To begin with, he made the hotel a cultural center for high society. Together with Escoffier as executive chef, he created a team that produced the finest cuisine in Europe in the most elegant of surroundings. He made evening dress compulsory and introduced orchestras to the restaurants. Cesar Ritz would spare no expense in order to create the lavish effect he sought. On one occasion he converted a riverside restaurant into a Venetian waterway, complete with small gondolas and gondoliers singing Italian love songs.[1]

Ritz considered the handling of people as the most important of all qualities for a hotelier. His imagination and sensitivity to people and their wants contributed to a new standard of hotel keeping. The Ritz name remains synonymous with refined, elegant hotels and service.[2] However, Ritz drove himself to the point of exhaustion, and at age 52, he suffered a nervous breakdown.

---

1. Richard A. Wentzel. "Leaders of the Hospitality Industry or Hospitality Management," *An Introduction to the Industry*, 6th ed. Dubuque, IA: Kendall/Hunt, 1991, p. 29.
2. Donald E. Lundberg, The Hotel and Restaurant Business, 4th ed. New York: Van Nostrand Reinhold, 1984, pp. 33–34.

- People skills
- Patience
- Ability to delegate effectively

A successful GM selects and trains the best people. A former GM of Chicago's Four Seasons Hotel deliberately hired division heads who knew more about what they were hired for than he did. The GM sets the tone—a structure of excellence—and others try to match it. Once the structure is in place, each employee works to define the hotel's commitment to excellence. General managers need to understand, empathize, and allow for the cultures of both guests and employees.

Management Structure

Management structure differs among larger, midscale, and smaller properties. The midscale and smaller properties are less complex in their management structures than the larger ones. However, someone must be responsible for each of the key result areas that make the operation successful. For example, a small property may not have a director of human resources, but each department head will have general day-to-day operating responsibilities for the human resources function. The manager will have the ultimate responsibility for all human resources decisions. The same scenario is possible with each of the following areas: engineering and maintenance, accounting and finance, marketing and sales, food and beverage management, and so on.

The Executive Committee

The general manager, using input from the **executive committee** (Figure 5–1), makes all the major decisions affecting the hotel. These executives, who include the directors of human resources, food and beverage, rooms division, marketing and sales, engineering, and accounting, compile the hotel's occupancy forecast together with all revenues and expenses to make up the budget. They generally meet once a week for one or two hours—although The Ritz-Carlton has a daily lineup at 9 A.M.— and might typically cover some of the following topics:

Guest satisfaction	Renovations
Employee satisfaction	Ownership relations
Total quality management	Energy conservation
Occupancy forecasts	Recycling
Sales and marketing plans	New legislation
Training	Profitability
Major items of expenditure	

Some GMs rely on input from the executive committee more than others, depending on their leadership and management style. These senior executives determine the character of the property and decide on the missions, goals, and objectives of the hotel. For a chain hotel, this will be in harmony with the corporate mission.

In most hotels, the executive committee is involved with the decisions, but the ultimate responsibility and authority rests with the GM. One major role of the committee is communicator, both up and down the line of authority. This helps build interdepartmental cooperation.

Executive Committee Chart for a 300 - plus-room Full Service Hotel

General Manager

| **Director of Human Resources** | **Director of Food and Beverage** | **Director of Rooms Division** | **Director of Marketing and Sales** | **Director of Engineering** | **Director of Accounting** |

Figure 5–1 *Executive Committee Chart*

The Departments

Rooms Division

The rooms division director is responsible to the GM for the efficient and effective leadership and operation of all the rooms division departments. They include concerns such as the following:

Financial responsibility for rooms division
Employee satisfaction goals
Guest satisfaction goals
Guest services
Guest relations
Security
Gift shop

The **rooms division** consists of the following departments: front office, reservations, housekeeping, concierge, guest services, security, and communications. Figure 5–2 shows the organizational chart for a 300-plus-room hotel rooms division.

The guest cycle in Figure 5–3 shows a simplified sequence of events that takes place from the moment a guest calls to make a reservation until he or she checks out.

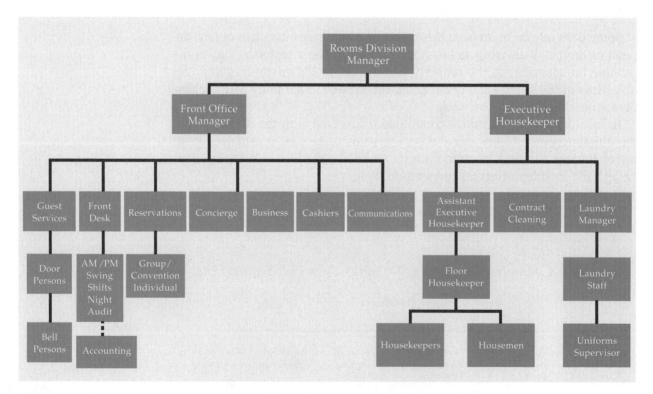

Figure 5–2 *Rooms Division Organizational Chart*

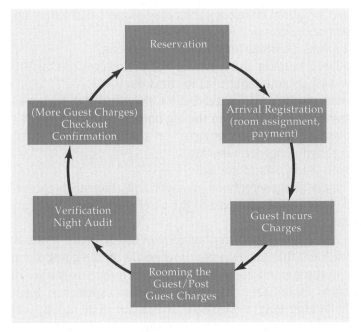

Figure 5–3 *The Guest Cycle*

Front Office

The front office manager's (FOM) main duty is to enhance guest services by constantly developing services to meet guest needs. An example of how some FOMs practice enhancing guest services is to have a guest service associate (GSA) greet guests as they arrive at the hotel, escort them to the front desk, and then personally allocate the room and take the guest and luggage to the room. This innovative way of developing guest services looks at the operation from the guest's perspective. There is no need to have separate departments for doorperson, bellperson, front desk, and so on. Each guest associate is cross-trained in all aspects of greeting and rooming the guest. This is now being done in smaller and midsized properties as well as specialty and deluxe properties. Guest service associates are responsible for the front desk, concierge, PBX, bellpersons, valet, and reservations.

During an average day in a hotel—if there is such a thing—the front office manager and his or her associates perform the following duties:

- Check night clerk report.
- Review previous night's occupancy.
- Review previous night's average rate.
- Look over market mix and determine what rooms to sell at what price.
- Handle checkouts and check-ins.
- Check complimentary rooms.
- Verify group rooms to be picked up for the next 30 days.
- Review arrivals and departures for the day.
- Politely and efficiently attend to guest inquiries.
- Review the VIP list and prepare preregistration.

- Organize any room changes guests may request and follow up.
- Arrange preregistrations for all arrivals.
- Attend rooms divisions and operations meeting.
- Advise housekeeping and room service of flowers/fruit for VIPs.
- Review arrivals and departures for next day.
- Make staffing adjustments needed for arrivals and departures.
- Note any important things in the log book.
- Check issuing and control of keys.
- Review scheduling (done weekly).
- Meet with lead GSAs (done daily).

In some hotels, the reservations manager and associates report to the director of sales. These positions report to the chief accountant: night auditor, night audit associates, and cashiers.

The front office has been described as the hub or nerve center of the hotel. It is the department that makes a first impression on the guest and one that the guest relies on throughout his or her stay for information and service. Positive first impressions are critical to the successful guest experience. Many guests arrive at the hotel after long, tiring trips. They want to be met by someone with a warm smile and a genuine greeting. If a guest should have a negative experience when checking into a hotel, he or she will be on guard in encounters with each of the other departments. The position description for a guest service agent details the work performed. Position descriptions for the three main functions of the front office are as follows:

1. *To sell rooms.* The hotel departments work like a team in a relay race. Sales or reservations staff make up room sales until the evening before the guest's arrival. At 6:00 P.M., when the reservations office closes, all the expected arrivals and available rooms are then handed over to the

A Front Office Manager about to Welcome Us

FOCUS ON ROOMS DIVISION

How to Have Fun Working at the Front Desk and Be Successful at the Same Time

William B. Martin
California State-Monterey Bay

If you are currently working at a front desk as a service provider or if you plan to do so in the near future, here are a few handy hints about being successful. Note that this list is only a beginning. By no means is it totally complete or does it cover all contingencies.

1. Get plenty of sleep the night before your shift. Arrive at work well rested.
2. Come to work early, in plenty of time to get all the change of shift information that you will need.
3. Approach each shift with a positive frame of mind.
4. Remember that when you are interacting with guests, you *are* the hotel.
5. Always keep in mind that delivering quality guest services is your first priority.
6. Smile a lot when interacting with guests and fellow service providers.
7. Keep in mind that your job is to service not only external customers (guests) but also internal customers—those people who also work at the hotel but who rely on you to get things done and perform your job well.
8. Remember that practicing quality guest service requires that you are good at procedural service as well as personal service. One is not sacrificed for the sake of the other. Both are emphasized and practiced.
9. Be genuinely enthusiastic about being a service provider. If you can't be, find another job.
10. Stay flexible. Be open to new demands and experiences.
11. When a large family checks into one room, anticipate that they may need extra towels or perhaps a hide-a-bed.
12. Take care of all requests for room repair and maintenance immediately.
13. Be willing to learn and open to learning new ways of doing things.
14. Try to tell a guest what you can do, not what you can't do. Keep it positive.
15. Always greet a guest with a smile.
16. When you are tired, don't show it, especially in front of guests.
17. Be an attitude catalyst. Infect others with your positive attitude.
18. Refer to a guest by name whenever and wherever you can. Especially during check-in, call the guest by name at least two or three times.
19. After check-in is complete, say, "Thank you, Mr./Ms. Doe. Have a great stay."
20. When passing a guest outside the front desk, in the hallway, or out on the patio, always smile and say hello.
21. Pre–room assign large tour groups and delegate key distribution to the tour director.
22. Always, always keep in constant touch with housekeeping, and say "thank you" to them a lot.
23. Look for cues such as age, attire, group mix, body language, or verbal abilities to determine any possible service needs a guest may have.
24. When booking reservations, get all needed information and ask about any special needs the guest may have.
25. Avoid the five forbidden phrases: "I don't know." "We can't do that." "You'll have to. . . ." "Hang on a second. I'll be right back." Saying "no" at the beginning of a sentence.
26. Anticipate guest needs. Be one step ahead of them so you can provide service without them having to ask.
27. Have plenty of toiletry supplies for guest emergencies available.
28. Genuinely enjoy working with guests, other service providers, and managers. Be a people person. If this is not you, find another job.
29. Remain guest focused. Constantly work toward understanding what it is that they need and helping them to feel welcome, comfortable, and important.
30. Smile, smile, smile!

front-desk P.M. shift. Reservations calls after 6:00 P.M. may either be taken by the front-desk staff or the 1-800 number. The front-desk team will try to sell out (achieve 100 percent occupancy) by selling the remaining rooms to call-in or walk-in guests—and of course the frantic calls from preferred guests who need a favor!

Upselling occurs when the guest service agent/front-desk clerk suggestively sells the features of a larger room, a higher floor, or perhaps a better view. Yield management originated in the airline industry where demand also fluctuates. Basically, a percentage of guests who book and send in a deposit in advance will be able to secure a room at a more reasonable price than someone booking a room with just three days' notice. The price will be even higher for the booking at three days' notice if demand is good.

Many other factors influence the hotel's ability to sell out. Chief among these are *demand*—the number of people needing rooms—and *supply*—the number of available rooms. A good example is the New York Hotel Convention and Trade Show. This event takes place in a city that has a high demand for hotel rooms in proportion to its inventory (number of available rooms). Because there is a fairly constant demand for rooms in New York, special events tend to increase demand to a point that forces up room rates. Another example comes from the airline industry, which always seems to raise prices at the peak travel times (Thanksgiving, Christmas, Easter, and the summer vacation times). They only give special fares when school is in session. Revenue management is explained in more detail later in this chapter.

2. *To maintain balanced guest accounts.* This begins with advance deposits, opening the guest folio (account), and posting all charges from the various departments. Most hotels have property management systems

A Rooms Division Manager Takes Care of a Guest Request

A Desk Clerk Ready to Welcome Us

(PMS) (property management systems are explained in more detail later in this chapter) and point-of-sale terminals (POS), which are online to the front office. This means that guest charges from the various outlets are directly debited to the guest's folio. Payment is either received on guest checkout or transferred to the **city ledger** (a special account for a company that has established credit with the hotel). This means that the account will be sent and paid within a specified time period.

3. *To offer services such as handling mail, faxes, messages, and local and hotel information.* People constantly approach the front desk with questions. Front desk employees need to be knowledgeable about the various activities in the hotel. The size, layout, and staffing of the front desk will vary with the size of the hotel. A busy 800-room city center property will naturally differ from a country inn. The front desk is staffed throughout the 24 hours by three shifts.

The evening shift duties are the following:

1. Check the log book for special items. (The log book is kept by guest contact; associates at the front office note specific and important guest requests and occurrences such as requests for room switches or baby cribs.)
2. Check on the room status, number of expected checkouts still to leave, and arrivals by double-checking registration cards and the computer in order to update the forecast of the night's occupancy. This will determine the number of rooms left to sell. Nowadays, this is all part of the capability of the PMS.
3. Handle guest check-ins. This means notifying the appropriate staff of any special requests guests may have made (e.g., nonsmoking room or a long bed for an extra-tall guest).
4. Take reservations for that evening and future reservations after the reservations staff have left for the day.

Figure 5–4 shows the types of **room rates** offered by hotels.

Major hotel chains offer a number of different room rates, including the following:

rack rate
corporate
association rate
government
encore
cititravel
entertainment cards
AAA
AARP (American Association of Retired Persons)
wholesale
group rates
promotional special

The rack rate is the rate that is used as a benchmark quotation of a hotel's room rate. Let us assume that the Hotel California had a rack rate of $135. Any discounted rate may be offered at a percentage deduction from the rack rate. An example would be a corporate rate of $110, an association rate of $105, and AARP rate of $95—certain restrictions may apply. Group rates may range from $95 to $125 according to how much the hotel needs the business.

Throughout the world there are three main plans on which room rates are based:

AP/American Plan—room and three meals a day
MAP/Modified American Plan—room plus two meals
EP/European Plan—room only, meals extra

Figure 5–4   *Types of Rates*

Night Auditor

A hotel is one of the few businesses that balances its accounts at the end of each business day. Because a hotel is open 24 hours every day, it is difficult to stop transactions at any given moment. The **night auditor** waits until the hotel quiets down at about 1:00 A.M. and then begins the task of balancing the guests' accounts receivable. Other duties include the following:

1. Post any charges that the evening shift was not able to post.
2. Pass discrepancies to shift managers in the morning. The room and tax charges are then posted to each folio and a new balance shown.
3. Run backup reports so if the computer system fails, the hotel will have up-to-date information to operate a manual system.
4. Reconcile point-of-sale and PMS to guest accounts. If this does not balance, then the auditor must do so by investigating errors or omissions. This is done by checking that every departmental charge shows up on guest folios.

The Night Audit Process in Simple Terms

1. The night audit team runs a preliminary reconciliation report that shows the total revenue generated from room and tax, banquets and catering, food and beverage outlets, and other incidentals (phone, gift shop, etc.).
2. All errors on the report are investigated.
3. All changes are posted and balanced with the preliminary charges.
4. A comparison of charges is carried out, matching preliminary with actual charges.
5. Totals for credit card charges, rooms operations, food and beverages, and incidentals are verified.
6. The team "rolls the date"—they go forward to the next day.

Corporate Profile: Hyatt Hotels

When Nicholas Pritzker emigrated with his family from the Ukraine to the United States, he began his career by opening a small law firm. His outstanding management skills led to the expansion of the law firm, turning it into a management company. The Pritzkers gained considerable financial support, which allowed them to pursue their goals of expansion and development. These dreams came into reality with the opening of the first Hyatt Hotel, inaugurated on September 27, 1957.

Today, Hyatt Hotel Corporation is a multibillion-dollar hotel management and development company; together with Hyatt International, they are among the leading chains in the hotel industry, with close to 8 percent of the market share.[1] Hyatt has earned worldwide fame as the leader in providing luxury accommodations and high-quality service, targeting especially the business traveler, but strategically differentiating its properties and services to identify and market to a very diverse clientele. This differentiation has resulted in the following types of hotels:

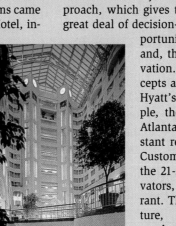

1. The *Hyatt Regency Hotels* represent the company's core product. They are usually located in business city centers and are regarded as five-star hotels.
2. *Hyatt Resorts* are vacation retreats. They are located in the world's most desirable leisure destinations, offering the "ultimate escape from everyday stresses."
3. The *Park Hyatt Hotels* are smaller, European-style, luxury hotels. They target the individual traveler who prefers the privacy, personalized service, and discreet elegance of a small European hotel.
4. The *Grand Hyatt Hotels* serve culturally rich destinations that attract leisure business as well as large-scale meetings and conventions. They reflect refinement and grandeur, and they feature state-of-the-art technology and banquet and conference facilities of world-class standard.
5. *Hyatt Vacation Club* offers vacation ownership, vacation rentals, and mini vacations
6. *U.S. Franchise Systems, Inc.* franchises Hawthorne Suites, Microtel, and Best Inns.
7. *Hyatt* has also acquired the upscale, limited-service AmeriSuites hotel chain, which are being repositioned under a new Hyatt brand called Hyatt Place.

Hyatt Hotels Corporation has been recognized by the *Wall Street Journal* as one of the 66 firms around the world poised to make a difference in the industries and markets. The effective management that characterized the company in its early years with the Pritzker family has continued through time. Hyatt Hotels Corporation is characterized by a decentralized management approach, which gives the individual general manager a great deal of decision-making power, as well as the opportunity to stimulate personal creativity and, therefore, differentiation and innovation. The development of novel concepts and products is perhaps the key to Hyatt's outstanding success. For example, the opening of the Hyatt Regency Atlanta, Georgia, gave the company instant recognition throughout the world. Customers were likely to stare in awe at the 21-story atrium lobby, the glass elevators, and the revolving rooftop restaurant. The property's innovative architecture, designed by John Portman, revolutionized the common standards of design and spacing, thus changing the course of the lodging industry. The atrium concept introduced there represented a universal challenge to hotel architects to face the new trend of grand, wide-open public spaces.

A further positive aspect of the decentralized management structure is the fact that the individual manager is able to be extremely customer responsive by developing a thorough knowledge of the guests' needs and thereby providing personalized service—fundamental to achieving customer satisfaction. This is, in fact, the ultimate innkeeping purpose, which Hyatt attains at high levels.

The other side of Hyatt's success is the emphasis on human resources management. Employee satisfaction, in fact, is considered to be a prerequisite to external satisfaction. Hyatt devotes enormous attention to employee training and selection. What is most significant, however, is the interaction among top managers and operating employees.

---

[1]The company operates 213 hotels and resorts in forty-three countries worldwide

*Night Auditor Verifying and
Balancing Guest Accounts*

5. Complete and distribute the daily report. This report details the previous day's activities and includes vital information about the performance of the hotel.
6. Determine areas of the hotel where theft could potentially occur.

The **daily report** contains some key operating ratios such as **room occupancy percentage (ROP),** which is rooms occupied divided by rooms available. Thus, if a hotel has 850 rooms and 622 are occupied, the occupancy percentage is 622 ÷ 850 = 73 percent. The ADR is, together with the occupancy percentage, one of the key operating ratios that indicates the hotel's performance.

The average daily rate is calculated by dividing the rooms revenue by the number of rooms sold. If the rooms revenue was $75,884 and the number of rooms sold was 662, then the ADR would be $114.63. See Figure 5–5 for an example of a daily report.

Room Occupancy Percentage (ROP):

If total available rooms are   850
And total rooms occupied are   622
Then:

$$\textbf{Occupancy percentage} = (622/850) \times 100 = 73\%$$

Average Daily Rate:

If rooms revenue is $75,884
And total number of rooms sold is   622
Then:

$$\textbf{Average daily rate} = \frac{75,884}{662} = \$ \, \textbf{114.63}$$

A more recent ratio to gauge a hotel rooms division's performance is the percentage of potential rooms revenue, which is calculated by determining potential rooms revenue and dividing the actual revenue by the potential revenue.

Clarion Hotel Bayview

| Daily Management Report Supplement January 2007 | | | Daily Report January 2007 | | | |

Occupancy%	Today	Avg or %	M–T–D Avg or %		Y–T–D Avg or %	
Rack Rooms	9	2.9%	189	3.37	189	3.37
Corporate Rooms	0	0.0%	103	1.83	103	1.83
Group Rooms	274	87.8%	2,379	42.36	2,379	42.36
Leisure Rooms	3	1.0%	395	7.03	395	7.03
Base Rooms	23	7.4%	348	6.14	345	6.14
Government Rooms	2	0.6%	32	.57	32	.57
Wholesale Rooms	1	0.3%	121	2.15	121	2.15
No-Show Rooms		0.0%	0	.00	0	.00
Comp Rooms	0	0.0%	37	.66	37	.66
Total Occ Rooms & Occ %	312	100%	3,601	64.12	3,601	64.12
Rack	$1,011	$112.33	17,207	91.04	17,207	91.04
Corporate	$0	ERR	8,478	82.31	8,478	82.31
Group	$22,510	$82.15	178,066	74.85	178,066	74.85
Leisure	$207	$69.00	24,985	63.25	24,985	63.25
Base	$805	$35.00	12,063	34.97	12,063	34.97
Govt	$141	$70.59	2,379	74.34	2,379	74.34
Wholesale	$43	$43.00	5,201	42.98	5,201	42.98
No-Show/Comp/Allowance	$0		−914	−24.69	−914	−24.69
Total Rev & Avg Rate	$24,717	$79.22	247,466	68.72	247,466	68.72

Hotel Revenue

Rooms	$24,717		247,466	77.46	247,466	77.46
Food	$1,400		37,983	11.89	37,983	11.89
Beverage	$539		9,679	3.03	9,679	3.03
Telephone	$547		5,849	1.83	5,849	1.83
Parking	$854		11,103	3.48	11,103	3.48
Room Svc II	$70		1,441	.45	1,441	.45
Other Revenue	$1,437		963	1.87	963	1.87
Total Revenue	$29,563		319,484	100.00	319,484	100.00

Figure 5–5   *Daily Report*

Clarion Hotel Bayview

Daily Management Report Supplement	Daily Report
January 2007	January 2007

Cafe 6th & K	Today	Avg or %	M–T–D Avg or %		Y–T–D Avg or %	
Cafe Breakfast Covers	88	57.1%	1,180	47.12	1,180	47.12
Cafe Lunch Covers	43	27.9%	674	26.92	674	26.92
Cafe Dinner Covers	23	14.9%	650	25.96	650	25.96
Total Cafe Covers	154	100.0%	2,504	100.00	2,504	100.00
Cafe Breakfast	$608	$6.91	7,854	6.66	7,854	6.66
Cafe Lunch	$246	$5.72	5,847	8.67	5,847	8.67
Cafe Dinner	$227	$9.86	4,309	6.63	4,309	6.63
Gaslamp Lounge Food			2,431	3.74	2,431	3.74
Total Rev/Avg Check	$1,081	$7.02	20,440	8.16	20,440	8.16

Banquets						
Banquet Breakfast Covers	0	ERR	154	13.24	154	13.24
Banquet Lunch Covers	0	ERR	134	11.52	134	11.52
Banquet Dinner Covers	0	ERR	254	21.84	254	21.84
Banquet Coffee Break Covers	0	ERR	621	53.40	621	53.40
Total Banquet Covers	0	ERR	1,163	100.00	1,163	100.00
Banquet Breakfast	$0	ERR	980	6.36	980	6.36
Banquet Lunch	$0	ERR	2,997	22.36	2,997	22.36
Banquet Dinner	$0	ERR	4,530	17.84	4,530	17.84
Banquet Coffee Break	$0	ERR	1,093	1.76	1,093	1.76
Total Rev/Avg Check	$0	ERR	9,600	8.25	9,600	8.25

Room Service						
Room Service Breakfast Covers	13	40.6%	324	48.00	324	48.00
Room Service Lunch Covers	3	9.4%	53	7.85	53	7.85
Room Service Dinner Covers	16	50.0%	298	44.15	298	44.15
Total Covers	32	100.0%	675	100.00	675	100.00
Room Service Breakfast	$119	$9.13	2,665	8.22	2,665	8.22
Room Service Lunch	$29	$9.77	418	7.89	418	7.89
Room Service Dinner	$171	$10.67	2,907	9.75	2,907	9.75
Total Rev/Avg Check	$319	$9.96	5,990	8.87	5,990	8.87

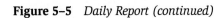

Figure 5–5   *Daily Report (continued)*

Larger hotels may have more than one night auditor, but in smaller properties these duties may be combined with night manager, desk, or night watchperson duties.

Hotel Information Technology Systems

Information technology has helped hotels reach one of the main goals of a hotel: to deliver exceptional guest satisfaction. Some hotels have utilized technology for many years. The first hotel to use a computer was the New York Hilton in 1963. This was the first computer-automated guest room management system, but it was very inefficient because front-desk clerks had to use key punch cards to record information and then process these cards in a batch at a later time.[1] Fortunately, hospitality information technology has progressed, and today several efficient systems are fast becoming industry standards.

Property Management Systems

The **property management system (PMS)** is the center of information processing in a hotel. A property management system is a computer-based lodging information system that relates to both the front- and back-office activities. Property management systems are used to help complete many tasks within a short period of time. Hotels with a large number of guests and employees to serve and inform predominantly use these systems. A PMS will aid a property to become more efficient with time, which is an important factor for guests who demand personal attention and fast service.

The property management system can interface with many other modules or applications. One application of the PMS in the front office is the **room management module,** which keeps the front office and   *A Popular Property Management System*

housekeeping informed about the status of rooms. The hotel room master in the PMS contains data on each room such as room number, room type, room features, room rates, locations and the status of each room. Knowing the status of each room definitely helps the housekeeping department know what work has to be done, what work is in progress, and what work has been completed.

Another front office module is a **guest accounting module.** A guest accounting module increases the hotel's control over guest accounts, makes them easily available at any time, and significantly shortens the night audit procedure. Other functions of a PMS are electronic locking systems, energy management systems, and call accounting systems.

There are many potential users of a PMS. Any manager making strategic decisions could utilize the information provided by a PMS. Some property management systems even offer microcomputer interfaces so that the information from the PMS can be downloaded onto a personal computer to be utilized by a number of business applications.

Some hotels use an express check-in process that allows guests to conveniently check in and out via a touch screen that interfaces with the hotel's property management system without associate assistance. A booth in the lobby allows guests to input their reservation details or provide data from an inserted card or touch-screen selections. Based on the information given, after obtaining an electronic signature, an electronic room key is then encoded and dispensed. A printout of guest stay information, including room type, rate, and departure date, is printed.[2] Guests may also use the booth to check out. Guest preferences are noted for future use and even airline boarding passes can now be issued.

The PMS system interfaces with the Internet to allow guests the capability to book rooms online. Hotels are now attempting to drive bookings to "their"

VingCard VISION is a full-featured, functionally rich access control system.

Web sites rather than pay commission to companies like hotels.com, Travelocity, and Expedia.

Perhaps the ultimate in guest convenience is the wireless curbside guest check-in made possible by the VingCard system. This recent technological advance allows guests to go right to their rooms from curbside. The system is capable of interfacing with existing PMS systems to fully integrate property management, reservations, and guest service functions. With a portable keycard encoder and MICROS's OPERA Palm, a wireless handheld device with real-time database access, the system works seamlessly to provide the ultimate guest convenience.[3]

Some property management systems use Microsoft Windows to move data between applications and to share information, a process called *information sharing*. Information sharing permits menu-driven interface with other systems, such as advanced reservations, room inventory, self-check-in/out, night audit, guest accounting, city ledger, group handling, travel agency accounting.[4] All these systems are designed to improve guest service. But beware: Management needs to ensure that the front-desk associate doesn't just look down while keying in the guest name and other details without ever really looking up at the customer. Yes, the hotels that will be successful in the next few years are the ones that go out of their way to make guests really feel welcome and offer high-tech yet high-touch service.

Hotel guests expect their rooms to be a home away from home, office, retreat, and even playroom. High-speed Internet is a given, but it is a challenge for hotel operators to select a service provider. Some of the older hotels have selected to go totally wireless using RoomLinx (**www.roomlinx.com**), a choice that gives guests high-speed Internet access not just from their rooms but also throughout the hotel, including meeting rooms.

Moderately priced Wingate Inns partners with Lodge Net (**www.lodgenet.com**) to offer guests high-speed Internet access in every room and a full array of entertainment options: movies, video games, and music. MGM Grand selected Cox Communications Hospitality Network (**www.Cox.com**) to deploy what will be the largest hotel wireless Internet network in the nation. Guests can purchase WiFi access or use the existing hospitality network wired Internet service from the convenience of their own rooms.

Web-enabled PDAs allow companies like Hyatt hotels to offer its Gold Passport guests a PDA-based program from Portable Internet (**www.portableinternet.com**) to deliver driving directions, shopping, restaurants, and entertainment information. Access is available to descriptions of the properties and their facilities and advanced reservations. At the Venetian Casino Resort in Las Vegas, guests can check in with their PDAs as soon as they walk in the door and make table reservations via Open Table. They may also select the in-room temperature and the room service menu.

High-speed Internet access (HSIA) is becoming a necessity. Hotels and restaurants that don't offer HSIA lose guests, as happened at one Holiday Inn Express that had not upgraded; guests moved across the street where their technology needs were met. Naturally, it did not take long for the Holiday Inn to install WiFi. Starbucks was the

High-Speed Internet Access for Hotel Guests

first restaurant chain to offer WiFi to guests, who can now enjoy a latté with their e-mail. Even some McDonald's have gone WiFi.

Energy Management Systems

Technology is used to extend guest in-room comfort by means of an energy management system. Passive infrared motion sensors and door switches can reduce energy consumption by 30 percent or more by automatically switching off lights and air conditioning, thus saving energy when the guest is out of the room. Additional features include:

- Room occupancy status reporting
- Automatic lighting control
- Minibar access reporting
- Smoke detector alarm reporting
- Central electronic lock control
- Guest control amenities

Due to increasing energy costs, some operators are installing software programs that will turn off nonessential equipment during the peak billing times of day (utility companies' charges are based on peak usage). Hospitality operators can save money by utilizing this type of energy-saving software to reduce their energy costs.

Call Accounting Systems

Call accounting systems (CAS) track guest room phone charges. Software packages can be used to monitor where calls are being made and from what phones on the property. To track this information, the CAS must work in conjunction with the PBX (telephone) and the PMS. Call accounting systems today can be used to offer different rates for local guest calls and long-distance guest calls. The CAS can even be used to offer discounted calling during off-peak hours at the hotel.

Guest Reservation Systems

Before hotels started using the Internet to book reservations, they received reservations by letters, telegrams, faxes, and phone calls. Airlines were the first industry to start using **global distribution systems (GDS)** for reservations (Figure 5–6). Global distribution systems are electronic markets for travel, hotel, car rental, and attraction bookings.

A **central reservation system (CRS)** houses the electronic database in the **central reservation office (CRO).** Hotels provide rates and availability information to the CRO usually by data communication lines. This automatically updates the CRS so that guests get the best available rate when they book through the central reservation office. Guests instantly receive confirmation of their reservation or cancellation.

The hotel benefits from using a central reservation system. With such a system, hotels can avoid overselling rooms by too large a margin. The CRS database can also be used as a chain or individual property-marketing tool because guest

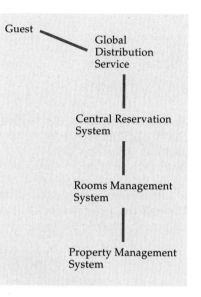

Figure 5–6 *Sequence and Relationships of a Hotel Guest Reservation*

information can easily be stored. A CRS can also provide yield management information for a hotel. The more flexible a central reservation system is, the more it will help with yield management. For example, when demand is weak for a hotel, rates will need to drop to increase reservations and profitability. When demand is higher, the hotel can sell room rates that are closer to the rack rate.

A CRS can be used in several areas of a hotel. If a hotel has a reservations department, the terminals or personal computers in that department can be connected to the central reservation system. It would also be important for front-desk employees to have access to the CRS. The reason for this is because they will need to know what the hotel has available because they may need to book rooms for walk-ins who don't have reservations. Constant communication back and forth is needed between the central reservation system and the front office and reservations department. Managers who are the decision makers in the hotel will also use the system to forecast and set pricing for rooms and different amenities.

Hotels can use other forms of technology to facilitate reservation systems. Several companies offer an **application service provider (ASP)** environment that can deliver a complete booking system tied to the hotel's inventory in real time via the Web. One operator, Paul Wood of the El Dorado Hotel in Santa Fe, New Mexico, says that he simply went to the ASP's Web site and put in a promotional corporate rate for the summer, and the same day he started seeing reservations coming in with that code. After a few months, bookings were up 3 percent over the previous year.

Billing Guests

Hospitality businesses today seek to obtain the most high-speed and reliable computer systems they can afford that allow them to bill their guests without delay. Fast access to guests' accounts is required by large hotels due to their high priority for guest satisfaction (no lineups at checkout).

Corporate Profile

McKibbon Hotel Management, Inc. Management Services (www.mckibbon.com/ManServ.htm)

M3 (**www.m3as.com/**) was created out of one of the oldest and most successful hospitality companies in the industry. This experience, coupled with its software development expertise, has allowed M3 to develop an integrated suite of hospitality products, including AccKnowledge, InnQuire, and LaborWatch. These products, utilizing Internet-based technology, allow owners, operators, and managers unsurpassed access to the information they need most.

M3 is the first ASP, or application service provider, in the hospitality industry. Hosting their applications in a professionally managed, centralized data center allows clients easy access to their information via the Internet. Clients do not have to purchase software; rather, they access it online. Included in the monthly fee is all the hardware, software support, maintenance, and upgrades necessary for clients to manage and grow their business. And there is no contract to sign.

In 1998, M3 became the first company in the world to offer hosted hospitality applications. By the end of 1999, 75 hotels subscribed to the M3 product suite. For the first time, many corporate executives could view their information online, first thing in the morning, without having to wait on anyone to fax or e-mail information to them or for someone to consolidate a report.

M3 Computer Room

It took M3 two years, over $1 million, and the advice of lots of experts to develop the initial product. Since that time, hundreds of enhancements have been made at no extra cost to clients, and the system is up every day.

What Is Hosting?

Hosting is application software that resides in a professionally managed third-party data center. The client subscribes to use the hardware, software, data security, and storage, as well as ongoing support, maintenance, and upgrades. The advantages of hosting are that data are secure and maintained by professionals, access is available 24 hours a day from anywhere in the world via the Internet, costs are typically 50 to 70 percent less than owning and managing your own system, there is no need to buy expensive equipment, hardware and software are updated at no additional cost, and contracts are not required.

M3 AccKnowledge links properties and corporate offices to a common site, where data are entered directly into the system at the property level. This reduces the cost, time, and inefficiency of two or more people handling the same paperwork. M3 AccKnowledge allows several partnerships to review information about their properties or lets corporate accounting staff see the daily report upon request. Companies that use M3 and similar systems save money by having immediate access to vital performance information. For example, if a company is being audited by a state agency or information on insurance or workers' compensation is required, this system can provide the required information in minutes.

Additional features of M3 AccKnowledge are: data are continuously backed up and stored, an efficient Windows-based user-friendly technology is used, access is available any time anywhere in the world, financial reports are user defined and can be created or changed to suite clients, updates to data are instantaneous, the system expands quickly to any size company, financial reporting across company lines is handled easily, checks can be printed for all the companies within your enterprise or in one batch, and daily reports are quickly and easily customized to accommodate the requirements of various owners, brands, and the client's staff.

M3 InnQuire is a Web-based data-mining tool that allows managers to write and run their own multiunit reports with unlimited statistics. InnQuire is a warehouse of information that consists of data from client's property-level daily reports. These data allow for comparison among brands, divisions, occupancy, rates, revenues, and labor costs. The features of M3 InnQuire include the use of historical data to predict future expectations; use of actual statistics to classify properties; use of data to find causal relationships that might otherwise be hidden; and direct deviation (clients can find anomalies in data that might not be clear from a consolidated report). The system allows clients to grow and can handle five or fifty units without having to increase their staff.

M3 LaborWatch is seamless payroll integration from time card to paycheck. M3 LaborWatch brings it all together to give clients a multiunit reporting of actual hours versus volume-adjusted standards and benchmark performance versus others in the industry. M3 LaborWatch keeps track of employees' time throughout their workday. This information is made available to managers on a daily basis. From these data, M3 LaborWatch lets clients design and produce their own reports; compare labor hours to standards, adjusted for volume; review by day,

week or month; review by job code or department; review by hotel or region; calculate hours per occupied room; and review overtime hours by job or department for any property. M3 LaborWatch allows clients to compare their labor statistics to similar hotels. The results help gauge productivity, rate of pay, overtime, and benchmark performance in key categories versus a group of hotels that are similar in size, location, and brand.

Meeting Matrix (**www.meetingmatrix.com**) provides software for the planning, diagramming, and modeling of meeting space. Winner of the Microsoft Retail Application Developer (RAD) award, Meeting Matrix can benefit meeting planners, conference centers, hotels, hospitals, universities, convention centers and trade show managers.

Billing guests has become much easier with the aid of computers. Billing guests can be a long process if information technologies are not used to complete transactions. Property management systems aid large hotels to make faster transactions and provide a more efficient service to their guests. These systems help the hospitality associates bill their guests within seconds.

Some hotels utilize software that enables guests to check and approve their bills by using the TV and remote, thus avoiding the need to line up at the cashier's desk to check out. A copy of their bill is then mailed to their home address.

Security

Each business in the hospitality industry offers some sort of security for their guests and employees. Peace of mind that the hotel or restaurant is secure is a key factor in increasing guest satisfaction. Security is one of the highest concerns of guests who visit hospitality businesses. Hospitality information technology systems include surveillance systems in which cameras are installed in many different areas of the property to monitor the grounds and help ensure guest safety. These cameras are linked directly to computers, televisions, and digital recorders, which helps security teams keep an eye on the whole property.

Recent technological advances have produced electronic door locking systems, some of which even offer custom configurations of security and safety. Guest room locks are now capable of managing information from both magstripe and smart cards simultaneously. From the hotel's point of view, a main advantage of this kind of key is that the hotel knows who has entered the room and at what time because the system can trace anyone entering the room.

In-room safes can now be operated by key cards. Both systems are an improvement on the old metal keys. Even smarter safes use biometric technology that includes the use of thumbprints or retina scans to verify a user's identity.

Electronic Lock

Guest Comfort and Convenience

Hotels provide guest comfort and convenience in order to maintain a home-away-from-home feeling for their guests. Hotels will receive recognition because they provide many additional in-room services and amenities for their guests, such as dining, television, telephones, Internet connections, minibars, and hygiene products. These amenities help provide a cozy experience for the guest. Many other services can be provided outside of the rooms, such as swimming pools, massages, fine dining, postal services, and meeting space. Other services are provided to suit the demands of all types of guests, a concierge and business center, for example.

Hotels communicate with many entities to provide services for their guests. Some companies offer creative solutions to hotels for enhanced in-room services for guests. Sprint InSite with KoolConnect Interactive Media has created a product that provides many services to the guest from just one supplier. Services include Internet access and e-mail; movies, music, and games on demand; hotel and concierge services; special promotions; advertising; travel planning; feedback from guests; and customer support. All these services aid hotels in fulfilling guest demands. Sprint states, "Build loyalty and promote business retention by enhancing the overall quality-of-visit for your guest."[5] Play Stations and video games are also a part of the technology-based guest amenities.

Revenue Management

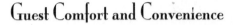

Revenue management is used to maximize room revenue at the hotel. It is based on the economics of supply and demand, which means that prices rise when demand is strong and drop when demand is weak. Thus, the purpose of yield management is to increase profitability. Naturally, management would like to sell every room at the highest rack rate. However, this is not reality, and rooms are sold at discounts on the rack rate. An example would be the corporate or group rate. In most hotels, only a small percentage of rooms are sold at rack rate. This is because of conventions and group rates and other promotional discounts that are necessary to stimulate demand. What yield management does is to allocate the right type of room to the right guest at the right price so as to maximize revenue per available room.[6]

Generally, the demand for room reservations follows the pattern of group bookings being made months or even years in advance of arrival and individual bookings, which mostly are made a few days before arrival. Figures 5–7 and 5–8 show the pattern of group and individual room reservations.

Group reservations are booked months, even years, in advance. Yield management will monitor reservations and, based on previous trends and current demand, determine the number and type of rooms to sell at what price to obtain the maximum revenue.

The curve in Figure 5–7 indicates the pattern of few reservations being made 120 days prior to arrival. Most of the individual room bookings are made in the last few days before arrival at the hotel. The yield management program will

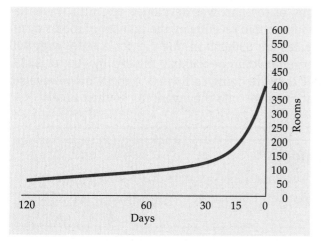

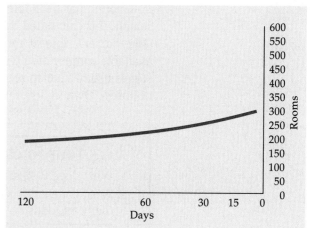

Figure 5–7 *Individual Room Booking Reservations Curve (Source: Jay R. Schrock, personal correspondence. August 18, 2005.)*

Figure 5–8 *Group Booking Curve*

monitor the demand and supply and recommend the number and type of rooms to sell for any given day, and the price for which to sell each room.

With yield management, not only will the time before arrival be an important consideration in the pricing of guest rooms, but also the type of room to be occupied. For example, there could be a different price for a double, queen, or king room when used for single occupancy. This rate could be above the single rack rate. Similarly, double and multiple room occupancy would yield higher room rates. It works as follows:

Suppose a hotel has 300 rooms and a rack rate of $150. The average number of rooms sold is 200 per night at an average rate of $125. The yield for this property would be

$$\text{Room occupancy percentage} = 200 \div 300 = 66.6\%$$

The rate achievement factor is

$$\$125 \div \$150 = 0.833$$

and the yield would be

$$0.666 \times 0.833 = 55.5\%$$

The application of yield management in hotels is still being refined to take into consideration factors such as multiple nights' reservations and incremental food and beverage revenue. If the guest wants to arrive on a high-demand night and stay through several low-demand nights, what should the charge be?

Yield management has some disadvantages. For instance, if a businessperson attempts to make a reservation at a hotel three days before arrival and the rate quoted in order to maximize revenue is considered too high, this person may decide to select another hotel and not even consider the first hotel when making future reservations.

Revenue per available room, or **rev par,** was developed by Smith Travel Research. It is calculated by dividing room revenue by the number of rooms available. For example, if room sales are $50,000 in one day for a hotel with 400 available rooms, then the formula would be $50,000 divided by 400, or $125. Hotels use rev par to see how they are doing compared to their competitive set of hotels. Owners use rev par to gauge who they want to run their hotels.

Check Your Knowledge

1. What does PMS stand for? What functions does this system perform?
2. What is revenue management? How is revenue management applied in the hotel industry?

Reservations

The reservations department is headed by the reservations manager who, in many hotels today, is on the same level as the front office manager and reports directly to the director of rooms division or the director of sales. This emphasizes the importance of the sales aspects of reservations and encompasses yield management. Reservations is the first contact for the guest or person making the reservation for the guest. Although the contact may be by telephone, a distinct impression of the hotel is registered with the guest. This calls for exceptional telephone manners and telemarketing skills. Because some guests may be shopping for the best value, it is essential to sell the hotel by emphasizing its advantages over the competition.

The reservation department generally works from 8:00 A.M. to 6:00 P.M. Depending on the size of the hotel, several people may be employed in this important department. The desired outcome of the reservations department is to exceed guest expectations when they make reservations. This is achieved by selling all of the hotel rooms for the maximum possible dollars and avoiding possible guest resentment of being overcharged. Reservations originate from a variety of sources:

1. Telephone to the same property
   a. Fax
   b. Letter
   c. Cable
2. Corporate/1-800 numbers
3. Travel agents
4. The Internet
5. Meeting planners
6. Tour operators
7. Referral from another company property
8. Airport telephone
9. Walk-in

*A Sheraton Reservations
Agent Taking a Booking*

Clearly, reservations are of tremendous importance to the hotel because of the potential and actual revenue realized. Many hotel chains have a 1-800 number that a prospective guest may call without charge to make a reservation at any of the company properties in the United States and internationally. The corporate **central reservations system** allows operators to access the inventory of room availability of each hotel in the chain. Once a reservation has been made, it is immediately deducted from the inventory of rooms for the duration of the guest stay. The central reservations system interfaces with the hotel's inventory and simultaneously allows reservations to be made by the individual hotel reservations personnel. A number of important details need to be recorded when taking reservations.

Confirmed reservations are reservations made with sufficient time for a confirmation slip to be returned to the client by mail or fax. Confirmation is generated by the computer printer and indicates confirmation number, dates of arrival and departure, type of room booked, number of guests, number of beds, type of bed, and any special requests. The guest may bring the confirmation slip to the hotel to verify the booking.

Guaranteed reservations are given when the person making the reservation wishes to ensure that the reservation will be held. This is arranged at the time the reservation is made and generally applies in situations when the guest is expected to arrive late. The hotel takes the credit card number, which guarantees payment of the room, of the person being billed. The hotel agrees to hold the room for late arrival. The importance of guaranteed reservations is that the guest will more likely cancel beforehand if unable to show up, which gives more accurate inventory room count and minimizes no-shows.

Another form of guaranteed reservations is advance deposit/advance payment. In certain situations, for example, during a holiday, in order to protect itself against having empty rooms (no-shows), the hotel requires that a deposit of either one night or the whole stay be paid in advance of the guest's arrival. This is done by obtaining the guest's credit card number, which may be charged automatically for the first night's accommodation. This discourages no-shows. Corporations that use the hotel frequently may guarantee all of their bookings

Communications plays a critical role in running a hotel.

so as to avoid any problems in the event a guest arrives late, remembering that in cities where the demand is heavy, hotels release any nonguaranteed or non-paid reservations at 4:00 P.M. or 6:00 P.M. on the evening of the guest's expected arrival.

Communications CBX or PBX

The communications CBX or PBX includes in-house communications; guest communications, such as pagers and radios; voice mail; faxes; messages; and emergency center. Guests often have their first contact with the hotel by telephone. This underlines the importance of prompt and courteous attention to all calls, because first impressions last.

The communications department is a vital part of the smooth running of the hotel. It is also a profit center because hotels generally add a 50 percent charge to all long-distance calls placed from guest rooms. Local calls cost about $0.75 to $1.25, plus tax.

Communications operates 24 hours a day, in much the same way as the front office does, having three shifts. It is essential that this department be staffed with people who are trained to be calm under pressure and who follow emergency procedures.

Guest Services/Uniformed Services

Because first impressions are very important to the guest, the guest service or uniformed staff has a special responsibility. The guest service department or **uniformed staff** is headed by a guest services manager who may also happen to be the bell captain. The staff consists of door attendants and bellpersons and the concierge, although in some hotels the concierge reports directly to the front office manager.

Door attendants are the hotel's unofficial greeters. Dressed in impressive uniforms, they greet guests at the hotel front door, assist in opening/closing

A Day in the Life of Ryan Adams

Guest Services Manager, Hotel del Coronado, San Diego, California

From what I gather there is supposed to be some sort of magical formula for how everything works out. You should have some plan with some kind of divine guidance; if you are spiritual, then you are on your way. However, I cannot rightly say that this has become known to me. I was lucky enough to develop a plan and have made some rather good decisions to get where I am.

I have been in the industry now for 11 years and I am always amazed at the magnetic draw this industry has on you. I always tell people, "It's not the job that is so hard, that is rudimentary; it is people that really make the challenge worth undertaking." I wake up at 5:30 A.M. every morning and prepare myself mentally before I go to work on how I am going to tackle the day.

My automatic coffee maker wakes me up and I establish my bearings as I proceed to take my shower and then turn on ESPN to catch sport highlights. I pour myself a cup of coffee and sit on the couch trying to figure out what I missed and memorize scores from the previous night's game. I then switch over to CNN to catch up on politics and headline news just in case there actually might be something of interest to my isolated world.

Picking out my suit for the day reflects my mood so I always take time to select the right color and style. I will choose blue if I feel like communicating well or brown if I am feeling emotional and warmhearted. If I am working a night shift I usually wear black with a red tie or some other kind of tie. I am a big tie fan. I believe ties are like the eyes of someone. They are the windows to the soul and express our mood or persona. I try to think of what I have to accomplish for the day as far as meetings or just pure operational work.

I usually roll into work at about 7 A.M. so I can see the graveyard bellman for a half hour and then the morning valet and cashiers. You learn a lot from the night crew. They see a lot of the nonsense that happens over the midnight hour. I touch base with the front desk and the concierge to see if they have any challenges starting off the day. I then retreat to my office.

As I get into my office it never fails that I have at least five voice mails and ten e-mails. I listen to my voice mails and print my e-mails and look at my calendar in Microsoft Outlook to see what meetings I have dedicated my time to. I then make a list of what I need to respond to and work on the pile of papers on my desk. I usually have a pile of papers from the night before as I get a lot of mail. I look at my 14-day forecast to see what events or groups we have in house and touch base with my bell phone receptionist who usually has good insight into the day's events.

My responsibilities are to oversee the functions of the bellman, elevator operators, doorman, valet runners, kiosk cashiers, mass transportation, parking control, and the concierge. I have two assistant guest services managers that come in at 11 A.M. and 2:30 P.M. to cover the other shifts. I also have a parking operations supervisor and a cashier supervisor. We hold a weekly meeting so I can share the vision of the company and my own. After all, I am not just a manager; I am a leader who has to take people somewhere where they would not have gone otherwise.

I spend most of my day in meetings. On Tuesdays I attend operations meetings. Our managing director and general manager speak to us about financial position and goals for the quarter. They also bring up special highlights or events. We hear from sales and convention management regarding groups and then catering for events. Room reservations personnel update us on their budget and how many rooms are going to be occupied for the next two weeks and then compare that to the forecasted level of occupancy. We then hear from accounting facilities, recreation, retail, guest services, and signature services. It is a very informative meeting and it also gives you a good read on the mood of upper management.

I try to spend as much face time with my associates as possible, getting feedback and safety suggestions and to let them vent frustrations as I try to win them over to the big picture. I spend a little time "shmoozing" clients who have porterages and deliveries to ensure my team is doing their best to impress. I attend their preconvention meetings to discover what the clients are about. We identify their needs and fulfill them with the kind of guest service that leaves their jaws dropped.

The funny thing about modern technology is how dependent you become on it. Gone are the days of the good ol' boy network when all you had to do was ask. Now you

Hotel del Coronado

have to set up a meeting in Microsoft Outlook, send e-mails, fill out tons of paperwork, and constantly check your voice mails and e-mails. The company has made it a little easier by supplying me with a Nextel phone, or "the leash" as we call it. This phone has walkie-talkie capability and allows the executive team to communicate on a network.

I know what you're thinking: Sounds tedious and problematic. Well it is. The challenge of making it all come together is what is so appealing to me. I usually get so involved that I forget to eat lunch, unless one of my teammates pulls me away for a bite and engages me in some endless banter about work. I stock my office refrigerator with candy bars and various beverages because I usually don't make the time to eat; it just gets too busy.

My days typically end about 5 P.M. or 6 P.M. I have by then passed on all information the night crews will need and delegated responsibilities to the two assistant guest services managers. I still have a big stack of papers to go through and file for tomorrow. I hop on my bicycle, ride by security to check in my keys, and then I am off to go home and see my lovely wife. This is the day in a life of a guest services manager.

automobile doors, removing luggage from the trunk, hailing taxis, keeping the hotel entrance clear of vehicles, and giving guests information about the hotel and the local area in a courteous and friendly way. People in this position generally receive many gratuities (tips); in fact, years ago, the position was handed down from father to son or sold for several thousand dollars. Rumor has it that this is one of the most lucrative positions in the hotel, even more than the general manager's.

The bellperson's main function is to escort guests and transport luggage to their rooms. Bellpersons also need to be knowledgeable about the local area and all facets of the hotel and its services. Because they have so much guest contact, they need a pleasant, outgoing personality. The bellperson explains the services of the hotel and points out the features of the room (lighting, TV, air conditioning, telephone, wake-up calls, laundry and valet service, room service and restaurants, and the pool and health spa).

Concierge

The **concierge** is a uniformed employee of the hotel who has her or his own separate desk in the lobby or on special concierge floors. The concierge is a separate department from the front office room clerks and cashiers.

Luxury hotels in most cities have concierges. New York's Plaza Hotel has 800 rooms and a battery of ten concierges who serve under the direction of Thomas P. Wolfe. The concierge assists guests with a broad range of services such as the following:

- Tickets to the hottest shows in town, even for the very evening on the day they are requested. Naturally, the guest pays up to about $150 per ticket.
- A table at a restaurant that has no reservations available
- Advice on local restaurants, activities, attractions, amenities, and facilities
- Airline tickets and reconfirmation of flights
- VIP's messages and special requests, such as shopping

Less frequent requests:

- Organize a wedding on two days' notice
- Arrange for a member of the concierge department to go to a consulate or embassy for visas to be stamped in guests' passports
- Handle business affairs

What will a concierge do for a guest? Almost anything, *Conde' Nast Traveler* learned from concierges at hotels around the world. Among the more unusual requests were the following:

1. Some Japanese tourists staying at the Palace Hotel in Madrid decided to bring bullfighting home. Their concierge found bulls for sale, negotiated the bulls' purchase, and had them shipped to Tokyo.

2. After watching a guest pace the lobby, the concierge of a London hotel, now operating the desk at the Dorchester, asked the pacer if he could help. The guest was to be married within the hour, but his best man had been detained. Because he was dressed up anyway, the concierge volunteered to substitute.

3. A guest at the Hotel Plaza Athenee in Paris wanted to prevent her pet from mingling with dogs from the "wrong side" of the boulevard while walking.

Concierges assist guests with a variety of services.

Madame requested that the concierge buy a house in a decent neighborhood so that her pampered pooch might stroll in its garden unsullied. Although the dog continued to reside at the hotel, Madame's chauffeur shuttled him to the empty house for his daily constitutional.

Concierges serve to elevate a property's marketable value and its image. They provide the special touch services that distinguish a "top property." To make sure they can cater to a guest's precise needs, concierges should make sure that they know precisely what the guest is looking for budget-wise, as well as any other parameters. Concierges must be very attentive and must anticipate guest needs when possible. In this age of highly competitive top-tier properties and well-informed guests, only knowledgeable concierge staff can provide the services to make a guest's stay memorable. As more properties try to demonstrate enhanced value, a concierge amenity takes on added significance.

The concierge needs not only a detailed knowledge of the hotel and its services, but also of the city and even international details. Many concierges speak several languages; most important of all, they must want to help people and have a pleasant, outgoing personality. The concierges' organization, which promotes high professional and ethical standards, is the UPPGH (Union Professionelle des Portiers des Grand Hotels), more commonly called the *Clefs d'Or* because of the crossed gold-key insignia concierges usually wear on the lapels of their uniforms.

Housekeeping

The largest department in terms of the number of people employed is housekeeping. Up to 50 percent of the hotel employees may work in this department. Due to the hard work and comparatively low pay, employee turnover is very high in this essential department. The person in charge is the executive housekeeper or director of services. Her or his duties and responsibilities call for exceptional leadership, organization, motivation, and commitment to maintaining high standards. The logistics of servicing large numbers of rooms on a daily basis can be challenging.

An executive housekeeper checks the desk in a hotel room. Attention to detail is important in maintaining standards.

The importance of the housekeeping department is underlined by guest surveys that consistently rank cleanliness of rooms number one.

The following are the ten rules for effective housekeeping leadership:

1. Utilize people power effectively. Spread responsibilities and tasks to get work done properly and on time.
2. Devise easy methods of reporting work that has to be done. Encourage feedback from all associates and continuous communication with the associates.
3. Develop standard procedures for routine activities. Help associates to develop consistent work habits.
4. Install **inventory controls.** Control costs for supplies and equipment.
5. Motivate housekeeping associates. Keep high morale, motivation, and understanding.
6. Accept challenges presented by guests and management. Remain unflappable in the face of any request.
7. Involve associates in planning. Encourage associates to use imagination to make the job easier and quicker without changing standards.
8. Increase educational level of staff. Support training, encouragement, and educational classes.
9. Set recruitment programs to develop management trainees. Give trainees opportunities to advance.
10. Cooperate and coordinate with other departments, such as front office, engineering and maintenance, and laundry.

The four major areas of responsibilities for the executive housekeeper are as follows:

1. Leadership of people, equipment, and supplies
2. Cleanliness and servicing the guest rooms and public areas
3. Operating the department according to financial guidelines prescribed by the general manager
4. Keeping records

An example of an executive housekeeper's day might be as follows:

7:45 A.M.   Walk the lobby and property with the night cleaners and supervisors
Check the housekeeping log book
Check the forecast house count for number of checkouts
Check daily activity reports, stayovers, check-ins, and VIPs to ensure appropriate standards
Attend housekeepers' meeting
Meet challenges
Train new employees in the procedures
Meet with senior housekeepers/department managers
Conduct productivity checks
Check budget
Approve purchase orders

Check inventories
Conduct room inspections
Review maintenance checks
Interview potential employees

6:00 P.M.   Attend to human resource activities, counseling, and employee development

Perhaps the biggest challenge of an executive housekeeper is the leadership of all the employees in the department. Further, these employees are often of different nationalities. Depending on the size of the hotel, the executive housekeeper is assisted by an assistant executive housekeeper and one or more housekeeping supervisors, who in turn supervise a number of room attendants or housekeeping associates (see Figure 5–9). The assistant executive housekeeper manages the housekeeping office. The first important daily task of this position is to break out the hotel into sections for allocation to the room attendants' schedules.

The rooms of the hotel are listed on the floor master. If the room is vacant, nothing is written next to the room number. If the guest is expected to check out, then SC will be written next to the room number. A stayover will have SS, on hold is AH, out of order is OO, and VIPs are highlighted in colors according to the amenities required.

If 258 rooms are occupied and 10 of these are suites (which count as two rooms), then the total number of rooms to be allocated to room attendants is 268 (minus any no-shows). The remaining total is then divided by 17, the number of rooms that each attendant is expected to make up.

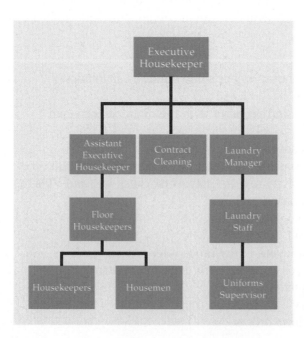

Figure 5–9   *Housekeeping Organization Chart*

Total number of rooms occupied	258
Add 10 for the suites	<u>10</u>
Total number of rooms and suites occupied	268
Less any no-shows	<u>3</u>
	265

Divide 265 by 17 (the number of rooms each attendant services) =
16 (the number of attendants required for that day)

Figure 5–10 shows a daily attendant's schedule. To reduce payroll costs and encourage room attendants to become "stars," a number of hotel corporations have empowered the best attendants to check their own rooms. This has reduced the need for supervisors. Notice in Figure 5–10 how the points are weighted for various items. This is the result of focus groups of hotel guests who explained the important things to them about a room. The items with the highest points were the ones that most concerned the guests.

The assistant executive housekeeper or administrative assistant will assist the executive housekeeper with a number of the duties and will be the anchor person in the housekeeping office. This is the central headquarters for all housekeeping operations. The following are some examples from the Hilton La Jolla, Torrey Pines, California:

1. All housekeeping associates report here.
2. Section assignments are given.
3. All housekeeping telephone calls are received here.
4. All checkout and in-order rooms are processed here.
5. All guest rooms that are not cleaned by a specified time are reported.
6. All household supplies are issued.
7. Commercial laundry, counting linen, and checking linen may be handled here.
8. Table linen may be issued here.
9. All uniforms and costumes may be issued here.
10. Working records are kept.
11. All housekeeping pass keys are kept and controlled.

Guest room supplies on housekeeping associates' carts are replaced during the night shift. It is suggested that the items given away to the customer are placed on the lower shelf of the cart to discourage guests from collecting souvenirs. Taking calls and relaying information about the rooms is a vital part of the communications necessary for the smooth operation of this busy department.

The evening assistant housekeeper or housekeeper supervisor will take over the office and allocate the turndown sections to the evening attendants. Each attendant has an allocation of 63 rooms to turndown and a turndown summary report to complete. The attendants also report back to the housekeeping office any discrepancies, which are in turn forwarded and communicated to the front office. The housekeeping associates clean and service between 15 and 20 rooms per day, depending on the individual hotel characteristics. Servicing a room takes longer in some older hotels than it does in some of the newer properties. Also, service time depends on the number of check-out rooms versus stayovers because servicing checkouts takes

Housekeepers Guest Room Self–Inspection Rating

Inspection Codes:

| P – POLISH | R – REPLACE | E – WORK ORDER | S – SOAP SCUM | SM – SMEAR |
| SA – STAIN | H – HAIR | D – DIRT | DU – DUST | M – MISSING |

PART I – GUEST ROOM		S		1	U	COMMENTS
Entry, door, frame, threshold, latch				1		
Unusual odor OR smoke smell				3		
CLOSET, doors, louvers–containing				1		
Hangers, 8 suits, 4 skirts, 2 bags w/ invoices				2		
Two (2) robes, with info card				2		
Extra TP & FACIAL				1		
One (1) luggage rack				1		
Current rate card				1		
VALET	Shoe Horn & Mitt			2		
DRESSER	LAMP/ SHADE/ BULB			2		
	ICE BUCKET, LID, TRAY			2		
	TWO (2) WINE GLASSES			2		
	Room Service MENU			2		
MINIBAR	TOP, FRONT, 2 Wine glasses/ price list			1		
SAFE	KEY IN SAFE, SIGN			5		
CHECK BEHIND DRESSER				2		
DRAWERS	BIBLE AND BUDDHIST BOOK			1		
	PHONE BOOKS, ATT DIRECTORY			1		
TELEVISION	ON & OFF, CH 19 BEHIND			1		
COFFEE TABLE	REMOTE CONTROL/TEST 1			2		
	T.V. LISTINGS/BOOK MARK			1		
	GLASS TOP/LA JOLLA BOOK			1		
CARPET	VACUUM, SPOTS?			2		
SOFA	UNDER CUSHION/ BEHIND			2		
3 W LAMP	BULB, SHADE, & CORD			1		
WINDOWS	GLASS, DOOR, LATCH—C BAR?			2		
CURTAINS	Pull — check seams			1		
PATIO	2 CHAIRS, TABLE & DECK			3		
DESK	2 CHAIRS, TOP, BASE, & LAMP/SHADE			5		
	GREEN COMPENDIUM			3		
	Waste paper can			1		
BED	Tight, Pillows, bedspread			5		
	Check Under/SHEETS, PILLOWS			3		
HVAC	Control, setting, vent			1		
SIDE TABLES	Lamps & shade			2		
	Telephone, MESSAGE LIGHT			1		
	Clock Radio CORRECT TIME?			1		
MIRRORS	LARGE MIRROR OVER DRESSER			1		
PICTURES	ROOM ART WORK			1		
WALLS	Marks, stains, etc.			3		

Figure 5–10 *Housekeepers Guest Room Self-Inspection*

Housekeepers Guest Room Self–Inspection Rating

Inspection Codes:

P – POLISH	R – REPLACE	E – WORK ORDER		S – SOAP SCUM	SM – SMEAR
SA – STAIN	H – HAIR	D – DIRT		DU – DUST	M – MISSING

PART II – BATHROOM		S			U		COMMENTS
BATH TUB/SHOWER							
	GROUT/TILE & EDGE			2			
	ANTISLIP GRIDS			2			
	SIDE WALLS			1			
	SHOWER HEAD			1			
	WALL SOAP DISH			1			
	CONTROL LEVER			1			
	FAUCET			1			
	CLOTHESLINE			1			
	SHOWER ROD, HOOKS			1			
	SHOWER CURTAIN/ LINER			2			
VANITY	TOP, SIDE, & EDGE			1			
	SINK, TWO FAUCETS			3			
	3 GLASSES, COASTERS			2			
	WHITE SOAP DISH			1			
	FACIAL TISSUE & BOX			1			
AMENITY BASKET							
	1 SHAMPOO			1			
	1 CONDITIONER			1			
	1 MOISTURIZER			1			
	2 BOXED SOAP			1			
	1 SHOWER CAP			1			
MIRROR	LARGE & COSMETIC			2			
WALLS, CEILING, & VENT				2			
TOILET	TOP, SEAT, BASE, & LIP			2			
OTHER	TOILET PAPER, fold			1			
	SCALE AND TRASH CAN			2			
	FLOOR, SWEPT AND MOPPED			3			
	TELEPHONE			1			
BATH LINENS, racks							
	THREE (3) WASH CLOTHS			1			
	THREE (3) HAND TOWELS			1			
	THREE (3) BATH TOWELS			1			
	ONE (1) BATH MAT			1			
	ONE (1) BATH RUG			1			
LIGHT SWITCH				1			
DOOR	FULL LENGTH MIRROR			1			
	HANDLE/LOCK			1			
	THRESHOLD			1			
	PAINTED SURFACE			1			

Figure 5–10 *Housekeepers Guest Room Self-Inspection (continued)*

A housekeeping associate makes up a room. What a positive outlook she has.

longer. Housekeeping associates begin their day at 8:00 A.M., reporting to the executive or assistant executive housekeeper. They are assigned a block of rooms and given room keys, for which they must sign and then return before going off duty.

The role of the executive housekeeper may vary slightly between the corporate chain and the independent hotel. An example is the purchasing of furnishings and equipment. A large independent hotel relies on the knowledge and experience of the executive housekeeper to make appropriate selections, whereas the chain hotel company has a corporate purchase agent (assisted by a designer) to make many of these decisions.

The executive housekeeper is responsible for a substantial amount of record keeping. In addition to the scheduling and evaluation of employees, an inventory of all guest rooms and public area furnishings must be accurately maintained with the record of refurbishment. Most of the hotel's maintenance work orders are initiated by the housekeepers who report the maintenance work order. Many hotels now have a computer linkup between housekeeping and engineering and maintenance to speed the process. Guests expect their rooms to be fully functional, especially at today's prices. Housekeeping maintains a perpetual inventory of guest room amenities, cleaning supplies, and linens.

Productivity in the housekeeping department is measured by the person hours per occupied room. The labor costs per person hour for a full service hotel ranges from $2.66 to $5.33, or 20 minutes of labor for every occupied room in the hotel. Another key ratio is the labor cost, which is expected to be 5.1 percent of room sales. Controllable expenses are measured per occupied rooms. These expenses include guest supplies like soap, shampoo, hand and body lotion, sewing kits, and stationery. Although this will vary according to the type of hotel, the cost should be about $2.00 per room. Cleaning supplies should be approximately $0.50 and linen costs $0.95, including the purchase and laundering of all linen. These budgeted costs are sometimes hard to achieve. The executive housekeeper may be doing a great job controlling costs, but if the sales department discounts rooms, the room sales figures may come in below budget. This would have the effect of increasing the costs per occupied room.

Another concern for the executive housekeeper is accident prevention. Insurance costs have skyrocketed in recent years, and employers are struggling to

A Room at the Mauna Lani Resort on the Kohala Coast Ready for Guests

increase both employee and guest safety. It is necessary for accidents to be carefully investigated. Some employees have been known to have an accident at home but go to work and report it as a work-related injury in order to be covered by workers' compensation. To safeguard themselves to some extent, hotels keep sweep logs of the public areas; in the event that a guest slips and falls, the hotel can show that it does genuinely take preventative measures to protect its guests.

The **Occupational Safety and Health Administration (OSHA),** whose purpose it is to ensure safe and healthful working conditions, sets mandatory job safety and health standards, conducts compliance inspections, and issues citations when there is noncompliance. Additionally, the U.S. Senate Bill 198, known as the **Employee Right to Know,** has heightened awareness of the storage, handling, and use of dangerous chemicals. Information about the chemicals must be made available to all employees. Great care and extensive training is required to avoid dangerous accidents.

The executive housekeeper must also maximize loss prevention. Strict policies and procedures are necessary to prevent losses from guest rooms. Some hotels require housekeeping associates to sign a form stating that they understand they may not let any guest into any room. Such action would result in immediate termination of employment. Although this may seem drastic, it is the only way to avoid some hotel thefts.

Laundry

Increasingly, hotels are operating their own laundries. This subdepartment generally reports to the executive housekeeper. The modern laundry operates computerized washing/drying machines and large presses. Dry cleaning for both guests and employees is a service that may also come under the laundry

Linen Management System

The Chicago Hilton and Towers has installed a semicustomized linen-management and inventory control system that is expected to save the 1,620-room property between $70,000 and $100,000 annually. The system reduces labor costs by eliminating the need to manually sort linen from the different properties that are served. In addition, because the system provides a perpetual inventory, needs can be anticipated better and overtime costs by housekeeping staff can be minimized.

department. Hotels are starting to get away from in-house dry cleaning due to environmental concerns.

Some hotels, especially the smaller and older ones, contract out the laundry service. This is because it is costly to alter an existing hotel to provide space for laundry. Even space itself costs money because the space might be otherwise used for revenue-producing purposes, such as meetings, functions, and so on. In addition, by contracting out, the hotel does not have to own its own linen. It may rent linen and be charged for each piece used. However, operators frequently complain that they receive inferior linen and inconsistent service. Another alternative is for the hotel to purchase its own linen and have it laundered by contract. In either case, the executive housekeeper must ensure that strict control is maintained over linen. Figure 5–11 lists some advantages for both types of systems.

Much of the heavy work in the housekeeping department is conducted by housepersons. They clean public areas using heavy floor polishers for marble or tile floors, vacuum the corridors on the guest room floors, do carpet shampooing and moving of furniture, and, on occasion, take the linen from the linen room to the floors. The houseperson may also assist the housekeepers with spring cleaning and the turning of mattresses.

Check Your Knowledge
1. What is a PBX or CBX?
2. What constitutes uniformed services? What is the role played by each staff member of uniformed service?
3. Name the characteristics an executive housekeeper should possess.

Advantages of an In-House Laundry
Twenty-four hour anytime laundry service available for guests
Smaller par-stock of linen can be maintained
Full control over quality of laundered linen

Advantages of Contract Laundry Service
No maintenance costs for equipment
No labor costs
Fixed projected expenses toward contract
Lower labor costs because no exclusive laundry staff is required
No trained staff required
Lower training costs
Lower overhead cost of energy and water

Figure 5–11 *In-House Laundry Service Versus Contract Laundry Service*

Security/Loss Prevention

Providing guest protection and loss prevention is essential for any lodging establishment regardless of size. Violent crime is a growing problem, and protecting guests from bodily harm has been defined by the courts as a reasonable expectation from hotels. The security/loss division is responsible for maintaining security alarm systems and implementing procedures aimed at protecting the personal property of guests and employees and the hotel itself.

A comprehensive security plan must include the following elements:

Security Officers
- Make regular rounds of the hotel premises including guest floors, corridors, public and private function rooms, parking areas, and offices.
- Duties involve observing suspicious behavior and taking appropriate action, investigating incidents, and cooperating with local law enforcement agencies.

Equipment
- Two-way radios between security staff are common.
- Closed-circuit television cameras are used in out-of-the-way corridors and doorways, as well as in food, liquor, and storage areas.
- Smoke detectors and fire alarms, which increase the safety of the guests, are a requirement in every part of the hotel by law.
- Electronic key cards offer superior room security. Key cards typically do not list the name of the hotel or the room number. So if lost or stolen, the key is not easily traceable. In addition, most key card systems record every entry in and out of the room on the computer for any further reference.

Safety Procedures
- Front-desk agents help maintain security by not allowing guests to reenter their rooms once they have checked out. This prevents any loss of hotel property by guests.
- Security officers should be able to gain access to guest rooms, store rooms, and offices at all times.
- Security staff develop **catastrophe plans** to ensure staff and guest safety and to minimize direct and indirect costs from disaster. The catastrophe plan reviews insurance policies, analyzes physical facilities, and evaluates possible disaster scenarios, including whether they have a high or low probability of occurring. Possible disaster scenarios may include fires, bomb threats, earthquakes, floods, hurricanes, and blizzards. The well-prepared hotel will develop formal policies to deal with any possible scenario and will train employees to implement chosen procedures should they become necessary.

Identification Procedures
- Identification cards with photographs should be issued to all employees.
- Name tags for employees who are likely to have contact with guests not only project a friendly image for the property, but are also useful for security reasons.

Trends in Hotel and Rooms Division Operations

- *Diversity of work force:* All the pundits are projecting a substantial increase in the number of women and minorities who will not only be taking hourly paid positions, but also supervising and management positions as well.
- *Increase in use of technology:* Reservations are being made by individuals via the Internet. Travel agents are able to make reservations at more properties. There is increasing simplification of the various property management systems and their interface with POS systems. In the guest room, the demand for high-speed Internet access, category 5 cables, and in some cases equipment itself is anticipated.
- *Continued quest for increases in productivity:* As pressure mounts from owners and management companies, hotel managers are looking for innovative ways to increase productivity and to measure productivity by sales per employee.
- *Increasing use of revenue management to increase profit by effective pricing of room inventory.*
- *Greening of hotels and guest rooms:* This includes an increase in recycling and the use of environmentally friendly products, amenities, and biodegradable detergents.
- *Security:* The survey by the International Hotel Association indicated that guests continue to be concerned about personal security. Hotels are constantly working to improve guest security. For example, one hotel has instituted a women-only floor with concierge and security.
- *Diversity of the guest:* More women travelers are occupying hotel rooms. This is particularly due to an increase in business travel.
- *Compliance with the ADA:* As a result of the Americans with Disabilities Act (ADA), all hotels must modify existing facilities and incorporate design features into new constructions that make areas accessible to persons with disabilities. All hotels are expected to have at least 4 percent of their parking space designated as "handicapped." These spaces must be wide enough for wheelchairs to be unloaded from a van. Guest rooms must be fitted with equipment that can be manipulated by persons with disabilities. Restrooms must be wide enough to accommodate wheelchairs. Ramps should be equipped with handrails, and meeting rooms must be equipped with special listening systems for those with hearing impairments.
- Hotel company's are trying to persuade guests to book rooms via the company Web site rather than via an Internet site like hotels.com because the hotel must pay about $20 for each room booking.
- Hotels are upgrading in-room technology.

CASE STUDY

Checking Out a Guest

A guest walked up to the front-desk agent in an up-scale hotel, ready to check out. As she would normally do when checking out a guest, the agent asked the guest what his room number was. The guest was in a hurry and showed his anxiety by responding, "I stay in a hundred hotel rooms and you expect me to remember my room number?"

The agent then asked for the guest's name, to which he responded, "My name is Mr. Johnstein." After thanking him, the agent began to look for the guest's last name, but the name was not listed in the computer. Because the man had a heavy accent and the agent assumed that she had misunderstood him, she politely asked the guest to spell his last name. He answered, "What? Are you an idiot? The person who checked me in last night had no problem checking me in." Again, the agent looked on the computer to find the guest.

The guest, becoming even more frustrated, said, "I have a plane to catch and it is ridiculous that it has to take this long to check me out. I also need to fax these papers off, but I need to have them photocopied first." The agent responded, "There is a business center at the end of the counter that will fax and photocopy what you need." The guest replied, "If I wanted your opinion, I would have asked you for it. Haven't you ever heard of customer service? Isn't this a five-star hotel? With your bad attitude, you should be working in a three-star hotel. I can't be-lieve they let you work here at the front desk. Haven't you found my name yet?"

The agent, who was beginning to get upset, asked the guest again to spell out his full name. The guest only replied, "Here are my papers I want faxed if you are capable of faxing them." The agent reached to take the papers, and the guest shouted, "Don't grab them from my hand! You have a bad attitude, and if I had more time, I would talk to someone about getting you removed from your position to a hotel where they don't require such a level of customer service." The agent was very upset, but kept herself calm in order to prevent the guest from getting angrier.

The agent continued to provide service to the guest, sending the faxes and making the photocopies he had requested. Upon her return, the agent again asked the guest to repeat his last name, since he had failed to spell it out. The guest replied by spelling out his name, "J-o-h-n-s-t-o-n-e." The agent was finally able to find his name on the computer and checked him out, while he continued to verbally attack her. The agent finished by telling the guest to have a nice flight.

Discussion Questions

1. Is it appropriate to have the manager finish the checkout? Or should the front-desk agent just take the heat?
2. Would you have handled the situation in the same manner?
3. What would you have done differently?

CASE STUDY

Overbooked: The Front-Office Perspective

Overbooking is an accepted hotel and airline practice. Many question the practice from various standpoints including ethical and moral. Industry executives argue that there is nothing more perishable than a vacant room. If it is not used, there is no chance to regain lost revenue. Hotels need to protect themselves because potential guests frequently make reservations at more than one hotel or are delayed and, therefore, do not show up.

The percentage of no-shows varies by hotel and location but is often around 5 percent. In a 400-room hotel, that is 20 rooms, or an average loss of approximately $2,600 per night. Considering these figures, it is not surprising that hotels try to protect themselves by overbooking.

Hotels look carefully at bookings: Whom they are for, what rates they are paying, when they were made, whether they are for regular guests or from a major account (a corporation who uses the hotel frequently), and so on.

Jill Reynolds, the front-office manager at the Regency La Jolla, had known for some time that the 400-room hotel would be overbooked for this one

continued

night in October. She prepared to talk with the front-desk associates as they came on duty at 7:30 in the morning, knowing it would be a challenge to sell out without "walking" guests. Seldom does a hotel sell out before having to walk a few guests.

The hotel's policy and procedure on walking guests enables the front-desk associates to call nearby hotels of a similar category to find out if they have rooms available to sell. If it is necessary to walk a guest, the associate explains to the guest that, regrettably, no rooms are available due to fewer departures than expected. The associate must explain that suitable accommodations have been reserved at a nearby hotel and that the hotel will pay for the room and transportation to and from the hotel. Normally guests are understanding, especially

when they realize that they are receiving a free room and free transportation.

On this particular day, the house count indicated that the hotel was overbooked by thirty rooms. Three or four nearby, comparable hotels had rooms available to sell in the morning. Besides walking guests, Jill considered other options—in particular "splitting" the 15 suites with connecting parlors. If the guests in the suites do not need the parlor, it is then possible to gain a few more "rooms" to sell separately; however, roll-away beds must be placed in the rooms. Fortunately, eight parlors were available to sell.

Discussion Question

1. If you were in the same situation, what would you do?

CASE STUDY

Overbooked: The Housekeeping Perspective

It is no secret that in all hotels the director of housekeeping must be able to react quickly and efficiently to any unexpected circumstances that arise. Stephen Rodondi, executive housekeeper at the Regency in La Jolla, California, usually starts his workday at 8:00 A.M. with a department meeting. These morning meetings help him, and the employees, to visualize their goals for the day. On this particularly busy day, Rodondi arrives at work and is told that three housekeepers have called in sick. This is a serious chal-

lenge for the hotel because it is overbooked and has all its 400 rooms to service.

Discussion Question

1. What should Stephen do to maintain standards and ensure that all the guest rooms are serviced?

Courtesy of Stephen Rodondi, Executive Housekeeper, Hyatt Regency, La Jolla, CA.

CAREER INFORMATION

Hotel and Rooms Division Operation

Hotel management is probably the most popular career choice among hospitality educational program graduating seniors. The reason for hotel management's popularity is tied to the elegant image of hotels and the prestige associated with being a general manager or vice-president of a major lodging chain. Managing a hotel is a complex balancing act that involves keeping employees, customers, and owners satisfied while overseeing a myriad of departments, including reservations, front desk, housekeeping, maintenance, accounting, food and beverage, security, concierge, and sales.

Becoming a GM means that a person needs to understand all of the various functions of a hotel and how

their interrelationship makes up the lodging environment. The first step down this career path is getting a job in a hotel while you are in college. Once you become proficient in one area, volunteer to work in another. A solid foundation of broad-based experience in the hotel will be priceless when you start your lodging career. Some excellent areas to consider are the front desk, night audit, food and beverage, and maintenance. Another challenging but very important place to gain experience is in housekeeping. It has been said that if you can manage the housekeeping department, the rest of lodging management is easy. An internship with a large hotel chain property can also be a powerful learning experience. There is simply no substitute for being

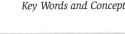

part of a team that operates a lodging property with several hundred rooms.

You may hear about graduates being offered "direct placement" or "manager in training" (MIT) positions. (There are several name variations for these programs.) Direct placement means that you will be offered a specific position at a property on graduation. An MIT program exposes you to several areas of the hotel over a period of time and then you are given an assignment based on your performance during training. Neither one is better than the other from a career standpoint.

Another important consideration of a lodging career is your wardrobe. Hotels are places where people are judged based on their appearance and a conservative, professional image is a key to success. Clothes are the tools of the lodging professional's trade, and they are not inexpensive. Begin investing in clothes while you are in school. Buy what you can afford but buy items of qual-

ity. Stay away from trendy or flashy clothes that will quickly be out of fashion.

When you take a position, you can expect to work from 50 to 60 hours per week. The times you work may vary. You can expect to have a starting salary of between $30,000 and $34,000. Some hotel chains will assist with moving expenses and may even offer a one-time signing bonus. However, try not to focus too much on money; instead try to find a company that you feel comfortable with and will allow you opportunities for advancement.

Related Web Sites

www.hoteljobs.com/—Careers in lodging
www.hyatt.com/—Hyatt Hotels
www.marriott.com/—Marriott International

Courtesy of Charlie Adams.

SUMMARY

1. A big hotel is run by a general manager and an executive committee, which is represented by the key executives of all the major departments, such as rooms division, food and beverage, marketing, sales, and human resources.
2. The general manager represents the hotel and is responsible for its profitability and performance. Because of increased job consolidation, he or she also is expected to attract business and to empathize with the cultures of both guests and employees.
3. The rooms division department consists of front office, reservations, housekeeping, concierge, guest services, and communications.
4. The front desk, as the center of the hotel, sells rooms and maintains balanced guest accounts, which are completed daily by the night auditor. The front desk constantly must meet guests' needs by offering services such as mailing, faxing, and messages.

5. The property management system, centralized reservations, and yield management have enabled a hotel to work more efficiently and to increase profitability and guest satisfaction.
6. The communications department, room service, and guest services (such as door attendants, bellpersons, and the concierge) are vital parts of the personality of a hotel.
7. Housekeeping is the largest department of the hotel. The executive housekeeper is in charge of inventory, cleaning, employees, and accident and loss prevention. The laundry may be cleaned directly in the hotel or by a hired laundry service.
8. The electric room key and closed-circuit television cameras are basic measures provided to protect the guests and their property.

KEY WORDS AND CONCEPTS

Application service provider (ASP)
Average daily rate (ADR)
Call accounting systems (CAS)
Catastrophe plans
Central reservation office (CRO)
Central reservation system (CRS)

City ledger
Confirmed reservations
Daily report
Employee Right to Know
Executive committee
Global distribution systems (GDS)
Guaranteed reservations
Guest accounting module
Inventory control

Night auditor
Occupational Safety and Health Administration (OSHA)
Productivity
Property management systems (PMS)
Revenue management
Rev par
Room management module

Room occupancy percentage (ROP)
Room rates
Rooms division
Uniformed staff

REVIEW QUESTIONS

1. Briefly define the purpose of a hotel. Why is it important to empathize with the culture of guests?
2. List the main responsibilities of the front office manager.
3. Explain the terms *sell out, American plan,* and *rack rate.*
4. What are the advantages and disadvantages of yield management?
5. Why is the concierge an essential part of the personality of a hotel?
6. Explain the importance of accident and loss prevention. What security measures are taken in order to protect guests and their property?

INTERNET EXERCISES

1. Organization: **Hyatt Hotel Corporation**
   Web site: **www.hyatt.com**
   Summary: Hyatt Hotel Corporation is a multibillion-dollar hotel management and company. Together with Hyatt International, the company has close to 10 percent of the hotel industry market share. Hyatt is recognized for its decentralized management approach, in which general managers are given a great deal of the management decision-making process.
   Click on the "Careers" icon and take a look at the Management Training Program that Hyatt has to offer.
   (a) What is Hyatt's management training program?
   (b) What requisites must applicants meet in order to qualify for Hyatt's management training program?

2. Organization: **Hotel Jobs**
   Web site: **www.hoteljobs.com**
   Summary: Hoteljobs.com is a Web site that offers information to recruiters, employers, and job seekers in the hospitality industry.
   (a) What different jobs are being offered under "Job Search" and which one, if any, interests you?
   (b) Post your résumé online.

APPLY YOUR KNOWLEDGE

1. If you were on the executive committee of a hotel, what kinds of things would you be doing to ensure the success of the hotel?

2. Your hotel has 275 rooms. Last night 198 were occupied. What was the occupancy percentage?

SUGGESTED ACTIVITY

Go to a hotel's Web site and find the price of booking a room for a date of your choice. Then go to one of the Web sites (Hotels.com, Expedia, Travelocity, etc.) that "sell" hotel rooms and see how the price compares.

ENDNOTES

1. Personal conversation with Rollie Teves. August 20, 2005.
2. **www.micros.com**
3. VingCard press kit. August 24, 2005.
4. **www.golbalaz.com/prod.02.htm#Fund%200for%20Yourself.**
5. **www.sprint.com**. August 25, 2005.
6. Personal correspondence with Jay R. Schrock, Ph.D. August 18, 2005.

WEB RESOURCES

Hyatt Hotels and Resorts
www.hyatt.com

Hilton
www.hilton.com

Hotel Plaza Athenee Paris
www.plaza-athenee-paris.com

New York Plaza Hotel
www.nyctourist.com/topten_plaza.htm

Hotel del Coronado
www.hoteldel.com

Micros
www.micros.com

VingCard
www.VingCard.com

Westin Hotels
www.westin.com

Disney
www.disney.go.com

National Concierge Association
www.nationalconciergeassociation.com

Les Clefs d'Or
www.lcdusa.org

Food and Beverage Operations

6

After reading and studying this chapter, you should be able to:

- Describe the duties and responsibilities of a food and beverage director and other key department heads.
- Describe a typical food and beverage director's day.
- State the functions and responsibilities of the food and beverage departments.
- Perform computations using key food and beverage operating ratios.

Food and Beverage Management

In the hospitality industry, the food and beverage division is led by the **director of food and beverage.** She or he reports to the general manager and is responsible for the efficient and effective operation of the following departments:

- Kitchen/Catering/Banquet
- Restaurants/Room Service/Minibars
- Lounges/Bars/Stewarding

Figure 6–1 illustrates a food and beverage organization chart.

The position description for a director of food and beverage is both a job description and a specification of the requirements an individual needs to do the job. (See Figure 2–4 for the duties and the average amount of time spent on each.)

In recent years, the skills needed by a food and beverage director have grown enormously, as shown by the following list of responsibilities:

- Exceeding guests' expectations in food and beverage offerings and service
- Leadership
- Identifying trends
- Finding and keeping outstanding employees
- Training
- Motivation
- Budgeting
- Cost control
- Finding profit from all outlets
- Having a detailed working knowledge of the front-of-the-house operations

These challenges are set against a background of stagnant or declining occupancies and the consequent drop in room sales. Therefore, greater emphasis has

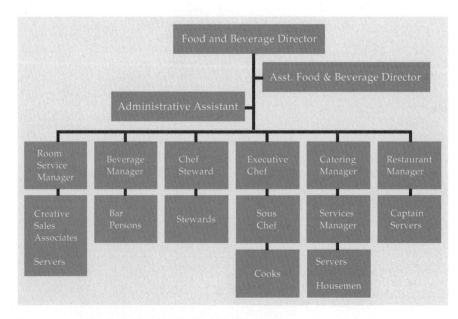

Figure 6–1 *Food and Beverage Division Organization Chart for a Large Hotel*

been placed on making food and beverage sales profitable. Traditionally, only about 20 percent of the hotel's operating profit comes from the food and beverage divisions. In contrast, an acceptable profit margin from a hotel's food and beverage division is generally considered to be 25 to 30 percent. This figure can vary according to the type of hotel. For example, according to Pannell Kerr Forster, an industry consulting firm, all-suite properties achieve a 7 percent food and beverage profit (probably because of the complimentary meals and drinks being offered to guests).

A typical food and beverage director's day might include the following:

8:30 A.M.	Check messages and read logs from outlets and security. Tour outlets, especially the family restaurant (a quick inspection). Check breakfast buffet, reservations, and shift manager. Check daily specials. Check room service. Check breakfast service and staffing. Visit executive chef and purchasing director. Visit executive steward's office to ensure that all equipment is ready. Visit banquet service office to check on daily events and coffee break sequence.
10:00 A.M.	Work on current projects: new summer menu, pool outlet opening, conversion of a current restaurant with a new concept, remodeling of ballroom foyer, installation of new walk-in freezer, analysis of current profit-and-loss (P&L) statements. Plan weekly food and beverage department meetings.
11:45 A.M.	Visit kitchen to observe lunch service and check the "12:00 line," including banquets. Confer with executive chef. Check restaurants and banquet luncheon service. Have working lunch in employee cafeteria with executive chef, director of purchasing, or director of catering.
1:30 P.M.	Visit human resources to discuss current incidents.
2:30 P.M.	Check messages and return calls. Telemarket to attract catering and convention business. Conduct hotel daily menu meeting.
3:00 P.M.	Go to special projects/meetings. Tour cocktail lounges. Check for staffing. Review any current promotions. Check entertainment lineup.
6:00 P.M.	Check special food and beverage requests/requirements of any VIPs staying at the hotel. Tour kitchen. Review and taste.
8:00 P.M.	Review dinner specials. Check the restaurant and lounges.

A food and beverage director's typical day starts at 8:00 A.M. and ends at 8:00 P.M., unless early or very late events are scheduled, in which case the working day is even longer. Usually, the food and beverage director works Monday through Saturday. If there are special events on Sunday, then she or he works on Sunday and takes Monday off. In a typical week, Saturdays are used to catch up on reading or specific projects.

The director of food and beverage eats in his or her restaurants at least twice a week for dinner and at least once a week for breakfast and lunch. Bars are generally visited with clients, at least twice per week. The director sees salespersons regularly, because they are good sources of information about what is going on in the industry and they can introduce leads for business. The director attends staff meetings, food and beverage meetings, executive committee meetings, interdepartmental meetings, credit meetings, and P&L statement meetings.

To become a food and beverage director takes several years of experience and dedication. One of the best routes is to gain work experience or participate in an internship in several food and beverage departments while attending college. This experience should include full-time, practical kitchen work for at least 1 to 2 years, followed by varying periods of a few months in purchasing, stores, cost control, stewarding,[1] and room service. Additionally, a year spent in each of the following work situations is helpful: restaurants, catering, and bars. After these departmental experiences, a person would likely serve as a department manager, preferably in a different hotel from the one in which the departmental experience was gained. This prevents the awkwardness of being manager of a department in which the person was once an employee and also offers the employee the opportunity to learn different things at different properties. Figure 6–2 shows a career path for a food and beverage director.

Check Your Knowledge

1. What are the skills and responsibilities of a food and beverage director?
2. Describe a food and beverage director's day.

Director of Food and Beverage Go-getters may rise to this position more quickly. It depends on the individual's capability, industry expansion, opportunities, and the labor market.	9 to 15 years
Assistant Food and Beverage Manager	3 to 5 years
Department Manager Kitchen restaurant, room service, stewarding, or cost control	3 to 5 years
Department Experience kitchens, restaurants, lounges, purchasing, cost control, stewarding, room service, and catering	3 to 5 years

Figure 6–2 *Career Ladder to Director of Food and Beverage*

Personal Profile: George Goldhoff

Vice President of Food & Beverage, Bean Rivage Resort and Casino, Biloxi, Mississippi

Being hired as the pot washer for the Old Homestead Country Kitchen at the early age of 15 hardly seemed to herald the beginnings of an auspicious career in the hospitality industry. But to George Goldhoff, with his high energy and natural leadership skills, he had found the perfect environment in which to excel. The sense of family and camaraderie between the staff members and the interaction with guests, mixed with the intensity of performance and deadlines, have never lost their appeal. Excellence in service would become his lifelong pursuit.

Fast forward 20 years later; as director of food and beverage at Bellagio of MGM/Mirage, Inc., in Las Vegas, George is responsible for the quality assurance, personnel development, and financial performance of seventeen restaurants and ten bars, comprised of 3,000 employees and over $200 million in revenues. His responsibilities may have increased since his pot washer days, but the core message in his service training remains intact: sincerity toward the guest and anticipation of their needs. His approach to service is simple: greet all guests with a smile, make sure they are comfortable, offer them something to eat and drink. These service basics, simple instructions given to him as a five-year-old by his parents, have stayed with him. Playing host at one of his parents' dinner parties he learned early on the power of a sincere smile and the rewarding experience of pleasing others. Little did he or his parents intuit that one day his child's play would evolve into a rewarding career in hospitality.

As one of the original members of the opening team for the Bellagio, George drew from his extensive and varied food and beverage background to make the Bellagio's opening a success. In 1983 George graduated from Schenectady County Community College as a dean's list student and recipient of an athletic scholarship award. He continued on to the University of Massachusetts where he earned his B.S. degree in hotel, restaurant and travel administration. His acceptance to these two institutions, after having dropped out of high school, instilled in George the self-confidence in his abilities and the technical skills necessary to achieve his goals. For a young man without a high school diploma who was often characterized as wild and rebellious, it was a revelation, an awakening to his potentials and the realization that he could accomplish great things. His introduction to corporate culture was as an assistant front office manager and Hyatt corporate trainee in Savannah, Georgia.

Upon completion of his training, he moved to beautiful Tahoe in 1988, where he was able to combine his love for restaurants and sports. An all-around athlete, adhering to the work hard, play hard principle, he pursued speed skiing competitions at the highest levels. He stayed on as general manager of Rosie's Café for two and a half years. However, growing tired of the small town confines of Tahoe City and with the singular challenges of Rosie's Café becoming undemanding, George acted on a friend's advice, contacted a mutual friend, and took a job on a 750-foot merchant ship. For the next six months George sailed around the world cooking breakfast, lunch, and dinner for a crew of twelve, while visiting ports in Gibraltar, Malta, Egypt, the United Arab Emirates, Kuwait, and Saudi Arabia. In 1990, aspiring to be a major player not just in skiing, but in the restaurant arena as well, he sought grander, more sophisticated restaurants to manage.

George's ambitions led him to the Plaza Hotel in New York, where he started as an assistant beverage director. George immersed himself in his new position with his usual high-voltage energy and infectious enthusiasm, earning him nicknames such as the Golden Boy and Mr. Hollywood. It did not take long for George to be recognized for his positive attitude and management abilities. Within six months, he was promoted to manager of the stately Oak Room, the youngest manager in the restaurant's 90-year history. Within a two-year period, he was promoted to managing four of the Plaza Hotel's five à la carte restaurants.

Holding to his personal belief that "you are the company you keep," he has always endeavored to associate with the highest quality restaurateurs and organizations. In 1993, he realized one of his dreams—the opportunity to work with the legendary Joe Baum—managing the famous Rainbow Room in Rockefeller Center. His commitment to service, the evident pride in his work, and his high standard of ethics earned George praise from Joe Baum as being his best maître d' ever. Such a high compliment could have gone to his head. However, George is not one to sit back and take it easy. Instead, he set even higher standards and focused his energies on new goals. He quotes his old boss and industry idol Joe Baum as saying "Values and standards are those you make for yourself.

continued

You don't have to be as good as the other guy. You have to be better—a lot better."

Against the advice of well-meaning family and peers, he left the Rainbow Room in 1997 to enroll in the MBA program at Columbia University. This was no easy decision, considering George was happily married at this point, with one child and another on the way. However, he has never been afraid to take risks, nor been one to fear taking on new challenges. In fact, his adventurous and go-getter nature revels in change. With the same self-confidence, resourcefulness, and ability to focus on multiple tasks, not surprisingly, he took first place in Columbia's Business Plan competition and was the recipient of the prestigious Eugene Lang Entrepreneurial Initiative Fund. Armed with his MBA degree and newly acquired business skills, he was ready for his next adventure.

Even before he had graduated, he was tapped by Stephen Rushmore, founder and president of Hospitality Valuation Services, to work with him as a consultant and valuation analyst. Here he was afforded the opportunity to incorporate his academic learning, fresh ideas, and extensive hotel background. He created the 1996 Hotel Valuation Index, which was later published in the *Cornell Quarterly*. Ever the entrepreneur, he left HVS in 1997 to establish his own venture, The Irish Coast, Inc., creating and implementing the Guinness Irish pub concept. He jumped into the task of perfecting the Irish pub ambience of warmth, comfort, and congeniality, the heart of hospitality. Hence, it was only a matter of time before he would find himself in Las Vegas, the "Hospitality Capital of the World." In 1998 he signed aboard with Mirage Resorts, Inc., to open the ultimate luxury resort and casino, Bellagio.

For George, it's all about service. Excellence in customer satisfaction and a genuine concern for his staff and coworkers have been his guiding principles. Characterized by colleagues as a dreamer, he has the rare ability to communicate his vision and to motivate and inspire others into executing that vision, making it a reality. The ability to instill in those around him the desire to strive beyond and stretch past their comfort zones is just one of his leadership characteristics. His motivational secret is to "constantly remind the staff that their job is precious, even if they've been doing it year after year." He maintains that the key to service is to "know one's job and to remember that a little kindness goes a long way to making people happy. A guest always knows if someone doesn't care."

In addition to starting up and overseeing the entire food and beverage operations for the hotel, he was chosen to represent Mirage Resorts in Focus Las Vegas, a leadership development program of the Las Vegas Chamber of Commerce. Making a difference in others' lives has always been one of the appealing factors about being in the hospitality field. He has always felt personally rewarded when he can give back to others, such as promoting a new busperson, building up someone else's self-esteem, watching them gain confidence in themselves and take pride in their work. He concedes he did not reach his position on his own, but with the assistance of many caring mentors. Always mindful and appreciative of those who have helped him throughout his career, he enjoys helping others discover their own potential. He considers human relations to be one of his strengths and regards staff development to be one of his greatest priorities as a leader. Empowering your frontline employees is essential to maintaining a restaurant's competitive edge. "Give them the tools and let them do the job."

George sets great expectations for himself and those around him and is not afraid of hard work. In fact, he works with a passion. The long hours and the intensity do not faze him. His adaptability toward different situations, his ability to relate to a variety of personalities and temperaments, and his keen sense of humor serve him well both in front and back of the house. With his winning smile and straightforward demeanor, he sets his sights on a promising future and the many adventures ahead.

Kitchen

A hotel kitchen is under the charge of the **executive chef** or chef in smaller or medium-sized properties. This person, in turn, is responsible to the director of food and beverage for the efficient and effective operation of kitchen food production. The desired outcome is to exceed guests' expectations in the quality and quantity of food, its presentation, taste, and portion size, and to ensure that hot food is served hot and cold food is served cold. The executive chef operates the kitchen in accordance with company policy and strives to achieve desired financial results.

The executive chef of a very large hotel manages the kitchen and may not do much cooking.

Some executive chefs are now called **kitchen managers;** they even serve as food and beverage directors in midsized and smaller hotels. This trend toward "right-sizing," observed in other industries, euphemistically refers to restructuring organizations to retain the most essential employees. Usually, this means cutting labor costs by consolidating job functions. For example, Michael Hammer is executive chef and food and beverage director at the 440-room Hilton La Jolla–Torrey Pines, California. Mike is typical of the new breed of executive chefs: His philosophy is to train his sous chefs, *sous* being a French word meaning "under," to make many of the operating decisions. He delegates ordering, hiring, and firing decisions; sous chefs are the ones most in control of the production and the people who work on their teams. By delegating more of the operating decisions, he is developing the chefs de partie (or stations chefs) and empowering them to make their own decisions. As he puts it, "No decision is wrong—but in case it is unwise, we will talk about it later."

Mike spends time maintaining morale, a vital part of a manager's position. The kitchen staff is under a great deal of pressure and frequently works against the clock. Careful cooperation and coordination is the key to success. He explains that he does not want his associates to "play the tuba"—he wants them to conduct the orchestra. He does not hold food and beverage department meetings; instead he meets with groups of employees frequently and problems are handled as they occur. Controls are maintained with the help of software that costs their standard recipes, establishes **perpetual inventories,** and calculates potential food cost per outlet. Today, executive chefs and food and beverage directors look past food cost to the actual profit contribution of an item. For example, if a pasta dish costs $3.25 and sells for

$12.95, the contribution margin is $9.70. Today, there are software programs like ChefTec, which offers software solutions for purchasing, ordering, inventory control, and recipe and menu costing, and ChefTec Plus, which also offers perpetual inventory, sales analysis, theoretical inventory reports, and multiple profit centers.

Controlling costs is an essential part of food and beverage operations and, because labor costs represent the most significant variable costs, staffing becomes an important factor in the day-to-day running of the food and beverage locations. Labor cost benchmarks are measured by covers-per-person-hour. For example, in stewarding, it should take no more than one person per hour to clean 37.1 covers. Mike and his team of outlet managers face interesting challenges, such as staffing for the peaks and valleys of guest needs at breakfast. Many guests want breakfast during the peak time of 7:00 to 8:30 A.M., requiring organization to get the right people in the right place at the right time to ensure that meals are prepared properly and served in a timely manner.

At the Hilton La Jolla–Torrey Pines, Executive Chef Hammer's day goes something like the following:

1. Arrive at 6:00 to 7:00 A.M. and walk through the food and beverage department with the night cleaners.
2. Check to make sure the compactor is working and the area is clean.
3. Check that all employees are on duty.
4. Ask people what kind of challenges they will face today.
5. Sample as many dishes as possible, checking for taste, consistency, feel, smell, and overall quality.
6. Check walk-ins.
7. Recheck once or twice a day to see where department stands production-wise—this eliminates overtime.
8. Approve schedules for food and beverage outlet.
9. Keep a daily update of food and beverage revenues and costs.
10. Forecast the next day's, week's, and month's business based on updated information.
11. Check on final numbers for catering functions.

Financial results are generally expressed in ratios, such as **food cost percentage**—the cost of food divided by the amount of food sales. In its simplest form, an example would be the sale of a hamburger for $1.00. If the cost of the food was $0.30 then the food cost percentage would be 30 percent, which is about average for many hotels. The average might be reduced to 27 percent in hotels that do a lot of catering. As discussed later in this section, in determining the food and beverage department's profit and loss, executive chefs and food and beverage directors must consider not only the food cost percentage, but also the **contribution margin** of menu items. The contribution margin is the amount contributed by a menu item toward overhead expenses and is the difference between the cost of preparing the item and its selling price.

Another important cost ratio for the kitchen is labor cost. The **labor cost percentage** may vary depending on the amount of convenience foods purchased versus those made from scratch (raw ingredients). In a kitchen, this

Corporate Profile: Four Seasons Regent Hotels[1]

In 1960, Isadore Sharp opened the first Four Seasons Hotel on Jarvis Street in downtown Toronto, Canada. Today, Four Seasons Hotels and Resorts manage sixty-five hotels in 29 countries, under the brand names Four Seasons and Regent.

Isadore Sharp's understanding of what modern travelers want from a hotel has positioned Four Seasons as the first choice of many business travelers. They can expect their check-in to be fast and efficient, the rooms to be luxurious, the laundry to be back on time, and the food to be very good. Genuinely caring about the needs of the guests has led to the introduction of many innovative services that have made Four Seasons a benchmark for quality and service. For example, the company was the first to introduce in-room amenities and company-wide concierge services.

Quality in every aspect of the business translates into excellent food and beverage. Each of the restaurants in all of the Four Seasons properties was designed to lead the local fine-dining market. Four Seasons successfully challenged the hotel food stigma. Its restaurants serve imaginative and attractive dishes that suit the tastes of both the local guests and the international clientele.

Once again, meeting the guests' needs was accomplished with the introduction of alternative cuisine—stylish and flavorful items prepared with an eye on proper nutrition—designed for the frequent business traveler who spends many nights in hotel rooms and would appreciate lighter menu options.

Alternative cuisine is a method of preparation that creates nutritionally balanced dishes with reduced levels of cholesterol and sodium, without sacrificing quality, originality, taste, or presentation. The principles of alternative cuisine are achieved by:

- *Reducing fats,* using low-fat content ingredients and avoiding high-fat dairy products, oils, mayonnaise, and so on

- *Reducing sodium* by reducing salt, high-sodium foods such as olives, pickles, and Parma ham, and by avoiding any unnatural flavoring
- *Reducing cholesterol* by carefully limiting animal meats, avoiding organ meats, skin of poultry, egg yolks, and so on

Instead, Four Seasons chefs emphasize the use of foods containing animal protein (fish, poultry, and selected meats such as veal, flank steaks, game), complex carbohydrates (vegetables, salads, starch), simple carbohydrates (fruits), and fiber (whole grain breads, rice, pasta, cereal). The results are pleasing to the health-conscious traveler. A typical two-course alternative cuisine lunch can have as few as 500 calories. A three-course dinner can count as little as 650.

These food and beverage innovations have contributed to Four Seasons-Regent Hotel restaurants ranking among the top restaurants in their respective cities. They reflect the company's single-minded commitment to quality and guest satisfaction in all aspects of the hotel experience.

The Four Seasons has recently won these awards:

1. *Fortune* magazine ranked the Four Seasons "one of the best companies to work for in America." They came in forty-eighth.
2. Eighteen Four Seasons Hotels were awarded top honors in the AAA Diamond Awards.
3. Eight different Four Seasons Hotels received the Mobile Five-Star Award.
4. *Gourmet* magazine's annual readers survey of "America's Top Tables" had a total of nine Four Season's restaurants rated in the top 20 listings of their respective cities.

---

1. www.fourseasons.com. August 22, 2005.

may be expressed as a **food sales percentage.** For example, if food sales total $1,000 and labor costs total $250, then labor costs may be expressed as a percentage of food sales by the following formula:

$$\frac{\text{Labor cost}}{\text{Food sales}} \quad \text{therefore} \quad \frac{\$250}{\$1,000} \quad = 25\% \text{ labor cost}$$

Labor management is controlled with the aid of programs like TimePro from Commeg Systems. TimePro is a time, attendance, and scheduling package that provides an analytical tool for managers and saves time on forecasting and scheduling.

An executive chef has one or more **sous chefs.** Because so much of the executive chef's time is spent on administration, sous chefs are often responsible for the day-to-day running of each shift. Depending on size, a kitchen may have several sous chefs: one or more for days, one for evenings, and another for banquets.

Under the sous chefs is the **chef tournant.** This person rotates through the various stations to relieve the **station chef** heads. These stations are organized according to production tasks, based on the classic "brigade" introduced by Escoffier. The **brigade** includes the following:

Sauce chef, who prepares sauces, stews, sautes, hot hors d'oeuvres
Roast chef, who roasts, broils, grills, and braises meats
Fish chef, who cooks fish dishes
Soup chef, who prepares all soups
Cold larder/pantry chef, who prepares all cold foods: salads, cold hors d'oeuvres, buffet food, and dressings
Banquet chef, who is responsible for all banquet food
Pastry chef, who prepares all hot and cold dessert items
Vegetable chef, who prepares vegetables (this person may be the fry cook and soup cook in some smaller kitchens)
(Soup, cold larder, banquets, pastry, and vegetable chefs' positions may be combined in smaller kitchens.)

Pastry chef Markus Farbinger adds the finishing touches to another fine pastry.

A Day in the Life of Jim Gemignani
Executive Chef, Marriott Hotel

Jim Gemignani is executive chef at the 1,500-room Marriott Hotel in San Francisco. Chef Jim, as his associates call him, is responsible for the quality of food, guest, and associate satisfaction and for financial satisfaction in terms of results. With more than 200 associates in eight departments, Chef Jim has an interesting challenge. He makes time to be innovative by researching food trends and comparative shopping. Currently, American cuisine is in, as are free-standing restaurants in hotels. An ongoing part of American cuisine is the healthy food that Chef Jim says has not yet found a niche.

Hotels are building identity into their restaurants by branding or creating their own brand name. Marriott, for example, has Pizza Hut pizzas on the room service menu. Marriott hotels have created their own tiers of restaurants. JW's is the formal restaurant, Tuscany's is a Northern Italian-themed restaurant, the American Grill has replaced the old coffee shop, and Kimoko is a Japanese restaurant. As a company, Marriott decided to go nationwide with the first three of these concepts. This has simplified menus and improved food quality and presentation, and yet regional specials allow for individual creativity on the part of the chef.

When asked about his personal philosophy, Chef Jim says that in this day and age, one needs to embrace change and build teams; the guest is an important part of the team. Chef Jim's biggest challenge is keeping guests and associates happy. He is also director of food service outlets, which now gives him a front-of-the-house perspective. Among his greatest accomplishments are seeing his associates develop—20 are now executive chefs—retaining 96 percent of his opening team, and being voted Chef of the Year by the San Francisco Chef's Association.

Chef Jim's advice: "It's tough not to have a formal education, but remember that you need a combination of 'hands on' and formal training. If you're going to be a leader, you must start at the bottom and work your way up; otherwise, you will become a superior and not know how to relate to your associates."

Check Your Knowledge

1. What is a food cost percentage and how is it calculated?
2. What is a contribution margin?
3. How is labor cost percentage calculated?

Food Operations

A hotel may have several restaurants or no restaurant at all; the number and type of restaurants varies as well. A major chain hotel generally has two restaurants: a signature or upscale formal restaurant and a casual coffee shop type of restaurant. These restaurants cater to both hotel guests and to the general public. In recent years, because of increased guest expectations, hotels have placed greater emphasis on food and beverage preparation and service. As a result, there is an increasing need for professionalism on the part of hotel personnel.

The dining room of the Bellagio Hotel's Picasso restaurant in Las Vegas features Mediterranian-style decor and paintings by Pablo Picasso.

Hotel restaurants are run by restaurant managers in much the same way as other restaurants. **Restaurant managers** are generally responsible for the following:

- Exceeding guest service expectations
- Hiring, training, and developing employees
- Setting and maintaining quality standards
- Marketing
- Banquets
- Coffee service
- In-room dining, minibars, or the cocktail lounge
- Presenting annual, monthly, and weekly forecasts and budgets to the food and beverage director

Some restaurant managers work on an incentive plan with quarterly performance bonuses. Hotel restaurants present the manager with some interesting challenges because hotel guests are not always predictable. Sometimes they will use the hotel restaurants, and other times they will dine out. If they dine in or out to an extent beyond the forecasted number of guests, problems can arise. Too many guests for the restaurants results in delays and poor service. Too few guests means that employees are underutilized, which can increase labor costs unless employees are sent home early. A restaurant manager keeps a diary of the number of guests served by the restaurant on the same night the previous week, month, and year.

The number (house count) and type of hotel guest (e.g., the number of conference attendees who may have separate dining arrangements) should also be considered in estimating the number of expected restaurant guests for any meal. This figure is known as the **capture rate,** which, when coupled with historic and banquet activity and hotel occupancy, will be the restaurant's basis for forecasting the number of expected guests.

Most hotels find it difficult to coax hotel guests into the restaurants. However, many continuously try to convert food service from a necessary amenity to a profit center. The Royal Sonesta in New Orleans offers restaurant coupons worth $5 to its guests and guests of nearby hotels. Another successful strategy, adopted by the Plaza Athenee in New York, is to show guests the restaurants

Bars are run by bar managers. The responsibilities of a bar manager include:

- Supervising the ordering process and storage of wines
- Preparing a wine list
- Overseeing the staff
- Maintaining cost control
- Assisting guests with their wine selection
- Proper service of wine
- Knowledge of beers and liquors and their service

Bar efficiency is measured by the **pour/cost percentage.** Pour cost is obtained by dividing the cost of depleted inventory by sales over a period of time.

Food and beverage directors expect a pour cost of between 16 and 24 percent. Generally, operations with lower pour costs have more sophisticated control systems and a higher-volume catering operation. An example of this would be an automatic system that dispenses the exact amount of beverage requested via a pouring gun, which is fed by a tube from a beverage store. These systems are expensive, but they save money for volume operations by being less prone to pilferage, overpouring, or other tricks of the trade. Their greatest savings comes in the form of reduced labor costs; fewer bartenders are needed to make the same amount of drinks. However, the barperson may still hand pour premium brands for show.

Hotel bars are susceptible to the same problems as other bars. The director of food and beverage must set strict policy and procedure guidelines and see to it that they are followed. In today's litigious society, the onus is on the operator to install and ensure **responsible alcoholic beverage service** (the NRA offers Serve Safe alcohol). If a guest becomes intoxicated and is still served alcohol or a minor is served alcohol and is involved in an accident involving someone else, then the server of the beverage, the barperson, and the manager may be liable for the injuries sustained by the person who was harmed, the third party.

Another risk bars encounter is **pilferage.** Employees have been known to steal or tamper with liquor. They could, for example, dilute it with water or colored liquids, sell the additional liquor, and pocket the money. There are several other ways to defraud a bar. One of the better known ways is to overcharge guests for beverages. Another is to underpour, which gives guests less for their money. Some bartenders overpour measures in order to receive larger tips. The best way to prevent these occurrences is to have a good control system, which should include **shoppers**—people who are paid to use the bar like regular guests, except they are closely watching the operation.

In a large hotel there are several kinds of bars:

Lobby bar: This convenient meeting place was popularized when Conrad Hilton wanted to generate revenue out of his vast hotel lobby. Lobby bars, when well managed, are a good source of income.

Restaurant bar: Traditionally, this bar is away from the hubbub of the lobby and offers a holding area for the hotel's signature restaurant.

Service bar: In some of the very large hotels, restaurants and room service have a separate backstage bar. Otherwise, both the restaurant and room

A Sheraton hotel bar in Australia gives guests an opportunity to mingle and relax.

service are serviced by one of the regular beverage outlets, such as the restaurant bar.

Catering and banquet bar: This bar is used specifically to service all the catering and banquet needs of the hotel. These bars can stretch any operator to the limit. Frequently, several cash bars must be set up at a variety of locations; if cash wines are involved with dinner, it becomes a race to get the wine to the guest before the meal, preferably before the appetizer. Because of the difficulties involved in servicing a large number of guests, most hotels encourage inclusive wine and beverage functions in which the guests pay a little more for tickets that include a predetermined amount of beverage service. Banquet bars require careful inventory control. The bottles should be checked immediately after the function, and, if the bar is very busy, the bar manager should pull the money just before the bar closes. The breakdown of function bars should be done on the spot if possible to help prevent pilferage.

The banquet bar needs to stock not only large quantities of the popular wines, spirits, and beers but also a selection of premium spirits and after-dinner liqueurs. These are used in the ballroom and private dining rooms in particular.

Pool bars: Pool bars are popular at resort hotels where guests can enjoy a variety of exotic cocktails poolside. Resort hotels that cater to conventions often put on theme parties one night of the convention to allow delegates to kick back. Popular themes that are catered around the pool might be a Hawaiian luau, a Caribbean reggae night, Mexican fiesta, or Country and Western events. Left to the imagination, one could conceive of a number of theme events.

Minibars: Minibars or honor bars are small, refrigerated bars in guest rooms. They offer the convenience of having beverages available at all times. For security, they have a separate key, which may be either included in the room key envelope at check-in or withheld according to the guest's preference. Minibars are typically checked and replenished on a daily basis. Charges for items used are automatically added to the guest folio.

Night clubs: Some hotels offer guests evening entertainment and dancing. Whether formal or informal, these food and beverage outlets offer a full beverage service. Live entertainment is very expensive. Many hotels are switching to operations with a DJ or where the bar itself is the entertainment (e.g., sports bar). Directors of food and beverage are now negotiating more with live bands, offering them a base pay (below union scale) and a percentage of a cover charge.

Sports bars: Sports bars have become popular in hotels. Almost everyone identifies with a sporting theme, which makes for a relaxed atmosphere that complements contemporary lifestyles. Many sports bars have a variety of games such as pool, football, bar basketball, and so on, which, together with satellite-televised sporting events, contribute to the atmosphere.

Casino bars: Casino bars and beverage service are there to keep people gambling by offering low-cost or free drinks. Some have lavish entertainment and light food offerings, which entice guests to enjoy the gaming experience, even when experiencing heavy losses.

Different types of bars produce revenue according to their location in the hotel and the kind of hotel itself. Nightclubs, sports bars, and the banqueting department see bulk consumption of alcoholic beverages; and restaurant bars usually see more alcohol consumption than minibars and lounge bars.

Check Your Knowledge

1. What departments does the food and beverage director oversee?
2. What are the responsibilities of a food and beverage director on a day-to-day basis?
3. Explain how the pour/cost percentage is used in a bar to measure efficiency.

Stewarding Department

The **chief steward** is responsible to the director of food and beverage for the following functions:

- Cleanliness of the back of the house (all the areas of the backstage that hotel guests do not see)
- Maintaining clean glassware, china, and cutlery for the food and beverage outlets

A Chief Steward Checking the Silver Inventory

- Maintaining strict inventory control and monthly stock check
- Maintenance of dishwashing machines
- Inventory of chemical stock
- Sanitation of kitchen, banquet isles, storerooms, walk-ins/freezers, and all equipment
- Pest control and coordination with exterminating company
- Forecasting labor and cleaning supplies

In some hotels the steward's department is responsible for keeping the kitchen(s) clean. This is generally done at night to prevent disruption of the food production operation. A more limited cleaning is done in the afternoon between the lunch and dinner services. The chief steward's job can be an enormous and thankless task. In hotels this involves cleaning up for several hundred people three times a day. Just trying to keep track of everything can be a headache. Some hotels have different patterns of glasses, china, and cutlery for each outlet. The casual dining room frequently has an informal theme, catering and banqueting a more formal one, and the signature restaurant, very formal place settings. It is difficult to ensure all the pieces are returned to the correct places. It is also difficult to prevent both guests and employees from taking souvenirs. Strict inventory control and constant vigilance help keep pilferage to a minimum.

Catering Department

Throughout the world's cultural and social evolution, numerous references have been made to the breaking of bread together. Feasts or banquets are one way to show one's hospitality. Frequently, hosts attempted to outdo one another with the extravagance of their feasts. Today, occasions for celebrations, banquets, and catering include the following:

- State banquets, when countries' leaders honor visiting royalty and heads of state
- National days
- Embassy receptions and banquets

- Business and association conventions and banquets
- Gala charity balls
- Company dinner dances
- Weddings

Catering has a broader scope than banquets. **Banquets** refers to groups of people who eat together at one time and in one place. **Catering** includes a variety of occasions when people may eat at varying times. However, the terms are often used interchangeably.

For example, catering departments in large, city-center hotels may service the following events in just one day:

- A Fortune 500 company's annual shareholders meeting
- An international loan-signing ceremony
- A fashion show
- A convention
- Several sales and board meetings
- Private luncheons and dinner parties
- A wedding or two

Naturally each of these requires different and special treatment. Hotels in smaller cities may cater the local chamber of commerce meeting, a high school prom, a local company party, a regional sales meeting, a professional workshop, and a small exhibition.

Catering may be subdivided into on-premise and off-premise. In off-premise catering, the event is catered away from the hotel. The food may be prepared either in the hotel or at the event. The organization chart in Figure 6–3 shows how the catering department is organized. The dotted lines show cooperative reporting relationships and continuous lines show a direct reporting relationship. For example, the banquet chef reports directly to the executive chef, but must cooperate with the director of catering and the catering service manager.

The **director of catering (DOC)** is responsible to the food and beverage director for selling and servicing, catering, banquets, meetings, and exhibitions in a way that exceeds guests' expectations and produces reasonable profit. The director of

A catering officer reviews an event order. Attention to detail is critical to ensure complete guest satisfaction.

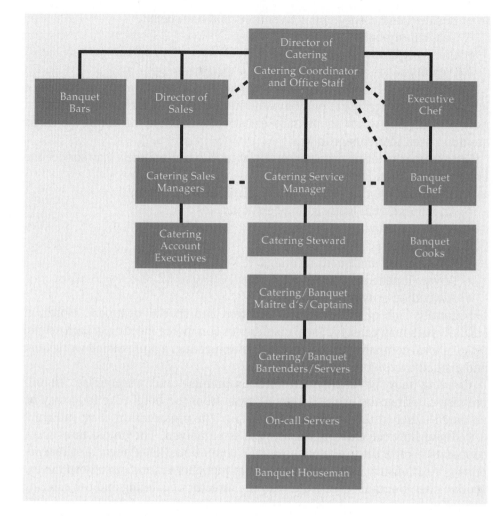

Figure 6–3 *Organization of the Catering Department*

catering has a close working relationship with the rooms division manager because the catering department often brings conventions, which require rooms, to the hotel. There is also a close working relationship with the executive chef. The chef plans the banqueting menus but the catering manager must ensure that they are suitable for the clientele and practical from a service point of view. Sometimes they work together in developing a selection of menus that will meet all the requirements, including cost and price.

The director of catering must be able to do the following:

1. Sell conventions, banquets, and functions.
2. Lead a team of employees.
3. Together with input from team members, make up departmental goals and objectives.
4. Set individual and department sales and cost budgets.
5. Set service standards.

6. Ensure that the catering department is properly maintained.
7. Be extremely creative and knowledgeable about food, wine, and service.
8. Be very well versed in the likes, dislikes, and dietary restrictions of various ethnic groups, especially Jewish, Middle Eastern, and European.

Position Profile

The director of catering is required to have a variety of skills and abilities as shown in the following:

Technical
- A thorough knowledge of food and beverage management, including food preparation and service
- Ability to sell conventions, functions, and banquets
- Ability to produce a profit
- Ability to develop individual and department sales and cost budgets

Leadership
- Lead a team of employees.
- Set departmental mission, goals, and objectives.
- Train the department members in all facets of operations.
- Set service standards.
- Ensure that the catering department is properly maintained.

The catering department is extremely complex and demanding; the tempo is fast and the challenge to be innovative is always present. The director of catering in a large city hotel should, over the years, build up a client list and an intimate knowledge of the trade shows, exhibitions, various companies, groups, associations, and SMERF organizations (social, military, education, religious, and fraternal market). This knowledge and these contacts are essential to the director of catering's success, as is the selection of the team members.

The main sales function of the department is conducted by the director of catering (DOC) and catering sales managers (CSMs). Their jobs are to optimize guest satisfaction and revenue by selling the most lucrative functions and exceeding guests' food and beverage and service expectations.

The DOC and catering sales managers obtain business leads from a variety of sources, including the following:

Hotel's director of sales: She or he is a good source of event bookings because she or he is selling rooms, and catering is often required by meetings and conventions.

General managers: These are good sources of leads because they are very involved in the community.

Corporate office sales department: If, for example, a convention were held on the East Coast one year at a Marriott hotel, and by tradition the association goes to the West Coast the following year, the Marriott hotel in the chosen city will contact the client or meeting planner. Some organizations have a selection of cities and hotels bid for major conventions. This ensures a competitive rate quote for accommodations and services.

Convention and visitors bureau: Here is another good source of leads because its main purpose is to seek out potential groups and organizations to visit that city. To be fair to all the hotels, they publish a list of clients and brief details of their requirements, which the hotel catering sales department may follow up on.

Reading the event board of competitive hotels: The event board is generally located in the lobby of the hotel and is frequently read by the competition. The CSM then calls the organizer of the event to solicit the business the next time.

Rollovers: Some organizations, especially local ones, prefer to stay in the same location. If this represents good business for the hotel, then the DOC and GM try to persuade the decision makers to use the same hotel again.

Cold calls: During periods of relative quiet, CSMs call potential clients to inquire if they are planning any events in the next few months. The point is to entice the client to view the hotel and the catering facilities. It is amazing how much information is freely given over the telephone.

Figure 6–4 shows the steps involved in booking a function. The most frequent catering events in hotels are the following:

- Meetings
- Conventions
- Dinners
- Luncheons
- Weddings

For meetings, a variety of room setups are available, depending on a client's needs. The most frequently selected meeting room setups are as follows:

Theater style: Rows of chairs are placed with a center group of chairs and two aisles. Figure 6–5 shows a theater-style setup with equipment cen-

---

Enquiry: Incoming calls
  From prospective clients
  Director of marketing and sales
  Corporate sales office
  Cold calls by catering sales manager to seek prospective clients
Check for space available in the "bible"* or the computer program.
Confirm availability and suggest menus and beverages. Invite clients to view hotel when it is set up for a similar function.
Catering prepares a contract and creates a proposal and a pro-forma invoice for client. This enables client to budget for all costs with no surprise.
Catering manager makes any modifications and sends client a contract detailing events, menus, beverages, and costs.
Client confirms room booking, menus, and beverages by returning the signed contract.

---

*The bible is the function book in which a permanent record is maintained of each function room's availability, tentative booking, or guaranteed booking.

Figure 6–4 *Booking a Function*

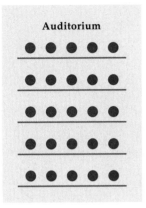

Figure 6–5 *Theater-Style Seating*

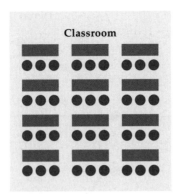

Figure 6–6 *Classroom-Style Seating*

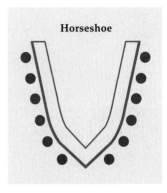

Figure 6–7 *Horseshoe-Style Seating*

tered on an audiovisual platform. Sometimes multimedia presentations, requiring more space for reverse image projections, reduce the room's seating capacity.

Classroom style: As the name suggests, tables, usually slim 18-inch ones, are used because meeting participants need space to take notes. Classroom-style setup usually takes about three times as much space as theater style and takes more time and labor to set up and break down. Figure 6–6 shows a classroom-style setup.

Horseshoe style: This type of meeting setup (Figure 6–7) is frequently used when interaction is sought among the delegates, such as training sessions and workshops. The presenter or trainer stands at the open end of the horseshoe with a black or white board, flip chart, overhead projector, and video monitor and projector.

Dinner style: Dinners are generally catered at round tables of eight or ten persons for large parties and on boardroom-style tables for smaller numbers. Of course, there are variations of this setup (see Figure 6–8).

Catering Event Order

A **catering event order (CEO),** which may also be called a **banquet event order (BEO),** is prepared/completed for each function to inform not only the client but also the hotel personnel about essential information (what needs to happen and when) to ensure a successful event.

The CEO is prepared based on correspondence with the client and notes taken during the property visits. Figure 6–9 shows a CEO and lists the room's layout and decor, times of arrival, if there are any VIPs and what special attention is required for them, that is, reception, bar times, types of beverages and service, cash or credit bar, time of meal service, the menu, wines, and service details. The catering manager or director confirms the details with the client. Usually, two copies are sent, one for the client to sign and return and one for the client to keep.

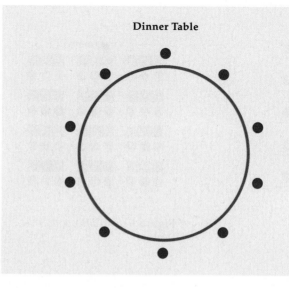

Figure 6–8 *Dinner-Style Seating*

An accompanying letter thanks the client for selecting the hotel and explains the importance of the function to the hotel. The letter also mentions the guaranteed-number policy. This is the number of guests the hotel will prepare to serve and will charge accordingly. The guaranteed number is given about seven days prior to the event. This safeguards the hotel from preparing for 350 people and having only 200 show up. The client, naturally, does not want to pay for an extra 150 people—hence the importance of a close working relationship with the client. Contracts for larger functions call for the client to notify the hotel of any changes to the anticipated number of guests in increments of ten or twenty.

Experienced catering directors ensure that there will be no surprises for either the function organizer or the hotel. This is done by calling to check on how the function planning is going. One mistake catering directors sometimes make is accepting a final guest count without inquiring as to how that figure was determined. This emphasizes the fact that the catering director should be a consultant to the client. Depending on the function, the conversion from invitations to guests is about 50 percent. Some hotels have a policy of preparing for about 3 to 5 percent more than the anticipated or guaranteed number. Fortunately, most events have a prior history. The organization may have been at a similar hotel in the same city or across the country. In either case, the catering director or manager will be able to receive helpful information from the catering director of the hotel where the organization's function was held previously.

The director of catering holds a daily or weekly meeting with key individuals who will be responsible for upcoming events. Those in attendance should be the following:

Director of catering
Executive chef and/or banquet chef
Beverage manager or catering bar manager

SHERATON GRANDE TORREY PINES
BANQUET EVENT ORDER

POST AS:	WELCOME BREAKFAST	CHERI WALTER
EVENT NAME:	MEETING	
GROUP:	CROCKER AND ASSOCIATES	
ADDRESS:	41 MAIN ST	**BILLING:**
	BOWLING GREEN, OHIO 43218	
PHONE:	(619) 635-4627	DIRECT BILL
FAX:	(619) 635-4528	
GROUP CONTACT:	Dr. Ken Crocker	**Amount Received:**
ON-SITE-CONTACT:	same	

DAY	DATE	TIME	FUNCTION	ROOM	EXP	GTE	SET	RENT
Wed	January 25, 2007	7:30 AM – 12:00 PM	Meeting	Palm Garden	50			250.00

BAR SET UP:

N/A

MENU:

7:30 AM CONTINENTAL BREAKFAST

Freshly Squeezed Orange Juice, Grapefruit Juice, and
    Tomato Juice
Assortment of Bagels, Muffins, and Mini Brioche
Cream Cheese, Butter, and Preserves
Display of Sliced Seasonal Fruits
Individual Fruit Yogurt
Coffee, Tea, and Decaffeinated Coffee

PRICE:_____

11:00 AM BREAK

Refresh Beverages as needed

WINE:

FLORAL:

MUSIC:

AUDIO VISUAL:
–OVERHEAD PROJECTOR/SCREEN
–FLIPCHART/MARKERS
–VCR/MONITORS

PARKING:

HOSTING PARKING, PLEASE PROVIDE VOUCHERS

LINEN:
HOUSE

SETUP:
–CLASSROOM-STYLE SEATING
–HEAD TABLE FOR 2 PEOPLE
–APPROPRIATE COFFEE BREAK SETUP
–(1) 6' TABLE FOR REGISTRATION AT ENTRANCE
    WITH 2 CHAIRS, 1 WASTEBASKET

All food and beverage prices are subject to an 18% service charge and 7% state tax. Guarantee figures, cancellations, changes must be given 72 hours prior or the number of guests expected will be considered the guarantee. To confirm the above arrangements, this contract must be signed and returned.

ENGAGOR SIGNATURE _____   DATE _____

BEO # 003069

Figure 6–9 *Catering Event Order (Courtesy of Sheraton Grande Torrey Pines)*

Catering managers
Catering coordinator
Director of purchasing
Chief steward
Audiovisual representative

The purpose of this meeting is to avoid any problems and to be sure that all the key staff know and understand the details of the event and any special needs of the client.

Catering Coordinator

The **catering coordinator** has an exacting job in managing the office and controlling the "bible" or function diary now on computer. She or he must see that the contracts are correctly prepared and check on numerous last-minute details, such as whether flowers and menu cards have arrived.

Web-enabled technology tools like Newmarket International's Delphi System (which is used at over 4,000 properties) is a leader in delivering group, sales, catering, and banquet software to global travel and entertainment groups. One of the latest hotels to adopt the Delphi System is the Wynn Las Vegas, which installed the sales and catering systems Delphi Diagrams, MeetingBroker, and e-Proposal. The Delphi system can keep inventory current in real time due to its ability to interface with the property management system. The suite of Delphi products allows function space to be clearly and concisely managed, which increases guest satisfaction and profitability.

An Elegant Banquet Room at a Ritz-Carlton Hotel

Catering Services Manager

The **catering services manager (CSM)** has the enormous responsibility of delivering higher-than-expected service levels to guests. The CSM is in charge of the function from the time the client is introduced to the CSM by the director of catering or catering manager. This job is very demanding because several functions always occur simultaneously. Timing and logistics are crucial to the success of the operation. Frequently, there are only a few minutes between the end of a day meeting and the beginning of the reception for a dinner dance.

The CSM must be liked and respected by guests and at the same time be a superb organizer and supervisor. This calls for a person of outstanding character and leadership—management skills that are essential for success. The CSM has several important duties and responsibilities, including the following:

- Directing the service of all functions
- Supervising the catering housepersons in setting up the room
- Scheduling the banquet captains and approving the staffing levels for all events
- Cooperating with the banquet chef to check menus and service arrangements
- Checking that the client is satisfied with the room setup, food, beverages, and service
- Checking last-minute details
- Making out client bills immediately after the function. Adhering to all hotel policies and procedures that pertain to the catering department. This includes responsible alcoholic beverage service and adherence to fire code regulations.
- Calculating and distributing the gratuity and service charges for the service personnel
- Coordinating the special requirements with the DOC and catering coordinator

Check Your Knowledge

1. What is the difference between banquets and catering?
2. What does SMERF stand for?
3. Where do the director of catering and the catering sales manager obtain their information?
4. What are the various styles used when setting up a meeting room? Give examples of when each style might be used.

Room Service/In-Room Dining

The term **room service** has for some time referred to all service to hotel guest rooms. Recently, some hotels have changed the name of room service to *in-room dining* to present the service as more upscale. The intention is to bring the dining experience to the room with quality food and beverage service.

A survey of members of the American Hotel & Lodging Association showed that 56 percent of all properties offer room service and that 75 percent of airport properties provide room service. Generally, the larger the hotel and the higher the room rate, the more likely it is that a hotel will offer room service.

Economy and several midpriced hotels avoid the costs of operating room service by having vending machines on each floor and food items like pizza or Chinese food delivered by local restaurants. Conversely, some hotels prepare menus and lower price structures that do not identify the hotel as the provider of the food. As a result, the guests may have the impression that they are ordering from an "outside" operation when they are in fact ordering from room service.

The level of service and menu prices will vary from hotel to hotel. The Hilton at Torrey Pines, California, has butler service for all guest rooms without additional charge.

A few years ago, room service was thought of as a necessary evil, something that guests expected, but which did not produce profit for the hotel. Financial pressures have forced food and beverage directors to have this department also contribute to the bottom line. The room service manager has a difficult challenge running this department, which is generally in operation between 16 and 24 hours a day. Tremendous effectiveness is required to make this department profitable. Nevertheless, it can be done. Some of the challenges in operating room service are as follows:

> Delivery of orders on time—this is especially important for breakfast, which is by far the most popular room service meal
> Making room service a profitable food and beverage department
> Avoiding complaints of excessive charges for room service orders

There are many other challenges in room service operation. One is forecasting demand. Room service managers analyze the front-desk forecast, which gives details of the house count and guest mix—convention, group, and others for the next two weeks. The food and beverage forecast will indicate the number of covers expected for breakfast, lunch, and dinner. The convention résumés will show where the convention delegates are having their various meals. For example, the number of in-house delegates attending a convention breakfast can substantially reduce the number of room service breakfast orders. Experience enables the manager to check if a large number of guests are from different time zones, such as the West or East Coasts or overseas. These guests have a tendency to either get up much earlier or much later. This could throw room

Butler service is offered at some upscale and luxury hotels as a special additional service to guests.

service demands off balance. Demand also fluctuates between weekdays and weekends; for example, city hotels may cater to business travelers, who tend to require service at about the same time. However, on weekends, city hotels may attract families, who will order room service at various times.

To avoid problems with late delivery of orders, a growing number of hotels have dedicated elevators to be used only by room service during peak periods. At the 565-room Stouffer Riviera Chicago, director of food and beverage Bill Webb has a solution: Rapid action teams (RAT) are designated food and beverage managers and assistants who can be called on when room service orders are heavy.

Westin Hotels recently introduced Service Express, an innovation that allows a customer to address all needs (room service, housekeeping, laundry, and other services) with a single call. In addition, new properties are designed with the room service kitchen adjacent to the main kitchen so that a greater variety of items can be offered.

The challenge of speedy and accurate communication is imperative to a successful room service operation. This begins with timely scheduling and ends with happy guests. In between is a constant flow of information that is communicated by the guest, the order taker, the cook, and the server.

Another challenge is to have well-trained and competent employees in the room service department. From the tone of voice of the order taker and the courteous manner with which the order is taken to the panache of the server for the VIP dinners, training makes the difference between ordinary service and outstanding service. With training, which includes menu tasting with wine and suggestive selling, an order taker becomes a room service salesperson. This person is now able to suggest cocktails or wine to complement the entree and can entice the guest with tempting desserts. The outcome of this is to increase the average guest check. Training also helps the setup and service personnel hone their skills to enable them to become productive employees who are proud of their work.

Trends in Food and Beverage Operations

- The use of branded restaurants instead of hotels operating their own restaurants.
- Hotels opting not to offer food and beverage outlets. These are usually smaller to midsized properties that may have restaurants on the same lot nearby.
- Making restaurants and beverage outlets more casual.
- Using themes for a restaurant. For example, one major hotel chain has adopted a Northern Italian theme in all its restaurants.
- Standardized menus for all hotel restaurants in a chain.
- Many hotels are converting one of the beverage outlets into a sports-themed bar.
- Technology is being used to enhance guest services and control costs in all areas of a hotel, including guest ordering and payment, food production, refrigeration, marketing, management control, and communication.
- More low-fat low-carb menu items.

CASE STUDY

Ensuring Guest Satisfaction

The Sunnyvale Hotel is operated by a major hotel management corporation. To ensure guest satisfaction, 300 survey forms each containing 65 questions are mailed to guests each month. Normally, about seventy of the forms are returned. The hotel company categorizes the guest satisfaction scores obtained into colored zones with green being the best, then clear and yellow, and red being the worst. Scores can be compared with those of equivalent hotels.

The most recent survey indicated a significant decline for the Sea Grill Restaurant with scores in the red zone. Guests' concerns were in the following areas: hostess attentiveness, spread of service, and quality of food.

Upon investigation, the director of food and beverage also realized that the name of the restaurant, Sea Grill, was not appropriate for the type of restaurant being operated. When asked, some guests commented that "it's a bit odd to eat breakfast in a fish place."

Discussion Question

1. What would you do, as director of food and beverage, to get the guest satisfaction scores back into the clear or green zones?

CASE STUDY

Friday Evening at the Grand Hotel's Casual Restaurant

Karla Gomez is the supervisor at the Grand Hotel's casual restaurant. Karla's responsibilities include overseeing five servers and two busers, seating guests, and taking reservations. One Friday evening, the restaurant was very busy—all 20 tables were occupied, there was a substantial wait-list, and there were people on standby. The service bar was almost full of guests and most of the seated guests in the dining area had finished their entrees or were just beginning their desserts. They were not leaving, however, in part because of cold, rainy weather outside. The guests did not seem to be in a rush to leave the restaurant, but several of the guests waiting for tables were complaining about the long wait.

Discussion Question

1. What can Karla do to solve the problem?

CAREER INFORMATION

Food and beverage (F&B) management careers within the hotel and resort segment of the hospitality industry offer an assortment of positions, from limited service properties that offer very simple food operations, to hotels and resorts that offer room service, banquet facilities, catering operations, and a variety of types of restaurants. Management positions can be as simple as a coffee shop manager or as complex as the director of food and beverage operations for a 5,000-room property.

Managing an F&B operation is similar to working in a restaurant with long hours and varied work schedules. Holidays tend to be the busiest time of the year, eliminating these as potential vacation periods for you. Lodging corporations either treat F&B outlets as a guest amenity working on a break-even premise or see them as profit centers. In either case, an F&B manager is required to balance the needs of the guest with the requirements of the employer.

Compensation is often less than for similar positions in chain restaurants, but lodging properties offer excellent benefits packages, and signing bonuses are not unusual. Another incentive of working for hotel chains is reduced or free lodging at associated properties. Those interested in a career in hotel management should note that most general managers have an F&B background.

Food service at hotels and resorts can be challenging, to say the least. Flexibility, quick thinking, and the willingness to meet and exceed guest expectations are essential components of a successful F&B career.

Related Web Sites

www.fourseasons.com/—Four Seasons Hotels & Resorts
www.eldoradohotel.com/—Eldorado Hotel

www.vine2wine.com/—Links to a variety of Web sites about wine
www.americanwineries.org/—site for the National Association of American Wineries
wineserver.ucdavis.edu/winegrape/index.htm—Winery education information and links to other sites
www.realbeer.com/—Great Web site for information on beer
hbd.org/brewery/—Information and links to brewing

www.abgbrew.com/—Brewing school
www.siebelinstitute.com/—For brewing school in Chicago
www.republicbeverage.com/—For Republic Beverage career information and links to other sites
www.starbucks.com/hom.asp—For Starbucks Coffee; includes employment information

Courtesy of Charlie Adams.

SUMMARY

1. The food and beverage department division is led by the director of food and beverage, who is responsible for the efficient operation of kitchen, catering, restaurants, bars, and room service; in addition, the director has to keep up with trends and preplan for special events.
2. A hotel kitchen is the responsibility of the executive chef, who is in charge of the quality and quantity of food, organization of the kitchen and his or her sous chefs, administrative duties, and careful calculation of financial results.
3. A hotel usually has a formal and a casual restaurant, which are either directly connected to the hotel or operated separately.
4. Bars are an important revenue source for a hotel, but they must adhere to strict guidelines to be profitable. Commensurate with its size, a hotel might have several kinds of bars, such as a lobby bar, restaurant bar, mini-bar, or even a night club.
5. The chief steward has the often unrewarded job of cleaning the kitchen, cutlery, plates, glasses, and backstage of the hotel and is in charge of pest control and inventory.
6. Catering is subdivided into on-premise and off-premise occasions, which may include meetings, conventions, dinners, luncheons, and weddings. According to the occasion, the type of service and room setup may vary. It involves careful planning and the interaction and cooperation of many people.
7. Room service offers the convenience of dining in the room, with quality food and beverage service, at a price acceptable to both the guest and the hotel.

KEY WORDS AND CONCEPTS

Banquet
Banquet event order (BEO)
Brigade
Capture rate
Catering
Catering coordinator
Catering event order (CEO)
Catering services manager (CSM)

Chef tournant
Chief steward
Classroom-style seating
Contribution margin
Dinner-style room seating
Director of catering (DOC)
Director of food and beverage
Executive chef

Food cost percentage
Food sales percentage
Horseshoe-style room seating
Kitchen manager
Labor cost percentage
Perpetual inventory
Pilferage
Pour/cost percentage

Responsible alcoholic beverage service
Restaurant manager
Room service
Shopper
Sous chef
Station chef
Theater-style room seating

REVIEW QUESTIONS

1. Briefly describe the challenges a food and beverage director faces on a daily basis.
2. List the measures used to determine the food and beverage department's profit and loss.
3. Explain the problems a hotel faces in making the following departments profitable: restaurants, bars, and room service.
4. Explain the importance of the catering department for a hotel and list the responsibilities of a catering sales manager.

INTERNET EXERCISES

1. Organization: **Foodservice**
   Web site: **www.foodservice.com**
   Summary: Foodservice.com is a Web site that focuses on the foodservice industry. It has links to employment, industry resources, foodservice, technology innovations, and much more.
   (a) Click on the "Forums and Chat" icon. Go to the "Chef and Cooks Corner" and take a look at some of the latest articles. Bring your favorite one to the table (discuss in class).
   (b) Look at the most current articles on food safety. What are the major concerns being addressed?

2. Organization: **National Restaurant Association**
   Web site: **www.restaurant.org**
   Summary: The National Restaurant Association is an organization devoted to representing, educating, and promoting the restaurant/hospitality industry.
   (a) Look under the "Education" icon. What does it mean to be "FMP Certified" and what are the eligibility requirements?
   (b) What are some of the upcoming events and what do they have to offer?

APPLY YOUR KNOWLEDGE

1. If a casual dining restaurant in a four-star hotel forecasts for 100 covers, how many servers, busers, hosts, and assistant managers would you schedule on that particular day? Calculate the labor cost of these associates for that day if the manager(s) work from 1:00 to 11:00 P.M., the server(s) work from 4:00 to 11:00 P.M., the buser(s) work from 4:30 to 11:30 P.M., and the host(s) works from 4:00 to 11:00 P.M. Use minimum wage of $5.75 for calculations. Use the rate of $12 per hour for the assistant manager(s) and $6.50 for hosts.

2. Kitchen labor costs are an important ratio used to determine the efficiency of the food and beverage department. The labor cost for a banquet meal is $126.45 and the revenue for the banquet is $505.80. What is the labor cost percentage?

SUGGESTED ACTIVITIES

Contact a bar manager in your area. Discuss with him or her how to monitor pilferage and overpouring. Ask what the expected and actual pouring cost percentage is and how the manager deals with any variances.

Visit a hotel restaurant in your area. Make a note of how busy the establishment is. Does it seem to be staffed with the appropriate number of employees? Are guests being served in a timely manner? Think about why this specific restaurant may be overly crowded or overly vacant. What could or should be done differently? What seems to be working well?

ENDNOTE

1. Stewarding is responsible for back-of-the-house areas such as dishwashing, issuing and inventory of china, glassware, and cutlery. Stewarding duties include maintaining cleanliness in all areas.

WEB RESOURCES

Pannell Kerr Forster Consulting Firm
http://www.pkf.com/

Bellagio Las Vegas
http://www.bellagio.com/

Hilton
www.hilton.com

Four Seasons
www.fourseasons.com

Marriott
marriott.com

part **3**

Restaurants and Managed Services

The Restaurant Business

7

After reading and studying this chapter, you should be able to:

- Describe the different characteristics of chain and independent restaurants.
- Identify some of the top chain and independent restaurants.
- List the classifications of restaurants.
- Differentiate characteristics of chain and independent restaurants.

The Restaurant Business

Classical Cuisine

North America gained most of its culinary legacy from France. Two main events were responsible for our culinary legacy coming from France. First was the French Revolution in 1793, which caused the best chefs of the day to lose their employment because their bosses lost their heads! Many chefs came to North America as a result, bringing with them their culinary talents. The second was Thomas Jefferson, who in 1784 spent five years as envoy to France and brought a French chef to the White House when he became president. This act stimulated interest in French cuisine and enticed U.S. tavern owners to offer better-quality and more interesting food.

No mention of classical cuisine can be made without talking about the founders: Mari-Antoine Careme (1784–1833), who is credited as the founder of classical cuisine, and Auguste Escoffier, who is profiled in this chapter. After learning all aspects of cooking, Careme dedicated his career to refining and organizing culinary techniques. His many books contain the first really systematic account of cooking principles, recipes, and menu making.

Source: Wayne Gisslen, *Professional Cooking*, 2nd ed. New York: John Wiley and Sons, 1989.

Restaurants are a vital part of our everyday lifestyles; because we are a society on the go, we patronize them several times a week to socialize, as well as eat and drink. Restaurants offer a place to relax and enjoy the company of family, friends, colleagues, and business associates, to restore our energy level before heading off to the next class or whatever. Actually, the word restaurant is from the word *restore*.

As a society we spend an increasing amount, approaching 50 percent, of our food dollar away from home. Restaurants are a multibillion-dollar business that employs about 11.5 million people and contributes to our social and economic well-being. This chapter looks at the different types of restaurants and classifies them into recognizable segments.

Culinary Arts

This is an exciting time to be involved with the culinary arts and restaurants. Not only are new restaurant concepts and themes to fit a variety of tastes and budgets appearing on the scene but the culinary arts are being developed by several creative and talented chefs. It is important to realize that in this industry, we are never far from food. So, let's take a look at the recent development of **culinary arts.**

The main "ingredient" in a restaurant is cuisine, and one of the main foundations of classical French

A group of friends enjoy a fine dining experience.

cooking, on which much of the American cuisine is based, is the five **mother sauces:** bechamel, velouté, espagnole, tomato, and hollandaise. These elaborate sauces were essential accompaniments for the various dishes on the menu. Until about 1900, all menus were written in French—some still are—and regardless of whether a person was dining in a good hotel or restaurant in London or Lisbon, the intention was that the dish should be prepared in the same manner and taste similar to the French version. The travelers of the day either spoke French or had a knowledge of menu French.

Classical French cuisine was in vogue until the late 1960s and early 1970s when **nouvelle cuisine** became popular. Nouvelle cuisine is a lighter cuisine than French and is based on simpler preparations—with the aid of processors, blenders, and juicers—using more natural flavors and ingredients. Instead of thickening a sauce with a flour-based **roux,** a **purée** of vegetables would be used instead. Fresh was in, and this included herbs for flavor. Nouvelle cuisine combined classical techniques and principles with modern technology and scientific research. "Simpler quicker" quickly became more stylish, with plate presentation becoming a part of the chef's art. North American cooking had arrived. The bounties of Canada and the United States provided the basis for regional cuisine to flourish nationally. **Infusion,** the blending of flavors and techniques from two cuisines, became popular. New England and Italian or Californian and Asian can be blended. For example, a Japanese recipe might be blended with a Mexican one to create a new hybrid recipe.

Many great chefs have influenced our recent culinary development. Among them are Julia Child, whose television shows did much to take the mystique out of French cooking and encourage a generation of homemakers to elevate their cooking techniques and skills, and more recently Emeril "Bam" Lagasse and Bobby Flay, who have popularized cooking via the Food Network on TV.

The culinary schools have done an excellent job of producing a new generation of chefs who are making significant contributions to the evolving culinary arts, including chefs like Alice Waters, who at Chez Panice, her restaurant in Berkeley, California, is credited with the birth of California cuisine. Waters uses only fresh produce bought from local farmers. Paul Prudhomme is another contemporary chef who has energized many aspiring chefs with his passion for basic cooking, especially cajun style.

Charlie Trotter, chef–owner of Charlie Trotter's in Chicago, who is considered

Chef Emeril Lagasse outside His New Orleans Restaurant at the MGM Grand, Las Vegas

Auguste Escoffier (1846–1935)

Auguste Escoffier is considered the patron saint of the professional cook. Called the "emperor of the world's kitchens," he is considered as a reference point and a role model for all chefs. His exceptional culinary career began at the age of 13, when he apprenticed in his uncle's restaurant. He worked until 1920, and retired to die quietly at home in Monaco in 1935. Uneducated, but a patient educator and diligent writer, he was an innovator who remained deeply loyal to the regional and bourgeois roots of French cookery. He exhibited his culinary skills in the dining rooms of the finest hotels in Europe, including the Place Vendome in Paris and the Savoy and Carlton hotels in London.

When the Prince of Wales requested something light but delicious as late dinner after a night in the casino in Monte Carlo, Auguste Escoffier responded with *poularde Derby*, a stuffed chicken served with truffles cooked in champagne, alternating with slices of butter-fried *foie gras*, its sauce basted with the juices from the chicken and truffles. Another interesting anecdote regarding the chef's originality in making sauces tells of a special dinner for the Prince of Wales and Kaiser Wilhelm. Escoffier was asked to create a special dish to honor such an occasion. Struggling with an apparent loss of creativity until the night before the event, the chef finally noticed a sack of overripe mangos, from which he created a sauce that he personally came out from the kitchen to serve. As he placed the plate on the table, he looked at the Kaiser and with a wicked smile said, "*zum Teufel*"—to the devil. Then was born sauce diabla, today a favorite classic sauce. Escoffier's insistence on sauces derived from the cooking of main ingredients was revolutionary at the time and in keeping with his famous instruction: *faités simple*—keep it simple.

In fact, in his search for simplicity, Escoffier reduced the complexity of the work of Careme, the "cook of kings and king of cooks," and aimed at the perfect balance of a few superb ingredients. In *Le Livre des Menus* (1912), Escoffier makes the analogy of a great dinner as a symphony with contrasting movements that should be appropriate to the occasion, the guests, and the season. He was meticulous in his kitchen, yet wildly imaginative in the creation of exquisite dishes. In 1903, Escoffier published *Le Guide Culinaire*, an astounding collection of more than 5,000 classic cuisine recipes and garnishes. Throughout the book, Escoffier emphasizes technique, the importance of a complete understanding of basic cookery principles, and ingredients he considers to be essential to the creation of great dishes.

Escoffier's refinement of Careme's *grand cuisine* has been so radical as to credit him with the development of a new cuisine referred to as *cuisine classique*. His principles have been reinstated by successive generations, most emphatically by the *novelle cuisine* brigade. Francois Fusero, *chef de cuisine* at the Hotel Hermitage, Monte Carlo, regards Escoffier as his role model, and he schools his chefs in Escoffier's style: No detail is left to chance.

by many to be America's finest chef–owner and king of infusion, said in one of his books:[1]

> After love there is only cuisine! It's all about excellence, or at least working towards excellence. Early on in your approach to cooking—or in running a restaurant—you have to determine whether or not you are willing to commit fully and completely to the idea of the *pursuit of excellence*. I have always looked at it this way: if you strive for perfection—an all out assault on total perfection—at the very least you will hit a high level of excellence, and then you might be able to sleep at night. To accomplish something truly significant, excellence has to become a life plan.

Chef Trotter brings his knowledge and exposure together into a coherent view on what the modern fine dining experience could be. He says "I thought the blend of European refinement regarding the pleasures of the table, American ingenuity and energy in operating a small enterprise, Japanese minimalism and poetic elegance in effecting a sensibility, and a modern approach to incorporating health and dietary concerns would encompass a spectrum of elements through which I could express myself fully. Several years later, I find I am even more devoted than ever to this approach."[2]

Paul G. Van Landingham, offers these insights: The term *culinarian* has taken on new meaning as we enter the twenty-first century. In the past, to be successful in the field of culinary arts, one would only have to be a good cook. Today, to meet the challenges of the industry, it is essential for the modern chefs to be well educated and highly diversified. Keeping current with food trends is not enough. Chefs today must be "change agents." Chefs also must be familiar with the world of science and technology. Great changes will have to be made in training of the chef of the future.

Charlie Trotter, One of America's Finest Restaurant Chef–Owners and King of Infusion

Culinary Practices (Courtesy of Mike Zema)

In this new millennium, we are seeing culinary education setting the pace for dining exploration. As you prepare for a career in the hospitality industry, you will find it imperative that you develop a strong culinary foundation. Within the structure of this you will need to develop skills that include cooking, strong employability traits, people skills, menu development, nutrition, sanitation/safety, accounting, and computer skills.

Before you can become a successful chef, you have to be a good cook. To be a good cook, you have to understand the basic techniques and principles of cooking. The art of cooking has not changed in thousands of years. And although the concept of cooking has not changed, science and technology have allowed us to improve the methods of preparation. We still use fire to cook with; grilling, broiling, and simmering are still popular methods of cooking.

Let's look at each of the skill areas that are important to becoming a successful chef.

Cooking

You will need to learn all of the basic cooking methods in order to understand flavor profiles. As you look at recipes to cook, try to enhance the basic ingredient list to improve the flavor. As an example, I tell my students to always try to substitute a flavored liquid if water is called for in a recipe. It is also important to understand basic ingredient flavors so we can improve flavor. The idea behind

Personal Profile: Chef Paul Prudhomme

Very rarely do we find such a fine cook who takes pride and joy in what he does and does it so perfectly. Meet Paul Prudhomme, best known as Chef Paul. His widely known special-blend herbs, cookbooks, and recipes have made him one of the most loved cooks of all time. What started as "just assisting" his mom in the kitchen has become a career for Chef Paul.

Chef Paul was born and reared on a farm near Opelousas in Louisiana's Acadiana country. He was the youngest of 13 children. When the youngest girl left home, there was no one left to help his mom cook for the family. Paul, then only seven, would assist his mom, and this is when he learned about using only the freshest ingredients while cooking. He knew at this time that he wanted to make preparing food his life's work. After completing school, his curiosity about life and cultural customs led him to leave Louisiana while in his early twenties and travel across the United States to experience every culinary environment possible. He worked as a cook in all kinds of restaurants and learned a lot about ingredients and styles of cooking in different parts of the country. He recalls, "Sometimes, when I thought the food was too bland, I'd sneak in a few dried herbs and spices. When customers complimented the dishes from my station, I'd try to remember exactly what I'd used, but that was hard, so I began keeping little notes on good mixes in my pockets. Sometimes, though, I'd get caught and this didn't make me popular with the head chefs."

In July 1979, Chef Paul and his late wife, K. Hinrichs Prudhomme, opened K-Paul's Louisiana Kitchen in New Orleans. This French Quarter restaurant attracted world travelers and continues to excite diners today. His blackened redfish and blackened steak attracted people to his kitchen. K-Paul's catering division satisfies palates in New Orleans and around the country.

In response to all of this, Chef Paul decided to reveal his seasoning secrets. He created his own line of all-natural herbs and spices. Chef Paul Prudhomme's Magic Seasoning Blends are distributed all around the United States and in over 30 countries around the world. Other cooking blends offered are his own seasoned and smoked meats (andouille and tasso) and pizza and pasta, which are available through mail order.

When someone appears on TV as a guest over and over again, we know that person has "hit it big." Chef Paul has been featured often on the three major television networks' prime time programs and has made guest appearances on NBC's *Today Show,* ABC's *Good Morning America,* CBS's *This Morning* and *Larry King Live,* and many others. But what has made Chef Paul famous is his best-selling cookbooks. He has also made several cooking videos, one of which made it to the top of the Billboard charts for fifty-three consecutive weeks. He has been featured in several articles in magazines such as *Life, Time, Newsweek, Bon Appétit,* and *Metropolitan Home.* Chef Paul has made appearances and given lectures and seminars all over Europe and Asia. He serves as a consultant to Team USA of the American Culinary Federation and participates actively at conventions, seminars, and food trade shows as a guest lecturer and in support of his seasoning blends. As for cooking for the famous, Chef Paul has cooked for heads of state as well as members of the U.S. Congress.

He spends a lot of time at universities giving educational seminars to students in all walks of life as well as charity work and benefits. He was the first chef to participate in the Robert Mondavi *Great Chefs of America* television series. He was one of the 12 chefs chosen from around the world to participate in the celebration of Jerusalem's 3,000-year anniversary, at which each chef created a Kosher dish that was served at the King David's Feast.

His great cooking skills and sweet success made Chef Paul the first American-born chef to receive the coveted Merite Agricole of the French Republic. The American Culinary Federation has honored him as "Culinarian of the Year."

Paul Prudhomme is always eager to learn. He still has the drive to travel, experiment, and make personal appearances and develop new recipes. He still uses only the earth's finest harvests, as did his mother. He has propelled the distinctive cuisine of his native Louisiana into the international spotlight and continues to push the limits by creating exciting, new American and international dishes.

Sources: This section was compiled from Chef Paul Prudhomme's biography from the www.foodlocker.com/chefpaulprud.html *and* magicseasoning. com/meet.html *Web sites.*

Personal Profile: Richard Melman

Chairman of the Board and Founder, Lettuce Entertain You Enterprises, Inc.

Richard Melman is founder and chairman of Lettuce Entertain You Enterprises, Inc., a Chicago-based corporation that owns and licenses nearly 50 restaurants nationwide and in Japan.

The restaurant business has been Melman's life work, beginning with his early days in a family-owned restaurant, and later as a teenager working in fast-food eateries and a soda fountain, and selling restaurant supplies. After realizing that he wasn't cut out to be a college student and failing to convince his father that he should be made a partner in the family business, Melman met Jerry A. Orzoff, a man who immediately and unconditionally believed in Melman's ability to create and run restaurants. In 1971, the two opened R. J. Grunts, a hip burger joint that soon became one of the hottest restaurants in Chicago. Here, Melman and Orzoff presented food differently and with a sense of humor, creating the youthful and fun restaurant that was a forerunner in the trend toward dining out as entertainment that swept this country in the early 1970s.

Melman and Orzoff continued to develop restaurant concepts together until Orzoff's death in 1981. Through his relationship with Orzoff, Melman formulated a philosophy based on the importance of partners, of sharing responsibilities and profits with them, and of developing and growing together.[1]

To operate so many restaurants well, Lettuce has needed to hire, train, and develop people, and then keep them happy and focused on excellence. Melman's guiding philosophy is that he is not interested in being the biggest or the best known—only in being the best he can be. He places enormous value on the people who work for Lettuce Entertain You Enterprises and feels tremendous responsibility for their continued success. Today, he has forty working partners, most of whom came up through the organization, and has 5,000 people working for him. Melman's personal life revolves around his family.

Over the years, Melman has stayed close to the guests by using focus groups and frequent diner programs. The group's training programs are rated among the best in the business, and Melman's management style is clearly influenced by team sports. He says, "There are many similarities between running a restaurant and a team sport. However, it's not a good idea to have ten all-stars; everybody can't bat first. You need people with similar goals—people who want to win and play hard."[2]

Papagus

---

[1]Marilyn Alva, "Does He Still Have It?" *Restaurant Business*, 93, 4. March 1, 1994, pp. 104–111.
[2]Personal communication with Richard Melman, June 8, 2004.

---

back-to-basic cooking means to evaluate your recipe and look for flavor improvement with each item.

Employability traits are those skills that focus on attitude, passion, initiative, dedication, sense of urgency, and dependability. These traits are not always traits that can be taught, but a good chef can demonstrate them by example. Most of the employers that contact me with job opportunities for students consider these skills to be more important than technical skills. The belief is that if you have strong employability traits, your technical skills will be strong.

One of the most important things I've learned about our industry is that *you can't do it alone.* Each person in your operation has to work together in order for you to be successful. The most important ingredient in managing people is to *respect them.*

Many words can be used to describe a manager (coach, supervisor, boss, mentor), but whatever term is used, you have to be in the game in order to be effective. Managing a kitchen is like coaching a football team—everyone must work together in order to be effective. The difference between a football team and a kitchen is that chefs/managers cannot supervise from the sidelines; we have to be in the game. One of my favorite examples of excellent people management skills is that of the general manager of a hotel who had the warewashing team report directly to him. When asked why, he indicated that they are the people who know what is being thrown in the garbage, they are the people who know what the customers are not eating, and they are the people most responsible for the sanitation and safety within an operation. There are many components to managing people—training, evaluating, nurturing, delegating, and so on—but the most important is respect.

Check Your Knowledge

1. From what country did North America gain most of its culinary legacy?
2. Define infusion cuisine and give an example.

Classifications of Restaurants

There is no single definition of the various classifications of restaurants, perhaps because it is an evolving business. Most experts would agree, however, that there are two main categories: **independent restaurants** and **chain restaurants.** Other categories include designations as full-service restaurants, casual restaurants, and quick-service restaurants. Some restaurants may even fall into more than one category—for instance, a restaurant can be both ethnic and quick service, such as Taco Bell.

The National Restaurant Association's figures indicate that Americans are spending an increasing number of food dollars away from home in various food-service operations. Americans are eating out more than ever—up to five times a week—and on special occasions like birthdays, anniversaries, Mother's Day, and Valentine's Day. The most popular meal eaten away from home is lunch, which brings in approximately 50 percent of fast-food restaurant sales.

Individual restaurants (also called indies) are typically owned by one or more owners, who are usually involved in the day-to-day operation of the business. Even if the owners have more than one store, each functions independently. These restaurants are not affiliated with any national brand or name. They offer the owner independence, creativity, and flexibility, but are accompanied by risk. Chain restaurants, on the other hand, are a group of restaurants, each identical in market, concept, design, service, food, and name. Part of the marketing strategy of a chain restaurant is to remove uncertainty from the dining experience. The same menu, food quality, level of service, and atmosphere can be found in any one of the restaurants, regardless of location. These are usually owned by family teams or other entrepreneurs.

Full-Service Restaurants

Restaurant types included in this category are fine dining, casual, theme, celebrity, steak houses, and some ethnic restaurants.

Fine Dining

A **fine dining restaurant** is one where a good selection of menu items is offered; generally at least 15 or more different entrees cooked to order, with nearly all the food being made on the premises from scratch using raw or fresh ingredients. Full-service restaurants may be formal or casual and may be further categorized by price, decor/atmosphere, level of formality, and menu. Most fine dining restaurants may be cross-referenced into other categories, as mentioned previously. Many of these restaurants serve **haute cuisine** (pronounced *hote*), which is a French term meaning "elegant dining," or literally" high food." Many of the fine restaurants in the United States are based on French or Northern Italian cuisine, which, together with fine Chinese cuisine, are considered by many Western connoisseurs to be the finest in the world.

Most fine dining restaurants are independently owned and operated by an entrepreneur or a partnership. These restaurants are in almost every city. Today, with value-conscious guests expecting more for their money, it is becoming increasingly more difficult to make a profit in this segment of the business because of strong competition from other restaurants.

Anthony Bourdain, owner and chef of Les Halles Restaurant, sits at one of its tables. Bourdain is the best-selling author of Kitchen Confidential and A Cook's Tour.

Restaurant Operations: The Challenge of the Intangibles

William B. Martin

Cal Tech—Monterey Bay

Does this situation sound familiar? You are sitting at home (studying, of course) and a friend or relative suggests that you should go out for dinner. That sounds good to you, so you say, "Okay." That is the easy part.

Next comes the more difficult part. Where should you go? And so you ask, "Where do you want to go?" Your friend (or relative) responds, "I don't know. Where do you want to go?" And so it goes, back and forth until finally you arrive at a decision as to where you will go.

Some time later you arrive at your chosen destination. You experience whatever the restaurant has to offer. Afterward, consciously or unconsciously, you decide whether you will return to that particular restaurant.

As we can see from this common scenario, from a customer's point of view, dining out involves three critical questions: (1) To eat out or not? (2) Where to go? and (3) Whether to return?

Let's take a closer look at typical restaurant consumer responses to each of these questions and see what we can learn.

To Eat Out or Not?

Why do people choose to dine out? What are the reasons? Multiple consumer surveys over the years have consistently reflected the following reasons. The rank order of importance may vary from survey to survey, but the reasons, themselves, remain fairly constant.

The top ten reasons consumers tend to dine out in a full-service restaurant include to celebrate a special occasion, relax, avoid cooking, have a family night out, be waited on, enjoy the atmosphere, enjoy a familiar place, have menu choices, meet friends, and try foods not eaten at home.

The reasons consumers tend to dine out in a fast-food restaurant are surprisingly similar with two variations, and they are to eat inexpensively and to eat quickly. All the other reasons for dining at a full-service restaurant are also cited for dining at a fast-food restaurant.

Now, let's take a minute and look carefully at this list of reasons for dining out—whether fast food or full service. What *don't* you see on this list? What is missing?

What is missing is that the reason for dining out is "to eat." What does this tell us? What it tells us is that people choose to dine out for lots of reasons in addition to the need to eat. Eating comes along with the experience, but the choice to dine out in the first place is made for more complicated reasons—most of which are psychological and social reasons: to celebrate, to meet friends, to enjoy, to experience something new, to relax, and so forth.

How can we interpret this? What can we learn? First, we have to distinguish between tangibles and intangibles because in the restaurant business we deal with both, and both are very important to our success.

Tangibles are those things that can be seen, smelled, touched, poked, prodded, weighed, or otherwise physically inspected. Food, of course, fits into this category.

Intangibles, on the other hand, can't be so easily weighed and measured. They deal with human characteristics such as emotions, physiological states of mind, and sociological and cultural influences. They are indeed varied and complex—and often elusive, because we can't inspect them, touch them, or smell them to know whether they are "right" or "wrong." Now here's the punch line. *The reasons that people decide whether or not to dine out are predominately intangible in nature.* As you can see from the list, the reasons tend to be primarily psychologically and sociologically based.

Where to Go?

You have decided to go out. Now, how do you choose a restaurant? How it looks? Type of food? Location? The amount of money in your pocket (or purse)? Reputation? A recommendation? An advertisement?

The answer is probably any one, all, or a combination of the above. If you have been to a restaurant be-

continued

fore, you may choose to return for a combination of liking the food, the ambience, the value (what you get for your money), and the service. Choosing a restaurant for the first time usually involves a different set of criteria, which usually includes type of food, location, and perceived pricing.

While the reasons for choosing a particular restaurant are varied and complex, the type of *food* desired plays an important role, if not *the* role, in making a choice. Whether it is fast food or full service, we tend to choose a particular restaurant because we want to eat the style or type of food that the restaurant serves.

Whether to Return?

So you have made a choice of where to eat. Among other factors, the type of food that is served has attracted you. Now, what determines whether you will return—or not?

Think about the last time you went out to eat in a restaurant. Once there, what happened? Was it a positive experience? How was the food? The service? The ambience? Did you have a good time? Would you go back? Why or why not?

If you had a bad or disappointing food experience, most likely you would tend not to go back. No doubt about it, food is a critical factor. But, there is more—much more. Let's go back to those *intangibles* that have influenced your decision to dine out in the first place. The decision to return is greatly influenced by how well your intangible expectations were met. Did you have a good time? Did you enjoy yourself? Were you treated well? These are questions that go way beyond food. They address your *total dining experience*. Simply put, when that *total* experience is positive, you tend to return. When it is not, you don't.

In short, a restaurant is much more than about food. Restaurant success is about creating a total positive atmosphere and dining experience.

We have addressed three questions: To eat out or not? Where to go? And, Whether to return? In two of the three questions intangibles remain *the* critical decisive factor. That is why in the restaurant business managing the intangibles is just as important as managing the tangibles. As you can readily see, in the restaurant business it's the intangibles that can make or break you.

In recent years, fine dining has become more fun. At places like Osteria del Circo in New York, operators are looking for guests who want spectacular meals without the fuss. Marco Maccioni, son of Sirio Maccioni of the famed Le Cirque, says that the sons did not want to simply clone Le Cirque. For the menu, they sought inspiration from Mama's home cooking—pizza, pasta, and comfortable, braised dishes.

Tavern on the Green in New York's Central Park is America's highest sales volume restaurant.

One famous restaurant in New Orleans is the Court of the Two Sisters. It has the names of prisoners from various wars inscribed on the walls of the entrance way.

Many cities have independent fine dining restaurants that pursue those who are not content with wings and deep-fried cheese. Chefs are therefore making approachable, yet provocative food; each course is expertly prepared and may be served with wine. The top independent restaurant in terms of sales is the Tavern on the Green in New York City, which opened in 1976. Tavern on the Green is one of the most financially successful restaurants. It has sales of more than $37.6 million from 1,000 seats—including banquets with an average dinner check of $63.40—and serves 55,000 people a year. Now that's cooking![3]

Other restaurants of interest are operated by celebrity chefs like Wolfgang Puck, co-owner of Spago and Chinois in Los Angeles, and Alice Waters of Chez Panisse in Berkeley, California. Both have done much to inspire a new generation of talented chefs. Alice Waters has been a role model for many female chefs and has received numerous awards and published several cookbooks, including one for children.

The level of service in fine dining restaurants is generally high, with a hostess or host to greet and seat patrons. Captains and food servers advise guests of special items and assist with the description and selection of dishes during order taking. If there is no separate sommelier (wine waiter), the captain or food server may offer a description of the wine that will complement the meal and assist with the order taking. Some upscale or luxury full-service restaurants have table-side cooking and French service from a gueridon cart.[4] The decor of a full-service restaurant is generally compatible with the overall ambiance and theme that the restaurant is seeking to create. These elements of food, service, and decor create a memorable experience for the restaurant guest.

Theme Restaurants

Many **theme restaurants** are a combination of a sophisticated specialty and several other types of restaurants. They generally serve a limited menu but aim to wow the guest by the total experience. Of the many popular theme restaurants, two stand out. The first highlights the nostalgia of the 1950s, as done in

A Day in the Life of Karen Harris
Hostess, The Ritz-Carlton Members Beach Club, Sarasota, Florida

I arrive at The Ritz-Carlton Members Beach Club Grill at 8:30 A.M. and change into uniform to begin my shift. At 9:00 A.M. my shift starts, and I spend my first hour getting the restaurant ready for lunch service. This includes checking the menus to ensure that they are clean and current, preparing the server assignments on Open Table, and entering guest preferences and special occasion notes into the client database.

At 10:00 A.M. the staff of The Members Beach Club hold a daily lineup to communicate information with each other. The lineup focuses on the daily "Commitment to Quality," which covers a basic of the day, story of excellence, guest information, events, special occasions, and so on. It is my responsibility as a hostess to enter guest information from the "CTQ" into Open Table.

At 11:00 lunch service begins, and the fun really starts! Depending on the day at hand, I may, for example, give tours of the property, take photographs for guests on the "sunset terrace," send faxes for guests, or look up local information or maps for guests on the Internet. In many ways my position has created the opportunity to function as both an ambassador for the Members Beach club and concierge in addition to my position as a hostess. I love the ability to interact with the guests and members throughout the day. Lunch is served from 11:00 A.M. to 5:00 P.M. daily, and during this time I am mainly stationed at the hostess stand, where it is my job to give guests and members the initial "warm welcome" as they enter the restaurant. During this time I also answer the telephone, seat tables in the restaurant as well as on the terrace, and offer the "fond farewell" as guests leave the building. It is my goal throughout the day to ensure that the guests are enjoying their stay with us. I offer information regarding activities both in and outside of the hotel and offer to make future reservations.

At around 4:00 P.M. I will either be preparing the table assignments for dinner, which is served 5:00 to 10:00 P.M. Thursday through Saturday, or I will be checking the restaurant to ensure that everything is in order for the next day. My shift generally ends around 5:00 P.M. during the week following lunch service and when the last guests leave the restaurant, or it may end at 10:00 P.M. following dinner service and when the last guests leave the restaurant and are given that fond farewell.

the T-Bird and Corvette diners. These restaurants serve all-American food such as the perennial meatloaf in a fun atmosphere that is a throwback to the seemingly more carefree 1950s. The mostly female food servers appear in short polka-dot skirts with gym shoes and bobby socks.

The second popular theme restaurant is the dinner house category; among some of the better known national and regional chains are TGI Friday's, Houlihan's, and Bennigan's. These are casual American bistro-type restaurants that combine a lively atmosphere created in part by assorted bric-a-brac to decorate the various ledges and walls. These restaurants have remained popular over the past 20 years. In a prime location, they can do extremely well.

People are attracted to theme restaurants because they offer a total experience and a social meeting place. This is achieved through decoration and atmosphere and allows the restaurant to offer a limited menu that blends with the theme. Throughout the United States and the world, numerous theme restaurants stand out for one reason or another. Among them are decors featuring airplanes, railway, dining cars, rock and roll, 1960s nostalgia, and many others.

Outback Steakhouse. This Australian-themed restaurant is a success story based on a "no rules–just right" philosophy.

Celebrity Restaurants

Celebrity-owned restaurants have been growing in popularity. Some celebrities, such as Wolfgang Puck, came from a culinary background, whereas others, like Naomi Campbell, Claudia Schiffer, and Elle Macpherson (owners of the Fashion Café), did not. A number of sports celebrities also have restaurants. Among them are Michael Jordan, Dan Marino, Junior Seau, and Wayne Gretzky. Television and movie stars have also gotten into the act. Oprah Winfrey was part owner of The Eccentric in Chicago for a number of years. Dustin Hoffman and Henry Winkler are investors in Campanile, a popular Los Angeles restaurant. Dive, in Century City (Los Angeles), is owned by Steven Spielberg; House of Blues, by Denzel Washington. Musicians Kenny Rogers and Gloria Estefan are also restaurant owners.

Celebrity restaurants generally have an extra zing to them—a winning combination of design, atmosphere, food, and perhaps the thrill of an occasional visit by the owner(s). For example, Fashion Café in New York invites the guest to literally step through the lens of a camera into the glamorous world of fashion. Guests are seated in the Milan, Paris, or New York rooms, where they are entertained with daily fashion shows.

Spago, one of Wolfgang Puck's Fine Dining Restaurants, Known for Its Innovative Cuisine and Stunning Dining Rooms

Corporate Profile: Outback Steakhouse

The founders of Outback Steakhouse have proved that unconventional methods can lead to profitable results. Such methods include opening solely for dinner, sacrificing dining-room seats for back-of-the-house efficiency, limiting servers to three tables each, and handing 10 percent of cash flow to the restaurants' general managers.

March 1988 saw the opening of the first Outback Steakhouse. Outback's founders, Chris Sullivan, Robert Basham, and Senior Vice-President Tim Gannon, know plenty about the philosophy "No rules, just right" because they have lived it since day one. Even the timing of their venture to launch a casual steak place came when many pundits were pronouncing red meat consumption dead in America.

The chain went public and has since created a track record of strong earnings. It was evident that the three founders were piloting one of the country's hottest restaurant concepts. The trio found themselves with 230 restaurants, instead of the 5 they originally envisioned.

Robert Basham, cofounder, president, and chief operating officer at Outback Steakhouse, was given the Operator of the Year award at MUFSO '96 (Multi-Unit Foodservice Operators Conference). He has helped expand the chain, a pioneer in the steak house sector of the restaurant business, to more than 650 restaurants in 2004 with some of the highest sales per unit in the industry in spite of the fact that it serves only dinner.

Perhaps the strongest indication of what this company is about lies in its corporate structure, or lack thereof. Despite its rapid growth, the company has no public relations department, no human resources department, and no recruiting apparatus. In addition, the Outback Steakhouse headquarters is very different from that of a typical restaurant company. There is no lavish tower—only modest office space in an average suburban complex. Instead of settling into a conservative chair and browsing through a magazine-lined coffee table (as is the case in most reception areas), at Outback you must belly up to an actual bar, brass foot rail and all, to announce your arrival.

Also, Outback's dining experience—large, highly seasoned portions of food for moderate prices—is so in tune with today's dining experience that patrons in many of its restaurants experience hour-long dinner waits seven nights a week. The friendly service is notable, from the host who opens the door and greets guests, to the well-trained servers, who casually sit down next to patrons in the booths and explain the house specialties featured on the menu.

Using such tactics and their "No rules, just right" philosophy, they have accomplished two main goals: discipline and solid growth. Good profits and excellent marketing potentials show just how successful the business has become. Outback also owns and operates Bonefish Grill, Flemming's Prime Steakhouse, Caraba's Italian Grill, Roy's, and Cheeseburger in Paradise.

Steak Houses

The steak restaurant segment is quite buoyant in spite of nutritional concerns. The upscale steak dinner houses, like Flemming's of Chicago, Ruth's Chris, and Houston's, continue to attract the expense account and "occasion" diners. Some restaurants are adding additional value-priced items like chicken and fish to their menus to attract more guests. Steak restaurant operators admit that they are not expecting to see the same customer every week but hopefully every two or three weeks. The Chart House chain is careful to market their menu as including seafood and chicken, but steak is at the heart of the business, with most of its sales from red meat.

Outback Steakhouse, which is profiled in this chapter, owns and operates about 1,000 Outback restaurants and about 30 Flemming's Prime Steakhouse and Wine Bars. Metromedia Restaurant Group operates and franchises more than 800 casual dining restaurants, including Bonanza and Ponderosa family steakhouses and Steak and Ale eateries, plus the 300-unit Bennigan's Irish American grill and Tavern chain.[5] Other restaurants in this segment include Stewart Anderson's Black Angus, Golden Corral, Western Sizzlin', and Ryan's Family Steak Houses which all have sales of more than $300 million each. In fact, chains have the biggest share of the segment.

Casual Dining and Dinner House Restaurants

The types of restaurants that can be included in the casual dining restaurants category are as follows:

Midscale casual restaurants
Family restaurants
Ethnic restaurants

As implied, **casual dining** is relaxed and could include restaurants from several classifications: chain or independent, ethnic, or theme. Hard Rock Cafe, TGI Friday's, The Olive Garden, Houston's, Romano's Macaroni Grill, and Red Lobster are good examples of casual dining.

Houston's is a leader in the casual restaurant segment with about $5.5 million in average per unit sales in its 35 restaurants. The menu is limited to about 40 items and focuses on American cuisine, with a $16 average per-person ticket for lunch and a cost of $35 to $45 for dinner. While encouraging local individuality in its restaurants and maintaining exceptional executive and unit general manager stability, it succeeds with no franchising and virtually no advertising.

Over the past few years, the trend in **dinner house restaurants** has been toward more casual dining. This trend merely reflects the mode of society. Dinner

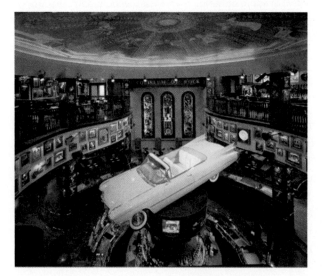

Hard Rock Cafe offers first-rate, moderately priced casual American Fare with, of course, a side of rock 'n' roll.

Guests Enjoying a Meal in a Family Restaurant

house restaurants have become fun places to let off steam. A variety of restaurant chains call themselves *dinner house restaurants.* Some of them could even fit into the theme category.

Many dinner house restaurants have a casual, eclectic decor that may promote a theme. Chart House, for example, is a steak and seafood chain that has a nautical theme.

Friday's is an American bistro dinner house with a full menu and a decor of bric-a-brac that contributes to the fun atmosphere. Friday's is a chain that has been in operation for nearly 40 years, so the concept has stood the test of time. Friday's is featured in Chapter 8, Restaurant Operations, as a corporation of excellence.

Family Restaurants

Family restaurants evolved from the coffee shop style of restaurant. In this segment, most restaurants are individually or family operated. Family restaurants are generally located in or with easy access to the suburbs. Most offer an informal setting with a simple menu and service designed to please all the family. Some of these restaurants offer alcoholic beverages, which mostly consist of beer, wine, and perhaps a cocktail special. Usually, there is a hostess/cashier standing near the entrance to greet and seat guests while food servers take the orders and bring the plated food from the kitchen. Some family restaurants have incorporated salad and dessert bars to offer more variety and increase the average check.

The lines separating the various restaurants and chains in the family segment are blurring as operators upscale their concepts. Flagstar Co.'s acquisition of Coco's and Carrow's family restaurant brands have created the high-end niche of family dining—somewhere between traditional coffee shops and the casual dining segment. The value-oriented operator in the family dining segment is Denny's, also owned by Flagstar. The more upscale family concepts include Perkins, Marie Callender's, and Cracker Barrel, all of which are sometimes referred to as the "relaxed" segment. These chains tend to have higher check averages than do traditional and value-oriented family chains, and compete not only with them, but also with moderately priced, casual-themed operators, such as Applebee's and TGI Friday's.

Applebee's is designed to be an attractive, friendly neighborhood restaurant featuring moderately priced high-quality food and beverages.

Karen Brennan, vice-president of marketing for the Coco's concept, says that people's use of restaurants is very different from five years ago. Consumers are thinking in terms of "meal solutions." The operators in this segment are seeking to capitalize on two trends affecting the industry as a whole: the tendency of families to dine out together more often and the quest among adults for higher-quality, more flavorful food offerings.

Ethnic Restaurants

The majority of **ethnic restaurants** are independently owned and operated. The owners and their families provide something different for the adventurous diner or a taste of home for those of the same ethnic background as the restaurant. The traditional ethnic restaurants sprang up to cater to the taste of the various immigrant groups—Italian, Chinese, and so on.

Perhaps the fastest growing segment of ethnic restaurants in the United States, popularity-wise, is Mexican. Mexican food has a heavy representation in the southwestern states, although, because of near-market saturation, the chains are spreading east. Taco Bell is the Mexican quick-service market leader with a 60 percent share. This *Fortune 500* company has achieved this incredible result with a value-pricing policy that has increased traffic in all units.

Guests Enjoying a Relaxing Evening at a Mexican Restaurant

There are more than 7,000 units with sales of about $5 billion. Other large Mexican food chains are Del Taco, Chi-Chi's, La Salsa, and El Torito. These Mexican food chains can offer a variety of items on a value menu. Our cities offer a great variety of ethnic restaurants, and their popularity is increasing. For example, in 1985 in San Diego, America's sixth largest city, there were no Thai restaurants. Today there are 22, in addition to new Afghan and Ethiopian restaurants.

Quick-Service (QSR) Fast-Food Restaurants

Quick-service restaurants consist of diverse operating facilities whose slogan is "quick food." The following types of operations are included under this category: hamburger, pizza, chicken, pancakes, sandwich shops, and delivery services.

The quick-service sector is the one that really drives the industry. Recently, the home-meal replacement and fast casual concepts have gained momentum.

Quick-service or fast-food restaurants offer limited menus featuring food such as hamburgers, fries, hot dogs, chicken (in all forms), tacos, burritos, gyros, teriyaki bowls, various finger foods, and other items for the convenience of people on the go. Customers order their food at a counter under a brightly lit menu featuring color photographs of food items. Customers are even encouraged to clear their own trays, which helps reduce costs. The following are examples of the different types of quick-service/fast-food restaurants:

Hamburger—McDonald's, Burger King, Wendy's
Pizza—Pizza Hut, Domino's, Godfather's
Steak—Bonanza, Ponderosa
Seafood—Long John Silver's
Chicken—KFC, Church's, Boston Market, Kenny Roger's, Popeye's
Sandwich—Subway
Mexican—Taco Bell, El Torito
Drive-Thru-In/Delivery—Domino's, Pizza Hut

A Pizza Hut waiter dishes out slices of steaming pan pizza.

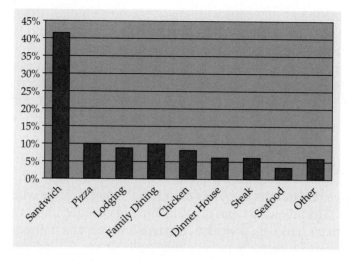

Figure 7–1 *Approximate Market Share of Restaurant Segments (Source: J. R. Schrock)*

Figure 7–1 shows the top 100 market shares by restaurant segment.

Quick-service restaurants have increased in popularity because of their location strategies. They are found in very convenient locations in every possible area. Their menus are limited, which makes it easy for customers to make quick decisions on what to eat. The world equates time with money these days, and most people do not want to spend time trying to look through long menus to make an eating decision. These restaurants deliver fast service and usually include self-service facilities, too. Such restaurants also use cheaper, processed ingredients, which allow them to have extremely low, competitive prices. Quick-service restaurants also require minimum use of both skilled and unskilled labor, which increases the profit margins.

In an attempt to raise flat sales figures, more quick-service restaurant (QSR) chains are using cobranding at stores and nontraditional locations, including highway plazas and shopping centers. It is hoped that the traffic-building combos will increase sales among the separate brands, such as Carl's Jr. and Green Burrito, as well as concepts like Triarc Co.'s Arby's, Zu Zu, P.T. Noodles, and T.J. Cinnamon brands. Many QSR chains are targeting international growth, mostly in the larger cities in a variety of countries.

Hamburgers

McDonald's is the giant of the entire quick-service/fast-food segment and serves nearly 50 million people daily.[6] This total is amazing because it is more than the next three megachains combined—Burger King, KFC, and Pizza Hut. McDonald's has individual product items other than the traditional burger—for example, chicken McNuggets and burritos as well as salads and fish, which all aim to broaden customer appeal. Customer appeal has also been broadened by the introduction of breakfast and by targeting not only kids but also seniors. Innovative menu introductions have helped stimulate an increase in per-store traffic.

Personal Profile: Ray Kroc

The world's greatest fast-food success story is undoubtedly McDonald's. Back in the 1950s, Ray Kroc was selling soda fountains. He received an order from Mr. McDonald for two soda fountains. Ray Kroc was so interested in finding out why the McDonald brothers' restaurant needed two machines (everyone else ordered one) that he went out to the restaurant. There he saw the now-familiar golden arches and the hamburger restaurant. Ray persuaded the McDonalds to let him franchise their operation. Billions of burgers later, the reason for the success may be summarized as follows: quality, speed, cleanliness, service, and value. This has been achieved by systemizing the production process and by staying close to the original concept—keeping a limited menu, advertising heavily, being innovative with new menu items, maintaining product quality, and being consistent.

Of all hospitality entrepreneurs, Ray Kroc has been the most successful financially. In 1982, he was senior chairman of the board of McDonald's, an organization intent on covering the earth with hamburgers. Among the remarkable things about Kroc is that it was not until age 52 that he embarked on the royal road to fame and fortune.

The original McDonald's concept was created by two brothers, Richard and Maurice, who had no interest in expanding. The McDonald brothers were content with their profitable yet singular restaurant in San Bernardino, California. However, the golden arches impressed Kroc, as did the cleanliness and simplicity of the operation.

Kroc's organizational skills, perseverance, and incredible aptitude for marketing were his genius. His talent also extended to selecting close associates who were equally dedicated and who added financial, analytical, and managerial skills to the enterprise. Kroc remained the spark plug and master merchandiser until he died in 1984, leaving a multimillion-dollar legacy.

Much of Kroc's $400 million has gone to employees, hospitals, and the Marshall Field Museum. It is distributed through Kroc's own foundation. Most importantly, Kroc developed several operational guidelines, including the concepts of "KISS"—Keep It Simple Stupid—and QSC&V—Quality, Service, Cleanliness, and Value. Kroc's "Never Be Idle a Moment" motto was also incorporated into the business.

Enterprises like McDonald's are not built without ample dedication and Ray Kroc certainly had a wealth of dedication. Today, an average McDonald's franchise can net more than $1 million annually thanks to Kroc's ingenious marketing strategies. In fact, McDonald's Corporation has become so affluent that it was named *Entrepreneur* magazine's number one franchise.

In recent years, because traditional markets have become saturated, McDonald's has adopted a strategy of expanding overseas. It is embarking on a rapid expansion in the world's most populous nation, China, with more than 12,000 restaurants nationwide. The reason for this expansion in China is a rapidly developing middle class with a growing appetite for Western culture and food. McDonald's is now in 119 countries and has a potential audience of 3.2 billion people. Of the company's roughly 32,000 restaurants, some 8,600 are outside the United States, serving 47 million people each day.

It is interesting to note that about 50 percent of total profits come from outside of the United States. More than two-thirds of new restaurants added by McDonald's are outside of the United States. McDonald's also seeks out nontraditional locations in the U.S. market, such as on military bases or smaller-sized units in the high-rent districts or gas stations.

McDonald's is taking another step toward being the most convenient foodservice operation in the world by striking deals with gasoline companies Chevron, U.S. Petroleum Star Enterprise, and Mobil Oil Corporation to codevelop sites.

It is very difficult to obtain a McDonald's franchise in the United States because they have virtually saturated the primary markets. It often costs between $1 million and $2 million to open a major brand fast-food restaurant. Franchises for lesser-known chains are available for less money (about $35,000 and for the 4 percent of sales royalty fee and 4 percent for advertising, but you need about $125,000 liquid and $400,000 net worth for an upscale, quick-service outlet, not counting land costs).

Each of the major hamburger restaurant chains has a unique positioning strategy to attract their target markets. Burger King hamburgers are flame broiled, and Wendy's uses fresh patties. Some smaller regional chains are succeeding in gaining market share from the big-three burger chains because they provide an excellent burger at a reasonable price. In-N-Out Burger, Sonic, and Rally's are good examples of this.

Pizza

The pizza segment continues to grow. By some estimates it is now a $21 billion market, with much of the growth fueled by the convenience of delivery. There are several chains: Pizza Hut, Domino's, Godfather's, Papa John's, and Little Caesar's. Pizza Hut, with 12,000 units and system-wide sales of $2,200 million,[7] has broken into the delivery part of the business over which, until recently, Domino's had a virtual monopoly. Pizza Hut has now developed system-wide delivery units that also offer two pizzas at a reduced price.

In response to the success of Pizza Hut's Stuffed Crust Pizza, Domino's highlights their Ultimate Deep Dish Pizza and their new Pesto Crust Pizza. They are currently stressing the quality of their advertising. With twelve toppings to choose from, people can have fun designing their own pizza.

Chicken

Chicken has always been popular and is likely to remain so because it is relatively cheap to produce and readily available and adaptable to a variety of preparations. It also is perceived as a healthier alternative to burgers.

Kentucky Fried Chicken (KFC), with a worldwide total of more than 12,000 units and annual sales of more than $120 billion, dominates the chicken segment. Even though KFC is a market leader, the company continues to explore new ways to get its products to consumers. More units now offer home deliv-

A KFC Restaurant

ery, and in many cities KFC is teaming up with sister restaurant Taco Bell, selling products from both chains in one convenient location.

Church's Chicken, with 1,500 units, is the second largest chicken chain. It offers a simple formula consisting of a value menu featuring Southern-style chicken, spicy chicken wings, okra, corn on the cob, coleslaw, biscuits, and other items. Church's focused on becoming a low-cost provider and the fastest to market. To give customers the value they expect day in and day out, it is necessary to have unit economies in order. System-wide, Church's now registers 34 percent in food costs and 25.9 percent labor costs.

Popeye's is another large chain in the chicken segment, with 1,818 units in 27 international markets. It is owned by AFC, the same parent company as Church's. Popeye's is a New Orleans–inspired "spicy chicken" chain operating more than 300 restaurants in Texas and Louisiana that is expanding into 11 markets around the country. The chain hopes to increase average-unit sales to $1 million.

There are a number of up-and-coming regional chains, such as El Pollo Loco, of Irvine, California. It focuses on a marinated, flame-broiled chicken that is a unique, high-quality product. Kenny Rogers and Cluckers are also expanding rotisserie chains.

Sandwiches

Indicative of America's obsession with the quick and convenient, sandwiches have achieved star status. Recently, menu debuts in the sandwich segment have outpaced all others. Classics, like melts and club sandwiches, have returned with a vengeance—but now there are also wraps and panini.

A sandwich restaurant is a popular way for a young entrepreneur to enter the restaurant business. The leader in this segment is Subway, which operates more than 24,054 units in 84 countries.[8] Cofounder Fred Deluca parlayed an initial investment of $1,000 into one of the largest and fastest-growing chains in the world. Franchise fees are $12,500, with a second store fee of $2,500.

The Subway strategy is to invest half of the chain's advertising dollars in national advertising. Franchise owners pay 2.5 percent of sales to the marketing fund. As with other chains, Subway is attempting to widen its core 18- to 34-year-old customer base by adding Kids Packs and Value 4-inch Round sandwiches aimed at teens and women. Sandwich restaurants stress the health value of their restaurants.

Bakery Café

The bakery café sector is headed up by Panera Bread, a 795-unit chain in 35 states, with the mission of "a loaf in every arm" and the goal of making specialty bread broadly available to consumers across America. Panera focuses on the art and craft of breadmaking with made-to-order sandwiches, tossed-to-order salads, and soup served in bread bowls.[9]

Check Your Knowledge

1. Describe the different types of restaurants, and give examples of each. Highlight some of the characteristics that make up the specific restaurant types.

Trends in the Restaurant Business

- Demographics: As the baby boomers move into middle age, a startling statistic will emerge in the early 2000s. Thirty-five- to 54-year-olds (the age group with the highest income) will make up almost one-third of the American population, as the 45- to 54-year-old bracket increases by an unprecedented 46 percent from 1990. Simply put, the largest demographic group will have the most money.
- Branding: Restaurant operators are using the power of branding, both in terms of brand name recognition from a franchising viewpoint and in the products utilized.
- Alternative outlets: Increased competition from convenience "c-stores" and home meal replacement outlets.
- Globalization: Continued transnational development.
- Continued diversification within the various dining segments.
- More twin and multiple locations.
- More points of service (e.g., Taco Bell at gas stations).
- More hypertheme restaurants.
- Chains vs. independents.

Food Trends and Practices

As the level of professionalism rises for the chef of the twenty-first century, chefs will need a strong culinary foundation with a structure that includes multiculture cooking skills and strong employability traits, such as passion, dependability, cooperation, and initiative. Additional management skills include strong supervisory training, sense of urgency, accounting, sanitation/safety, nutritional awareness, and marketing/merchandising.

The term *back-to-basic cooking* has been redefined to mean taking classical cooking methods and infusing modern technology and science to create healthy and flavorful dishes. Some examples of this include:

- Thickening soups and sauces by processing and using the food item's natural starches instead of traditional thickening methods
- Redefining the basic mother sauces to omit the béchamel and egg-based sauces and add or replace with coulis, salsas, or chutneys
- Pursuing more cultural culinary infusion to develop bold and aggressive flavors
- Experimenting with sweet and hot flavors
- Taking advantage of the shrinking globe and disappearing of national borders to bring new ideas and flavors to restaurants
- Evaluating recipes and substituting ingredients for better flavor; that is, flavored liquid instead of water, infused oils and vinegars instead of nonflavored oils and vinegars
- Substituting herbs and spices for salt
- Returning to one-pot cooking to capture flavors

This is truly an exciting time to enter the hospitality industry and particularly the culinary arts. Today, being a chef is considered a real profession that offers a variety of opportunities in every segment of the hospitality industry and anywhere in the world.

CAREER INFORMATION

Opening your own restaurant as an entrepreneur can be an exciting prospect. For the winners, the restaurant business is fun—lots of people coming and going. The business is always challenging because other restaurant owners are striving to attract your guests—but with the right location, menu, atmosphere, and management, the winners continue to attract the market. The successful restaurant offers a high return on investment. One restaurant, then two, perhaps a small chain. Retire wealthy. It happens.[1]

In addition to ownership in the restaurant business there are a number of career paths in the supply sector of the industry. Someone has to consult, plan, design, construct, and outfit each restaurant. The larger chain restaurants all have marketing, human resources, financial, and accounting positions.

For those interested in a career in the restaurant business, it is a good idea to gain experience in all facets of restaurant operations. As one famous restauranteur once said to me, "John, first you must know how to steal the chicken before you can stop someone else stealing the chicken." Culinary experience is a must to protect yourself in case your chef/cook walks out. Obviously, front-of-the-house experience is a must and a good way of financing college.

[1] John R. Walker and Donald E. Lundberg. *The Restaurant from Concept To Operation,* 4th ed., John Wiley and Sons, New York, 2005, p. 5.

SUMMARY

1. Restaurants offer the possibility of excellent food and social interaction. In general, restaurants strive to surpass an operating philosophy that includes quality food, good value, and gracious service.
2. To succeed, a restaurant needs the right location, food, atmosphere, and service to attract a substantial market. The concept of a restaurant has to fit the market it is trying to attract.
3. The location of a restaurant has to match factors such as convenience, neighborhood, parking, visibility, and demographics. Typical types of locations are downtown, suburban, shopping mall, cluster, or standalones.
4. The menu and pricing of a restaurant must match the market it wants to attract, the capabilities of the cooks, and the existing kitchen equipment.
5. The main categories of restaurants are fine dining and specialty, independent, and chain. Further distinctions can be made: quick-service, ethnic, dinner house, occasion, and casual. In general, most restaurants fall into more than one category.

KEY WORDS AND CONCEPTS

Actual market share
Casual dining
Celebrity-owned restaurant
Chain restaurant
Culinary arts

Dinner house restaurant
Ethnic restaurant
Family restaurant
Fine dining restaurant
Haute cuisine

Independent restaurant
Infusion
Mother sauces
Nouvelle cuisine
Purée

Quick-service restaurant
Roux
Theme restaurant

REVIEW QUESTIONS

1. Describe the evolution of American Culinary Arts.
2. What are the five mother sauces?
3. Name some of America's finest chefs.
4. How are restaurants classified?
5. Explain why there is no single definition of the various classifications of restaurants; give examples.

INTERNET EXERCISES

1. Organization: **Charlie Trotter**
   Web site: **charlietrotters.com/restaurant**
   Summary: Charlie Trotter is regarded as one of the finest chefs in the world. Chef Trotter's restaurant has received numerous awards, yet chef Trotter is always seeking new opportunities.
   (a) What are Chef Trotter's recent activities?
2. Organization: **Olive Garden Restaurant**
   Web site: **www.olivegarden.com/**
   Summary: The Olive Garden is a multiunit chain that primarily serves exquisite Italian food. They are currently operated by Darden Restaurants, Inc. and have about 534 restaurants in the United States and Canada.

Olive Garden strives to create a feeling of warmth and caring for every guest, which extends beyond the walls of the restaurants into the community. Olive Garden participates in civic community service, such as delivering meals during times of crisis, sponsoring charity events, and hosting school tours of the restaurants.
   (a) What kind of restaurant does the name Olive Garden represent?
   (b) What is the Garden Fare? How is its menu different from the design and layout of the lunch menu?

APPLY YOUR KNOWLEDGE

In groups, evaluate a restaurant and write out a list of weaknesses. Use the headings outlined in the restaurant chapters. Then, for each of the weaknesses, decide on what actions you would take to exceed guest expectations.

SUGGESTED ACTIVITIES

1. Identify a restaurant in your neighborhood and identify its catchment area. How many potential guests live and work in the catchment area?
2. Search the Web for examples of four great restaurant web sites. Compare them and share your findings in class.

ENDNOTES

1. Charlie Trotter, *Charlie Trotter.* Berkeley, CA: Ten Speed Press, 1994, p. 11.
2. Ibid., p. 12.
3. **http://www.foodservice411.ljmrimag/ archives/2005/04a/top100-list.asp**. August 14, 2005.
4. A wheelable cart that is used to add flair to tableside service. It is also used for flambé dishes.
5. **www.metromedia.com**. August 30, 2005.
6. **www.mcdonalds.com**. August 30, 2005.
7. **www.hoovers.com**. August 28, 2005.
8. **www.subway.com**. September 1, 2005.
9. **www.Panerabread.com**. September 1, 2005.

WEB RESOURCES

Steak and Shake
www.steaknshake.com

Lettuce Entertain You
www.leye.com

National Restaurant Association
www.restaurant.org

Les Halles Restaurant
www.leshalles.net

Osteria del Circo
www.osteriadelcirco.com

Le Cirque
www.lecirque.com

Tavern on the Green
web.tavernonthegreen.com

Spago
http://www.wolfgangpuck.com

Chez Pannise
www.chezpanisse.com

Prairie Grass Café
www.prairiegrasscafe.com

TGI Friday's
www.tgifridays.com

Outback Steakhouse
www.outbacksteakhouse.com

Morton's of Chicago
www.mortons.com

Ruth's Chris
www.ruthschris.com

Chart House
www.chart-house.com

Houston's
www.houstons.com

Ponderosa/Bonanza
www.ponderosasteakhouses.com

Hard Rock Cafe
www.hardrock.com

Olive Garden
www.olivegarden.com

Romanos Macoroni Grill
www.macaronigrill.com

Red Lobster
www.redlobster.com

Friday's
www.fridays.com

Applebee's
www.applebees.com

KFC
www.kfc.com

Pizza Hut
www.pizzahut.com

Restaurant Operations

After reading and studying this chapter, you should be able to:

- Describe restaurant operations for the front of the house.
- Explain how restaurants forecast their business.
- Outline back of the house operations.
- Identify key elements of an income statement.
- Name the key restaurant operating ratios.
- Outline the functional areas and tasks of a restaurant manager's job.

Front of the House

Restaurant operations are generally divided between what is commonly called **front of the house** and **back of the house.** The front of the house includes anyone with guest contact from the hostess to the busperson. The sample organization chart in Figure 8–1 shows the differences between the front and back of the house areas.

The restaurant is run by the general manager, or restaurant manager. Depending on the size and sales volume of the restaurant, there may be more managers with special responsibilities, such as kitchen manager, bar manager, and dining room manager. These managers are usually cross-trained in order to relieve each other.

In the front of the house, restaurant operation begins with creating and maintaining what is called **curbside appeal,** or keeping the restaurant looking attractive and welcoming. Ray Kroc of McDonald's once spent a couple of hours in a good suit with one of his restaurant managers cleaning up the parking lot of one of his restaurants. Word soon got around to the other stores that management begins in the parking lot and ends in the bathrooms. Most restaurant chains have checklists that each manager uses. In the front of the house, the parking lot, including the flower gardens, need to be maintained in good order. As guests approach the restaurant, hostesses may hold the door open and welcome them to the restaurant. At the 15th Street Fisheries restaurant in Ft. Lauderdale, hostesses welcome the guests by assuring them that "we're glad you're here!"

Once inside, the **hostess** or, as T.G.I. Friday's calls them, "smiling people greeters" (SPGs), greets guests appropriately, and, if seating is available, escorts them to a table. If there is a wait, the hostess will take the guests' names and ask for their table preference.

Aside from greeting the guests, one critical function of the hostess is to rotate arriving guests among the sections or stations. This ensures an even and timely

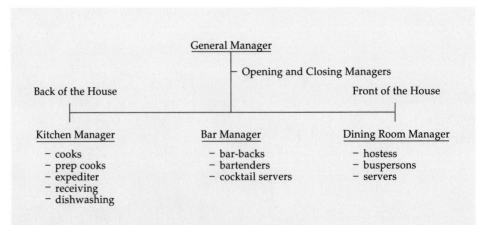

Figure 8–1 *Restaurant Organization Chart*

A manager visits with guests at a Cheesecake Factory.

distribution of guests—otherwise one section may get overloaded. Guests are sometimes asked to wait a few minutes even if tables are available. This is done to help spread the kitchen's workload.

The hostesses maintain a book, or chart, showing the sections and tables so they know which tables are occupied. Hostesses escort guests to the tables, present menus, and may explain special sales promotions. Some may also remove excess covers from the table.

In some restaurants, servers are allocated a certain number of tables, which may vary depending on the size of the tables and the volume of the restaurant. Normally, five is the maximum. In other restaurants, servers rotate within their section to cover three or four tables.

The server introduces himself or herself, offers a variety of beverages and/or specials, or invites guests to select from the menu. This is known as suggestive selling. The server then takes the entree orders. Often, when taking orders, the server begins at a designated point and takes the orders clockwise from that point. In this way, the server will automatically know which person is having a particular dish. When the entrees are ready, the server brings them to the table. He or she checks a few minutes later to see if everything is to the guests' liking and perhaps asks if they would like another beverage. Good servers are also encouraged, when possible, to prebus tables.

Busers and servers may clear the entree plates, while servers suggestively sell desserts by describing, recommending, or showing the desserts. Coffee and after-dinner cocktails are also offered. Suggestions for steps to take in table service include the following:

- Greet the guests.
- Introduce and suggestively sell beverages.
- Suggest appetizers.
- Take orders.
- Check to see that everything is to the guests' liking within two bites of the entrees.
- Ask if the guests would like another drink.
- Bring out dessert tray and suggest after-dinner drinks and coffee.

In addition to the seven steps of the table service, servers are expected to be NCO—neat, clean, and organized—and to help ensure that hot food is served hot, and cold food is served cold.

For example, during the lunch hour, servers may be scheduled to start at 11:00 A.M. The opening group of two or three people is joined by the closing group of the same number at around 11:45 P.M. If the restaurant is quiet, servers may be phased out early. When the closing group comes in, there is a quick shift meeting, or "alley rally." This provides an opportunity to review recent sales figures, discuss any promotions, and acknowledge any items that are "86'ed"—the restaurant term for a menu item that is not available. Recognition is also given to the servers during the meetings, serving as morale boosters.

Restaurant Forecasting

Most businesses, including restaurants, operate by formulating a budget that projects sales and costs for a year on a weekly and monthly basis. Financial viability is predicted on sales, and sales budgets are forecasts of expected business.

Forecasting restaurant sales has two components: guest counts or covers and the average guest check. **Guest counts** or **covers** are the number of guests patronizing the restaurant over a given time period—a week, month, or year. To forecast the number of guests for a year, the year is divided into 13 periods: twelve of 28-day and one 29-day accounting period. This ensures that accounting procedures are able to compare equal periods rather than months of unequal days. The accounting periods are then broken down into four 7-day weeks. Restaurant forecasting is done by taking into consideration meal period, day of week, special holidays, and previous forecast materializations.

In terms of number of guests, Mondays usually are quiet; business gradually builds to Friday, which is often the busiest day. Friday, Saturday, and Sunday frequently provide up to 50 percent of revenue. This, however, can vary according to type of restaurant and its location.

The **average guest check** is calculated by dividing total sales by the number of guests. Most restaurants keep such figures for each meal. The number of guests forecast for each day is multiplied by the amount of the average food and beverage check for each meal to calculate the total forecast sales. Each day, actual totals are compared with the forecasts. Four weekly forecasts are combined to form one accounting period; the thirteen accounting periods, when totaled, become the annual total.

Restaurant forecasting is used not only to calculate sales projections but also for predicting staffing levels and labor cost percentages. Much depends on the accuracy of forecasting. Once sales figures are determined, all expenditures, fixed and variable, have to be deducted to calculate profit or loss.[1]

Service

More than ever, what American diners really want when they eat out is good service. Unfortunately, all too often, that is not on the menu. With increased competition, however, bad service will not be tolerated in American restaurants.

Focus on Restaurant Operations

Service and the Restaurant Industry

Linda Hoops

At the end of the day, for most restaurants that serve practically the same menu items, service is all that matters. Service is the only competitive advantage. Those who are smart enough to realize that their future success lies in providing consistent good customer service along with good food will progress and remain in business. I am reminded of what a former colleague in academia once told me. She takes her elderly mother every Saturday to breakfast to the same restaurant, even though there are several other breakfast diners around. She is served burned toast and bacon every time, but she is greeted with a smile and called by her first name. She admits that at least there are no surprises; the food is consistently bad, but she does not mind because the wait staff makes her feel welcome when they mention her name and give her the smile. Although we all crave food that tastes good, sometimes we excuse mediocre food if the service is exceptional. But we would rather have both.

As competition accelerates, market share becomes tougher and sometimes service is compromised for the short-term bottom line in order to stay in business. Today, customers have the upper hand; they know they have choices and they are prepared to take their business elsewhere if they are not satisfied. As much as I travel as a consultant, I cannot get enough good customer service and neither should you. I am passionate about good service and keep hoping to be surprised by excellent service every time I dine out. When I get good service anywhere, I become a repeat customer and I rave about the service to everyone I know. By the same token, when I get bad service, not only do I not go back, but I tell everyone about the service and treatment I received.

Consistent customer service is about more than the dollar earned; it is about satisfying customer needs and exceeding their expectations. When you let waitstaff know how long you waited to have your order taken or for the food to be served, they are often horrified and try to make excuses. Worse yet, they may ignore you and walk away. Perhaps the waitstaff is having a bad day. You are not really interested in their problems; you came because you wanted to have a good meal along with good service. Any member of an establishment with a bad attitude who cannot be reasoned with will have a very limited life in any restaurant that wants to grow and be profitable.

The key to customer service is identifying customer expectations and then meeting, and even exceeding, their expectations. These are strong points that need to be reinforced in every employee of the restaurant. Customer service is a commitment that has to start from the top and work its way through the whole organization team. Everyone who works in the restaurant needs to know what the establishment wants to achieve and the level of service expected from everyone. A restaurant can have great menus and quality food, but it can be let down by one member of the waitstaff whose attitude belies customer service.

I have a strong belief in the value of customer service and the important role it can play in having a stable business, happier employees, and satisfied customers. I impressed on my former students my passion for customer service and, in jest, I warned them that if I ever walk into their restaurants and my expectations are not met and I walk away unsatisfied, I would recall their grades.

Just as American cuisine came of age in the 1970s and 1980s, service is showing signs of maturing in the twenty-first century.

A new American service has emerged. A less formal—yet professional—approach is preferred by today's restaurant guests. The restaurants' commitment to service is evidenced by the fact that most have increased training for new employees. For example, at Splendido in San Francisco's Embarcadero, the amount

A server as a salesperson, explaining a dish on the menu to a guest.

of time new servers spend in training has increased from 40 to 100 hours. Servers are not merely order takers; they are the salespeople of the restaurant. A server who is undereducated about the menu can seriously hurt business. One would not be likely to buy a car from a salesperson who knew nothing about the car; likewise, guests feel uneasy ordering from an unknowledgeable waiter.

Restaurants in the United States and Canada and many other parts of the world all use American service, in which the food is prepared and appealingly placed onto plates in the kitchen, carried into the dining room, and served to guests. This method of service is used more than Russian service because it is quicker and guests receive the food hot as presented by the chef.

At Posterio, servers are invited to attend a one and a half-hour wine class in the restaurant; about three-quarters of the 40-member staff routinely benefit from this additional training. The best employees are also rewarded with monthly prizes and with semi-annual and annual prizes, which range from $100 cash, a limousine ride, dinner at Posterio, or a night's lodging at the Prescott Hotel to a week in Hawaii. Servers at other San Francisco restaurants role play the various elements of service such as greeting and seating guests, suggestive selling, correct methods of service, and guest relations to ensure a pos-

With American service, the food is plated in the kitchen and quickly brought to the table by servers.

itive dining experience. A good food server in a top restaurant in many cities can earn $50,000 or more a year.

Good servers quickly learn to gauge the guests' satisfaction levels and to be sensitive to guests' needs; for example, they check to ensure guests have everything they need as their entree is placed before them. Even better, they anticipate guests' needs. For example, if the guest had used the entree knife to eat the appetizer, then a clean one should automatically be placed to the guest's right side. In other words, the guest should not receive the entree and then realize he or she needs another knife.

Another example of good service is when the server does not have to ask everyone at the table who is eating what. The server should either remember or do a seating plan so that the correct dishes are automatically placed in front of guests.

Danny Meyer, owner of New York City's celebrated Union Square Cafe and recipient of both the Restaurant of the Year and Outstanding Service Awards from the James Beard Foundation, gives each of the restaurant's 95 employees—from busperson to chef—a $600 annual allowance ($50 each a month) to eat in the restaurant and critique the experience.[2]

At the critically acclaimed Inn at Little Washington in Washington, Virginia, servers are required to gauge the mood of every table and jot a number (one to ten) and sometimes a description ("elated, grumpy, or edgy") on each ticket. Anything below a seven requires a diagnosis. Servers and kitchen staff work together to try to elevate the number to at least a nine by the time dessert is ordered.

Suggestive Selling

Suggestive selling can be a potent weapon in the effort to increase food and beverage sales. Many restaurateurs cannot think of a better, more effective, and easier way to boost profit margins. Servers report that most guests are not offended or uncomfortable with suggestive selling techniques. In fact, customers may feel special that the server is in tune with their needs and desires. It may be that the server suggests something to the guest that he or she has never considered before. The object here is to turn servers into sellers. Guests will almost certainly be receptive to suggestions from competent servers.

On a hot day, for example, servers can suggest frozen margaritas or daiquiris before going on to describe the drink specials. Likewise, servers who suggest a bottle of Mondavi fumé blanc to complement a fish dish or a Mondavi pinot noir or cabernet sauvignon to go with red meat are likely to increase their restaurant's beverage sales.

Upselling takes place when a guest orders a "well" drink like a vodka and tonic. In this case, the server asks if the guests would like a Stoli and tonic. (Stoli is short for Stolichnaya, a popular brand of vodka.)

An example of the benefits of upselling is a server who describes a menu item like this: "Our special tonight is a slow-roasted aged prime Angus beef ribroast, served with roasted potatoes and a medley of fresh vegetables." Now, if this entrée cost $10 more than another beef dish on the menu, and the same thing happens with suggestions for guests to select from fish, seafood and other meat or vegetarian items, the table's check will increase by $50 to $75. We know that a server receives about 15 percent in tips and does four or five tables that can turn twice each per night. You do the math: 15% of $50 = $7.50, and say the server does four tables = $4 \times \$7.50 \times 2 =$ an additional $60 in tips.

Check Your Knowledge

1. What is considered the front of the house?
2. Define curbside appeal.
3. Suggest methods for remembering who ordered what on a table for a large party.
4. Name some of the responsibilities and duties of an assistant restaurant manager.
5. Briefly explain American service.

Front-of-the-House Restaurant Systems

Point-of-Sale Systems

Point-of-sale (POS) systems are very common in restaurants and other foodservice settings, such as a stadium, theme park, airport, or cruise ship. These systems are used by hotel properties that have food and beverage and retail outlets. They are used to track food and beverage charges and other retail charges that may occur at a hotel or restaurant. A point-of-sale system is made up of a number of POS terminals that interface with a remote central processing unit. A POS terminal may be used as an electronic cash register, too.

MICROS, a leading software, hardware, and enterprise systems provider, offers Restaurant 3000, a modular suite of applications that encompasses front-of-the-house, back-of-the-house, and enterprise systems. The popular 3700 POS is a Windows-based touch-screen system where client terminals are networked to a central POS server. Transactions are rung at the terminal and posted into the database for later analysis and reporting. The 3700 POS will support a network of kitchen printers so that orders can be presented to line cooks and chefs for food preparation. This POS system also supports use of a wireless personal digital assistant as an order-taking device so that servers can take orders directly from the guest tableside. Mobile handheld devices can greatly speed the processing of orders to the kitchen and ultimately increase revenues due to faster table turns.

Point-of-Sale System

Kitchen Display Systems

Kitchen display systems further enhance the processing of orders to and in the kitchen. Printers in the kitchen are replaced with video monitors and present orders to kitchen associates along with information on how long orders are taking to be prepared. Orders change color or flash on the monitor, which alerts kitchen associates to orders that are taking too long. Kitchen monitors are widely used in quick-service restaurants but are also gaining momentum in table service restaurants. Kitchen video systems also post order preparation times to a central data base for later reporting and analysis by management to determine how the kitchen is performing.

Guest Services Solutions

Guest services solutions are applications that are designed to help a restaurateur develop a dining relationship with guests. Applications include a frequent-diner management program, delivery management with caller ID interface, and guest accounts receivable to manage home accounts and gift certificate management. All these applications are accessed through the POS system and give restaurateurs the opportunity to offer their guests convenience, while allowing the restaurateurs to track who their best customers are. Guest activity is posted into the central database and management can develop targeted marketing programs based on this information.

Wireless POS System

Peter Perdikakis is the owner of two Skyline fast-casual restaurants in Cincinnati. The restaurants are unusual in that the kitchen is open and visible to diners. Servers used to simply yell the orders across the steam table. Peter says, "You eat off china and have silverware, but it's very fast—typically you get your order about two minutes after it's ordered. Other POS systems slowed this process down, because the servers had to go over to a terminal and write down the order," which is why Peter became interested in wireless. When he wanted to expand his operations, he selected a Pocket POS system from PixelPoint, consisting of two primary fixed terminals (one at a drive-through window and one at the check-out station), three handheld units for use on the dining floor, and another fixed unit for the back office.

The PixelPoint wireless POS system allows the servers to use a handheld PDA, which operates on the Windows CE platform, to send orders to the kitchen. Given that wireless POS systems speed up orders, their use in restaurants is likely to be on the increase.

Check Your Knowledge

1. What do front-of-the-house systems entail?
2. Briefly define guest services solutions.

Back-of-the-House Restaurant Systems

Back-of-the-house systems are also known as product management systems and include inventory control and food costing, labor management, and financial reporting features. SoftCafe develops software for restaurants and foodservice operations allowing them to create menus on personal computers. SoftCafe MenuPro creates professional menus at a fraction of the cost of print shop menus, with over 1,000 predesigned menu styles, hundreds of food illustrations, menu backgrounds, over 50 font types, and a culinary spell-checker.[3] Beverage inventory systems are discussed in Chapter 10.

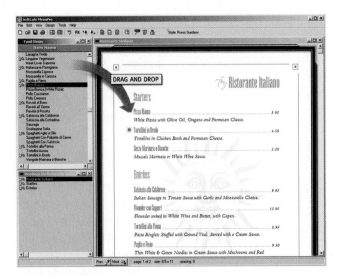

One of the Menu-Creation Programs Available from MenuPro

Labor Management

Most front-of-the-house systems have the ability to track employee working time. A back-of-the-house labor management package adds the ability to manage all of a restaurant's payroll and human resource information. A labor management system includes a human resources module to track hiring, employee personal information, vacation, I-9 status, security privileges, tax status, availability, and any other information pertinent to employees working at the restaurant. A labor management system would also include scheduling capability so that managers can create weekly schedules based on forecasted business. Schedules would then be enforced when employees check in and out so that labor costs can be managed.

The labor management package also presents actual work time and pay rates to a payroll processor so that paychecks can be cut and distributed. It also collates tips data and receipt data from the front of the house so that proper tip allocations can be reported according to IRS guidelines.

Financial Reporting

Back-of-the-house and front-of-the-house systems post data into a relational database located on the central server. The restaurant manager uses these data for reporting and decision making. Profit and loss reports, budget variances, end-of-day reports, and other financial reports are generated from the central database. Financial management reporting needs to be flexible so that restaurant operators can manipulate it in ways that are useful to them. It is also important to get reports during the day in real time as the day unfolds so that restaurateurs can make decisions before profit is lost. Some reporting packages provide a graphical representation of the financial data displayed continuously on a monitor so that critical restaurant data are always available. This type of reporting provides restaurants with a real-time "heartbeat" for their operations.

Both back-of-the-house and front-of-the-house systems must be reliably linked so that POS food costs, labor costs, service times, and guest activity can be analyzed on the same reports. Restaurant management can then make critical business decisions armed with all necessary information. Technology is also used to collect data throughout the day for real-time budget control and "on-the-fly" management of labor effectiveness. Budgets are tight, and this is a way for management to watch, in real-time, where their labor costs are at all times.

Personal Digital Assistants

Personal digital assistants (PDAs) help hospitality businesses stay effective and efficient by improving time management and helping with faster service. For example, computer systems are used today in restaurants to transmit orders to the kitchen and to retrieve and post guest payments. These actions took extra time in the past, when the computer systems were placed at a distance from the server. PDAs have been created to allow servers to control their business with their fingertips.

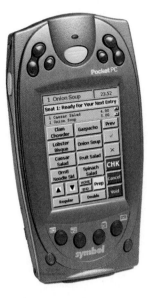

Pocket PC Used in Restaurants

One leading software provider to restaurant operators is Restaurant Technology, Inc. (RTI). RTI was founded by two restaurant owners who understand the accounting applications that operate from a central platform known as the Restaurant Financial System. Working together, their accounting programs form an integrated system, with these modules:

* Accounts payable
* Check reconciliation
* Daily store reporting
* General ledge
* Payroll
* Time keeping

PDAs can also be used in the hotel setting. Often, PDAs can be integrated with a PMS to give housekeepers real-time information about which rooms need to be cleaned and which rooms are not occupied. In the same way, as housekeepers complete the cleaning of a room, they can send a wireless signal to the front desk to affirm that the room is ready to be occupied.

Check Your Knowledge

1. Explain in what ways advances in technology aid the inventory process in restaurants.
2. What are back-of-the-house systems also known as?
3. What are the benefits of using a PDA?

Back of the House

The back of the house is generally run by the kitchen manager and refers to all the areas that guests do not normally come in contact with. This includes purchasing, receiving, storing/issuing, food production, stewarding, budgeting, accounting, and control.

One of the most important aspects to running a successful restaurant is having a strong back-of-the-house operation, particularly in the kitchen. The kitchen is the backbone of every full-service restaurant; thus it must be well managed and organized. Some of the main considerations in efficiently operating the back of the house include staffing, scheduling, training, food cost analysis, production, management involvement, management follow-up, and employee recognition.

Food Production

Planning, organizing, and producing food of a consistently high quality is no easy task. The kitchen manager, cook, or chef begins the production process by determining the expected volume of business for the next few days. The same period's sales from the previous year will give a good indication of the expected volume and the breakdown of the number of sales of each menu item. As described earlier, ordering and receiving will have already been done for the day's production schedule.

The **kitchen manager** checks the head line cook's order, which will bring the prep (preparation) area up to the par stock of prepared items. Most of the prep work is done in the early part of the morning and afternoon. Taking advantage of slower times allows the line cooks to do the final preparation just prior to and during the actual meal service.

The kitchen layout is set up according to the business projected as well as the menu design. Most full-service restaurants have similar layouts and designs for their kitchens. The layout consists of the back door area, walk-ins, the freezer, dry storage, prep line, salad bar, cooking line, expediter, dessert station, and service bar area.

The **cooking line** is the most important part of the kitchen layout. It might consist of a broiler station, window station, fry station, salad station, saute station, and pizza station—just a few of the intricate parts that go into the setup of the back of the house. The size of the kitchen and its equipment are all designed according to the sales forecast for the restaurant.

A Chef and Kitchen Team in "Full Swing"

A Day in the Life of James Lorenz
Kitchen Manager, T.G.I. Friday's, La Jolla, California

7:00 A.M.: Arrive. Check the work of cleaning crew (such as clogs in burners, stoves/ovens, etc.) for total cleanliness

7:15–7:40: Set production levels for all stations (broiler/hot sauce/expediter, cold sauce, vegetable preparation, baker preparation, line preparation: saute/noodles, pantry, fry/seafood portioning)

8:00: The first cooks begin arriving; greet them and allocate production sheets with priority items circled

9:00: On a good day, the produce arrives at 9:00 A.M. Check for quality, quantity, accuracy (making sure the prices match the quotation sheet) and that the produce is stored properly

9:30–11:00: Follow up on production. The sauté cook, who is last to come in, arrives. He or she is the closing person for the morning shift.

- Follow up on cleanliness, recipe adherence, production accuracy.
- Check the stations to ensure the storage of prepped items (e.g., plastic draining inserts under poultry and seafood), the shelf life of products, general cleanliness, and that what is in the station is prepared correctly (e.g., turkey diced to the right size and portioned and dated correctly).

10:45: Final check of the line and production to ensure readiness. Did everyone prepare enough?

11:00–2:30: All hands on deck. Jump on the first ticket. Pretoast buns for burgers and hold in heated drawers. Precook some chicken breasts for salads. Monitor lunch until 2:30 P.M.

- Be responsible for cleanliness.
- Determine who needs to get off the clock.
- Decide what production is left for the remainder of the day.
- Focus on changing over the line, change the food pan inserts (BBQ sauce, etc.).

2:30–3:15: Complete changeover of the line and check the stocking for the P.M. crew

- Final prep portioning.
- Check the dishwasher area and prep line for cleanliness.
- Check that the product is replaced in the store walk-in or refrigerator.
- Reorganize the produce walk-in. Check the storage of food, labels, and day dots, lids on.
- Thank the A.M. crew and send them home.

4:00–4:15: Welcome the P.M. crew

- Place produce order (as a double-check, ask the P.M. crew what they might need).
- 5:00: Hand over to P.M. manager.

The kitchen will also be set up according to what the customers prefer and order most frequently. For example, if guests eat more broiled or sauteed items, the size of the broiler and saute must be larger to cope with the demand.

Teamwork, a prerequisite for success in all areas of the hospitality and tourism industry, is especially important in the kitchen. Due to the hectic pace, pressure builds, and unless each member of the team excels, the result will be food that is delayed, not up to standard, or both.

While organization and performance standards are necessary, it is helping each other with the prepping and the cooking that makes for teamwork. "It's just like a relay race; we can't afford to drop the baton," says Amy Lu, kitchen manager of China Coast restaurant in Los Angeles. Teamwork in the back of the house is like an orchestra playing in tune, each player adding to the harmony.

Another example of organization and teamwork is T.G.I. Friday's five rules of control for running a kitchen:

1. Order it well.
2. Receive it well.
3. Store it well.
4. Make it to the recipe.
5. Don't let it die in the window.

It is amazing to see a kitchen line being overloaded, yet everyone is gratified when the team succeeds in preparing and serving quality food on time.

Kitchen/Food Production

Staffing and Scheduling

Practicing proper staffing is absolutely crucial for the successful running of a kitchen. It is important to have enough employees on the schedule to enable the restaurant, as a whole, to handle the volume on any given shift. Often it is better to overstaff the kitchen, rather than understaff it, for two reasons. First, it is much easier to send an employee home than it is to call someone in. Second, having extra employees on hand allows for cross-training and development, which is becoming a widely used method.

Problems can also be eliminated if a staffing plan is created to set needed levels. These levels should be adjusted according to sales trends on a monthly basis.

Also crucial to the smooth running of the kitchen is having a competent staff. This means putting the best cooks in the appropriate stations on the line, which will assist in the speed of service, the food quality, and the quality of the operations.

Training and Development

Implementing a comprehensive training program is vital in the kitchen, due to a high turnover rate. Trainers should, of course, be qualified and experienced in the kitchen. Often, the most competent chefs are used to train new hires. Such trainings are usually done on the job and may include study material. Some restaurants may even require new hires to complete a written test, evaluating the skills acquired through the training process.

Ensuring adequate training is necessary because the success of the business lies in the hands of the trainer and the trainee. If employees are properly trained when they begin their employment, little time and money will need to be spent on correcting errors. Thorough training also helps in retaining employees for longer periods of time.

Training, however, does not stop after passing a test. Developing the skills of all the employees is critical to the growth and success of the kitchen and, ultimately, the restaurant. A development program may consist of delegating duties or projects to the staff, allowing them to expand their horizons within the kitchen and the restaurant business. Such duties include projections of sales, inventory, ordering, schedule writing, and training.

A Chef in "Full Swing"

This will help management get feedback on the running of the kitchen and on how well the development program works in their particular operation. Also, this allows for internal growth and promotion.

Production Procedures

Production in the kitchen is key to the success of a restaurant since it relates directly to the recipes on the menu and how much product is on hand to produce the menu. Thus, controlling the production process is crucial. To undertake such a task, **production control sheets** are created for each station, for example, broiler, saute, fry, pantry, window, prep, dish, and dessert. With the control sheets, levels are set up for each day according to sales.

The first step in creating the production sheets is to count the products on hand for each station. Once the production levels are determined, the amount of product required to reach the level for each recipe is decided. Once these calculations are completed, the sheets are handed to the cooks. It is important to make these calculations before the cooks arrive, considering the amount of prep time that is needed in order to produce before business is conducted. For instance, if a restaurant is open only for lunch and dinner, enough product should be on hand by 11:00 A.M. to ensure that the cooks are prepared to handle the lunch crowd.

When determining production, par levels should be changed weekly according to sales trends. This will help control and minimize waste levels. Waste is a large contributor to food cost; therefore, the kitchen should determine the product levels necessary to make it through only one day. Products have a particular shelf life, and if the kitchen overproduces and does not sell the product within its shelf life, it must be thrown away. More importantly, this practice allows for the freshest product to reach the customers on a daily basis.

After the lunch rush, the kitchen checks to see how much product was sold and how much is left for the night shift. (Running out of a product is unacceptable and should not happen. If proper production procedures are followed, a restaurant will not have to "86" anything on the menu.) After all production is completed on all stations, the cooks may be checked out. It is essential to check out the cooks and hold them accountable for production levels. If they are not checked out, they will slide on their production, negatively impacting the restaurant and the customer.

The use of production sheets is critical, as well, in controlling how the cooks use the products, since production plays a key role in food cost. Every recipe has a particular "spec" (specification) to follow. When one deviates from the recipe, quality goes down, consistency is lost, and food cost goes up. That is why it is important to follow the recipe at all times.

Management Involvement and Follow Up

As in any business, management involvement is vital to the success of a restaurant. Management should know firsthand what is going on in the back of the house. It is also important that they be "on the line," assisting the staff in the preparation of the menu and in the other operations of the kitchen, just as they should be helping when things are rushed. When management is visible to the staff, they are prone to do what they need to be doing at all times, and food quality is more apparent and consistent. Managers should constantly be walking and talking food cost, cleanliness, sanitation, and quality. This shows the staff how serious and committed they are to the successful running of the back of the house. Figure 8–2 is a job description for a typical assistant restaurant manager.

As management spends more time in the kitchen, more knowledge is gained, more confidence is acquired, and more respect is earned. Employee–management interaction produces a sense of stability and a strong work ethic among employees, resulting in higher morale and promoting a positive working environment. To ensure that policies and standards are being upheld, management follow-up should happen on a continual basis. This is especially important when cooks are held accountable to specifications and production and when other staff members are given duties to perform. Without follow-up, the restaurant may fold.

Employee Recognition

Employee recognition is an extremely important aspect of back-of-the-house management. Recognizing employees for their efforts creates a positive work environment that motivates the staff to excel and to ultimately produce consistently better quality food for the guests.

Recognition can take many different forms, from personally commending a staff person for his or her efforts to recognizing a person in a group setting. By recognizing employees, management can make an immediate impact on the quality of operations. This can be a great tool for building sales, as well as assisting in the overall success of the restaurant.

Check Your Knowledge

1. Explain the following terms: guest counts/covers, product specification, production control sheets.

POSITION TITLE: *Assistant Manager*
REPORTS TO: *Manager*

POSITION OVERVIEW:
Under the general supervision of the manager, subject to the Service Policy and Procedure Manual, assures constantly and consistently the creation of maximal guest satisfaction and dining pleasure.

RESPONSIBILITIES AND DUTIES:
A. Planning and organizing
 1. Studies past sales experience records, confers with manager, keeps alert to holidays and special events, and so on; forecasts loads and prepares work schedules for service employees in advance to meet requirements.
 2. Observes guest reactions and confers frequently with servers to determine guest satisfactions, dissatisfactions, relative popularity of menu items, and so on and reports such information with recommendations to the manager.
 3. Observes daily the condition of all physical facilities and equipment in the dining room, making recommendations to the manager for correction and improvements needed.
 4. Anticipates all material needs and supplies and assures availability of same.
 5. Inspects, plans, and assures that all personnel, facilities, and materials are in complete readiness to provide excellent service before each meal period.
 6. Anticipates employment needs, recommending to the manager plans for recruitment and selection to meet needs as they arise.
 7. Discusses menu changes with servers in advance to assure full understanding of new items.
 8. Conducts meetings of service employees at appropriate times.
 9. Defines and explains clearly for servers and buspersons their responsibilities for relationships
    ✔ with each other
    ✔ with guests
    ✔ with the hostess/host
    ✔ with the manager
    ✔ with the cashier
    ✔ with the kitchen personnel
B. Coordinating
 1. Ensures that servers are fully informed as to all menu items—how they are prepared, what they contain, number of ounces per portion.
 2. Periodically discusses and reviews with employees company objectives, and guest and personnel policies.

 3. Keeps manager informed at all times about service activities, progress, and major problems.
C. Supervising
 1. Actively participates in employment of new servers and buspersons, suggests recruitment sources, studies applications, checks references, and conducts interviews.
 2. Following an orientation outline, introduces new employees to the restaurant, restaurant policies, and fellow employees.
 3. Using a training plan, trains new employees and current employees in need of additional training.
 4. Promptly corrects any deviations from established service standards.
 5. Counsels employees on job issues and personal problems.
 6. Follows established policy in making station assignments for servers.
 7. Establishes, with approval of manager, standards of conduct, grooming, personal hygiene, and dress.
 8. Prepares, in consultation and with approval of the manager, applied standards of performance for servers and buspersons.
 9. Recommends deserving employees for promotion, and outstanding performers for special recognition and award.
 10. Strives at all times through the practice of good human relations and leadership to establish esprit de corps—teamwork, unity of effort, and individual and group pride.
 11. Remains constantly alert to the entire dining room situation—is sensitive to any deviation or problem and assists quickly and quietly in its correction, alleviating guests' complaints.
 12. Greets and seats guests cordially and courteously, to assure a sincere welcome and to express a genuine interest in their dining pleasure.
D. Controlling
 1. Controls performance, conduct, dress, hygiene, sanitation, and personal appearance of employees according to established policies, standards, and procedures.
 2. Studies all evidence of waste of time and materials, and makes recommendations for preventing further waste.
E. Other
 1. In emergency situations, may serve guests, act as cashier, or perform specifically assigned duties of the manager.
 2. Personifies graciousness and offers hospitality to guests and employees by showing "we're glad you're here" and "we're proud to serve you."

Figure 8–2 *Job Description for Assistant Restaurant Manager*

Personal Profile: Ruth Fertel

There is no accolade or award for "the former first lady of American restaurants," but if there were, Ruth Fertel, founder of Ruth's Chris Steak House, would surely qualify for it.

Ruth's Chris Steak House is the nation's largest upscale restaurant chain with fifty-nine operations—54 in the United States and Puerto Rico, and 5 internationally—selling more than 11,000 steaks daily and grossing more than $200 million annually. By virtue of this volume, Ruth Fertel was the country's most successful woman restauranteur until her death in 2002.

The Ruth's Chris's success story began on a hunch and a gamble. Born in New Orleans in 1927, Fertel earned a degree in chemistry with a minor in physics at Louisiana State University at the age of nineteen. She taught briefly at McNeese Junior College in Lake Charles, Louisiana, but left to marry and raise a family. Fourteen years later, and by then divorced, she reentered the workforce as a lab technician at Tulane Medical School. After four years, she was convinced that she could not earn enough to send her two sons to college and so, in 1965, she decided to go into business for herself. While scanning the classified section of the local newspaper, Fertel found an ad for a steak house that was

for sale. Although she had no prior experience and limited funds, she decided to try it despite the advice of her lawyer, her banker, and her best friend to the contrary. She mortgaged her home to buy the small restaurant, which was then called Chris Steak House.

Fertel compensated for her lack of experience with plain hard work. In the first six months, she more than doubled her previous annual salary. Her restaurant soon became popular with the city's media personalities, political leaders, sports figures, and businesspeople. The name "Ruth's Chris" became synonymous with fine, quality steaks.

In 1977, at the urging of a loyal customer, Fertel granted her first franchise for a locally owned Ruth's Chris Steak House. Today, twenty-four restaurants are company owned and thirty-five are franchised.

Fertel attributed her success to the way she treated her customers and associates—as she would want to be treated—and to her basic "gut feeling" that has been responsible for successful decisions throughout the years.

The consistent quality of the meat she serves has also contributed to her success. Through the years, she stuck with the same suppliers and served nothing but the finest foods on the market.

Purchasing

Purchasing for restaurants involves procuring the products and services that the restaurant needs in order to serve its guests. Restaurant operators set up purchasing systems that determine the following:

- Standards for each item (**product specification**)
- Systems that minimize effort and maximize control of theft and losses from other sources
- The amount of each item that should be on hand (par stock and reorder point)
- Who will do the buying and keep the purchasing system in motion
- Who will do the receiving, storage, and issuing of items[4]

It is desirable for restaurants to establish standards for each product, called *product specification*. When ordering meat, for example, the cut, weight, size, percentage of fat content, and number of days aged are all factors that are specified by the purchaser.

Establishing systems that minimize effort and maximize control of theft may be done by computer or manually. However, merely computerizing a system does not make it theft-proof. Instead, employing honest workers is a top priority because temptation is everywhere in the restaurant industry.

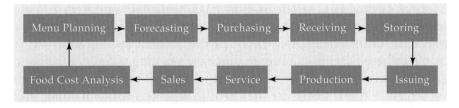

Figure 8–3   *Food Cost Control Process*

An efficient and effective system establishes a stock level that must be on hand at all times. This is called a **par stock.** If the stock on hand falls below a specified reorder point, the computer system automatically reorders a predetermined quantity of the item.

In identifying who will do the buying, it is most important to separate task and responsibility between the person placing the order and the person receiving the goods. This avoids possible theft. The best way to avoid losses is to have the chef prepare the order; the manager or the manager's designee place the order; and a third person, responsible for the stores, receive the goods together with the chef (or the chef's designee).

Commercial (for-profit) restaurant and foodservice operators who are part of a chain may have the menu items and order specifications determined at the corporate office. This saves the unit manager from having to order individually; specialists at the corporate office cannot only develop the menu but also the specifications for the ingredients to ensure consistency. Both chain and independent restaurants and foodservice operators use similar prepurchase functions (Figure 8–3).

- Plan menus.
- Determine quality and quantity needed to produce menus.
- Determine inventory stock levels.
- Identify items to purchase by subtracting stock levels from the quantity required to produce menus.
- Write specifications and develop market orders for purchases.

Professor Stefanelli at the University of Nevada, Las Vegas, suggests a formal and an informal method of purchasing that includes the following steps.[5]

Formal	**Informal**
Develop purchase order	Develop purchase order
Establish bid schedule	Quote price
Issue invitation to bid	Select vendor and place order
Tabulate and evaluate bids	
Award contract and issue delivery order	
Inspect/receive deliveries, inventory stores, and record transactions in inventory	Receive and inspect deliveries, store, and record transaction
Evaluate and follow up	Evaluate and follow up
Issue food supplies for food production and service	Issue food supplies for food production and service

The formal method is generally used by chain restaurant operators and the informal one by independent restaurant operators.

A **purchase order** comes as a result of the product specification. As it sounds, a purchase order is an order to purchase a certain quantity of an item at a specific price. Many restaurants develop purchase orders for items they need on a regular basis. These are then sent to suppliers for quotations, and samples are sent in for product evaluations. For example, canned items have varying amounts of liquid. Normally, it is the drained weight of the product that matters to the restaurant operator. After comparing samples from several vendors, the operator can choose the supplier that best suits the restaurant's needs.

Receiving

When placing an order, the restaurant operator specifies the day and time (for example, Friday, 10:00 A.M. to 12:00 noon) for the delivery to be made. This prevents deliveries from being made at inconvenient times.

Receiving is a point of control in the restaurant operation. The purpose of receiving is to ensure the quantity, quality, and price are exactly as ordered. The quantity and quality relate to the order specification and the standardized recipe. Depending on the restaurant and the type of food and beverage control system, some perishable items are issued directly to the kitchen, and most of the nonperishable items go into storage.

Storing/Issuing

Control of the stores is often a problem. Records must be kept of all items going into or out of the stores. If more than one person has access to the stores, it is difficult to know where to attach responsibility in case of losses.

Items should only be issued from the stores on an authorized requisition signed by the appropriate person. One restaurateur who has been in business for many years issues stores to the kitchen on a daily basis. No inventory is kept in the production area and there is no access to the stores. To some, this may be overdoing control, but it is hard to fault the results: a good food cost percentage. All items that enter the stores should have a date stamp and be rotated using the first in-first out (FIFO) system.

First in–first out is a simple but effective system of ensuring stock rotation. This is achieved by placing the most recent purchases, in rotation, behind previous purchases. Failure to do this can result in spoilage.

Obviously restaurants should maintain strict controls. Among the better-known controls are taking inventory regularly; calculating food and beverage cost percentages; having receiving done by a person other than the person who orders; using a "par stock" reordering system; using one entrance/exit for employees and not permitting employees to bring bags into the restaurant with them; employing a good accountant; and, yes, checking the garbage!

Restaurant managers also need to spend time with staff members.

Budgeting

Budgeting costs fall into two categories: fixed and variable. **Fixed costs** are constant regardless of the volume of business. Fixed costs are rent/lease payments, interest, and depreciation. **Variable costs** fluctuate with the volume of business. Variable costs include controllable expenses such as payroll, benefits, direct operating expense, music and entertainment, marketing and promotion, energy and utility, administrative, and repairs and maintenance.

Regardless of sales fluctuations, variable or controllable expenses vary in some controllable proportion to sales. For example, if a restaurant is open on a Monday it must have a host, server, cook, dishwasher, and so on. The volume of business and sales total may be $750. However, on Friday that sales total might be $2,250 with just a few more staff. The controllable costs increased only slightly in proportion to the sales, and the fixed costs did not change.

Restaurant Accounting

To operate any business efficiently and effectively, it is necessary to determine the mission, goals, and objectives. One of the most important goals in any enterprise is a fair return on investment, otherwise known as profit. In addition, accounting for the income and expenditures is a necessary part of any business enterprise. The restaurant industry has adopted a uniform system of accounts.

The **uniform system of accounts** for restaurants (USAR) outlines a standard classification and presentation of operating results. The system allows for easy comparison among restaurants because each expense item has the same schedule number.

Balance Sheet

A **balance sheet** for a restaurant, or any business, reflects how the assets and liabilities relate to the owner's equity at a particular moment in time. The balance

Corporate Profile: T.G.I. Friday's® Restaurant

In the spring of 1965, Alan Stillman, a New York perfume salesman, opened a restaurant located at First Avenue and 63rd Street. The restaurant boasted striped awnings, a blue exterior, and yellow supergraphics reading T.G.I. Friday's. Inside were wooden floors covered with sawdust, Tiffany-style lamps, bentwood chairs, red-and-white tablecloths, and a bar area complete with brass rails and stained glass.

T.G.I. Friday's was an immediate success. The restaurant on Manhattan's upper east side became the meeting place for single adults. In fact, *Newsweek* and the *Saturday Evening Post* called the opening of T.G.I. Friday's "the dawn of the singles' age."

In 1971, franchisee Dan Scoggin opened a T.G.I. Friday's in Dallas and in four other sites around the country. The success was instant; thus, began the company that is Friday's today.

By 1975, there were ten T.G.I. Friday's in eight states, but the great success that the company had seen was starting to diminish. Dan Scoggin began a countrywide tour to visit each restaurant; he talked with employees, managers, and customers to isolate the roots of successes and failures. This was the critical turning point for the company. The focus shifted from being just another restaurant chain to giving guests exactly what they wanted. The theories and philosophies Scoggin developed are the principles by which Friday's now does business.

T.G.I. Friday's goal was to create a comfortable, relaxing environment where guests could enjoy food and drink. Stained glass windows, wooden airplane propellers, racing sculls, and metal advertising signs comprised the elegant clutter that greeted guests when they entered a T.G.I. Friday's. Nothing was left to chance. Music, lights, air conditioning, decor, and housekeeping were all designed to keep guests comfortable. Employees were encouraged to display their own personalities and to treat customers as they would guests in their own homes.

As guests demanded more, T.G.I. Friday's provided more—soon becoming the industry leader in menu and drink selection. The menu expanded from a slate chalkboard to an award-winning collection of items representing every taste and mood.

T.G.I. Friday's also became the industry leader in innovation—creating the now-famous Jack Daniel's® Grill. This was the first restaurant chain to offer stone ground whole wheat bread, avocados, bean sprouts, and Mexican appetizers across the country. As guests' tastes continued to change, T.G.I. Friday's introduced pasta dishes, brunch items, and fettucine.

America owes the popularization of frozen and ice cream drinks to T.G.I. Friday's, where smooth, alcoholic and nonalcoholic drinks were made with fresh fruit, juices, ice cream, and yogurt. These recipes were so precise that T.G.I. Friday's drink glasses were scientifically designed for the correct ratio of each ingredient. These specially designed glasses have since become popular throughout the industry.

Through the years, T.G.I. Friday's success has been phenomenal. More than 750 restaurants have opened in 49 states and 55 countries. With average gross revenues of $3.5 million per year at each location, it has the highest per unit sales volume of any national casual dining chain.

T.G.I. Friday's is privately owned by Carlson Companies, Inc., of Minneapolis—one of the largest privately held companies in the country. Today, T.G.I. Friday's has come to be known as a casual restaurant where family and friends meet for great food, fun, and conversation. Everyone looks forward to T.G.I. Friday's!

What does it take to be successful in the restaurant business, and what does it take to be a leader? The answers to these questions are crucial to success as a restaurant company. The essentials of success in business are as follows:

1. Treat everyone with respect for their dignity.
2. Treat all customers as if they are honored guests in your home.
3. Remember that all problems result from either poor hiring, lack of training, unclear performance expectations, or accepting less than excellence.
4. Remember that management tools are methods, not objectives.

As you can see, these are principles to guide decision making as opposed to step-by-step actions. However, I would submit that if these principles are not followed, then actions have very short term effects. And if you do choose to follow them, they form a base on which you can easily decide which specific actions are necessary in any given situation.

The basics of leadership are as follows:

1. Hire the right people.
2. Train everyone thoroughly and completely.
3. Be sure that everyone clearly understands the performance expectations.
4. Accept only excellence.

Here we are dealing with the very basics of how to provide strong, clear leadership. However, once again we are talking about only the minimum requirements, not all the qualities necessary to be a good leader. Individual success and that of the company, T.G.I. Friday's Inc., are predicated on understanding and following the essentials of success in business and the basics of leadership. Whether you are an hourly employee or a manager, it is critical that you manage your part of the business using these philosophies.

One thing that makes T.G.I. Friday's unique is the philosophies and theories. These are principles that each employee understands to ensure everyone stays focused on the same goals. T.G.I. Friday's philosophies and theories were first conceived in the mid-1970s. They are used to solve existing problems and enable management to be proactive to problems experienced in the past.

The Guest Focus

At most companies, it appears that senior management runs the company. The employees consider senior management to be the most important people with whom they interact. As a result, decisions are made in an effort to please senior management, and decisions that affect people lower in the hierarchy are viewed as less important. T.G.I. Friday's success is dependent on inverting the typical management pyramid. Guests are the most important element in the organization; immediately following them are the employees who are closest to the guests—those people who have the greatest impact on the guests' experience. The livelihood of each employee depends on one group of people: guests. It is critical to determine what guests' needs are and fill those needs. To the extent that this objective is accomplished, the needs of each person in the pyramid will be fulfilled. Every decision at T.G.I. Friday's is made with guests in mind.

The "Five Easy Pieces Theory" stresses T.G.I. Friday's deep concern for the guests' satisfaction. T.G.I. Friday's will always cheerfully go out of their way to serve a quality product prepared to individual tastes. In the movie ti-

tled *Five Easy Pieces,* the star, Jack Nicholson, goes to a restaurant and orders a side order of whole wheat toast. The waitress makes it clear that they do not serve whole wheat toast. Nicholson notes on the menu that the chicken salad sandwich comes on whole wheat bread. The annoyed waitress points to a sign in the restaurant that reads "No substitutions" and "We reserve the right to refuse service to anyone." Jack Nicholson orders a chicken salad sandwich on whole wheat toast, but tells the waitress to hold the mayo, hold the lettuce, hold the chicken salad, and just bring him the whole wheat toast. Unwisely, she asks where she should hold the chicken salad. Nicholson sarcastically responds, "Between your knees!" On that note, he leaves, a very dissatisfied guest. T.G.I. Friday's managers and employees are responsible for honoring any guest request within realistic possibilities. Many managers take a guest's request even further and get them exactly what they want—even if the ingredients are not in the restaurant.

The "Triangle Theory" explains the need to balance and expand upon the goals of the guest, employee, and company, and maximize the results to each. Managers make many decisions and must always consider the effect of those decisions on all three sides of the triangle—the guest, the employee, and the company. Some decisions can cause one side of the triangle to prosper (temporarily) at the expense of the other two. For example, if a company overprices its menu items, it can greatly improve the bottom line. However, guests will object to being cheated and will not return. This will ultimately result in lower staffing and will eventually kill the company. Management's responsibility is to balance the results among the three sides so all sides thrive. But this is only the first step. To grow and expand the business, decisions must be made that maximize or expand all three sides of the triangle at the same time.

These are just a few of the philosophies and theories on which T.G.I. Friday's is based.

Expectations of the General Manager

The expectations of the general manager are different in each restaurant; however, there are certain commonalities as well. Some of these commonalities are as follows:

- General managers answer directly to the owner or to regional directors for major corporations.
- General managers are expected to run good numbers for the periods. The numbers analyzed are food cost, labor cost, beverage cost. These areas are controlled in order to produce sufficient profit for the restaurant.
- General managers promote good morale and teamwork in the restaurant. Having a positive environment in the restaurant is of utmost importance. This will not

continued

only keep the employees happy, but it will also contribute to providing better service to the guests.

Duties and Responsibilities

The general manager of a restaurant is directly in charge of all the operations in the restaurant. General managers are also in charge of the floor managers, kitchen manager, and all the remaining employees in the restaurant.

The general manager should always check on the floor managers to ensure that all policies and regulations are being met. This will keep operations running smoothly.

Another important duty is to organize and control the staffing of the restaurant. The floor managers usually write the employee schedule; however, the general manager is still directly responsible for proper staffing for the period. This will help keep labor costs to about 20 percent of sales. The general manager is also in charge of conducting employee reviews and training.

Qualifications for a General Manager

To be hired as a general manager, the following qualifications are necessary:

- The general manager should be very knowledgeable in the restaurant business.
- He or she should have previously worked all the stations in a restaurant and be very familiar with them.
- The general manager should be able to get along with all people, be fair with all employees, and not discriminate.
- Having a degree is not the most important thing in becoming a general manager. However, a degree is very useful in moving up the ladder in a company to regional manager, regional director, and so on.

Budgeted Costs in a Restaurant

Running a good pace in the restaurant is of absolute importance. Every restaurant has different numbers to make. The following numbers came from a T.G.I. Friday's restaurant. These numbers reflect their goals versus actual numbers run for a given week.

	Goal	Actual	Variance
Food Cost	27.0	27.2	+0.2
Labor Cost	19.9	20.8	+0.9
Beverage Cost	19.0	18.2	−0.8

As can be seen, this T.G.I. Friday's did well with the beverage cost; however, the food cost and the labor cost are two areas to focus on for the upcoming week.

Making good percentages for the restaurant is the most important focus, simply because this is where the restaurant makes or does not make a profit. When the general manager runs good numbers, then he or she will receive a large bonus check for contributing to the profit of the restaurant. This is why it is so important to focus on these three key areas.

Scheduling the Restaurant

Appropriate scheduling plays a key role in the success of the restaurant. For one thing, overscheduling and underscheduling have a direct effect on the labor cost. If there are too many employees working on a shift for the business acquired, then the labor cost will be high. In contrast, if there are not enough employees working, then the service will suffer and overtime will increase the labor cost.

T.G.I. Friday's values are summed up in the Carlson Credo, shown below.

The Carlson Credo

Whatever you do, do it with INTEGRITY.
Wherever you go, go as a LEADER.
Whomever you serve, serve with CARING.
Whenever you dream, dream with your ALL.
And never, ever give up.

—Curt Carlson

---

sheet is mainly used by owners and investors to verify the financial health of the organization. Financial health may be defined in several ways—for example, liquidity, which means having a sufficient amount of cash available to pay bills when they are due, and debt leverage, which is the percentage of a company's assets owned by outside interests (liabilities).

Restaurants are one of the few, fortunate types of businesses to operate on a cash basis for income receivables. There are no outstanding accounts receivable because all sales are in cash—even credit cards are treated as cash because of their prompt payment. Normally, restaurants invest significant funds in assets, such as equipment, furniture, and building (if they own it). The balance sheet will reflect how much of the cost of these assets has been paid for, and is thus owned by the company (owner's equity), and how much is still due to outsiders (liability). Furthermore, the balance sheet will show the extent to which the company has depreciated these assets, thus providing owners and investors with an indication of potential future costs to repair or replace existing assets.

Operating or Income Statement

From an operational perspective, the most important financial document is the operating statement. Once a sales forecast has been completed, the costs of servicing those sales are budgeted on an income statement. Figure 8–4 shows an example of an income statement for a hypothetical restaurant.

The **income statement,** which is for a month or a year, begins with the food and beverage sales. From this total the cost of food and beverage is deducted; the remaining total is **gross profit.** To this amount any other income is added (e.g., cigarettes, vending machines, outside catering, and telephone income). The next heading is controllable expenses, which includes salaries, wages, employee benefits, direct operating expenses (telephone, insurance, accounting and legal fees, office supplies, paper, china, glass, cutlery, menus, landscaping, and so on), music and entertainment, marketing, energy and utility, administrative and general, repairs and maintenance. The total of this group is called total controllable expenses. Rent and other occupation costs are then deducted from the total, leaving income before interest, depreciation, and taxes. Interest and depreciation are deducted leaving a total of net income before taxes. From this amount income taxes are paid leaving the remainder as net income.

Managing the money to the bottom line requires careful scrutiny of all key results, beginning with the big ticket controllable items like labor costs, food costs, and beverages, on down to related controllable items. Additionally, management may wish to compare several income statements representing operations over a number of different periods. The ideal method for comparing is to compute every component of each income statement as a percentage of its total sales. Then compare one period's percentage to another to determine if any significant trends are developing. For example, a manager could compare labor as a percent of total sales over several months, or years, to assess the impact of rising labor rates on the bottom line. Notice how Figure 8–4 has columns for budgeted, actual, percentage of sales, variance (+/−) last period, and same period last year. This really gives management good decision-making information.

Operating Ratios

Operating ratios are industry norms that are applicable to each segment of the industry. Experienced restaurant operators rely on these operating ratios to indicate

	Budgeted	Actual Amount	Percentage	Variance + (–)	Last Period	Same Period Last Year
Sales						
Food						
Beverage						
Others						
Total sales		____	100			
Cost of Sales						
Food						
Beverage						
Others						
Total cost of sales		____				
Gross profit		____				
Controllable Expenses						
Salaries and wages						
Employee benefits						
Direct operating expenses[a]						
Music and entertainment						
Marketing						
Energy and utility						
Administrative and general						
Repairs and maintenance						
Total controllable expenses		____				
Rent and other occupation costs						
Income before interest, depreciation, and taxes						
Interest						
Depreciation						
Net income before taxes						
Income taxes		____				
Net Income		____				

[a]Telephone, insurance, legal, accounting, paper, glass, china, linens, office supplies, landscaping, cleaning supplies, etc.

Figure 8–4   *Sample Income Statement*

the restaurant's degree of success. Several ratios are good barometers of a restaurant's degree of success. Among the better known ratios are the following:

- ✓ Food cost percentage
- ✓ Contribution margin
- ✓ Labor cost percentage
- ✓ Prime cost
- ✓ Beverage cost percentage

Food Cost Percentage

The basic **food cost percentage,** for which the formula is cost/sales $\times$ 100 = the food cost percentage, is calculated on a daily, weekly, or monthly basis. The procedure works in the following manner:

1. An inventory is taken of all the food and the purchase price of that food. This is called the *opening inventory.*
2. The purchases are totaled for the period and added to the opening inventory.
3. The closing inventory (the inventory at the close of the week or period for which the food cost percentage is being calculated) and returns, spoilage, complimentary meals, and transfers to other departments are also deducted from the opening inventory plus purchases.
4. This figure is the cost of goods sold. The cost of goods sold is divided by the total sales. The resulting figure is the food cost percentage.

The following example illustrates the procedure:

Food Sales	$3,000
Opening Inventory	−1,000
Add Purchases	−500
	1,500
Less Spoilage and Complimentary Meals	−100
Less Closing Inventory	−500
Cost of Goods Sold	$900

$$\frac{\text{Food Cost (\$900)}}{\text{Sales (\$3,000)}} \times 100 = 30\% \text{ Food Cost Percentage}$$

The food cost percentage calculations become slightly more complicated when the cost of staff meals, management meals and entertaining (complimentary meals), and guest food returned are all properly calculated.

Food cost percentage has long been used as a yardstick for measuring the skill of the chef, cooks, and management to achieve a predetermined food cost percentage—usually 28 to 32 percent for a full-service restaurant and a little higher for a high-volume, fast-food restaurant.

Controlling food costs begins with cost-effective purchasing systems, a controlled storage and issuing system, and strict control of the food production and sales. The best way to visualize a food cost control system is to think of the food as money. Consider a $100 bill arriving at the back door: If the wrong people get their hands on that money, it does not reach the guest or the bottom line.

Contribution Margin

More recently, attention has focused not only on the food cost percentage but also on the contribution margin. The **contribution margin** is the amount that a menu item contributes to the gross profit, or the difference between the cost of the item and its sales price. Some menu items contribute more than others;

therefore, restaurant operators focus more attention on the items that produce a higher contribution margin. It works like this:

The cost of the chicken dish is $2.00, and its selling price is $9.95, which leaves a contribution margin of $7.95. The fish, which costs a little more at $3.25, sells for $12.75 and leaves a contribution of $9.50. The pasta cost price of $1.50 and selling price of $8.95 leave a contribution margin of $7.45. Under this scenario it would be better for the restaurants to sell more fish because each plate will yield $1.55 more than if chicken were sold.

Labor Cost Percentage

Labor costs are the highest single cost factor in staffing a restaurant. Fast-food restaurants have the lowest **labor costs percentage** (about 16 to 18 percent) with family and ethnic restaurants at about 22 to 26 percent, and upscale full-service restaurants at about 30 to 35 percent.

Labor costs include salaries and wages of employees, employee benefits, and their training. Food service is a highly labor intensive industry, depending on the type of restaurant. Quick-service restaurants have a lower payroll cost primarily due to their limited menu and limited service. Good managers try to manage their labor costs by accurate hiring and scheduling of staff according to the restaurant's cover turnover.

Prime Cost

Combined food and labor costs are known as **prime cost.** To allow for a reasonable return on investment, prime cost should not go above 60 to 65 percent of sales.

There are various methods of control, beginning with effective scheduling based on the expected volume of business. In reality, because of the high cost of labor, today's restaurateur manage by the minute. Once a rush is over, the effective manager thanks employees for doing a great job and looks forward to seeing them again. This may appear to be micromanagement, but an analysis of restaurant operations does not leave any alternatives.[6]

Beverage Cost Percentage

The **beverage cost percentage** is calculated like the food cost percentage. The method used most often is to first determine the unit cost and then mark up by the required percentage to arrive at the selling price. This is rounded up or down to a convenient figure. The actual beverage cost percentage is then compared with the anticipated cost percentage; any discrepancy is investigated.

The National Restaurant Association publishes guidelines for restaurant operations. These valuable documents help provide a guide for operators to use when comparing their restaurants with other similar establishments. If the costs go above the budgeted or expected levels, then management must investigate and take corrective action.

Therefore, if we are operating a casual Italian restaurant, industry comparisons would show the following:

Labor costs at 20 to 24 percent of sales
Food costs at 28 to 32 percent of food sales
Beverage costs at 18 to 24 percent of beverage sales

Personal Profile: Sarah Stegner

Chef-Owner, Prairie Grass Café

Sarah Stegner, forty, opened Prairie Grass Café in Northbrook, Illinois, with her partner, former executive chef George Bumbaris of The Ritz-Carlton Chicago, in 2004. A little history . . .

The Evanston, Illinois, native grew up in a family devoted to food. Her grandmother was a caterer "before women did those kinds of things," and her grandfather was an avid backyard vegetable gardener. The table was the center of the family and was where Stegner's passion for food emerged.

After a year spent studying classical guitar at Northwestern University, Stegner followed her heart and enrolled at the Dumas Pere Cooking School. She graduated with a chef's certificate one year later and was hired as an apprentice at The Ritz-Carlton Chicago.

In 1990, after six years of working in various culinary capacities (including a first job of cleaning fish for 12 hours a day), Stegner was promoted to chef of The Dining Room. She worked for years under the guiding hands of Fernand Gutierrez, former executive chef and director of food and beverage at The Ritz-Carlton Chicago, and current food and beverage director at Four Seasons Mexico City. Since then, Stegner has distinguished herself as one of America's most creative young chefs.

As a result of her talents, she has captured many national honors. Chef Stegner was named Best Chef of the Midwest in 1998 by the prestigious James Beard Foundation and The Dining Room was named One of the Top 5 Restaurants in Chicago in 1999 by Gourmet magazine and received four stars from the Chicago Tribune. In addition, it was rated best Hotel Dining Room in Chicago in 1999 by the prestigious Zagat Chicago Restaurant Guide and was named Best Restaurant in Chicago in 1996 by *Gourmet;* One of the Top 13 Hotel Dining Rooms in the U.S. in 1996 by *Bon Appétit;* and One of the Top 10 Hotel Restaurants in the World in 1996 by *Hotels* magazine.

Chef Stegner is recipient of the 1995 Robert Mondavi Culinary Award of Excellence and captured the national title of 1994 Rising Star Chef of the Year in America by the James Beard Foundation. She also holds the title of Prix Culinaire International Pierre Taittinger 1991 U.S. Winner, where she represented America in the finals in Paris and was the only female chef present at the global competition.

In recent years, Chef Stegner has enjoyed periodic training in France, under the expertise of Chef Pierre Orsi at his two-star Michelin Pierre Orsi Restaurant in Lyon, France, and with chefs Bertolli and Berard Bessin in Paris.

She also finds time to donate her talents to charitable causes. Six years ago, she founded The Women Chefs of Chicago, comprising the city's top female chefs who donate cuisine for numerous events throughout the city to raise money for charity. Under her direction, The Women Chefs of Chicago have helped raise over $500,000 for Chicagoland charities in the past few years.

Sarah's support of her state's agriculture is reflected in her food: she uses the finest seasonal produce from Midwest vegetable farmers and cheesemakers. She works with her husband, Rohit Nambiar, who manages the front of house at Prairie Grass Café. Her mother, Elizabeth Stegner, makes the pies served at Prairie Grass Café. Sarah feels right at home in her new restaurant.

Lease and Controllable Expenses

Lease Costs

Successful restaurant operators will ensure that the restaurant's lease does not cost more than 5 to 8 percent of sales. Some chain restaurants will search for months or even years before they find the right location at the right price. Most leases are triple net, which means that the lessee must pay for all alterations, insurance, utilities, and possible commercial fees (e.g., landscaping or parking upkeep, security, etc.).

The best lease is for the longest time period with options for renewal and a sublease clause. The sublease clause is important because if the restaurant is not successful, the owner is still liable for paying the lease. With the sublease clause the owner may sublease the space to another restaurant operator or any other business.

Many leases are quoted at a dollar rate per square foot per month. Depending on the location, rates may range from $2.25 per square foot up to as much as $16.00 or more per square foot.

Some restaurants pay a combination of a flat amount based on the square footage and a percentage of sales. This helps protect the restaurant operator in the slower months and gives the landlord a bit extra during the good months.

Once a lease contract is signed, it is very difficult to renegotiate even a part of it. Only in dire circumstances is it possible to renegotiate lease contracts. The governing factor in determining lease rates is the marketplace. The marketplace is the supply and demand. If there is strong demand for space, then rates will increase. However, with a high vacancy rate, rates will be driven down by the owners in an effort to rent space and gain income.

Controllable Expenses

Controllable expenses are all the expenses over which management and ownership has control. They include salaries and wages (payroll) and related benefits; direct operating expenses such as music and entertainment; marketing, including sales, advertising, public relations, and promotions; heat, light, and power; administrative and general expenses; and repairs and maintenance. The total of all controllable expenses is deducted from the gross profit. Rent and other occupation costs are then deducted to arrive at the income before interest, depreciation, and taxes. Once these are deducted, the **net profit** remains.

Successful restaurant operators are constantly monitoring their controllable expenses. The largest controllable expense is payroll. Because payroll is about 24 to 28 percent of a restaurant's sales, managers constantly monitor their employees, not by the hour but by the minute. Bobby Hays, general manager of the Chart House Restaurant in Solana Beach, California, says that he feels the pulse of the restaurant and then begins to send people home. Every dollar that Bobby and managers like him can save goes directly to the bottom line and becomes profit.

The actual sales results are compared with the budgeted amounts—ideally with percentages—and variances investigated. Most chain restaurant operators monitor the key result areas of sales and labor costs on a daily basis. Food and beverage costs are also monitored closely, generally on a weekly basis.

Check Your Knowledge

1. What is the back of the house?
2. Create a recognition program that would encourage restaurant employees.
3. What is the storing/issuing process? Why is it important?
4. Briefly explain the term *contribution margin.*

Restaurant Manager Job Analysis

The National Restaurant Association (NRA) has formulated an analysis of the foodservice manager's job by functional areas and tasks, which follows a natural sequence of functional areas from human resources to sanitation and safety.

Human Resource Management

Recruiting/Training

1. Recruit new employees by seeking referrals.
2. Recruit new employees by advertising.
3. Recruit new employees by seeking help from district manager/supervisors.
4. Interview applicants for employment.

Orientation/Training

1. Conduct on-site orientation for new employees.
2. Explain employee benefits and compensation programs.
3. Plan training programs for employees.
4. Conduct on-site training for employees.
5. Evaluate progress of employees during training.
6. Supervise on-site training of employees that is conducted by another manager, employee leader, trainer, and so on.
7. Conduct payroll signup.
8. Complete reports or other written documentation on successful completion of training by employees.

Scheduling for Shifts

1. Review employee work schedule for shift.
2. Determine staffing needs for each shift.
3. Make work assignments for dining room, kitchen staff, and maintenance person(s).
4. Make changes to employee work schedule.
5. Assign employees to work stations to optimize employee effectiveness.
6. Call in, reassign, or send home employees in reaction to sales and other needs.
7. Approve requests for schedule changes, vacation, days off, and so on.

Supervision and Employee Development

1. Observe employees and give immediate feedback on unsatisfactory employee performance.
2. Observe employees and give immediate feedback on satisfactory employee performance.
3. Discuss unsatisfactory performance with an employee.
4. Develop and deliver incentive for above-satisfactory performance of employees.

5. Observe employee behavior for compliance with safety and security.
6. Counsel employees on work-related problems.
7. Counsel employees on nonwork-related problems.
8. Talk with employees who have frequent absences.
9. Observe employees to ensure compliance with fair labor standards and equal opportunity guidelines.
10. Discipline employees by issuing oral and/or written warnings for poor performance.
11. Conduct employee and staff meetings.
12. Identify and develop candidates for management programs.
13. Put results of observation of employee performance in writing.
14. Develop action plans for employees to help them in their performance.
15. Authorize promotion and/or wage increases for staff.
16. Terminate employment of an employee for unsatisfactory performance.

Financial Management

Accounting

1. Authorize payment on vendor invoices.
2. Verify payroll.
3. Count cash drawers.
4. Prepare bank deposits.
5. Assist in establishment audits by management or outside auditors.
6. Balance cash at end of shift.
7. Analyze profit and loss reports for establishment.

Cost Control

1. Discuss factors that impact profitability with district manager/supervisor.
2. Check establishment figures for sales, labor costs, waste, inventory, and so on.

Administrative Management

Scheduling/Coordinating

1. Establish objectives for shift based on needs of establishment.
2. Coordinate work performed by different shifts—for example, cleanup, routine maintenance, and so on.
3. Complete special projects assigned by district manager/supervisor.
4. Complete shift readiness checklist.

Planning

1. Develop and implement action plans to meet financial goals.
2. Attend off-site workshops and training sessions.

Communication

1. Communicate with management team by reading and making entries in daily communication log.

2. Prepare written reports on cleanliness, food quality, personnel, inventory, sales, food waste, labor costs, and so on.
3. Review reports prepared by other establishment managers.
4. Review memos, reports, and letters from company headquarters/main office.
5. Inform district manager/supervisor of problems or developments that affect operation and performance of the establishment.
6. Initiate and answer correspondence with company, vendors, and so on.
7. File correspondence, reports, personnel records, and so on.

Marketing Management

1. Create and execute local establishment marketing activities.
2. Develop opportunities for the establishment to provide community services.
3. Carry out special product promotions.

Operations Management

Facility Maintenance

1. Conduct routine maintenance checks on facility and equipment.
2. Direct routine maintenance checks on facility and equipment.
3. Repair or supervise the repair of equipment.
4. Review establishment evaluations with district manager/supervisor.
5. Authorize the repair of equipment by outside contractor.
6. Recommend upgrades in facility and equipment.

Food and Beverage Operations Management

1. Direct activities for opening establishment.
2. Direct activities for closing establishment.
3. Talk with other managers at beginning and end of shift to relay information about ongoing problems and activities.
4. Count, verify, and report inventory.
5. Receive, inspect, and verify vendor deliveries.
6. Check stock levels and submit orders as necessary.
7. Talk with vendors concerning quality of product delivered.
8. Interview vendors who wish to sell products to establishment.
9. Check finished product quality and act to correct problems.
10. Work as expediter to get meals served effectively.
11. Inspect dining area, kitchen, rest rooms, food lockers, storage, and parking lot.
12. Check daily reports for indications of internal theft.
13. Instruct employees regarding the control of waste, portion sizes, and so on.
14. Prepare forecast for daily or shift food preparation.

Service

1. Receive and record table reservations.
2. Greet familiar customers by name.

3. Seat customers.
4. Talk with customers while they are dining.
5. Monitor service times and procedures in the dining area.
6. Observe customers being served in order to correct problems.
7. Ask customers about quality of service.
8. Ask customers about quality of the food product.
9. Listen to and resolve customer complaints.
10. Authorize complimentary meals or beverages.
11. Write letters in response to customer complaints.
12. Telephone customers in response to customer complaints.
13. Secure and return items left by customers.

Sanitation and Safety

1. Accompany local officials on health inspections on premise.
2. Administer first aid to employees and customers.
3. Submit accident, incident, and OSHA reports.
4. Report incidents to police.
5. Observe employee behavior and establishment conditions for compliance with safety and security procedures.

Trends in Restaurant Operations

- More flavorful food
- Increased takeout meals, especially at lunch and more home meal replacement (for dinner)
- Increased food safety and sanitation
- Guests becoming more sophisticated and needing more things to excite them
- More food court restaurants in malls, movie theater complexes, and colleges and universities where guests line up (similar to a cafeteria), select their food (which a server places on a tray), and pay a cashier
- Steak houses are becoming more popular
- With more restaurants in each segment, the segments are splitting into upper, middle, and lower tiers
- Twin and multirestaurant locations
- Quick-service restaurants (QSRs) in convenience stores
- Difficulty in finding good employees

CASE STUDY

Short Staffed in the Kitchen

Sally is the general manager of one of the best restaurants in town, known as The Pub. As usual, at 6:00 P.M. on a Friday night, there is a 45-minute wait. The kitchen is overloaded, and they are running behind in check times, the time that elapses between the kitchen getting the order and the guest receiving his or her meal. This is critical, especially if a complaint is received because a guest has waited too long for a meal to be served.

Sally is waiting for her two head line cooks to come in for the closing shift. It is now 6:15 P.M. and she receives phone calls from both of them. Unfortunately, they are both sick with the flu and are not able to come to work.

As she gets off the phone, the hostess tells Sally that a party of 50 is scheduled to arrive at 7:30 P.M. Sally is concerned, knowing that they are currently running a six-person line with only four cooks. The productivity is very high, but they are running extremely long check times. How can Sally handle the situation?

Discussion Questions

1. How would you handle the short-staffing issue?
2. What measures would you take to get the appropriate cooks in to work as soon as possible?
3. What would you do to ensure a smooth, successful transition for the party of 50?
4. How would you manipulate your floor plan to provide great service for the party of 50?
5. How would you immediately make an impact on the long check times?
6. What should you do to ensure that all the guests in the restaurant are happy?

CASE STUDY

Shortage in Stock

It is Friday morning at 9:30 at The Pub. Product is scheduled to be delivered at 10:00. Sally specifically ordered an exceptional amount of food for the upcoming weekend because she is projecting it to be a busy holiday weekend. Sally receives a phone call at 10:30 from J&G groceries, stating that they cannot deliver the product until 10:00 A.M. on Saturday morning. She explains to the driver that it is crucial that she receives the product as soon as possible. He apologizes; however, it is impossible to have delivery made until Saturday morning.

By 1:00 P.M., they are beginning to run out of product, including absolute necessities such as steaks, chicken, fish, and produce. The guests are getting frustrated because the staff are beginning to 86 a great deal of product. In addition, if they do not begin production for the P.M. shift soon, they will be in deep trouble.

On Friday nights, The Pub does in excess of $12,000 in sales. However, if the problem is not immediately alleviated, the restaurant will lose many guests and a great amount of profits.

Discussion Questions

1. What immediate measures would you take to resolve the problem?
2. How would you produce the appropriate product as soon as possible?
3. Who should you call first, if anyone, to alleviate the problem?
4. What can you do to always have enough product on hand?
5. Is it important to have a back-up plan for a situation like this? If so, what would it be?

CAREER INFORMATION

Restaurant Operations

Choosing a management career in restaurant operations means you have just selected the area of hospitality that offers college graduates enormous opportunity, the highest starting salaries in the hospitality industry, and the best opportunities for advancement. Opportunities range from fast-food to five-star dining. Salaries range from $32,000 to over $40,000 for entry-level management positions. Where you will be on that continuum depends on the skills you acquired while in the restaurant industry during college and your ability to sell yourself. (The type

of operation, sales volume, and location of the establishment also affect salaries.)

Higher salaries mean a more competitive environment for jobs. In the last few years, salaries have started to increase, reflecting the restaurant industry's willingness to hire experienced young talent. Recruiters refer to these graduates sometimes as grade A candidates or thoroughbreds. Recruiters want graduates who are confident in their skills and have a work record that shows a genuine interest in restaurant management.

Possessing confidence and skill is necessary to complete the management training programs and to get through your first year as a manager. Typically, restaurant managers work 50 to 60 hours a week, including weekends and holidays. It is a physically demanding job that requires being constantly on your feet and working under pressure in a fast-paced environment.

However, this kind of challenge has tremendous rewards. As a manager, you will work in an atmosphere that offers endless opportunities to delight customers and motivate employees. Few things are more gratifying than a genuinely satisfied customer or sharing in the pleasure of the restaurant crew's successfully completed shift. Restaurant operations typically pay people based strictly on performance. It is not uncommon for restaurant general managers to make six-figure incomes from restaurants that generate $5 million-plus in sales.

Related Web Sites

www.edfound.org/ —NRA educational foundation
www.restaurant-careers.com/ —Career Bulletin Board
www.brinker.com/htm/006_Employment_framesource.htm —Brinker International employment opportunities
www.houstons.com/html/benefits.htm —Houston's Restaurants employment opportunities
www.darden.com/darden.html —Darden Restaurants employment opportunities
www.careeradviser.com/all/Restaurant_and_food_service_managers.htm —opportunity for career advice
www.ranw.com/books/careers.html —foodservice books on careers

Courtesy of Charlie Adams.

SUMMARY

1. Most restaurants forecast a budget on a weekly and monthly basis that projects sales and costs for a year in consideration of guest counts and the average guest check.
2. To operate a restaurant, products need to be purchased, received, and properly stored.
3. Food production is determined by the expected business for the next few days. The kitchen layout is designed according to the sales forecasted.
4. Good service is very important. In addition to taking orders, servers act as salespersons for the restaurant.

5. The front of the house deals with the part of the restaurant having direct contact with guests, in other words, what the guests see—grounds maintenance, hosts/hostesses, dining and bar areas, bartenders, busers, etc.
6. The back of the house is generally run by the kitchen manager and refers to all areas guests normally do not come in contact with. This includes purchasing, receiving, storing/issuing, food production, stewarding, budgeting, accounting, and control.

KEY WORDS AND CONCEPTS

Average guest check	Employee recognition	Labor costs percentage	Production control sheets
Back of the house	First in–first out	Net profit	Purchase order
Balance sheet	Food cost percentage	Operating ratios	Receiving
Beverage cost percentage	Front of the house	Par stock	Restaurant forecasting
Budgeting costs	Gross profit	Personal digital assistants (PDAs)	Suggestive selling
Contribution margin	Guest counts or covers	Point-of-sale (POS) systems	Uniform system of accounts
Controllable expense	Hostess	Prime cost	Variable costs
Cooking line	Income statement	Product specification	
Curbside appeal	Kitchen manager		

REVIEW QUESTIONS

1. Briefly describe the two components of restaurant forecasting.
2. Explain the key points in purchasing, receiving, and storing.
3. Why is the kitchen layout an important aspect of food production?
4. Explain the purpose of suggestive selling. What characteristics make up a good server?
5. Accounting is important in order to determine the profitability of a restaurant. Briefly describe the following terms:

   a. Controllable expenses
   b. Uniform system of accounts
   c. Prime cost
6. What is the point-of-sales system, and why is a control system important for a restaurant operation?
7. What are the differences between the back of the house and the front of the house?
8. What steps must one take in preparing production sheets?

INTERNET EXERCISES

1. Organization: **National Restaurant Association (NRA)**
   Web site: **www.restaurant.org/**
   Summary: The NRA is the business association of the food industry. It consists of 400,000 members and over 170,000 restaurants. Member restaurants represent table service and quick-service operators, chains, and franchises. The NRA helps international restaurants receive the benefits of the association and gives guidance for success to nonprofit members.
   (a) List the food-borne diseases listed on the NRA site. Find out about each disease and how the National Restaurant Association suggests you can prevent it.
   (b) What kinds of careers are available in the restaurant and hospitality industry?
   (c) What legal issues does this site advise you on if you want to start your own restaurant?

2. Organization: **Chili's Grill and Bar**
   Web site: **chilis.com**
   Summary: Chili's is a fun and exciting place to have burgers, fajitas, margaritas, and chili. Established in 1975 in Dallas, the chain now has more than 637 restaurants in the United States and twenty other countries.
   (a) What requirements must you meet to open a Chili's franchise? From what you have learned about the issues involved in starting your own business, how is setting up your own business different from having a franchise?
   (b) What is the "Chilihead culture"?

APPLY YOUR KNOWLEDGE

In a casual Italian restaurant, sales for the week of September 15 are as follows:

Food sales	$10,000
Beverage sales	2,500
Total	$12,500

1. If the food cost is 30 percent, how much did the food actually cost?
2. If the beverage cost is 25 percent of beverage sales, how much did the beverages cost?
3. If the labor cost is 28 percent, how much money does that represent and how much is left over for other costs and profit?

SUGGESTED ACTIVITIES

1. Get in groups of two and assign the roles of guest and server. Role-play using the concept of suggestive selling and upselling.
2. Create an income statement for an imaginary restaurant.

ENDNOTES

1. This section draws on John R. Walker, and Donald E. Lundberg, *The Restaurant from Concept to Operation,* 4th ed. New York: John Wiley and Sons, 2005, pp. 86–87.
2. Personal conversation with Danny Meyer. January 14, 2004.
3. **www.softcafe.com**.
4. This section draws on John R. Walker and Donald E. Lundberg, *The Restaurant from Concept to Operation,* 4th ed. New York: John Wiley and Sons, 2005, p. 275.
5. Ibid.
6. Personal conversation with Bobby Hays, general manager, Chart House Restaurant, Solana Beach, California, January 1994.

WEB RESOURCES

McDonald's
www.mcdonalds.com

15th Street Fisheries Ft Lauderdale
www.15streetfisheries.com

T.G.I. Friday's
www.tgifridays.com

Union Square Café
www.unionsquarecafe.com

Inn at Little Washington
www.theinnatlittlewashington.com

Mondavi Winery
www.robertmondavi.com

National Restaurant Association
www.restaurant.org

Ruth's Chris Steak House
www.ruthschris.com

Managed Services 9

After reading and studying this chapter, you should be able to:

- Outline the different managed services segments.
- Describe the five factors that distinguish managed services operations from commercial ones.
- Explain the need for and trends in elementary and secondary school foodservice.
- Describe the complexities in college and university foodservice.
- Identify characteristics and trends in health care, business and industry, and leisure and recreation foodservices.

Overview

Managed services consists of all foodservice operations as follows:

- Airlines
- Military
- Elementary and secondary schools
- Colleges and universities
- Health care facilities
- Business and industry
- Leisure and recreation
- Conference centers
- Airports
- Travel plazas

Several features distinguish managed services operations from **commercial foodservices:**

1. In a restaurant, the challenge is to please the guest. In managed services, it is necessary to meet both the needs of the guest and the client (i.e., the institution itself).

2. In some operations, the guests may or may not have alternative dining options available to them and are a captive clientele. These guests may be eating at the foodservice operation only once or on a daily basis.

3. Many managed operations are housed in host organizations that do not have foodservice as their primary business.

4. Most managed services operations produce food in large-quantity batches for service and consumption within fixed time periods. (For example, **batch cooking** means to produce a batch of food to serve at 11:30 A.M., another batch to serve at 12:15 P.M., and a third batch to serve at 12:45 P.M., rather than putting out all the food for the whole lunch period at 11:30 A.M. This gives the guests who come to eat later in the serving period as good a quality meal as those who came to eat earlier.

5. The volume of business is more consistent and therefore easier to cater. Because it is easier to predict the number of meals and portion sizes, it is easier to plan, organize, produce, and serve meals; therefore, the atmosphere is less hurried than that of a restaurant. Weekends tend to be quieter than weekdays in managed services and, overall, the hours and benefits may be better than those of commercial restaurants.

A company or organization might contract its food- or other services for the following reasons:

- Financial
- Quality of program
- Recruitment of management and staff
- Expertise in management of service departments
- Resources available: people, programs, management systems, information systems
- Labor relations and other support
- Outsourcing of administrative functions[1]

Airlines and Airports

In-Flight and Airport Foodservice

When airlines do provide meals, they either come from their own *in-flight* business or have the service provided by a contractor. In-flight food may be prepared in a factory mode at a facility close to but outside of the airport. In these cases, the food is prepared and packaged; then it is transported to the departure gates for the appropriate flights. Once the food is loaded onto the aircraft, flight attendants take over serving the food and beverages to passengers.

In-flight foodservice is a complex logistical operation: The food must be able to withstand the transport conditions and the extended hot or cold holding period from the time it is prepared until the time it is served. If a food item is to be served hot, it must be able to rethermalize well on the plate. The meal should also look appetizing and taste good. Finally, all food and beverage items must be delivered on time and correctly to each departing aircraft.

Gate Gourmet International is the largest in-flight foodservices provider, operating in 27 countries on six continents from more than 140 catering facilities and producing over 250 million meals on average annually. It is estimated that sales will exceed $2 billion supported by more than 26,000 employees. Another major player in the in-flight food service market is Sky Chefs, headquartered in Dallas, Texas. The in-flight foodservice management operators plan the menus, develop the product specifications, and arrange the purchasing contracts. Each airline has a representative who oversees one or more locations and checks on the quality, quantity, and delivery times of all food and beverage items. Airlines regard in-flight foodservice as an expense that needs to be controlled. The cost for the average in-flight meal is just over $6. The cost had been higher, but in order to trim costs, many airlines now offer snacks instead of meals on a number of short flights and flights that do not span main meal times. Some airlines are experimenting with optional meals paid for by the passenger.

In-Flight Coffee Service

Food Being Prepared, Loaded, and Served on an Aircraft

International airlines try to stand out by offering superior food and beverages in hopes of attracting more passengers, especially the higher-paying business and first-class passenger. Others reduce or eliminate foodservice as a strategic decision to support lower fares. Due to the length of the flight, and the higher price paid for the ticket, international flights have better-quality food and beverage service.

On board, each aircraft has two or three categories of service, usually coach, business, and first class. First- and business-class passengers usually receive free beverages and upgraded meal items and service. These meals may consist of items like fresh salmon or filet mignon; the rest of us get those "carry-on doggie-bags"!

A number of smaller regional and local foodservice operators contract to a variety of airlines at hundreds of airports. Most airports have caterers or foodservice contractors who compete for airline contracts. With several international and U.S. airlines all using U.S. airports, each airline must decide whether to use its own foodservice (if it has one) or to contract with one of several independent operators.

Airport restaurants such as Chili's serve passengers meals that they no longer get on board.

Corporate Profile: Sodexho

Sodexho is a North American leading food and facilities management services company. This company is also a member of the international Sodexho Alliance that was founded in 1966 by a Frenchman named Pierre Bellon with its first service provider in Marseille, France. Primarily serving schools, restaurants, and hospitals, the company soon became internationally successful by signing deals with Belgian foodservice contractors. In 1980 after considerable success in Europe, Africa, and the Middle East, Sodexho Alliance decided to expand its reach into North and South America. In 1997 the company joined with Universal Ogden Services, a leading U.S. remote-site service provider. The empire grew a year later when Sodexho Alliance and Marriott Management Services merged. The merger created a new company called Sodexho Marriott Services. Listed on the New York Stock Exchange, the new company became the market leader in food and management services in the United States. At that time, Sodexho Alliance was the biggest shareholder, holding 48.4 percent of shares on the company's capital. In 2001, however, Sodexho Alliance acquired 53 percent of the shares in Sodexho Marriott Services, which changed its name to simply Sodexho.

Today, Sodexho Alliance has over 313,000 employees at 24,900 sites in 76 countries. In the United States there are 120,000 employees. The goal of Sodexho is to improve the quality and life of customers and clients all over the

United States and Canada. They offer outsourcing solutions to the health care, corporate, and education markets. This includes the following services: housekeeping, groundskeeping, foodservice, plant operation and maintenance, and integrated facilities management.

Sodexho's mission is to create and offer services that contribute to a more pleasant way of life for people wherever and whenever they come together. Its challenge is to continue to make its mission and values come alive through the way in which employees work together to serve the clients and customers. The values of Sodexho are service spirit, team spirit, and spirit of progress.

A leading provider of food and facilities management services in North America, Sodexho provides their services at more than 6,000 locations, including corporations, colleges and universities, health care organizations, and school districts. They are always looking to develop talent. Sodexho offers internships in foodservice and facilities management businesses as well as in staff positions such as finance, human resources, marketing, and sales. Sodexho believes that workforce diversity is essential to the company's growth and long-term success. By valuing and managing diversity at work, Sodexho can leverage the skills, knowledge, and abilities of all employees to increase employee, client, and customer satisfaction.

This feature draws on Sodexho USA home page, http://www.sodexhousa.com/about_us.html.

As airlines have decreased their in-flight foodservice, airport restaurants have picked up the business. Popular chain restaurants like T.G.I. Friday's and Chili's are in several terminals, along with the quick-service restaurants like Pizza Hut. These restaurants supplement airport foodservice offered by local restaurants.

Check Your Knowledge

1. What are managed services?
2. Why would companies use contract management?

Military

Military foodservice is a large and important component of managed services. There are about 1.5 million soldiers, sailors, and aviators on active duty in the United States. Even with the military downsizing, foodservice sales top $6 billion per year. Base closings have prompted many military foodservice organizations to rediscuss services and concepts in order to better meet the needs of their personnel.

Recent trends in military foodservice call for services such as officers' clubs to be contracted out to foodservice management companies. This change has reduced military costs because many of the officers' clubs lost money. The clubs now have moved the emphasis from fine dining to a more casual approach with family appeal. Many clubs are renovating their base concept even further, restyling according to theme concepts, such as sports or country western, for example. Other cost-saving measures include menu management, such as the use of a single menu for lunch and dinner (guests seldom eat both meals at the clubs). With proper plating techniques and portion size manipulation, a single menu can be created for lunch and dinner, meaning one inventory for both meals and less stock in general. To make this technique work successfully, the menu features several choices for appetizers, entrees, and desserts.

Another trend is the testing of prepared foods that can be reheated and served without much labor. Technological advances mean that field troops do not eat out of tin cans anymore; instead, they receive their food portions in plastic-and-foil pouches called meals ready-to-eat (MREs). Today, mobile field kitchens can be run by just two people, and bulk food supplies have been replaced by preportioned, precooked food packed in trays, which then are reheated in boiling water.

Feeding military personnel includes feeding troops and officers in clubs, dining halls, and military hospitals, as well as in the field. As both the budget and the numbers of personnel decrease, the military is downsizing by consolidating responsibilities. With fewer people to cook for, fewer cooks are required.

A model for such downsizing is the U.S. Marine Corps, who contracts out foodservice. With smaller numbers, they could not afford to take a marine away from training to work in the dining facilities without affecting military operations. Sodexho has the contract for the U.S. Marine Corps Serving on seven bases in 55 barracks, plus clubs and other related services. In addition, fast-food restaurants like McDonald's and Burger King have opened on well over 150 bases; they are now installing Express Way kiosks on more bases. The fast-food restaurants on base offer further alternatives for military personnel on the move. One problem that may arise as a result of the downsizing and contracting out of military foodservice is that it is not likely that McDonald's could set up on the front line in a combat situation. The military will still have to do their own foodservice when it comes to mobilization.

Elementary and Secondary Schools

The United States government enacted the National School Lunch Act of 1946. The rationale was that if students received good meals, the military would have healthier recruits. In addition, such a program would make use of the surplus food that farmers produced.

Each day, millions of children are fed breakfast or lunch, or both in approximately 98,000 schools.[2] Many challenges currently face elementary and secondary school foodservice. One major challenge is to balance salability with good nutrition. Apart from cost and nutritional value, the broader social issue of the universal free meal arises. Proponents of the program maintain that better nourished children have a better attention span, are less likely to be absent from school, and will stay in school longer. Offering free meals to all students also removes the poor kid stigma from school lunch. Detractors from the universal program say that if we learned anything from the social programs that were implemented during the 1960s, it was that throwing money at problems is not always the best answer.

Both sides agree that there is serious concern about what young students are eating. A U.S. Department of Agriculture survey found that school lunches, on average, exceeded dietary guidelines for fat by 25 percent, for saturated fat by 50 percent, and for sodium by 85 percent. Equally shocking is the percentage of children who eat one serving or less of fruits and vegetables each day (excluding french fries), as shown in Figure 9–1.

The preparation and service of school foodservice meals varies. Some schools have on-site kitchens where the food is prepared and dining rooms where the food is served. Many large school districts operate a central commissary that prepares the meals and then distributes them among the schools in that district. A third option is for schools to purchase ready-to-serve meals that require only assembly at the school.

Schools may decide to participate in the **National School Lunch Program (NSLP)** or operate on their own. In reality, most schools have little choice because

Getting kids to eat proper food is a challenge.

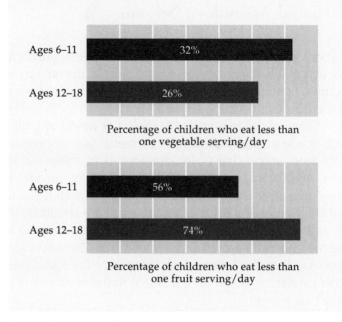

Figure 9–1 *Numbers of Servings of Fruit and Vegetables that Children Eat (Source: National Cancer Institute)*

participating in the program means that federal funding is provided in the amount of approximately $2.19 per meal per student. Contract companies such as ARA-MARK and Sodexho are introducing more flexibility in choices for students.

Meeting dietary guidelines is also an important issue. Much work has gone into establishing the nutritional requirements for children. It is difficult to achieve a balance between healthy food and costs, taking children's eating habits into account. Under the NSLP regulations, students must eat from what is commonly known as the type A menu. All the items in the type A menu must be offered to all children at every meal. The children have to select a minimum of three of the five meal components in order for the school to qualify for funding. However, USDA regulations have established limits on the amount of fat and saturated fat that can be offered. Fat should not exceed 30 percent of calories per week, and saturated fat was cut down to 10 percent of calories per week.

The government-funded NSLP, which pays over $7 billion per year for the meals given or sold at a discount to schoolchildren, is a huge potential market for fast-food chains. Chains are extremely eager to penetrate into the elementary and secondary school markets, even if it means a decrease in revenues. "We do reduce the price of our product, and we do make less margin than in our normal operations," says Joy Wallace, national sales director/nontraditional sales for Pizza Hut. However, they believe that it is to their benefit to introduce Pizza Hut to young people very early—in other words, the aim is to build brand loyalty. For example, in Duluth, Minnesota, James Bruner, foodservice director for the city schools, was forced into offering branded pizza in several junior high and high schools. The local principals, hungry for new revenue, began offering Little Caesar's in direct competition to the cafeteria's frozen pizzas.

Taco Bell is in nearly 3,000 schools, Pizza Hut is in 4,500, and Subway is in 650. Domino's, McDonald's, Arby's, and others are well established in the market as well. Despite the positives, although it is not hard to convince the children, chains need to convince the adults. Much debate has arisen as to whether chains should enter the schools or not. Many parents feel that the school environment should provide a standard example of what sound nutrition should be, and they believe that with fast food as an option, that will not be the case.

At a school lunch challenge at the American Culinary Federation (ACF) conference, chefs from around the country developed nutritious menus geared to wean children away from junk food to healthy foods. An 80-cent limit on the cost of raw ingredients was placed on the eleven finalists. Innovation and taste, as well as healthfulness, were the main criteria used to evaluate the winning entry: turkey taco salad, sausage pizza bagel, and stuffed potatoes.

Nutrition Education Programs

Nutrition education programs are now a required part of the nation's school lunch program. As a result of this program, children are learning to improve their eating habits, which, it is hoped, will continue for the rest of their lives. To support the program, nutritional education materials are used to decorate the dining room halls and tables. Perhaps the best example of this is the food pyramid developed by the Food and Nutrition Service of the U.S. Department of Agriculture. Figure 9–2 shows this food pyramid, which shows what to eat each day for a healthy diet.

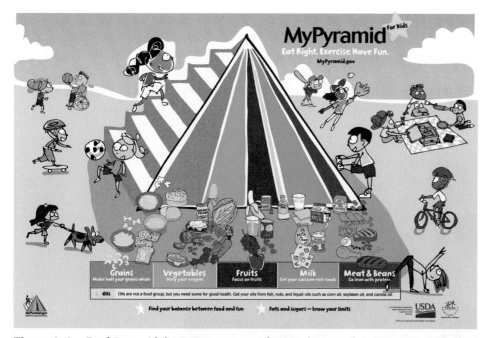

Figure 9–2   *Food Pyramid (U.S. Department of Agriculture and U.S. Department of Health and Human Services)*

Colleges and Universities

College and university foodservice operations are complex and diverse. Among the various constituents of foodservice management are residence halls, sports concessions, conferences, cafeterias/student unions, faculty clubs, convenience stores, administrative catering, and outside catering.

On-campus dining is a challenge for foodservice managers because, as you well know, the clients live on campus and eat most of their meals at the campus dining facility. If the manager or contractor is not creative, students, staff, and faculty will quickly become bored with the sameness of the surroundings and menu offerings. Most campus dining is cafeteria style, offering cyclical menus that rotate every 10 or 14 days.

However, a college foodservice manager does have some advantages when compared with a restaurant manager. Budgeting is made easier because the on-campus students have already paid for their meals and their numbers are easy to forecast. When the payment is guaranteed and the guest count is predictable, planning and organizing staffing levels and food quantities are relatively easy and should ensure a reasonable profit margin. For instance, the **daily rate** is the amount of money required per day from each person to pay for the foodservice. Thus, if foodservice expenses for one semester of 98 days amount to $650,000 for an operation with 1,000 students eating, the daily rate will be

$$\frac{\$650,000 \div 98 \text{ (days)}}{1000} = \$6.63$$

College foodservice operations now offer a variety of meal plans for students. Under the old board plan, when students paid one fee for all meals each day—whether they ate them or not—the foodservice operator literally made a profit from the students who did not actually eat the meals they had paid for. More typically now, students match their payments to the number of meals eaten: Monday–Friday, breakfast, lunch, dinner; dinner only; and prepaid credit cards that allow a student to use the card at any campus outlet and have the value of the food and beverage items deducted from his or her credit balance.

College Foodservice

Personal Profile: Manuel Lorenzo

Manuel Lorenzo is a supervisor for Sodexho Food Services and arrives at Alliant International University (AIU) to begin his shift at 9:00 A.M. Manuel's first duty is to check the catering board, where he will find a list of scheduled catering events for the day. Manuel then plans the food preparation and starts gathering the necessary equipment.

By 10:00 A.M., Manuel goes around to all the foodservice outlets that are open during the night hours and collects money and receipts. The cash must then be immediately transported to the bank for deposit. The figures must also be entered into the company computer.

After Manuel completes handling the money, he talks with Richard Nargi, the general manager of foodservices at AIU. He keeps him abreast of information for the day. This is the time any problems or concerns can be addressed. At 11:00 A.M., Manuel walks around to make sure the cafeteria is ready to serve lunch. Manuel supervises the lunch operation until it ends at 1:30. After lunch, he continues working on catering functions and makes sure everything flows and is ready for dinner.

Before leaving for the day, Manuel must check to see that all catering vehicles are tanked and running properly. Then the storerooms must be cleaned and organized. The general manager will also have a list of pro-

jects for Manuel to complete. These tasks usually consist of maintaining sanitation standards. Last, Manuel checks staffing levels for the rest of the week and deals with basic human resource functions.

Manuel sees time management as one of the major challenges of his career. Events are constantly pending, and he has only a very limited amount of time to plan, organize, and carry out those functions. Manuel contends that the only way to be successful, in this respect, is to be highly organized. Manuel says that success requires one to be a "people-person." This skill helps him deal with employees effectively and helps him understand the people he serves, so that he can serve them better.

Keeping the customer satisfied is another challenge for Manuel. University foodservice operations have the unique and difficult task of keeping long-term boarding residents happy with food quality. Manuel solves this problem by serving a wide variety of entrees, yet keeping consistent with daily staples.

Each catering event is different because of the variety in food served. With each new function, Manuel learns something about food and/or culture. Mr. Lorenzo admits that this is one of the most interesting, exciting, and rewarding aspects of his job.

Leaders of the National Associations of College Auxiliary Services (NACAS), who represents 1,200 member institutes, have noticed that on-campus services and activities are undergoing continuous change. The environment has become a critical part of policy and implementation that transcends parochial interests for those that best meet the needs of the institution and, ultimately, its students.

The driving forces of change on campuses are the advent and growth of branded concepts, privatization, campus cards, and computer use. A college foodservice manager today must have greater skills in retail marketing and merchandizing as students are given more discretion in how they may spend their money for food on campus.

Student Unions

As you know, the college student union offers a variety of managed services that caters to the needs of a diverse student body. Among the services offered are cafeteria foodservice, beverage services, branded quick-service restaurants, and take-out foodservice.

The cafeteria foodservice operation is often the "happening" place in the student union where students meet to socialize as well as to eat and drink. The cafeteria is generally open for breakfast, lunch, and dinner. Depending on the volume of business, the cafeteria may be closed during the nonmeal periods and weekends, and the cafeteria menu may or may not be the same as the residence foodservice facility. Offering a menu with a good price value is crucial to the successful operation of a campus cafeteria.

On campuses at which alcoholic beverage service is permitted, beverage services mainly focus on some form of a student pub where beer and perhaps wine and spirits may be offered. Not to be outdone, the faculty will undoubtedly have a lounge that also offers alcoholic beverages. Other beverages may be served at various outlets such as a food court or convenience store. Campus beverage service provides opportunities for foodservice operators to enhance profits.

In addition, many college campuses have welcomed branded, quick-service restaurants as a convenient way to satisfy the needs of a community on the go. Such an approach offers a win–win situation for colleges. The experience and brand recognition of chain restaurants like Pizza Hut, McDonald's, Subway, and Wendy's attract customers; the restaurants pay a fee, either to the foodservice management company or the university directly. Obviously, there is a danger that the quick-service restaurant may attract customers that the cafeteria might then lose, but competition tends to be good for all concerned.

Take-out foodservice is another convenience for the campus community. At times, students—and staff—do not want to prepare meals and are thankful for the opportunity to take meals with them. And it is not just during examination time that students, friends, and staff have a need for the take-out option. For example, tailgate parties prior to football and basketball games or concerts and other recreational/sporting events allow entrepreneurial foodservice operators to increase revenue and profits. The type of contract that a managed services operator signs varies depending on the size of the account. If the account is small, a fee generally is charged. With larger accounts, operators contract for a set percentage (usually about 5 percent) or a combination of a percentage and a bonus split. Figure 9–3 shows a typical college menu for the dining hall where students usually eat on campus.

As with all types of contract services, there are advantages and disadvantages. Here are both from a client's (that would be your college) perspective:

Advantages	Disadvantages
• Experience in size and types of operations	• Some segments perceived as institutionalized
• Use contracted department as a model for rest of institution	• Potential for lost contracts
• Variety of services	
• Resource and support available	
• Hold contractor to a higher level of performance	

WEEK 1

	MONDAY	TUESDAY	WEDNESDAY	THURSDAY	FRIDAY

Breakfast - Cold cereal, fruit and yogurt bar, toast, juices, milks, coffee, tea, hot chocolate and fresh fruit

	MONDAY	TUESDAY	WEDNESDAY	THURSDAY	FRIDAY
Bakery:	Quick Coffee Cake	Assorted Danish	Cinnamon Coffee Cake	Sticky Top Roll	Banana Nut Muffins
Hot Cereal:	Oatmeal	Malt-O-Meal	Cream of Wheat	Grits	Oatmeal
Entrees:	Buttermilk Pancakes	Waffles	French Toast	Oatmeal Pancakes	Waffles w/Peaches
	Scrambled Eggs	Scrambled Eggs	Scrambled Eggs	Scrambled Eggs	Scrambled Eggs
	Sausage Gravy	Egg O'Muffin w/Bacon	Ham & Cheese	Chorizo & Eggs	Egg Burrito
	& Biscuits	Hearty Fried Potatoes	Omelette	Cottage Fries	Home Fries
	Cottage Fries	Bacon	Hash Browns	Sausage Links	

Lunch - Salad Bar, Rice & Chili Bar, Cereal, Build-Your-Own-Sandwich Bar & Fresh Fruit

	MONDAY	TUESDAY	WEDNESDAY	THURSDAY	FRIDAY
Soup:	Beef Barley	Italian Minestrone	Chicken Gumbo	Chicken Noodle	New England Clam Chowder
Entrees:	Baked Seafood & Rice	Chicken Tortilla	Fishwich	Cheesy Mushroom	BBQ Ham Sandwich
	Grilled Ham & Cheese	Casserole	Spanish Macaroni	Burger	Ground Beef &
	Potato Salad	Patty Melt	Ranch Beans	Hamburger	Potato Pie
	Wax Beans	French Fries	Italian Green Beans	Grilled Cheese	Whipped Potatoes
	Mixed Vegetables	Hominy	Braised Carrots &	Onion Rings	Italian Green Beans
		Spinach	Celery	Carrots	Beets
				Oriental Veg. Blend	
Dessert:	Chocolate Pudding	Applesauce Cake	Peanut Butter	Coconut Cake	Vanilla Pudding
	Soft Serve Ice Cream	Soft Serve Ice Cream	Cookies		

Dinner - Salad Bar, Cereal, & Fresh Fruit (Tortillas served at Breakfast & Dinner)

	MONDAY	TUESDAY	WEDNESDAY	THURSDAY	FRIDAY
Soup:	Beef Barley	Italian Minestrone	Chicken Gumbo	Chicken Noodle	New England Clam Chowder
Entrees:	Oven Broiled Chicken	Beef Fajitas	Roast Turkey w/Gravy	Egg Roll Over Rice	Pizza! Pizza! Pizza!
	Grilled Liver & Onions	Fried Perch	Old Fashion Beef Stew	Grilled Pork Chop	Curly Fries
	Parsley Potatoes	Spanish Rice	Whipped Potatoes	Rice	Broccoli
	Corn	Asparagus	Corn Cobbettes	Beets	Mixed Vegetables
	Zucchini	Carrots	Brussel Sprouts	Cauliflower au Gratin	
Dessert:	Chocolate Chip Cookies	Spicy Whole Wheat Bar	Chocolate Mayo Cake	Peach Cobbler	Best Ever Cake

Figure 9–3   *Sample College Menu (Courtesy Sodexho Foodservice Management)*

Responsibilities in Managed Services

A foodservice manager's responsibilities in a small or midsize operation are frequently more extensive than those of managers of the larger operations. This is because larger units have more people to whom to delegate certain functions, such as human resources. For example, following are some of the responsibilities that the foodservice manager in a small or midsize operation might have in addition to strictly foodservice responsibilities:

Employee Relations
- Team development
- Rewards/recognition
- Drug alcohol abuse/prevention
- Positive work environment
- Coaching/facilitating vs. directing

Human Resource Management
- Recruitment/training/evaluating
- Wage/salary administration
- Benefits administration
- Compliance with federal/state laws/EEO/Senate Bill 198
- Harassment/OSHA
- Disciplinary actions/terminations
- Unemployment/wrongful disclosure

Financial/Budgeting
- Project budgets
- Actual vs. budget monitoring (weekly)
- Controlling food cost, labor, expenses, and so on
- Record keeping requirements/audit
- Monitoring accounts payable/receivable
- Billing/collecting
- Compliance to contracts
- Cash procedures/banking

Safety Administration
- Equipment training/orientation
- Controlling workers compensation
- Monthly inspections/audits (federal/state/ OSHA requirements/Senate Bill 198)

Safety Budget
- Work on the expensive injuries
- Reduce lost time frequency rate and injury frequency rate

Food Production/Service
- Menu/recipe development
- Menu mix vs. competition

Personal Profile: Regynald G. Washington

Vice-President and General Manager for Disney Regional Entertainment and Vice-President of New Business Initiatives for Walt Disney Parks and Resorts

For a student majoring in hotel and restaurant management, being a general manager, president, or even chief executive officer in the food industry is a goal to be achieved. For Regynald G. Washington, not only has it been a goal reached, but a dream realized. His bright smile spells success. As a child growing up in a middle-income family in the town of Marathon in the Florida Keys, working was mandatory. At the early age of 13, he was introduced to the food industry. His first job consisted of waiting on and busing tables and doing other chores in the Indies Inn Resort and Yacht Club. He took this on as an exciting and new challenge.

For Regynald, attitude is everything. His positive attitude toward being the best that he can be was derived from a phrase his parents used to repeat to him: "A chip on your shoulder earns a lack of respect from colleagues, friends, and family." His great energy and pride in his work is what makes him stand out among many other leaders in the food industry. He has a quality and people-oriented mind that keeps him focused on any task he wishes to accomplish.

Regynald graduated from Florida International University with a degree in hotel and restaurant administration. He continued to work for Indies Inn Resort, but by this time he was running the food and beverage operation. This was the beginning of the long career road for Regynald G. Washington.

In the years that followed, Regynald worked as a restaurant general manager and at Concessions International, an airport food and beverage, duty free, gifts, and magazine organization in Atlanta. He was promoted to executive vice president in 1990. He then formed Washington Enterprises and developed Sylvia's Restaurant in Atlanta, which turned out to be very successful.

A few years later though, a major entertainment company executive recruiter offered Washington an opportunity to join the new and creative food and beverage approach that the company was aiming to develop.

Regynald's secret to managing 2,500 employees and satisfying Epcot's customers is simply organization and care. Having organization and direction in your work eliminates stress and makes time for fun. Making sure that all the staff know what they are doing and that they are doing it well and serving guests hot food hot and cold food cold is all it takes. He uses a back-to-basics formula, which requires that everything go well, from making guests happy to proper staffing. Not only has his ambition and energy helped him climb to the top, but he also has great concern for others and wants to help his employees learn new things and move forward in their careers. He is very well focused on quality and precision in anything and everything he does. One of his number one concerns is food safety.

To make sure everything is intact and going well, Regynald and his support team perform unannounced inspections every quarter. A specific food and beverage facility is concentrated on and fully evaluated for its table turns, guest service, food quality, and training programs. Specialists act as the guests and observe and report anything that seems less than perfect. Epcot executive chefs check the kitchen food as well as the menu. In-house sanitarians evaluate the level of sanitation at the facility. The goal of these inspections is to make sure nothing is less than perfect. Excellence is the goal for Regynald. He admires and respects the people who work with him and has ranked them as being the best food and beverage people.

Mr. Washington is a frequent guest lecturer in educational forums and has served on the advisory boards of a number of universities for their hospitality management programs. His board service includes being a trustee of the National Restaurant Association Educational Foundation.

Regynald believes that he has achieved a lot and has had many successes during his career. His career is exciting and motivating and he has the opportunity to make a difference is people's lives every single day. This is what he always wanted and now he has it. He says, "My parents really wanted me to become a lawyer, physician, or architect. They didn't believe you could reach the top and do exciting things in the restaurant industry."

Source: This profile draws on Whit Smyth, "Regynald Washington, EPCOT's Chief of Food and Beverage. "Says Pleasing Customers Is No Mickey Mouse," Nation's Restaurant News, 33, 4, January 25, 1999, p. 28–30 and personal correspondence. April 6, 2005.

A Subway Quick-Service Outlet on Campus at UCLA, La Jolla, California

- Food waste/leftovers utilization
- Production records
- Production control
- Presentation/merchandising

Sanitation/FBI Prevention
- FBI (food-borne illness) prevention
- Sanitation/cleaning schedule
- Proper food handling/storage
- Daily prevention/monitoring
- Monthly inspection
- Health department compliance

Purchasing/Recruiting
- Ordering/receiving/storage
- Food and beverage specifications/quality
- Inventory control
- Vendor relation/problems

Staff Training/Development
- On-the-job vs. structured
- Safety/sanitation/food handling and so on
- Food preparation/presentation
- Guest service

There are a number of support staff positions that offer career opportunities not only within managed services but also in all facets of hospitality operations and arrangements. They include sales, marketing, controller/audit, financial analysis, human resources, training and development, affirmative action/EEO compliance, safety administration, procurement/distribution, technical services (recipes, menus, product testing), labor relations, and legal aspects.

DESCRIPTION		%	STUDENT UNION	%	TOTAL	%
SALES						
FOOD REGULAR	$ 951,178				951,178	
FOOD SPECIAL FUNCTIONS	40,000				40,000	
PIZZA HUT EXPRESS			$ 100,000		100,000	
BANQUET & CATERING	200,000				200,000	
CONFERENCE	160,000				160,000	
BEER			80,000		80,000	
SNACK BAR			300,000		30,000	
A LA CARTE CAFE	60,000				60,000	
** TOTAL SALES	$1,411,178		$ 480,000	100.0%	$1,891,178	100.0%
PRODUCT COST						
BAKED GOODS	$ 9,420		$ 4,700		$ 14,120	
BEVERAGE	10,000		8,000		18,000	
MILK & ICE CREAM	11,982		2,819		14,801	
GROCERIES	131,000		49,420		180,420	
FROZEN FOOD	76,045		37,221		113,266	
MEAT, SEAFOOD, EGGS & CHEESE	129,017		48,000		177,017	
PRODUCE	65,500		26,000		91,500	
MISCELLANEOUS					0	
COLD DRINK	0		0		0	
** TOTAL PRODUCT COST	$ 432,964		$ 176,160	36.7%	$ 609,124	32.2%
LABOR COST						
WAGES	$ 581,000		$ 154,000		$ 735,000	
LABOR—OTHER EMPLOYEES	101,500		545,000		156,000	
BENEFITS + PAYROLL TAXES	124,794		50,657		175,451	
MANAGEMENT BENEFITS	58,320		6,000		64,320	
WAGE ACCRUALS	0				0	
** TOTAL LABOR COST	$ 865,614		$ 265,157	55.2%	$1,130,771	59.8%
FOOD OPERATING COST-						
CONTROLLABLE						
CLEANING SUPPLIES	$ 24,000		$ 6,000		$ 30,000	
PAPER SUPPLIES	9,000		46,000		55,000	
EQUIPMENT RENTAL					0	
GUEST SUPPLIES					7,000	
PROMOTIONS	4,500		2,500		40,000	
SMALL EQUIPMENT	35,000		5,000		0	
BUSINESS DUES & MEMBERSHIP					3,000	
VEHICLE EXPENSE	3,000				4,300	
TELEPHONE	3,600		700		$ 22,000	
	$ 17,000		$ 5,000			

continued

Figure 9–4   *Sample Operating Statement*

A sample operating statement is shown in Figure 9–4. It shows a monthly statement for a college foodservice operation.

Managed Services Career Paths

A typical career path in managed services for a college graduate includes the following positions:

- *Assistant foodservice director:* Salary range of $30,000 to $35,000 plus benefits, which can be about 30 percent of salary and include a pension plan. If you already have experience in a variety of foodservice operations/positions, upon graduation, it is possible to gain this type of position. It is

DESCRIPTION		%	STUDENT UNION	%	TOTAL	%
LAUNDRY & UNIFORMS					0	
MAINTENANCE & REPAIRS	$ 1,200		$ 200		$ 1,400	
FLOWERS	10,000		4,000		140,000	
TRAINING					0	
SPECIAL SERVICES	18,000		3,000		21,000	
MISCELLANEOUS						
** TOTAL CONTROLLABLE SUPPLIES	$ 125,300	8.9%	$ 72,400	15.1%	$ 197,700	10.5%
OPERATING COSTS-NONCONTROLLABLE						
AMORTIZATION & DEPRECIATION	$ 13,500		$ 7,000		$ 20,500	
INSURANCE	55,717		14,768		70,485	
MISCELLANEOUS EXPENSE	12,400		4,100		16,500	
ASSET RETIREMENTS					0	
RENT/COMMISSIONS	48,000		40,000		88,000	
PIZZA HUT ROYALTIES			7,000		7,000	
PIZZA HUT —						
LICENSING MARKETING			7,000		7,000	
TAXES, LICENSE & FEES	5,000		500		5,500	
VEHICLE —						
DEPRECIATION & EXPENSE	4,000				4,000	
ADMINISTRATION & SUPERVISION						
** TOTAL NONCONTROLLABLE COST	$ 138,617	9.8%	$ 80,368	16.7%	$ 218,985	11.6%
** TOTAL COST OF OPERATIONS	$1,562,495	110.7%	$ 594,085	123.8%	$2,156,580	114.0%
EXCESS OR (DEFICIT)	(151,317)	(10.7%)	(114,085)	(23.8)	(265,402)	(14.0%)
PARTICIPATION-CONTRACTOR						
*** NET EXCESS OR (DEFICIT)						
STATISTICS						
CUSTOMER COUNT						
HOURS WORKED						
AVERAGE FOOD-SALES/CUSTOMER						

Figure 9–4 *continued*

possible that you would move to a larger operation or a different type of account to broaden your experience and knowledge before moving up to the next level.

- *Foodservice director:* $35,000 to $80,000 plus benefits. It is likely that you would begin at one account and then move to a larger one after a few years.
- *General manager:* $50,000 to $100,000 plus benefits. After spending a few years at one location, it is likely that you would move to another possibly larger one. For example, you may be GM of a $4 million account and go to a $10 million account.
- *District manager:* $75,000 to $125,000 plus benefits. The district manager is responsible for several accounts; other responsibilities include making proposals to gain new accounts and negotiating contracts with clients.

Check Your Knowledge

1. In your own words, define in-flight foodservice.
2. What are some of the challenges faced by in-flight foodservice operators? What can be done to solve these problems?
3. Name the foodservice operations that constitute managed services.
4. How is each foodservice operation characterized?
5. In small groups, discuss the differences between the foodservice operations; then share with the class.

Health Care Facilities

Health care managed services operations are remarkably complex because of the necessity of meeting the diverse needs of a delicate clientele. Health care managed services are provided to hospital patients, long-term care and assisted-living residents, visitors, and employees. The service is given by tray, cafeteria, dining room, coffee shop, catering, and vending.

The challenge of health care managed services is to provide many special meal requirements to patients with very specific dietary requirements. Determining which meals need to go to which patients and ensuring that they reach their destinations employs especially challenging logistics. In addition to the patients, health care employees need to enjoy a nutritious meal in pleasant surroundings in a limited time (usually 30 minutes). Because employees typically work five days in a row, managers must be creative in the development of menus and meal themes.

The main focus of hospital foodservice is the **tray line.** Once all the requirements for special meals have been prepared by a registered dietitian, the line is set up and menus color coded for the various diets. The line begins with the tray, a mat, cutlery, napkin, salt and pepper, and perhaps a flower. As the tray moves along the line, various menu items are added according to the color code for the particular patient's diet. Naturally, each tray is double- and triple-checked, first at the end of the tray line and then on the hospital floor. The line generally goes floor by floor at a rate of about five trays a minute; at this rate, a large hospital with 600 beds can be served within a couple of hours. This is time consuming for the employees, because three meals a day represent up to 6 hours of line time. Clearly, health care foodservice is very labor intensive, with labor accounting for about 55 to 66 percent of operating dollars. In an effort to keep costs down, many operators have increased the number of help-yourself food stations, buffets, salads, desserts, and topping bars. They also focus on increasing revenues through catering and retail innovations. Operators must also contend with the fact that food costs are not totally covered by Medicare.

Hospital foodservice has evolved to the point where the need for new revenue sources has changed the traditional patient and nonpatient meal-service ratios at many institutions. This situation was imposed by the federal

*The All-Important Tray Line
in Health Care Foodservice*

government when it narrowed the treatment-reimbursement criteria; originally 66 percent of a typical acute-care facility's foodservice budget went toward patients' meals, with the remainder allocated for feeding the employees
and visitors. In the past few years, as cash sales have become more important, the 66/33 percent ratio has reversed.

Experts agree that because economic pressures will increase, foodservice managers will need to use a more high-tech approach, incorporating labor-saving sous-
vide and cook–chill methods. This segment of the industry, which currently is
dominated by self-operated managed services, will continue to see contract specialists, such as Sodexho, Compass, and ARAMARK Services, increase their market share at the expense of self-operated health care managed services. One reason
for this is that the larger contract companies have the economy of scale and a more
sophisticated approach to quantity purchasing, menu management, and operating systems that help to reduce food and labor costs. A skilled independent foodservice operator has the advantage of being able to introduce changes immediately
without having to support layers of regional and corporate employees.

Another trend in health care managed services is the arrival of the major
quick-service chains. McDonald's, Pizza Hut Express, Burger King, and Dunkin'
Donuts are just a few of the large companies that have joined forces with the
contract managed services operators. Using branded quick-service leaders is a
win–win situation for both the contract foodservice operator and the quick-
service chain.

The chains benefit from long-term leases at very attractive rates compared with a restaurant site. Chains assess the staff size and patient and visitor count to determine the size of unit to install. Thus far, they have found that weekday lunches and dinners are good, but the numbers on weekends are disappointing.

In contrast, several hospitals are entering the pizza-delivery business: They hook up phone and fax ordering lines, and they hire part-time employees to deliver pizzas made on the premises. This ties in with the increasing emphasis on customer service. Patients' meals now feature "comfort foods," based on the concept that the simpler the food is, the better. Hence, the resurgence of meat loaf, pot pies, meat and potatoes, and tuna salad, which contributes to customer satisfaction, and makes them feel at home and comfortable.

Business and Industry

Business and industry (B&I) managed services is one of the most dynamic segments of the managed services industry. In recent years, B&I foodservice has improved its image by becoming more colorful, with menus as interesting as commercial restaurants.

There are important terms to understand in B&I foodservice:[3]

1. **Contractors:** Companies that operate foodservice for the client on a contractual basis. Most corporations contract with managed services companies because they are in manufacturing or some other service industry. Therefore, they engage professional managed services corporations to run their employee dining facilities.
2. **Self-operators:** Companies that operate their own foodservice operations. In some cases, this is done because it is easier to control one's own operation; for example, it is easier to make changes to comply with special nutritional or other dietary requests.
3. **Liaison personnel:** A liaison is responsible for translating corporate philosophy to the contractor and for overseeing the contractor to make certain that he or she abides by the terms of the contract.

Contractors have approximately 80 percent of the B&I market. The remaining 20 percent is self-operated, but the trend is for more foodservice operations to be contracted out. The size of the B&I sector is approximately 30,000 units. To adapt to corporate downsizing and relocations, the B&I segment has offered foodservice in smaller units, rather than huge full-sized cafeterias. Another trend is the necessity for B&I foodservice to break even or, in some cases, make a profit. An interesting twist is the emergence of multitenant buildings, the occupants of which may all use a central facility. However, in today's turbulent business environment, there is a high vacancy rate in commercial office space. This translates into fewer guests for B&I operators in multitenant office buildings. As a result, some office buildings have leased space to commercial branded restaurants.

A Business and Industry Account of Sodexho

B&I managed services operators have responded to requests from corporate employees to offer more than the standard fastfood items of pizza and hamburgers; they want healthier foods offered, such as make-your-own sandwiches, salad bars, fresh fruit stations, and ethnic foods.

Most B&I managed services operators offer a number of types of service. The type of service is determined by the resources available: money, space, time, and expertise. Usually these resources are quite limited, which means that most operations use some form of cafeteria service.

B&I foodservice may be characterized in the following ways:

1. Full-service cafeteria with *straight line, scatter* or *mobile systems*
2. *Limited-service cafeterias* offering parts of the full-service cafeteria, fast-food service, cart and mobile service, fewer dining rooms, and executive dining rooms

An ARAMARK Business and Industry Foodservice Account

Focus on Managed Services

Mega-Event Management—the Olympics—Going for the Gold

Fred J. DeMicco
Professor and ARAMARK Chair of Hotel, Restaurant & Institutional Management, University of Delaware, and Penn State Walter J. Conti Professor of HRIM

ARAMARK is a world leader in providing global managed services, including food, facility, and other support services. ARAMARK has leadership positions serving the business, education, health care, sports, entertainment, and recreation management segments. Related to sports, entertainment, and food service is "serving the world" at the Olympics.

ARAMARK has a long and rich history with the Olympic Games, dating back to 1968 when it served at the Mexico City Summer Games, the largest in history at the time. Since then, the company has managed services at more Olympic Games than any other company, earning its own "gold medal" performance at both the summer and winter games over the past four decades, including the 1976 Summer Olympic Games in Montreal, Canada; the 1980 Winter Olympic Games in Lake Placid, New York; the 1984 Winter Olympic Games in Sarajevo, Yugoslavia; the 1984 Summer Olympic Games in Los Angeles, California; the 1988 Winter Olympic Games in Calgary, Canada; the 1988 Summer Olympic Games in Seoul, South Korea; the 1992 Summer Olympic Games in Barcelona, Spain; the 1994 Winter Olympic Games in Lillehammer, Norway; the 1996 Centennial Olympic Games in Atlanta, Georgia; the 1998 Winter Olympic Games in Nagano, Japan; the Summer Olympic Games in Sydney, Australia, in 2000, and the Summer Olympic Games in Athens, Greece.

ARAMARK chefs and nutritionists develop a World Menu with over 550 recipes designed to meet the needs of athletes from 200 different countries, with different ethnic and religious backgrounds and varying nutritional needs, to help them achieve their best during their Olympic performances.

For the third time, Mr. DeMicco is taking students to the Olympic Village to work for ARAMARK. In 1996, his students worked the summer games in Atlanta, and they traveled to Sydney to work in the 2000 summer games.

With 1,500 different menu items available, 24 hours a day, the students will have their work cut out for them. Some of the stranger dishes that appeared on athletes' plates during the 2000 Sydney Olympics included kangaroo prosciutto, smoked emu, grilled mako shark, and goat vindaloo.

"The exposure to this type of event provides more learning than any other food service venture," Jerome Bill, of ARAMARK, said. "Usually a small city is built, operated for approximately 33 days, and then is taken down just as fast. The logistics are tremendous."

ARAMARK recruits and trains more than 6,500 persons to prepare and serve more than 5 million meals during the 33 days the Olympics and Para-Olympics take place. The grocery list for such an event is enormous. In Atlanta in 1996, some of the major ingredients that ARAMARK used included 576,000 eggs, 34,000 pounds of rice, 32,800 pounds of margarine, and 9,057 pounds of shredded cheddar cheese.

"Where else can you welcome 15,000 of the best in the world into your home for dinner? It is truly the ultimate display of blending one's background, classroom experience, and human nature into an unforgettable learning environment. Students learn more than just serving and cooking; they reach the brink of fully understanding the true meaning of hospitality," said Marc Bruno, MBA ARAMARK.

The students were able to interact with elite athletes in the world in a fast-paced and constantly changing environment. They were able to be part of providing foodservice that met the unique cultural and nutritional needs of athletes from over 200 countries. They went in every day knowing that their jobs were critical to each athlete's peak performance.

According to a student participant, "The Olympics allowed me to get an inside view of how a mega event was run, the problems that came up, and how they were overcome. Being in the Olympic Village introduced me to working with people of many different cultures. I am currently working for NBC Olympics in the Games Services department. I am really looking forward to being part of another Olympic Games."

Managed Services Other Than Food

Many companies like Sodexho have recognized the potential to increase their market opportunities by developing service capabilities beyond food. This also offers hospitality managers the opportunity to expand their career paths as well. Typically, hospitals, colleges, schools, and businesses outsource other service departments the same as they do food. Companies on the cutting edge are able to offer clients broader packages of services. These services often come under the area of facilities management[4] and offer the following services:

- Housekeeping/custodial/environment services
- Maintenance and engineering
- Grounds and landscaping
- Procurement and materials management
- Office and mail services
- Concierge services
- Patient transportation services (hospitals)

Many colleges and universities recognize that this is an area for career opportunities and are developing courses and programs surrounding the area of facilities management. Managers who work in the managed services segment of the industry have the advantage of learning about several disciplines, similar to hotels. In doing so, they increase their career growth potential and can find career paths similar to those available in the lodging segment of the industry.

Leisure and Recreation

The leisure and recreation[5] segment of managed services may be the most unique and the most fun part of the foodservice industry in which to work.

Leisure and recreation foodservice operations include stadiums, arenas, theme parks, national parks, state parks, zoos, aquariums, and other venues where food and beverage are provided for large numbers of people. The customers are usually in a hurry, so the big challenge of the foodservice segment is to offer their product in a very short period of time. The average professional sporting event only lasts for two to three hours of actual playing time.

What makes this segment unique and fun is the opportunity to be part of a professional sporting event, a rock concert, a circus, or other event in a typical stadium or arena. There is also the choice of working in a national or state park and being part of the great outdoors, if that is to your liking. The roar of the crowd and the excitement of the event make this a very stimulating place to work. Imagine *getting paid* to see the Super Bowl versus *paying* to see the Super Bowl.

Stadium Points of Service

Leisure and recreation facilities usually have several points of service where food and beverage are provided. In the typical stadium a vendor is yelling, "Here, get your hot dog here!" to the fans in the stands, while on the concourse other fans get their food and beverage from concession stands. These stands offer everything from hot dogs and hamburgers to local cuisine. For example, in Philadelphia the cheesesteak sandwich is popular, whereas in Baltimore crab-cake sandwiches are favored by fans. Another place for people to get food is in a restaurant, which most stadiums have as a special area. In some cases, fans must be members of the restaurant; in other cases, fans can buy special tickets that provide them with access to this facility. These restaurants are like any other except that they provide unobstructed views of the playing area.

The other major point of service is the food and beverage offered in the premium seating areas known as superboxes, suites, and skyboxes. These premium seating areas are usually leased by corporations to entertain corporate guests and customers. In each of these areas, food and beverage service is provided for the guests. These facilities are capable of holding 30 to 40 guests and usually have an area where the food is set up buffet style and a seating area where the guest can see the sporting or other event. In a large, outdoor stadium, there could be as many as 60 to 70 of these superbox-type facilities.

In summary, a large stadium/arena could have vendors in the stands, concession outlets, restaurants, and superboxes all going at once and serving upward of 60,000 to 70,000 fans. Feeding all these people takes tremendous planning and organization on the part of the foodservice department. The companies that have many of the contracts for these stadiums and arenas are ARAMARK, Fine Host, Sodexho, Compass Group, and Delaware North.

Other Facilities

Besides stadiums and arenas, food and beverage service is provided in several other types of facilities by the same major managed service companies that service stadiums. Most of the U.S. national parks are contracted to these companies. These parks have hotels, restaurants, snack bars, gift shops, and a myriad of other service outlets where tourists can spend their money. In addition to these parks, other venues where food and beverage is offered include zoos, aquariums, tennis tournaments like the U.S. Open in New York, and PGA golf tournaments. All these events involve big numbers of people. For example, a PGA event, which lasts a week including practice time, will have upward of 25,000 spectators per day watching the pros play. These tournament events are similar to stadiums and arenas because they also include concession stands, food and beverage areas for the fans, and "corporate tents" for special catering and company guests.

Advantages and Disadvantages

A foodservice career in this segment has several advantages, which include the unique opportunity to see professional and amateur sporting events to your heart's delight, to hear the "roar of the crowd," to be in rural, scenic areas and enjoy the great outdoors, to provide a diverse set of services for the guests or fans, and to have a set work schedule.

The disadvantages of this segment include very large crowds of people to serve in a short time; a work schedule of weekends, holidays, nights; impersonal service; less creativity with food; seasonal employees; and an on-season/off-season work schedule.

Leisure and recreation foodservice is a very exciting, unique part of the hospitality industry that offers employees very different opportunities from standard hotel and restaurant jobs. With the current trend toward building new stadiums and arenas around the country, this segment offers many new career openings.

Trends in Managed Services

- College and university foodservice managers face increasing challenges. *Restaurants and Institutions* magazine asked several managers to identify some of those challenges. In general, managers mentioned trying to balance rising costs with tighter dollars. Bill Rigan, foodservice center manager at Oklahoma State University, Stillwater, pointed out two main challenges: the reduction of revenues from board-plan sales in addition to increased costs such as food and utilities. He dealt with these challenges by recognizing that, inasmuch as he could not change the utilities or hourly rates for employees, he would have to maximize purchasing potential. He also made optimal usage of "from scratch" cooking, convenience foods, and more efficient labor scheduling.
- Martha Willis, foodservice director at Tennessee Technological University, Cookesville, sees declining enrollment and a reduction in state funding as challenges. This translates to a cutback in services and more pressure to produce a bigger bottom line. Martha intends to achieve this by filling vacant full-time positions with part-time and student employees. The savings made by not paying full-time employee benefits can amount to 30 percent of a person's wage.
- Increased use of campus cards (declining balance or debit cards)
- Increased use of food-to-go—for instance, before sporting events
- Increased use of carts at vantage points
- Dueling demands for foodservice managers—from students who want more freshly prepared foods in convenient locations and from administrators who want more revenue from existing sources
- Twenty-four-hour foodservice
- Increased business in health care and nursing homes
- Proliferation of branded concepts in all segments of managed services, including military, school and college, business and industry, health care, and airport
- Development of home meal replacement options in each segment of the managed services sector, as a way to increase revenue
- Increasing use of fresh product

CAREER INFORMATION

Managed Services

Management careers in the field of managed services offer college graduates a vast array of opportunities. A tremendous advantage to this type of career is that as a manager you have more control over your time because of the structured nature of the environment. Airlines, schools, and health care foodservice, as well as college and university dining, usually work on a set schedule that is based on a menu rotation. There are no late nights unless you are supervising a catering event or special function. Within the educational environment, summers and school breaks allow managers time to get caught up on projects and/or take vacations.

If you are looking for a managed services career, these areas offer a rare opportunity for a quality of life that is often not available in foodservice.

Military dining operations can offer a more restaurant or club-oriented career path. Working as a civilian for the military means competitive salaries, excellent benefits, and the opportunity to travel.

Business and industry dining is the most diverse career segment of institutional foodservice. It draws from all aspects of the industry. Hours are usually longer but still defined, and there is a greater potential for bonuses and advancement.

Institutional foodservice is enjoying unprecedented growth as a multibillion dollar industry. It has expanded to include services outside the hospitality industry, such as groundskeeping, maintenance, janitorial services, and vending machine sales.

Related Web Sites

www.sodexhousa.com/ —Sodexho
www.aramark.com/ —ARAMARK foodservice

Courtesy of Charlie Adams.

CASE STUDY

Gas Leak

The kitchen at a major corporation's managed service business account includes several gas and electric stoves, ovens, broilers, steamers, grills, and other appliances. On average, the kitchen serves 500 lunches. At 10:15 A.M., on a Tuesday in December, a gas leak prompts the gas company to cut off the gas supply.

Question

1. What can be done to offer the best possible lunch food and service?

CASE STUDY

Chaos in the Kitchen

Jane is the foodservice director at an on-campus dining service that feeds 800 students per meal for breakfast, lunch, and dinner. Jane arrives at her office at 7:00 A.M. (half an hour before breakfast begins) only to find many problems.

After listening to her phone messages, she finds that her breakfast cashier and one of her two breakfast dishroom employees have called in sick. The cashier position is essential, and the second dishroom person is necessary at 8:15 A.M. when the students leave to go to their 8:30 A.M. classes.

Shortly after listening to the messages, the executive chef tells Jane that one of their two walk-in refrigerators is not working properly, so some of the food is above the safe temperature of 40°F.

The lead salad person later comes to her, saying that one of the three ice machines is not working. Hence, there will not be enough ice to ice down the salad bars and to use for cold beverages at lunch.

Last, the catering supervisor tells Jane that he has just found out that there was a misunderstanding with the bakery that supplies their upscale desserts. The desserts were requested by the president of the university for a luncheon he is having that day; however, because the employee at the bakery wrote the wrong delivery date, the desserts would not be delivered. This will cause the president to be angry.

Questions

1. How should Jane handle being short a cashier and a dishroom person at breakfast?
2. What should Jane do with the food in the defective refrigerator? Should the food that is measured to be above 40°F be saved?
3. What are Jane's options concerning the ice shortage?
4. How should Jane handle the president's function, knowing that the requested desserts have not been delivered?
5. If the special dessert cannot be purchased in time, how should the catering supervisor approach this situation when speaking with the president's office?
6. What can be done to ensure that mistakes, such as the one made by the bakery employee, do not happen again?

SUMMARY

1. Managed services operations include segments such as airlines, military, schools and colleges, health care facilities, and businesses.
2. Food has become scarce on short and median domestic flights. Most airlines have food prepared by a contractor, such as Dobbs International or Sky Chefs.
3. Service to the military includes feeding troops and officers in clubs, dining halls, and hospitals as well as out in the field. Direct vendor delivery, menu management, prepared foods, and fast-food chains located on the base have met new trends in military foodservice.
4. Schools are either equipped with on-site kitchens and dining rooms or receive food from a central commissary. They try to balance salability with good nutrition. Today, nutrition education is a required subject in school.
5. College and university managed services operations include residence halls, cafeterias, student unions, faculty clubs, convenience stores, and catering.
6. The responsibilities of a foodservice manager are very complex. He or she is in charge of employee relations, human resource management, budgeting, safety administration, sanitation, and inventory.
7. Health care managed services operations need to provide numerous special meals to patients with very specific dietary requirements and nutritious meals in a limited time period for employees. The main areas of concern for health care managed services operations are tray lines and help-yourself food stations.
8. Business and industry managed services operations either operate with a full-service cafeteria or limited-service cafeteria. The type of service is determined by money, space, and time available.
9. Leisure and recreation foodservice offers yet more career opportunities. It is often available at several points of service.

KEY WORDS AND CONCEPTS

Batch cooking
Commercial foodservice
Contractors
Daily rate

Liaison personnel
Managed services
National School Lunch
   Program (NSLP)

Nutrition education
   programs

Self-operators
Tray line

REVIEW QUESTIONS

1. What are managed services operations?
2. List and explain features that distinguish managed services operations from commercial ones.
3. Describe the issues that schools are currently facing concerning school food service.
4. Explain the term *National School Lunch Program* (NSLP).
5. Identify recent trends in college foodservice management.
6. What are the pros and cons concerning fast-food chains on campus?
7. Briefly explain the complex challenges for health care managed services operations.

INTERNET EXERCISES

1. Organization: **ARAMARK**
   Web site: **www.aramark.com**
   Summary: ARAMARK is "a global leader in managed services" according to its Web site. ARAMARK is an outsourcing company that provides services ranging from everyday catering to corporate apparel.
   (a) Click on "*Careers.*" Who is ARAMARK's star of the month? What is his or her position and responsibilities?
   (b) What are some of the characteristics that make a star of the month?

2. Organization: **SODEXHO**
   Web site: **www.sodexhousa.com**
   Summary: Sodexho offers a full range of outsourcing solutions and is a leading food and facilities management services company in North America.
   (a) What corporate services does Sodexho offer?
   (b) Look at the current opportunities (at Sodexho or ARAMARK) within your area.

APPLY YOUR KNOWLEDGE

1. From the sample operating statement (Figure 9–4), calculate the labor cost percentage by taking total labor cost and dividing by total sales × 100. Remember the formula:

$$\frac{\text{Cost}}{\text{Sales}} \times 100$$

2. Consider a retail operation at a local college where a grilled chicken combo, which consists of a grilled chicken breast, fries, and a 20-oz. soda, is on the menu. Cost out the ingredients by writing out everything needed for the combo, including its service. What is your cost price? How much would you charge customers for it to make a reasonable profit?

SUGGESTED ACTIVITY

Create a sample menu for a day at an elementary or high school. Then compare your items to the food guide pyramid and the recommended daily servings. How does your menu measure up?

ENDNOTES

1. Personal conversation with Susan Pillmeier, ARAMARK, and John Lee, Sodexho, July 28, 2005.
2. **www.fns.usda.gov/fns/services.htm**. September 2, 2005.
3. Personal correspondence with John Lee, Director of college and External Relations, Sodexho. September 13, 2005.
4. Ibid.
5. Courtesy of David Tucker.

WEB RESOURCES

Aramark
www.aramark.com

Gate Gourmet International
www.gategourmet.com

Sky Chefs
www.lsg-skychefs.com

Sodexho
www.sodexhousa.com

T.G.I. Friday's
www.tgifridays.com

Pizza Hut
www.pizzahut.com

Chili's
www.chilis.com

Marriott
marriott.com

Department of Defense
www.defenselink.mil

U.S. Marine Corps
www.marines.com

Restaurants and Institutions Magazine
www.foodservice411.com/rimag

Beverages

10

After reading and studying this chapter, you should be able to:

- List and describe the main grape varieties.
- Suggest appropriate pairings of wine with food.
- Identify the various types of beer.
- List the types of spirits and their main ingredients.
- Explain a restaurant's liability in terms of serving alcoholic beverages.

This chapter offers an overview of alcoholic and nonalcoholic beverages in the hospitality industry. Be sure that you realize the utmost importance of responsible beverage consumption and service. Arrange for a designated driver if you intend to have a drink. If you do drink alcoholic beverages, then stay with the same drink—don't mix them (two different types are grape and grain—that is, wine and spirits). That's when trouble really begins and hangovers are bad. Remember that moderation is the key to enjoying beverages, whether it is a get-together with friends at a local restaurant or a getaway for spring break. Examine the tragic alcohol-related auto and other accidents that too many people are involved in each year. Enjoy, but do not overindulge.

Serving beverages is traditional throughout the world. According to his or her culture, a person might welcome a visitor with coffee or tea—or bourbon. Beverages are generally categorized into two main groups: alcoholic and nonalcoholic. **Alcoholic beverages** are further categorized as wines, beer, and spirits. Figure 10–1 shows these three categories.

Wines

Wine is the fermented juice of freshly gathered ripe grapes. Wine may also be made from other sugar-containing fruits, such as blackberries, cherries, or elderberries. In this chapter, however, we will confine our discussion to grape wines. Wine may be classified first by color: red, white, or rose. Wines are further classified as light beverage wines, still, sparkling wines, fortified wines, and aromatic wines.

Light Beverage Wines

White, red, or rose table wines are "still" light beverage wines; such still table wines may come from a variety of growing regions around the world. In the United States, the premium wines are named after the grape variety, such as

A bottle of champagne. Remember not to point the cork at anyone when opening the bottle; point it at the ceiling. In fact, a napkin should be placed over the cork, which is then held there and the bottle is gently twisted open.

Wine	Beer	Spirits
Still	Top fermenting	Grapes/fruit
Natural	Lager	Grains
Fortified	Bottom fermenting	Cactus
Aromatic	Ale	Sugar cane/molasses
Sparkling	Stout	
	Lager	
	Pilsner	
	Porter	

Figure 10–1 *Alcoholic Beverages*

chardonnay and cabernet sauvignon. This proved so successful that Europeans are now also naming their wines after the grape variety and their region of origin, such as Pouilly Fuisse and Chablis.

Sparkling Wines

Champagne, sparkling white wine, and sparkling rose wine are called the **sparkling wines.** Sparkling wines sparkle because they contain carbon dioxide. The carbon dioxide may be either naturally produced or mechanically infused into the wine. The best known sparkling wine is champagne, which has become synonymous with celebrations and happiness.

Champagne became the drink of fashion in France and England in the seventeenth century. Orig-

Champagne is served chilled in fluted glasses, which help keep the bouquet and effervessence longer.

inating in the Champagne region of France, the wine owed its unique sparkling quality to a second fermentation—originally unintentional—in the bottle itself. This process became known as *methode champenoise.*

The Benedictine monk, Dom Perignon (1638–1715), was the cellar master for the Abbaye Hautvilliers and an exceptional wine connoisseur. He was the first to experiment with blending different wines to achieve the so-called *cuvee* (the basis of champagne production). He also revolutionized wine by retaining the resulting carbon dioxide in the bottles. Dom Perignon's methods were refined throughout the centuries and led to the modern method used in champagne production.

Champagne may, by law, only come from the Champagne region of France. Sparkling wines from other countries have *methode champenoise* written on their labels to designate that a similar method was used to make that particular sparkling wine.

Figure 10–2 explains how to handle and serve champagne.

Check Your Knowledge

1. Why is champagne served in fluted glasses?
2. How are alcoholic beverages categorized?
3. Why should you avoid mixing grape (wine) and grain (spirits) drinks?
4. Where should you point the cork of a champagne bottle when opening it?

Champagne should be stored horizontally at a temperature between fifty and fifty-five degrees Fahrenheit. However, it should be served at a temperature between forty-three and forty-seven degrees Fahrenheit. This is best achieved by placing the bottle in an ice bucket.

When serving champagne, there are some recommended steps to take to achieve the best results, as listed below.

1. If the bottle is presented in a champagne cooler, it should be placed upright in the cooler, with fine ice tightly packed around the bottle.
2. The bottle should be wrapped in a cloth napkin. Remove the foil or metal capsule to a point just below the wire, which holds the cork securely.
3. Hold the bottle firmly in one hand at a forty-five degree angle. Unwind and remove the wiring. With a clean napkin, wipe the neck of the bottle and around the cork.
4. With the other hand, grasp the cork so that it will not fly out. Twist the bottle and ease the cork out.
5. When the cork is out, retain the bottle at an angle for about five seconds. The gas will rush out and carry with it some of the champagne if the bottle is held upright.
6. Champagne should be served in two motions: pour until the froth almost reaches the brim of the glass. Stop and wait for the foam to subside. Then finish filling the glass to about three-quarters full.

Figure 10–2 *Handling and Serving Champagne*

Sherry can be dry (Fino), medium, or sweet. Pictured here are bottles of dry sherry with a glass. The lighter the color, the dryer the sherry.

Fortified Wines

Sherries, ports, madeiras, and marsalas are **fortified wines,** meaning that they have had brandy or wine alcohol added to them. The brandy or wine alcohol imparts a unique taste and increases the alcohol content to about 20 percent. Most fortified wines are sweeter than regular wines. Each of the groups of fortified wines have several subgroups with myriad tastes and aromas.

Aromatic Wines

Aromatized wines are fortified and flavored with herbs, roots, flowers, and barks. These wines may be sweet or dry. Aromatic wines are also known as aperitifs, which generally are consumed before meals as digestive stimulants. Among the better known brands of aperitif wines are Dubonnet Red (sweet), Dubonnet White (dry), vermouth red (sweet), vermouth white (dry), Byrrh (sweet), Lillet (sweet), Punt e Mes (dry), St. Raphael Red (sweet), and St. Raphael White (dry).

The History of Wine

Wine has been produced for centuries. The ancient Egyptians and Babylonians recorded the fermentation process. The very first records about wine making date back about 7,000 years. The Greeks received the vine from the Egyptians,

Port wines are generally red, fortified, and sweet. Vintage port is the most prized by port lovers. Port is normally served with cheese and biscuits at the end of a meal.

and later the Romans contributed to the popularization of wine in Europe by planting vines in the territories they conquered.

The wine produced during these times was not the cabernet or chardonnay of today. The wines of yesteryear were drunk when they were young and likely to be highly acidic and crude. To help offset these deficiencies, people added different spices and honey, which made the wine at least palatable. To this day, some Greek and German wines have flavoring added.

The making of good wine is dependent on the quality of the grape variety, type of soil, climate, preparation of vineyards, and method of wine making. Thousands of grape varieties exist, thriving in a variety of soil and climatic conditions. Different plants thrive on clay, chalky, gravelly, or sandy soil. The most important wine-making grape variety is the vitis vinifera, which yields cabernet sauvignon, gamay, pinot noir, pinot chardonnay, and riesling.

Making Wine

Wine is made in six steps: crushing, fermenting, racking, maturing, filtering, and bottling. Grapes are harvested in the autumn, after they have been scientifically tested for maturity, acidity, and sugar concentration. The freshly harvested grapes are taken to pressing houses where the grapes are destemmed and crushed. The juice that is extracted from the grapes is called **must.**

The second step of the process is **fermentation** of the must, a natural phenomenon caused by yeasts on the skin of the grapes. Additional yeasts also are added either environmentally or by formula. When exposed to air in the proper environment, the yeast

Est! Est! Est!

In Europe, during the Middle Ages, it was considered a good thing to make a pilgrimage to Rome once in a lifetime. There is a delightful story of a German bishop who liked his wine and food so much that he sent a servant to seek out the best tavern. (The tavern door was to be marked *est*, meaning it is.) *Est* was painted on the best tavern door in the town they would reach that evening. After traveling across Germany and into northern Italy, the bishop's group came across a tavern door with *Est! Est! Est!* painted on it. Well, the bishop liked the wine and food at that tavern so much he never actually made it to Rome.

White grapes make white wines, and the main white grapes are chardonnay, sauvignon blanc, riesling, pinot blanc, and gewurztraminer.

Red grapes make red wine, and the main red grapes are cabernet sauvignon, merlot, merlot/cabernet sauvignon, pinot noir, and shiraz.

multiplies. Yeast converts the sugar in the grapes to ethyl alcohol, until little or no sugar remains in the wine. The degree of sweetness or dryness in the wine can be controlled at the end of the fermentation process by adding alcohol, removing the yeast by filtration, or adding sulphur dioxide.

Red wine gains its color during the fermentation process from the coloring pigments of the red grape skins, which are put back into the must.

After fermentation has ceased, the wine is transferred to racking containers, where it settles before being poured into oak barrels or large stainless steel containers for the maturing process. Some of the better wines are aged in oak barrels, from which they acquire additional flavor and character during the barrel aging. Throughout the aging process, red wine extracts tannin from the wood, which gives longevity to the wine. Some white wine and most red wine is barrel-aged for periods ranging from months to more than two years. Other white wines that are kept in stainless steel containers are crisp, with a youthful flavor; they are bottled after a few months for immediate consumption.

After maturing, the wine is filtered to help stabilize it and remove any solid particles still in the wine. This process is called **fining.** The wine is then **clarified** by adding either egg white or bentonite, which sinks to the bottom of the vat. The wine then is bottled.

Fine **vintage** wines are best drunk at their peak, which may be a few years— or decades—away. Red wines generally take a few more years to reach their peak than do white wines. In Europe, where the climate is more variable, the good years are rated as vintage. The judgment of experts determines the relative merits of each wine-growing district and awards merit points on a scale of 1 to 10.

Matching Wine with Food

The combination of food and wine is one of life's great pleasures. We eat every day, so a gourmet will seek out not only exotic foods and vintage wines, but also simple food that is well prepared and accompanied by an unpretentious, but quality wine.

Over the years, traditions have developed a how-to approach to the marrying of wines and food. Generally, the following traditions apply:

* White wine is best served with white meat (chicken, pork, or veal), shellfish, and fish.
* Red wine is best served with red meat (beef, lamb, duck, or game).
* The heavier the food, the heavier and more robust the wine should be.
* Champagne can be served throughout the meal.
* Port and red wine go well with cheese.
* Dessert wines best complement desserts and fresh fruits that are not highly acidic.
* When a dish is cooked with wine, it is best served with that wine.
* Regional food is best complemented by wines of the region.
* Wines should never accompany salads with vinegar dressings, or curries; the tastes will clash or be overpowering.
* Sweet wines should be served with foods that are not too sweet.

Figure 10–3 matches some of the better known varietal wines with food.

WINE	SMELL AND TASTE ASSOCIATED WITH WINE	FOOD PAIRING
Gewurztraminer (Alsace in France)	grapefruit, apple, nectarine, peach, nutmeg, clove, cinnamon	Thai, Indian, Tex-Mex, Szechwan, ham, sausage, curry, garlic
Chardonnay Chablis (Burgundy in France)	citrus fruit, apple, pear, pineapple, other tropical fruit	pork, salmon, chicken, pheasant, rabbit
Sauvignon Blanc Sancerre (Loire in France)	citrus fruit, gooseberry, bell pepper, black pepper, green olives, herbs	goat cheese, oysters, fish, chicken, pork, garlic
Pinot Blanc	citrus fruit, apple, pear, melon	shrimp, shellfish, fish, chicken
Pinot Noir Cote d' Or (Burgundy in France)	strawberry, cherry, raspberry, clove, mint, vanilla, cinnamon	duck, chicken, turkey, mushrooms, grilled meats, fish and vegetables, pork
Merlot Gamay (Beaujolais in France)	cherry, raspberry, plum, pepper, herbs, mint	beef, lamb, duck, barbecued meats, pork ribs
Cabernet Sauvignon Medoc (Bordeaux in France)	cherry, plum, pepper, bell pepper, herbs, mint, tea, chocolate	beef, lamb, braised, barbecued and grilled meats, aged cheddar, chocolate
Late harvest white wines	citrus fruit, apple, pear, apricot, peach, mango, honey	custard, vanilla, ginger, carrot cake, cheesecake, cream puffs, apricot cobbler

Figure 10–3 *Matching Wine with Food (Courtesy of Jay R. Schrock)*

Focus on Wines

Wine and Food Pairing

Jay R. Schrock
University of South Florida

The combination of food and wine is as old as the making of wine. It is truly one of the great pleasures in life. Food and wine are natural accompaniments and enhance the flavor and enjoyment of each other. The flavor of a wine consumed by itself will taste different than when it is imbibed with food. Much of the wine taste experience is actually perceived from the nose; hence you will hear that "the wine has a good nose." In fact, wine experts, called *sommeliers,* say that 80 percent of the taste comes from the nose. The nose is where the flavors described as nuts, oak, fruits, herbs, spices, and all the others that describe wine come from. To improve the smell and taste of wine, we often decant it and serve it in stemware with large openings. The wine taster often swirls the wine to increase the aromas entering the nose.

Over the years, traditions have developed as to how to approach **wine and food pairing.** Remember these are traditions and that food and wine pairing is a highly subjective and an inexact process. The traditional rules basically state that red wines are served with red meat and white wines are served with fish and poultry. These rules are still generally valid; but they don't take into consideration the complexity of today's multiethnic fusion cuisines, with their wide range of flavors, and the corresponding wide range of wines from around the world that are now readily available to everyone. Today you are more likely to hear of food and wine pairing suggestions, rather than the hard and fast traditional rules of the past.

The new tradition has begun:

1. When serving more than one wine at a meal, it's best to serve lighter wines before full-bodied ones. The dryer wines should be served before sweeter wines. The exception is if a sweet flavored food is served early in the meal. Serve wines with lower alcohol content before wines with higher alcohol content.
2. Pair *light-bodied wines* with lighter food and *fuller-bodied wines* with heaver, richer, or more flavorful ones. This is a restatement of the old red wine with red meat and white wine with fish and chicken.
3. Match flavors. A *pinot noir* goes well with duck, prosciutto, and mushrooms and *gewürztraminer* is a well-suited accompaniment for ham, sausage, curry, and Thai and Indian food. Beware of pairing a wine with food that is sweeter than the wine. Most people agree that chocolate is the one exception. It seems to go with almost anything.
4. Delicately flavored foods that are poached or steamed should be paired with delicate wines.
5. Match regional wines with regional foods; they have been developed together and have a natural affinity for each other. The red sauces of Tuscany and the Chianti wines of the Tuscany region in Italy are an unbeatable combination.
6. Soft cheese like Camembert and Brie pair well with a variety of red wine, including *cabernet sauvignon,* zinfandel, and red burgundy. Cabernet sauvignon also goes well with sharp, aged cheddar cheese. Pungent and intensely flavored cheeses, such as a blue cheese, are better with the sweeter *eis* wine or late harvest dessert wines. Sheep and goat cheeses pair well with dry white wines, while red wine with fruit flavors goes best with milder cheeses.

Many of your restaurant guests may want to have wine with their dinner but are intimidated by the process or are afraid of the price. Set your guests' minds at ease when they are ordering wine. The know-it-all attitude will not work here; you are not trying to sell a used car or life insurance. You are trying to improve your guests' experience, the check average, and your tip. Make an honest suggestion, and try to explain the differences in wine choices. If guests are pondering two wines by the glass, do not just suggest the more expensive one; bring two glasses and let them taste. They will decide for themselves.

Food and wine are described by texture and flavor. Textures are the qualities in food and wine that we feel in the mouth, such as softness, smoothness, roundness, richness, thickness, thinness, creaminess, chewiness, oiliness, harshness, silkiness, coarseness, and so on. Textures correspond to sensations of touch and temperature, which can be easy to identify—for example, hot, cold, rough, smooth, thick, or thin. Regarding the marrying of food and wine, light food with light wine is always a reliable combination. Rich food with rich wine can be wonderful as long as the match is not too rich. The two most important qualities to consider when choosing the appropriate wine are richness and lightness.

Flavors are food and wine elements perceived by the olfactory nerve as fruity, minty, herbal, nutty, cheesy, smoky, flowery, earthy, and so on. A person often determines flavors by using the nose as well

Sniffing the Bouquet of the Wine

as the tongue. The combination of texture and flavor is what makes food and wine a pleasure to enjoy; a good match between the food and wine can make occasions even more memorable. Figure 10–4 suggests the steps to be taken in wine tasting.

Check Your Knowledge

1. What are the names of the main white and red grape varieties used to make wine?
2. Cabernet sauvignon is best served with _____.
3. Chardonnay is best served with _____.
4. Why does a wine taster swirl the wine around the glass before tasting it?
5. What is the general guideline for serving wine with food?

Many restaurants have introduced **wine tastings** as special marketing events to promote the restaurant itself, or a particular type or label of wine. Wine tasting is more than just a process—it is an artful ritual. Wine offers a threefold sensory appeal: color, aroma, and taste. Wine tasting, thus, consists of three essential steps.

1. Hold the glass to the light. The color of the wine gives the first indication of the wine's body. The deeper the color, the fuller the wine will be. Generally, wines should be clear and brilliant.
2. Smell the wine. Hold the glass between the middle and the ring finger in a "cuplike" fashion and gently roll the glass. This will bring the aroma and the bouquet of the wine to the edge of the glass. The bouquet should be pleasant. This will tell much about what the taste will be.
3. Finally, taste the wine by rolling the wine around the mouth and by sucking in a little air—this helps release the complexities of the flavors.

Figure 10–4 *Wine Tasting*

Major Winegrowing Regions of Europe and North America

Europe

Germany, Italy, Spain, Portugal, and France are the main European wine-producing countries. Germany is noted for the outstanding Riesling wines from the Rhine and Moselle river valleys. Italy produces the world-famous Chianti. Spain makes good wine, but is best known for sherry. Portugal also makes good wine, but is better known for its port.

France is the most notable of the European countries, producing not only the finest wines but also champagne and cognac. The two most famous wine-producing areas in France are the Bordeaux and Burgundy regions. The vineyards, villages, and towns are steeped in the history of centuries devoted to the production of the finest quality wines. They represent some of the most beautiful countryside in Europe and are well worth visiting.

In France, wine is named after the village in which the wine is produced. In recent years, the name of the grape variety is also used. The name of the wine grower is also important; because the quality may vary, reputation understandably is very important. A vineyard might also include a chateau in which wine is made.

Within the Bordeaux region, wine growing is divided into five major districts: Medoc, Graves, St. Emilion, Pomerol, and Sauternes. The wine from each district has its own characteristics.

There are several other well-known wine-producing regions of France, such as the Loire Valley, Alsace, and Cotes du Rhone. French people regard wine as an important part of their culture and heritage.

Wine and Health

A glass of wine may be beneficial to health. This perspective was featured in the CBS news magazine program *60 Minutes,* which focused on a phenomenon called the French paradox. The French eat 30 percent more fat than Americans, smoke more, and exercise less, yet they suffer fewer heart attacks—about one-third as many as Americans. Ironically, the French drink more wine than people of any other nationality—about 75 liters per person a year. Research indicates that wine attacks platelets, which are the smallest of the blood cells and that cause the blood to clot, preventing excess bleeding. However, platelets also cling to the rough, fatty deposits on arterial walls, clogging and finally blocking arteries and causing heart attacks. Wine's flushing effect removes platelets from the artery wall. After the *60 Minutes* program was broadcast, sales of wine, particularly red wine, in the United States increased dramatically.

United States

In California, viticulture began in 1769 when Junipero Serra, a Spanish friar, began to produce wine for the missions he started. At one time the French considered California wines to be inferior. However, California is blessed with a near perfect climate and excellent vine-growing soil. In the United States, the name of the grape variety is used to name the wine, not the village or chateau used by the French. The better known varietal white wines in the United States are chardonnay, sauvignon blanc, riesling, and chenin blanc; varietal red wines are cabernet sauvignon, pinot noir, merlot, syrah, and zinfandel.

California viticulture areas are generally divided into three regions:

1. North and central coastal region
2. Great central valley region
3. Southern California region

The north and central coastal region produces the best wines in California. A high degree of use of mechanical methods allows for efficient, large-scale

Personal Profile: Robert Mondavi

Since its founding in 1966, the Robert Mondavi Winery has established itself as one of the world's top wineries. Robert Mondavi, now in his eighties, still continues his activity as wine's foremost spokesperson, having greatly contributed to the wine industry throughout his successful life.

Robert Mondavi was born in 1913 to an Italian couple who had emigrated from the Marche region of Italy in 1910. His father, Cesare, became involved in shipping California wine grapes to fellow Italians. Extremely pleased with California, Cesare Mondavi decided to move to the Napa Valley and set up a firm that shipped fruit east. Robert Mondavi grew up among wines and vines and remained in his father's business.

Robert began by improving the family enterprise, adding to it the management, production, and marketing skills he learned at Stanford University, from which he graduated in 1936. Robert acknowledged the great business potential of the Napa Valley in the broader context of the California wine industry. What the firm needed was to be upgraded with innovations in technology, to keep up with the changes in the overall business environment.

Mondavi had an ambitious dream that was realized when the Charles Krug Winery was offered for sale in 1943. The facility was purchased, and Robert knew that the strategy for success included well-planned marketing as well as the crucial wine-making expertise that the family already had.

Mondavi understood also the importance of the introduction of innovative processes that could place the winery in a competitive position. From the 1950s to the 1960s, he performed many experiments and introduced pivotal innovations. For example, Robert popularized new styles of wine, such as the chenin blanc, which was

previously known as white pinot and was not doing well in the market. Mondavi changed the fermentation, turning it into a sweeter, more delicious wine. The name was also changed, and sales increased fourfold the following year.

Similarly, he noticed that the sauvignon blanc was a slow-selling wine. He began producing it in a drier style, called it fumé blanc, and turned it into an immediate success. Although the winery's operations were successful, Mondavi was still looking for a missing link in the chain. A trip to Europe, designed to study the finest wineries' techniques, convinced him to adopt a new, smaller type of barrel to age the wine, which he believed added a "wonderful dimension to the finished product."

In 1966, Robert Mondavi opened the Robert Mondavi Winery, which represented the fulfillment of the family's vision to build a facility that would allow them to produce truly world-class wines. In fact, since its establishment, the winery has led the industry, standing as an example of continuous research and innovation in wine making, as well as a "monument to persistence in the pursuit of excellence."

Throughout the years of operation, the original vision remained constant: to produce the best wines that were the perfect accompaniments to food and to provide the public with proper education about the product. As a matter of fact, the Robert Mondavi Winery sponsors several educational programs, such as seminars on viticulture, a totally comprehensive tour program in the Napa Valley wineries, and the great chefs program.

The Robert Mondavi Corporation has been acquired by Constellation Brands, a leading international producer and marketer of beverages, selling nearly 90 million cases annually.

---

production of quality wines. The two best known areas within this region are the Napa and Sonoma valleys. The wines of the Napa and Sonoma valleys resemble those of Bordeaux and Burgundy. In recent years, the wines from the Napa and Sonoma valleys have rivaled and even exceeded the French and other European wines. The chardonnays and cabernets are particularly outstanding.

The Napa and Sonoma valleys are the symbols as well as the centers of the top-quality wine industry in California.

A worker picks grapes in a Napa Valley vineyard.

Several other states and Canadian provinces provide quality wines. New York, Oregon, and Washington are the other major U.S. wine-producing states. In Canada, the best wineries are in British Columbia's Okanagan Valley and southern Ontario's Niagara peninsula. Both of these regions produce excellent wines.

Australian Wines

Australia has been producing wines for about 150 years, but it is only in the last half-century that they have achieved the prominence and recognition they rightly deserve. Australian winemakers traveled to Europe and California to perfect the wine-making craft. Unlike France, with many rigid laws controlling wine growth and production, Australian wine makers use high technology to produce excellent wines, many of which are blended to offer the best characteristics of each wine.

Australia has about 60 winegrowing regions, with diverse climates and soil types, mostly in the southeastern part of the continent, in New South Wales, Victoria, and South Australia, all within easy reach of the major cities of Sidney, Melbourne, and Adelaide. There are about 1,120 wineries in Australia. One of the larger and more popular wineries is Lindemans, which regularly receives accolades for its consistent quality and value. The leading wines are red, cabernet sauvignon, cabernet-shiraz blends, cabernet-merlot blends, merlot, shiraz, white, chardonnay, semillon, sauvignon blanc, and semillon chardonnay. Among the better-known wine-growing areas is Hunter Valley in New South Wales, which produces semillon. When mature, this wine has a honey, nut, and butter flavor. The chardonnay is complex with a peaches-and-cream character. In recent years, Australian wines have shown exceptional quality and value, leading to increased sales in Europe, the United States, and Asia.

Wine also is produced in many other temperate parts of the world, most notably New Zealand, Chile, Argentina, and South Africa.

Beer

Beer is a brewed and fermented beverage made from malted barley and other starchy cereals, and flavored with hops. Beer is a generic term, for a variety of mash-based, yeast-fermented brewed malt beverages with an alcohol content varying from 3 to 16 percent.[1] The term **beer** includes the following:

- Lager, the beverage that is normally referred to as beer, is a clear light-bodied refreshing beer.
- Ale is fuller bodied and more bitter than lager.
- Stout is a dark ale with a sweet, strong, malt flavor.
- Pilsner is not really a beer. The term *pilsner* means that the beer is made in the style of the famous beer brewed in Pilsen, Czech Republic.

The Brewing Process

Beer is brewed from water, **malt, yeast,** and **hops.** The brewing process begins with water, an important ingredient in the making of beer. The mineral content and purity of the water largely determine the quality of the final product. Water accounts for 85 to 89 percent of the finished beer.

Next, grain is added in the form of malt, which is barley that has been ground to a course grit. The grain is germinated, producing an enzyme that converts starch into fermentable sugar.

The yeast is the fermenting agent. Breweries typically have their own cultured yeasts, which, to a large extent, determine the type and taste of the beer.

Mashing is the term for grinding the malt and screening out any bits of dirt. The malt then goes through a hopper into a mash tub, which is a large stainless steel or copper container. Here the water and grains are mixed and heated.

The liquid is now called **wort** and is filtered through a mash filter or lauter tub. This liquid then flows into a brewing kettle, where hops are added and the mixture is boiled for several hours. After the brewing operation, the hop wort is filtered through the hop separator or hop jack. The filtered liquid then is pumped through a wort cooler and flows into a fermenting vat where pure-culture yeast is added for fermentation.[2] The brew is aged for a few days prior to being barreled for draught beer or pasteurized for bottled or canned beer.

Spirits

A **spirit** or **liquor** is made from a liquid that has been fermented and distilled. Consequently, a spirit has a high percentage of alcohol, gauged in the United States by its proof content. **Proof** is equal to twice the percentage of alcohol in

A Bottle of Sterling Vineyards Chardonnay, One of Napa Valley's Best Known and Respected Vineyards

A Bottle of Franciscan Napa Valley Cabernet Sauvignon, One of Napa Valley's Best

A Day in the Life of Shane Dudley
Bar Manager, Tupelo American Restaurant, San Diego, California

Shane arrives at the bar at 1:30 P.M. and for the next couple of hours he meets with wine and liquor representatives. The representatives advise Shane of any new products and give information about them. Tupelo American prides itself on being a "breaking ground" restaurant. As such, so that he can offer guests the most up-to-date product, Shane tastes the wine and spirits and gives training sessions for the restaurant employees. Shane has assembled the best stocked bar in San Diego. This includes a great selection of single-malt scotch whiskies, single-barrel bourbons, cognacs, and vodkas. Shane checks the bar for stock to ensure that he is ready for the "Happy Hour" rush. He orders and receives stock twice a week.

During the service time, Shane takes care of the regular guests, of which there are many. The barstools are all occupied, and there is a buzz in the atmosphere. On busy nights, a second bartender takes care of the restaurant servers. Shane cross-trains the barbacks so they can step into a bartender's position in an emergency. At closing time, Shane does the banking and checks the restaurant before locking the doors.

The signature cocktail of the bar is the martini. Shane has brought the martini back from the dead—he has created 300 different martinis with 55 on the list at a time. No wonder three-quarters of the beverage orders are for martinis. This presents Shane with the challenge of coming up with new martini recipes.

Lager in a Beer Glass

the beverage; therefore, a spirit that is 80 proof is 40 percent alcohol. Spirits traditionally are enjoyed before or after a meal, rather than with the meal. Many spirits can be consumed straight or neat, or they may be enjoyed with water, soda water, juices, or cocktail mixes.

Fermentation of spirits takes place by the action of yeast on sugar-containing substances, such as grain or fruit. Distilled drinks are made from a fermented liquid that has been put through a distillation process.

Whiskies

Among the better known spirits is whisky, which is a generic name for the spirit first distilled in Scotland and Ireland centuries ago. The word *whisky* comes from the Celtic word *visgebaugh* meaning *water of life*. Whisky is made from a fermented mash of grain to which malt, in the form of barley, is added. The barley contains an enzyme called diastase that converts starch to sugars. After fermentation, the liquid is distilled. Spirits naturally are white or pale in color, but raw whisky is stored in oak barrels that have been charred (burnt). This gives whisky its caramel color. The whisky is stored for a period of time, up to a maximum of 12 to 15 years. However, several good whiskies reach the market after 3 to 5 years.

Most whiskies are blended to produce a flavor and quality that is characteristic of the brand. Not surprisingly, the blending process at each distillery is a closely guarded secret. There are four distinct whisky types that have gained a

Checking the Color of Johnnie Walker Scotch that is Maturing in Barrels

worldwide acknowledgment throughout the centuries: Scotch whisky, Irish whisky, bourbon whisky, and Canadian whisky.

Scotch Whisky

Scotch whisky, or Scotch, has been distilled in Scotland for centuries and has been a distinctive part of the Scots' way of life. From its origins in remote and romantic Highland glens, Scotch whisky has become a popular and international drink, its flavor appreciated throughout the world. Scotch became popular in the United States during the days of **Prohibition** (1919 to 1933) when it was smuggled into the country from Canada. It is produced like other whiskies, except that the malt is dried in special kilns that give it a smoky flavor. To be legally called scotch whisky, the spirit must conform to the standards of the Scotch Whisky Act. Only whisky made with this process can be called scotch whisky. Some of the better-known quality blended Scotch whiskies are Chivas Regal and Johnnie Walker Black, Gold, and Blue Labels.[3]

Irish Whisky

Irish whisky is produced from malted or unmalted barley, corn, rye, and other grains. The malt is not dried like the scotch whisky, which gives Irish whisky a milder character, yet an excellent flavor. Two well-known Irish whiskies are Old Bushmill's Black Bush and Jameson's 1780.[4]

Bourbon Whisky

Liquor was introduced in America by the first settlers, who used it as a medicine. Bourbon has a peculiar history. In colonial times in New England, rum was the most popular distilled spirit. After the break with Britain, settlers of Scottish and Irish background predominated. They were mostly grain farmers and distillers, producing whisky for barter. When George Washington levied a tax on this whisky, the farmers moved south and continued their whisky production. However, the rye crop failed, so they decided to mix corn, particularly abundant in Kentucky, with the remaining rye. The result was delightful. This experiment occurred in Bourbon County—hence the name of the new product.

Bourbon whisky is produced mainly from corn; other grains are also used, but they are of secondary importance. The distillation processes are similar to those of other types of whisky. Charred barrels provide bourbon with its distinctive taste. It is curious to note that barrels can only be used once in the United States to age liquor. Aging, therefore, occurs in new barrels after each distillation process. Bourbon may be aged up to six years to improve its mellowness. Among the better-known bourbon whiskies are Jack Daniels, Makers Mark, and George Dickle.

Canadian Whisky

Like bourbon, Canadian whisky is produced mainly from corn. It is characterized by a delicate flavor that nonetheless pleases the palate. Canadian whisky must be at least four years old before it can be bottled and marketed. It is distilled at 70 to 90 percent alcohol by volume. Among the better-known Canadian whiskies are Seagram's and Canadian Club.

White Spirits

Gin, rum, vodka, and tequila are the most common of the spirits that are called **white spirits.** Gin, first known as Geneva, is a neutral spirit made from juniper berries. Although gin originated in Holland, it was in London that the word *Geneva* was shortened to gin, and almost anything was used to make it. Often gin was made in the bathtub in the morning and sold in hole-in-the-wall dram shops all over London at night. Obviously, the quality left a lot to be desired, but the poor drank it to the point of national disaster.[5] Gin also was widely produced in the United States during Prohibition. In fact, the habit of mixing something else with it led to the creation of the cocktail. Over the years, gin became the foundation of many popular cocktails (e.g., martini, gin and tonic, gin and juice, and Tom Collins).

Rum can be light or dark in color. Light rum is distilled from the fermented juice of sugarcane, and dark rum is distilled from molasses. Rum comes mainly from the Caribbean Islands of Barbados (Mount Gay), Puerto Rico (Bacardi), and Jamaica (Myers). Rums are mostly used in mixed frozen and specialty drinks such as rum and Coke, rum punches, daiquiris, and piña coladas.

Tequila is distilled from the agave tequilana (a type of cactus), which is called *mezcal* in Mexico. Official Mexican regulations require that tequila be made in the area around the town of Tequila, because the soil contains volcanic ash, which is especially suitable for growing the blue agave cactus. Tequila may be white, silver, or golden in color. The white is shipped unaged, silver is aged up to three years, and golden is aged in oak from two to four years. Tequila is mainly used in the popular margarita cocktail or in the tequila sunrise (made popular in a song by the Eagles rock group).

Vodka can be made from many sources, including barley, corn, wheat, rye, or potatoes. Because it lacks color, odor, and flavor, vodka generally is combined with juices or other mixers whose flavors will predominate.

Other Spirits

Brandy is distilled from wine in a fashion similar to that of other spirits. American brandy comes primarily from California, where it is made in column stills and aged in white-oak barrels for at least two years. The best-known American brandies are made by Christian Brothers and Ernest and Julio Gallo. Their brandies are smooth and fruity with a touch of sweetness. The best brandies are served as after-dinner drinks, and ordinary brandies are used in the well for mixed drinks.

Cognac is regarded by connoisseurs as the best brandy in the world. It is only made in the Cognac region of France, where the chalky soil and humid climate combine with special distillation techniques to produce the finest brandy. Only

A Glass of Cognac

brandy from this region may be called cognac. Most cognac is aged in oak casks from two to four years or more. Because cognacs are blends of brandies of various ages, no age is allowed on the label; instead, letters signify the relative age and quality.

Brandies labeled as *VSOP* must be aged at least four years. All others must be aged in wood at least five years. Five years, then, is the age of the youngest cognac in a blend; usually several others of older age are added to lend taste, bouquet, and finesse. About 75 percent of the cognac shipped to Canada and the United States is produced by four companies: Courvoisier, Hennessy, Martell, and Remy Martin.

Cocktails

The first cocktails originated in England during the Victorian Era, but it wasn't until the 1920s and 1930s that cocktails became popular.

Cocktails are usually drinks made by mixing two or more ingredients (wines, liquors, fruit juices), resulting in a blend that is pleasant to the palate, with no single ingredient overpowering the others. Cocktails are mixed by stirring, shaking, or blending. The mixing technique is particularly important to achieve the perfect cocktail. Cocktails are commonly divided into two categories according to volume: short drinks (up to 3.5 ounces) and tall drinks (generally up to 8.5 ounces).

A Martini Cocktail Served in a Martini Glass

The secret of a good cocktail lies in several factors:

- The balance of the ingredients.
- The quality of the ingredients. As a general rule, cocktails should be made from a maximum of three ingredients.
- The skill of the bartender. The bartender's experience, knowledge, and inspiration are key factors in a perfect cocktail.

A good bartender should understand the effect and the "timing" of a cocktail. It is not a coincidence that many cocktails are categorized by when they are best served. There are aperitifs, digestifs, corpse-revivers, pick-me-ups, and so on. Cocktails can stimulate an appetite or provide the perfect conclusion to a fine meal.

Check Your Knowledge

1. Describe the different types of beer.
2. Describe the various spirits.

Nonalcoholic Beverages

Nonalcoholic beverages are increasing in popularity. The 1990s and on into the 2000s have seen a radical shift from the free love 1960s and the singles bars of the 1970s and early 1980s. People are, in general, more cautious about the consumption of alcohol. Lifestyles have become healthier, and organizations like MADD (Mothers Against Drunk Driving) have raised the social conscience about responsible alcohol consumption. Overall consumption of alcohol has decreased in recent years, with spirits declining the most.

From Goji juice to passion fruit green tea, the nonalcoholic beverage world has been innovative in creating flavored teas and coffees and an ever-increasing variety of juices to satisfy all our tastes.

In recent years, several new beverages have been added to the nonalcoholic beverage list.

Nonalcoholic Beer

Guinness, Anheuser-Busch, and Miller, along with many other brewers, have developed beer products that have the same appearance as regular beer but have a lower calorie content and approximately 95 to 99 percent of the alcohol removed, either after processing or after fermentation. The taste, therefore, is somewhat different from regular beer.

Coffee

Coffee is the drink of the present. People who used to frequent bars are now patronizing coffee houses. Sales of specialty coffees exceed $4 billion. The Specialty Coffee Association of America estimates that there are more than 17,400 coffee cafes nationwide.[6]

*Coffee Beans Growing on
a Coffee Tree*

Coffee first came from Ethiopia and Mocha, which is in the Yemen Republic. Legends say that Kaldi, a young Abyssinian goatherd, accustomed to his sleepy goats, noticed that after chewing certain berries, the goats began to prance about excitedly. He tried the berries himself, forgot his troubles, lost his heavy heart, and became the happiest person in "happy Arabia." A monk from a nearby monastery surprised Kaldi in this state, decided to try the berries too, and invited the brothers to join him. They all felt more alert that night during prayers![7]

In the Middle Ages, coffee found its way to Europe via Turkey but not without some objections. In Italy, priests appealed to Pope Clement VIII to have the use of coffee forbidden among Christians. Satan, they said, had forbidden his followers, the infidel Moslems, the use of wine because it was used in the Holy Communion and had given them instead his "hellish black brew." Apparently, the pope liked the drink, for his reply was "Why, this Satan's drink is so delicious that it would be a pity to let the infidels have exclusive use of it!" So his Holiness decided to baptize the drink, after which it quickly became the social beverage of Europe's middle and upper classes.[8]

In 1637, the first European coffeehouse opened in England; within 30 years, coffeehouses had replaced taverns as the island's social, commercial, and political melting pots.[9] The coffeehouses were nicknamed *penny universities,* where

*A casual coffeehouse, offers
coffee and related beverages
and snacks.*

Coffee shops are a major part of the "cafe society" where people gather and enjoy nonalcholic beverages.

any topic could be discussed and learned for the price of a pot of coffee. The men of the period not only discussed business but actually conducted business. Banks, newspapers, and the Lloyd's of London Insurance Company began at Edward Lloyd's coffeehouse.

Coffeehouses were also popular in Europe. In Paris, Cafe Procope, which opened in 1689 and still operates today, has been the meeting place of many a famous artist and philosopher, including Rousseau and Voltaire (who are reputed to have drunk 40 cups of coffee a day).

The Dutch introduced coffee to the United States during the colonial period. Coffeehouses soon became the haunts of the revolutionary activists plotting against King George of England and his tea tax. John Adams and Paul Revere planned the Boston Tea Party and the fight for freedom at a coffeehouse. This helped established coffee as the traditional democratic drink of Americans.

Brazil produces more than 30 percent of the world's coffee, most of which goes into canned and instant coffee. Coffee connoisseurs recommend beans by name, such as arabica and robusta beans. In Indonesia, coffee is named for the island on which it grows; the best is from Java and is rich and spicy with a full-bodied flavor. Yemen, the country in which coffee was discovered, names its best coffee for the port of Mocha. Its fragrant, creamy brew has a rich, almost chocolatey aftertaste. Coffee beans are frequently blended by the merchants who roast them; one of the best blends, mocha java, is the result of blending these two fine coffees.

Coffee may be roasted from light to dark according to preference. Light roasts are generally used in canned and institutional roasts, and medium is

Espresso roast coffee beans have a strong, pungent flavor.

the all-purpose roast most people prefer. Medium beans are medium brown in color, and their surface is dry. Although this brew may have snappy, acidic qualities, its flavor tends to be flat. Full, high, or Viennese roast is the roast preferred by specialty stores, where balance is achieved between sweetness and sharpness. Dark roasts have a fancy rich flavor, with espresso the darkest of all roasts. Its almost black beans have shiny, oily surfaces. All the acidic qualities and specific coffee flavor are gone from espresso, but its pungent flavor is a favorite of espresso lovers.

Decaffeinating coffee removes the caffeine with either a solvent or water process. In contrast, many specialty coffees have things added. Among the better-known specialty coffees are café au lait or caffe latte. In these cases, milk is steamed until it becomes frothy and is poured into the cup together with the coffee. Cappuccino is made by adding steamed hot milk to an espresso, which may then be sprinkled with powdered chocolate and cinnamon.[10]

Beverage Management Technology

Technology for beverage management has improved with companies like Scanbar (**www.scanbar.com**) that offer beverage operators a system that accounts for every ounce, with daily, weekly, or monthly results. The ongoing real-time inventory allows viewing results at any time and place with tamperproof reliability interfaced with major POS systems.

The Scanbar liquor module has a bar-coded label on each bottle, making it easy to track bottles from purchase to recycle bin. Each bottle variety has the same ribbon, allowing for easy calibration. The bar coded ribbon is used as a measuring tool to give accurate results. Inventory taking is done with a portable handheld radio-frequency bar code reader. Once the label is scanned, the level of alcohol in the bottle is recorded and the data are sent from the user's handheld reader to the computer in the office for real-time results.[11]

The wine module keeps control of all wines by region, variety, or vintage. Once the wines have been configured within the directory, the procedure is that, when a wine is received, the variety is identified by scanning the bar code already on the bottle or selected directly from the portable hand-held radio-frequency bar code reader. A bar-coded tag is placed around the collar, which creates a unique identity for each bottle. Once the bottle is ready to be served, either at the table or at the bar, the bar-coded tag is removed from the bottle and scanned out of inventory. Scanning the tag around the neck of the bottle accomplishes inventory taking.[12]

The beverage system from AZ Bar America (**www.azbaramerica.com**) offers a POS system that runs the operations behind the bar. It rings up the charge as the beverage is being poured while automatically removing the product from inventory.

Instead of holding up bottles and guessing what is left in them or even weighing each bottle at the end of shifts, the AZ2000 controller can at any time give a report of what was sold, who completed the transaction, how the system was used, and actual profits by brand, transaction, or product group. The system can be remotely monitored from home or vacation by dialing into the location and inventory for making price changes or monitoring sales activity.

The AZ2000 is the heart of a dispensing system that interfaces with a variety of products: "spouts," a cocktail tower, beer, wine, juice, soft drink machines, and soda guns. The system even runs cocktail programming, so if the bartender does not know what goes into a certain drink, he on she can hit the cocktail button, and it will even tell them what liquor bottle to pick up and control the recipe pour amounts.[13]

Product management applications provide restaurateurs with the ability to track all aspects of their inventory. Food cost menu items sold through the POS system are linked to recipes, which are made up of inventory items. Each time an item is sold, the appropriate inventory items are automatically depleted through the software application. For example, when a hamburger is sold, the inventory is depleted by one hamburger patty, one bun, one slice of tomato, one ounce of lettuce, and one ounce of onion. The system can automatically determine when inventory levels are low and it is time to place an order. Restauranteurs can set par levels for stock based on forecasted business to allow the system to generate the proper reorder quantities.

Restaurant managers periodically take a physical inventory count and enter that into the system to determine if there are any variances. Variances occur due to spoilage, waste, improper recipes, or theft. Inventory variance reports are critical to analyzing the profitability of a restaurant. When new items are received into inventory, they are entered into the system and, along with information about the cost of those items, the systems allow restaurants to then determine the food cost of their menu items.

In the restaurant and foodservice industry, inventory control must be accurate and monitored in a timely fashion. Inventory must be carefully managed due to the various types of foods restaurants handle. Perishable and nonperishable foods must be properly handled to provide fresh dishes on the menu. Information systems provide inventory control software to help foodservice associates manage their supply. Computer-based software determines reorder points to help eliminate low inventory levels, which can lead to inadequate service for restaurant guests. Companies purchasing stock and materials must determine proper stock levels, accurate ordering points, and approved vendor lists. This is all a part of the reorder process and can be handled by any number of available ISs.

Tea

Tea is a beverage made by steeping in boiling water the leaves of the tea plant, an evergreen shrub, or a small tree native to Asia. Tea is consumed as either a hot or cold beverage by approximately half of the world's population, yet it is second to coffee in commercial importance because most of the world's tea crop is consumed in the tea-growing regions. Tea leaves contain 1 to 3 percent caffeine. This means that weight for weight, tea leaves have more than twice as much caffeine as coffee beans. However, a cup of coffee generally has more caffeine than a cup of tea because one pound of tea leaves makes 250 to 300 cups of tea, whereas one pound of coffee makes only 40 cups.

Corporate Profile: Starbucks Coffee Company

Operations

Starbucks Coffee Company (named after the first mate in Herman Melville's Moby-Dick) is the leading retailer, roaster, and brand of specialty coffee in North America. More than 7 million people visit Starbucks stores each week. In addition to its more than thousand retail locations, the company supplies fine dining, foodservice, travel, and hotel accounts with coffee and coffee-making equipment and operates a national mail-order division.

Locations and Alliances

Starbucks currently has thousands of stores in 50 U.S. states and in 34 countries.

Starbucks Coffee Company and U.S. Office Products announced an agreement to distribute Starbucks fresh-roasted coffee and related products through U.S. Office Products extensive North American distributorship.

Starbucks has strategic alliances with United Airlines and is now the exclusive supplier of coffee on every United flight.

In addition, Specialty Sales and Marketing supplies coffee to the health care, business and industry, college and university, and hotel and resort segments of the food service industry; to many fine restaurants throughout North America; and to companies such as Costco, Nordstrom, Starwood, Barnes & Noble, Inc., Hilton Hotels, Sodexho ARAMARK, Compass, Wyndham, Borders, Radisson, Sysco, Safeway, Albertson's, Kraft Foods, Pepsico and Marriott International.

Product Line

Starbucks roasts more than 30 varieties of the world's finest arabica coffee beans. The company's retail locations also feature a variety of espresso beverages and locally made fresh pastries. Starbucks specialty merchandise includes Starbucks private-label espresso makers, mugs, plunger pots, grinders, storage jars, water filters, thermal carafes, and coffee makers. An extensive selection of packaged goods, including unique confections, gift baskets, and coffee-related items are available in stores, through mail order, and through a site in the Marketplace section of America Online.

Starbucks introduced Frappuccino® blended beverages, a line of low-fat, creamy, iced coffee drinks. This product launch was the most successful in Starbucks history. They also have a bottled version of Frappuccino®, which is currently being distributed on a national basis

and is available in grocery stores and in many Starbucks retail locations.

A long-term joint venture between Starbucks Coffee and Breyer's Grand Ice Cream dishes up a premium line of coffee ice creams, with national distribution of several different flavors to leading grocery stores in, Starbucks has become the number one brand of coffee ice cream in the United States. Currently, ice cream lovers can choose from eight delectable flavors or two ice cream bars.

Starbucks and Capitol Records joined forces to produce Blue Note Blend, a compact disc featuring classic jazz recordings. It was played in Starbucks locations and was the first item to be sold to customers both over the counter and by mail order. The album was so successful that the company has subsequently released several other CDs, covering a wide range of tastes and moods, including Chicago blues, rhythm and blues, legendary female vocalists, an eclectic mix from the late 1960s and early 1970s, jazz, and opera.

Community Involvement

Starbucks contributes to a variety of organizations that benefit AIDS research, child welfare, environmental awareness, literacy, and the arts. The company encourages its partners (employees) to take an active role in their own neighborhoods.

Starbucks fulfills its corporate social responsibility mission by reducing its environmental footprint on the planet. The company addresses three high-impact areas: sourcing of coffee, tea, and paper; transportation of people and products; and design and operations (energy, water, waste reduction, and recycling). Starbucks has developed relations with organizations that support the people and places that grow their coffee and tea, such as Conservation International, CARE, Save the Children, and the African Wildlife Foundation. Additionally, Starbucks has entered into a partnership with the U.S. Agency for International Development (USAID) and Conservation International to improve the livelihoods of small-scale coffee farmers by private sector approaches within the coffee industry that are environmentally sensitive, socially responsible, and economically viable. In 2005 Starbucks received the World Environment Center's Gold Medal for International Corporate Achievement in Sustainable Development.

Starbucks has received numerous awards for quality innovation, service and giving.

The following list shows where the different types of tea originate:

China—Oolong, Orange pekoe
India—Darjeeling, Assams, Dooars
Indonesia—Java, Sumatra

Carbonated Soft Drinks

Coca-Cola and Pepsi have long dominated the carbonated soft drink market. In the early 1970s, Diet Coke and Diet Pepsi were introduced and quickly gained in popularity. The diet colas now command about a 10 percent market share. Caffeine-free colas offer an alternative, but they have not, as yet, become as popular as diet colas.

Inasmuch as U.S. market sales tend to grow at around 2 percent, companies are expanding internationally with a 5 percent growth. Indeed, almost 66 percent of Coca-Cola's sales come from international sales.[14]

Juices

Popular juice flavors include orange, cranberry, grapefruit, mango, papaya, and apple. Nonalcoholic versions of popular cocktails made with juices have been popular for years and are known as virgin cocktails.

Juice bars have established themselves as places for quick, healthy drinks. Lately, "smart drinks" that are supposed to boost energy and improve concentration have become popular. The smart drinks are made up of a blend of juices, herbs, amino acids, caffeine, and sugar and are sold under names such as Energy Plasma Blast and IQ Booster.

Other drinks have jumped on the healthy drink bandwagon, playing on the consumer's desire to drink something refreshing, light, and healthful. Often, these drinks are fruit flavored, giving the consumer the impression of drinking

Juice Bar

something healthier than sugar-filled sodas. Unfortunately, these drinks usually just add the flavor of the fruit and rarely have any nutritional value whatsoever.

Also, some drinks are created by mixing different fruit flavors to arrive at new, exotic flavors such as Passion-Kiwi-Strawberry and Mango-Banana Delight. Some examples of such drinks are Snapple and Tropicana Twister.

Sport enthusiasts also find drinks available in stores that professional athletes use and advertise. These specially formulated isotonic beverages help the body regain the vital fluids and minerals that are lost during heavy physical exertion. The National Football League sponsors Gatorade and encourages its use among its athletes. The appeal of being able to drink what the professionals drink is undoubtedly one of the major reasons for the success of Gatorade's sales and marketing. Other brands of isotonic beverages include Powerade and All Sport, which is sponsored by the National Collegiate Athletics Association.

Bottled Water

Bottled water was popular in Europe years ago when it was not safe to drink tap water. In North America, the increased popularity of bottled water has coincided with the trend toward healthier lifestyles.

In the 1980s, it was chic to be seen drinking Perrier (a sparkling water) or some other imported bottled water. Perrier, which comes from France, lost market share a few years ago when an employee tampered with the product. Now the market leader is Evian (a spring water), which is also French. Domestic bottled water is equally as good as imported and is now available in various flavors that offer the consumer a greater selection.

Bottled waters are available as sparkling, mineral, and spring waters. Bottled water is a refreshing, clean-tasting, low-calorie beverage that will likely increase in popularity as a beverage on its own or to accompany another beverage such as wine or whisky.

Bars and Beverage Management

From an operating perspective, bar and beverage management follows much the same sequence as does food management, as shown in the following list:

- Forecasting
- Determining what to order
- Selecting the supplier
- Placing the order
- Receiving the order
- Storing
- Issuing
- Serving
- Accounting
- Controlling

A bar allows guests to meet and socialize.

Bar Setup

Whether a bar is part of a larger operation (restaurant) or a business in its own right, the physical setup of the bar is critical to its overall effectiveness. There is a need to design the area in such a way that it is not only pleasing to the eye but is also conducive to a smooth and efficient operation. This means that bar stations, where drinks are filled, are located in strategic spots, and that each station has everything it needs to respond to most, if not all, requests. All *well liquors* should be easily accessible, with popular call brands not too far out of reach. The brands that are less likely to be ordered (and more likely to be high priced) can be farther away from the stations. The most obvious place for the high-priced, premium brands is the back bar, a place of high visibility. Anyone sitting at the bar will be looking directly at it, giving the customers a chance to view the bar's choices.

As for beer coolers, their location depends on the relative importance of beer to the establishment. In many places, beer is kept in coolers under the bar or below the back bar, and sample bottles or signs are displayed for customers. However, in many places beer is their biggest seller, and they may offer numerous brands from around the world. In such places, other setups may be used, such as stand-up coolers with glass doors so that customers can easily see all the varieties available. This is also true for draft beers.

Inventory Control

The beverage profitability of an organization is not a matter of luck. Profits are due largely to the implementation and use of effective **inventory controls** by management and employees. Training is also important to ensure that employees treat inventory as cash and that they handle it as if it were their own money. Management's example will be followed by employees. If employees sense a lax management style, they may be tempted to steal. No control system can guarantee the prevention of theft completely. However, the better the control system, the less likely it is that there will be a loss.[15]

To operate profitably, a beverage operation manager needs to establish what the expected results will be. For example, if a bottle of gin contains twenty-five 1-ounce measures, it would be reasonable to expect twenty-five times the selling price in revenue. When this is multiplied for each bottle, the total revenue can be determined and compared to the actual revenue.

One of the critical areas of bar management is the design, installation, and implementation of a system to control possible theft of the bar's beverage inventory. Theft may occur in a number of ways including

1. Giving away drinks
2. Overpouring alcohol
3. Mischarging for drinks
4. Selling a call liquor at a well price
5. Outright stealing of bar beverages by employees

As is the case with the food operations, there is an anticipated profit margin based on the ratio of sales generated to related beverage costs. Bar management must be able to account for any discrepancies between expected and actual profit margins.

All inventory control systems require an actual physical count of the existing inventory that may be done on a weekly or monthly basis, depending on the needs of the management. This physical count is based on units. For liquor and wine, the unit is a bottle, either 0.750 or 1.0 liter; for bottled beer, the unit is a case of 24 bottles; and for draft beer, the unit is one keg. The results of the most current physical count are then compared to the prior period's physical count to determine the actual amount of beverage inventory consumed during the period. This physical amount is translated into a cost or dollar figure by multiplying the amount consumed for each item times its respective cost per unit. The total cost for all beverages consumed is compared to the sales it generated to result in a profit margin that is compared to the expected margin.

Management should design forms that can be used to account for all types of liquor, beer, and wine available at the bar. The listing of the items should follow their actual physical setup within the bar to facilitate easy accounting of the inventory. The forms should also have columns where amounts of each inventory item can be noted. A traditional way to account for the amount of liquor in a bottle is by using the "10" count, where the level of each bottle is marked by tenths; thus, a half-full bottle of well vodka would be marked on the form as a ".5." Similarly, for kegs of draft beer, a breakdown of 25, 50, 75, and 100 percent may be used to determine its physical count.

Personnel Procedures

Another key component of internal control is having procedures in place for screening and hiring bar personnel. Employees must be experienced in bartending and cocktail serving and also must be honest, since they have access to the bar's beverage inventory and its cash.

Bar managers may also implement several other procedures to control inventory and reduce the likelihood of employee theft. One popular method is the use of *spotters,* who are hired to act like normal bar customers, but are actually observing the bartenders and/or cocktailers for inappropriate behavior, such as not taking money from customers or overpouring. Another method for checking bar personnel is to perform a bank switch in the middle of the shift. In some cases, employees steal from the company by taking money from customers without ringing it up on the register. They keep the extra money in the cash drawer until the end of the shift when they are cashing out, at which point they retrieve the stolen funds. To do a bank switch, the manager must "z-out" a bartender's cash register, take the cash drawer, and replace it with a new bank. The manager then counts the money in the drawer, subtracts the starting bank, and compares that figure to the one on the register's tape. If there is a significant surplus of funds, it is highly likely that the employee is stealing. If there is less than what is indicated on the tape, the employee may be honest but careless when giving change or hitting the buttons on the register. Either way, there is a potential for loss.

Restaurant and Hotel Bars

In restaurants, the bar is often used as a holding area to allow guests to enjoy a cocktail or aperitif before sitting down to dinner. This allows the restaurant to space out the guests' orders so that the kitchen can cope more effectively; it also increases beverage sales. The profit margin from beverages is higher than the food profit margin.

In some restaurants, the bar is the focal point or main feature. Guests feel drawn to having a beverage because the atmosphere and layout of the restaurant encourages them to have a drink. Beverages generally account for about 25 to 30 percent of total sales. Many restaurants used to have a higher percentage

The Banyan Court bar at the Moana Hotel is a perfect venue for a "sundowner."

of beverage sales, but the trend toward responsible consumption of alcoholic beverages has influenced people to decrease their consumption.

Bars carry a range of each spirit, beginning with the *well* package. The well package is the least expensive pouring brand that the bar uses when guests simply ask for a "scotch and water." The *call* package is the group of spirits that the bar offers to guests who are likely to ask for a particular name brand. For example, guests may call for Johnnie Walker Red Label. An example of a premium scotch is Johnnie Walker Black Label, and a super premium scotch is Chivas Regal.

A popular method of costing each of the spirits poured is calculated according to the following example:

A premium brand of vodka such as Grey Goose costs \$32.00 per liter and yields twenty-five $1\frac{1}{4}$-oz. shots that each sell for \$5.50. So the bottle brings in \$137.50. The profit margins produced by bars may be categorized as follows:

Liquor Pouring Cost % (approx.)	12
Beer	25
Wine	38

When combined, the sales mix may have an average pouring cost of 16 to 20 percent.

Most bars operate on some form of par stock level, which means that for every spirit bottle in use, there is a minimum par stock level of one, two, or more bottles available as a backup. As soon as the stock level falls to a level below the par level, more is automatically purchased.

Nightclubs

Nightclubs have long been a popular place to go to get away from the stresses of everyday life. From the small club in a suburban neighborhood to the world famous clubs of New York, Las Vegas, and Miami's South Beach, all clubs have one thing in common: People frequent them to kick back, relax, and, more often than not, enjoy a wild night of dancing and partying with friends and strangers alike.

Night clubs offer fun, excitement, and socialization.

Like restaurant ownership, starting up a nightclub is very risky business. But with the right education and proper planning, nightclub ownership can be a very profitable endeavor. As with most businesses in the hospitality industry, many believe that experience is more important than education and that you can learn as you go. However, when embarking on a journey as involved as owning a nightclub, a person with a degree and a high level of education is well ahead of the game.

The ability to read the market is key in developing a nightclub. When investing anywhere from $300,000 to $1 million in start-up costs, it is of utmost importance to be sure that the right spot is chosen and that a relevant market is within reach. Great nightclubs result from an accurate and calculated read of a marketplace, not by virtue of good luck. In fact, the number one cause of early nightclub failure stems from an inaccurate read on the marketplace. For example, if an entrepreneur is interested in opening up a country line dancing nightclub in an urban neighborhood, he or she may want to do extensive market research to be sure that members of the community even like country music.

When considering the prospect of a new nightclub, it is important to invest considerable time in the study of demographics, market attitude, and social dynamics of the proposed target. Many people tend to come up with a concept they are dead set on pursuing without really digging into the market. One should take all markets into account, even if the other markets may not seem relevant at the time. In the future it may be these same markets that are being divided to come to the newer clubs that have just opened.

A new and exciting concept is a highly important factor in creating a nightclub. Some people feel that if one nightclub is doing well down the street, they will open the same type and be equally successful. This is not true. Variety is one of the keys to successful business. By offering patrons a fresh new opportunity, one can draw clientele away from the old clubs and into the new club.

Budgeting is another big factor in developing a nightclub. While such an undertaking can be very costly, cutting corners in building and design will only hurt the business later. It is better to spend the money now and do it right than to have to spend more money for repairs later. Creating a budget should include all aspects of the operation, including, but not limited to, food and beverage costs, staffing and labor, licenses, building ramifications, décor, lighting, and entertainment.

Be sure to know all the legal issues that come with running a nightclub. For example, many laws exist for the sale and distribution of alcohol. In many instances, if a problem occurs involving a patron who was last drinking at the club, the problem can be considered the fault of the operation's management. Lawsuits can arise fairly easily, and it is highly important to be aware of such possibilities.

Nightclubs can be great experiences for both the patrons and the owner, as revenues can be very high. However, it is important to remember the risks involved and work to minimize them.

Although this is only a brief discussion of the creation of a nightclub, the points are quite important to successful operation. As with all business endeavors, the more one knows about the industry that he or she is getting involved with, the better off the business will be. For more information regarding the nightclub industry, go to **www.nightclub.com** or **www.nightclubbiz.com**.

Microbreweries/Brewpubs

Brewpubs are a combination brewery and pub or restaurant that brews its own fresh beer onsite to meet the taste of local customers. Microbreweries are craft breweries that produce up to 15,000 barrels (or 30,000 kegs) of beer a year. The North American microbrewery industry trend revived the concept of small breweries serving fresh, all-malt beer. Although regional breweries, micro-breweries, and brewpubs account for only a small part of the North American brewing industry in terms of total beer production (less than 5 percent), they have a potential growth rate. One reason for the success of microbreweries and brewpubs is the wide variety of styles and flavors of beer they produce. On one hand, this educates the public about beer styles that have been out of production for decades and, on the other hand, helps brewpubs and restaurants meet the individual tastes and preferences of their local clientele.

Starting a brewpub is a fairly expensive venture. Although brewing systems come in a wide range of configurations, the cost of the equipment ranges from $200,000 to $800,000. Costs are affected by factors such as annual production capacity, beer types, and packaging. The investment in microbreweries and brewpubs is well justified by the enormous potential for returns. Microbreweries can produce a wide variety of ales, lagers, and other beers, the quality of which depends largely on the quality of the raw materials and the skill of the brewer. There are several regional brewpub restaurants of note, including Rock Bottom, which built its foundation on a tradition of fresh handcrafted beers and a diverse menu. It promotes itself as a place to gather with friends, drink the best beer around, enjoy a great meal, and share good times. John Harvard's has a famous selection of ales and lagers brewed on the premises according to the old English recipes brought to America in 1637 by John Harvard, after whom Harvard University is named. Gordon Biersch has several excellent brewery restaurants also offering handcrafted ales and beers along with a varied menu.

Sports Bars

Sports bars have always been popular but have become more so with the decline of disco and singles bars. They are places where people relax in the sporting atmosphere, so bar/restaurants like Trophies in San Diego or Characters at Marriott hotels have become popular "watering holes." Satellite television coverage of the top sporting events helps sports bars to draw crowds. Sports bars have evolved over the years into much more than a corner bar that features the game of the week. In the past, sports bars were frequented by die-hard sports fans and rarely visited by other clientele. Today the original sports bar is more of an entertainment concept and is geared toward a more diverse base of patrons.

Sports bars were originally no more than a gathering spot for local sports fans when the home team played on TV. Now such places have been transformed into mega-sports adventures, featuring musical entertainment, interactive games, and hundreds of TVs tuned in to just about every sport imaginable. According to National Restaurant Association research, sales at bars and taverns increased about $3 million from 1990 to 2000, largely because of the continued growth of sports bars.[16] "There are no more watering holes," says Zach Strauss,

New York Yankees fans cele-brate in a sports bar.

general manager of Sluggers World Class Sports Bar in Chicago. "Things have changed. People are more health conscious; nobody really drinks, drinks, drinks anymore. . . . You have to offer more than booze. People expect sports bars to have more personality, better food, and better service."

Today's sports bars are attracting a much more diverse clientele. Sports bars were once a destination for mainly male sports fans. Now more women and families are frequenting these venues, which provides a new prospect for revenue for bar owners. Scott Estes, founding partner of Lee Roy Selmon's restaurant in Tampa, Florida, has recognized that women are an increasing revenue force in the industry and has made adjustments to his restaurant to be sure to capitalize on this rapidly expanding market. "A lot of women are very involved in sports, and we wanted women to feel comfortable coming here. We used certain colors and treatments to make it feel less masculine," Estes says. "We wanted to be nongender-specific friendly." Sports bars are also making changes in their establishments to become more family oriented. Lee Roy Selmon's main dining room, for example, is a television-free environment. Many families go into sports bars and request a room with no TVs, so, recognizing that, an increasing number of owners have chosen to set aside a special place where families can eat uninterrupted by the noise of TV.

Another method of attracting bar patrons on slower nights is to offer games and family friendly menus. Frankie's Food, Sports, and Spirits in Atlanta attracts families by hosting a sports-trivia game for teens. For the younger crowd, the restaurant provides a kids' menu every day and serves each pint-sized meal on upside-down Frisbees, which children can take home as souvenirs. Sports bars have also become the latest version of the traditional arcade. Many bars offer interactive video games where friends and families can compete against one another. Virtual reality games such as Indy 500 and other sports games are available at many establishments. Some venues have even gone a step farther and offer batting cages, bowling alleys, and basketball courts for their patrons to enjoy.

Another aspect of the sports bar that has changed drastically is the menu. Sports bars have a reputation for serving spicy chicken wings, hamburgers, and other typical bar fare. But just as sports bars have evolved in their entertainment offerings, so too have their menus. People's tastes have changed, causing sports bars to offer a more diverse menu. Today guests can dine on a variety of foods, from filet mignon, to fresh fish, to gourmet sandwiches and pizza. Now people frequent sports bars as much for the great meal they will have as for the entertainment. In the past, sports bars usually had a few TVs that showcased games that would appeal to the area and big games such as the Super Bowl. The sudden increase in technology and TV programming available have made game viewing very different. The popularity of satellites and digital receivers has allowed bars to tune in to virtually dozens of events at any given time. Bars now have hundreds of televisions, and fans can watch games featuring every sport, team, and level of play around the world at any time of the day or night.

Burbank, California-based ESPN Zone has about 200 televisions in each of its locations so that fans can catch all the action, even in the restrooms. A handful of televisions are placed in the restaurant's bathrooms, because "we don't want you to miss a second," says Nina Roth, marketing manager for ESPN Zone in New York City. "If you have to go at the last minute, you're not going to miss the end of the game." The evolution of sports bars has turned the smoky corner bar into an exciting dining and sports experience. Customers who once rarely frequented the establishments, such as women and families, are now some of the biggest patrons, increasing both attendance and revenue at sports bars. "We have something for everyone," says ESPN Zone's Roth. "We serve a great meal, and you don't have to be a diehard sports fan to want to come."

Coffee Shops

Another fairly recent trend in the beverage industry in the United States and Canada is the establishment of coffeehouses, or coffee shops. Coffeehouses originally were created based on the model of Italian bars, which reflected the deeply rooted espresso tradition in Italy. The winning concept of Italian bars lies in the ambiance they create, which is suitable for conversation of a personal, social, and business nature. A talk over a cup of coffee with soft background music and maybe a pastry is a typical scenario for Italians. Much of the same concept was recreated in the United States and Canada, where there was a niche in the beverage industry that was yet to be acknowledged and filled. The original concept was modified, however, to include a much wider variety of beverages and styles of coffee to meet the tastes of their consumers, who have a tendency to prefer a greater selection of products. Consequently, the typical espresso/cappuccino offered by Italian bars has been expanded in North America to include items such as iced mocha, iced cappuccino, and so forth.

Students as well as businesspeople find coffeehouses a place to relax, discuss, socialize, and study. The success of coffee houses is reflected in the establishment of chains, such as Starbucks, as well as family-owned, independent shops.

Cyber cafes are a recent trend in the coffeehouse sector. Cyber cafes offer the use of computers, with Internet capability, for about $6 per hour. Guests can enjoy coffee, snacks, or even a meal while online. Reasonable rates allow regular guests to have e-mail addresses.

> ## Check Your Knowledge
> 1. Describe the bar setup.
> 2. How is inventory control conducted?
> 3. What is the average beverage pouring cost percentage?
> 4. What is a trend in sports bars?

Liquor Liability and the Law

Owners, managers, bartenders, and servers may be liable under the law if they serve alcohol to minors or to persons who are intoxicated. The extent of the liability can be very severe. The legislation that governs the sale of alcoholic beverages is called **dram shop legislation.** The dram shop laws, or civil damage acts, were enacted in the 1850s and dictated that owners and operators of drinking establishments are liable for injuries caused by intoxicated customers.[17]

Some states have reverted back to the eighteenth-century common law, removing liability from vendors except in cases involving minors. Nonetheless, most people recognize that as a society we are faced with major problems of underage drinking and drunk driving.

To combat underage drinking in restaurants, bars, and lounges, a major brewery distributed a booklet showing the authentic design and layout of each state's drivers licenses. Trade associations, like the National Restaurant Association and the American Hotel & Lodging Association, have, together with other major corporations, produced a number of preventive measures and programs aimed at responsible alcohol beverage service. The major thrust of these initiatives is awareness programs and mandatory training programs like Serve Safe for Alcohol that promote responsible alcohol service. Serve Safe for Alcohol is sponsored by the National Restaurant Association and is a certification program that teaches participants about alcohol and its effects on people, the common signs of intoxication, and how to help customers avoid drinking too much.

Other programs include designated drivers, who only drink nonalcoholic beverages to ensure that friends return home safely. Some operators give free nonalcoholic beverages to the designated driver as a courtesy.

One positive outcome of the responsible alcohol service programs for operators is a reduction in the insurance premiums and legal fees that had skyrocketed in previous years.

Highway Deaths and Alcohol

Each year thousands of people are killed on the highways in the United States. Many of these accidents can be prevented, as they are a result of carelessness and bad decision making while drinking. The National Highway Traffic Safety Administration is committed to decreasing the number of alcohol-related highway deaths. "You Drink & Drive, You Lose" and "Friends Don't Let Friends Drive

Drunk" are national slogans created to discourage impaired driving and are familiar to millions of Americans. On the positive side, the message is getting through to the public. In 1982, 57 percent of motor vehicle fatalities were alcohol related. In 2002, that number had fallen to 41 percent.[18] However, the battle with drunk driving is far from over.

In 2002, 14,409 people died in motor vehicle crashes in which alcohol was a factor. Thousands more were injured. Alcohol-related crashes are painful and expensive. Costs to treat the injured are passed on to taxpayers in the form of increased public health costs and higher insurance premiums. When it comes to impaired driving, everyone loses.

The National Highway Traffic Safety Administration (NHTSA) and its partners have a mission to reduce the annual number of fatalities attributed to impaired driving. To achieve this mission, states across the country are involving themselves in a coordinated and sustained driving under the influence enforcement effort and media campaign.

Impaired driving is a public safety problem and requires attention and the implementation of proven countermeasures. Based on facts, data analysis, experience and research, NHTSA pulled together a team of experts that in turn identified five distinct approaches to combat the impaired driving problem. They include prevention, intervention, enforcement, adjudication, and treatment. Specific information on these approaches can be obtained from your NHTSA regional office.

NHTSA is divided into ten regions across the country. Each region consists of several states, and each has a focus area in which it hopes to increase awareness. For example, region 4 is the southern region and consists of Florida, Georgia, Alabama, Louisiana, Tennessee, North and South Carolina, and Kentucky.

Region 4 is dedicated to reducing the number of fatalities and injuries due to impaired driving within our eight southern states. This is accomplished through ongoing contact with the states and promoting effective alcohol enforcement efforts, including conducting sobriety checkpoints, training police officers on driving while intoxicated (DWI) detection, and a variety of public information and education campaigns. Each state within the region has a high-visibility alcohol enforcement program that emphasizes multiagency partnerships to share resources and conduct large-scale enforcement efforts. These efforts, coupled with strong publicity about the enforcement efforts, provide the framework to change the public's attitude about drinking and driving.

In addition to the enforcement campaign, region 4 is finalizing a community assessment tool to help communities improve their DWI system in five critical areas: enforcement, prosecution, adjudication, treatment, and evaluation. This system improvement strategy is based on best practices and successful models already existing in states. The initiative focuses on establishing improvements at the local level that will ultimately reduce the number of repeat offenders and DWI offenders with high blood alcohol content (BAC) levels.

Through its constant efforts to increase state and regional awareness of the destructiveness of driving under the influence, NHTSA hopes to continue to decrease the number of alcohol-related highway deaths.

Underage Drinking

In addition to being illegal, underage drinking poses a high risk to both the individual and society. For example, the rate of alcohol-related traffic crashes is greater for drivers ages 16 to 20 than for drivers age 21 and older. Teenagers are also more vulnerable to alcohol-induced brain damage, which could contribute to poor performance at school or work. In addition, underage drinking is associated with an increased likelihood of developing alcohol abuse or dependence later in life. Early intervention is essential to prevent the development of serious alcohol problems among youth between the ages of 12 and 20. If not prevented or treated correctly, underage drinking will escalate out of control.

The statistics regarding underage drinking are staggering:

- By the time they reach the eighth grade, nearly 50 percent of teenagers have had at least one drink, and over 20 percent report having been drunk.
- Approximately 20 percent of eighth graders and almost 50 percent of twelfth graders have consumed alcohol within the past 30 days.
- Among twelfth graders, almost 30 percent report drinking on three or more occasions per month.
- Approximately 30 percent of twelfth graders engage in heavy episodic drinking, now popularly termed binge drinking—that is, having at least five or more drinks on one occasion within the past 2 weeks—and it is estimated that 20 percent do so on more than one occasion.[19]

Underage drinking is more likely to kill adolescents than all illegal drugs combined. Motor vehicle crashes are the leading cause of death for teens between 15 and 20 years old. This demographic is already at risk on the roads due to their low level of driving experience. Combine this lack of experience with alcohol and deadly results occur. In fact, in 2002, 3,827 drivers ages 15 to 20 died in automobile crashes. Twenty-four percent of the drivers in this age range who died had a BAC of 0.08 or higher.[20]

Alcohol use also increases teenagers' likelihood for depression and other emotional illnesses. More often than many people realize, this depression leads to suicide or thoughts of suicide, which is the third leading cause of death among people ages 14 to 25. In one study, 37 percent of eighth grade females who drank heavily reported attempting suicide, compared with 11 percent who did not drink.[21]

Teenagers who consume alcohol are also at higher risk for sexual assault and unsafe sex practices. Sexual assault and rape occur most among adolescent and young adult girls. When either the accuser or the victim is using alcohol, the likelihood of assault is much greater. Because their clarity of thinking is impaired when using alcohol, many teens also engage in sexual activities in which they would not partake if sober. The link between high-risk sex and drinking is directly affected by the quantity of alcohol consumed. The probability of sexual intercourse is increased by drinking amounts of alcohol sufficient to impair judgment, and the probability of unsafe sex or sex with multiple partners is much greater.

Alcohol has a huge effect on a teenager's brain because at a young age the brain is still in the developmental stage. Alcohol-induced learning impairments can affect academic and occupational achievement. One study that evaluated short-term memory skills in alcohol-dependent and nondependent adolescents ages 15 to 16 found that the alcohol-dependent youth had greater difficulty remembering words and simple geometric designs after a 10-minute interval.[22]

Not only is early alcohol use a problem in the present, but it can also lead to long-term dependency. People who begin drinking before age 15 are four times more likely to develop alcohol dependence at some time in their lives compared with those who have their first drink at age 20 or older.[23] While some evidence indicates that genetic factors may contribute to the relationship between early drinking and subsequent alcoholism, environmental factors may also be involved. These factors are especially prevalent in alcoholic families, where children may start drinking earlier because of easier access to alcohol in the home, family acceptance of drinking, and lack of parental monitoring.

Underage drinking has many causes. One thing that most encourages teens to drink is advertising. Teenagers are exposed to alcohol advertisements everywhere, in magazines, newspapers, television, and movies. Fifty-six percent of students in grades 8 to 12 say that alcohol advertising encourages them to drink.[24] Beer and liquor commercials are everywhere during popular television programs, and these ads promote drinking as part of a fun and exciting lifestyle.

Easy access to alcohol is another big factor in underage drinking. Many teens have access to alcohol in their homes. While there are laws prohibiting the sale of alcohol to teens that are underage, many of these laws are loosely followed. The ease of gaining fake identification is also relatively simple due to increases in technology. Bars who allow access to patrons younger than 21 years of age also encourage underage drinking. While patrons under 21 are not legally allowed to drink, it is impossible for establishments to monitor the activities of every person in the bar.

Because of recent increases in underage drinking, bars have been greatly encouraged to crack down on such practices. Bouncers are expected to know the signs of a fake ID and must confiscate such. In many areas the establishment will be fined if underage patrons are found to have been let in the door with a fake ID. It is also common practice to reward bar owners for confiscating fake IDs. Many places in the United States have a system of undercover police who monitor and stop underage drinking in bars. For example, in Tallahassee, Florida, the Alcohol, Tobacco, and Firearms unit of the police department travels to bars and parties disguised as regular partygoers. When underage drinking is spotted, teens can be fined, have their drivers' licenses revoked, and even be arrested.

The key to stemming underage drinking is to take a preventive approach. Many schools have such programs in place, starting while children are very young, to discourage negative behavior in the future. Strong family relationships that enforce healthy lifestyles also greatly reduce the probability that a teenager will drink in the first place.

Trends in the Beverage Industry

- The comeback of cocktails
- Designer bottled water
- Microbreweries
- More wine consumption
- Increase in coffeehouses and coffee intake
- Increased awareness and action to avoid irresponsible alcoholic beverage consumption

CASE STUDY

Hiring Bar Personnel

As bar manager of a popular local night club, it is your responsibility to interview and hire all bar personnel. One of your friends asks you for a job as a bartender. Since he has experience, you decide to help him out and give him a regular shift. During the next few weeks, you notice that the overall sales for his shifts are down slightly from previous weeks with other bartenders. You suspect he may be stealing from you.

Questions

1. What are your alternatives for determining whether your friend is, in fact, stealing?
2. If you determine that he has been stealing, how do you handle it?

CASE STUDY

Java Coffee House

Michelle Wong is manager of the Java Coffee House at a busy location on Union Street in San Francisco. Michelle says that there are several challenges in operating a busy coffeehouse, such as training staff to handle unusual circumstances. For example, one guest consumed a cup of coffee and ate two-thirds of a piece of cake and then said he didn't like the cake.

Another problem is suppliers who quote good prices to get her business and then, two weeks later, raise the price of some of the items.

Michelle says that the young employees she has at the Java Coffee House are her greatest challenge of all. According to Michelle, there are four kinds of employees—lazy; good, but not responsible; those who steal; and great ones who are no trouble.

Questions

1. What are some suggestions for training staff to handle unusual circumstances?
2. How do you ensure that suppliers are delivering the product at the price quoted?
3. What do you do with lazy employees?
4. What do you do with irresponsible employees?
5. How do you deal with employees who steal?

CAREER INFORMATION

Beverages

A career in beverage management includes everything from coffee shops and restaurants to bars and nightclubs to wineries and breweries. Careers can involve production of the product or selling and marketing it to customers.

Winery or brewery careers are very specialized. A great way to explore this career option is to work at a winery or brewpub in your area while you are attending college. If you discover that this is what you want to do, try taking some related courses at a college or university in your area. Taking courses in viticulture and enology can help develop your knowledge about grapes and wine making in order to help you decide if this is a career path you wish to pursue. *Viticulture* is the science of growing grapes and *enology* is the science of making wine. Knowledge in these areas is becoming so important that some universities are offering specialized degrees in both areas. Brewery schools offer brewer certification programs and associate degrees in malting and brewing science or brewing technology.

Selling wine or spirits for a distributor can also be a very lucrative and interesting career. If you enjoy meeting people and like the idea of working on a commission, this may be an option you want to consider. As with any type of selling you need to be a person who is motivated, organized, and outgoing. You will also be selling a product that requires you to have very specialized knowledge. When you are hired your employer will spend time and money training you; however, it is advantageous to develop your knowledge of "adult beverages" while you are in college. Beverage management courses, seminars, and working for liquor distributors are great ways to develop this expertise.

Beverage management in nightclubs and restaurants involves late nights and sometimes long hours. Establishments can keep their bars open until well into the morning hours. Serving alcohol requires understanding hospitality law and dealing with your customers responsibly. While you are in school you should take courses in beverage management and hospitality law and also work as a barback, bartender, or part-time manager. Upon becoming a manager you will experience late nights, intoxicated people, and the constant temptation of substance abuse. It takes self-control to work the long, irregular hours and not join your customers for a good time. If you are a disciplined person, who likes being where the action is and can handle the late hours, then this could be your type of hospitality career.

Coffee shops emerged during the 1990s and have become a separate segment of the hospitality business. Well-managed coffee bars offer a relaxed environment where customers can enjoy themselves with a good cup of coffee while reading a book or talking with friends. Coffee shops foster close relationships between customers and managers. It is not uncommon for people to visit a coffee bar several times each month. If you enjoy personal relationships and a low-stress environment, this career is worth checking out.

Related Web Sites

cocktails.about.com/food/cocktails/?once=true& — gives information on liquor
www.geocities.com/Paris/5289/cocktail.html—bartending and liquor
www.vine2wine.com/—links to a variety of Web sites about wine
www.americanwineries.org/—National Associations of American Wineries
www.wineserver.ucdavis.edu/winegrape/index.htm—winery education information and links to other sites
www.realbeer.com/—great Web site for information on beer
hbd.org/brewery/—information and links to brewing
www.abgbrew.com/—brewing school
www.siebelinstitute.com/—brewing school in Chicago
www.republicbeverage.com/—Republic Beverage career information and links to other sites
www.starbucks.com/home.asp—Starbucks Coffee employment information

Courtesy of Charlie Adams.

SUMMARY

1. Beverages are categorized into alcoholic and nonalcoholic beverages. Alcoholic beverages are further categorized into spirits, wines, and beer.
2. Wine is the fermented juice of ripe grapes. It is classified as red, white, and rose, and we distinguish between light beverage wines, sparkling wines, and aromatic wines.
3. The six steps in making wine are crushing, fermenting, racking, maturing, filtering, and boiling. France, Germany, Italy, Spain, and Portugal are the main European wine-producing areas, and California is the main American wine-producing area.
4. Beer is a brewed and fermented beverage made from malt. Different types of beer include ale, stout, lager, and pilsner.
5. Spirits have a high percentage of alcohol and are served before or after a meal. Fermentation and distillation are

parts of their processing. The most popular white spirits are rum, gin, vodka, and tequila.

6. Today people have become more health conscious about consumption of alcohol; nonalcoholic beverages such as coffee, tea, soft drinks, juices, and bottled water are increasing in popularity.

7. Beverages make up 20 to 30 percent of total sales in a restaurant, but managers are liable if they serve alcohol to minors. Programs such as designated driver and TIPS and the serving of virgin cocktails have increased.

8. Close to 18,000 people die each year in the United in alcohol-related auto accidents.

9. Underage drinking leads to significant personal and social problems.

KEY WORDS AND CONCEPTS

Alcoholic beverage	Fermentation	Must	White spirits
Beer	Fining	Nonalcoholic beverage	Wine
Brandy	Fortified wines	Prohibition	Wine and food pairing
Champagne	Hops	Proof	Wine tasting
Clarify	Inventory control	Sparkling wine	Wort
Cognac	Malt	Spirit (liquor)	Yeast
Dram shop legislation	Mashing	Vintage	

REVIEW QUESTIONS

1. What is the difference between fortified and aromatic wines? In what combination is it suggested to serve food and wine and why?

2. Describe the brewing process of beer. What is the difference between a stout and a pilsner?

3. Name and describe the main types of spirits.

4. Why have nonalcoholic drinks increased in popularity and what difficulties do bar managers face when serving alcohol?

5. Describe the origin of coffee.

6. Describe the proper procedure for handling and serving champagne.

7. Describe the origin of cocktails. What constitutes a cocktail?

8. Describe a typical bar setup.

9. What are the problems relating to underage alcoholic beverage drinking?

INTERNET EXERCISES

1. Organization: **Clos Du Bois**
   Web site: **www.closdubois.com**
   Summary: Clos Du Bois is one of America's well-known and loved wineries and is premier producer of wines from Sonoma County in California. The winery was started in 1974 and since then has acquired many more vineyards and a name for itself. It now sells about a million cases of premium wine annually.
   (a) Take a look at the detailed food and wine pairings. What can you serve with the Clos Du Bois Sonoma County sauvignon blanc? Compare it to what you already know about what to eat with sauvignon blanc.
   (b) The Clos Du Bois has been named Wine of the Year for nine years by *Wine & Spirits*. What is it about this wine that makes it so different from others?

2. Organization: **Siebel Institute of Technology**
   Web site: **www.siebelinstitute.com**
   Summary: Siebel Institute of Technology is recognized for its training and educational programs in brewing technology.
   (a) What are some of the services that the Institute of Technology offers its students?
   (b) List the career path options available through Siebel Institute of Technology.

APPLY YOUR KNOWLEDGE

1. In groups, do a blindfold taste test with cans of Coke and Pepsi. See if your group can identify which is which and who likes Coke or Pepsi the most.
2. Complete the class survey and share the results with your classmates.
3. Demonstrate the correct way of opening and serving a bottle of nonalcoholic wine.
4. What type of wine would be recommended with the following:

a. Pork
b. Cheese
c. Lamb
d. Chocolate cake
e. Chicken

5. Mothers Against Drunk Driving (MADD) is a nonprofit organization working to stop drunk drivers and support victims of drunk drivers. Find out what impact MADD has had on society.

SUGGESTED ACTIVITIES

1. Search the Internet for underage drinking statistics and related highway deaths in your state.
2. Create an outline for a sports bar concept.

ENDNOTES

1. **www.cookingvillage.com**. September 2005.
2. Budweiser Brewing Company Presentation. University of South Florida, September 7, 2004.
3. **www.en.wikipedia.org/wiki/Scotch_whisky**. September 17, 2005.
4. **www.en.wikipedia.org/wiki/Scotch_whisky**. September 17, 2005.
5. C. Katsigris and M. Porter, *The Bar and Beverage Book*, 3rd ed. New York: John Wiley & Sons, 2002, p. 139.
6. Personal conversation with Susan Davis of the Specialty Association of America. August 26, 2005.
7. **www.ancora-coffee.com/history-goats.asp**. July 2005.
8. Ibid.
9. **www.thebeanshop.com**. July 2005.
10. **www.scanbar.com/eng/liquor.html**. August 28, 2005.
11. **www.scanbar.com/eng/wine.html**. August 28, 2005.
12. **www.azabaramerica.com/products/controller.html**. August 28, 2005.
13. Coca-Cola's 2004 annual report.
14. Personal correspondence with Kenneth E. Crocker. September 19, 2005.
15. **www.restaurant.org/rusa/magArticle.cfm**? ArticleID=515.
16. **www.3.madd.org/laws/law.cfm**? LawID = DRAM.
17. **http://www.nhtsa.dot.gov/nhtsa/whatis/regions/Region04/04alcohol.html**.
18. L. D. Johnston, P. M. O'Malley, and J. G. Bachman. Monitoring the Future: National Results on Adolescent Drug Use. Overview of Key Findings, 2002. NIH Pub. No. 03–5374. Bethesda, MD: National Institute on Drug Abuse (NIDA), 2003.
19. U.S. Department of Transportation. National Highway Traffic Safety Administration. 400 Seventh Street, S. W. Washington, DC 20590, November 2003.
20. M. Windle, C. Miller-Tutzauer, and D. Domenico. Alcohol use, suicidal behavior, and risky activities among adolescents. *Journal of Research on Adolescence* 2(4): 317–330, 2003.
21. **www.teendrugabuse.us/teensandalcohol.html**. July 2005.
22. Ibid.
23. **www.focuoas.com/alchol.html**. July 2005.
24. Ibid.

WEB RESOURCES

University of South Florida
www.usf.edu

Robert Mondavi
www.robertmondavi.com

Napa Valley
www.napavalley.com

Sonoma Valley
www.sonomovalley.com

Sterling Vineyards
www.sterlingvineyards.com

Chivas Regal
www.chivas.com

Johnnie Walker
www.johnniewalker.com

Madd
www.madd.org

Anheuser-Busch
www.anheuser-busch.com

Miller
www.millerbrewing.com

The Specialty Coffee Association of America
www.scaa.com

Starbucks Coffee Company
www.starbucks.com

Coca Cola
www.cocacola.com

Pepsi
www.pepsi.com

The National Football League
www.nfl.com

Gatorade
www.gatorade.com

National Collegiate Athletics Association
www2.ncaa.org

Perrier
www.perrier.com

Evian
www.evian.com

Trophies Sports Bar-Star City Casino
http://www.starcity.com

National Highway Traffic Safety Administration
www.nhtsa.dot.gov

ESPN Zone
espnzone.com

Sluggers World Class Sports Bar
www.sluggersbar.com

Recreation, Theme Parks, and Clubs

11

After reading and studying this chapter, you should be able to:

- Discuss the relationship of recreation and leisure to wellness.
- Explain the origins and extent of government-sponsored recreation.
- Distinguish between commercial and noncommercial recreation.
- Name and describe various types of recreational clubs.
- Identify the major U.S. theme parks.
- Describe the operations of a country club.

Recreational activities include all kinds of sports, both team and individual. Baseball, softball, football, basketball, volleyball, tennis, swimming, jogging, skiing, hiking, aerobics, rock climbing, and camping are all active forms of recreation. Passive recreational activities include reading, fishing, playing and listening to music, gardening, playing computer games, and watching television or movies. **Recreation** is an integral part of our nation's total social, economic, and natural resource environment. It is a basic component of our lives and well being.[1]

Recreation, Leisure, and Wellness

As postindustrial society has become more complex, life has become more stressed. The need to develop the wholeness of the person has become increasingly important. Compared to a generation ago, the stress levels of business executives are much higher. The term *burnout*—and indeed the word *stress*—have only become a part of our everyday vocabulary in recent years. Recreation is all about creating a balance, a harmony in life that will maintain wellness and wholeness.

Recreation allows people to have fun together and to form lasting relationships built on the experiences they have enjoyed together. This recreational process is called *bonding.* Bonding is hard to describe, yet the experience of increased interpersonal feeling for friends or business associates as a result of a recreational pursuit is common. These relationships result in personal growth and development.

The word *recreation* is defined as "any activity that a person chooses to participate in during his or her free time for enjoyment or relaxation."[2] Recreation is synonymous with lifestyle and the development of a positive attitude. An example of this is the increased feeling of well-being experienced after a recreational activity. Some people make the mistake of trying to pursue happiness as a personal goal. It is not enough for a person to say, "I want to be happy; therefore, I will recreate." Nathaniel Hawthorne wrote in the mid-nineteenth century: "Happiness in this world, when it comes, comes incidentally. Make it the object

Canoeing is active recreation.

Windsurfing is definitely an active recreational activity.

of pursuit, and it leads us on a wild goose chase, and it is never attained. Follow some other object, and very possibly we may find that we have caught happiness without dreaming of it."[3]

Recreation is a process that seeks to establish a milieu conducive to the discovery and development of characteristics that can lead to happiness. Happiness and well-being, therefore, are incidental outcomes of recreation. Thus, happiness may be enhanced by the pursuit of recreational activities. The setting of personal recreational goals is equally as important as any other business or personal goal. These goals might include running a mile in under six minutes or maintaining a baseball batting average above 0.300. The fact that a person sets and strives to achieve goals requires personal organization. This helps improve the quality of life.

Leisure is best described as time free from work, or discretionary time. Some recreation professionals use the words *leisure* and *recreation* interchangeably, while others define leisure as the "productive," "creative," or "contemplative" use of free time. History shows again and again a direct link between leisure and the advancement of civilization. Hard work alone leaves no time for becoming civilized. Ironically, however, the opportunity to be at leisure is the direct result of increased technological and productivity advancements.

Hiking is a great exercise and an ideal way to get back to nature.

Government-Sponsored Recreation

Various levels of government that constitute **government-sponsored recreation** are intertwined, yet distinct, in the parks, recreation, and leisure services. The founding fathers of America said it best when they affirmed the right to life, liberty, and the pursuit of happiness in the Declaration of Independence. Government raises revenue from income taxes, sales taxes, and property taxes. Additionally, government raises special revenue from recreation-related activities such as automobile and recreational vehicles, boats, motor fuels, **transient occupancy taxes (TOT)** on hotel accommodations, state lotteries, and others. The monies are distributed among the various recreation- and leisure-related organizations at the federal, state/provincial, city, and town levels. Recreation and leisure activities are extremely varied, ranging from cultural pursuits like museums, arts and crafts, music, theater, and dance to sports (individual and team), outdoor recreation, amusement parks, theme parks, community centers, playgrounds, libraries, and gardens. People select recreational pursuits based on their interests and capabilities.

Park and recreation leaders confront daunting challenges at a time when leisure and recreational resources are highly valued community assets. Yet, securing adequate funding for staff and services can be a juggling act.[4] The following are some of the issues recreation professionals must deal with:
- Comprehensive recreation planning
- Land classification systems
- Federal revenue sharing
- Acquisition- and development-funding programs
- Land-use planning and zoning
- State and local financing
- Off-road vehicle impacts and policy
- Use of easements for recreation
- Designation of areas (such as wilderness, wild and scenic rivers, national trails, nature preserves)
- Differences in purposes and resources (of the numerous local, state/provincial, and federal agencies that control more than one-third of the nation's land, much of which is used for recreation)

National Parks in the United States

National Parks are the best idea we ever had. Absolutely American, absolutely democratic, they reflect us at our best rather than our worst.

—Wallace Stegner

The prevailing image of a **national park** is one of grand natural playgrounds, such as Yellowstone National Park; but there is much more to it than that. The United States has designated 367 national park units throughout the country, comprising a rich diversity of places and settings. The **National Parks Service** was founded in 1916 by Congress to conserve park resources and to provide for their use by the public in order to leave them unimpaired for the enjoyment of

The New York Marathon brings thousands of people to the city and thousands more in economic impact.

future generations. In addition to the better-known parks such as Yellowstone and Yosemite, the Parks Service also manages many other heritage attractions, including the Freedom Trail in Boston, Independence Hall in Philadelphia, the Antietam National Battlefield in Sharpsburg, Maryland, and the USS *Arizona* Memorial at Pearl Harbor in Hawaii. The Parks Service is also charged with caring for myriad cultural artifacts, including ancient pottery, sailing vessels, colonial-period clothing, and Civil War documents.

> *There is nothing so American as our National Parks. . . . The fundamental idea behind the parks . . . is that the country belongs to the people.*
>
> —Franklin D. Roosevelt

The ever-expanding mandate of the Parks Service also calls for understanding and preserving the environment. It monitors the ecosystem from the Arctic tundra to coral atolls, researches the air and water quality around the nation, and participates in global studies on acid rain, climate change, and biological diversity. The idea of preserving exceptional lands for public use as national parks arose after the Civil War when America's receding wilderness left unique national resources vulnerable to exploitation. Recent years have seen phenomenal growth in the system, with three new areas created in the last 20 years. These include new kinds of parks, such as urban recreational areas, free-flowing rivers, long-distance trails, and historic sites honoring our nation's social achievements. The system's current roster of 367 areas covers more than 80 million acres of land, with individual areas ranging in size from the 13-million-acre Wrangell–St. Elias National Park and Preserve in Alaska to the Thaddeus Kosciuszko National Memorial (a Philadelphia row house commemorating a hero of the American Revolution), which covers two one-hundredths of an acre.

The splendor of nature awaits us in our national parks.

More than 272 million visitors go to the parks each year and take advantage of the full range of services and programs. The focus once placed on preserving the scenery of the most natural parks has shifted as the system has grown and changed. Today emphasis is placed on preserving the vitality of each park's ecosystem and on the protection of unique or endangered plant and animal species.[5]

Public Recreation and Parks Agencies

During the early part of the nineteenth century in the United States, the parks movement expanded rapidly as a responsibility of government and voluntary organizations. By the early 1900s, 14 cities had made provisions for supervised play facilities, and the playground movement gained momentum. Private initiative and financial support were instrumental in convincing city government to provide tax dollars to build and maintain new play areas.

About the same time, municipal parks were created in a number of cities. Boston established the first metropolitan park system in 1892. In 1898, the New England Association of Park Superintendents (predecessor of the American Institute of Park Executives) was established to bring together park superintendents and promote their professional concerns. Increasingly, the concept that city governments should provide recreation facilities, programs, and services became widely accepted. Golf courses, swimming pools, bathing beaches, picnic areas, winter sports facilities, game fields, and playgrounds were constructed.

Golf is a leisurely sport that can be enjoyed by young and older people.

Street basketball is a great team sport.

Check Your Knowledge

1. Explain the importance of taxes to government-sponsored recreation.
2. Name a few parks in the United States and in Canada. What are some characteristics that make the parks you named special?
3. Name your favorite park. Share with your classmates why it is your favorite.

Commercial Recreation

Recreation management came of age in the 1920s and 1930s, when recreation and social programs were offered as a community service. Colleges and universities began offering degree programs. Both public and private sector recreation management has grown rapidly since 1950.

Commercial recreation, often called eco- or adventure tourism, provides residents and visitors with access to an area's spectacular wilderness through a variety of guided outdoor activities. Specifically, commercial recreation is defined as outdoor recreational activities provided on a fee-for-service basis, with a focus on experiences associated with the natural environment.[6] Commercial recreation includes theme parks, attractions, and clubs.

Theme Parks

Visiting **theme parks** has always been a favorite tourist activity. Theme parks attempt to create an atmosphere of another place and time, and they usually emphasize one dominant theme around which architecture, landscape, rides, shows, foodservices, costumed personnel, and retailing are

Corporate Profile

Busch Gardens

Busch Gardens is the ultimate family adventure park, featuring an unparalleled combination of exotic animal encounters, world-class thrill rides, and innovative live entertainment. The adventure park is recognized among the top zoos in North America, with award-winning natural habitats that provide more diverse ways to get up close and personal to animals than any other place outside of Africa. With a unique blend of thrilling rides, one of the country's best zoos with more than 2,000 animals, live shows, restaurants, shops, and games, Busch Gardens provides unrivaled excitement for guests of every age.

SheiKra, which opened in May 2005, is North America's first dive coaster. It sends riders through a breathtaking three-minute journey 200 feet up, then 90 degrees straight down at 70 miles per hour — and that's just the beginning. The name SheiKra evokes the power and speed of an African hawk as it twists, turns, and plunges — giving guests over-the-edge excitement unrivaled by any coaster in the world. SheiKra is the first dive coaster to incorporate an Immelmann loop (a simultaneous loop and roll), a second 90-degree, 138-foot drop into an underground tunnel, and a stunning water feature, all packed into more than half a mile of steel track. This one-of-a-kind coaster will serve as the centerpiece of Busch Gardens' newly themed Stanleyville area, which also includes the new Zambia Smokehouse restaurant, which is situated on the coaster's perimeter to allow guests to be a part of the action while dining.

"KaTonga: Musical Tales From the Jungle" takes you on a journey to the heart of Africa in a 35-minute musical celebration of animal folklore. The show follows a day in the lives of aspiring storytellers, called Griots, as they strive to become masters of their craft. To accomplish this rite of passage, the performers evoke traditional African stories that mesmerize and entertain! Masterful puppet design, magical folklore, energetic original music, and spectacular African-inspired dance combine to create the first theme park show of Broadway-production caliber.

Families can challenge the curves, drops, and corkscrews of Cheetah Chase, the seventh addition to the adventure park's family of world-class coasters. With its top speed of 22 mph and 46-inch height requirement, Cheetah Chase is the perfect ride for a child's first coaster experience. The five-story "wild mouse" style family coaster makes its home in Timbuktu.

---

orchestrated. In this definition, the concept of *themes* is crucial to the operation of the parks, with rides, entertainment, and food all used to create several different environments.[7]

Theme parks and attractions vary according to theme, which might be historical, cultural, geographical, and so on. Some parks and attractions focus on a single theme, like the marine zoological Sea World parks. Other parks and attractions focus on multiple themes, like King's Island in Ohio, a family entertainment center divided into six theme areas: International Street, October First, River-Town, Hanna-Barbera Land, Coney Mall, and Wild Animal Habitat. Another example is Great America in California, a 100-acre family entertainment center that evokes North America's past in five themes: Home Town Square, Yukon Territory, Yankee Harbor, Country Fair, and Orleans Place.[8]

There are an abundance of theme parks located throughout the United States. These parks have a variety of attractions, from animals and sea life, to thrill rides and motion simulators. There are parks with educational themes and parks where people go to simply have a good time.

Many of the country's most well known parks are located in Florida. Walt Disney World, Sea World, Water Mania, Wet 'N' Wild, and Universal Studios are just a few of the many parks located in Orlando. Busch Gardens and Adventure Island are both in Tampa.

One theme park that differs greatly from the other parks in the area is Sea World in Orlando. It is based on the creatures of the sea. Guests can pet dolphins and other fish; watch shows featuring Shamu, the famous killer whale; and learn all about the mysteries of the sea. Several rides are also available at Sea World, and countless exhibits feature everything from stingrays to penguins. Sea

A seven-story water slide at Water Mania Theme Park in Kissimmee, Florida, is an example of a single-themed park.

World also has parks located in San Diego, California, and San Antonio, Texas.

Busch Gardens, located in both Tampa, Florida, and Williamsburg, Virginia, is perhaps the most well known of the animal-themed parks. Busch Gardens is like a zoo with a twist. It features equal amounts of thrill rides and animal attractions. Guests can take a train ride through the Serengeti Plains, where zebras and antelope run wild, hop aboard a giant tube ride through the Congo River rapids or ride on one of the parks' many world-record-holding roller coasters.

Killer whales entertain the crowds at Sea World.

Mardi Gras revellers crowd about a parade float in New Orleans.

Many cities in the United States are well known for their festivals, which bring in droves of vacationers year after year. One of the most well known is Mardi Gras (Fat Tuesday) in New Orleans, Louisiana. Mardi Gras began over 100 years ago as a carnival and has evolved into a world-renowned party. Mardi Gras takes place every year in February, the day before Ash Wednesday, the beginning of Lent. The days leading up to Fat Tuesday are filled with wild parades, costume contests, concerts, and overall partying. The famous Bourbon Street is home to most of the partygoing crowd, and it is often too crowded to even walk around. Beads are big at Mardi Gras, and thousands are given out each year. The culture of New Orleans greatly adds to the festiveness of Mardi Gras, as traditional jazz and blues can always be heard on most street corners.

Another famous site of interest is the Grand Ole Opry in Nashville, Tennessee. The Grand Ole Opry is a live radio show in which country music guests are featured. Started over 75 years ago, the Grand Ole Opry is what made Nashville "Music City." Since the Opry's start, Nashville has created a theme park, Opryland, and a hotel, the Opryland Resort. Famous musicians come from all over the world to showcase their talents, and tourists flock from everywhere to hear the sounds of the Opry and see the sites that Nashville has to offer.

Walt Disney: A Man with a Vision

To all who come to this happy place: Welcome! Disneyland is your land; here, age relives fond memories of the past, and here youth may savor the challenge and promise of the future.

Disneyland is dedicated to the hard facts that have created America, with the hope that it will be a source of joy and inspiration to all the world.

—Disneyland Dedication Plaque, July 17, 1955

Walt Disney World

In 1923, at the age of 21, Walt Disney arrived in Los Angeles from Kansas City to start a new business. The first endeavor of Walt Disney and his brother Roy was a series of "shorts" called *Alice Comedies,* which featured a child actress playing with animated characters. Realizing that something new was needed to capture the audience, Walt Disney conjured up the concept of a mouse. In 1927, Disney began a series called *Oswald the Lucky Rabbit.* It was well received by the public, but Disney lost the rights due to a dispute with his distributor.

Mickey and Minnie Mouse first appeared in *Steamboat Willie,* which also incorporated music and sound, on November 18, 1928. Huge audiences were ecstatic about the Disney Brothers, who became overnight successes.

During the next few years, Walt and Roy made many Mickey Mouse films, which earned them enough to develop other projects, including full-length motion pictures in Technicolor.

According to Disney, "Disneyland really began when my two daughters were very young. Saturday was always Daddy's Day, and I would take them to the merry-go-round and sit on a bench eating peanuts while they rode. And sitting there alone, I felt there should be something built, some kind of family park where parents and children could have fun together."[9]

Walt's original dream was not easy to bring to reality. During the bleak war years, not only was much of his overseas market closed, but the steady stream of income that paid for innovation dried up. However, even during the bleak years, Walt never gave up. Instead, he was excited to learn of the public's interest in movie studios and the possibility of opening the studios to allow the public to visit the birthplace of Snow White, Pinocchio, and other Disney characters.

Disneyland had its growing pains—larger than expected opening day crowds, long lines at the popular rides, and a cash flow that was so tight that the cashiers had to rush the admission money to the bank in order to make payroll. Fortunately, since those early days, Disneyland and the Disney characters have become a part of not only Walt Disney, but also of the American dream.

By the early 1960s, Walt had turned most of his attention from film to real estate. Because he was upset when cheap motels and souvenir shops popped up around Disneyland, for his next venture, Walt Disney World, he bought 27,500 acres around the park. The center of Walt Disney World was to be the Experimental Prototype Community of Tomorrow (Epcot). Regrettably, Epcot and Walt Disney World were his dying dreams, as Walt Disney succumbed to cancer in 1966.

The ensuing years have given Disney phenomenal successes with Epcot, movies, a TV station, the Disney Channel, Disney stores, and Disney-MGM Studios theme park. In April 1992, EuroDisneyland, now Disneyland Paris, opened near Paris. For a variety of reasons (location, cost, climate, and culture) it was initially a failure, until his Royal Highness Prince Al Waleed Bin Talal Bin Abdula of Saudi Arabia purchased 25 percent of the EuroDisney Paris Resort. Tokyo Disneyland continues to be successful; since its opening in 1983, millions have enjoyed the happiest place on earth. Disneyland Hong Kong, China, opened in 2005 and promises to draw millions if not billions to the magical kingdom.

Both Walt Disney World and Disneyland have excellent college programs that enable selected students to work during the summer months in a variety of hotel, foodservice, and related park positions. Disney has also introduced a faculty internship that allows faculty to intern in a similar variety of positions.

Walt Disney World is composed of four major theme parks: Magic Kingdom, Epcot, Disney's Animal Kingdom, and Disney-MGM Studios, with more than 100 attractions, 22 resort hotels themed to faraway lands, spectacular nighttime entertainment, and vast shopping, dining, and recreation facilities that cover thousands of acres in this tropical paradise.

Walt Disney World includes 25 lighted tennis courts, 99 holes of championship golf, marinas, swimming pools, jogging and bike trails, water skiing, and motor boating. The resort also offers a unique zoological park and bird sanctuary on Discovery Island in the middle of Bay Lake that is alive with birds, monkeys, and alligators; 226 restaurants, lounges, and food courts; a nightclub metropolis to please nearly any musical palate; a starry-eyed tribute to 1930s Hollywood; and even bass fishing. Walt Disney World is always full of new surprises: It now features the world's most unusual water adventure park, a "snow-covered" mountain with a ski resort theme called Blizzard Beach.

Three new Disney hotels are architecturally exciting and more affordable than ever. The funfilled Disney's All-Star Sports Resort and Disney's colorful All-Star Music Resort are categorized as value-class hotels. Disney's Wilderness Lodge is one of the park's jewels, with its impressive tall-timber atrium-lobby and rooms built around a Rocky Mountain geyser pool. For nighttime fun, there are the Pleasure Island nightclubs. In all, the park has a cast of 37,000 hosts, hostesses, and entertainers famous for their warm smiles and commitment to making every night an especially good one for Disney guests.

There is more to enjoy than ever in ExtraTERRORestrial Alien Encounter, developed in collaboration with George Lucas, and Transportarium in New Tomorrowland. Already open are Fantasyland's Legend of the Lion King; Epcot's INNOVENTIONS; the mind-blowing 3D adventure, Honey, I Shrunk the Audience, in Future World; and, at the Disney-MGM Studios, the ultimate thriller, The Twilight Zone Tower of Terror™.

Magic Kingdom

The heart of Walt Disney World and its first famous theme park is the Magic Kingdom—the "happiest land on earth"—where "age relives fond memories" and "youth may savor the challenge and promise of the future." It is a giant theatrical stage where guests become part of exciting Disney adventures. It is also the home of Mickey Mouse, Snow White, Peter Pan, Tom Sawyer, Davy Crockett, and the Swiss Family Robinson.

More than 40 major shows and ride-through attractions, not to mention shops and unique dining facilities, fill its seven lands of imagination. Each land carries out its theme in fascinating detail—architecture, transportation, music, costumes, dining, shopping, and entertainment are designed to create a total atmosphere where guests can leave the ordinary world behind. The seven lands include the following:

Main Street USA—Turn-of-the-century charm with horsedrawn streetcars, horseless carriages, Penny Arcade, and grand-circle tour on Walt Disney World Steam Railroad

Adventureland—Explore with Pirates of the Caribbean, wild animal Jungle Cruise, Swiss Family Treehouse, Tropical Serenade by birds, flowers, and tikis

Frontierland—Thrills on Splash Mountain and Big Thunder Mountain Railroad, musical fun in Country Bear Jamboree, Shooting Gallery, Tom Sawyer Island caves and raft rides

Liberty Square—Steamboating on the Rivers of America, mystery in the Haunted Mansion, whooping it up in Diamond Horseshoe Saloon, viewing the impressive Hall of Presidents with the addition of President Bill Clinton in a speaking role

Fantasyland—Cinderella Castle is the gateway to the new Legend of The Lion King plus Peter Pan's Flight, Snow White's Adventure, Mr. Toad's Wild Ride, Dumbo the Flying Elephant, Alice's Mad Tea Party, musical cruise with doll-like dancers in It's a Small World, Cinderella's Golden Carousel, and Skyway cable car to Tomorrowland

Mickey's Toontown Fair—Mickey's House, Grandma Duck's Farm, Mickey's Treehouse playground, and private photo session in Mickey's Dressing Room

New Tomorrowland—Sci-fi city of the future, new frightening Alien Encounter, Transportarium time machine travels in Circle-Vision 360, new whirling Astro-Orbiter, speedy Space Mountain, new production of Carousel of Progress, Grand Prix Raceway, elevated Transit tour, new Disney Character show on Tomorrowland Stage

Epcot

Epcot is a unique, permanent, and ever-changing world's fair with two major themes: Future World and World Showcase. Highlights include Illumi-Nations, a nightly spectacle of fireworks, fountains, lasers, and classical music.

Future World shows an amazing exposition of technology for the near future for home, work, and play in INNOVENTIONS. The newest consumer products

The monorail zips past Spaceship Earth at Walt Disney's Epcot Center in Orlando, Florida.

are continually added. Major pavilions exploring past, present, and future are shown in the Spaceship Earth story of communications. The Universe of Energy giant dinosaurs help explain the origin and future of energy. There are also the Wonders of Life with spectacular Body Wars, Cranium Command and other medical health subjects, the World of Motion soon-to-be test track, Journey into Imagination, The Land with spectacular agricultural research and environmental growing areas, and The Living Seas, the world's largest indoor ocean with thousands of tropical sea creatures.

Around the World Showcase Lagoon are pavilions where guests can see world-famous landmarks and sample the native foods, entertainment, and culture of 11 nations:

Mexico—Mexico's fiesta plaza and boat trip on El Rio Del Tiempo plus San Angel inn for authentic Mexican cuisine
Norway—Thrilling Viking boat journey and Restaurant Akershus
China—Wonders of China Circle-Vision 360 film tour from the Great Wall to the Yangtze River plus Nine Dragons Restaurant
Germany—Authentic Biergarten restaurant
Italy—St. Mark's Square street players and L'Originale Alfredo di Roma Ristorante
United States—The American Adventure's stirring historical drama
Japan—Recreating an Imperial Palace plus Teppanyaki Dining Rooms
Morocco—Morocco's palatial Restaurant Marrakesh
France—Impressions de France film tour of the French countryside, Chefs de France
United Kingdom—Shakespearean street players plus Rose & Crown Pub
Canada—Halifax to Vancouver Circle-Vision 360 tour.
Each showcase has additional snack facilities and a variety of shops featuring arts, crafts, and merchandise from each nation.

Disney–MGM Studios

With fifty major shows, shops, restaurants, ride-through adventures, and backstage tours, the Disney–MGM Studios combines real working motion picture, animation, and television studios with exciting movie attractions. The newest

*Crowds flock to the
Disney–MGM Studios, Florida.*

adventure in the Sunset Boulevard theater district is the Twilight Zone™ Tower
of Terror, with a stunning 13-story elevator fall. The famous Chinese Theater on
Hollywood Boulevard houses The Great Movie Ride.

Other major attractions include a Backstage Studio Tour of production facilities, Catastrophe Canyon, and New York Street; a tour of Walt Disney Animation Studios, Florida; exciting shows at Indiana Jones™ Epic Stunt
Spectacular and Jim Henson's Muppet Vision 3D; plus a thrilling space flight
on Star Tours.

Especially entertaining for movie and TV fans are the SuperStar Television
and Monster Sound Show, where audience members take part in performances.
Favorite Disney films become entertaining stage presentations in the Voyage of
the Little Mermaid theater and in Beauty and the Beast, a live, 25-minute musical revue at Theater of the Stars. The best restaurants include the Hollywood
Brown Derby, 1950s Prime Time Cafe, Sci-Fi Dine-In Theater, Mama Melrose's
Ristorante Italiano, and the Studio Commissary.

All this and much more are what help make Walt Disney World the most popular destination resort in the world. Since its opening in 1971, more than 500
million guests, including kings and celebrities from around the world and all six
U.S. presidents in office since the opening, have visited the parks. What causes
the most comment from guests is the cleanliness, the friendliness of its cast, and
the unbelievable attention to detail—a blend of showmanship and imagination
that provides an endless variety of adventure and enjoyment.[10]

The Animal Kingdom is the newest edition to Walt Disney World. The Animal
Kingdom focuses on nature and the animal world around us. Guests can go on
time-traveling rides and come face to face with animals from the prehistoric past
to the present. Shows are put on featuring Disney's most popular animal-based
films, such as *Lion King* and *A Bug's Life*. Safari tours that bring guests up close
and personal with live giraffes, elephants, and hippopotamuses are also offered at
Animal Kingdom.

Walt Disney World's two water parks are Blizzard Beach and Typhoon Lagoon. Blizzard Beach has a unique ski resort theme, while Typhoon Lagoon is
based on the legend that a powerful storm swept through, leaving pools and
rapids in its wake. Both parks offer a variety of slides, tube rides, pools, and
moving rivers that drift throughout the parks.

Clubs

Private clubs are places where members gather for social, recreational, professional, or fraternal reasons. Members enjoy bringing friends, family, and business guests to their club. Their club is like a second home, but with diverse facilities and staff to accommodate the occasion. It can be more impressive than inviting them to their homes, and there is still a level of the same personal atmosphere as there would be if they were invited home. Many of today's clubs are adaptations of their predecessors, mostly from England and Scotland. For example, the North American Country Club is largely patterned after the Royal and Ancient Golf Club of St. Andrews, Scotland, founded in 1758 and recognized as the birthplace of golf. Many business deals are negotiated on the golf course. A few years ago, country clubs were often considered to be bastions of the social elite.

Historically, the ambiance of these clubs attracted the affluent. Their character transcended generations. Their etiquette and mannerisms were developed over years to a definable point by which they could recognize each other through subtleties, and those not possessing the desired qualities were not admitted.

Today there are more affluent people than ever, and their number continues to grow. The new rich are now targeted and recuited for a variety of new hybrids that also call themselves clubs. The newer clubs cost of initiation and membership may be considerably less than at some of the more established clubs. The stringent screening process and lengthy membership applications are now simplified, and cash is the key to admittance.

New clubs are born when a developer purchases a tract of land and builds a golf course with a clubhouse surrounded by homes or condominiums. The homes are sold and include a membership to the club. Once all the homes are sold, the developer announces he will be selling the golf course and clubhouse to an investor who wishes to open it up to the public. The homeowners rush to purchase the clubhouse and golf course to protect their investment. A board is formed, and the employees of the developer and all operations are usually transferred to and become the responsibility of the new owners or members.

Club Management

Club management is similar in many ways to hotel management, both of which have evolved in recent years. The general managers of clubs now assume the role of chief operating officer and in some cases chief executive officer of the corporation. They may also have responsibility for management of the homeowners' association and all athletic facilities, including the golf courses. In addition they are responsible for planning, forecasting and budgeting, human resources, food and beverage operations, facility management, and maintenance. The main difference between club management and hotel management is that with clubs the guests feel as if they are the owners (in many cases they are) and frequently behave as if they are the owners. Their emotional attachment is stronger than that of hotel guests who do not use hotels with the same frequency that members use clubs. Another difference is that most clubs do not offer sleeping accommodations.

Club members pay an initiation fee to belong to the club and annual membership dues thereafter. Some clubs also charge a set utilization fee, usually related to food and beverages, which is charged whether or not those services are used. There are approximately 14,000 private clubs in America, including both country and city clubs.

The Club Manager's Association of America (CMAA) is the professional organization to which many of the club managers of the 6,000 private country clubs belong. The association's goal is to advance the profession of club management by fulfilling the educational and related needs of the club managers. The association provides networking opportunities and fosters camaraderie among its member managers through meetings and conferences held locally and nationally. These gatherings keep managers abreast of current practices and procedures and new legislation. The general managers who join CMAA subscribe to a code of ethics.

Club Management Structure

The internal management structure of a club is governed by the corporation's articles of incorporation and bylaws. These establish election procedures, officer positions, a board of directors, and standing committees. Guidance and direction also are provided for each office and committee and how it will function. The general manager will usually provide an orientation for the new directors and information to help them in their new role. The members elect the officers and directors of the club. The officers represent the membership by establishing policies by which the club will operate. Many clubs and other organizations maintain continuity by having a succession of officers. The secretary becomes the vice-president and the vice-president becomes the president. In other cases the person elected president is simply the person believed to be the most qualified person to lead the club for that year. Regardless of who is elected president, the club's general manager must be able to work with that person and the other officers.

The president presides at all official meetings and is a leader in policy making. The vice-president is groomed for the role of president, which is usually eminent, and will in the absence of the president perform the presidential duties. If the club has more than one vice-president, the title first, second, third, and so on, may be used. Alternatively, vice-presidents may be assigned to chair

Country clubs offer some of the finest golf courses for members and guests to play on.

Personal Profile: Edward J. Shaughnessy CCM, MBA, CHE

For Ed Shaughnessy, working in a country club is not just a job but a passion. Clubs feature great recreational facilities, including some fabulous golf courses, gourmet dining, the finest entertainment, and clientele who are more like family than customers. Shaughnessy has worked for three prestigious clubs in his career. He began working in clubs at the tender age of 14 as a busboy. Shortly after graduating from high school, he accepted a full-time evening bar manager position at Sleepy Hollow Country Club in New York. He worked full time at nights while attending college full time until he received his AAS degree. Upon graduation he was promoted to food and beverage manager, but continued his education, taking two or three courses every semester until he earned and received his BBA. He was subsequently promoted to assistant general manager.

After 14 years at the same club and on his twenty-ninth birthday, he was offered and accepted the general manager's position at Belle Haven Country Club in Alexandria, Virginia. He began an active role in the National Capital Club Manager's Association and was elected president. He continued his education and earned his Certified Club Manager (CCM) designation and his Certified Hospitality Educator (CHE) designation through the Club Manager's Association of America. He stayed at Belle Haven Country Club for 8 years, but wanted to live closer to sunny beaches in a warmer climate.

An opportunity at the prestigious Belleair Country Club was brought to Shaughnessy's attention by John Sibbald, a top recruiter in the club industry, and in 1997 Ed Shaughnessy accepted the position of general manager/chief operating officer at the Belleair Country Club. He continued his education, earning his MBA in International Hotel and Tourism Management from Schiller International University, where he now teaches a variety of hospitality-related courses. Shaughnessy is still active with the Club Managers Association and serves on the Club Foundation Allocation Committee. This committee reviews scholarship and grant applications and recommends the awarding of funds to promote education. He also serves as the ethics chair for the Florida's Chapter Club Managers Association.

Shaughnessy believes that there are two stages in life, growth and decay, and that we are all in one of these stages. For him, to be in the growth stage is the preferred view in life. He believes we are all given the choice to change our environment, and he enjoys catering to those with the highest expectations. It appears that people will always recognize and be willing to pay for great value and quality. Meticulous attention to detail and proactively providing what the customer desires before they have to ask is the key to success.

No two days are the same or predictable for a general manager. One day you could be developing a strategic plan, the next you may be invited to fly on a private Lear jet to see the Super Bowl. You have to make a conscious effort to balance work and family life. A general manager should remember that, although you enjoy many of the same privileges as the elite, you are still an employee and must always set an exemplary role as a professional. A general manager's people skills are very important, as well as a comprehensive understanding of financial statements.

The challenge for the future is finding talented and service-oriented people who are needed to exceed the constantly increasing expectations of sophisticated and discriminating club members. Shaughnessy has discovered some time ago that it may be necessary to grow one's own talent among his employees, and this gives him the confidence that he will be ready to serve his customers well. Shaughnessy has a high concern for the welfare of his loyal and dedicated employees. They could lose their jobs if the club is mismanaged. These people and their families count on him to operate the club efficiently. He also recognizes that he must take proactive steps to ensure the growth and success of his club. With two waterfront golf courses, a marina, and the amenities of a full-service country club, Ed Shaughnessy is taking steps to be sure he positions the club for continued success.

CMAA Code of Ethics

We believe the management of clubs is an honorable calling. It shall be incumbent upon club managers to be knowledgable in the application of sound principles in the management of clubs, with ample opportunity to keep abreast of current practices and procedures. We are convinced that the Club Managers Association of America best represents these interests and, as members thereof subscribe to the following CODE OF ETHICS.

We will uphold the best traditions of club management through adherence to sound business principles. By our behavior and demeanor, we shall set an example for our employees and will assist our club officers to secure the utmost in efficient and successful club operations.

We will consistently promote the recognition and esteem of club management as a profession and conduct our personal and business affairs in a manner to reflect capability and integrity. We will always honor our contractual employment obligations.

We shall promote community and civic affairs by maintaining good relations with the public sector to the extent possible within the limits of our club's demands.

We will strive to advance our knowledge and abilities as club managers, and willingly share with other Association members the lessons of our experience and knowledge gained by supporting and participating in our local chapter and the National Association's educational meetings and seminars.

We will not permit ourselves to be subsidized or compromised by any interest doing business with our clubs.

We will refrain from initiating, directly or through an agent, any communications with a director, member, or employee of another club regarding its affairs without the prior knowledge of the manager thereof, if it has a manager.

We will advise the National Headquarters, whenever possible, regarding managerial openings at clubs that come to our attention. We will do all within our power to assist our fellow club managers in pursuit of their professional goals.

We shall not be deterred from compliance with the law, as it applies to our clubs. We shall provide our club officers and trustees with specifics of federal, state and local laws, statutes, and regulations to avoid punitive action and costly litigation.

We deem it our duty to report to local or national officers any willful violations of the CMAA CODE OF ETHICS.

Source: Club Manager's Association of America.

certain committees, such as membership. Board members usually chair one or more committees.

Committees play an important part in the club's activities. If the committees are effective, the operation of the club is more efficient. The term of committee membership is specified, and committee meetings are conducted in accordance with Robert's Rules of Order, which are procedural guidelines on the correct way to conduct meetings. Standing committees include the following: house, membership, finance/budget, entertainment, golf, green tennis, pool, and long-range planning. The president may appoint additional committees to serve specific functions commonly referred to as ad hoc.

The treasurer obviously must have some financial and accounting background, because an integral part of his or her duties is to give advice on financial matters, such as employing external auditors, preparing budgets, and installing control systems. The general manager is responsible for all financial matters and usually signs or cosigns all checks.

It is the duty of the secretary to record the minutes of meetings and take care of club-related correspondence. In most cases the general manager prepares the document for the secretary's signature. This position can be combined with that of treasurer, in which case the position is titled secretary–treasurer. The secretary may also serve on or chair certain committees.

The Club Managers Association of America (CMAA) has reexamined the role of club managers and, due to ever-increasing expectations, the role of the general manager has changed from the traditional managerial model to a leadership model. (This is discussed in more detail in Chapter 14.) The new CMAA model is based on the premise that general managers or COOs are more than a chief operating officers responsible for operating assets and investments and club culture.

Figure 11-1 shows the core competencies of a general manager or COO as private club management, food and beverage, accounting and financial management,

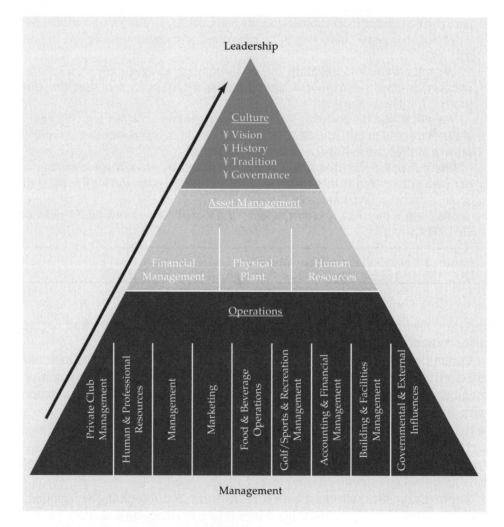

Figure 11–1 *Management to Leadership*

human and professional resources, building and facilities management, external and governmental influences, management, marketing, and sports and recreation.

The second tier of the model is mastering the skills of asset management. Today's general manager or COO must be able to manage the physical property, the financial well-being, and the human resources of the club. These facets of the manager's responsibility are equally as important as managing the operations of the club.

The third and final tier of the new model is preserving and fostering the culture of the club, which can be defined as the club's traditions, history, and vision. Many managers or COOs intrinsically perform this function; however, it is often an overlooked and underdeveloped quality. A job description for club manager is given in Figure 11–2. The Club Management Competencies are shown in Figure 11–3.

Country Clubs

Nearly all **country clubs** have one or more lounges and restaurants, and most have banquet facilities. Members and their guests enjoy these services and can be billed monthly. The banquet facilities are used for formal and informal parties, dinners, dances, weddings, and so on, by members and their personal guests. Some country clubs charge what might seem to be an excessive amount for the initiation fee in order to maintain exclusivity—as much as $250,000 in some cases.

Country clubs have two or more types of membership. Full membership enables members to use all the facilities all the time. Social membership only allows members to use the social facilities: lounges, bars, restaurants, and so on, and perhaps the pool and tennis courts. Other forms of membership can include weekday and weekend memberships.

Tiger Woods playing at the Westchester Country Club.

I. **Position:** General Manager

II. **Related Titles:** Club Manager; Club House Manager

III. **Job Summary:** Serves as chief operating officer of the club; manages all aspects of the club including its activities and the relationships between the club and its board of directors, members, guests, employees, community, government, and industry; coordinates and administers the club's policies as defined by its board of directors. Develops operating policies and procedures and directs the work of all department managers. Implements and monitors the budget, monitors the quality of the club's products and services, and ensures maximum member and guest satisfaction. Secures and protects the club's assets, including facilities and equipment

IV. **Job Tasks (Duties):**

1. Implements general policies established by the board of directors; directs their administration and execution

2. Plans, develops, and approves specific operational policies, programs, procedures, and methods in concert with general policies

3. Coordinates the development of the club's long-range and annual (business) plans

4. Develops, maintains, and administers a sound organizational plan; initiates improvements as necessary

5. Establishes a basic personnel policy; initiates and monitors policies relating to personnel actions and training and professional development programs

6. Maintains membership with the Club Managers Association of America and other professional associations. Attends conferences, workshops, and meetings to keep abreast of current information and developments in the field

7. Coordinates development of operating and capital budgets according to the budget calendar; monitors monthly and other financial statements for the club; takes effective corrective action as required

8. Coordinates and serves as ex-officio member of appropriate club committees

9. Welcomes new club members; meets and greets all club members as practical during their visits to the club

10. Provides advice and recommendations to the president and committees about construction, alterations, maintenance, materials, supplies, equipment, and services not provided in approved plans and/or budgets

11. Consistently ensures that the club is operated in accordance with all applicable local, state, and federal laws

12. Oversees the care and maintenance of all the club's physical assets and facilities

13. Coordinates the marketing and membership relations programs to promote the club's services and facilities to potential and present members

14. Ensures the highest standards for food, beverage, sports and recreation, entertainment, and other club services

15. Establishes and monitors compliance with purchasing policies and procedures

16. Reviews and initiates programs to provide members with a variety of popular events

17. Analyzes financial statements, manages cash flow, and establishes controls to safeguard funds; reviews income and costs relative to goals; takes corrective action as necessary

18. Works with subordinate department heads to schedule, supervise, and direct the work of all club employees

19. Attends meetings of the club's executive committee and board of directors

20. Participates in outside activities that are judged as appropriate and approved by the board of directors to enhance the prestige of the club; broadens the scope of the club's operation by fulfilling the public obligations of the club as a participating member of the community

V. **Reports to:** Club President and Board of Directors

VI. **Supervises:** Assistant General Manager (Club House Manager); Food and Beverage Director; Controller; Membership Director; Director of Human Resources; Director of Purchasing; Golf Professional (Director of Golf); Golf Course Superintendent; Tennis Professional; Athletic Director; Executive Secretary

Source: Club Managers Association of America

Figure 11–2   *Job Description, Club Manager*

City Clubs

City clubs are predominantly business oriented, although some have rules prohibiting the discussion of business and the reviewing of business-related documents in dining rooms. They vary in size, location, type of facility, and services offered. Some of the older, established clubs own their own buildings; others

Private Club Management	Accounting and Finance in the Private Club	

Private Club Management
History of Private Clubs
Types of Private Clubs
Membership Types
Bylaws
Policy Formulation
Board Relations
Chief Operating Officer Concept
Committees
Club Job Descriptions
Career Development
Golf Operations Management
Golf Course Management
Tennis Operations Management
Swimming Pool Management
Yacht Facilities Management
Fitness Center Management
Locker Room Management
Other Recreational Activities

Food and Beverage Operations
Sanitation
Menu Development
Nutrition
Pricing Concepts
Ordering/Receiving/Controls/Inventory
Food and Beverage Trends
Quality Service
Creativity in Theme Functions
Design and Equipment
Food and Beverage Personnel
Wine List Development

Accounting and Finance in the Private Club
Accounting and Finance Principles
Uniform System of Accounts
Financial Analysis
Budgeting
Cash Flow Forecasting
Compensation and Benefit Administration
Financing Capital Projects
Audits
Internal Revenue Service
Computers
Business Office Organization
Long-Range Financial Planning

Human and Professional Resources
Employee Relations
Management Styles
Organizational Development
Balancing Job and Family Responsibilities
Time Management
Stress Management
Labor Issues
Leadership vs. Management

Building and Facilities Management
Preventive Maintenance
Insurance and Risk Management
Clubhouse Remodeling and Renovation

Contractors
Energy and Water Resource Management
Housekeeping
Security
Laundry
Lodging Operations

External and Governmental Influences
Legislative Influences
Regulatory Agencies
Economic Theory
Labor Law
Internal Revenue Service
Privacy
Club Law
Liquor Liability
Labor Unions

Management and Marketing
Communication Skills
Marketing Through In-House Publications
Professional Image and Dress
Effective Negotiation
Member Contact Skills
Working with the Media
Marketing Strategies in a Private Club Environment

Source: Club Managers Association of America

Figure 11–3 *Club Management Competencies*

lease space. Clubs exist to cater to the wants and needs of members. Clubs in the city fall into the following categories:

- Professional
- Social
- Athletic
- Dining
- University
- Military
- Yachting
- Fraternal
- Proprietary

Professional clubs, as the name implies, are clubs for people in the same profession. The National Press Club in Washington, D.C., the Lawyer's Club in New York City, and the Friars Club for actors and other theatrical people in Manhattan are good examples.

Social clubs allow members to enjoy one another's company; members represent many different professions, yet they have similar socioeconomic backgrounds. Social clubs are modeled after the famous men's social clubs in London, such as Boodles, St. James's, and White's. At these clubs, it is considered bad form to discuss business. Therefore, conversation and social interaction focus on companionship or entertainment unrelated to business.

The oldest social club in America is thought to be the Fish House in Philadelphia, founded in 1832. To ensure that the Fish House would always be socially oriented rather than business oriented, it was formed as a men's cooking club, with each member taking turns preparing meals for the membership. Other social clubs exist in several major cities. The common denominator is that they all have upscale food and beverage offerings and club managers to manage them.

Athletic clubs give city workers and residents an opportunity to work out, swim, play squash and/or racquetball, and so on. Some of the downtown athletic clubs provide tennis courts and running tracks on the roof. Athletic clubs also have lounges, bars, and restaurants at which members may relax and interact socially. Some athletic clubs also have meeting rooms and even sleeping accommodations. The newest feature is known as the executive work-out. This begins with a visit to the steam room, followed by a trip to the Jacuzzi, then sauna, a massage, and nap in the resting room before showering and returning to work.

Dining clubs are generally located in large city office buildings. Memberships are often given as an inducement to tenants who lease space in the office building. These clubs are always open for lunch and occasionally for dinner.

University clubs are private clubs for alumni or alumnae. University clubs are generally located in the high-rent district and offer a variety of facilities and attractions focusing on food and beverage service.

Military clubs cater to both NCOs (noncommissioned officers) and enlisted officers. Military clubs offer similar facilities as other clubs for recreation and entertainment and food and beverage offerings. Some military clubs are located on base. The largest membership club in the country is the Army Navy Country Club in Arlington, Virginia. The club has over 6,000 members, 54 holes of golf, 2 clubhouses, and a host of other facilities. Many of these clubs in recent years have given over their club management to civilians.

Yacht clubs provide members with moorage slips, where their boats are kept secure. In addition to moorage facilities, yacht clubs have lounge, bar, and dining facilities similar to other clubs. Yacht clubs are based on a sailing theme and attract members with various backgrounds who have sailing as a common interest.

Fraternal clubs include many special organizations, such as the Veterans of Foreign Wars, Elks, and Shriners. These organizations foster camaraderie and often assist charitable causes. They generally are less elaborate than other clubs, but have bars and banquet rooms that can be used for various activities.

Proprietary clubs operate on a for-profit basis. They are owned by corporations or individuals; individuals wanting to become members purchase a membership, not a share in the club. Proprietary clubs became popular with the real estate boom in the 1970s and 1980s. As new housing developments were planned, clubs were included in several of the projects. Households paid a small initiation fee and monthly dues between $30 and $50, allowing the whole family to participate in a wide variety of recreational activities.

Clearly, the opportunities for recreation and leisure abound. The goal must be to achieve a harmony between work and leisure activities and to become truly professional in both giving and receiving these services. The next few years will see a substantial increase in the leisure and recreational industries.

Focus on Recreation

Hospitality and Recreation: Inextricably Intertwined

Bart Bartlett
Penn State

Americans have more leisure time than ever before, and as leisure time has grown, leisure activities have evolved and grown as well. As this chapter points out, opportunities today for recreation and for careers in recreation management are vast and multifaceted. These include positions in commercial recreation (resorts, themed resorts, the ski industry), in noncommercial recreation (federal or state parks and community recreation), in clubs and sports venues, and in recreation with special populations.

Although the focus of this text is hospitality management, in many situations recreation and hospitality go hand in hand. When a ski trip incorporates recreation on the slopes with food and beverage services in the lodge or when a hotel guest uses the hotel's business services and the spa, recreation and hospitality are both involved. When a convention center hotel provides rooms, food, and beverage; coordinates meetings and breakout sessions; and also organizes recreation and group activities during the conference, hospitality and recreation begin to merge. In fact, because our guests' total experience often involves a combination of lodging, food and beverage, and recreation, we do not want to distinguish, but instead want to ensure guest satisfaction by seamlessly integrating these different elements into the total package.

As growth in leisure travel continues to outstrip growth in business travel, the growing leisure travel market will create an increasing emphasis on recreation as an integral part of hospitality. Furthermore, though hospitality and recreation may involve different emphases, the critical customer focus and customer service skills that we love about our industry are common to all aspects of hospitality and recreation.

Resorts and resort hotels are the prototypical combination of hospitality and recreation. A mega-resort such as Walt Disney World provides an ideal example of a venue that integrates hospitality and recreation skills and services. On a Disney vacation, a family may enjoy lodging and food and beverage services provided by hotel staff and management trained in hospitality, go into the park itself to enjoy attractions and shows arranged and managed by a recreation specialist, take a break to enjoy foodservice provided by a hospitality provider, and at the end of the day enjoy dinner provided by the hospitality staff and entertainment or dancing arranged by a recreation professional.

The golf industry provides other examples. At a typical golf club, the director of golf operations is primarily involved with managing recreation activities, including scheduling and supervising play, course maintenance, and the pro shop. The clubhouse manager, meanwhile, is responsible for hospitality functions, including food and beverage operations, catering events, and membership. If either were missing, the club simply could not meet guests' and members' overall expectations.

Finally, as cruise ships are essentially floating resort hotels with many features of land-based resorts, both hospitality and recreation are required. On a cruise ship, the purser and food and beverage manager are responsible for hospitality functions, while the cruise director provides recreation programming. Both are critical parts of the cruise experience, thus providing the all-around good time guests desire and deserve.

Through this text you have learned about hotels, restaurants, and managed services and about the knowledge and skills involved in managing these operations. This chapter talks about recreation and the opportunities to apply your hospitality skills in recreation settings. Across the spectrum, from business travelers to family vacationers, from golfing outings to business banquets, from back-country adventures to haute cuisine dining, from white sand Caribbean beaches to black diamond ski slopes, customer service and a focus on customer satisfaction are constants, and both hospitality and recreation skills are critical to providing a memorable guest experience. The commonalities in settings, service, and focus on guest satisfaction indicate that hospitality and recreation are indeed inextricably intertwined!

Check Your Knowledge

1. Name all types of clubs discussed here and briefly describe their functions.
2. List the important duties of a club manager.
3. Describe the operations of a country club.

Noncommercial Recreation

Noncommercial recreation includes voluntary organizations, campus, armed forces, and employee recreations, as well as recreation for special populations.

Voluntary Organizations

Voluntary organizations are nongovernmental, nonprofit agencies, serving the public-at-large or selected elements with multiservice programs that often include a substantial element of recreational opportunity. The best known voluntary organizations include the Boy Scouts, Girl Scouts, YMCA, YWCA, and YM–YWHA.

In the early 1900s, YMCAs began to offer sporting facilities and programs. The Ys, though nonprofit, were pioneers in basketball, swimming, and weight training. Later, commercial health clubs also began to evolve, offering men's and women's exercise. As the sports and fitness movement grew, clubs appealed to special interests. Now clubs can be classified as follows: figure salons, health clubs, body-building gyms, tennis clubs, rowing clubs, swim clubs, racquetball centers, or multipurpose clubs.

A multipurpose club has more exclusive recreation programs than a health club. Leagues, tournaments, and classes are common for racquet sports, and most clubs offer several types of fitness classes. Some innovative clubs offer automatic bank tellers, stock market quote services, computer matching for tennis competition, auto detailing, laundry and dry cleaning services, and wine-cellar storage.

Club revenue comes from membership fees, user fees, guest fees, food and beverage sales, facility rental, and so on. Human resources accounts for about 66 percent of expenses at most clubs.

It is amazing to realize that in the center of a city there may be several voluntary organizations, each serving a particular segment of the population.

Richard Kraus writes that a study of the city of Toronto that examined various land uses and leisure programs in the city's core found the following organizations: a Boy's Club, a mission, the Center of the Metropolitan Association for the Retarded, a Catholic settlement house, a day care center, an Indian center, a YM-YWHA, a service center for working people, a Chinese center, a Ukrainian center, and several other organizations meeting special needs and interests. These were all in addition to public parks, recreation areas, and nineteen churches.

A Day in the Life of Luis Azucena
Recreation Director, Dolores Park, San Francisco, California

A recreation director doesn't just look over the park and make sure everything is running well; that may well be the duty of most other kinds of directors but not a recreation director.

The park we are talking about isn't just any park, it's Dolores Park. This park is one of San Francisco's best, most romantic, and peaceful places to be. Its beautiful view, grassy hills, and shade trees make for a bucolic refuge from urban life. The park's greatest asset, no doubt, is the sublimely peaceful view of downtown. The director of all this is none other than Luis Azucena.

Luis Azucena loves what he does. He is able to do what he wants to do in his job. For a typical day, Luis works afternoons and evenings usually from about 1 P.M. to 10 P.M.

Dolores Park is a large city-owned park that consists of a club house, soccer fields, tennis courts, and computer rooms. When Luis comes in, he looks through paperwork that has to be completed. He does the cleaning himself to make sure everything is tidy and neat. From 1:30 P.M. to about 3:00 P.M., Luis is involved in giving adult tennis lessons along with another director, Mr. Lou Maunaupau. Luis usually coaches about ten players. Some of them are young. After doing this, it's time for Luis's lunch break.

After lunch, at about 4:00 P.M., Luis goes to the soccer field and meets with his summer soccer league players,

who are kids from the community area. He organizes this league. He helps them get their uniforms and ID cards and then they warm up. This game is recreational, so Luis strives to teach them good sportsmanship. For instance, his players end games with handshakes. In winter or when the weather isn't favorable, Luis arranges indoor games. He helps put teams together for the community.

After all this, Luis helps kids with their homework and plays board games with them. While he does this, people from around the community come to the park to have picnics or to attend community political, recreational, or just-for-fun events. Dolores is a center of attraction for people, especially on the weekends and holidays.

Volunteers often come in to help with activities that go on in the park. This is called "workcreation." They work with the community and its kids, helping with games, activities, or even schoolwork. Luis's day comes to an end at about 10 P.M. He goes home feeling satisfied and positive about what he is doing.

Luis loves sports and fitness. He works with the school districts around the community to help kids become more involved in sports and also have time for schoolwork. He has worked at his job for several years and is very happy to be where he is now.

Campus, Armed Forces, and Employee Recreation

Campus Recreation

North America's colleges and universities provide a major setting for organized leisure and recreational programs with services involving millions of participants each year. The programs include involvement by campus recreation offices, intramural departments, student unions, residence staffs, or other sponsors. People spend much of their leisure time participating in a wide variety of organized recreational activities, such as aerobics, arts and crafts, the performing arts, camping, and sports. Recreation and fitness workers plan, organize, and direct these activities in local playgrounds and recreation areas, parks, community centers, health clubs, fitness centers, religious organizations, camps, theme parks, and tourist attractions. Increasingly, recreational and fitness workers also are found in workplaces, where they organize and direct leisure activities and athletic programs for employees of all ages.[11]

The various recreational activities help in maintaining good morale on campus. Some use recreational activities such as sports or orchestras or theater companies as a means of gaining alumni support. Students look for an exciting and interesting social life. For this reason, colleges and universities offer a wide range of recreational and social activities that may vary from campus to campus.

Armed Forces Recreation

It is the official policy of the Department of Defense to provide a well-rounded welfare and recreational program for the physical, social, and mental well-being of its personnel. Each service sponsors recreational activities under the auspices of the Morale, Welfare, and Recreation Program (MWR), which reports to the Office of the Assistant Secretary of Defense for Manpower, Reserve Affairs, and Logistics. MWR activities are provided to all military personnel and civilian employees at all installations.

MWR programs include the following types of activities:
- Sports, including self-directed, competitive, instructional, and spectator programs
- Motion pictures
- Service clubs and entertainment
- Crafts and hobbies
- Youth activities for children of military families
- Special interest groups such as aero, automotive, motorcycle, and power boat clubs, as well as hiking, skydiving, and rod and gun clubs
- Rest centers and recreation areas
- Open dining facilities
- Libraries

Recreation is perceived as an important part of the employee benefits package for military personnel, along with the G.I. Bill, medical services, commissaries, and exchanges.

Employee Recreation

Business and industry have realized the importance of promoting employee efficiency. Human resource experts have found that workers who spend their free time at constructive recreational activities have less absenteeism resulting from emotional tension, illness, excessive use of alcohol, and so on. Employee recreation programs may also be an incentive for a prospective employee to join a company.

In the United States and Canada, almost all the leading corporations have an employee recreation and wellness program. Some companies include recreation activities in their team-building and management-development programs.

Recreation for Special Populations

Recreation for special populations involves professionals and organizations who serve groups such as the mentally ill, mentally retarded, or physically challenged. In recent years, there has been increased recognition of the need to provide recreational programs for special populations. These programs, developed for each of the special population groups, use therapeutic recreation as a form of treatment.

One sports program for people with disabilities that has received considerable attention in recent years is the Special Olympics, an international year-round program of physical fitness, sports training, and athletic competition for children and adults with mental retardation. The program is unique because it accommodates competitors at all ability levels by assigning participants to competition divisions based on both age and actual performance.[12]

Today, the Special Olympics serves more than 1.4 million individuals in the United States and more than seventy other countries. Among the official sports are track and field events, swimming, diving, gymnastics, ice skating, basketball, volleyball, soccer, softball, floor hockey, bowling, Frisbee disk, downhill skiing, cross-country skiing, and wheelchair events. The National Parks and Recreation Association and numerous state and local agencies and societies work closely with Special Olympics in promoting programs and sponsoring competitions.[13]

Trends in Recreation and Leisure

- An increase in all fitness activities
- An increase in personal leisure time devoted to computer activities
- A surge in travel and tourism
- In addition to a continuation of traditional recreation and leisure activities, special programs targeted toward at-risk youths and latchkey children are also being developed
- Several additional products in the commercial sector
- Additional learning and adventure opportunities for the elderly, such as Elderhostel

CASE STUDY

Service Proposal for Guests

You recently joined the front desk of a nice resort hotel in New England and your hotel manager has complimented you on your guest service ability. She has asked you to develop a walking/jogging trail for the guests.

Question

1. What would be some of the key elements to consider in developing a proposal for your hotel guests?

CASE STUDY

Overpopulation of National Parks

Our national parks are under serious threat from a number of sources, including congestion resulting from overvisitation, consequent environmental degradation, and pollution.

There are too many people and too many vehicles in the most popular national parks. Many bring their city life-style, leaving garbage lying around, listening to loud music, and leaving the trails in worse shape.

Question

1. List the recommendations you have for the park superintendents to help save the parks.

CAREER INFORMATION

Recreation and Leisure

The recreation and leisure areas cover a broad range of potential career paths. There are options in the parks and recreation field as well as careers to be had in club and resort management. Working in a country club may sound exciting, but it actually entails long, difficult hours spent dealing with demanding members. A recent survey of club general managers revealed that, on average, they are 30- to 40-year-old males who work more than 60 hours per week managing a club with more than 600 members.

Many of you may wish to pursue a career in club management because you do not want to work in a hotel or restaurant. However, 81 percent of the general managers surveyed above stated that they came from a food and beverage background. Historically, many general managers have worked their way up from a dining room server at a private club, with the average having spent 10 to 15 years in the industry and more than 7 years at their current club.

Regardless of what type of club you wish to work in—city, country, athletic or social—clubs fall into two categories: equity clubs, which are owned by the members, or nonequity clubs, which are owned by individuals or corporations. ClubCorp is one of the largest corporate owners of clubs and it operates more than 220 country clubs, business clubs, and golf resorts. Recent expansions in corporate ownership have made it slightly easier to enter the club management profession.

If you are serious about a career in club management, you should join a local student chapter of the Club Managers Association of America (CMAA). CMAA meetings are a great place for networking in order to gain access to a summer job or internship. Experience gained during your college tenure will provide you with the knowledge you need to begin your career in the recreation and leisure industries.

Related Web Sites

www.clubcorp.com —ClubCorp
www.cmaa.org —Club Managers Association of America
www.nps.gov —National Parks Service
www-p.afsv.af.mil —United States Air Force Services

Courtesy of Charlie Adams.

SUMMARY

1. Recreation is free time that people use to restore, rest, and relax their minds and bodies. Recreational activities can be passive or active, an individual or a group activity.
2. Recreational activities range from cultural pursuits such as museums or theaters, to sports or outdoor recreation such as amusement parks, community centers, playgrounds, and libraries. These services involve various levels of government.
3. National parks preserve exceptional lands for public use, emphasizing the protection of their ecosystems and endangered plant and animal species and honoring historical sites. Two of the best known of the cur-

rent 367 parks in the United States include Yellowstone and Yosemite national parks.

4. Today, city governments are increasingly expected to provide recreational facilities such as golf courses, swimming pools, picnic areas, and playgrounds as a community service.

5. Commercial recreation—for example, theme parks, clubs, and attractions—involves a profit for the supplier of the recreational activity.

6. Clubs are places where members gather for social, recreational, professional, or fraternal reasons. There are many different types of clubs such as country clubs or city clubs, according to the interests they represent to their members.

7. Noncommercial recreation includes governmental and nonprofit agencies, such as voluntary organizations, campus, armed forces, employee recreation, and recreation for special populations, such as the physically challenged.

KEY WORDS AND CONCEPTS

City clubs
Club management
Commercial recreation
Country clubs
Government-sponsored recreation

Leisure
National parks
National Parks Service
Noncommercial recreation

Recreation
Recreation for special populations
Theme parks

Transient occupancy taxes (TOT)
Voluntary organizations

REVIEW QUESTIONS

1. Define recreation and its importance to human wellness. What factors affect an individual's decision to participate in recreational activities?

2. Describe the origin of government-sponsored recreation in consideration of the origin and purpose of national parks.

3. Briefly describe the difference between commercial and noncommercial recreation.

4. Briefly explain the purpose of a theme park and the purpose of clubs.

5. Explain the concept of recreation for special populations.

INTERNET EXERCISES

1. Organization: **Del Mar Fairgrounds**
   Web site: **www.delmarfair.com**
   Summary: The Del Mar Fairgrounds is an indoor and outdoor, multiuse public assembly facility with an emphasis on agriculture, education, entertainment, and recreation in a fiscally sound and environmentally conscientious atmosphere. For more than half a century, the Del Mar Fairgrounds has been located in San Diego where it has been a great tourist attraction.
   (a) What kinds of facilities are offered by Del Mar Fairgrounds?
   (b) What does the fair do to promote the ecosystem?

2. Organization: **Prestonwood Country Club**
   Web site: **www.prestonwoodcc.com**
   Summary: Prestonwood is a full-service country club that offers activities and fine food.
   (a) What kinds of activities are offered at the Prestonwood Country Club?
   (b) Parents may wish to take their kids on vacations. In these situations, what might this country club offer those kids?

APPLY YOUR KNOWLEDGE

1. Create your own personal recreation goals and make a plan to reach them.

2. Describe the features of commercial versus noncommercial recreation.

SUGGESTED ACTIVITIES

1. Research the history of Mardi Gras on the Internet. Write a one-page description of the event and its cultural roots.

2. Look up your favorite theme park on the Web. Think about what kind of position you would like to have at the park. If the site has job listings, do any of them appeal to you?

ENDNOTES

1. Personal correspondence with Jay Sullivan, October 4, 2004.
2. **http://www.adelaidecitycouncil.com/council/publications/Strategies/Recreation_Sport_Plan.pdf**. July 2005.
3. Ibid., p. 66.
4. **http://www.peopleassets.net/cprs/reports/samplereport.htm**. July 2005.
5. This section draws on information supplied by the National Parks Service.
6. **http://lwbc.bc.ca/02land/tenuring/commercialrecreation/**. 2004.
7. **Temporal Aspects of Theme Park Choice Behavior http://alexandria.tue.nl/extra2/200013915.pdf**. July 29, 2005.
8. Other prominent theme parks and attractions are Knott's Berry Farm, Universal Studios, and Six Flags over America.
9. **http://savedisney.com/news/features/fe071505.1.asp**. July 29, 2005.
10. **http://www.atlastravelweb.com/waltdisneyworldpackages.shtml**. Atlas Cruise and Tours, 2005.
11. **http://www.collegegrad.com/careers/servi19.shtml**. July 29, 2005.
12. **www.specialolympics.org/special+olympics+public+website/English/About_us/default.htm**
13. Ibid.

WEB RESOURCES

National Parks Service
www.nps.gov

Yellowstone Park
www.yellowstone-natl-park.com

Yosemite Park
www.yosemitepark.com

Wrangell-St. Elias National Park and Preserve
wrangellstelias.areaparks.com

New England Association of Park Superintendents
http://www.newenglandparks.org/about/about.html

Sea World
www.seaworld.com

Kings Island
www.pki.com

Walt Disney World
disney.go.com

Water Mania
www.watermania-florida.com

Wet 'N' Wild
www.wetnwild.com

Universal Studios
www.universalstudios.com

Busch Gardens
www.buschgardens.com

Adventure Island
www.adventure-island.com

Mardi Gras New Orleans
www.mardigrasneworleans.com

Grand Ole Opry
www.opry.com

Royal and Ancient Golf Club of St. Andrews
www.randa.org

Club Managers Association of America
www.cmaa.org

The National Press Club
npc.press.org

Friars Club
www.friarsclub.org

Boodles
http://www.victoriahinshaw.com/london_regency.html

Penn State
www.psu.edu

Army Navy Country Club
www.ancc.org

Veterans of Foreign War
www.vfw.org

Elks
www.elks.org

YMCA
www.ymca.com

YWCA
www.ywca.org

YM-YWHA
www.ymywha.com

Boy's Club
www.bgca.org

Department of Defense
www.defenselink.mil

Special Olympics
www.specialolympics.org

National Parks and Recreation Association
www.nrpa.org

Morale, Welfare, and Recreation Program
www.mwr.navy.mil

Gaming Entertainment

After reading and studying this chapter, you should be able to:

- Outline the history of the gaming entertainment industry.
- Describe the various activities related to gaming entertainment.
- Explain how gaming entertainment is converging with other aspects of the hospitality business.
- Discuss the controversies surrounding the gaming entertainment industry.

One of the most significant developments in the hospitality industry during the past two decades has been the astounding growth of the casino industry and its convergence with the lodging and hospitality industries. What has emerged from this development is an entirely new arena of hospitality known as the gaming entertainment industry. With its rapid expansion in North America and throughout the world, new opportunities have been created for hospitality careers. This chapter explores the gaming entertainment industry and details exciting developments yet to come in this dynamic and controversial segment of the hospitality business.

Gaming Entertainment Defined

For the purposes of this chapter, the term **gaming entertainment** refers to one subset of the gaming industry, that is, the casino industry. What used to be known as the casino business is now known as gaming entertainment. The dramatic growth of this part of the hospitality business has brought with it significant changes in how businesses in this industry operate and what they offer their guests. The changes have been so great that a new name needed to be created to accurately describe all the amenities this industry provides.

The gaming industry includes 432 casinos in 11 states (both land-based and riverboats),[1] card rooms, charitable games, lottery-operated games, and wagering on greyhound and horse races. The gaming industry as a whole is larger than most people can believe. Approximately $70 billion is **wagered,** or **bet,** on games or races every year.

That is more than seven times what is spent on movie tickets. The total amount bet is called the **handle** in the gaming industry, and it is often a misunderstood concept. When a customer places a bet in any type of gaming activity, sometimes that customer wins and sometimes he or she loses. The total amount of all bets is the handle, and the net amount of spending by the customer is termed **win** by the gaming industry.

What is the difference between gambling and gaming? **Gambling** is playing a game of risk for the thrill of the "action" and the chance of making money. True gamblers spend a great deal of time learning and understanding a favorite game of risk and enjoying its subtle attributes, and they find an enjoyable challenge in trying to "beat the house," or win more than they lose from a casino.

A gambler has little interest in anything other than the casino floor and the games it offers. It is true that the 48 million visitors who come to Las Vegas and the 33 million to Atlantic City and the hundreds of thousands who frequent other casino operations love the green felt tables, the whirling roulette wheels, the feel of the chips, and the thrill of the game. The rows of colorful **slot machines** sounding out musical tones and flashing lights, the distant sounds of someone hitting a jackpot, and bells ringing and guests shouting creates an environment of excitement and anticipation that can only be found on the casino floor. The gaming industry has exploded from just two jurisdictions in 1976 to some form of legal gambling in 48 states.

Not long ago, the presence of a slot machine or a blackjack table was all that was needed to bring in the visitors. However, with the rapid spread of

A Themed Gaming and Slot Machine Area in a Casino

casinos throughout North America, this is no longer true. The competitive nature of the casino business has created a bigger, better product to meet the needs of their guests. As Steve Wynn, former Mirage Resorts CEO and now owner of the Wynn Las Vegas, puts it, the casino floor is "a thing that people pass on their way to visit the things that really matter to them." The product that has evolved over the past decade is what is called gaming entertainment.

Gaming entertainment offers games of risk only as part of a total package of entertainment and leisure time activities. Gaming entertainment serves a customer base of "social gamblers," customers who play a game of risk as a form of entertainment and a social activity, combining gambling with many other activities during their visit. Social gamblers, by this definition, are interested in many of the amenities of the gaming entertainment operation and take part in many diverse activities during a stay.

Gaming entertainment refers to the casino gaming business and all its aspects, including hotel operations, entertainment offerings, retail shopping, recreational activities, and other types of operations in addition to wagering on the gaming floor. The heart of gaming entertainment is what Glen Schaeffer, president of Circus Circus, has dubbed the "entertainment megastore," with thousands of rooms; dynamic, interesting exterior architecture; and nongaming attractions—that is, it's a building someone can design a vacation around, with 100,000 square feet or more of casino at its core. Schaeffer has said this product "is to tourism what the Pentium chip is to technology," a dynamic new tourism product that serves as a destination attraction. Gaming entertainment is the business of hospitality and entertainment with a core strength in casino gaming, also known as the global hospitality–gaming–entertainment market.

According to this definition, a gaming entertainment business always has a casino floor area that offers various games of risk and that serves as the focal point for marketing to and attracting guests. Next in importance to the guests is high-quality food and beverage operations.

Gaming entertainment is one of the last hospitality concepts to support the full-service, table-side gourmet restaurant, in addition to the lavish buffet offerings that many casino locations offer. The number of foodservice concepts is wide and diverse—from signature restaurants featuring famous chefs, to ethnic offerings, to quick-service, franchised outlets. The gaming entertainment industry offers unlimited career opportunities in restaurant management and the culinary arts that were unheard of just a decade ago.

Gaming entertainment also goes hand in hand with the lodging industry, because hotel rooms are part of the package. Full-service hotels are part and parcel of gaming entertainment. Rooms, food and beverage, convention services, banquet facilities, health spas, recreation, and other typical hotel amenities support gaming entertainment. Most of the largest and most complex hotels in the world are found in gaming entertainment venues, a number of which are described in detail later in this chapter.

So far we have discussed gaming entertainment as a place to gamble on the casino floor, eat and drink, have a place to sleep and relax, and maybe do some business. But gaming entertainment offers much more. The entertainment offerings range from live performances by the most famous entertainers to production shows that use the latest high-tech wizardry. Gaming entertainment includes theme parks and thrill rides, museums, and cultural centers. The most popular gaming entertainment destinations are designed around a central theme that includes the hotel and the casino operations.

Unlike its predecessor, the casino business, the gaming entertainment business has numerous revenue-generating activities. Gaming revenue is produced from casino win, or the money guests spend on the casino floor. The odds of any casino game favor the house, some more than others. Casino win is the cost of gambling to guests, who often win over the house in the short run, and are therefore willing to place bets and try their luck.

The Flamingo Hilton, a Popular Casino Hotel for Many Years

The Development of Two Corporate Cultures in Casinos

Kathryn Hashimoto
University of New Orleans

In America, the history and evolution of casinos have created two very strong corporate cultures. A corporate culture could be described as the personality of the organization. Like a person, a business can be weak or strong, conservative or daring, or even stodgy or innovative. Corporate cultures are very important because they set the boundaries for behavior of managers and employees. The stronger the culture, the easier it is for employees to know what they should do when the formal rules are not available. In a casino, there are always new situations and problems that must be addressed, and a strong corporate culture sets the  tone and guidelines for the problem solving and ultimate solution. In the case of casinos, the traditional casino culture is still evolving into a more corporate one.

Traditional Casino Culture

When casinos first developed in America, ownership was by a single individual who could lose that enterprise on a toss of the dice. It was the owner's "luck of the draw," not his management ability, that determined his length of stay. As a result, owners were superstitious and they trusted only their own instincts. This resulted in the "monopoly on brains" syndrome—the fact that only the owner, not employees, could make a great decision. Fear of management was what kept the employees honest. According to the traditional school of casino culture attitudes, employees should be constantly reminded that their jobs were a privilege, not a right. Their jobs could be taken away at any time. Therefore, promotion came to employees who were loyal to management. To prove their knowledge and loyalty, employees had to learn the trade from the ground up, starting as a dealer.

Employees showed their loyalty by doing whatever they could to help the owner. In some cases, employees were asked to violate rules and regulations in order to favor the house or accommodate a high roller's desires. Even though a guest might make unreasonable requests, operators would agree because the customer might take his business elsewhere. For example, at one casino a high roller requested that he have a male dealer instead of the woman who was currently at the table. The management complied, knowing that it was discriminatory. However, in their view it was cheaper to pay the class action suit that followed than to antagonize the player. Another example of the traditional casino culture was the emphasis on superstition and luck in decision making. Dealers were perceived to be personally responsible for the outcome of games. Any dealer who lost money had "bad karma" and was instantly fired—no questions asked. Without rational decision-making guidelines, superstition and one man's idea of common sense ruled the casino operation.

Shift to Corporate Culture in Casinos

During the 1960s and 1970s, there was a shift in casino management styles and decision making. Some say it was Howard Hughes who began this movement. The story goes that Hughes liked staying in the penthouse suite of a particular casino, so he paid his bill and lived there. However, the casino management was very concerned that he wasn't gambling enough, and they wanted the penthouse for a high roller, so they ordered him to vacate the premises. Hughes didn't want to leave. So what did he do? He bought the casino and changed the rules. Under the new management, the casino began to function like a large corporation. Superstitions were replaced by well-researched facts. Teams of managers replaced the individual owner. The idea that a dealer was responsible for table losses was replaced by probability theory. The casino made money and this encouraged other corporate giants like Baron Hilton to invest in casinos.

These giants of corporate America started a new trend in casino management styles and corporate cultures. The casino was divided into two parts: the casino side and the administration side. The casino side revolved around what happened on the casino floor: the daily grind of securing the casino and tracking the money. The administration side handled the

continued

marketing, accounting, human resources, and the like. With this split, new emphasis was placed on education credentials such as MBAs. People with no background in gambling began to work on marketing plans and run the financial enterprise. Computers and statistics became the guiding decision makers. For example, the authority for "comping" decisions switched from floor people to computers. When this old school of traditional casino managers lost their "comping" privileges to a computer, it was a confusing time. How could a computer know who were the right people to comp? How could a machine build a rapport with the players so that they would come back? Old-time supervisors issued comps to whomever they pleased. It gave them power. But now the computer decided.

Two Cultures Collide

The clash of traditional culture versus new corporate culture was inevitable. The traditional casino culture was characterized by statements like "The guys upstairs don't know the business" and "How can an MBA know anything about the way a casino works?" By the same token, the new culture examined these traditional views and found them lacking. The new corporate culture became characterized by statements like "The traditional managers want to micro-manage and keep everything to themselves" and "Managers do not want anyone else to know what is going on" and "What does a dealer know about marketing or accounting?" The collision between these two cultures would lead to inevitable changes.

However, it wasn't just the ownership switch that altered the traditional corporate culture. When Las Vegas and Atlantic City found themselves inundated with new kinds of gaming venues, the competition for employees became intense. Finding trained employees was a big problem. Anyone with any qualifications or experience quickly climbed the corporate ladder. Employees always had the enticement from the next casino or riverboat for higher wages. There were too many jobs and not enough workers. As a result, the casino employment department changed into human resources to reflect an emphasis on improving employee–employer relationships. Instead of hiring, disciplining, and firing, their responsibility shifted to keeping employees. "Employee satisfaction" became the new buzz words. Now retention and motivation have become the new service management foci. Empowering, educating, and recognizing workers improve the chances for a company to build employee loyalty and reduce the costs of turnover.

Instead of the traditional casino view that "your job is a privilege," the new corporate culture view is that a casino should strive to "be the place of choice." Instead of looking for abilities, the new corporate culture searches for personality first: someone who is friendly, personable, and stable. A person can learn many skills, but he or she cannot be taught to be outgoing and friendly. These new views in corporate culture reflect the emphasis on the satisfied employee. As researchers study the best corporations, they are finding that good service management pays. There is a strong relationship between employees who like their jobs and customers who are treated with both enthusiasm and awareness of bottom-line profits. Understanding this connection is the key to winning a competitive slot in today's business environment.

Nongaming revenue comes from sources that are not related to wagering on the casino floor. As the gaming entertainment concept continues to emphasize activities other than gambling, nongaming revenue is increasing in importance. This is what gaming entertainment is truly about: hospitality and entertainment based on the attraction of a casino.

What forms does gaming entertainment take? The megaresorts of Las Vegas and Atlantic City garner the most publicity as the meccas of the gaming entertainment industry. However, there are smaller properties throughout Nevada and other casino-based businesses in 48 states and seven Canadian provinces. These casinos take the form of commercially operated businesses, both privately and publicly held. Some are land based, meaning the casinos are housed in regular buildings. Others are riverboats that cruise up and down a river, or barges that are moored in water and do not cruise, called dockside casinos.

Casinos are also operated by Native American tribes on their reservations and tribal lands. These are land-based casinos and are often as complex as any operation in Las Vegas. Gaming entertainment is also popular on cruise ships as

The Las Vegas Strip

part of the cruise vacation product or on what are called "cruises to nowhere," where gaming and entertainment on board the ship are the main attraction.

There is strong support for gaming in the marketplace as an entertainment activity. Twenty-six percent or 51.2 million U.S. households gamble in casinos. U.S. households make 300 million visits annually to casinos. According to market research, more than 90 percent of U.S. adults say casino entertainment is acceptable for themselves or others.[2]

The demographic makeup of the typical gaming entertainment guest has remained consistent during the past several years. In comparison to the average American, casino players tend to have higher levels of income and education and are more likely to hold white-collar jobs. The customer profile of Las Vegas has gotten younger, and people who spend money want a total entertainment experience.

Gaming entertainment operators are becoming more retail driven and try to bring people in with a new hotel, magic shop, exclusive restaurants, or other shops. And guests have responded to these efforts. According to the latest Las Vegas Visitor Profile Study, the average visitor to Las Vegas stays 3.4 nights, budgets $503 for gambling, and spends $75 per night on lodging, $193 on food and drink, $51 on local transportation, $83 on shopping, $45 on shows, and another $9 on sightseeing.

Knowing the customers and their preferences is becoming critical in the gaming entertainment business. For example, Harrah's Entertainment, aiming to become America's first national-brand casino, created a Total Gold players' card. Gamblers accumulate points for their computer-monitored play. The card is then used to dispense cash back to players or vouchers good for complimentary rewards at any of its 26 U.S. casinos in 13 states.[3]

Most casino companies have similar players' clubs that operate like the airlines' frequent-flier programs. But Harrah's Entertainment became the first gaming entertainment chain to "comp," or redeem, those points systemwide. For instance, players can earn cash-value points gambling in Kansas City and then cash them in toward the price of a hotel room at Harrah's Las Vegas casino. Harrah's believes that linking the Total Gold card to a computer database of its millions of customers nationwide elevates the gaming entertainment firm to a new level of marketing sophistication.[4]

The bankruptcy court has approved Donald J. Trump's plan to save his casino empire (Trump Marina, Trump Taj Mahal, and Trump Plaza in Atlantic City). The reorganization plan gives bondholders an equity stake in the casino company in exchange for $575 million of debt. The plan would reduce Trump's stake in the company from 56 percent to about 27 percent and will reduce its debt by $400 million and save about $98 million annually in interest payments. Trump will still be at the top of the company and be its largest individual stockholder. The plan allows Trump Hotels to spruce up its tired Atlantic City casinos to compete with cash-rich competition like Borgata, Harrah's Atlantic City, and Caesar's Entertainment's three properties.[5]

Historical Review of Gaming Entertainment

Las Vegas. The name alone summons images of millions of neon lights, elaborate shows, outrageous performers, and bustling casinos, where millions are won and lost every night. Las Vegas is all of that, but much more. This city represents the American dream. A dusty watering hole less than 70 years ago, it has been transformed into one of the most elaborate cities in the world and one of the hottest vacation spots for the entire family. Las Vegas is second only to Walt Disney World as the favorite vacation destination in the United States.

The gaming entertainment business has its roots in Las Vegas. From the early 1940s until 1976, Las Vegas had a monopoly on the casino business, not the gaming entertainment business. Casinos had no hotel rooms, entertainment, or other amenities. The hotels that existed were just a place to sleep when a guest was not on the casino floor.

To reduce the amount of dollars being spent in Atlantic City, the Pennsylvania State Legislature passed the Pennsylvania Slot Law, which provides for licensing and placing of slot machines within the commonwealth. It also created the Pennsylvania State Gambling Commission, providing powers and duties and enforcement agents. Lawmakers get to decide what forms of gaming will be allowed and how many licenses to issue.

Gambling is a general term used for different types of games. Gambling is any behavior involving the risk of money or valuables on the outcome of a game, contest, or other event which is partially or totally dependent on chance or skill). Today the precise origin of gambling is still unknown. Chinese records show the first official account of the practice as far back as 2300 B.C. The Romans were also gamblers. They placed bets on chariot races, cockfights, and dice throwing. This eventually led to problems, and gambling, or "the games of chance," was banned except during the winter festival of Saturnalia. In the seventeenth century, casino-style gaming clubs existed in England, Italy, and Central Europe. A public gambling house was legalized for the first time in 1626 in Venice, Italy. Soon the upper class gathered in so-called *casinis* to socialize and gamble. In the first half of the nineteenth century organized gaming casinos started to appear. The first casino, the Bellevue, was officially opened on August 10, 1901.

Las Vegas is rich with tales of **Benjamin Hymen Siegelbaum,** better known as Bugsy Siegel. Bugsy was born on February 28, 1906, in Brooklyn, New York, to a

A Day in the Life of Richard Duke
Former Casino Shift Manager, Las Vegas Hilton Hotel and Casino, Las Vegas, Nevada

I arrive at work at approximately 9:30 A.M. My first task is to update myself on the previous day's operations. This includes how much the casino won or lost, what customers are gambling at our property, and how they are doing.

Prior to the beginning of each shift (graveyard, days, or swing), we conduct a shift meeting. This meeting takes approximately 20 minutes. The casino shift manager going off duty will conduct the meeting and the incoming shift manager along with his or her pit managers will attend. In the meeting we pass on to the next shift any pertinent information relevant to the day's operations. We also discuss those customers currently gambling in our casino, their credit lines, betting limits, and activities.

After the shift meeting, I go out onto the casino floor and evaluate our current level of casino business. I discuss with my pit managers how many casino games we will need for the expected day's business. We also determine at this time whether we will need any private games for our high limit customers.

Once these accommodations are decided on, the remainder of the day consists of keeping abreast as to who is gambling in our casino, managing employees, and monitoring casino activities. I continually visit with our established customers and meet and welcome new ones. This means knowing who they are, what casino games they play, what their casino credit limit is, and how much is still available and whether they are winning or losing.

Customer problems and complaints fall within my authority as well. If they are casino customers, I pretty much handle it myself. If they are hotel guests only and they come to me with their problem, I usually team up with the hotel manager and we resolve the situation together. We spend a lot of time and exhibit concern when it comes to customer problems or complaints. We always try to find a way to say "yes" to customer requests and try to reach an equitable agreement to problems.

I also spend a lot of time each day managing and monitoring employees. Those that fall within my realm of authority are dealers, box supervisors, floor supervisors, and pit managers. Good employee relations are a big concern of mine. I feel a happy employee is the key to good customer service. This in turn makes my job easier and generates revenue for the company.

Toward the end of the day, I prepare a report as to the status of the casino. Then I conduct a shift meeting with the incoming managers.

I usually leave the property at approximately 6:30 P.M.

Courtesy of Las Vegas Hilton.

poor Austrian Jewish family. It is said that Siegel began his career at a very young age by extorting money from pushcart peddlers. Eventually he turned to a life of bootlegging, gambling rackets, and murder-for-hire operations. In 1931 Bugsy was one of four men who executed Joe "the Boss" Masseria. Several years later he was sent west to develop rackets. In California Siegel successfully developed gambling dens and ships. He also took part in narcotics smuggling, blackmail, and other questionable operations. After developing nationwide bookmakers' wire service, Bugsy moved on to build the well-known Flamingo Hotel and Casino in Las Vegas. Upon completion, the Casino ended up costing $6 million which forced Siegel to skim profits. This angered the eastern bosses, and Bugsy died at his Beverly Hills home the evening of June 20, 1947, hit by a barrage of bullets fired through his living-room window. At the same time, three henchmen walked into the Flamingo Hotel and announced that they were the new owners.

Casino gambling, seen as a desperate remedy for Atlantic City's severe economic situation at the time, was approved by a voter referendum in a statewide ballot in November 1976.[6] Following the referendum, casino gambling was legalized in the state of New Jersey by the Casino Control Act. The state looked to the casino hotel industry to invest capital, create jobs, pay taxes, and attract tourists, thus revitalizing the economy and creating a financial environment in which urban redevelopment could occur.

The act initiated a number of fees and taxes specific to the casino hotel business that would provide revenues to support regulatory costs, to fund social services for the disabled and the elderly throughout the state, and to provide investment funds for the redevelopment of Atlantic City. The Casino Control Act created the Casino Control Commission, whose purpose was not only to ensure the success and integrity of the Atlantic City casino industry, but also to carry out the objective of reversing the city's economic fortunes.

Sensing that the objectives of the Casino Control Act were being fulfilled in New Jersey and wanting similar benefits for their state, but not wanting land-based casino gambling, Iowa legalized riverboat casinos 13 years later. They were followed in rapid succession by Illinois, Mississippi, Louisiana, Missouri, and Indiana. With the spread of the casino industry throughout the United States and Canada, the competitive nature of the industry began to create a need for what is now known as gaming entertainment with the addition of noncasino attractions. Gaming entertainment is, therefore, a natural evolution of the casino industry.

Native American Gaming

In *California* v. *Cabazon Band of Mission Indians et al.* (1987), the Supreme Court decided 6 to 3 that once a state has legalized any form of gambling, the Native Americans in that state have the right to offer and self-regulate the same games, without government restrictions. The state of California and the county of Riverside had sought to impose local and state regulations on card and bingo clubs operated by the Cabazon and Morongo bands of Mission Indians. These court decisions were unequivocal in their recognition of the rights of tribes with regard to certain gaming activities.

Congress, which some observers say was alarmed by the prospect of tribal gaming going out of control, responded to these court decisions by passing the **Indian Gaming Regulatory Act of 1988 (IGRA)**. The IGRA provides a framework by which games are conducted to protect both the tribes and the general public. For example, the IGRA outlines criteria for approval of casino management contracts entered into by tribes and establishes civil penalties for violation of its provisions. The act clearly is a compromise in that it balances the rights of sovereign tribal nations to conduct gaming activities with the rights of the federal and state governments to regulate activities within their borders.

The three objectives of the IGRA were to (1) provide a statutory basis for the operation of gaming by Native American tribes as a means of promoting tribal economic development, self-sufficiency, and strong tribal governments; (2) pro-

The gaming industry is clearly an important provider of jobs.

vide a statutory basis for the regulation of gaming by a Native American tribe adequate to shield it from organized crime and other corrupting influences; and (3) establish an independent regulatory authority, the National Indian Gaming Commission (NIGC), for governing gaming activity on Native American lands.

IGRA defines three different kinds, or classes, of Native American gaming activities: (1) class I gaming, consisting of social games played solely for prizes of minimum value or traditional forms of Native American gaming; (2) class II gaming, consisting of bingo, games similar to bingo, and card games explicitly authorized by the laws of the state; and (3) class III gaming, consisting of all forms of gaming that are neither class I nor class II gaming, and therefore including most of what are considered casino games.

The significance of the definition of class III gaming activity is that it defines the games that (1) must be located in a state that permits such gaming for any purpose by any person, organization, or entity and (2) are conducted in conformance with a compact that states are required to negotiate "in good faith" with the tribes.

While the federal gaming law precludes state taxation, the tribes in several states have made voluntary payments and also negotiated payments to state governments under certain circumstances. Often tribes give local governments voluntary payments in recognition of services the tribe receives, and some pay revenues in exchange for permission to maintain a casino gambling monopoly in a state. In Michigan, Connecticut, and Louisiana, tribes have agreed to make payments to the state as part of their comprehensive compacts for casino gambling. In almost all the states, the tribes make payments to the state for state costs incurred in the process of regulation of the casinos as provided for in the negotiated agreements.

There are 281 gaming facilities on reservation lands in 32 states, and Native American gaming has been the fastest-growing sector of casino gaming in the United States. Additional Native American gaming is conducted by the First Nations Bands of Canada.

Check Your Knowledge

1. Define the following:
   a. Wagered
   b. Bet
   c. Handle
   d. Win
   e. Action
   f. Beat the house
   g. Social gambler
2. Briefly describe the history of the gaming industry.
3. What does the Indian Gaming Regulatory Act of 1988 consist of?

Size and Scope of Gaming Entertainment

Recently, a merging frenzy has occurred in the gaming industry. There are four large casino operators—Caesar's Entertainment, Inc.; MGM Grand, Inc.; Harrah's Entertainment, Inc.; and Mandalay Resort Group. These four hold all the cards in the gaming industry, so to speak!

Why is the gaming/entertainment industry growing so quickly? Basically, because people like to wager and, historically, there has been more demand than supply for wagering opportunities. As public acceptance of legalized gaming has grown, and state and local governments have permitted gaming entertainment establishments to open, supply is beginning to meet demand.

The gaming entertainment industry pays billions of dollars per year in gambling privilege taxes to state governments. Casino development has been credited with revitalizing economies through new capital investment, job creation, new tax revenue, and increased tourism.

Casino gaming has created thousands of direct and indirect jobs with billions paid in wages. When unemployment is high and an area is in economic despair, casinos create jobs.

Casino gaming companies pay an average of 12 percent of total revenues in taxes. Casino gaming companies contribute to federal, state, and local governments through gaming-related and other taxes. Direct taxes include property, federal/state income, and construction sales and use taxes, which all industries pay, and gaming taxes, which are levied only on the gaming industry at rates ranging from 6.25 to 20 percent of gaming revenues.

Key Players in the Industry

Until recently the leading participants in the gaming entertainment business were Venetian, Mirage Resorts, Harrah's Entertainment, Hilton Hotels Corporation, ITT Corporation, Bellagio, and MGM Grand. Today, there are only four industry giants: Caesers Entertainment, MGM Mirage, Harrah's, and Mandalay Resorts Group. Changes in the industry happen in the wink of an eye. They all have diverse property portfolios and solid business practices and are well respected by Wall Street.

Mandalay Resorts Group owns five premier hotel/casinos in Las Vegas: Mandalay Bay, Luxor, Excalibur, Monte Carlo, and Circus Circus. In addition, they own properties in several other Nevada locations, as well as in Tunica, Mississippi; Elgin, Illinois; and Detroit, Michigan.

Harrah's Entertainment operates casinos in major gaming markets throughout the United States. Its casinos are located in Reno, Lake Tahoe, Las Vegas, and Laughlin, Nevada; and Atlantic City, New Jersey. One of the most geographically diverse casino companies, it also operates riverboat and dockside casinos in Illinois, Louisiana, Missouri, and Mississippi, and Native American reservation casinos in Arizona and Washington. In all, the company operates more than 700,000 square feet of gaming space. Although Harrah's also operates nearly 6,500 hotel rooms and more than 50 restaurants, it derives nearly 80 percent of its revenues from its casinos.

Harrah's Entertainment, Inc., is the premier name in casino entertainment. The Harrah's brand was born in Reno, Nevada, in the late 1930s and has since grown to become the largest casino entertainment company in North America. Harrah's history is a rich combination of casino expertise and quality, which was launched in northern Nevada and expanded across the continent. Today, Harrah's is a $1.5 billion company, publicly traded on the New York Stock Exchange. The gaming division of the former Promus Companies is now

The Venetian and the Mirage: Two Popular Casino Resort Hotels

The Bellagio and MGM Grand: Two Successful Casino Resort Hotels

a separate, publicly traded company, with 26 properties in 13 states and one foreign country, and 23,000 employees.

Hilton owns, manages, and/or franchises more than 220 hotels around the world. Hilton, with its $3 billion purchase of Bally Entertainment, is the nation's largest gambling business. U.S. gaming operations include three casino hotels in Las Vegas, two in Atlantic City, two in Reno, and one in Laughlin; a riverboat casino in New Orleans; and interest in a Canadian casino.

The New Caesars Entertainment, Inc., is one of the world's largest gaming companies with 29 properties in five countries on four continents, featuring 29,000 hotel rooms, 2 million square feet of casino space, and 54,000 employees. The new Caesars Entertainment represents the union of four legendary gaming organizations: Caesars World, Hilton gaming, Bally's, and Grand Casinos.

MGM Mirage, one of the world's leading and most respected hotel and gaming companies, owns several casino resorts in Nevada, Mississippi, Michigan, and Australia. Included in the impressive portfolio are The Bellagio, MGM Grand Las Vegas, The Mirage, Treasure Island, New York–New York Boardwalk Hotel and Casino, and several others.

MGM Mirage prides itself on operating the world's largest hotel/casino. The MGM Grand Hotel, located on 113 acres along the Las Vegas strip, has more than 5,000 rooms and a 171,500-square-foot casino with some 3,700 slot machines, about 160 table games, some 50 shops, a theme park, and a special-events center featuring superstar acts. Across the strip is the 2,000-room New York–New York Hotel and Casino, MGM Grand's 50 percent joint venture with Primadonna Resorts. The Bellagio's lobby ceiling contains a breathtaking display of 2,000 hand-blown glass flowers created by world-renowned artist Dale Chihuly. A water ballet in front of the resort offers viewers a musical and visual spectacle performed by Bellagio's acclaimed water fountains. MGM Grand also runs a hotel/casino in northern Australia that caters to Asian gamblers. The company has agreed to develop casinos in Atlantic City, New Jersey, and South Africa.

Personal Profile: Stephen A. Wynn

Chairman of the Board and Chief Executive Officer Wynn Resorts, Limited

"Steve Wynn has done more for Nevada than any business leader in history. He turns his dreams into works of art. Las Vegas is his canvas."

—U.S. Senator Harry Reid at Wynn Las Vegas groundbreaking, October 2002

Casino Developer Stephen A. Wynn is widely credited with transforming Las Vegas into a world-renowned resort and convention destination. As chairman of the board, president, and chief executive officer of Mirage Resorts, Inc., Mr. Wynn envisioned and built the Mirage, Treasure Island, and Bellagio—boldly conceived resorts that set progressively higher standards for quality, luxury, and entertainment. Now, as chairman of the board and chief executive officer of Wynn Resorts, Limited, Mr. Wynn is developing Wynn Las Vegas, intended to be among the world's preeminent luxury hotel resorts when it opened on the Las Vegas Strip and Wynn Macau, which is scheduled to open in 2006.

Mr. Wynn began his career in 1967 as part owner, slot manager, and assistant credit manager of the Frontier Hotel. Between 1968 and 1972 he also owned and operated a wine and liquor importing company. But it was an entrepreneurial real estate transaction with Howard Hughes in 1971 that produced sufficient profits for a major investment in the landmark Golden Nugget Casino. Once known only as a "gambling joint," Mr. Wynn transformed the Golden Nugget into a four-diamond resort known for elegance and personal service. By 1973, at age 31, Mr. Wynn controlled the property and began developing the Golden Nugget as a complete hotel resort.

In 1978, Mr. Wynn used profits from the Golden Nugget in Las Vegas to build the 506-room Golden Nugget Hotel & Casino on the Boardwalk in Atlantic City. The resort became known for its elegant facilities, television ads featuring Frank Sinatra, and its impressive lineup of superstar entertainment. From its opening in December 1979 until its sale in 1986, the Atlantic City property dominated the market in revenues and profits in spite of its smaller size.

In 1987, Mr. Wynn sold the Atlantic City Golden Nugget, which had cost $160 million, to Bally for $450 million and turned his creativity to developing what would become the company's flagship property: the Mirage. Opened in November 1989, the elegant hotel, with its imaginative erupting volcano and South Seas theme, ignited a $12 billion building boom that catapulted Las Vegas to America's number one tourist destination and fastest-growing city. In 1991, Golden Nugget Incorporated was renamed Mirage Resorts, Incorporated.

In October 1993, Mr. Wynn opened Treasure Island, establishing a new paradigm by which casino theme resorts are designed. At the front corner of the resort, the Battle of Buccaneer Bay was acted out on a full-size pirate ship. Inside, the four-diamond property, with its romantic tropical theme, is one of the city's most electrifying casino resorts.

In October 1998, Mr. Wynn raised the bar again when he opened the opulent Bellagio, a $1.6 billion resort considered among the world's most spectacular hotels. With its sumptuous guest rooms, high-end retail stores, and traditional European feel, Bellagio appealed to an audience that long overlooked Las Vegas as a vacation destination. Today, visitors line the street in front of the hotel to watch another Steve Wynn attraction: the "Dancing Waters" — shooting fountains, choreographed to music, that "dance" on the hotel's 8.5-acre manmade lake. In 1999, Mr. Wynn brought Mirage Resorts' standard of style to beautiful and historic Biloxi, Mississippi, where he oversaw development of the 1,835-room Beau Rivage. Blending Mediterranean beauty with southern hospitality, the resort was the centerpiece of a building boom that established Biloxi as a regional tourism center along the Mississippi Gulf Coast.

In June 2000, Mr. Wynn sold Mirage Resorts, Incorporated, to MGM for $6.6 billion and purchased Las Vegas's legendary Desert Inn Resort and Casino. The

continued

Desert Inn was closed in August 2000, and on the site Mr. Wynn began developing Wynn Las Vegas, a 2,700-room luxury casino resort that has inspired yet another wave of development on the Strip. Concurrently, Wynn Resorts is developing its Asian flagship casino resort in Macau, where the company has been awarded a 20-year concession by the Macau government.

Today Mr. Wynn is active in the community and has received honorary doctorate degrees from the University of Nevada, Las Vegas, and Sierra Nevada College in northern Nevada. He is chairman of the University of Utah's Moran Eye Institute; a trustee of his alma mater, the University of Pennsylvania; and a member of the board of the George Bush Presidential Library.

Two other gaming entertainment companies, Boyd Gaming and Grand Casinos, Inc., are expanding rapidly into markets across the United States.

Boyd Gaming operates ten gaming and hotel facilities in four states. The company's six Las Vegas properties are The Stardust Resort and Casino, Sam's Town Hotel and Gambling Hall, the Eldorado Casino, the Joker's Wild Casino, the California Hotel and Casino, and the Fremont Hotel and Casino. Outside Nevada, Boyd operates the Sam's Town Hotel and Gambling Hall, a dockside gaming and entertainment complex in Tunica County, Mississippi; Sam's Town Casino, a Kansas City, Missouri, casino complex; and the Silver Star Hotel and Casino, a land-based gaming and entertainment facility owned by the Choctaw Indians.

Grand Casinos, Inc., is a casino entertainment company that develops, constructs, and manages land-based and dockside casinos in emerging gaming markets. Grand Casinos, Inc., has been a publicly traded company since 1991 and is listed on the New York Stock Exchange under the trading symbol GND. The company currently owns and operates the three largest casino hotel resorts in the state of Mississippi, manages two land-based casinos in Louisiana, and manages two casino hotel resorts in Minnesota.

Exciting Gaming Entertainment Projects

The Mirage megaresort on the Las Vegas strip has a volcano that erupts every few minutes and a tropical rain forest with soaring palms and sparkling waterfalls. Guests checking into the hotel face a giant aquarium where live sharks swim. The pool is a tropical paradise of waterfalls and connected lagoons. The property contains a European shopping boulevard and a wide variety of themed food and beverage operations. There is meeting and convention space for up to 5,000 attendees. The resort is also the home of a family of Atlantic bottlenose dolphins.

Station Casino Kansas City is one of the largest floating casino operations in the world. The 140,000-square-foot, two-barge casino is home to 3,000 slot machines and 190 table games. In addition to the casino, the facility includes 12 restaurants, 11 lounges, a 200-room hotel, a 1,400-seat special events arena, a microbrewery, an arcade, a child-care center, and an 18-screen movie theater. The attractions at Station Casino are coordinated through a Victorian theme, including a cobblestone street that winds through a recreation of Victorian-era Kansas City, complete with antiques and a handpainted sky.

New York New York in Las Vegas is an eye-catching property with 12 hotel towers, each a replica of a Manhattan skyscraper. There is a Coney Island–style amusement area, a casino that feels like Central Park at dusk, a food court designed to simulate a Little Italy neighborhood, a 300-foot-long replica of the Brooklyn Bridge, and a 150-foot-tall model of the Statue of Liberty at the front of the resort. The property is jointly owned by MGM Grand and Primadonna Resorts.

Star Trek: The Experience attraction and outer space–themed SpaceQuest casino located in the Las Vegas Hilton is a $70 million joint venture of Hilton Corp. and the Paramount Parks Division of Viacom International Inc. The project targets baby boomers and generation X customers interested in science fiction and space-related entertainment. The SpaceQuest, separate from the main casino, simulates a ride aboard a space station. Television screens create an illusion of space flight. Gaming equipment unique to the 20,000-square-foot SpaceQuest casino includes slot machines activated by breaking a light beam.

Wild Wild West Casino at Bally's Park Place in Atlantic City, New Jersey, is the city's first highly themed, entertainment-oriented, technologically advanced casino entertainment product. The casino has an 1880s frontier mining town, mountain scapes, model trains, animatronic characters, and colorful storefronts. There is a 50-foot-high canyon with waterfalls, a talking gold prospector, and a wisecracking vulture perched on a twelve-foot-high cactus.

The Masquerade Village at the Rio Hotel & Casino in Las Vegas is a Tuscany village-themed retail area with twenty stores and six restaurants, including a wine cellar tasting room. Its Masquerade Show in the Sky features five themed floats suspended from the ceiling that parade above the casino via an overhead track. Costumed entertainers and musicians perform from atop the floats and from other posts inside the casino during free shows throughout the day. Guests are invited to ride on the floats and participate in the shows.

Luxor Las Vegas, operated by Circus Circus, was constructed as a 30-story pyramid and houses the world's largest atrium, measuring 29 million cubic feet. It also features a beam of light emanating from its peak that is so intense it can be seen as far away as Los Angeles, California. The 4,500 rooms are appointed

Bally's and Caesars Casinos line the Boardwalk mimicking various architectural styles in Atlantic City.

in Egyptian architecture. The lobby area includes a life-sized replica of the great Temple of Ramses II and large Egyptian murals. The resort includes a museum containing reproductions of the items found in King Tutankhamen's tomb, which was discovered in 1922 by Howard Carter. The items are positioned exactly as they were found, according to records maintained by the Carter expedition. The resort also has a Theater of Time, the site of an IMAX 3D theater using the IMAX Personal Sound Environment headset, an advanced liquid crystal display technology for three-dimensional viewing.

Grand Casino Tunica, with the largest dockside casino between Las Vegas and Atlantic City, is located in Tunica County, Mississippi, just south of Memphis. The three-story, 140,000-square-foot gaming area is unlike any in the area. With more than 3,000 slot machines and 108 table games, guests can enjoy the atmosphere of the San Francisco Gold Rush, the New Orleans Mardi Gras, the Great American West of the 1870s, or an 1890s Mississippi riverboat town. Six restaurants, two entertainment lounges, a Kids Quest, a Grand Arcade, and a luxury hotel are located on this 2,000-acre site. There are plans to develop it into a premier destination resort.

The Monte Carlo Pub & Brewery, located in the Monte Carlo Resort & Casino in Las Vegas, is one of the largest brewpubs in the United States. Six different styles of Monte Carlo-labeled beer are regularly produced, including a light beer, an India pale ale, and an American-style, unfiltered wheat ale. The pub also features a traditional Irish stout, a rich amber ale, and a regular brewer's special. Gourmet, brick-oven pizzas and sausage platters and a full line of salads and sandwiches are on the menu. Huge copper beer barrels and antique furnishings add to the brewpub's atmosphere. The hotel offers a meeting room and function area from which guests can get a bird's-eye view of the entire operation. The brewpub also features an outdoor patio that overlooks the lavish 21,000-square-foot Monte Carlo pool area, which includes a wave pool and an easy river ride.

The pirate battle in front of the Treasure Island megaresort draws thousands of guests to Las Vegas to watch this show every 90 minutes in front of the hotel entrance.

Treasure Island megaresort's entrance is across a long wooden bridge that traverses the waters of Buccaneer Bay. Every 90 minutes each evening, cannon and musket fire are exchanged in a dramatic pyrotechnic battle between the pirate ship *Hispañiola* and the British frigate HMS *Britannia* in the middle of the bay. The showroom in this property is home to the world-famous performance troupe Cirque du Soleil and features an unusual circus act with no animals, but an overabundance of imagination.

Forum Shops at Caesars Palace draws an estimated 50,000 people a day and makes an average of $1,200 per square foot, far above the industry norm of $400. The Roman streetscape–themed, half-million-square-foot retail area features the Festival Fountain Plaza, which incorporates animatronic stat-

*The Fremont Street
Experience in the downtown
area of Las Vegas consists of
a four-block-long pedestrian
mall light and sound show,
with sky parades that take
place every two hours.*

ues of gods, such as Bacchus, Apollo, and Venus, with a fountain and light show. Another main feature is the Atlantic attraction, a fountain featuring animatronic figures that come to life during the Lost City of Atlantis laser light show that includes fire and other special effects. The backdrop for this attraction is a 50,000-gallon aquarium that can support 650 fish from 25 fish families. The Race for Atlantis ride uses a giant screen IMAX 3D motion simulator, the first of its kind to combine IMAX's large format film making with 3D computer animation, sound engineering, and motion simulation. The result is a multisensory experience that takes riders on an exhilarating chariot race through the legendary kingdom of Atlantis. Upscale retailers include Christian Dior, Versace, Niketown, a Virgin Megastore, and Wolfgang Puck's Spago restaurant. The FAO Schwarz store is the company's largest and features a 46-foot animatronic Trojan Horse.

Fremont Street Experience consists of a four-block-long pedestrian mall light and sound show with sky parades that take place every two hours. A canopy known as a space frame, which is really a giant video-quality animation screen, covers the entire area. The light shows are broadcast on 2 million-plus light bulbs from end to end that can produce 40,000 shades of color. There is virtually no image, animated or actual, that cannot be produced. The clarity and depth are close to movie quality. Digital sound accompaniments come from a 54,000-watt sound system pumped through clusters of exposed speakers, 40 in each block.

Foxwoods Resort Casino, near Ledyard, Connecticut, only a several-hour drive from New York City, is one of the largest gaming entertainment operations in the world. It is owned and managed by the Mashantucket Pequot Tribal Nation. There are two full-service hotels, restaurants and lounges, retail stores, amusement rides, and a museum and research center supporting the Pequot community.

The Aladdin opened in 2000. It is a $1 billion-plus hotel and casino. It has 2,567 rooms, 116,000-square-foot casino, 21 restaurants, a 500,000-square-foot mall with 135 stores, a 1,200-seat show room, a 33,000-square-foot spa, and 75,000 square feet of meeting and convention space. The Aladdin's 50-foot genie golden lamp centerpiece and its theme, the classic Arabian tale of the thousand and one nights, appeal to all.

Bellagio is a megaresort that appeared on the Las Vegas strip at a cost of more than $1.5 billion, which is more than the initial construction cost of Walt Disney

World. The 3,000-room hotel is fronted with a nine-acre lake featuring 2,200 fountains that perform a choreographed water dance several times each evening. The lobby includes an art gallery containing $150 million in fine art, including works by Picasso, Renoir, and Rembrandt. The signature showroom is home to a $70-million creation by Cirque du Soleil performed on a stage submerged in water, and a 15,000-square-foot conservatory featuring a massive flower display with classical gardens and European fountains and pools.

Caesars Riverboat at Bridgeport, Indiana, is located on the Indiana side of the Ohio River, just west of Louisville, Kentucky. The vessel is 450 feet long and 104 feet wide, with more than 80,000 square feet of casino space on four decks. The casino has 3,000 slot machines and 150 table games. The site of the new riverboat megaresort is a 232-acre tract of riverfront property that includes a 500-room convention-style Sheraton hotel, upscale shopping mall, sports arena, IMAX theater, Magical Empire, attractions, and an 18-hole golf course. The terminal for the riverboat is 130,000 square feet and houses four restaurants and an adjacent children's theme park. To facilitate visits from Louisville across the river, the company is developing a "Caesars Chariots" gondola system that will transport customers up and over the Ohio River in sky cars. The people mover can carry 1,000 persons per hour.

The MGM Grand, a 5,000-room megaresort in Las Vegas, is themed out as the "City of Entertainment." An area called the Studio Walk resembles a Hollywood sound stage and features a number of Hollywood landmarks, five restaurants, a food court, six retail stores, and a nightclub. The entrance to the resort is graced by a "liquid gold," six-story lion entry, fronting 80-foot entertainment walls that run multimedia and light shows continuously.

The Beau Rivage megaresort is the most magnificent resort on the Mississippi Gulf Coast and, perhaps, in the entire Southeast. This 32-story, 1,780-room resort, with its stately oak-tree-lined entrance, cascading fountains, lush formal gardens, and fragrant magnolias, graces acres of white sand beach overlooking the Gulf. As the newest Mirage Resorts property, Beau Rivage features twelve distinctive restaurants, an 85,000-square-foot casino, a 1,500-seat showroom, an elegantly appointed spa and salon, a shopping esplanade, and a 30,000-square-foot conference and convention center for banquets and business meetings, all under one roof.

Hilton Hotel Paris Casino Resort, is a $700 million, 3,000-room operation inspired by the prominent landmarks of Paris, France, a city that draws about one-third as many visitors annually as Las Vegas. The project includes a half-sized, 50-story replica of France's Eiffel Tower and an 85,000-square-foot casino. It has 130,000 square feet of casino space, a half-acre health spa, and a retail complex supplied by several French companies. An existing monorail that links the MGM Grand Hotel and Bally's Las Vegas (owned by Hilton) stops at a replica of a Paris Metro Station.

Las Vegas Sand's Venetian resort, casino, and convention complex is the largest megaresort ever planned. The $2 billion project includes 6,000 suites, each with 700 square feet of space, including sunken living rooms, two-line phones, and in-room fax machines. Inspired by the canals, bridges, and ancient architecture of Venice, Italy, the property includes a 1,200-foot replica of

Venice's Grand Canal, which fronts 150 stores. The Venetian has two casinos of 100,000 square feet each.

The MGM Grand Detroit megaresort is an art deco complex constructed in downtown Detroit. In addition to a spacious 100,000-square-foot gaming area with 40-foot-high ceilings, the complex includes a 36-story, 800-room hotel designed to be the midwest's premier resort hotel; a diverse array of signature restaurant and retail facilities; a state-of-the-art, five-screen movie theater; approximately 70,000 square feet of convention, ballroom, and meeting facilities; a 1,200-seat showroom theater; and a climate-controlled parking garage.

Le Jardin is Atlantic City's newest megaresort with 2,000 rooms and three acres of vaulted glass atriums. Lush horticultural gardens change with the seasons. It will be springtime 365 days a year, taking the seasonality out of the Atlantic City gaming entertainment market.

The Borgata, a $1 billion joint venture between Boyd Gaming and MGM Mirage, was the first new casino hotel to open in Atlantic City in 13 years. The property has 2,002 rooms and 125,000 square feet of gaming space.[7]

Check Your Knowledge

1. What impact does the gambling industry have on crime?
2. Briefly describe the following gaming entertainment projects:
   a. New York New York
   b. The Monte Carlo Pub & Brewery
   c. Treasure Island
   d. Forum Shops at Caesars Palace
   e. Bellagio
   f. MGM Grand

Positions in Gaming Entertainment

Careers in the gaming entertainment industry are unlimited. Students of the industry who understand the multidisciplinary needs of the business find five initial career tracks in hotel operations, food and beverage operations, casino operations, retail operations, and entertainment operations.

Hotel Operations

The career opportunities in gaming entertainment hotel operations are much like the career opportunities in the full-service hotel industry, with the exception that food and beverage can be a division of its own and not part of hotel operations. The rooms and guest services departments offer the most

Corporate Profile: Caesars Entertainment

Caesars Entertainment, Inc. is one of the world's leading gaming companies. With $4.5 billion in annual net revenue, 27 properties in five countries on four continents, 26,000 hotel rooms, 2 million square feet of casino space, and 52,000 employees, the Caesars portfolio is unmatched in the industry. The company has its corporate headquarters in Las Vegas, Nevada, where it operates Caesars Palace and three other major casino resorts. Caesars Entertainment adopted its new corporate name in 2004, but the company traces its roots back more than 50 years. The new Caesars Entertainment represents the union of four legendary gaming organizations: Caesars World, Hilton Gaming, Bally's, and Grand Casinos.

Caesars brands are among the most respected and best recognized in the world: Caesars, Paris, Bally's, Flamingo, Hilton, and Grand Casinos. Each Caesars Entertainment property creates a unique experience for its guests, from the Roman glory of Caesars Palace to the old-world romance of Paris Las Vegas to the southern charm of the Grand Casino resorts to the beach party excitement of the Flamingo.

In addition to world-class casinos, Caesars resorts feature more than 170 distinctive restaurants and cafes; 70 theaters, showrooms, and amphitheaters; 18 luxurious spas; five championship golf courses; a best-in-class sports shooting range; easy access to skiing; boating, deep-sea fishing, and other outdoor adventures; and the most alluring shopping destinations in the world. Caesars resorts surround their guests with entertainment — live performances by the world's most popular recording artists and comedians, championship boxing, celebrity golf, and world-class tennis — as well as exquisite dining, elegant shopping, pampering spas, challenging golf courses, and the most exciting gaming tables and slot floors in the world.

opportunities for students of hospitality management. Because gaming entertainment properties have hotels that are much larger than nongaming hotels, department heads have a larger number of supervisors reporting to them and more responsibilities. Reservations, front desk, housekeeping, valet parking, and guest services can all be very large departments with many employees.

Food and Beverage Operations

Gaming entertainment has a foundation of high-quality food and beverage service in a wide variety of styles and concepts. Some of the best foodservice operations in the hospitality industry are found in gaming entertainment operations. There are many career opportunities in restaurant management and the culinary arts. As with hotel operations, gaming entertainment properties are typically very large and contain numerous food and beverage outlets, including a number of restaurants, hotel room service, banquets and conventions, and retail outlets. Many establishments support gourmet, high-end signature restaurants. It is not unusual to find many more executive-level management positions in both front- and back-of-the-house food and beverage operations in gaming entertainment operations than in nongaming properties.

Casino Operations

Casino operations jobs fall into five functional areas. Gaming operations staff include slot machine technicians (approximately one technician for 40 machines), table-game dealers (approximately four dealers for each table game), and table-game supervisors. Casino service staff includes security, purchasing, and maintenance and facilities engineers. Marketing staff includes public relations, market research, and advertising professionals. Human resources staff includes employee relations, compensation, staffing, and training specialists. Finance and administration staff includes lawyers, accounts payable, audit, payroll, and income control specialists.[8]

While there was little organized dealer training as recently as a decade ago, the explosive growth of the gaming industry has increased the need for trained dealers skilled at working a variety of table games including **blackjack, craps, roulette, poker,** and **baccarat.** Now, through the use of textbooks and videotapes combined with hands-on training at a mock casino, future dealers learn the techniques and fine points of dealing at classes offered by both colleges and private schools.

Retail Operations

The increased emphasis on nongaming sources of revenues in gaming entertainment business demands an expertise in all phases of retail operations, from store design and layout to product selection, merchandising, and sales control. Negotiating with concession subcontractors may also be a part of the overall retail activities. Retail operations often support the overall theme of the property and can often be a major source of revenue; however, retail management careers are often an overlooked career path in the gaming entertainment industry.

Entertainment Operations

Because of the increased competition, gaming entertainment companies are creating bigger and better production shows to turn their properties into destination attractions. Some production shows have climbed into the $30 million to $90 million range and require professional entertainment staffs to produce and manage them. Gaming entertainment properties often present live entertainment of all sorts, with headline acts drawing huge audiences. For example, at the MGM Grand, there are three entertainment showcases. These include the 15,000-seat Grand Arena, used for professional boxing matches and for superstars like Tina Turner; the smaller 1,700-seat theater that houses an elaborate production show called EFX; and a 700-seat theater that plays host to other stars.

As a result of this emphasis on entertainment, career opportunities exist for those interested in stage and theater production, lighting and box office management, and talent management and booking.

Trends in the Gaming Entertainment Industry

- Gaming entertainment is depending less on casino revenue and more on room, food and beverage, retail, and entertainment revenue for its profitability and growth.
- The gaming entertainment industry and lodging industry are converging as hotel room inventory is rapidly expanding in gaming entertainment properties.
- Gaming entertainment, along with the gaming industry as a whole, will continue to be scrutinized by government and public policy makers as to the net economic and social impact of its activities.
- As the gaming entertainment industry becomes more competitive, exceptional service quality will become an increasingly important competitive advantage for success.
- The gaming entertainment industry will continue to provide management opportunities for careers in the hospitality business.

CASE STUDY

VIP

A frequent guest of the casino makes a last-minute decision to travel to your property for a weekend stay. The guest enjoys gaming as a leisure activity and is one of the casino's better customers. When he arrives at the casino, he is usually met by a casino host and treated as a very important person due to his level of wagering at the blackjack tables. This guest is worth approximately $50,000 in casino win per year to the hotel. Due to his last-minute arrangements, however, the guest cannot notify a casino host that he is on his way to the hotel. Upon arriving, he finds a very busy registration desk. He must wait in line for 20 minutes, and when he tries to check in, he is told that the hotel is full. The front-desk clerk acts impatient when the guest says that he is a frequent customer. In a fit of frustration, the would-be guest leaves the hotel and makes a mental note that all casinos have similar odds at the blackjack table and maybe another property will give him the respect he deserves.

Question

1. What systems or procedures could you institute to make sure this type of oversight does not happen in your property?

CASE STUDY

Negotiating with Convention Groups

Your convention sales department receives a call from a trip director for a large convention group. The group will use many function rooms for meetings during the day and will generate a substantial amount of convention services revenue. Likewise, their food and beverage needs are quite elaborate and will be great for the food and beverage department budget. However, the group is very sensitive concerning room price and is willing to negotiate the time of week for their three-night stay.

Question

1. What are the considerations that a gaming entertainment property must take into account when determining room rates for convention groups?

CAREER INFORMATION

Gaming Industry

The multibillion-dollar gaming entertainment industry is growing throughout the world. America will continue to see significant growth in the industry, but the extraordinary growth will occur internationally. Career opportunities will abound due to the gaming industry's growth, continuous operation, and labor-intensive nature.

Gaming entertainment offers careers in casino gambling, entertainment, foodservice, and lodging. Each area is an essential part of the gaming entertainment experience but it is important to remember that casinos still make the majority of their revenue from gambling! The other areas are designed to attract the customer and then keep them in the casino.

Management careers can be very different depending on your focus. If your interest is gaming management, it is important that you take courses in finance, law, human resources, management, and gambling. You also need to work in the gaming industry while in college so that you can open doors for yourself through networking. Casinos

still believe in promoting from within, so you will have to work your way up the corporate ladder. You also need to understand that because of the continuous operation of a casino, your work schedule will vary. It is not uncommon to work several 12-hour days straight, but the rewards for dedication and hard work can be very worthwhile. Casinos are exhilarating places where the rich and famous come to play and be entertained.

Related Web Sites

extranet.casinocareers.com/jobs/index.cfm —career bulletin board
www.casinoemployment.com/ —employment bulletin board
www.parkplace.com/ —gaming company information
www.mirage.com/ —gaming company information
www.harrahs.com/ —gaming company information and employment

Courtesy of Charlie Adams.

SUMMARY

1. The casino industry has developed into a new business called gaming entertainment with the introduction of full-service hotels, retail, and entertainment offerings.
2. To operate gaming entertainment businesses, it is necessary to understand the relationship between the casino and other departments in the operation.
3. Gaming entertainment is strictly regulated by state governments, and the integrity developed over time

by these regulations is necessary for the survival of the industry.
4. Nongaming revenue is increasing as a percentage of total revenue of gaming entertainment businesses.
5. Native American gaming entertainment businesses are a means for economic self-development by tribal people.

KEY WORDS AND CONCEPTS

Baccarat
Bet
Blackjack
Casino

Gambling
Gaming entertainment
Handle

Indian Gaming Regulatory Act (IGRA)
Poker
Roulette

Slot machine
Wager
Win

REVIEW QUESTIONS

1. Briefly describe the history of legalized gaming in the United States.
2. What defines a gaming entertainment business?
3. Explain the attraction of gaming entertainment to the destination of a tourist.
4. Why is it necessary for strict regulations to be in force on the casino floor?
5. How are hotel operations in a gaming entertainment business different from hotel operations in a nongaming environment?

INTERNET EXERCISES

1. Organization: **Wynn Las Vegas**
   Web site: **www.wynnlasvegas.com**
   Summary: Wynn Las Vegas is the latest casino from Steve Wynn. Check out the Web site and compare – contrast it with Caesars Entertainment or other related sites.
2. Organization: **Caesars Entertainment**
   Web site: **www.caesars.com**
   Summary: Caesers Entertainment is one of the largest and most diversified gaming companies in the world.

This site gives information on the company and the gaming business as a whole.
   (a) How many gaming properties and brand names worldwide does Caesars Entertainment serve?
   (b) What are your views on the gaming industry in Nevada now that gaming is permitted on Native American reservations?

APPLY YOUR KNOWLEDGE

1. Name the major gaming entertainment hotels in Las Vegas.

2. Give examples of nongaming revenue.

SUGGESTED ACTIVITIES

1. Pick a casino in Las Vegas and look it up on the Internet. What does it offer that sets it apart from other casinos in Las Vegas and in other areas of the United States? In what areas is it similar to other casinos?

2. Research careers in the gaming entertainment industry. Are there more opportunities than you realized? Do any of the careers interest you?

ENDNOTES

1. **www.aga.org**.
2. E. M. Christiansen, The Gross Annual Wager of the United States. **www.cca-1.com**.
3. Summary **www.lasvegas24hours.com**.
4. **www.harrahs.com**.
5. John Curran, Associated Press, *San Diego Union.* October 22, 2004; and *Gaming News,* May 19, 2005.
6. C. G. Braunlich, "Lessons from the Atlantic City Casino Experience," *Journal of Travel Research,* 34, 3, pp. 46–56.
7. *Internatinal Gaming & Wagering Business,* 24:11, 13, 17.
8. K. Hashimoto, S. Fried Kline, and G. G. Fenich, *Casino Management.* Dubuque, IA: Kendall/Hunt, 1995.

WEB RESOURCES

Caesars
www.caesars.com

MGM Grand
www.mgmgrand.com

Wynn Hotel and Resort
www.wynnlasvegas.com

Harrahs
www.harrahs.com/our_casinos

MGM Mirage
www.mgmmirage.com

Meetings, Incentive Travel, Conventions, Exhibitions (MICE), and Event Management

13

After reading and studying this chapter, you should be able to:

- Name the main hospitality industry associations.
- Describe the various types of meetings.
- Explain the difference between meetings, expositions, and conventions.
- Describe the role of a meeting planner.
- Explain the primary responsibilities of a convention and visitors bureau or authority.
- List the steps in event management.

Historical Review

People have gathered to attend meetings, conventions, and expositions since ancient times, mainly for social, sporting, political, or religious purposes. As cities became regional centers, the size and frequency of such activities increased, and various groups and associations set up regular expositions.

Associations go back many centuries to the Middle Ages and before. The guilds in Europe were created during the Middle Ages to secure proper wages and maintain work standards. Associations began in the United States at the beginning of the eighteenth century, when the Rhode Island candle makers organized themselves.

Today, according to the American Society of Association Executives (ASAE), in the United States with 23,000 members, about 6,000 associations operate at the national level, and a 100,000 more function at the regional, state, and local levels. The association business is big business. Associations spend billions holding thousands of meetings and conventions that attract millions of attendees.

The hospitality and tourism industry itself consists of a number of associations, including the following:

- The American Hotel & Lodging Association
- The National Restaurant Association
- The International Association of Convention and Visitors Bureaus
- Hotel Sales and Marketing Association International
- Meeting Planners Association
- Association for Convention Operation Management
- Club Managers Association of America
- Professional Convention Management Association

Associations are the main independent political force for industries like hospitality, offering the following benefits:

- Governmental/political voice
- Marketing avenues
- Education
- Member services
- Networking

*Participants at an
Association Meeting*

Thousands of associations hold annual conventions at various locations across North America and the rest of the world. Some associations alternate their venues from east to central to west; others meet at fixed locations, such as the National Restaurant Association (NRA) show in Chicago or the American Hotel & Lodging Association (AH&LA) convention and show in New York.

Types of Meetings

Meetings are conferences, workshops, seminars, or other events designed to bring people together for the purpose of exchanging information. Meetings can take any one of the following forms:

Clinic: A workshop-type educational experience in which attendees learn by doing. A clinic usually involves small groups interacting with each other on an individual basis.

Forum: An assembly for the discussion of common concerns. Usually experts in a given field take opposite sides of an issue in a panel discussion, with liberal opportunity for audience participation.

Seminar: A lecture and a dialogue that allow participants to share experiences in a particular field. A seminar is guided by an expert discussion leader, and usually 30 or fewer persons participate.

Symposium: An event at which a particular subject is discussed by experts and opinions are gathered.

Workshop: A small group led by a facilitator or trainer. It generally includes exercises to enhance skills or develop knowledge in a specific topic.

Meetings are mostly organized by corporations, associations, or social, military, educational, religious, and fraternal groups **(SMERF).** The reasons for having a meeting can range from the presentation of a new sales plan to a total quality management workshop. The purpose of meetings is to affect behavior. For example, as a result of attending a meeting, a person should know or be able to do certain things. Some outcomes are very specific; others may be less so. For instance, if a meeting were called to brainstorm new ideas, the outcome might be less concrete than for other types of meetings. The number of people attending a meeting can vary.

Successful meetings require a great deal of careful planning and organization. In a major convention city, convention delegates spend approximately $423 per day, almost twice that of vacation travelers. Figure 13–1 shows convention delegates' spending in a convention city.

Meetings are set up according to the wishes of the client. The three main types of meeting setups are *theater style, classroom style,* and *boardroom style.* Theater style generally is intended for a large audience that does not need to make a lot of notes or refer to documents. This style usually consists of a raised platform and a lectern from which a presenter addresses the audience. Classroom setups are used when the meeting format is more instructional and participants need to take detailed notes or refer to documents. A workshop-type meeting often uses this

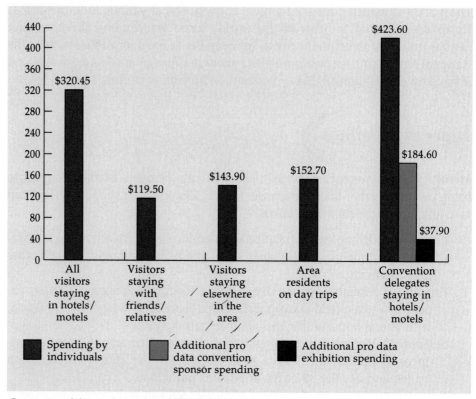

Convention delegates' spending in San Francisco

Figure 13–1 *Average Daily Visitor Spending at a Convention*

format. Boardroom setups are made for small numbers of people. The meeting takes place around one block rectangular table.

Expositions are events that bring together sellers of products and services at a location (usually a convention center) where they can show their products and services to a group of attendees at a convention or trade show. Exhibitors are an essential component of the industry because they pay to exhibit their products to the attendees. Exhibitors interact with attendees with the intention of making sales or establishing contacts and leads for follow-up. Expositions can take up several hundred thousand square feet of space, divided into booths for individual manufacturers or their representatives. In the hospitality industry, the two largest expositions are the AH&LA's annual New York show (held in November at the Javits Center) and the NRA's Annual Exposition (held every May in Chicago). Both events are well worth attending.

Conventions are generally larger meetings with some form of exposition or trade show included. A number of associations have one or more conventions per year. These conventions raise a large part of the association's budget. A typical convention follows a format like this:

- Welcome/registration
- Introduction of president
- President's welcome speech, opening the convention
- First keynote address by a featured speaker

NRA Show

- Exposition booths open (equipment manufacturers and trade suppliers)
- Several workshops or presentations on specific topics
- Luncheon
- More workshops and presentations
- Demonstrations of special topics (e.g., culinary arts for a hospitality convention)
- Vendors' private receptions
- Dinner
- Convention center closes

Figure 13–2 shows a convention event profile for a trade show.

Conventions are not always held in convention centers; in fact, the majority are held in large hotels over a three- to five-day period. The headquarters hotel is usually the one in which most of the activity takes place. Function space is allocated for registration, the convention, expositions, meals, and so on.

Associations used to be viewed as groups that held annual meetings and conventions with speeches, entertainment, an educational program, and social events. They have changed in activity and perception.

Check Your Knowledge

1. Define the five types of meetings.
2. What are the purposes of associations?
3. Name the major hospitality associations.
4. Describe the main types of meeting room setups.

Meetings, Incentives, Conventions, and Exhibitions

Meetings, incentive travel, conventions, and exhibitions (MICE)[1] represent a segment of the tourism industry that has grown dramatically in recent years. Gone are the days when a meeting planner's activities centered around organizing a wedding or an annual corporate dinner. Meeting planners in the

16:15:28   *San Diego*   Page: 1
                    Convention Center Corporation   9506059
                         EVENT PROFILE

EVENT STATISTICS

Event Name:	/6/San Diego Apartment Association Trade Show
Sales Person:	Joy Peacock
Event Manager:	Trish A. Stiles
ConVis Contact:	
Food Person:	
Event Tech.:	
Event Attend.:	
Nature of Event:	LT Local Trade Show
Event Parameter:	60 San Diego Convention Center
Business Type 1:	41 Association
Business Type 2:	91 LOCAL
Booking Status:	D Definite
Rate Schedule:	III Public Show, Meetings and Location
Open to Public:	No
Number Sessions:	1
Event Sold By:	F Facility (SDCCC)
Abbrev. Name:	/6/Apartment Assn
Est Bill Amount:	Rent - 6,060.00 Equip –
Last Changed On:	8/20/05 in: Comment Maintenance

ID:	9506059
Initial Contact:	8/3/2005
Move In Date:	6/22/2007
Move In Day:	Wednesday
Move In Time:	6:01 am
First Event Date:	6/23/2005
First Event Day:	Thursday
Start Show Time:	6:01 am
End Show Time:	11:59 pm
# of Event Days:	1
Move Out Date:	6/23/2005
Move Out Day:	Thursday
Out Time:	11:59 pm
Date Confirmed:	8/3/2004
Attend per Sesn:	3000
Tot Room Nights:	15
Public Release:	Yes
0.00 Food –	0.00

By – Joy Peacock

This Event has been in the facility before

CLIENT INFORMATION

Company: San Diego Apartment Assn, a non-profit Corporation
Contact Name: Ms. Leslie Cloud, Sales and Marketing Coord.
1011 Camino Del Rio South, Suite 200, San Diego, CA 92108
Telephone Number: (619) 297-1000
Fax Number: (619) 294-4510
Alternate Number: (619) 294-4510

ID: SDAA

Company: San Diego Apartment Assn, a non-profit Corporation
Alt Contact Name: Ms. Pamela A. Trimble, Finance & Operations Director
1011 Camino Del Rio South, Suite 200, San Diego, 92108
Telephone Number: (619) 297-1000
Fax Number: (619) 297-4510

EVENT LOCATIONS

ROOM	MOVE IN	IN USE	ED	MOVE OUT	BS	SEAT	RATE	EST. RENT	ATTEND
A	6/22/05 6:01 am	6/23/07	1	6/23/05 11:59 pm	D	E	III	6,060.00	5000
AS	6/22/05 6:01 am	6/23/07	1	6/23/05 11:59 pm	D	E	III	0.00	10
R01	6/22/05 6:01 am	6/23/07	1	6/23/05 11:59 pm	D	T	III	0.00	450
R02	6/22/05 6:01 am	6/23/07	1	6/23/05 11:59 pm	D	T	III	0.00	350
R03	6/22/05 6:01 am	6/23/07	1	6/23/05 11:59 pm	D	T	III	0.00	280
R04	6/22/05 6:01 am	6/23/07	1	6/23/05 11:59 pm	D	T	III	0.00	280
R05	6/22/05 6:01 am	6/23/07	1	6/23/05 11:59 pm	D	T	III	0.00	460

FOOD SERVICES

ROOM	DATE	TIME	BS ATTEND	EST. COST FOOD SERVICE

There are No Food Services booked for this event

Figure 13–2   *Convention Program* (Courtesy San Diego Convention Center)

San Diego
Convention Center Corporation
EVENT PROFILE

EVENT EQUIPMENT/SERVICES

ROOM   MOVE IN   IN USE   ED MOVE OUT   QUANTITY EQUIPMENT
There is No Equipment booked for this event

FOLLOW-UP/CHECKLIST ITEMS

FOLLOW-UP	DATE	ITEM	COMPLETED DATE	ASSIGN TO
	9/26/05	C DUE/date contracted		Vincent R. Magana
	8/22/05	c from sales	8/23/05	Sonia Michel
	8/22/05	c to licensee	8/23/05	Sonia Michel
	8/22/05	date c 1st printed	8/22/05	Sonia Michel

EVENT COMMENTS

8/3/05–JMP–This is a very strong hold for this group. CAD is pursuing a release of Hall A from Group Health and then this will be confirmed on a first option. Also holding an alternate date in April until this is released. All other rooms are clear.

200 BOOTHS – have used Carden in the past.
This is a trade show for the Apartment industry — products and services needed to keep a rental property in shape. Use Rooms 1–5 as seminar rooms. Trish has been the Event Coordinator for 2000 – 01.

8/18/05 - JMP-CAD has been able to clear Hall A on a first option for move-in on 22nd from Group Health. Made definite and requested Sonia produce a contract. NOTE TO SONIA: Contract should be signed and mailed to alternate contact Pam Trimble. Meeting logistics only will go through Leslie. Note to housekeeping: we did the cleaning for the 2003 show.

LICENSE AGREEMENT REQUEST

EVENT COMMENTS

Requested:	Saturday, 08/20/07, 2:56 pm
License #:	9506059
Sales Person:	JMP
Nature of Event:	Local Trade
Full Legal Name of Licensee:	Yes
Insurance Y/N:	Yes
Deposit Schedule:	50-50
Special Arrangements or Directions:	Contract should be signed and sent to alternate contact Pam Trimble. Leslie is responsible for meeting logistics only.
Gross Revenues F/B Revenue:	$1000 concessions
In House A/V Revenue:	$600
Security Revenue:	$200
Telecom. Revenue:	$220

(Below, identify MI/MO or event days and attendance for each event).
Other business in Center: GROUP HEALTH, definite, Hall B-1 (m/o 22nd), 3000ppl; ALCOHOLICS ANON, definite, Hall B, move-in; SECURITY EXPO, tentative, Hall C (m/i 22nd, show 23rd), 6600ppl; ENTRP. EXPO, contracted, Ballroom (m/i 23rd), 2000ppl.

Figure 13–2   *(continued)*

twenty-first century are required to have strong business and organizational skills to plan detail-driven, high-visibility events.

The MICE segment of the tourism industry can be especially lucrative. Industry statistics point to the fact that the average MICE tourist spends about twice the amount of money that other tourists spend.[2]

Increasingly meeting planners are under pressure to show a strong return on investment (ROI). This reflects a shift in this segment of the tourism industry to an important revenue source for organizations. Whether a meeting planner is organizing a meeting, a convention, or exhibition, the primary sources of revenue are as follows:

- Attendee registration fees
- Exhibit space rentals
- Sponsorship fees
- Conference program advertising fees

The pricing strategy for organizing events varies. Considerations include whether it is a consumer event or a trade event. For example, when organizing an event in which a large public attendance is desired, it may be best to keep attendance fees low in an effort to attract the largest number of attendees. In that case, the meeting planners would attempt to attract corporate sponsors, exhibitors, or advertisers to make up the difference in revenue.

Several factors are evaluated when determining the site. Considerations include facility location and service level, accessibility, hotel room availability, conference room availability, price, city, restaurant service and quality, personal safety, local attractions and geographic location, and hospitality.[3]

Meetings

Meetings are primarily conducted by either the corporate or nonprofit industries. Corporations in the medical, financial, and entertainment fields hold an extensive number of meetings—both for their employees and the public. Meetings are held primarily for the purposes of education, training, decision making, research, change, sales, team building, new product introduction, problem solving, strategy, or reorganization.

Meetings are often held as a marketing tool as well as a revenue source by associations, nonprofit entities, museums, performing arts organizations, and educational institutions. Estimates put association meeting expenditures collectively approaching $15 billion, while corporate expenditures are calculated at $10 billion. Meetings are generally held in hotels, conference centers, universities, corporate offices, or resorts, but more and more we find meetings housed in unique venues such as historic sites. With today's executives spending anywhere from 25 to 70 percent of their days in meetings, it is no wonder that the meeting planning profession has become such a high-growth career.

Whether a meeting is held as an in-house training event for internal employees or is designed as a mega-meeting attracting high-level international delegates, the average lead time required for organizing a meeting is three to six months. An effective meeting plan begins with defining a specific meeting objective. This objective will serve as a framework for determining the various choices that need to be made in organizing a meeting. The public statement of a meeting objective

FOCUS ON SECURITY

Meeting and Conference Safety

Hank and Lynne Christen

Corporations and organizations spend millions of dollars each year on conferences, meetings, trade shows, and other special events and both organizers and attendees expect and demand a safe and secure environment for their event.

While terrorism is a continuing national and international concern, criminal incidents, accidents, fires, and natural disasters are more common risks that create enormous liability for the facility hosting an event. Although these liabilities cannot be completely eliminated, there are considerations and precautions that lower the risks and minimize the consequences if an unforeseen problem occurs.

The following are some important steps for improving conference and meeting security at your hospitality facility:

- Safety and security are key parts of conference or event proposals and preplanning. It is critical that initial meetings and preconference security specifications clearly detail who, what, when, where, why, and how organizers and attendees will be protected.
- Once a conference or meeting is scheduled, develop a specific two-part crisis plan for the event. Begin by addressing preparation and prevention. The second part of the plan should focus on "what if" scenarios and establish contingency plans and strategies for reducing the impact of incidents on the guests and the event.
- Consider the international, national, and local political climate during an event. What is the national alert level? Is there local unrest or planned demonstrations? What is the current union–labor climate?
- Appoint a meeting and conference security specialist as the liaison between your facility and the meeting planners or organizers. If a problem or crisis occurs, leadership and communication are critical factors in handling the situation effectively.

- Provide attendees with personal safety guidelines and commonsense information that guests tend to overlook. Briefly outline emergency evacuation and bomb threat procedures.
- Remember that security extends beyond the actual event hours. Setup, breakdown, and overnight security are areas of vulnerability for security breaches.
- Today's attendees expect to see uniformed security. Professional and well-trained security guards or off-duty police officers help to deter crime and increase personal comfort levels.
- Conduct a thorough facility assessment prior to the event. Be alert for possible security breaches.
- Establish a relationship with local law enforcement and fire agencies. They can be valuable resources in your security assessment.
- Recognize the increased risks when high-profile politicians, religious leaders, and celebrities are present. Many VIPs have advance teams that are very proficient in security planning. Protecting high-profile guests requires protocols such as personal security, alias registration, medical coordination, and media planning.
- Establish an access control policy for employees and guests. Studies show that prominent identification deters unwanted guests and reduces security problems.
- Every employee is part of your event security team. Hold employee briefings, conduct frequent training, mandate a security exercise at least once a year to increase awareness, and reinforce responsibilities.

Realistically all conferences, meetings, and events involve some level of risk to your organization. There is no 100 percent way to prevent all problems; however, proactive safety and security planning and preparation greatly increase the odds for a successful, crisis-free event.

A speaker addresses a meeting at a convention center.

may differ from the internally defined objective. For example, a nonprofit association could serve as host of a conference to provide the public with information on a specific subject. At the same time, this nonprofit entity may count on this conference as a major fund-raising source. Goals for meetings are developed by the need to:

- Increase awareness of a particular issue
- Raise money for an activity or organization
- Provide information to colleagues or clients

Increase Awareness For associations and nonprofit entities, a frequent objective of meetings is to heighten awareness of the organization and gain public recognition and support.

Raise Money If the goal is to raise money, most decisions regarding the meeting will be driven by that goal. Meeting planners are increasingly concerned with ROI in organizing meetings. This is true whether the planner works for a private corporation or a nonprofit organization.

Provide Information In the information age, dissemination of information has become one of the major challenges in a changing, dynamic environment. Both public and private organizations are increasingly concerned with providing their employees with information on new products and services. This is a common motivation for meetings.

Incentives Over half of all meeting planners are involved in organizing incentive travel. The **incentive market** of MICE continues to experience rapid growth as meeting planners and travel agents organize incentive travel programs for corporate executives to reward them for reaching specific sales targets. Incentive trips generally vary from three to six days in length and can range from a moderate trip to an extremely lavish vacation for the employee and spouse. The most popular destination for incentive trips is Europe, followed closely by the Caribbean, Hawaii, Florida, and California.

Conventions Conventions are annual gatherings of a group of individuals, with no limit of numbers, who meet for a common interest. Conventions can vary from 75 people who meet on an annual basis to exchange information on a specific topic, such as collecting antique pottery, to the more than 50,000 individuals who annually gather at the Southern Baptist Convention.

Most conventions are housed in hotels, but conventions with the largest attendance are frequently held in city convention centers. Today conventions generally include an exhibition component, although it is not mandatory that they do so.

Exhibitions Just as meetings and conventions may be housed in a variety of types of venues, so may exhibitions. Large, state-of-the-art exhibitions are found at convention centers, but exhibition space may also be provided by large "convention" hotels as well as universities.

An exhibition may simply be a few table-top booths designed to display goods and services or an exhibition can be an elaborate, hallmark event such as the biannual Paris Air Show or Comdex. Comdex is the largest U.S. exhibition and is held annually in Las Vegas to showcase new computer products and services.

Today's exhibitions frequently include live demonstrations and seminars in addition to exhibit booths. **Convention centers** throughout the world compete to

Gamers in the Play Station Exhibit Area at the Electronic Entertainment Expo

host the largest exhibitions, which can be responsible for adding several million dollars in revenue to the local economy. As a result of this intense competition for housing of the most visible events, convention centers are under intense pressure to provide state-of-the-art technology, equipment, and service to exhibitors and meeting planners. Typically, exhibitions are either **consumer shows** or **trade shows.** Consumer shows such as a Boat Show or Auto Show are open to the general public. On the other hand, a trade show such as the Gift Show is available only to people employed by retail establishments selling gift items. Attendance at trade show events requires precertification and registration to participate. The convention industry has grown as more and more cities have added facilities to accommodate conventions, trade shows, and meetings. The increased number of centers has led to overbuilding and fiecer competition to attract conventions.

Forecast

The advent of technology and the Internet has dramatically affected the way tourism information is obtained for this business sector. Data are now available on virtually every aspect of business—from finance and investment to lifestyles and entertainment. The demand for this information has driven the increase in the numbers of meetings, conventions, and exhibitions.

While it was expected that information provided through technology would diminish the number of "live" or "face-to-face" meetings, the opposite has been the practice. In fact, the need for establishing personal contact has become more pronounced.

The nature of delivering meetings, however, has been impacted by technology in that data are now available in real time, via teleconferencing and satellite conferences. Another way that technology has influenced the delivery of meetings is from the perspective of the audience member, who increasingly expects a presentation to include illuminating, visual data.

New technology continues to drive changes in the industry. Planners utilize technology as a means of producing meetings more efficiently. Many organizational tasks are routinely managed by technology such as attendee registration, marketing, travel and housing, as well as delivering program proceedings. Other changes to appear during the next two years include the planning of more international meetings; increased family attendance at meetings; heightened security measures for attendees; shorter meetings due to financial constraints; more targeted; focused meetings, and testing the loyalty of attendees.[4]

Special Events and Off-Premise Catering[5]

The **special events** facet of the hospitality industry is the business of conceiving, designing, developing and producing ideas. Likewise, it is the business of details, timing, logistics, spacial mechanics, and organization. Typically, it includes teamwork and a dependence on vendor relationships. It also requires patience, flexibility, clear communication via written documents, and excellent listening and speaking skills. A sense of humor goes a long way also.

What is considered a special event? Special events come in many different sizes and markets:

Sporting events: golf tournaments, football tournaments, baseball tournaments, tennis tournaments, car races, balloon races
Festivals: arts and crafts, music
Corporate: incentive programs, grand openings, anniversaries, product launches
Convention: Spouse programs, incentive programs, sailing regattas, receptions and dinners, awards programs, team building
Social: birthdays, weddings, bar/bat mitzvahs, anniversaries, themed events, and just because

A special event incorporates the services of many vendors and suppliers. A special event organizer, producer, or coordinator will call on any one or several of the following services: florists, design and production houses, prop companies, transportation companies (buses and limousine, valet, or parking directors), bar catering services, rental companies, audiovisual experts, game and activity companies, entertainment agencies, printers and stationers, and temporary staffing agencies.

It is the *off-premise catering* consultant or special event consultant that conceives, develops, and expedites a vision. The vision takes on a life of its own via a theme that runs throughout the large picture of an event. The large picture includes the total ambiance: colors, fabrics and textiles, sizes and shapes (down to the type of dining chair), music and entertainment, functional and atmospheric lighting, and, of course, great food served graciously and expediently.

Catering, whether provided by a hotel, restaurant, or off-premise caterer, is central to the success of a special event. Quality, quantity, and timing are the key ingredients to the success of the food service. All the creativity and magnificence of an event may soon be forgotten if the execution of food service is less than excellent. Excellent catering requires a well-organized team that is able to anticipate the needs of the guests.

Know Your Client

An expert catering consultant will solicit information from the meeting planner to provide and satisfy the specific needs of a group. Significant information required to build a successful event includes, but is not limited to, the following:

- Group demographics: gender mix, age, profession, regional location, religious doctrine
- Conference/convention purpose
- Event date in relation to the rest of the meeting program
- Dietary preferences, restrictions, and special requests
- Meal and menu program for entire convention
- Past events held by the group
- Expected attendance number
- Event budget

All these are of equal importance, however, the budget carries the most weight. Knowing the budget before you go to the drawing board provides the consultant with the parameters by which you can design an event. The proposal process is now ready to begin.

The Special Event Job Market

Becoming a special event consultant or an off-premise catering/event specialist requires a delicate balance of many skills. Experience gained from several avenues will propel you to the heights of success. As with any career, an "experience ladder" must be climbed.

First, allow yourself to gain all the experience you can in the food and beverage aspect of the hospitality industry. If time and resources permit, it is highly recommended that you gain knowledge from a culinary arts program. Second, experience gained as a banquet food server in a high-volume convention or resort hotel property is invaluable. Also, paying your dues as a guest service agent at a hotel front desk or as a concierge provides you with the opportunity to hone your customer service skills. Promote yourself to a banquet manager or a CSM (convention service coordinator), which provides the opportunity to learn and perfect organizational skills—to which end is the ability to multitask and deal with hundreds of details simultaneously. After all, the business of special events is the business of managing details.

Events like weddings require detailed planning and organizing.

The next step is obtaining a sales position. An excellent appointment to aspire to is an executive meeting manager, sometimes called a small meeting manager, in a convention or conference hotel. Here, you are responsible for booking small room blocks (usually 20 rooms or fewer), making meeting room arrangements, meal plans, and audiovisual requirements. On a small scale, hundreds of details are coordinated for several groups at any one time. From this position, you may laterally move to a catering sales position within a hotel.

The catering sales position in a hotel will expose you to many different kinds of events: weddings, reunions, corporate events, holiday events, and social galas and balls. In this position, one either coordinates or has the opportunity to work with various vendors. This is where the florists, prop companies, lighting experts, entertainment agencies, rental companies, and audiovisual wizards come into play. Two to three years in this capacity grooms you for the next rung on the ladder.

Now, you can pursue several different angles: a promotion to a convention service manager within a hotel, moving into off-premise catering as a sales consultant, joining a production company, or perhaps affiliating yourself with a destination management company (DMC). Typically, without sales experience within a DMC, your first experience with them will be as an operations manager. Once proficient in this capacity, you then join the sales team.

After another two years creating and selling your heart out, you will be ready for the big leagues. The palette is now yours to paint your future. How about aspiring to be the next Super Bowl halftime creator and producer? Or perhaps creating the theme and schematics for the Olympics is in your future. Many avenues are available for exploring. Call on your marketing ideas, your business sense, your accounting skills, your aptitude for design, or your discriminating palette for creating unique entertaining and dining concepts. Continually educating yourself and discovering fresh ideas through adventurous experiences is essential to designing and selling special events. Don't forget to embark on as many internships as you can in the name of gaining knowledge and experience. Show your enthusiasm for what is different and unconventional. Know that creativity has no boundaries. Visualize the big picture and go for it!

Personal Profile: Carol C. Wallace

President and CEO, San Diego Convention Center Corporation

Carol Wallace was destined to be in charge from the time she was 12 years old. One of four children who grew up in a single-parent household, she was called upon at an early age to help out. Her mother, who finished high school only after her own children were grown, influenced her life tremendously. Often, she and her mother would sit down and talk about plans for the family's future, setting the stage for the rest of her life.

Carol adopted her mother's tough-love philosophy that "crying won't get me what I need, but hard work will." She earned a degree in English from Ohio State University in 1974. She married while in college and gave birth to two children. She would later divorce, becoming a single mother herself for several years.

Fresh out of college and eager to prove herself, she accepted a position with the Ohio Lung Association. During that time she had an opportunity to travel to Dallas, Texas, and loved the city so much that she moved there with her children. She immediately found an entry-level position with the Dallas Convention Center as an event manager. It took her less than a decade to rise through the ranks from event manager to the number two position, assistant general manager.

Just when it seemed as if she could go no further, the Denver Convention Center contacted her about a planned convention center expansion and offered her the number one position. This offer came as no surprise to those who knew Carol. By now, her reputation for being a leader and visionary was growing among industry movers and shakers.

In 1989, she moved her family to Denver and accepted the position as Executive Director of the Colorado Convention Center, then under construction. She joined the construction team, developed a management program, hired staff, and successfully opened the 960,000-square-foot facility in 1990.

Dallas and Denver proved to be the critical stepping stones that would lead Carol to her present position as President and CEO of the San Diego Convention Center Corporation. In 1991, San Diego city officials approached her with an offer to head up the San Diego Convention Center and an expansion that would double the size of the existing facility. She accepted the job and credits her successful career with her love of the industry and a willingness to take risks.

Since 1991, she has worked at the San Diego Convention Center Corporation and is responsible for a $27.7 million budget and overseeing three facilities: the world-class San Diego Convention Center, San Diego Concourse, and San Diego Civic Theater.

Under her leadership, the San Diego Convention Center opened a $216 million expansion in September 2001. The highly successful facility has twice been named one of the top three convention facilities in the world. It is also one of San Diego's most powerful engines, generating $4.5 million in economic impact and $24.8 million in operating revenues annually.

As the corporation's president and CEO, Carol exudes confidence as a leader and sets high expectations for herself—she's not afraid of hard work. As someone who worked her way to the top from the bottom, she enjoys working hard in an industry that she loves.

Carol is active in a variety of industry groups. She is the past president of the International Association of Assembly Managers. Recently she was selected as one of nine industry commissioners for the Accepted Practices Exchange Commission. She currently holds a board position for the International Association for Exhibition Management. Other professional affiliations include the Professional Convention Management Association, the American Society of Association Executives, and the International Convention Center Association.

Carol is the recipient of numerous awards. In October 2000, she received The Manpower Balance Award at the Women Who Mean Business Awards Dinner, making her the first woman in the convention industry to receive this recognition for her commitment to her family, community, and profession.

She serves on the board of directors for Alliant International University, San Diego and Narobi, Africa; the San Diego Hotel-Motel Association; the San Diego Convention and Visitors Bureau; the San Diego Rotary Club; and the San Diego Chamber of Commerce.

Key Players in the Industry

The need to hold face-to-face meetings and attend conventions has grown into a multibillion dollar industry. Many major and some smaller cities have convention centers with nearby hotels and restaurants.

The major players in the convention industry are convention and visitors bureau (CVBs) meeting planners and their clients, the convention centers, specialized services, and exhibitions. The wheel diagram in Figure 13–3 shows the number of different people and organizations involved with meetings, conventions, and expositions.

Meeting Planners

Meeting planners may be independent contractors who contract out their services to both associations and corporations as the need arises or they may be full-time employees of corporations or associations. In either case, meeting planners have interesting careers. There are thousands of full- and part-time meeting planners who work in the United States.

The professional meeting planner not only makes hotel and meeting bookings but also plans the meeting down to the last minute, always remembering to check to ensure that the services contracted for have been delivered. In recent years, the technical aspects of audiovisual and simultaneous translation equipment have added to the complexity of meeting planning.

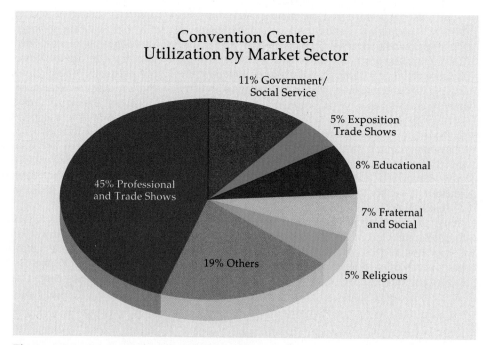

Figure 13–3   *Major Players in the Convention Industry*

The meeting planner's role varies from meeting to meeting, but may include some or all of the following activities:[6]

Premeeting Activities

- Plan meeting agenda
- Establish meeting objectives
- Predict attendance
- Set meeting budget
- Select meeting site
- Select meeting facility
- Select hotel(s)
- Negotiate contracts
- Plan exhibition
- Prepare exhibitor correspondence and packet
- Create marketing plan
- Plan travel to and from site
- Arrange ground transportation
- Organize shipping
- Organize audiovisual needs

On-Site Activities

- Conduct pre-event briefing
- Prepare executive plan
- Move people in/out
- Troubleshoot
- Approve invoices

Postmeeting Activities

- Debrief
- Evaluate
- Provide recognition and appreciation
- Arrange shipping
- Plan for next year

The meeting planner has several critical interactions with hotels, including negotiating the room blocks and rates. Escorting clients on site inspections gives the hotel an opportunity to show their level of facilities and service. The most important interaction is normally with the catering/banquet/conference department associates, especially the services manager, maître d', and captains; these front-line associates can make or break a meeting. For example, meeting planners often send boxes of meeting materials to hotels expecting the hotel to automatically know which meeting they are for. On more than one occasion, they have ended up in the hotel's main storeroom, much to the consternation of the meeting planner.

Fortunately for most meeting planners, once they have taken care of a meeting one year, subsequent years typically are very similar.

Convention centers and hotels provide meeting space and accommodations as well as food and beverage facilities and service. The convention center and a hotel team from each hotel capable of handling the meeting will attempt to impress the meeting planner. The hotel sales executive will send particulars of the

Meeting Planners at Site Inspection

hotel's meeting space and a selection of banquet menus and invite the meeting planner for a site inspection. During the site inspection, the meeting planner is shown all facets of the hotel, including the meeting rooms, guest sleeping rooms, the food and beverage outlets, and any special facility that may interest the planner or the client.

Convention and Visitors Bureaus

Convention and visitors bureaus (CVBs) are a major player in the meetings, conventions, and expositions market. The International Association of Convention and Visitors Bureaus (IACVB) describes a CVB as a not-for-profit umbrella organization that represents an urban area that tries to solicit business- or pleasure-seeking visitors.

The convention and visitors bureau comprises a number of visitor industry organizations representing the various industry sectors:

- Transportation
- Hotels and motels
- Restaurants
- Attractions
- Suppliers

The bureau represents these local businesses by acting as the sales team for the city. A bureau has four primary responsibilities:

1. To encourage groups to hold meetings, conventions, and trade shows in the area it represents
2. To assist those groups with meeting preparations and to lend support throughout the meeting
3. To encourage tourists to partake of the historic, cultural, and recreational opportunities the city or area has to offer
4. To develop and promote the image of the community it represents[7]

The outcome of these four responsibilities is for the cities' tourist industry to increase revenues. Bureaus compete for business at trade shows, where interested visitor industry groups gather to do business. For example, a tour wholesaler who is promoting a tour will need to link up with hotels, restaurants, and attractions to package a vacation. Similarly, meeting planners are able to consider several locations and hotels by visiting a trade show. Bureaus generate leads (prospective clients) from a variety of sources. One source, associations, have national/international offices in major cities like Washington, D.C. (so that they can lobby the government), New York, Chicago, and San Francisco.

Check Your Knowledge

1. What are the primary sources of revenue for meetings, conventions, or exhibitions?
2. Describe the incentive market.
3. What is the difference between a consumer and a trade show?
4. Explain what a CVB is.

A number of bureaus have offices or representatives in these cities or a sales team who will make follow-up visits to the leads generated at trade shows. Alternatively, they will make cold calls on potential prospects, such as major associations, corporations, and incentive houses. The sales manager will invite the meeting, convention, or exposition organizer to make a **familiarization (FAM) trip** to do a site inspection. The bureau assesses the needs of the client and organizes transportation, hotel accommodations, restaurants, and attractions accordingly. The bureau then lets the individual properties and other organizations make their own proposals to the client. Figure 13–4 shows the average expenditure per delegate per stay by the convention type. Figure 13–5 indicates the percentage of each item of an expenditure.

Convention Centers

Convention centers are huge facilities where meetings and expositions are held. Parking, information services, business centers, and food and beverage facilities are all included in the centers.

Usually convention centers are corporations owned by county, city, or state governments and operated by a board of appointed representatives from the various groups having a vested interest in the successful operation of the center. The board appoints a president or general manager to run the center according to a predetermined mission, and goals and objectives.

Convention centers have a variety of exposition and meeting rooms to accommodate both large and small events. The centers generate revenue from the rental of space, which frequently is divided into booths (one booth is about 100 square feet). Large exhibits may take several booths' space. Additional revenue is generated by the sale of food and beverages, concession stand rentals, and vending machines. Many centers also have their own subcontractors to handle staging, construction, lighting, audiovisual, electrical, and communications.

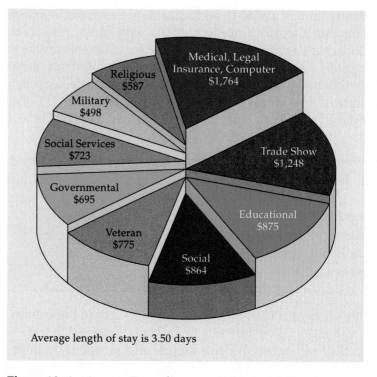

Average length of stay is 3.50 days

Figure 13–4   *Average Expenditure per Delegate per Stay by Convention Type*

In addition to the megaconvention centers, a number of prominent centers also contribute to the local, state, and national economies. One good example is the Rhode Island Convention Center. The $82 million center, representing the second largest public works project in the state's history, is located in the heart of downtown Providence, adjacent to the 14,500-seat Providence Civic Center. The 365,000-square foot center offers a 100,000-square-foot main exhibit hall, a 20,000-square-foot ballroom, 18 meeting rooms, and a full-service kitchen that can produce 5,000 meals per day. The exhibit hall divides into four separate halls, and the facility features its own telephone system, allowing individualized

Where do attendees spend their money?		
Lodging and Incidentals	$126.45	(47.6%)
Food and Beverage	$76.16	(28.7%)
Entertainment/Recreation	$8.29	(3.1%)
Retail	$29.16	(11.0%)
Transportation	$25.30	(9.5%)
Other	$0.17	(0.1%)
Total daily spend for delegates:	$265.53	

Figure 13–5   *Where do Attendees Spend Their Money?*

A Day in the Life of Kathleen Doeller
Director of Catering, The Estancia LaJolla Hotel and Spa, San Diego, CA

Every day is different, but much is the same. I do have a routine operations meeting every morning at 9:00 A.M., a sales meeting with my team every Friday morning at 7:45 A.M., and a 2:00 P.M. meeting with the banquet managers every day. On the other days, after returning from the gym, I meditate for thirty minutes and review my daily appointment calendar. I dress according to the day's schedule of appointments and events. Unfortunately, the San Diego freeways are jammed early, so with a jumbo mug of java in hand, I'm out the door without any delay by 6:00 A.M.

Upon my arrival at the hotel, I make my rounds and greet all my team members in the laundry, the kitchen, purchasing, banquets, sales and convention services. I immediately get connected on a two-way radio and listen to the status of the day's activities. I then retreat to my office, check my voicemail (yes, clients and employees do leave messages at all hours of the night), check my e-mail, and then review my To Do list. Checking the night manager's report and the engineering report on e-mail gives me a good idea of the state of the hotel. If I have groups or a contact in house, I find them in their assigned meeting room and greet them and inquire as to whether there is anything I can do to enhance their day.

I process anywhere from one to five creative proposals per day. It takes an immense amount of brain juice to creatively customize themes, schemes, and details for various clients. Predominantly, I handle the social market: weddings, religious celebrations, charitable galas, and some corporate events. And, in this day of technology, everybody wants it *now!* I do have an open-door policy, which sometimes is construed as "come on in anytime." Needless to say, interruptions do occur. In addition to responding to inquiries and requests for proposals, a schedule of follow-up calls is made in an attempt to close a sale. Plus, vendor purchases and operational details are worked out on those accounts that have gone definite (i.e., the sale has closed).

As well as wearing a "sales consultant's hat," I handle the marketing for the catering department. Therefore, in the course of a day, I schedule and coordinate trade shows, attend trade association meetings, serve on committees, participate on educational panels, counsel personnel, draw event diagrams, and meet with prospective clients for walk-site tours of the hotel. As The Estancia LaJolla is a new resort conference center—open since June of 2004—there are many curious people who want a private tour of the ten-acre hotel and spa property.

On the days that I have events and clients on the property, I am well ahead of event time and checking the timing of the event, the room set, vendor arrivals, and reviewing last-minute details with the banquet manager. Once the catering captain and his or her staff arrive, I pass the baton to them. I confer with the Front Desk Manager regarding valet for the event, check garden and walkway lighting, confer with housekeeping as to attendants' schedules for events and public space, and ensure that the event room is picture-perfect for guest arrival.

Financial responsibility also falls into my role. I review our sales pace report and definite bookings report on a daily basis, and I review these reports with my staff on Friday mornings. It is at these meetings that I also coach and mentor my team to learn new ways to improve their performance and resolve any challenges they may be facing with regard to sales and operations.

Being organized and a guru of time management is mandatory in this position. Patience, a passion for customer service, and continual diligence in doing better than your best are common denominators in succeeding with a great, high-end hotel company. Excellence is made up of consistency, a positive attitude, open-mindedness, motivation to exceed your previous best, and a willingness to help others along the way.

The common denominator in my life is *balance*. Balance requires an ever-present state of mind, and I do actually schedule quiet time and self-time. I do my meditation in my beautiful garden, I exercise regularly, and I treat myself to dining experiences at new restaurants with friends and family. Random getaways are also important to renew my spirit, mind, and body. A change of scenery is good for everyone, in my opinion. Jaunts to the cool pines in the mountains as well as experiencing cosmopolitan cities refresh all of my senses. The world has so much to offer and experience, if only I could see and do it all!

I have learned that the course a life takes is based on choices. Responsibility is always attached to a choice. Knowing that and accepting the responsibility—and the outcome of the choice—are the growing and learning steps of life. Blending responsibilities with pleasure, spirituality, family, and friends, and proceeding by keeping one's values and ethics in check will yield balance and a zest for great things in one's life. I mix and blend this recipe every day . . . knowing that it works . . . knowing that it keeps me strong . . . knowing that it is all in the course of a day.

A registration area at the Jacob K. Javits Convention Center in New York City

billing. A special rotunda function room at the front of the building features glass walls that offer a panoramic view of downtown Providence for receptions of up to 365 people. Extensive use of glass on the facade of the center provides ample natural light throughout the entrance and prefunction areas.

A convention center can draw millions of new dollars into the economy of the city in which it is located.

Event Management

Event management can be as small as an office outing to something larger like a music festival and on up to a Super Bowl or even the Olympics. Events can be on-off, annual or perennial (happening each year), or every four years, as for the Olympics. Things just do not happen by themselves; it takes a great deal of preparation to stage a successful event. To hold a successful event, the organizer should have a vision and leader–manager skills in the key result areas: marketing, financial, operational, and legal. Getting good sponsorship is a big help. Sponsors provide money or in-kind contributions and receive recognition as a sponsor of the event, including use or display of their logo in the events promotion. Sponsors expect to get something in return for their sponsorship, so give them something tangible that will help their corporation or organization. Each year thousands go to festivals and events of all kinds, and most, if not close to all, receive some sponsorship, because it is too costly to stage an event without sponsorship.

Event management requires special skills in marketing and sales (attracting the business in the first place); planning (to ensure all details are covered and that everything will be ready on time); organization (to make sure all the key staff know what to do, why, when, where, and how); financial (a budget needs to be made and kept to); human resources and motivation (the best people need to be selected and recruited, trained and motivated); and lots of patience and attention to details and endless checking up on them.

To gain business, event managers prepare a proposal for the client's approval and contract signature. There are some important how-to's in preparing an event proposal: Find out as much information as possible about the event (if it has been previously held) or what the client really has in mind. Ask organizers, attendees, providers, and others what went right and what went wrong or could be improved on next time the event is organized. Write the proposal in business English, no verbal foliage. Get creative—do something different and better and give them something to talk about; finally, do the numbers—nobody wants a surprise—do a pro-forma invoice so the client will know the costs, and surprise them by being on time and on budget.

An event can be costly to put on; in addition to advertising there is a location charge, security costs, labor costs, and production costs (this may be food, beverage, and service, but also the staging and decor). Usually, the event manager has a good estimate of the number of ticket sales expected. She then budgets the costs to include the entertainment and all other costs, leaving a reasonable profit.

Event management also takes place at convention centers and hotels, where event managers handle all the arrangements after the sales manager has completed the contract.

The larger convention center events are planned years in advance. As stated earlier, the convention and visitors bureau is usually responsible for the booking of conventions more than 18 months ahead. Obviously, both the convention and visitors bureau and the convention center marketing and sales teams work closely with each other. Once the booking becomes definite, the senior event manager assigns an event manager to work with the client throughout the sequence of pre-event, event, and postevent.

The *booking manager* is critical to the success of the event by booking the correct space and working with the organizers to help them save money by

The Providence Convention Center

Corporate Profile: Las Vegas Convention and Visitors Authority

The Las Vegas Convention and Visitors Authority (LVCVA) is one of the top convention and visitors bureaus, charged with the following mission: "To attract to the Las Vegas area a steadily increasing number of visitors to support the hotel and motel room inventory in Clark County."

The Las Vegas Convention and Visitors Authority hosts hundreds of conventions attended by more than a million delegates. The LVCVA is organized in the following way: State law establishes the number, appointment, and terms of the authority's board of directors. A 12-member board provides guidance and establishes policies to accomplish the LVCVA mission.

Seven members are elected officials of the county, and each represents one of the incorporated cities therein; the remaining five members are nominated by the Las Vegas

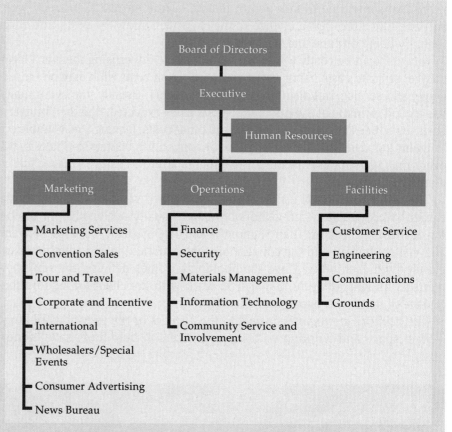

Organizational Chart, Las Vegas Convention and Visitors Authority

Chamber of Commerce and represent different segments of the industry. The board is one of the most successful public/private partnerships in the country. Under the presidency of Manuel J. Cortez, the Las Vegas Convention and Visitors Authority and its board of directors have received numerous awards, among them the following:

- World's Leading Tourist and Convention Board
- World's Leading Conference and Convention Center
- World's Leading Gaming Destination
- Top North American Tourist and Convention Board

The Las Vegas Convention and Visitors Authority's organizational structure is shown above. The board of directors employs a president (executive) to serve as chief executive officer. Other members of the executive staff are vice-president marketing, vice-president operations, and vice-president facilities. The marketing division's first priority is to increase the number of visitors to Las Vegas and southern Nevada. The division is composed of eight teams that specialize in various market segments to increase the number of visitors and convention attendance. The teams are also shown above.

The marketing services team is responsible for providing visitor services including research, registration, convention housing, hotel/motel reservations, and visitor information. The research team tracks the dynamics of the Las Vegas and Clark County tourism marketplace, along with the competitive gaming and tourism environment. The registration department coordinates and provides temporary help for conventions and trade shows being held in Las Vegas. The housing division receives and processes hotel and motel housing forms from convention and trade show delegates, forwarding the reservations to participating hotels daily. The reservations department operates toll-free telephone lines, transferring the calls of travel agents, tourists, conventioneers, and special event attendees to hotels and motels within a requested location and price range.

Five visitor centers operate in Jean, Boulder City, Mesquite, Laughlin, and Las Vegas seven days a week and serve more than 38,000 visitors a month. A brochure room supports the visitor centers by answering thousands of telephone calls and letters requesting a variety of information on Las Vegas including recreation, weddings, entertainment, and special events. The staff sends out posters, brochures, and other information.

The convention sales team coordinates convention sales efforts at the Authority and contributes to the success of convention sales citywide by providing sales leads to the hotels. Sales managers travel throughout the United States and the world, meeting with association meeting planners to sell the benefits of holding conventions in Las Vegas. Members of the team also attend numerous conventions and trade shows where they host or sponsor special events and functions to entice conventions and trade shows to Las Vegas.

With a market share of 88 percent of leisure travelers visiting Las Vegas, travel promotion is vital to the LVCVA. The tour and travel team is responsible for positioning Las Vegas as a complete and affordable destination, and the preeminent gaming and entertainment capital of the world. Because 30 percent of all leisure travelers use a travel agent, the tour and travel team aggressively markets Las Vegas with travel agents.

Familiarization trips for travel agents are conducted by team members to generate enthusiasm and excitement around Las Vegas bookings. Travel agent presentations are also scheduled in both primary and selected secondary airline market cities. Similar events are also scheduled for Laughlin, which also advertises a 1–800 number for tourism information.

The corporate and incentive markets are traditionally considered the high end of the travel industry. These buyers are extremely sophisticated and value conscious and are looking for the highest-quality facilities and amenities. Corporate and incentive team members attend various trade shows throughout the United States and Canada, as well as selected cities in Europe and Asia, promoting Las Vegas as a complete, value-oriented, flexible, and accessible resort destination for corporate meetings.

With increases in visitation from almost every country, the LVCVA's international team is charged with maintaining a high profile in the international marketplace, positioning Las Vegas and southern Nevada as the preferred destination and the gateway to the West. Team members travel throughout the world, from the Pacific Rim countries of Japan, Korea, and Taiwan to the European countries of Germany, Switzerland, France, and Austria, as well as to Canada and South America. Team sales executives provide information, brochures, and sales material in foreign languages emphasizing Las Vegas as a world-class, full-service resort destination.

In recent years, wholesale travel has been one of the fastest growing segments of the Las Vegas tourism market. During the past three years, the wholesale market has increased more than 75 percent, and the wholesaler team positions Las Vegas as a destination without limits on the variety of packages and activities that can be arranged. To provide education on the variety of activities offered by Las Vegas, the wholesaler team plans and implements several annual familiarization tours for wholesalers.

Annual Special Events

- Las Vegas Senior Classic
- Las Vegas Invitational
- National Finals Rodeo
- Big League Weekend
- Las Vegas Bowl
- Laughlin River Days
- Laughlin River Flight
- Laughlin Rodeo Days

In recent years, special event planners have also showed increased interest in Las Vegas and Laughlin as event destinations. Team members travel to several special event trade shows and conferences to maximize the opportunities for special events to be held in Las Vegas. The team works in cooperation with Las Vegas Events and the Laughlin Marketing Partners to aggressively pursue events that provide television exposure and draw large numbers of participants, spectators, and visitors.

Las Vegas Territory Matching Grant Funds

The Las Vegas Territory grants program provides funding for the advertising and promotion of special events in rural Clark County to attract visitors to the outlying areas. These events create a more enhanced vacation experience and provide a variety of additional activities for the Las Vegas visitor. Some examples are Boulder City Art in the Park, Henderson Industrial Days, Mesquite Arts Festival, NLV Parade of Many Cultures, and Mt. Charleston Festival in the Pines.

Travelers responded to the new advertising theme—"A World of Excitement in One Amazing Place"—and the Las Vegas tourism and convention business continues to flourish.

The advertising team is responsible for developing the general marketing strategy that provides a blueprint for the development of specific marketing initiatives, advertisements, and public relations efforts. These strategies are incorporated into each division of the marketing department.

The Las Vegas News Bureau is a part of the LVCVA. The news bureau provides information about Las Vegas and southern Nevada through direct contact with national and international freelance journalists and working members of print and broadcast media. The bureau also maintains a complete photographic collection of Las Vegas, depicting the resort and entertainment growth of the area over a period of almost 50 years.

The operations department provides administrative support services to the marketing and facilities divisions, as well as security for the entire authority.

Finance

The finance division maintains a general accounting system for the authority to ensure accountability in compliance with legal provisions and in accordance with generally accepted accounting principles. Finance is composed of financial services, accounting, and payroll activities. Additional responsibilities include the preparation of the authority's annual financial report (CAFR) and the annual budget. The CAFR has received the Government Finance Officers Association (GFOA) Excellence in Financial Reporting Award a number of times in recent years.

Materials Management

Materials management supports the marketing, operations, and facilities divisions by providing for purchasing of materials, services, and goods needed to meet its goals and objectives. Materials management is responsible for the storage and distribution of various supply items through an extensive warehousing program, as well as through printing and mail distribution.

Security

The security division provides protection of authority property, equipment, employees, and convention attendees 24 hours a day, 365 days a year, and also oversees

```
                        /Finance
                        /Security
OPERATIONS — Materials Management
                        /Information Technology
                        /Community Service and Involvement
```

Activities within Operations Department

paid parking and fire safety functions. The team patrols both the convention center and Cashman Field properties and is trained in first aid assistance. Several officers have been recognized by the authority board and convention organizations for providing life-saving measures to convention attendees.

Information Technology

The information technology division (ITD) is responsible for efficiently and effectively meeting the automation and information needs of the authority. ITD sustains a staff of technically competent professionals to design, maintain, implement, and operate the systems necessary to support the goals of the authority.

Rental Waiver Program

The LVCVA successfully runs an annual rental waiver program that provides $100,000 in grant money for in-kind use of Cashman Field facilities and equipment. Dozens of legitimate, registered Nevada nonprofit groups use the facility each year, transforming Cashman Field into a virtual civic center.

The LVCVA's research division tracks trends and statistics that give an accurate picture of the tremendous growth in southern Nevada from 1984 through 2004. The LVCVA's unique structure—housing both the building management and marketing teams within the same organization—has produced significant operational efficiencies and resulted in the optimal use of facilities.

Funding for the bureau comes mainly from the transient occupancy tax (TOT). This is a tax on hotel accommodations that the city charges all its visitors. The amount of the tax varies from about 10 to 19.25 percent. Over a year, this adds up to millions of dollars. Only a part of the TOT tax goes to the CVB; most of it goes into the city's general fund or to fund specific projects. The balance of the bureau's budget comes from members fees and promotions.

The author gratefully acknowledges that this section draws on information given by the Las Vegas Convention and Visitors Authority.

allocating only the space really needed and allowing the client to begin setting up on time. A contract is written based on the event profile. The event profile stipulates in writing all the client's requirements and gives relevant information, such as which company will act as decorator subcontractor to install carpets and set up the booths.

The contract requires careful preparation because it is a legal document and will guarantee certain provisions. For example, the contract may specify that the booths may only be cleaned by center personnel or that food may be prepared for samples only, not for retail. After the contract has been signed and returned by the client, the event manager will from time to time make follow-up calls until about 6 months before the event when arrangements such as security, business services, and catering will be finalized.

The event manager is the key contact between the center and the client. She or he will help the client by introducing approved subcontractors who are able to provide essential services. Figure 13–6 shows a job description for an event manager.

Two weeks prior to the event, an event document is distributed to department heads. The *event document* contains all the detailed information that each department needs to know in order for the event to run smoothly. About ten days before the event, a WAG meeting (week at a glance) is held. The WAG meeting is one of the most important meetings at the convention center because it provides an opportunity to avoid problems—like two event groups arriving at the same time or additional security for concerts or politicians. About this same time, a preconvention or pre-expo meeting is held with expo managers and their contractors—shuttle bus managers, registration operators, exhibit floor managers, and so on.

Once the setup begins, service contractors marshall the eighteen-wheeler trucks to unload the exhibits by using radio phones to call the trucks from a nearby depot. When the exhibits are in place, the exposition opens and the public is admitted. Figure 13–7 shows an event document for the Sixth International Boat Show at the San Diego Convention Center. It gives information regarding the exact amount of space allocated, the contact person, and the schedule of events.

Specialized Services

A number of companies offer specialized services such as transportation, entertainment, audiovisual, escorts and tour guides, convention setup, and destination management.

Check Your Knowledge

1. What are the functions of a meeting planner?
2. Explain a FAM trip.
3. Describe the functions of a booking manager.

SAN DIEGO CONVENTION CENTER

EVENT MANAGER

DEFINITION

Under moderate direction from the services manager, plans, directs, and supervises assigned events and represents services manager on assigned shifts.

KEY RESPONSIBILITIES

- Plans, coordinates, and supervises all phases of the events to include set-ups, move ins and outs, and the activities themselves
- Prepares and disseminates set-up information to the proper departments well in advance of the activity, and ensures complete readiness of the facilities
- Responsible for arranging for all services needed by the tenant
- Coordinates facility staffing needs with appropriate departments
- Acts as a consultant to tenants and the liaison between in-house contractors and tenants
- Preserves facility's physical plant and ensures a safe environment by reviewing tenants' plans; requests and makes certain they comply with facility, state, county, and city rules and regulations
- Prepares accounting paperwork of tenant charges, approves final billings, and assists with collection of same
- Resolves complaints, including operational problems and difficulties
- Assists in conducting surveys, gathering statistical information, and working on special projects as assigned by services manager
- Conducts tours of the facilities

MINIMUM REQUIREMENTS

- Bachelor's degree in hospitality management, business, or recreational management from a fully accredited university or college, plus two (2) years of experience in coordinating major conventions and trade shows
- Combination of related education/training and additional experience may substitute for bachelor's degree
- An excellent ability to manage both fiscal and human resources
- Knowledge in public relations; oral and written communications
- Experienced with audiovisual equipment

225 Broadway, Suite 710 • San Diego, CA 92102 • (619) 239-1989
FAX (619) 239-2030
Operated by the San Diego Convention Center Corporation

Figure 13–6 *Job Description for an Event Manager (Courtesy San Diego Convention Center)*

EVENT DOCUMENT
REVISED COPY
/6/SAN DIEGO INTERNATIONAL BOAT SHOW
Tuesday, January 4, 2005–Tuesday, January 11, 2005

SPACE: Combined Exhibit Halls AB, Hall A - How Manager's Office, Box Office by Hall A, Hall B –
Show Manager's Office, Mezzanine Room 12, Mezzanine Room 13, Mezzanine Rooms 14 A&B, AND
Mezzanine Rooms 15 A&B

CONTACT: Mr. Jeff Hancock
National Marine Manufacturers Association, Inc.
4901 Morena Blvd.
Suite 901
San Diego, CA 92117
Telephone Number: (619) 274-9924
Fax Number: (619) 274-6760
Decorator Co.:   Greyhound Exposition Services
Sales Person: Denise Simenstad
Event Manager: Jane Krause
Event Tech.:   Sylvia A. Harrison

SCHEDULE OF EVENTS:

Monday, January 3, 2005   5:00 am–6:00 pm   Combined Exhibit Halls AB
Service contractor move in GES,
Andy Quintena

Tuesday, January 4, 2005   8:00 am–6:00 pm   Combined Exhibit Halls AB
Service contractor move in GES,
Andy Quintena

12:00 pm–6:00 pm   Combined Exhibit Halls AB
Exhibitor move in

Wednesday, January 5, 2005   8:00 am–6:00 pm   Combined Exhibit Halls AB
Exhibitor move in
Est. attendance: 300

Thursday, January 5, 6005   8:00 am–12:00 pm   Combined Exhibit Halls AB
Exhibitor final move in

11:30 am–8:30 pm   Box Office by Hall A
OPEN: Ticket prices, Adults $6, Children 12 & under $3

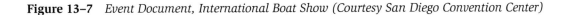

Figure 13–7   *Event Document, International Boat Show (Courtesy San Diego Convention Center)*

Trends in Conventions, Meetings, and Expositions

- *Globalization/international participation:* More people are going abroad to attend meetings.
- *The cloning of shows:* Some international shows do not travel very well (i.e., agricultural machinery). Thus, organizations such as Bleinheim or Reed Exposition Group airlift components and create shows in other countries.
- *Competition:* Competitiveness has increased among all destinations. Convention centers will expand and new centers will come online.
- *Technology:* The industry needs to be more sophisticated. The need for fiber optics is present everywhere.
- Shows are growing at a rate of 5 to 10 percent per year.
- Compared to a few years ago, large conventions are not as well attended, and the regional conventions have more attendees.
- Boom in the number of convention centers

CASE STUDY

Double-Booked

The convention bureau in a large and popular convention destination has jurisdiction over the convention center. A seasoned convention sales manager, who has worked for the bureau for seven years and produces more sales than any other sales manager, has rebooked a 2,000-person group for a three-day exposition in the convention center. The exposition is to take place two years from the booking date.

The client has a 15-year history of holding conventions, meetings, and expositions in this convention center and has always used the bureau to contract all space and services for them. In fact, the sales manager handling the account has worked with the client for 7 of the 15 years. The bureau considers this client a "preferred customer."

The convention group meeting planner also appears in a magazine ad giving a testimony of praise for the convention bureau, this particular sales manager, and the city as a destination for conventions.

Shortly after the meeting planner rebooks this convention with the bureau, the bureau changes sales administration personnel, not once, but three times. This creates a challenge for the sales managers in terms of producing contracts, client files, and event profiles, and in the recording and distribution of information. The preferred customer who re-booked has a contract, purchase orders for vendor services, a move in and setup agenda, and an event profile, all supplied by the sales manager. The sales manager has copies of these documents as well. The two hotels where the group will be staying also have contracts for the VIP group.

As is the nature of this particular bureau, other sales managers have been booking and contracting space for the same time period as the group that rebooked. In fact, the exhibit hall has been double-booked, as have the break-out rooms for seminars, workshops, and food and beverage service. The groups that were contracted later are all first-time users of the facility.

This situation remains undetected until ten days prior to the groups' arrival. It is brought to the attention of the bureau and the convention center only when the sales manager distributes a memo to schedule a preconvention meeting with the meeting planner and all convention center staff.

Due to the administrative personnel changes, necessary information was not disseminated to key departments and key personnel. The convention center was never notified that space had been contracted for the preferred customer. The preferred customer has been told about this potentially catastrophic situation. Now there is a major dilemma to rectify.

Discussion Questions

1. Ultimately, who is responsible for decision making with regard to this situation?
2. What steps should be taken to remedy this situation?
3. Are there fair and ethical procedures to follow to provide space for the preferred customer? If so, what are they?
4. What measures, if any, should be taken in handling the seasoned sales manager?
5. What leverage does the meeting planner have to secure this and future business with the bureau?
6. List five ramifications if the preferred customer is denied space and usage of the convention center.
7. How can this situation be avoided in the future?

CASE STUDY

Not Enough Space

Denise is the sales manager of a large convention center. A client has requested an exhibition that would not only bring excellent revenue but is an annual event that several other convention centers would like to host.

Exhibitions typically take one or two days to set up, with three or four days of exhibition, and one day to break down. Professional organizations handle each part of the set-up and breakdown.

When Denise checks the space available on the days requested for the exhibition, she notices that another exhibition is blocking a part of the space needed by her client.

Question

1. What can Denise do to get this exhibition to use the convention center without inconveniencing either exhibition too much?

CAREER INFORMATION

Meetings, incentive travel, conventions, and expositions (the MICE segment) offer a broad range of career paths. Successful meeting planners are detail-oriented, organized people who not only plan and organize meetings, but also negotiate hotel rooms and meeting space in hotels and convention centers.

Incentive travel includes aspects of organizing high-end travel, hotels, restaurants, attractions and entertainment. With big budgets this can be an exciting career for those interested in a combination of travel and hotels in exotic locations.

Conventions and convention centers have several career paths from assistants to sales managers, sales managers for a special type of account (e.g., associations) or for a territory. Senior sales managers are expected to book large conventions and expositions—yes, everyone has their quota. Event managers plan and organize the function/event with the client once the contract has been signed. Salaries range from $35,000 to $70,000 for both assistants on up to sales or event managers.

Careers are also possible in the companies that services the MICE segment. Someone has to equip the convention center and ready it for an exposition. Someone has to supply all the food and beverage items, and so on. Off-premise catering and special events also offers careers for creative people who like to create concepts and orchestrate themes around which an event or function may be planned.

For all the career paths, it is critical to gain experience in the areas of your interest. Request people you respect to be your mentor and ask questions. By showing your enthusiasm, people will respond with more help and advice.

SUMMARY

1. Conventions, meetings, and expositions serve social, political, sporting, or religious purposes. Associations offer benefits such as a political voice, education, marketing avenues, member services, and networking.

2. Meetings are events designed to bring people together for the purpose of exchanging information. Typical forms of meetings are conferences, workshops, seminars, forums, and symposiums.

3. Expositions bring together purveyors of products, equipment, and services in an environment in which they can demonstrate their products. Conventions are meetings that include some form of exposition or trade show.

4. Meeting planners contract out their services to associations and corporations. Their responsibilities include premeeting, on-site, and postmeeting activities.

5. The convention and visitors bureaus are nonprofit organizations that assess the needs of the client and or-

ganize transportation, hotel accommodations, restaurants, and attractions.

6. Convention centers are huge facilities, usually owned by the government, where meetings and expositions are held. Events at convention centers require a lot of planning ahead and careful event management. A contract based on the event profile and an event document are parts of effective management.

7. Event management can range from being as small as an office outing to as large as a music festival. These events just don't happen by themselves; it takes a great deal of preparation to stage a successful event, and this is where event management comes into play. To hold a successful event, the organizer should have a vision and leader–manager skills in the key result areas of marketing, financial, operational, and legal. It is helpful for event manager's to receive sponsorship.

KEY WORDS AND CONCEPTS

Associations	Convention center	Incentive market	SMERF
Consumer show	Exposition	Meeting	Special event
Convention	Familiarization (FAM) trip	Meeting planner	Trade show
Convention and visitors bureaus (CVBs)			

REVIEW QUESTIONS

1. What are associations and what is their purpose?
2. Explain the term SMERF.
3. Describe the main types of meeting setups.
4. What are a workshop and a seminar?
5. Explain the difference between an exposition and a convention.
6. What is a convention center?
7. List the duties of CVBs.
8. Conventions require careful planning. Explain the purpose of an event profile and an event document.
9. Discuss the different promotional tools, how they relate to each other, and their relationship to the marketing mix.

INTERNET EXERCISES

1. Organization: **The Massachusetts Convention Center Authority**
   Web site: **www.mccahome.com/meeting-plan.html**
   Summary: The Massachusetts Convention Center Authority operates the Boston Convention Center. Opened in 2004, this spectacular new facility on the South Boston waterfront dramatically increases Boston's ability to handle events of size and scope. The 516,000 square feet of contiguous exhibit space, 160,000 square feet of flexible meeting space, 82 state-of-the-art meeting rooms and 42,020-square-foot ballroom with stunning views of the city skyline and harbor all make for an ideal convention center.
   (a) Go to the Web site and click on the meeting planner near the top and scroll down to the Boston Convention and Event Center; then click on Event Planning Guide and go to page 13 and check the Information Guideline. How far out are contracts signed? Enjoy the site!

2. Organization: **M & C Online**
   Web site: **www.meetings-conventions.com**
   Summary: This excellent Web site offers in-depth information on meetings and conventions from different perspectives, ranging from legal issues to unique themes and concepts.
   (a) Go to the Web site and click on Breaking News. Pick a topic for class discussion.
   (b) Click on Planner's Portfolio and scroll down to checklist: save it for future reference.

APPLY YOUR KNOWLEDGE

Make a master plan with all the steps necessary for holding a meeting or seminar on careers in hospitality management.

SUGGESTED ACTIVITY

Contact meeting planners in your area and, with the permission of your professor, invite them to speak to the class about their work and how they do it. Prepare questions in advance so that they may be given to the speaker ahead of time.

ENDNOTES

1. Courtesy of Karen Smith, Claudia Green, and Andrea Sigler.
2. Personal correspondence, Karen Smith. July 14, 2004.
3. Personal conversation with Karen Smith. August 14, 2004.
4. MPI/ASAE Meetings Outlook Survey.
5. Courtesy of Kathleen A. Doeller.
6. Rhonda J. Montgomery and Sandra K. Strick, *Meetings, Conventions, and Expositions: An Introduction to the Industry*. New York: Van Nostrand Reinhold, 1995, p. 13.
7. Montgomery and Strick, p. 19.

WEB RESOURCES

American Society of Association Executives (ASAE)
www.asanet.org

Hospitality Sales and Marketing Association International (HSMAI)
www.hsmai.org

Meetings Planners International
www.mpiweb.org

Professional Convention Management Association (PCMA)
www.pcma.org

International Association of Convention and Visitors Bureaus/Destination Marketing Association International
www.iacvb.org

Las Vegas Convention and Visitors Association
www.lvcva.com

Leadership and Management

14

After reading and studying this chapter, you should be able to:

- Identify the characteristics and practices of leaders and managers.
- Define *leadership* and *management*.
- Describe the key management functions.
- Differentiate between leadership and management.

Leadership

Our fascination with **leadership** goes back many centuries. Lately, however, it has come into prominence in the hospitality, tourism, and other industries as they strive for perfection in the delivery of services and products in an increasingly competitive environment. Leaders can and do make a difference when measuring a company's success.

One person working alone can accomplish few tasks or goals. You have probably already experienced being part of a group that had good leadership. It might have been with a school, social, sporting, church, or other group in which the leader made a difference. The reverse might also be true: You may have been in a group with ineffective leadership. Few groups can accomplish much without an individual who acts as an effective leader. The leader can and often does have a significant influence on the group and its direction.

Characteristics and Practices of Leaders

So what are the ingredients that result in leadership excellence? If we look at the military for examples of leadership excellence, we see that leaders can be identified by certain characteristics. For example, the *U.S. Guidebook for Marines* lists the following leadership traits:

- Courage
- Decisiveness
- Dependability
- Endurance
- Enthusiasm
- Initiative
- Unselfishness
- Integrity
- Judgment
- Justice
- Knowledge
- Loyalty
- Tact

A Marine officer would likely choose integrity as the most important trait. Integrity has been defined as "doing something right even though no one may be aware of it."

In addition to these leadership traits, the following identifiable practices are common to leaders:

1. *Challenge the process:* Be active, not passive; search for opportunities; experiment and take risks.
2. *Inspire a shared vision:* Create a vision; envision the future; enlist others.
3. *Enable others to act:* Do not act alone; foster collaboration; strengthen others.
4. *Model the way:* Plan; set examples; strive for small wins.
5. *Encourage the heart:* Share the passion; recognize individual contributions; celebrate accomplishments.

Definitions of Leadership

Because of the complexities of leadership, the different types of leadership, and individual perceptions of leaders, leadership has several definitions.

Personal Profile: Herb Kelleher

Herb Kelleher, who recently gave up the titles of chairman and CEO to two other Southwest executives, is the living embodiment of the phrase "one of a kind." With his charismatic personality, he is a person who leaves a distinctive mark on whatever he does. Since the birth of Southwest Airlines in 1971 (actually, Rollin W. King, a banking client of Herb's at the time, conceived Southwest Airlines after he had drawn, on a cocktail napkin, a triangle connecting Texas's three major cities: Dallas, Houston, and San Antonio), Herb Kelleher—"Herb" to even his most distant acquaintances—nurtured Southwest Airlines into the seventh largest airline. The company has been profitable every year since 1973. When other carriers lost billions or were struggling with bankruptcy, Southwest was the only company that remained consistently profitable—a record unmatched in the U.S. airline industry—cheerfully pursuing its growth plans by buying more planes, expanding into new cities, and hiring personnel. Southwest is also a model of efficiency: It is a multiple-time winner of the U.S. Department of Transportation's Triple Crown, a monthly citation for the best on-time performance, fewest lost bags, and fewest overall complaints. Kelleher's operation, based on flights covering relatively short distances for prices that are sometimes shockingly low, is likely to experience rapid growth and become even more of a leading power.

One of the keys to this success lies in the company's mission. Southwest Airlines aims at providing cheap, simple, and focused airline service. Kelleher devoted enormous attention to thousands of small decisions, all designed to achieve simplicity. Among these small but tremendously strategic decisions were the removal of closets at the front of the planes to improve passengers' speed in boarding and departing and no onboard food, except snacks, which is justified by the number of short flights (about 400 miles). Southwest also refused full participation on computerized reservations systems used by travel agents. More than 80 percent of all Southwest tickets are sold directly to customers, saving the company millions annually. There is no assigned seating and no first-class seating. Planes have been standardized: Southwest only operates one type of aircraft, the 737, which simplifies flight crew training and maintenance personnel training.

These relatively minor privations have their positive counterpart in the fact that Southwest ground crew can turn around a plane at the gate in about 20 minutes! The airline's customers especially appreciate its low fares and on-time schedules.

Who is behind all this? The airline's success is credited to Kelleher's unorthodox personality and entrepreneurial management style. Born and raised in New Jersey, he was the son of the general manager of Campbell Soups Inc. He began to show leadership qualities as student body president both in high school and in college. From his original idea of becoming a journalist, Kelleher shifted his goal to the practice of law. By the mid-1960s, he was successfully practicing in San Antonio, Texas, his wife's hometown. However, he was always seeking the possibility of starting a venture of his own. The big chance came in 1966 when a banker client, Rollin King, suggested that Texas needed a short-haul commuter airline. That was the trigger: Southwest was born in 1971.

While CEO, Herb directly supervised his business, personally approving expenses over $1,000. His outstanding hands-on efforts also led to unusually good labor-management relations, on the basis of the motto "People are the most important of resources." In fact, he managed to establish a strong bond of loyalty between employees and their company that may have disappeared elsewhere in the American corporate environment.

He still represents some sort of a father figure to SWA, as well as the jester, and the "Lord of Ha-Ha." The effort that he was able to get out of his employees made the real difference. Unlike workers at most other carriers, Southwest employees are willing to pitch in no matter what the task. For example, a reservations sales clerk in Dallas took a call from an anxious customer who was putting his 88-year-old mother aboard a flight to St. Louis. The woman was quite frail, the fellow explained, and he wasn't quite sure she could handle the change of planes in Tulsa. "No sweat!" replied the clerk. "I'll fly with her as far as Tulsa and make sure she gets safely on the St. Louis flight."

Kelleher's outstanding leadership ability is also demonstrated by his long-term thinking. He gathered a top-rank team of successors, which will guarantee the airline's future prosperity. Kelleher is the leader who inspires, the amiable uncle to consult, the cheerleader who motivates, and the clown who spreads cheer. There are many great stories about Herb Kelleher; this is one of the most popular: Southwest was being threatened by an aviation services company over the advertising slogan "Plane Smart." Instead of incurring huge attorneys' fees and dealing with months-long litigation, the two CEOs agreed to settle the matter with an arm-wrestling contest. Herb actually lost the contest, but the other CEO had so much fun that the lawsuit was dropped. Both companies saved a bundle in legal fees.

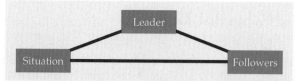

Figure 14–1   *Transactional Leadership Model*

Many definitions share commonalities, but there are also differences. In terms of hospitality leadership, the following definition is appropriate: "Leading is the process by which a person with vision is able to influence the activities and outcomes of others in a desired way."

Leaders know what they want and why they want it—and they are able to communicate those desires to others to gain their cooperation and support. Leadership theory and practice has evolved over time to a point where current industry practitioners may be identified as transactional or transformational leaders.[1]

Transactional Leadership

Transactional leadership is viewed as a process by which a leader is able to bring about desired actions from others by using certain behaviors, rewards, or incentives. In essence, an exchange or transaction takes place between leader and follower. Figure 14–1 shows the transactional leadership model. This concept illustrates the coming together of the leader, the situation, and the followers. A hotel general manager who pressures the food and beverage director to achieve certain goals in exchange for a bonus is an example of someone practicing transactional leadership.

Transformational Leadership

Leadership involves looking for ways to bring about longer-term, higher-order changes in follower behavior. This brings us to transformational leadership. The term **transformational leadership** is used to describe the process of eliciting performance above and beyond normal expectations. A transformational leader is one who inspires others to reach beyond themselves and do more than they originally thought possible; this is accomplished by raising their commitment to a shared vision of the future.

Transformational leaders practice a hands-on philosophy, not in terms of performing the day-to-day tasks of subordinates, but in developing and encouraging their followers individually. Transformational leadership involves three important factors:

1. Charisma
2. Individual consideration
3. Intellectual stimulation

Of course, it is also possible to be a charismatic transformational leader as well as a transactional leader. Although this does involve a measurable amount of effort, these leaders are guaranteed to rake in success throughout their careers.

Examples of Excellence in Leadership

Dr. Martin Luther King, Jr. was one of the most charismatic transformational leaders in history. King dedicated his life to achieving rights for all citizens by nonviolent methods. His dream of how society could be was shared by millions of Americans. In 1964 Dr. King won the Nobel Peace Prize.

Another transformational leader was Herb Kelleher, former president, CEO, and current board member of Southwest Airlines, who is profiled in this chapter. He was able to inspire his followers to pursue his corporate vision and reach beyond themselves to give Southwest Airlines that something extra that set it apart from its competitors.

Martin Luther King, Jr., One of the Most Charismatic Transformational Leaders of the Twentieth Century

Kelleher recognized that the company did not exist merely for the gratification of its employees. He knew that Southwest Airlines must perform and must be profitable. However, he believed strongly that valuing individuals for themselves was the best way to attain exceptional performance. Passengers who have flown Southwest Airlines may have seen Herb Kelleher because he traveled frequently and was likely to be found serving drinks, fluffing pillows, or just wandering up and down the aisle, talking to passengers. The success of Southwest and the enthusiasm of its employees indicate that Herb Kelleher achieved his goal of weaving together individual and corporate interests so that all members of the Southwest family benefited. Kelleher was a great transformational leader who was able to lead by visioning, inspiring, empowering, and communicating.[2]

In their fascinating book *Lessons in Leadership: Perspectives for Hospitality Industry Success,* Bill Fisher, former president and CEO of the American Hotel and Lodging Association and currently Darden Chair at the University of Central Florida, and Charles Bernstein, editor of *Nation's Restaurant News,* interviewed more than 100 industry leaders and asked each to give advice in an up-close-and-personal manner. Here are some of their answers:

"Experience is a hard teacher. It gives the test first, and then you learn the lesson." Richard P. Mayer, former chairman and CEO of Kentucky Fried Chicken and president of General Foods Corporation, says that the key traits and factors that he looks for in assessing talent included the following:

* Established personal goals
* The drive and ambition to attain those goals, tempered and strengthened with integrity
* Proven analytical and communications skills
* Superior interpersonal capabilities
* A sense of humor
* An awareness and appreciation of the world beyond her or his business specialty
* Receptivity to ideas (no matter the source)
* A genuine, deep commitment to the growth and profitability of the business

The essence of success has as many meanings as there are people to ponder it. One concept of success is to couple one's personal and family interests, dreams, and aspirations with a business or professional career such that they complement and fortify each other. Another aspect of leadership is the ability to motivate others in a hospitality working environment; decision making is also essential. These are discussed later in the chapter.

Leadership—The Basis for Management
William Fisher

The concept and practice of leadership as it applies to management carries a fascination and attraction for most people. We all like to think we have some leadership qualities and we strive to develop them. We look at leaders in all walks of life, seeking to identify which qualities, traits, and skills they possess so that we can emulate them. A fundamental question remains: What is the essence of leadership that results in successful management as opposed to failed management? At least part of the answer can be found within the word itself.

1. *Loyalty.* Leadership starts with a loyalty quadrant: loyalty to one's organization and its mission, loyalty to organizational superiors, loyalty to subordinates, and loyalty to oneself. Loyalty is multidirectional, running up and down in the organization. When everyone practices it, loyalty bonds occur, which drives high morale. Loyalty to oneself is based on maintaining a sound body, mind, and spirit so that one is always "riding the top of the wave" in service to others.

2. *Excellence.* Leaders know that excellence is a value, not an object. They strive for both excellence and success. Excellence is the measurement you make of yourself in assessing what you do and how well you do it; success is an external perception that others have of you.

3. *Assertiveness.* Leaders possess a mental and physical intensity that causes them to seek control, take command, assume the mantle of responsibility, and focus on the objective(s). Leaders do not evidence self-doubt as they are comfortable within themselves that what they are doing is right, which, in turn, gives them the courage to take action.

4. *Dedication.* Leaders are dedicated in mind, body, and spirit to their organization and to achievement. They are action oriented, not passive, and prefer purposeful activity to the status quo. They possess an aura or charisma that sets them apart from others with whom they interact, always working in the best interest of their organization.

5. *Enthusiasm.* Leaders are their own best cheerleaders on behalf of their organization and people. They exude enthusiasm and instill it in others to the point of contagion. Their style may be one of poise, stability, clear vision, and articulate speech, but their bristling enthusiasm undergirds their every waking moment.

6. *Risk management.* Leaders realize that risk taking is part of their management perch. They manage risk, rather than letting it manage them, knowing full well that there are no guaranteed outcomes, no foregone conclusions, no preordained results when one is dealing with the future. Nonetheless, they measure risk, adapt to it, control it, and surmount it.

7. *Strength.* Leaders possess an inner fiber of stamina, fortitude, and vibrancy that gives them a mental toughness, causing them to withstand interruption, crises, and unforeseen circumstances that would slow down or immobilize most people. Leaders become all the more energized in the face of surprises.

8. *Honor.* Leaders understand they will leave a legacy, be it good, bad, or indifferent. True leaders recognize that all their relationships and actions are based on the highest standards of honor and integrity. They do the right things correctly, shun short-term, improper expediency, and set the example for others with high-mindedness, professional bearing, and unassailable character.

9. *Inspiration.* Leaders don't exist without followers. People will follow leaders who inspire them to reach beyond the normal and ordinary to new levels of accomplishment, new heights of well-being, and new platforms for individual, organizational, and societal good. Inspiration is what distinguishes a leader from a mere position holder, as the leader can touch the heart, mind, and soul of others.

10. *Performance.* At the end of the day, leader–managers rise or fall on the most critical of all measurements: their performance. Results come first, but the ways in which results are achieved are also crucial to sustaining a leader's role. Many dictators don't last despite results, and many charismatics don't last despite personal charm.

Putting the ten elements together spells LEADERSHIP! Always remember, if you want to develop a leadership quality, act as though you already possess it!

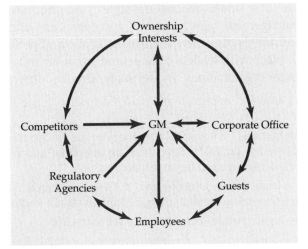

Figure 14–2 *Dynamics of Demands on General Managers in the Hospitality Industry*

Demands Placed on Leaders

Demands on a leader in the hospitality industry include those made by owners, the corporate office, guests, employees, regulatory agencies, and competitors (Figure 14–2). In response to many demands, the leader must balance two additional forces: how much energy to expend on getting results and how much to expend on relationships (Figure 14–3).

Applied social scientists like Peter Drucker, powerful industry leaders like Bill Marriott, and public service leaders like former New York mayor Rudolph Giuliani all seem to have common traits, among which are the following:

1. High ego strength
2. Ability to think strategically
3. Orientation toward the future
4. A belief in certain fundamental principles of human behavior
5. Strong connections that they do not hesitate to display
6. Political astuteness
7. Ability to use power both for efficiency and for the larger good of the organization

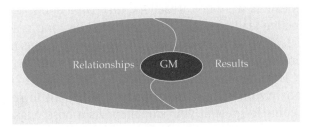

Figure 14–3 *Amount of Energy the General Manager Needs to Spend on Getting Results and Maintaining Relationships.*

Leaders vary in their values, managerial styles, and priorities. Peter Drucker, the renowned management scholar, author, and consultant of many years, has discussed with hundreds of leaders their roles, goals, and performance. These discussions took place with leaders of large and small organizations, with for-profit and volunteer organizations. Interestingly, Drucker observes:

> All the leaders I have encountered—both those I worked with and those I watched—realized:
>
> 1. The only definition of a leader is someone who has followers. Some people are thinkers. Some are prophets. Both roles are important and badly needed. But without followers, there can be no leaders.
> 2. An effective leader is not someone who is loved or admired. She or he is someone whose followers do the right things. Popularity is not leadership. Results are.
> 3. Leaders are highly visible. They therefore set examples.
> 4. Leadership is not about rank, privileges, titles, or money. It is about responsibility.[3]

Drucker adds that regardless of their enormous diversity with respect to personality, style, abilities, and interests, effective leaders all behave in much the same way:

> 1. They did not start out with the question "What do I want?" They started out asking, "What needs to be done?"
> 2. Then they asked, "What can and should I do to make a difference?" This has to be something that both needs to be done and fits the leader's strengths and the way she or he is most effective.
> 3. They constantly asked, "What are the organization's mission and goals? What constitutes performance and results in this organization?"
> 4. They were extremely tolerant of diversity in people and did not look for carbon copies of themselves. It rarely even occurred to them to ask, "Do I like or dislike this person?" But they were totally—fiendishly—intolerant when it came to a person's performance, standards, and values.
> 5. They were not afraid of strength in their associates. They gloried in it. Whether they had heard of it or not, their motto was the one Andrew Carnegie wanted to have put on his tombstone: "Here lies a man who attracted better people into his service than he was himself."
> 6. One way or another, they submitted themselves to the mirror test—that is, they made sure the person they saw in the mirror in the morning was the kind of person they wanted to be, respect, and believe in. This way they fortified themselves against the leader's greatest temptations—to do things that are popular rather than right and to do petty, mean, sleazy things.[4]

Finally, these leaders were not preachers; they were doers.

The most effective leaders share a number of skills, and these skills are always related to dealing with employees. The following suggestions outline an approach to becoming a hotel leader rather than just a manager:

- *Be decisive.* Hotel managers are confronted with dozens of decisions every day. Obviously, you should use your best judgment to resolve the decisions that come to roost at your doorstep. As a boss, make the decisions that best meet both your objectives and your ethics and then make your decisions known.

Corporate Profile: Carlson Companies

With operations in more than 140 countries, Carlson Companies is one of the largest privately held corporations in the United States and a leader in providing hospitality management, franchising, and direct-to-consumer services.[5]

Led by chairperson and chief executive officer Marilyn Carlson, Carlson Companies continues to build on a cornerstone set by her father, Curt Carlson, nearly 65 years ago: developing long-lasting relationships with clients.

The history of Carlson Companies is one of the classic business success stories in the American free enterprise system. Starting in 1938 with merely an idea and $55 of borrowed capital, entrepreneur Curtis L. Carlson founded the Gold Bond Stamp Company in his home city of Minneapolis, Minnesota. His trading stamp concept, designed to stimulate sales and loyalty for food stores and other merchants, proved to be right for the times and swept the nation in a wave of dramatic growth.

Through the years, Carlson diversified into hotels, travel, and other related businesses. In the 1960s, Carlson and several other partners collectively bought an interest in the original Radisson Hotel in downtown Minneapolis. Eventually, Carlson became sole owner of the hotel brand and expanded it around the globe. Today, there are 435 Radissons in 61 countries.

To reflect the company's growing diversification, its name was changed in 1973 from the Gold Bond Stamp Company to Carlson Companies. Four hotel brands are part of Carlson Hospitality Worldwide, one of Carlson's major business groups. They are Regent International Hotels, Radisson Hotels and Resorts, Country Inns & Suites by Carlson, and Park Plaza and Park Inn hotels. In addition, Carlson hospitality brands include T.G.I. Friday's and Pick Up Stix restaurants and Radisson Seven Seas Cruises.

Carlson Hospitality Worldwide encompasses more than 1,570 hotel, resort, restaurant, and cruise ship operations in 81 countries. Lodging operations include more than 810 locations in 63 countries. Restaurant operations include more than 753 locations in 55 countries, and cruise operations include 6 luxury ships with an additional vessel under construction.

These hospitality group brands and services, combined with sister companies Carlson Marketing Group, Carlson Wagonlit Travel, and other travel industry companies and consumer incentive programs, provide employment for more than 190,000 people around the world.

In addition to global business success, Carlson Companies is also recognized as a top employer. Both *Fortune* and *Working Mother* magazines have rated the company as one of their "100 Best Places to Work in America."

Marilyn is a regular on *Fortune* magazine's list of "Most Powerful Women in Business" and has been selected by *Business Week* as one of the "Top 25 Executives in Business." Marilyn has been ranked annually by *Travel Agent* magazine as the "Most Powerful Woman in Travel." She has served as chair of the National Women's Business Council. The council serves as an independent source of advice and counsel to the president, Congress, the U.S. Small Business Administration, and the Interagency Committee on Women's Business.

Marilyn has also served as national chair of the Travel Industry Association of America and is a member of the Council of the World Economic Forum and serves on the forum's board of governors for travel and tourism.

Among the hospitality industry-related honors she has received are the Cutting Edge Award by American Hotel & Lodging Association and the Stephen W. Brener Lodging Hospitality Silver Plate Award presented at the Annual New York University Hospitality Industry Investment Conference. She has been named "Hospitality Executive of the Year" by the Penn State Hotel and Restaurant Society.

Marilyn graduated from Smith College with a degree in international economics and attended the Sorbonne in Paris and the Institute des Hautes Etudes Economiques Politiques in Geneva, Switzerland, studying political science and international economics.

- *Follow through.* Never promise what you can't deliver, and never build false hopes among your employees. Once expectations are dashed, respect for and the reputation of the boss are shot.
- *Select the best.* A boss, good or bad, is carried forward by the work of his or her subordinates. One key to being a good boss is to hire the people who have the best potential to do what you need them to do. Take the time and effort to screen, interview, and assess the people who have not only the skills that you require, but also the needed values.
- *Empower employees.* Give people the authority to interact with the customer. The more important people feel, the better they work.
- *Enhance career development.* Good bosses recognize that most of their people want to improve themselves. However, career development is a two-edged sword: If we take the initative to train and develop our people properly, then the competition is likely to hire them. The only way a boss can prevent the loss of productive workers looking for career development is to provide opportunities for growth within the organization.

In recent years, the role of the hotel general manager has changed from that of being a congenial host, knowledgeable about the niceties of hotelmanship, to that of a multigroup pleaser. Guests, employees, owners, and community should all be not only satisfied but delighted with the operation's performance.

Many general managers are so bogged down with meetings, reports, and "putting out fires" that they hardly have any time to spend with guests. One GM who makes time is Richard Riley, GM of the fabulous Shangri-La hotel Makati in Manila, the Philippines. Richard extends an invitation for guests to visit with him in the hotel lobby between 5:00 and 7:00 P.M. every Thursday. As GM of a luxury Caribbean resort in Barbados, West Indies, the author personally greeted every guest to the property. Obviously, there is a difference between a small resort and a large city hotel. Resort guests stay for at least two, sometimes four, weeks in high season, so they need the individual attention.

Check Your Knowledge

1. What three factors does transformational leadership involve?
2. Define leadership.
3. Describe some examples of leadership.
4. Explain the demands placed on leaders.

Hospitality Management

Managers plan, organize, make decisions, communicate, motivate, and control the efforts of a group to accomplish predetermined goals. Management also establishes the direction the organization will take. Sometimes this is done with the help of employees or outside consultants, such as marketing research specialists. Managers obtain the necessary resources for the goals to be accom-

A Day in the Life of Steve Pinetti

Steve Pinetti is the senior vice-president of Sales and Marketing for Kimpton Hotels and Restaurants. Steve oversees branding efforts, sales, distribution, CRM, Internet presence, public relations, strategic partnerships, and new hotel openings. Steve has an interesting challenge, since both existing large hotel chains and new hotel companies claim to be the "boutique hotel" leader. In fact, Kimpton invented the concept in 1981: a unique, independent boutique hotel paired with a chef-driven/specialty restaurant. Says Steve, "The need to stay ahead of the growing competition as well as on top of our own game is never ending. We stay tuned to our customers' behavior, needs, and purchasing process to better understand where consumer thinking, influences and spending are headed."

Since word of mouth is the number one source of our business, we need to stay close to what our guests want, need, say, and do. We have developed a skill set around niche marketing. Since the advent of search on the Net, we have been able to get out from the shadow of the large bully brands and market to consumers who put value on personal preferences and individual style in all they do—especially travel. Since 9/11 we have found that there is a movement toward thinking about today versus the future. People are focusing their thinking on what's important to me today. What is that "thing" I keep putting off—now is the time to do it. Wellness, pampering, learning nuggets of information (how to read a painting), and discovery skills (cooking classes) are what are becoming more important. These are the types of people looking for and staying at Kimpton Hotels. The biggest project on Steve's plate is the recent rollout of the new Kimpton brand. "Getting every employee to understand the Kimpton brand, its promise, and the guests' expectations around our promise is proving to be a very large, ongoing project. The other half of this proposition is making sure every guest in every hotel each day knows he or she is in a hotel that is part of a larger collection—Kimpton Hotels.

"You need to do the basics in order for your business to survive, but you also need to take calculated risks in order to outdistance and separate yourself from the competition as well as gain notice by the unchained shopper. Taking risks is not in one's human nature, but it is something we highly value at Kimpton. By taking risks we have come up with some of the firsts in our industry. They include social wine hour every night in every Kimpton hotel, tall rooms for tall travelers, complimentary goldfish, first company to offer complimentary high-speed access, celebrity suites (Jerry Garcia, Carlos Santana), specialty suites with workout equipment, and Eco Floors.

Advice

Anything that requires the understanding and implementation of employees needs to be fully communicated well before being instituted operationally. The communication process around understating why and how as well as the benefits to all involved is more important than the actual action. It creates buy-in and buy-off. It ensures the people who are going to be responsible for implementing it or designing the process versus inheriting some program cooked up from the corporate offices.

Thoughts:

Success comes from involving and harnessing all the technical and human resources available.

It's vital to keep a balance in ones life between home, work, and self.

Need to continue to maintain the basics yet reinvent oneself to keep up with trends and times.

Steve grew up in the San Francisco Bay area, worked for Hilton and Hyatt, taught at all the San Francisco Bay area colleges and universities, founded his own marketing company, and was one of Bill Kimpton's first partners in founding Kimpton Hotels and Restaurants.

---

plished, and then they supervise and monitor group and individual progress toward goal accomplishment.

Managers, such as presidents and chief executive officers, who are responsible for the entire company, tend to focus most of their time on strategic planning and the organization's mission. They also spend time organizing and controlling the activities of the corporation. Most top managers do not get involved in the day-to-day aspects of the operation. These duties and responsibilities fall to the middle and supervisory management. In hospitality lingo, one would not expect Bill Marriott to pull a shift behind the bar at the local Marriott hotel. Although capable, his time and expertise are used in shaping the company's future. Thus, although the head bartender and Bill Marriott may both be considered management, they require slightly different skills to be effective and efficient managers.

What Is Management?

Management is simply what managers do: plan, organize, make decisions, communicate, motivate, and control. Management is defined as "the process of working with and through others to accomplish organizational goals in an efficient and effective way." In looking at this statement, we can see that the functions of management and working with and through the work of others are ongoing. Additionally, management involves getting efficient and effective results.

Efficiency is getting the most done with the fewest number of inputs. Manager's work with scarce resources: money, people, time, and equipment. You can imagine the rush in the kitchen to be ready for a meal service. But it's not enough to just be efficient; management is also about being effective. **Effectiveness** is "doing the right thing." As an example, cooks do the right thing when they cook the food correctly according to the recipe and have it ready when needed.

Who Are Managers?

The changing nature of organizations and work has, in many hospitality organizations, blurred the lines of distinction between managers and nonmanagerial employees. Many traditional jobs now include managerial activities, especially when teams are used. For instance, team members often develop plans, make decisions, and monitor their own performance. This is the case with total quality management.

So how do we define who managers are? A manager is someone who works with and manages others' activities to accomplish organizational goals in an efficient and effective way. Managers are often classified into three levels: **front-line managers** are the lowest-level managers; they manage the work of line employees. They may also be called supervisors. A front-office supervisor, for example, takes charge of a shift and supervises the guest service agents on the shift.

Middle managers are akin to department heads; they fall between front-line managers and top management. They are responsible for short- to medium-range plans, and they establish goals and objectives to meet these goals. They manage the work of front-line managers.

Top managers are responsible for making medium- to long-range plans and for establishing goals and strategies to meet those goals. Ali Kasiki is a top-level manager. He holds the title of managing director and is involved in creating and implementing broad and comprehensive changes that affect the entire or-

| Top Managers |
| Middle Managers |
| Front-line Managers |
| Nonmanagerial Associates |

Figure 14–4 *Three Levels of Management Plus Nonmanagerial Associates*

ganization. Figure 14–4 shows the three levels of management plus nonmanagerial employees.

Key Management Functions

The key management functions are planning, organizing, decision making, communicating, human resources and motivating, and controlling. These management functions are not conducted in isolation; rather they are interdependent and frequently happen simultaneously or at least overlap. Figure 14–5 shows the key management functions leading to goal accomplishment.

Hospitality companies exist to serve a particular purpose, and someone has to determine the vision, mission, goals, and strategies to reach or exceed the goals. That someone is management. The **planning** function involves setting the company's goals and developing plans to meet or exceed those goals. Once plans are complete, **organizing** is the process of deciding what needs to be done, who will do it, how the tasks will be grouped, who reports to whom, and who makes decisions.

Decision making is a key management function. The success of all hospitality companies, whether large, multinational corporations or sole proprietorships, depends on the quality of the decision making. Decision making includes determining the vision, mission, goals, and objectives of the company. Decision making also includes scheduling employees, determining what to put on the menu, and responding to guest needs. The chapter on decision making details long- and short-range decisions, centralized and decentralized decisions, programmed and nonprogrammed decisions, and the steps in the decision-making process.

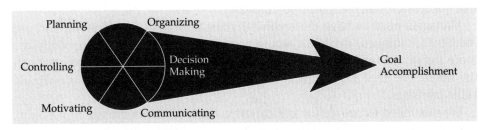

Figure 14–5 *Key Management Functions Leading to Goal Accomplishment*

Company management discusses time management, productivity, and communication.

Communication with and motivation of individuals and groups are required to get the job done. **Human resources and motivating** involves attracting and retaining the best employees and keeping morale high.

Controlling is the final management function that brings everything full circle. After the goals are set and the plans formulated, management then organizes, communicates, and motivates the resources required to complete the job. Controlling includes the setting of standards and comparing actual results with these standards. If significant deviations are seen, they are investigated and corrective action taken to get performance back on target. This scientific process of monitoring, comparing, and correcting is the controlling function and is necessary to ensure there are no surprises and that no one is guessing.

Managerial Skills

In addition to the management functions of forecasting, planning, organizing, communicating, motivating, and controlling, managers also need other major skills: conceptual, interpersonal, and technical.

Conceptual skills enable top managers to view the corporation as a complete entity and yet understand how it is split into departments to achieve specific goals. Conceptual skills allow a top manager to view the entire corporation, especially the interdependence of the various departments.

Managers need to lead, influence, communicate, supervise, coach, and evaluate employees' performances. This necessitates a high level of interpersonal human skills. The ability to build teams and work with others is a human skill that successful managers need to cultivate.

Managers need to have the technical skills required to understand and use modern techniques, methods, equipment, and procedures. These skills are more important for lower levels of management. As a manager rises through the ranks, the need for technical skills decreases and the need for conceptual skills increases.

We next need to realize the critical importance of the corporate philosophy, culture, and values, and a corporation's mission, goals, and objectives. Figure 14–6 shows the degree of managerial skills required by top managers, middle managers, and supervisory managers.

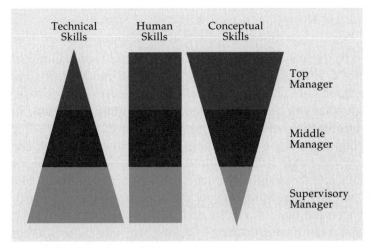

Figure 14–6   *Management Skill Areas*

The Manager's Changing Role

Managers may still have subordinates, but today's successful manager takes more of a team leader/coach approach. There are, of course, other ways to "slice and dice" what managers do. For example, managers don't just plan, organize, make decisions, communicate, motivate, and control. They wear a variety of hats, including the following:

- *Figurehead role.* Every manager spends some time performing ceremonial duties. For example, the president of a corporation might have to greet important business guests or clients or represent the corporation by attending dinners.
- *Leader role.* Every manager should be a leader, coaching, motivating, and encouraging employees.
- *Liaison role.* Managers spend a lot of time in contact with people in other departments both within the organization and externally. An example would be the sales manager liaising with the room's division director.
- *Spokesperson role.* The manager is often the spokesperson for the organization. For example, a manager may host a college class visit to the property.
- *Negotiator role.* Managers spend a lot of time negotiating. For example, the head of a company along with qualified lawyers may negotiate with a union representative to establish wages and benefits for employees.

These roles, together with the management functions, encompass what managers do. Remember, managers need to be many things—often in quick succession—even to the point of wearing two or more hats at once.

Twenty-first-century managers face not only a more demanding and increasingly complex world, but also a more dynamic and interdependent one. The "global village" is a reality, and sociocultural traditions and values must be understood and diversity respected and encouraged by future managers. The two most important changes going on right now are the technological advances and the internationalization of hospitality and tourism. The extent to which

You, Too, Are a Manager

Your classmates have just voted you to be the leader–manager of the summer study-abroad trip to France. None of you knows much about France or how to get there, what to do when you get there, and so on. Where would you start? (Resist the temptation to delegate the whole trip to a travel agent, please.)

You might start by thinking through what you need to do in terms of planning, organizing, deciding, communicating, motivating, and controlling. What sort of plans will you need? Among other things, you'll need to plan the dates your group is leaving and returning, the cities and towns you'll visit, the airline you'll take there and back, how the group will get around France, and where you'll stay when you're there. As you can imagine, plans like these are very important: You would not want to arrive at Orly Airport with a group of friends who are depending on you and not know what to do next.

Realizing how much work is involved—and that you cannot do it all and still maintain good grades—you get help. You divide up the work and create an organization by asking someone to check airline schedules and prices, another person to check hotel prices, and someone else the sites to see and the transportation needs. However, the job won't get done with the group members simply working by themselves. Each person requires guidance and coordination from you: The person making the airline bookings can't confirm the bookings unless she knows what city and airport the trip will originate in. Similarly, the person making the hotel arrangements can't make any firm bookings until he knows what cities are being visited. To improve communications, you could set up regular meetings with e-mail updates between meetings. Leadership and motivation could be a challenge because two of the group members do not get along well. So ensuring that everyone stays focused and positive will be a challenge.

Of course, you'll have to make sure the whole project remains "in control." If something can go wrong, it often will, and that's certainly the case when groups of people are traveling together. Everything needs to be double-checked. In other words, managing is something we do almost every day, often without even knowing it.

Adapted from Gary Dessler, *A Framework for Management.* Upper Saddle River, NJ: Prentice Hall, 2002, p. 8.

you as a future **leader–manager** can master these events and functions will determine your future.

The manager's role is not only internal but also external. For instance, a manager must be responsive to market needs and income generation. Managers must continually strive to be innovative by realizing efficiencies in their respective areas of responsibility through process improvement—for example, by determining how to reduce long check-in lines at airports and hotels. Some companies use innovative and creative ways to streamline the check-in procedures to make the process a more worthwhile experience for the guests. Disney, for instance, uses the creative approach of sending Mickey and the gang to entertain the guests while they stand in line.

A General Manager's Survival Kit

Ali Kasiki of the Peninsula Beverly Hills, California, offers his list:[6]

- Know yourself, your own core competencies, and your values.
- Hire a seasoned management team.

- Build barriers of entry; that is, make yourself indispensable.
- Be very flexible.
- Get close to your guests and owners to define reality versus perception.
- Show leadership, from both the top and the bottom.
- Delegate. There is no way you can survive without delegation.
- Appeal to trends.
- Trust your instincts.
- Take risks and change the ground rules.
- Don't become overconfident.
- Look successful, or people will think you're not.
- Manage the future—it is the best thing you can do. Bring the future to the present.

Distinction Between Leadership and Management

Managing is the formal process in which organizational objectives are achieved through the efforts of subordinates. Leading is the process by which a person with vision is able to influence the behavior of others in some desired way. Although managers have power by virtue of the positions they hold, organizations seek managers who are leaders by virtue of their personalities, their experience, and so on. The differences between management and leadership can be illustrated as follows[7]:

Managers	Leaders
Working in the system	Working on the system
React	Create opportunities
Control risks	• Seek opportunities
Enforce organizational rules	• Change organizational rules
Seek and then follow direction	Provide a vision to believe in and strategic alignment
Control people by pushing them in the right direction	Motivate people by satisfying basic human needs
Coordinate effort	Inspire achievement and energize people

Check Your Knowledge

1. What is management and what are the three management skill areas?
2. Explain levels of management.
3. Describe the key management functions.
4. What is the distinction between leadership and management?

Trends in Leadership and Management

- Leading a more diverse group of associates
- Many entry-level employees do not have basic job skills
- An increasing need for training
- The need to create leaders out of line managers
- Managing sales revenue all the way to the bottom line
- Establishing independent business units to make their own profit, or subcontracting out that department
- Instead of keeping a person on payroll for a function that is only needed occasionally, outsourcing that service to specialists
- Cutting down on full-time employees and hiring more part-time employees to avoid paying benefits
- An increasing challenge to keep up with technological advances and their benefits
- Social and environmental issues continue to increase in importance
- A greater emphasis is being placed on ethics

CASE STUDY

Performance Standards

Charles and Nancy both apply for the assistant front-office manager position at a 300-room upscale hotel. Charles has worked for a total of eight years in three different hotels and has been with this hotel for three months as a front-office associate. Initially, he had a lot of enthusiasm. Lately, however, he has been dressing a bit sloppily and his figures, cash, and reports have been inaccurate. In addition, he is occasionally "rattled" by demanding guests.

Nancy recently graduated from college, with honors, with a degree in hospitality management. While attending college, she worked part-time as a front-desk associate at a budget motel. Nancy does not have a lot of experience working in a hotel or in customer service in general, but she is quite knowledgeable as a result of her studies and is eager to begin her career.

It appears that Charles would have been considered a prime candidate for the office manager position because of his extensive experience in other hotels and his knowledge of the hotel's culture. In view of his recent performance, however, the rooms division manager will need to sit down with Charles to review his future career development track.

Questions

1. What are the qualifications for the job that should be considered for both applicants?
2. How should the discussion between the rooms division manager and Charles be handled? Make specific recommendations for the rooms division manager.
3. Who would be the better person for the job? Why?

CASE STUDY

Reluctant to Change

You have just been appointed assistant manager at an old, established, but busy, New York restaurant. Your employees respond to your suggested changes with "We have always done it this way." The employees really do not know any other way of doing things.

Question

1. How should you handle this situation?

CAREER INFORMATION

Leadership and Management

As a college graduate, you will be expected to fill a leadership role when you complete your education. It is more than likely that you will be working with hourly wage employees ranging from minimum-wage employees to skilled professionals. These are people who may have been working for the company for years and are extremely good at what they do.

So are we all leaders, and can we develop our leadership skills? We all have leadership capabilities, and, yes, we can develop our leadership skills. Leadership begins with each of us. We need to define our vision, mission, goals, and objectives. However, leadership is more than just defining goals; it is how we go about doing this. But you've got to know where you're going and how to get there. Then it's just a matter of becoming a believer. Leading these employees is your challenge as a manager. This means gaining their confidence and trust. Unless you know what you are doing, it is difficult—if not impossible—to accomplish. Part of being an effective leader is not asking anybody to do anything that you would not do yourself. Motivating employees is much easier when you have a real appreciation for their jobs, and this is where your work experience in college will pay off. You will have a much keener insight into your employees' jobs if you have done what they are doing. Your experience will help you with the difficult and challenging task of keeping your employees motivated and working together as a team. Your college education is important, but a valuable part of that education comes from your work experience while in college. Upon graduation, if your experience reflects your desire, you will possess the necessary skills and ability to excel as a manager for the hospitality industry.

Source: Courtesy of Charlie Adams.

SUMMARY

1. Leadership is defined as the process by which a person is able to influence the activities and outcomes of others in a desired way.
2. Contemporary leadership includes transactional and transformational types of leadership.
3. Increased demands placed on hospitality leaders include ownership, corporate, regulatory, employee, environmental, and social interests. Leaders must balance results and relationships.
4. Managing is the process of coordinating work activities so that they are completed efficiently and effectively with and through other people.
5. Leaders, according to Drucker, realized four things and behaved in much the same way.
   (a) A leader is someone who has followers—some people are thinkers, and some are prophets.
   (b) An effective leader is not someone who is loved or admired, but rather someone whose followers do the right things. Popularity is not leadership; results are.
   (c) Leaders are highly visible. Leaders set examples.
   (d) Leadership is not about rank, privileges, titles, or money. It is about responsibility.
6. There are six key management functions: planning, organizing, decision making, communicating, motivating, and controlling. However, in addition to these functions, managers occasionally have to fill roles such as figurehead, leader, spokesperson, or negotiator.
7. The difference between management and leadership is that the former is the formal process in which organization objectives are achieved through the efforts of subordinates, and the latter is the process by which a person with vision is able to influence the behavior of others in some desired way.

KEY WORDS AND CONCEPTS

Communication
Controlling
Decision making
Effectiveness
Efficiency

Front-line managers
Human resources and
   motivating
Leader–managers
Leadership

Management
Middle managers
Organizing
Planning
Top managers

Transactional leadership
Transformational leadership

REVIEW QUESTIONS

1. What kind of leader–manager will you be?
2. Give examples of the management functions as they apply to the hospitality industry.
3. Discuss the changing role of managers.
4. Define leadership and name the essential qualities of a good leader.
5. Distinguish between transactional and transformational leadership.

INTERNET EXERCISES

1. Organization: **Wet Feet.com**
   Web site: **www.wetfeet.com**
   Summary: Wet Feet.com is an organization dedicated to helping you make smarter career decisions. Wet Feet.com provides inside insight on jobs and careers for both job seekers and recruiters. By all means, take the time to check this one out!
   Click on the "Careers" icon and scroll down to "General Management." Answer the following questions.
   (a) What are the requirements for becoming a GM, and what tips does Wet Feet.com have to offer?
   (b) The "Career Overview" section illustrates several attributes that managers have in common. In groups, list these attributes and discuss their significance.

2. Organization: **American Management Association**
   Web site: **www.amanett.org**
   Summary: The American Management Association (AMA), a practitioner-based organization, offers a wide range of management development programs for managers and organizations.

   Find the section entitled "AMA Research." Choose two current reports. Read through these and make a bulleted list of the key information. Then write a description of how this information might affect the way a hospitality manager plans, organizes, makes decisions, communicates, motivates, and controls.

3. Organization: **Ritz-Carlton Hotel Company**
   Web site: **www.ritzcarlton.com**
   Summary: Ritz-Carlton hotels are known for their superior luxury and service in the hospitality industry. This particular Web exercise illustrates how the Ritz-Carlton maintains its culture of service excellence. Let's take a look at the Ritz-Carlton Leadership Center.
   Click on the "About Us" icon. Then click on "Other Ritz-Carlton Businesses." Now go to the "Ritz-Carlton Leadership Center" and answer the following questions.
   (a) What is Ritz-Carlton's Leadership Orientation?
   (b) What are the seven habits of highly effective people?

APPLY YOUR KNOWLEDGE

1. Your resort has management vacancies for the following positions: executive chef, executive housekeeper, and front-office manager. List the traits and characteristics that you consider essential and desirable for these positions.

SUGGESTED ACTIVITY

Think of someone you admire as a leader. Make a list of the qualities that make him or her a good leader.

ENDNOTES

1. For a more detailed review of the many leadership theories, consult one of the many texts on the topic.
2. Jay R. Schrock, Presentation to University of South Florida students and faculty. May 2, 2005.
3. This draws on Peter F. Drucker, "Foreword." In F. Hesselbein et al., Eds. *The Leader of the Future*. San Francisco: Josey-Bass, 1996, pp. xii–xiii.
4. Ibid., p. ix.

5. **www.carlson.com/press_07_29_05cfm**, August 20, 2005.

6. Personal correspondence with Ali Kasiki.

7. Vadim Kotelnikov, Ten3 Business e-Coach. **http://www.1000ventures.com**. Version 2005a.

WEB RESOURCES

Carlson Companies
www.carlson.com

Kimpton Hotels
www.kimptonhotels.com

Planning

15

After reading and studying this chapter, you should be able to:

- Describe the importance of planning.
- Discuss the merits of the different types of planning.
- Explain how goals and strategies are set and give examples
- Identify the seven steps in operational planning.

What Is Planning?

Things don't just happen by themselves—well, at least not the way we'd like them to. Remember the time, on a hot day, when you walked into an ice cream store and ordered your favorite flavor, only to be told they were out if it. You were expecting to be delighted but instead were disappointed. A lack of planning was the root cause of this negative experience. Someone forgot to order or did not order the flavor of ice cream in time for you to enjoy it. This is an example of simple but important planning. There are, as we shall see, more complex forms of planning.

Planning involves selecting the various **goals** that the organization wants to achieve and the actions (**strategies**) to be taken that will ensure those goals are accomplished. In organizations, executives determine where the organization is and where it wants to go. Goals are established for each of the **key operating areas.** In the hospitality industry these would include guest satisfaction, employee satisfaction, productivity, food and beverage preparation and service, marketing and sales, operating ratios, human resources, physical property, security, and finances. Strategies are then planned to ensure that the goals are met or exceeded. All managers do some form of planning, whether informal or formal. With informal planning, nothing is written down, and there is little or no sharing of goals with others in the organization. The owner has a vision of what she or he wants to accomplish and just goes ahead and does it. This is frequently the situation in small businesses; however, informal planning also goes on even in larger organizations. The problem with informal planning is that it lacks continuity.

Formal planning occurs when specific goals covering a period of up to several years are identified and shared with all associates and strategies are developed stating how each goal will be reached. When planning is discussed in this chapter, we are referring to formal planning. Several types of planning exist, but we will examine the main ones used in the hospitality industry.

Executive Committee Planning the Future Direction and Performance of "their" Property

Think back to the summer trip to France that was introduced in the previous chapter. Your plans might include the following: how you plan to get to the airport, your airline and flight times, the airport of arrival, how you'll get into Paris, your hotel, and the itinerary of what to do each day in each city visited. Think for a moment: What if you didn't plan? The group would not know what flight to take or, on arrival in France, how to get into central Paris and then how and where to find a place to stay. This would be chaotic and stressful, to say the least. Now think of your career plans. Perhaps your goal is to have a successful career in one of the many areas of hospitality management. Successfully completing your degree along with work experience would be the strategies that would facilitate your goal accomplishment. So we can see that planning provides direction and a sense of purpose.[1] Remember the wonderful line in *Alice in Wonderland* when Alice is lost and asks the Mad Hatter which way to go? The Mad Hatter asks her where she wants to go. Alice replies, "I don't know— anywhere." The Mad Hatter then explains, "If you don't know where you're going, any path will get you there."

Planning can also help identify potential opportunities and threats. Planning helps facilitate the other functions of management—organization, decision making, communication, motivation, and especially control—because planning establishes what needs to be done and how it is to be done, and control looks at how well we have done compared to how well we expected to do.[2]

The Purpose of Planning

Planning gives direction not only to top management but to all associates as they focus on goal accomplishment. The purpose of planning is to determine the best strategies and goals to achieve organizational goals. Figure 15–1 shows the hierarchy of planning in organizations. Notice how top executives do most of the strategic planning and first-line managers do most of the operational planning.

Planning provides the road map of where the organization is going. Planning also helps coordinate the efforts of associates toward goal accomplishment. Planning assists in risk reduction by forcing managers to look ahead and anticipate change so they can plan scenarios to react to those potential changes.

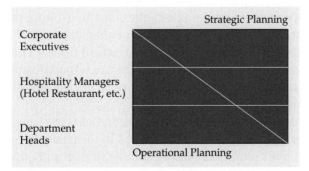

Figure 15–1 *The Hierarchy of Planning in Organizations*

Strategic Planning

The two main categories of plans are strategic (long-term) plans and operational (short-term) plans. Associated with strategic plans are business plans or feasibility studies, which deal with the structure of the plan and provide the details necessary for obtaining finance or other approvals for the operation. At the other end of the planning spectrum is, for example, the short-term operational plan for a function at a convention center. The services manager plans the layout of the room for client approval and then plans the method of service in accordance with client needs. Given that strategic plans are the long-range plans for an organization, let us begin with those.

Strategic Planning and Strategic Management

Strategic planning creates the long-range plans that steer an organization toward its goals in the accomplishment of its mission and vision. The strategic planning process involves top management, who, in simple terms, identify where the organization is and where it wants to go. There is a strong link between strategic planning and strategic management. The planners figure out what to do and management implements the plan.

How does a large hotel or restaurant company with the mission of being a global entity determine which markets to focus on? Should they focus on expansion in Canada, Europe, Latin America, or Asia? Which market would be more beneficial? And can they enter more than one market at a time? What will the method of entry into these markets be? Will a strategy appropriate for one country work in another? Pick up a copy of the *Wall Street Journal, Business Week*, a hospitality trade magazine, or a major newspaper, and you are bound to find an article on or reference made to business strategy. In the hospitality industry, strategies are devised that become the road map of how to succeed in increasing guest satisfaction, gaining market share, increasing profits, and so on.

Strategic management develops the mission, goals, and strategies by identifying the business of the corporation today and the business it wants for the future, and then identifying the course of action it will pursue, given its strengths, weaknesses, opportunities, and threats (internal and external environments).

Strategic management is a critical part of planning and the management process. There are three main strategic management tasks: (1) developing a vision and mission statement, (2) translating the mission into strategic goals, and (3) crafting a strategy (course of action) to move the organization from where it is today to where it wants to be.

Given the frequency of change in the environment, managers must conduct effective strategic planning in order to respond to the challenges of managing in a highly competitive environment. For example, the terrorist attack of September 11, 2001, highlighted the need for business to craft effective strategic plans that allow them to respond to such surprises. In other words, a good strategic plan should include detailed prescriptions of how a business wishes to implement its mission in the highly competitive environment coupled with allowances for responding to extraordinary events.

A direct link exists between the mission of the organization and strategic management—they complement each other. Strategic planning involves creating the long-term strategy for how the organization will meet its mission. The job of strategic management is to translate the mission into strategic goals.

The difference between strategic planning and strategic management is that strategic planning is a systematic process whereby the top management of an organization charts the future course of the enterprise. Strategic management is the process of guiding the organizational strategic plan and acquiring the necessary resources and capabilities to ensure successful implementation of the plan in the context of emergent situations caused by the level of environmental turbulence.[3]

A strategy is the "how to" action necessary to accomplish goals and missions. In the hospitality industry, for instance, there are six steps to strategic planning:[4]

1. Build your vision.
2. Understand your customers.
3. Examine your operating environment.
4. Determine the key issues.
5. Identify strategies for the future.
6. Create your action plan.

Strategic Planning Process

Most of the strategic planning that takes place at the top management level is called *corporate-level strategy*. Figure 15–2 shows the strategic management process. Notice how it begins with identifying the organization's mission, goals, and objectives. It then goes on to analyze the environment and the organization's resources and to identify strengths, weaknesses, opportunities, and threats. The organization then formulates strategies, implements them, and evaluates the results.

Check Your Knowledge

1. Name four purposes of planning.
2. What are the two main categories of planning?
3. What are the three main strategic management tasks?

Corporate-Level Strategies

At the highest corporate level many organizations consist of a portfolio of several businesses or divisions. For instance, Disney's portfolio includes movies, theme parks, and the ABC network. Hilton Hotels' portfolio includes Conrad Hotels, Doubletree, Embassy Suites and Hotels, Hampton Inn and Hampton Inns and Suites, Hilton Hotels, Hilton Garden Inn, and Homewood Suites by

A Day in the Life of Jessica Leibovich
Chef/Owner, Entree Nous, "Best Personal Chef" San Diego Magazine

I begin planning my day as a personal chef the night before I cook for a client. Using a program called Mastercook, a recipe database software, I begin menu planning and customize a menu for the clients that I will be cooking for the following day. I usually choose five entrees and side dishes, trying to keep a variety of one seafood, two chickens, one beef or pork, and one vegetarian selection. The side dishes are combinations of fresh vegetables, whole grains, and starches. This combination of meals may change based on the likes and dislikes of each client along with any special diets that they may be on. After the menu planning, I enter the recipes, using Mastercook, into a shopping list and create a shopping list for my cook date. This is all done the previous night before a cook date.

The day I am going to cook, I start my workday at approximately 8:30 A.M. I begin at my computer by printing out the shopping list for the day along with each of the recipes I will be preparing for my client. I also type up heating instructions for the client. Before I leave the house, I go through the shopping list for the day and place all of the nonperishable items I have already in my rolling cooler. Then I go through the list and identify which stores I will need to shop for each of the items.

Before leaving, I load my car with my cooler and my portable kitchen kit. I make sure to bring my shopping list, recipes, and heating instructions. I am in my car, ready to leave around 9:15 A.M.

I usually need to go to at least three stores: one store for my dry goods, one store for my meat and produce, and one for seafood. Occasionally, I may need to visit a store if I cannot locate something I need at the others. As I shop, I check off my shopping list as I go.

I am finished shopping around 10:00 A.M. and begin to drive to my client's home. Each day, I go to a different client's house. Some of my clients I cook for every week, and others may only be once a month. Once I arrive, I bring in all of the groceries, my cooler from home, my portable kitchen kit, and the recipes and heating instructions.

Once everything is in from the car, I remove it from the bags and place it on the counters. I put all perishable items such as meat and dairy in the refrigerator. I then set up a cutting board and knife and wash my hands. I quickly go over my recipes and decide which ones need the longest cooking time and need to be started first. I also need to decide on the rotation of the items in the oven so I will not have more than two things in the oven at any given time. Eventually, I get in a rhythm and cook for about four to five hours, preparing each entrée and side dish. My day cooking is spent washing, cutting, and trimming vegetables and meat. Then I may sauté, braise, roast, bake, or stew any particular dish, depending on what the menu selections are for that day. Sometimes I am preparing desserts and will need to bake as well. Fresh salads are also often requested sometimes so the blender may be buzzing with homemade salad dressings. At one time, there may be items on three burners while two different items are in the oven. One thing I always make sure to do is to clean as I go. Otherwise, I would have quite a mess at the end of the day. As I am finished with an item, I clean it up and set it aside to dry.

As I finish preparing items, I place them in ovenproof Pyrex and Corningware containers to store them in the refrigerator or freezer, depending on the client. As each item cools, I place a label identifying what each item is along with the date and number of servings on a sealable lid. I leave the items to cool briefly and then place them in the refrigerator. If the client will not be eating them within the next two days, they place it in the freezer to enjoy at a later date.

At the end of the day, it all comes together, and the full menu is completed. As I am finished with an item, I place it back in my cooler. That way, when I am completed, there will be no more items left on the counters. Once all the cooking is complete, I carefully clean the kitchen and leave it exactly the way it was when I arrived. I then load up my car with my portable kitchen and rolling cooler. This is usually at about 3:00 P.M.

When I arrive back home, about 4:00 P.M., I bring in my things and unload my cooler. I place everything back in its place in the cabinets. That evening I will prepare the menu and shopping list and begin again for the next day.

For more information, including menus and background information, please visit my web site at **www.chefjessica.com**.

Figure 15–2   *Strategic Management Process*

Hilton. These and other companies need a corporate-level strategy to plan how to best meet the mission of the company. A few years ago, both Hilton and Marriott, after careful strategic planning, decided, in the case of Hilton, to form a separate company made up of their gaming entertainment hotels and, in the case of Marriott, sell their foodservice operations to Sodexho. This allowed both corporations to focus on best meeting their mission with their lodging operations. Hilton found that operating casino hotels was very different from operating their other hotel brands. Marriott decided that growing their hotel brands was their best strategy.

Corporations choose the number of areas of business in which they want to operate. McDonald's and KFC are focused in one area, but Hilton, Marriott, and others have several brands, ranging from full-service hotels and extended-stay hotels all the way to vacation ownership and senior living. Most companies want to grow, and they must plan a strategy for that growth. There are four growth strategies. **Market penetration** aims to increase market share by promoting sales aggressively in existing markets. **Geographic expansion** is a strategy in which a company expands its operations by entering new markets—this is in addition to concentrating on existing markets. An example would be Hilton entering and enhancing its position in the Chinese market by entering into an agreement with Air China, China's leading air carrier. The agreement allows for cross-participation in Hilton Honors, Hilton's guest reward program, and Air China's Companion Club. The aim of the partnership between one of the world's most recognized hotel brands and China's leading airline is to provide enhanced global service for the increasing number of business travelers in China and to address the strong competitive situation with international airlines in the local business travel market after China's entry into the World Trade Organization.[5]

The third form of growth strategy is **product development,** such as Hilton's Garden Inn or a new restaurant menu item. The fourth type of growth strategy is **horizontal integration,** which is the process of acquiring ownership or control of competitors with similar products in the same or similar markets. Hilton's purchase of Promus Corporation (Embassy Suites) was an example of horizontal integration.

Strategic alliances or **joint ventures** are yet other methods for a corporation to fulfill its mission. They work like this: American Airlines has as its mission "to be the world's leading airline by focusing on industry leadership in the areas of safety, service, network, product, technology, and culture." They wanted to expand operations into Asia and Europe—the two main air travel growth areas—but lacked the resources necessary for opening up routes to several additional countries, and they were not allowed to do so anyway by foreign governments because of the competition it would bring to national airlines. So American Airlines formed a "One World" alliance with several other airlines including Air Lingus, British Airways, Cathay Pacific, Finnair, Iberia Airlines, Lan-Chile, and Qantas and more than 20 affiliate carriers to feed each other passengers, code share some flights, and share resources, thus saving money and offering the consumer a better deal with the economy of scale.

Another strategy is **diversification,** where companies expand into other types of business—related or unrelated. Celebrity chef Emeril "Bam" Lagasse's expansion into TV dinners is an example of diversification.

Strengths, Weaknesses, Opportunities, and Threats Analysis

A major strategic planning technique that is widely used in the hospitality and tourism industry is a SWOT analysis: an analysis of *s*trengths, *w*eaknesses, *o*pportunities, and *t*hreats. A SWOT analysis is used to assess the company's internal and external strengths and weaknesses, to seek out opportunities, and to be aware of and avoid threats. A **SWOT analysis** is conducted in comparison with a company's main competitors. This makes it easier to see the competitors' strengths, weaknesses, opportunities, and threats. It also makes it easier to plan a successful strategy. Each operator can decide what the key points are for inclusion in the SWOT analysis. The four *P's* of marketing—place (or location), product, price, and promotion—are a good place to begin. All plans need to be implemented; Figure 15–3 shows how plans follow goals and strategy. Strategic plans are implemented through action plans, operating plans, and standing plans.

Environmental Scanning and Forecasting

Environmental scanning is the process of screening large amounts of information to anticipate and interpret changes in the environment. Environmental scanning creates the basis for forecasts. **Forecasting** is the prediction of future outcomes. Information gained through scanning is used to form scenarios. These, in turn, establish premises for forecasts, which are predictions of future outcomes. The two main types of outcomes that managers seek to forecast are

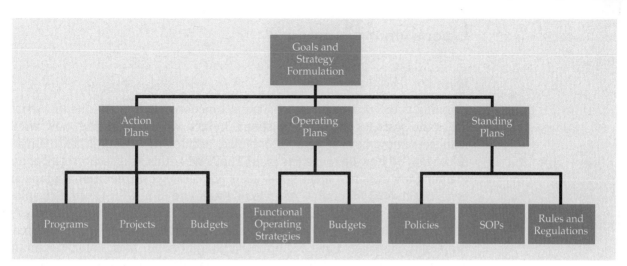

Figure 15–3   *How Plans Follow Goals and Strategies*

future revenues and new technology breakthroughs. However, any component in the organization's general or specific environment may receive further attention. Both Marriott International and Magic Mountain's sales levels drive purchasing requirements, production goals, employment needs, inventories, and numerous other decisions. Similarly, your university's income from tuition and state appropriations will determine course offerings, staffing needs, salaries, and the like. These examples illustrate that predicting future revenue is a crucial first step in planning for success.

As you can imagine, the forecasting done by the president of Hilton Hotels is very different from the forecasting done by a restaurant manager or department head. The president of Hilton needs to assess the broad economic, political, social, cultural, technological, and financial implications that might impact any forecast. For instance, should Hilton open a hotel in Providence, Rhode Island, or a different city? The desire of Hilton to have a presence in these markets must be considered along with the economic and other environmental factors in each market location. The president must also consider the probability of success of the new property. Another scenario is that of the president of a major chain restaurant corporation trying to forecast in a changing business environment. What if minimum wage were to be increased? What if health care were mandated? How would these changes affect the corporation?

Check Your Knowledge

1. Briefly explain the four growth strategies of corporations: (a) market penetration, (b) geographic expansion, (c) product development, and (d) horizontal integration.
2. What does SWOT analysis stand for?
3. What is environmental scanning?

Operational Planning

How Do Managers Plan?

Planning is the first of the management functions, so it is the one that establishes the basis for the other functions. In fact, without planning, how would managers know how or what to organize, decide on, communicate, motivate, or control? So how do managers plan? That's what this next section is all about. Planning involves two main parts: goals and strategies. **Operational plans** are generally created for periods of up to one year and fit in with the strategic plan. We have seen that strategic planning takes place at the top management level; now we look at the operational midlevel and supervisory level and see that most hospitality managers have a shorter planning horizon. Most hotel, restaurant, and other hospitality managers plan for periods from hourly, daily, weekly, monthly, and up to 90 days. A hotel department head meeting is a typical example of midlevel managers planning the various topics that make a hotel run successfully.

Operational plans provide managers with a step-by-step approach to accomplish goals. The overall purpose of planning is to have the entire organization moving harmoniously toward the goals. These are the seven steps in operational planning:

1. *Setting goals.* The first step in planning is identifying expected outcomes—that is, the goals. The goals should be specific, measurable, and achievable.
2. *Analyzing and evaluating the environment.* This involves analyzing political, economic, social, and other trends that may affect the operation. The level of turbulence is evaluated in relation to the organization's present position and the resources available to achieve goals.
3. *Determining alternatives.* This involves developing courses of action that are available to a manager to reach a goal. Input may be requested from all levels of the organization. Group work is normally better than individual input.
4. *Evaluating alternatives.* This calls for making a list of advantages and disadvantages of each alternative. Among the factors to be considered are resources and effects on the organization.
5. *Selecting the best solution.* This analysis of the various alternatives should result in determining one course of action that is better than the others. It may, however, involve combining two or more alternatives.
6. *Implementing the plan.* Once the best solution is chosen, the manager needs to decide the following:
   - Who will do what?
   - By when?
   - What resources are required?
   - At what benefit?
   - At what cost?

A Hotel Department Head Meeting Planning for Special Events

- What reporting procedures will there be?
- What authority will be granted to achieve goals?
7. *Controlling and evaluating results.* Once the plan is implemented, it is necessary to monitor progress toward goal accomplishment.

Operational Goal Setting

Goal setting is the process of determining outcomes for each area and associate. In Chapter 1, we looked at organizational vision, mission, goals, and objectives. Once the vision and mission have been determined, organizations set goals in order to meet the mission. The goals are set for each of the key operating areas mentioned earlier. No one can work effectively without specific goals and monthly evaluation reports to assess progress toward goal accomplishment or whether adjustments must be made to change course.[6] Examples of the goals and information a sales department should record and analyze each month follow:

Group Room Nights
- Booked this month and year-to-date by market segment and salesperson
- Actual consumed room nights this month and year-to-date by month, by market segment, and on the books for months to come
- Actual average group room rates by month, year-to-date and on the books for months to come

Individual Room Nights
- Actual room nights booked by month and year-to-date by market segment
- Local corporate clients—actual individual and group room nights booked by month and year-to-date
- Occupancy—actual by month and year-to-date and same time last year
- REV PAR—actual by month and year-to-date and same time last year
- Packages—number sold for each type by month, year-to-date, and zip code origin[7]

Another example would be setting productivity goals. Productivity refers to the amount of labor it takes to do a particular task. Productivity is measured in labor costs, which are expressed as a percentage of sales, for each department. Because labor costs are the highest of the operational costs, it is critical to keep them in line with budget. Productivity and labor costs can be compared from one operation to another so we can determine which is more efficient. So the goal for a family restaurant's labor costs is 23 percent of sales. Now, if sales goes up, then so too can the labor cost—but proportionately. But what if sales go down? Then, so will labor costs—again, proportionately. The skill of management is to operate efficiently and effectively. It is easy to operate a hospitality business when it is busy; the skill comes in running a hospitality business that is only operating at, say, 50 to 60 percent capacity or, worse still, even less.

Expressing goals in specific, measurable terms is important because that allows us to measure our progress toward goal accomplishment. Goals are set for each of the key result areas; an example would be profit of $100,000 per month, using the area to be measured, such as sales, and then a yardstick, such as sales revenue. A time by which the goal is to be met is also identified, as is the individual who is to be responsible for its accomplishment.

Planning expert George Morrisey presents a four-point model for use in formulating goals:[8]

Morrisey's Four-Point Model

To (1) Action/Verb	The (2) Single Measurable Result
By (3) Target Date/Time Span	At (4) Cost in Time and Energy

Operational Objectives

Objectives state how the goals will be met. One example is to achieve a food cost percentage of 28.5 percent by October 15 and maintain it until further notice at a cost not to exceed $100 or ten working hours, the food and beverage director and executive chef must do the following:

- Cost all menu items to achieve the desired food cost percentage by having the menu items priced and their costs calculated.
- Control portion sizes by establishing an exact portion for each menu item and watching to see that it is adhered to.
- Ensure that regular and spot checks are done on inventory and the food cost is calculated correctly. Take a physical count of all food items accurately, including all items in the freezers, in the kitchen, the storeroom, banquet kitchen, and so on, and calculate their costs accurately.
- Ensure that all sales and food costs are included in the calculations. Check that all guest food charges are included in the calculations—especially any functions for the day of the inventory if the food is included—and that the sales are also included.

Personal Profile: Tim Mulligan

Meet Tim Mulligan, area director of human resources for the Sheraton Hotels, San Diego, California. Mr. Mulligan feels that the important elements in planning are knowing what the desired outcome will be, having the proper information followed by organization, and being a good time manager to help ensure goal attainment.

Goal setting can be divided into two types: the annual goals for managers, which have to be in line with career growth, annual bonuses, and so forth, and annual goals for employees, which need to be stated in terms of individual development. According to Mr. Mulligan, the objectives need to be in line with the company objectives, with the individual hotel objectives, and with the personal growth objectives.

- *Operational plans* are important to meet the financial goals (profit), guest satisfaction goals, and employee satisfaction goals.
- *Specific plans* are important to reach day-to-day success with goals and objectives (i.e., check-in, recruiting, hiring process, room cleaning).
- *Single-use plans* are used only for special events, such as holiday parties or HR receptions.
- *Standing plans* are annual plans, such as benefit enrollment and management screening plans. They are also used for company policies, such as tuition reimbursement or training programs.

Mr. Mulligan gave these examples for contingency factors in planning. If the occupancy of the hotel decreases, the HR department has a plan for layoffs. On the other hand, if a need to hire a significant amount of new staff exists, then the HR department has a plan in place for a mass-hiring action.

Forecasting in the HR department differs from forecasting in other departments, according to the HR director. In the HR field, there is a need for more accurate information on a business level, to determine needs on a staffing level, and the need for dollar amounts for advertising, recruiting, background checks, drug tests, training, and so forth.

In response to a question about which benchmarking practices he believes are the most successful, Mr. Mulligan named turnover rates, employee retention, the employee satisfaction index, and the guest satisfaction index.

In the field of technology, a new trend in planning is the optimal business model. This model works with drivers and is based on the business practice. As an example, this model can determine the amount of hours available for scheduling and the maximum amount of money you can spend to stay within a budget. Two more trends are an online employee evaluation model and a goal-setting process called the performance management process.

- Use any leftover food within 48 hours.
- Maintain a vigilant loss prevention program with security. Conduct checks on bags leaving the property and do not allow any bags in the kitchen.
- Ensure that all food sales are accounted for by checking that food sales are recorded and paid for.

Collectively, these objectives will ensure that the goal will be met. Each goal needs to have step-by-step objectives written that state how they will be met.

We can see from the preceding examples that it makes sense if the associates who are going to be responsible for achieving the goals are also the ones involved in setting them. Some years ago this concept lead to **management by objectives (MBO),** a managerial process that determines the goals of the organization then plans the objectives, that is, the how-tos of reaching the goals.

With MBO, associates usually establish the goals and objectives and review them with management. MBO works because associates have been involved with the goal and objective setting and are likely to be motivated to see them successfully achieved. The MBO process consists of six steps:

1. *Set organizational goals.* Top management sets goals for the company in each key result area.
2. *Set departmental goals.* Department heads and their team members jointly set supporting goals for their departments' key result areas.
3. *Present goals.* Department heads present goals and gain approval from senior management.
4. *Discuss department goals.* Department heads present department goals and ask all team members to develop their own individual goals.
5. *Set individual goals.* Team members set their own goals with their supervisor and timetables are assigned for accomplishing those goals.
6. *Give feedback.* The supervisor and team members meet periodically to review performance and to assess progress toward goals.

MBO goals need to be specific and measurable, challenging but attainable, just as any other goals. The main purpose of an MBO program is to integrate the goals of the organization and the goals of the associates so that they are in focus. Over the years MBO has proved very successful and has, in some organizations, been superseded by **total quality management (TQM),** which was described in Chapter 1. TQM involves not only planning but also touches on the other functions of management. The idea of improving efficiency and increasing productivity while placing a larger emphasis on quality has caught on fast. Originally designed by Japanese businesses to help reconstruct the economy after WWII, today TQM is widely applied in most industrialized countries. The hospitality industry has embraced quality management with open arms, asking for input from all levels of employees and calling for teamwork. Ultimately the customer rates the team on quality, values, and product—and the customer does not lie. An example of TQM is that of a group of associates being asked to suggest ways to improve the guest experience by addressing specific challenges (actually problems, but industry professionals prefer to be positive and call them challenges) that the hospitality operation has in delivering exceptional service.

Take guest check-in as an example. The TQM team would include members from the front office and guest services (bellpersons, etc.) who identify lineups for check-in during the 4:00 to 7:00 P.M. time period. The group writes a challenge or problem statement and various ways of improving the situations are presented. They might include:

- Using a special desk for airport check-ins
- Handling convention and group guest check-ins in another location (the rooming list is made up in advance and rooms allocated with keys encoded and ready for distribution to guests)
- Cross-training and utilizing associates from other departments to assist with the check-ins

- Adopting an "all hands on deck" approach to have members of management available to assist with check-ins in various ways
- Having additional help available for housekeeping to get the rooms ready more quickly

An example of TQM in the restaurant industry is asking servers in a restaurant for help solving the challenge of reducing the guests' waiting time for a table by turning tables more quickly during the rush periods. Once the problem or challenge statement is written, the TQM team can focus on ways to improve the guest experience by suggesting ideas to reduce the guest waiting time. The head chef might automatically take on the role of coach, as opposed to that of supervisor. Implementing TQM will have the natural outcome of teamwork because one employee cannot improve quality on his or her own. The chef uses motivation and inspiration to keep his team in high spirits, and each employee is important in their own way. Emphasis is placed on recruiting, training, and keeping quality employees to ensure that the TQM approach will be a success.

Benchmarking is a concept that identifies the best way of doing something and which companies excel in that area (best practices companies). The best practice is noted and emulated or even improved on by other companies. In the spirit of cooperation, companies are expected to share information so you need to give as well as receive.

The history of benchmarking begins with the 1970s.[9] Japanese companies would take trips to industrialized nations to study their large, successful industrial companies and take that knowledge home to apply to their local companies. By aggressively copying others, they were able to supersede the company being copied by improving on the success strategy. Meanwhile, benchmarking has become a global trait. Some companies are even copying companies outside of their own industry. For example, IBM carefully studied Las Vegas casinos to apply their strategy of reducing employee theft at IBM.

How do you benchmark? First of all, a team is formed. The duty of this team is to identify companies to be benchmarked. Next, they must determine the best possible way of collecting the data, which can be collected internally as well as externally. Once collected, it must be analyzed to determine where the success lies and where the differences lie. The last step is to create an action plan on how to improve on the newly gained data—that is, what steps need to be taken to implement it.

The question to be answered is "How do these companies obtain internal information on other companies they are benchmarking?" An initial team is formed, the members of which may have contacts among customers, suppliers, or employees of the company they are planning on benchmarking. Companies often are glad to swap success stories and information with others, not only informing them but being informed about others as well. Successful companies can often be identified by the number of quality awards they have won. Also, trade associations typically know who the successful companies are, and analyzing financial data will help you determine which companies to benchmark. Using employees who will actually implement the benchmarked changes helps ensure their commitment to service or product improvement.

Focus on Service

Disaster and Emergency Planning

Hank Christen and Paul Maniscalco

Unconventional Concepts, George Washington University Inc.

It is unrealistic to expect any level of success in disaster operations without a formal, comprehensive emergency management plan (CEMP). A hospitality industry CEMP must meet two important objectives:

- Support emergency response agencies. Hospitality companies have facilities, personnel, and supplies that enhance emergency response efforts.
- Provide support and direction to facility recovery. Returning to normal operations is the goal; the CEMP must address the human, financial, and material resources needed for effective recovery.

An effective hospitality industry CEMP is divided into seven major functions: (1) threat assessment, (2) vulnerability analysis, (3) management, (4) operations, (5) logistics, (6) planning, and (7) administration and finance.

The threat assessment and vulnerability analysis functions are similar to the SWOT analysis (strengths, weaknesses, opportunities, and threats) discussed in this chapter. Threats are categorized into three groups: (1) natural threats: severe weather, wild land fires, earthquakes, disease outbreaks; (2) technological threats: chemical spills, utility failures, explosions, urban fires, transportation accidents, cyber failure; and (3) manmade threats: terrorism, cyber attacks, violence, criminal activities, bomb threats, arson.

Vulnerability analysis is the identification of weaknesses or deficiencies relating to a specific threat. For example, a resort in a wilderness area is vulnerable to wildfires.

The management section of the CEMP identifies the incident manager (the person in charge) during disaster operations. The incident manager may or may not be the chief executive of the organization. He or she is responsible for directing team members as well as ensuring a direct liaison between the hospitality facility and the local on-scene incident commander.

Operations are the direct and hands-on activities of hospitality industry personnel that support emergency operations and/or assist the hospitality facility in returning to normalcy. Operations cover a wide spectrum, from evacuation and security procedures to restoration of guest services and rehabilitation of the facility.

Logistics play a vital role; by definition, a disaster exhausts the resources of responders. Logistics includes facilities (buildings), communications, supplies, utilities, fuel/maintenance, food, and water. A climate-controlled room with telephones, computers, and a fax machine serves as an ideal incident command post for fire, law enforcement, and EMS command officers. Food and hot coffee from the facility's restaurants provides rehabilitation to fire fighters. Construction materials and equipment are needed during long-term rescue efforts.

A planning section is established to monitor the CEMP and develop action plans during disaster operations to facilitate response to real-time issues and surprises that emerge during disasters. Action plans are usually updated on a 12-hour or full-day cycle as needs dictate and are less formal than the CEMP.

Administration and finance relates to the tracking of all documents and expenditures relating to the disaster event, including employee-related issues such as salary, overtime, and workmen's compensation. Documents may include computer records, video, and photographs, as well as paper files.

Sources of low-cost disaster planning expertise include county or city emergency management office, fire departments, law enforcement crime prevention officers, the Internet, the American Red Cross, EMS offices, and the Federal Emergency Management Agency (FEMA). Conduct at least one internal exercise a year to test your plan. Evaluate your plan and make appropriate changes continuously.

Critical Factors

- A disaster plan is a formal document.
- The sections of a comprehensive emergency management plan (CEMP) include a threat assessment, vulnerability analysis, management, operations, logistics, planning, and administration/finance.
- A CEMP must be coordinated with local emergency agencies.

Corporate Profile: Choice Hotels International

This awesome story began in 1968 when Gerald Petitt, a Dartmouth engineering and business student, was seeking summer employment with IBM.[1] He blew the roof off the company's pre-employment test scores. The test scores were brought to the attention of Robert C. Hazard, Jr., who at that time was in charge of the Coors Brewery account. This had an appeal for the ski-bum in Petitt, who was originally from Denver. Robert Hazard says that Jerry Petitt did more in one summer for IBM's efforts to design a production system for the brewery than a team of five engineers did in two years.

Robert Hazard decided then, more than 25 years ago, to keep this talented person. They progressed in their careers with spells at American Express, Best Western, and eventually went on to Silver Spring, Maryland, where they would take a sleepy, stagnating lodging company called Quality Inns from 300 properties to more than 5,000 hotels in 48 countries and territories. Because they had been so successful at Best Western, they were enticed to join Quality in 1980 for equity plus $500,000 annual salaries.

Bob and Jerry brought to Quality a combination of engineer-builders and entrepreneur-marketers. They quickly set about changing the mausoleum management style—"where you don't get creative thinking, where you try to pit good minds against each other." Instead, you get "What will the chairman think?" and "We can all go along with it—or look for another job."[2]

To illustrate the change of management style, Bob Hazard draws the upside-down management organization, where the bosses are the millions of guests, at 5,000 hotels worldwide. He and Jerry Petitt, of course, were on the bottom.[3]

The strategy of changing the corporate culture, of taking advantage of emerging technological and management trends with emphasis on marketing-driven management over operations has worked for Choice hotels. The development of brand segmentation was perhaps their best move. Choice Hotels International is now an international hotel franchisor consisting of eight brands: Sleep, Comfort, Quality, Clarion, Friendship, Econo Lodge, Mainstay, and Rodeway.

More recently, under President Charles Ledsinger, Choice has reorganized, creating market area management teams strategically placed so that licensees can be closer to support staff. Each field staff manager has 45 properties and helps with sales, training, quality assurance reviews, and operations consolidations.

---

[1]This draws on Philip Hazard, *The Bob and Jerry Show: Lodging*, 19, 4, December 1993, pp. 37–41.
[2]Ibid., p. 58.
[3]www.choicehotels.com. July 27, 2005.

Benchmarking is an operational tool that can be used to guide the corporate strategy as well as the operations strategies.[10] The process in an ideal setting is to compare company operations with those of other companies that exhibit best practices. Note that often, best practices would be found outside our industry grouping. The FAA has contracted with Disney to help reduce the long lines at the airports occasioned by more severe security measures due to the threat of terrorism. In many instances, the best practices adopted from outside the hospitality industry sometimes must be modified to fit our context.

Policies, Procedures, and Rules

Policies, procedures, and rules are examples of standing plans. **Policies** set broad guidelines for associates to use when making decisions. For example, it is the policy of most hotels to pay the room and tax at another hotel and provide a taxi/hotel limo when "walking" a guest.

Procedures specify what to do in given situations. An example would be when a former classmate calls you to request a room for the next weekend. However, the hotel is forecasting 94 percent occupancy, and company procedures, unfortunately for your friend, state that no employees or their friends may stay at complimentary or discounted rates if the hotel is forecast to be more than 90 percent occupied. Policy and procedures often go together. A **rule** is a very specific action guide that associates must follow. Consider this example: Under no circumstances shall an employee serve alcoholic beverages to minors or intoxicated guests.

Developed by General Electric, Six Sigma is a disciplined, data-driven approach and methodology for eliminating defects. To achieve Six Sigma, a process must not produce more than 3.4 defects per million opportunities. A Six Sigma defect is anything outside of customer or guest expectations. The real goal of the Six Sigma methodology is the implementation of a measurement-based strategy that focuses on process improvement projects. This is accomplished by the use of two Six Sigma methods: DMAIC and DMADV. The Six Sigma DMAIC process (define, measure, analyze, improve, control) is an improvement system for existing processes falling below specification and looking for incremental improvement. The Six Sigma DMADV (define, measure, analyze, design, verify) is an improvement system used to develop new processes or products at Six Sigma quality levels. Both Six Sigma processes are executed by Six Sigma Green Belts and Six Sigma Black Belts and are overseen by Six Sigma Master Black Belts. Since General Electric saved millions of dollars with Six Sigma, thousands of companies have installed a Six Sigma process.

Budgeting

Most of us are familiar with budgets; we learned about them when we received our first "allowance." Remember how often we had it spent before the week was up? That's why organizations plan the use of their financial resources. A **budget** is a plan allocating money to specific activities. There are budgets for revenues (sales) and costs (expenses) for capital equipment—equipment that has an expected life of several years.

Budgets are popular because they force managers to anticipate expected sales and budget expenses accordingly—that is, not to spend it all before the week is up! Budgets are used extensively in all levels of hospitality organizations from the corporate level to the smallest departments. Once an estimation of a particular department's revenues is determined, the costs are then budgeted, leaving a portion for profit. This is also called the bottom line. Here's an example of a budget: A restaurant expects 750 guests in a given week; at an average check of $15, this means sales of $39,250 for the week. This allows management to budget labor costs, usually to a predetermined percentage of sales (normally between 18 and 24 percent, depending on the type of restaurant). Food, beverage, and other costs are budgeted in the same way. Figure 15–4 shows a detailed restaurant budget listing all the items of expenditure. Note that the column on the right-hand side is for the percentage of sales to which the dollar amount refers. This percentage is help-

Restaurant Operational Budget

	Budget (Thousands)	%	Actual Variance +(–)
Sales			
Food	750.0	75	
Beverage	250.0	25	
Others	0.0		
Total Sales	1,000.0	100	
Cost of Sales			
Food	225.0	30.0	
Beverage	55.0	22.0	
Others	0.0		
Total Cost of Sales	280.0	28.0	
Gross Profit	720.0	72.0	
Controllable Expenses			
Salaries and wages	240.0	24.0	
Employee benefits	40.0	4.0	
Direct operating expenses	60.0	6.0	
Music and entertainment	10.0	1.0	
Marketing	40.0	4.0	
Energy and utility	30.0	3.0	
Administrative and general	40.0	4.0	
Repairs and maintenance	20.0	2.0	
Total Controllable Expenses	480.0	48.0	
Rent and other occupation costs	70.0	7.0	
Income before interest, depreciation, and taxes	170.0	17.0	
Interest	10.0	1.0	
Depreciation	20.0	2.0	
Net Income before Taxes	140.0	14.0	

Figure 15–4 *Restaurant Operational Budget*

ful in that it can be easily compared with other similar restaurant operations. In fact, restaurant companies use percentages to check on a manager's performance. If one restaurant manager gets a food cost percentage of 28.5 and another gets 33 percent, then the corporate office will be asking the latter manager questions!

Budgets are popular because they are applicable to a variety of applications and they can be used all over the world in any country. Budgets are planning techniques that force managers to be fiscally responsible. Notice that the actual and variance columns have no entries in them as yet. As soon as the period (usually monthly) is over, the results can be totaled and any variances recorded.

Budgets are created by department heads once a year and revised monthly or as necessary. First, the projected revenue is forecasted, and then all fixed and variable costs are allocated to ensure the required profit is attained. Forecasting revenues is not easy—there are so many variables—but it has to be done. If the business was operating the previous year(s), there is a history. For a new business it's the operator's experience, plus any information from similar operations, plus calculated guesswork, equals a "guestimate" of sales.

Budgets intertwine with scheduling—because scheduling equals labor costs—the largest controllable budget item; purchasing—because that contributes to food, beverage, and other costs; and controlling—because we want to compare budget to actual revenue and expenditure results.

Check Your Knowledge

1. What is the difference between operational planning and strategic planning?
2. Define benchmarking.
3. Why is it important to have a budget?
4. Give an example of goal setting.
5. What are the four points of Morrisey's model to formulate goals?
6. Briefly describe the five steps of the MBO process.

Scheduling

Scheduling of associates is a planning activity that involves taking the business forecast and allocating an appropriate number of staff to give the necessary level of service. Due to the increasing cost of labor and benefits, schedules must be planned very carefully to avoid being over- or understaffed. Because the hospitality industry is operating 24/7, we need to staff all departments, with appropriate coverage day and night.

In Chapter 1, we briefly introduced the main shifts as early or opening, middle or swing, and late or closing plus the night shift. Staffing each area or department with a necessary group of associates costs money and is necessary just to open the doors. For example, a restaurant needs a host person to greet and seat guests, a server or two, a prep cook or two, a cook or two, a dishwasher, a bartender, and a manager. This is the minimum acceptable staffing level regardless of the number of guests. The same holds true for all areas of the hospitality industry. The problem is that we never know exactly how many guests we will have, and one day can be busy and the next quiet. That's why accurate forecasting, as discussed earlier, is so important.

Now, obviously the level of service will vary from one lodging operation to another. A full-service hotel may have 24-hour bell service, whereas a limited service hotel will not offer it. An amusement park is open up to 12 hours a day and will need at least two shifts. A restaurant is open for up to 12 hours a day and may need two shifts, depending on whether it serves breakfast, lunch, and dinner. The hospitality industry, in order to keep costs down and remain competitive, uses a large number of part-time employees. Many hospitality departments have a skeleton staff of full-time employees, which are augmented by several part-time ones, as the business needs them.

Project Management

Project management means exactly that—managing a project. Project management is the task of completing the project on time and within budget. In the hospitality industry, we have a variety of projects at each level of the corporation. At the corporate level, there is, for instance, the construction of a new hotel or restaurant. At the unit level, there is the alteration or renovation of an existing building, and at the department level, there is the installation of a new piece of equipment or a new point-of-sale system. But project management is broader than these examples. What about the senior prom? That's a project, too. So are most of the catering functions that take place at convention centers and hotels.

Hospitality companies are increasingly using project management because the approach fits well with the need for flexibility and rapid response to perceived market opportunities. Sometimes an organization has a specific need for a project that does not fit into a regular planning schedule so they use project management. Project management works like this: Say the project is to become more environmentally friendly. A hospitality organization will create a team of associates from various departments and challenge them to come up with a plan to accomplish the goal of becoming more environmentally friendly. Figure 15–5 shows the steps in the project planning process.

The process begins by clearly defining the project's goals. This step is necessary because the manager and team need to know exactly what's expected. All

Step 1:	**Define Project Goals**
Step 2:	**Identify Resources and Activities Needed**
Step 3:	**Decide on Completion Sequence**
Step 4:	**Schedule Project Completion Activities**
Step 5:	**Assign Task and Budgetary Responsibilities**

Figure 15–5 *Steps in the Project Planning Process*

activities and the resources needed to do them must then be identified. What labor and materials are needed to complete the project? Once the activities have been identified, the sequence of completion needs to be determined. What activities must be completed before others can begin? Which can be done simultaneously? This step is actually done using flowchart-type diagrams such as a Gantt chart or a PERT network. Next, the project activities need to be scheduled. Time estimates for each activity are done, and these estimates are used to develop an overall project schedule and completion date.[11]

Check Your Knowledge
1. Describe the minimum acceptable staffing level for a restaurant as it relates to scheduling.
2. What are the steps in project management?

Trends in Planning

Given today's hospitality business environment of rapid change, planning needs to be done quickly and adjusted when necessary. Technology, especially the Internet, can be used to overcome time and distance, allowing for more people to have input into the planning process. Associates can contribute to the planning process online instead of going to meetings.

CASE STUDY

Shell's Seafood Restaurant also caters to weddings and other events in a small New England town. The following is an overview of the planning—or lack of planning that took place last summer. Jason, the restaurant's general manager, together with the wedding couple, planned the garden wedding and reception in a town park near the restaurant. At first, it seemed as if there were so many choices and decisions to be made, but as they went through the lists they had prepared, they were all pleased with the arrangements.

They chose a wedding ceremony time of 2 PM followed by a reception at 2:30 PM. The wedding couple and their families wanted it to be a special occasion but did not want to spend a fortune, so they decided to use Shell's Seafood Restaurant because

they had enjoyed meals there in the past. Jason prepared a menu which the couple liked: Cream of Asparagus Soup, Chicken Fricassée, Potatoes au gratin, Cauliflower Mornay, and for dessert: Crème Brûlé. Jason also suggested a white and red house wine with an allocation of 3/4 bottle per person. The wedding couple's aunt made the cake and it was delivered to the park, but when Jason's staff assembled it, the weight of the top two tiers, caused the cake to sink into the thin layer of icing and fall over.

The wedding ceremony was a success but as you can imagine the reception was not.

Discussion Question

1. Please list the planning errors that were made.

CAREER INFORMATION

Planning is an integral part of any career. Someone has to plan the strategic direction of all hospitality corporations. Likewise, middle- and lower-level managers, in order to be successful, need to plan and reevaluate plans. The larger corporations have planning departments, but operational experience is necessary before moving up to the corporate planning level.

SUMMARY

1. Planning involves selecting the various goals that the organization wants to achieve and the actions (objectives) that will ensure the organization accomplishes the goals.
2. Goals are set for each of the key operating areas.
3. Planning gives direction, not only to top managers, but to all associates as they focus on goal accomplishment.
4. Strategic (long-term) planning and strategic management involve the process of identifying the business of the corporation and the business it wants for the future, and then identifying the course of action it will pursue, given its strengths, weaknesses, opportunities, and threats.
5. There are three main strategic management tasks: developing a vision and mission statement, translating the mission into strategic goals, and creating a strategy or course of action to move the organization from where it is today to where it wants to be.
6. Strategic planning and management take place at the higher levels of management. This is known as corporate-level strategy.
7. There are four growth strategies: market penetration, geographic expansion, product development, and horizontal integration.
8. A strengths, weaknesses, opportunities, and threats (SWOT) analysis is a key strategic management technique.
9. Environmental scanning is the process of assessing information about the economic, social, political, and technological environment to anticipate and interpret changes in the environment.
10. Operational plans are generally for periods of up to one year and dovetail with the strategic plan.
11. There are seven steps in operational planning: setting objectives, analyzing and evaluating the environment, determining alternatives, evaluating alternatives, selecting the best solution, implementing the plan, and controlling and evaluating results.
12. Benchmarking is a concept that identifies the best way of doing something and which companies excel in the area under study.
13. Policies, procedures, and rules are examples of standing plans. Policies set broad guidelines, procedures specify what to do in given situations, and rules are very specific action guides that associates must follow.
14. Budgets are plans allocating money for specific activities. They are popular because they force managers to anticipate expected sales and budget expenses accordingly.
15. Goal setting is determining the outcomes for the organization and associates.
16. Objectives state how the goals will be met. Management by objectives is a managerial process that determines the goals of the organization then plans the objectives.
17. Project management is the task of completing a project on time and within budget.

KEY WORDS AND CONCEPTS

Benchmarking
Budget
Diversification
Environmental scanning
Forecasting
Geographic expansion
Goal setting
Goals
Horizontal integration

Joint ventures
Key operating areas
Management by objectives (MBO)
Market penetration
Objectives
Operational plans
Policies
Procedures

Product development
Programs
Project management
Rule
Scheduling
Standing plans
Strategic alliances
Strategic management
Strategic planning

Strategy
SWOT (strengths, weaknesses, opportunities, and threats) analysis
Total quality management (TQM)

REVIEW QUESTIONS

1. What does planning involve?
2. How are goals and objectives different?
3. What is strategic planning?
4. What is the distinction between SWOT analysis and environmental screening analysis?
5. Why do companies use policies, procedures, and rules?

INTERNET EXERCISE

Organization: Your restaurant chain.
 Web site: None
 Summary: Fast food chains need to know what their competitors are doing or going to do.

In this exercise you select fast food company Web sites and see what you can find out about your competitors.

APPLY YOUR KNOWLEDGE

1. Benchmarking can be an important tool and source of information for managers. It can also be useful to students, as you'll see in this team-based exercise. In your small group, discuss study habits that each of you has found to be effective from your years of being in school. As a group, come up with a bulleted list of at least eight effective study habits in the time allowed by your professor. When the professor calls time, each group should combine with one other group and share ideas, again in the time allowed by the professor. In this larger group, be sure to ask questions about suggestions that each small group had. Each small group should make sure it understands the suggestions of the other group with which it is working. When the professor calls time, each small group will then present and explain the study habit suggestions of the other group it was working with. After all groups have presented their suggestions, the class will come up with what it feels are the "best" study habits of all the ideas presented.

2. In groups of four, develop a plan for your formal class graduation dinner with a prominent guest speaker.[14]

ENDNOTES

1. This draws on Gary Dessler, *A Framework for Management*, 2/e. Upper Saddle River, NJ: Prentice Hall, 2002, p. 99.
2. Ibid., p. 100.
3. Personal conversation with Kenneth E. Crocker. May 15, 2005.
4. www.cleggsassociates.com. 2005.
5. http://www.apn.btbtravel.com/s/Editorial-Hotels-And-Resorts.asp?ReportID531401.
6. Personal conversation with Stephen Deuker. June 18, 2005.
7. Ibid.
8. Dessler, *Framework*, p. 108.
9. Robbins and Mary Coulter, *Management*, 8/e. Upper Saddle River, NJ: Prentice Hall, 2005, pp. 228–230.
10. Personal conversation with Kenneth E. Crocker. June 15, 2005.
11. Robbins and Coulter, *Management*, p. 240.

WEB RESOURCES

American Planning Association
www.planning.org

United States Small Business Administration (SBA)
www.sba.gov

Organizing

After reading and studying this chapter, you should be able to:

- Describe organizational structure and organizational design.
- Explain why structure and design are important to an organization.
- Identify the key elements of organizational structure.
- Differentiate between mechanistic and organic organizational designs.
- Explain team-based structures and why organizations use them.
- Describe matrix structures, project structures, independent business units, and boundaryless organizations.

From Planning to Organizing

Howard Schultz, head of Starbucks Corporation,[1] knows that with more than 2,200 Starbucks stores in the United States, organizing the company is no easy task. Such an organization needs training departments to turn college students into café managers (who know, for example, that every espresso must be pulled within 23 seconds or be thrown away), departments that sell coffee to United Airlines and supermarkets, and a way to manage stores in locations as far away as the Philippines and China. How to organize is, therefore, not an academic issue to Howard Schultz. He has discovered that planning and organizing are inseparable. When his company was small, its strategy focused on high-quality coffee drinks provided by small neighborhood coffeehouses. This strategy in turn suggested the main jobs for which Schultz had to hire lieutenants—for example, store management, purchasing, and finance and accounting. Departments then grew up around these jobs.

As Schultz's strategy evolved to include geographic expansion across the United States and abroad, his organization also had to evolve. Regional store management divisions were established to oversee the stores in each region. Today, with Starbucks coffee also sold to airlines, bookstores, and supermarkets, the company's structure is evolving again, with new departments organized to sell to and serve the needs of these new markets. What Schultz discovered is that the organization is determined by the plan; that is, strategy determines structure.

The Purpose of Organizing

The purpose of **organizing** is to get a job done efficiently and effectively by completing these tasks:

- Divide work to be done into specific jobs and departments.
- Assign tasks and responsibilities associated with individual jobs.
- Coordinate diverse organizational tasks.

Howard Schultz inviting guests into one of the new Starbucks.

- Cluster jobs into units.
- Establish relationships among individuals, groups, and departments.
- Establish formal lines of authority.
- Allocate and deploy organizational resources.

This chapter covers these important aspects of organization, but first we need to know what organization is. *Organization* refers to the arrangement of activities so that they systematically contribute to goal accomplishment. No one person can do all the things necessary for a hospitality organization to be successful. Imagine just one person trying to do all the different tasks that make a restaurant meal memorable.

Defining Organizational Structure

In the past few years, organizational structures have changed quite a bit. Traditional approaches were questioned and reevaluated as managers searched for structures that would best support and facilitate employees doing the organization's work. The structure needs to be efficient but also have the flexibility that is so necessary in today's dynamic environment. The challenge for managers is to design an organizational structure that allows employees to efficiently and effectively do their work.

An **organizational structure** is like a skeleton in that it lends support to the various departments in an organization. It provides the total framework by which job tasks are divided, grouped, and coordinated. In today's leaner and meaner hospitality business environment, organizations are flatter, meaning they have fewer levels of managers. They are also structured to better fulfill the needs of the guests. A typical example is the change of mind-set that turned the traditional organizational chart upside down, as shown in Figure 16–1. The general manager used to be at the top of the organizational chart and the frontline associate at the bottom—the guest never appeared on the chart! Now we have the guest at the top of the inverted pyramid and the general manager at the bottom. Given higher labor costs, there are also fewer associates to do the same amount of work. Organizations have had to become more flexible in their desire to delight the guest. Some hotels have created rapid reaction teams of associates who respond to urgent guest needs. These teams are from several different departments but come together in an effort to please the guest. More about this type of team and other teams are discussed later in this chapter.

Work Specialization and Division of Labor

You may recall the humble beginnings of Marriott International as a Hot Shoppe. Mr. and Mrs. Marriott probably decided what was going to be on the menu, then they purchased the food, cooked it, and served it. They also collected the money and made sure everything was to their guests' liking. It's fun and stimulating to have your own business and see the results of food well prepared and served and gratified guests returning. Now consider the organizational structure of Marriott International today.

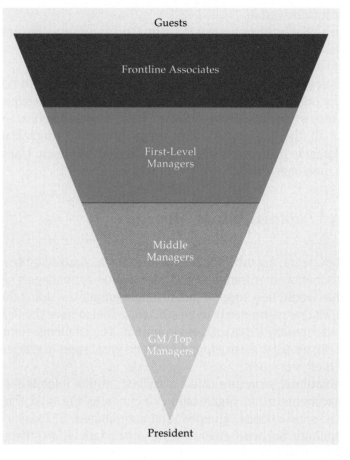

Figure 16–1   *The New "Upside-Down" Organizational Chart*

Today, **work specialization** is used to describe the extent to which jobs in an organization are divided into separate tasks. One person does not do the entire job. Instead, it is broken down into steps and a different person completes each step. In the hospitality industry, we use work specialization in various departments but not to the extent that heavy industry does. The reason is that in the hospitality industry we are not producing a commodity, so the line cook is likely to continue to prepare a variety of different dishes. However, the concept does apply to a banquet kitchen when a line is created to plate the food. In such a situation, each person will add a particular part of the meal to the plate, and someone will check it and place it in the heated rolling cart. In other departments, such as housekeeping, work specialization has some application: In making up guest rooms, housekeepers may work in pairs, with each specializing in a particular task. However, because the tasks are very repetitive, housekeepers prefer to do more than one task to avoid boredom.

Work specialization allows professionals to focus on their specialty.

Departmentalization

We are all familiar with governmental departments such as the Department of Motor Vehicles and Department of Labor, and your college probably has departments of admissions, financial aid, and student affairs, to name just a few. Once jobs have been divided up by work specialization, they have to be grouped back together so that the common tasks can be coordinated. This is called departmentalization. Every organization has its own form of **departmentalization** according to its needs. The organization's structure is shown in its **organization chart** (Figure 16–2).

Departments are created to coordinate the work of several associates in a given area. An example is housekeeping in a hotel or marketing and sales for a convention center. The main question facing company presidents is "What

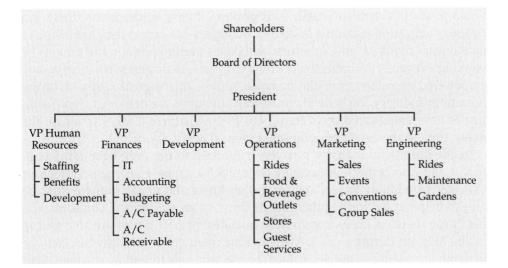

Figure 16–2 *Organization Chart for a Theme Park*

form of organization will best meet the organization's goals?" Should it be organized by function, product, service, guest, or territory, or by a combination of these?

The simplest form of departmentalization is by **function.** A large hotel rooms division has a reservations department, uniformed service department, front desk, communications department, concierge, housekeeping, and so on—each with its own specialized function.

Choice Hotels International departmentalizes its lodging properties by **product** in the form of brands: Comfort Inns, Comfort Suites, Quality Hotels, Sleep Inns, Clarion, MainStay Suites, Econo Lodge, and Roadway Inns. Each brand attracts a slightly different target market and offers slightly different services and is managed independently.

Sodexho and ARAMARK, both huge multinational corporations with billions of dollars in sales, departmentalize by **guest** needs. They have departments or divisions for education, business and industry, health care, and so on. The sales department of a convention and visitors bureau may departmentalize itself by market served: travel industry, medical, legal, insurance, leisure travel, incentive travel, or military.

Many of the larger companies departmentalize by **territory** when they have representation in several states, provinces, and countries. Avis car rental has representation in a number of states, provinces, and countries. They recognize that each geographic market has its own nuances.

Authority and Responsibility

Authority is closely associated with chain of command because it gives the right to managers to exercise their power in a given situation. Authority should be commensurate with responsibility. In other words, managers should only exercise power in accordance with their position. In any organization, there is a two-way obligation regarding authority: Managers can expect their associates to do the work required, and, in return, associates need to perform their duties by working efficiently and effectively. In recent years, managers have increasingly empowered associates to make more decisions—this is particularly so in the hospitality industry. We have to ensure that our guests are delighted. Some companies have empowered their employees to do whatever it takes to please the guest, even to the extent of **comping** a room if necessary.

In the hospitality industry it is very important to not only have formal authority but also respect. Associates are quick to gauge a new supervisor's or manager's credibility to see how much they know and to determine if they are able to help out by "getting their hands dirty" in an emergency. Someone who has "been there" is likely to gain the associates' respect if they are able to step in and help out during a crisis. Managers are often given authority but lack the in-depth knowledge of the department to really be able to lead by example. Simply put: "You've got to know your onions." Without credibility and therefore respect, it is much more difficult for associates to work with managers to get the job done. Thus many companies require that a newly appointed manager have experience in the area or at least an accelerated apprenticeship in the area he or she will be responsible for, thus building up the credibility of the new manager.

When authority is delegated, so also should commensurate **responsibility** be delegated. That means that you are responsible for the performance of your operation and the associates who work with you. That can sometimes be a big responsibility. What if an associate serves an alcoholic drink to a guest who is intoxicated and that guest later drives off and has an accident, injuring not only himself but also another innocent party. Are you responsible? Yes! As manager of the department or restaurant you are not only responsible but liable as well.

Check Your Knowledge

1. Why is organizing important?
2. What are the drawbacks of work specialization?
3. Describe ways managers can departmentalize work activities.

Chain of Command

Organization charts not only show the structure and size of the organization but also the **chain of command** (Figure 16–3). Departments are clearly indicated, and titles may be used to show each associate's position. The chain of command begins at the top of the organization—in the case of a large publicly traded company like Marriott International with the board of directors, who are elected by

Chain of Command for a Hotel

Board of Directors
↑ ↓
CEO/President
↑ ↓
Top Executives (CFO, VP, etc.)
↑ ↓
Regional/Area Vice Presidents
↑ ↓
General Manager
↑ ↓
Directors (Director of Rooms Division,
Director of Food and Beverage, etc.)
↑ ↓
Department Heads (Executive Chef, etc.)
↑ ↓
Supervisors
↑ ↓
Frontline Associates

Figure 16–3 *An Example of a Hotel's Chain of Command*

The Guest Is God

An industry consultant was once in Japan giving a seminar with another colleague. The colleague began by saying that in business today the guest is king, and as he was saying that a gentleman rushed down from the back row and grabbed the microphone and told the audience that the guest is not king but God! The gentleman was the company president. Reflecting on this unusual happening, the consultant realized just how much the Japanese revere their guests.

the shareholders. The board of directors select a president (chief executive officer, CEO), and the president selects the top executives like the chief financial officer (CFO), vice president of marketing, and so on. The president and the executive team develop plans that are presented to the board for approval and then implement those plans. The chain of command is helpful for associates who have questions or need advice because they will know whom to ask. Similarly, they know to whom they are responsible for their work performance. The chain of command should flow from the top to the bottom of the organization and up from bottom to top. This is usually illustrated by lines of authority that indicate who is responsible for what or over whom.

Increasing Span of Control

The question is often asked, "How many associates can a manager supervise?" The answer used to be between 8 and 12. Now, however, the answer is likely to be 12 to 18. The reason for this increase in span of control is that organizations needed to become more competitive with not only other U.S. companies but foreign ones, too. Consider the cost savings realized by eliminating levels of management: If there are two organizations, both with 4,000 employees, and one organization has a span of control of, say, 10, and the other, 15, the wider span of control will have fewer levels of management and lower costs because there will be fewer managers. But how much will that save? Well, if the average manager makes $65,000 a year, then the total savings would be $8.66 million. Having said that many hospitality corporations have increased their span of control, it is also fair to say that they realize that there is a point when the number of people reporting to them overburdens associates. At that point, managers don't have the time to give advice, nor do they have time to properly supervise their associates, so standards decline. So what factors determine the appropriate span

Empowerment allows associates to own the guest request and check to see that it has been fulfilled.

A Day in the Life of Andrea Kazanjian
The Ritz-Carlton Members Club, Sarasota

Andrea Kazanjian serves as Director of Membership for The Ritz-Carlton Members Club, Sarasota. In her role, Kazanjian is charged with developing and implementing strategies that shape the membership experience for this unique and exclusive luxury tier brand extension.

A day in the life of Andrea Kazanjian consists of conducting membership training workshops, developing professional and successful Membership Sales Executive and Members Services teams, designing all membership collateral and messaging, and managing a number of marketing campaigns. These are just a few of the techniques she will utilize to assist the organization in meeting the aggressive membership recruitment and sales goals outlined by the Ownership.

Kazanjian earned a B.S. in Hotel, Restaurant, and Travel Administration from the University of Massachusetts, Amherst, on a swimming scholarship as Division I Swimmer and Team Captain. A native of Albany, New York, she is a board member on the Sarasota Chamber of Commerce's Young Professionals Group and volunteer for the community outreach subcommittee, member of the Junior League of Sarasota, representative of the Sarasota Chamber of Commerce Leadership Luncheon Series, member of the United Way of Sarasota, and leader of The Ritz-Carlton, Sarasota, campaign.

An extension of The Ritz-Carlton Hotel Company, L.L.C., The Ritz-Carlton Members Club is a luxury tier nonequity membership that combines the benefits of a private social club with the tradition of personalized Ritz-Carlton services and world-class amenities designed to compliment the Sarasota lifestyle. Memberships have the opportunity to access the Members Beach Club, on Lido Key, the Members Spa Club, and the Tom Fazio–designed Members Golf Club.

of control? It depends on the type of work being done. Is it straightforward or complex? Are the associates highly skilled and well trained, or is there a training need? Other factors include the degree to which standardized procedures are in place, the information technology available, the leadership style of the manager, and how experienced the manager is in the area of concern.

Empowerment

Given the increasing span of control, **empowerment** has become an industry norm. As managers delegate more authority and responsibility, associates have become empowered to do whatever it takes to delight the guest. Frontline associates are in a better position to know guests' wants and needs than management, so it makes sense to empower them to take care of delighting guests. In the old days, associates had to check with management before making a decision to ensure guest delight. Let's look at an example. A guest and his wife check into a hotel that advertises a room rate that includes a buffet breakfast. Unfortunately, the wife catches a nasty virus and is not well enough to go down to enjoy the buffet breakfast. Her husband says that he will call her to let her know what's offered at the buffet, so she can choose something and he can bring it up for her. He goes down to the restaurant and dutifully calls her to tell her what's available. She tells him what she wants: scrambled eggs and bacon.

When the husband explains to a server that his wife is sick and not able to come down for the buffet and requests a tray to carry up her breakfast, the server listens and goes to consult a more senior server, but not the manager. The husband then explains all over again and once more asks for a tray. This time he is told that food cannot be taken upstairs. The husband then says, "My wife is sick and needs something to eat and drink. We've already paid for it. . . . Get the manager here now!" The server later comes over to say that the duty manager says the husband can choose anything from the cold section of the buffet but not the hot part. That does it. The guest demands that the general manager, not the duty manager, be summoned. You get the picture. All of this could have been avoided if only the associates had been empowered to use a little discretion.

Centralization and Decentralization

Some organizations make most of the decisions at the corporate office and inform unit managers of them. This process is called **centralization.** If the top managers make the organization's key decisions with little or no input from subordinates, then the organization is centralized. Other organizations make most of the decisions at the unit level or with input from associates. This is **decentralization.** In reality, organizations are never completely centralized or decentralized because they could not function if all decisions were made by the CEO, nor could they function properly if all decisions were made at the lowest level. Figure 16–4 illustrates the difference between a centralized and a decentralized organization.

Many companies have become more centralized in an effort to save costs and improve service to associates. Due to the rapid changes in the hospitality business, organizations are becoming more flexible and responsive. This means the organizations are becoming more decentralized. A good example is Choice Hotels' restructuring of their franchise services. They have centralized franchising services under one umbrella and created one brand management position that

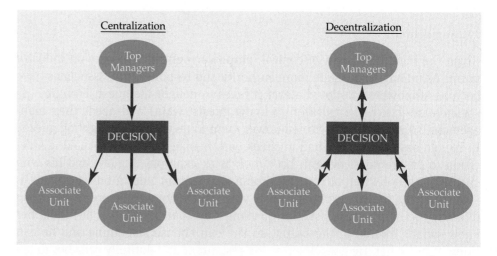

Figure 16–4 *Centralization versus Decentralization in an Organization*

oversees the company's eight brands. As a result, the company closed five market offices. In large companies especially, lower-level managers who are "closer to the action" and typically have more detailed knowledge about problems and how best to solve them are empowered to delight the guest.

Check Your Knowledge

1. How are the chain of command and span of control used in organizing?
2. Describe the factors that influence greater centralization and those factors that influence greater decentralization.

Organizational Design Decisions

Organizations are structured in different ways, depending on which structure best suits their needs. A company with 20 associates will look very different from one with 10,000 associates. But even organizations of comparable size don't necessarily have similar structures. What works for one organization may not work for another. How do managers decide which is the best structure for them? That decision depends on certain contingency factors that we are about to discuss.

Mechanistic and Organic Organizations

Mechanistic and organic organizations are described in Figure 16–5. The **mechanistic organization** is a rigid and tightly controlled structure. It is characterized by a relatively high degree of job specialization, rigid departmentalization, many layers of management, narrow spans of control, high formalization, centralized decision making, a limited information network (mostly downward communication), and little participation in decision making by lower associates. This combination of elements results in what is called a *tall organizational structure.*[2]

With mechanistic organizations, there is a strong adherence to the unity of command principle and a formal hierarchy of authority, with each person controlled and supervised by one supervisor. Keeping the span of control small at increasingly

Mechanistic Organization	*Organic Organization*
High specialization	Division of labor
Rigid departmentalization	Adaptive, flexible departmentalization
Narrow span of control	Few formal rules, little supervision
High formalization	Low in formalization
Limited information network	Low in complexity
Centralization	Decentralization

Figure 16–5 *Mechanisitic and Organic Organizations*

higher levels in the organization creates tall impersonal structures. As the distance between the top and bottom of the organization expands, top management increasingly imposes rules and regulations. Top management substitutes rules and regulations because they cannot easily enforce control. It is top management's aim for mechanistic organizations to be well oiled by rules, regulations, and routinization. The intention is to minimize the impact of personalities and judgments that might allow inefficiencies. Standardization is expected to lead to stability and predictability because confusion and ambiguity are eliminated.

In the hospitality industry, none of the organizations is completely mechanistic in structure; however, some are predominantly mechanistic—you may be working or have worked in the past for one of them. They are not necessarily all bad, but they are not the preferred type of organizational structure in today's rapidly changing environment.

An **organic organization** is in direct contrast with the mechanistic form. It is low in complexity, low in formalization, and decentralized. The organic organization is a highly adaptive form that is as loose and flexible as the mechanistic organization is rigid and stable. The loose structure allows it to change rapidly as needs require. Organic organizations use division of labor, but the jobs are not standardized. Associates are professionals who are technically proficient and trained to handle diverse problems. They need very few formal rules and little direct supervision because their training has installed in them standards of professional conduct. For instance, when given a recipe a competent professional chef does not need to be given procedures on how to use it. Most problems can be solved after conferring with colleagues. Professional standards guide associates' behavior. The organic organization is low in centralization in order for the professional to respond quickly to problems and because top management cannot be expected to possess the expertise to make necessary decisions.

Most hospitality organizations are based on a combination of the two organizational structures. It is also likely that the larger an organization becomes, the more mechanistic it will be. An independent restaurant is more likely to use associates' opinions and be adaptable. Communication is likely to be more informal, and to some extent authority may be decentralized. A larger restaurant chain is more likely to have more rigid hierarchical relationships, fixed duties, formal communication channels, and centralized decision making.

Coordination of Activities

When there are only a few associates in an operation, everyone can catch up quickly, but as the business expands, problems can and do occur unless there is good **coordination of activities.** The hospitality business is fast paced—guests want something now or even sooner! Departments need to communicate quickly and often to keep up with guest requests. You may have experienced an occasion when something did not go as planned—perhaps it was the checkout delay at your hotel or there were charges on your folio that were not yours—but now you're in a rush to get to the airport. You get the picture—someone made a mistake!

Coordination of different functions and areas is critical in exceeding guest expectations—an event coordinator goes over the event plan with service associates.

Contingency Planning

Top managers give a lot of thought to designing an appropriate structure. What that appropriate structure is depends on the organization's strategy, size, technology, and degree of environmental uncertainty. Structure should follow strategy and be closely linked.

An organization's size generally affects its structure. Larger organizations tend to have more specialization, departmentalization, centralization, and rules and regulations than do small organizations. If there are 30 associates at one hospitality company and 300 at another, then the one with 300 will have more departments and be more mechanistic.

Every organization has some form of technology that relates to structure. Consider a hotel company that has a central reservations center. It can hold the inventory of all the hotels in the chain and be far more efficient in offering available rates and rooms to callers and also make the inventory available to travel agents and Internet travel organizations. A central reservations center can also do a better job of controlling and maximizing revenue for the available rooms than a bunch of decentralized centers.

Technology has enabled restaurant chains to transfer data and store menus and operations and training manuals via the Internet. In some cases this has led to a change in organizational structure. In the hospitality industry, technology has tended to aid the existing structure to perform better—sometimes with fewer associates. A convention center may have the latest software program for reserving and allocating space, but it will not significantly change the organization's structure; someone must take the guest requests and enter them into the program.

Contingency factors deal with what hospitality organizations refer to as the *what-ifs.* What if "such and such" happens? The company plans and organizes for several possible outcomes. After the terrorist attack on September 11, 2001, many hospitality companies immediately planned and organized for a drastic drop in business. Departments were greatly reduced, reorganized, or even closed in an effort to reduce the losses.

Contemporary Organizational Designs

Team-Based Structures

In response to competitive market demands for being lean, flexible, and innovative, managers are finding creative ways to structure and organize work and to make their organizations more responsive to guest needs. The first of the contemporary designs is a **work team structure;** either the complete organization or a part of it is made up of teams that perform the duties necessary to delight the guest (Figure 16–6). This concept is, like many, borrowed from business but has relevance for hospitality managers. Perhaps the best use of this concept for hospitality managers is with TQM, which you may remember we introduced in Chapter 1. Basically, teams of mostly frontline associates take on the challenge of improving guest services and products. At first, these teams are often made up of associates from one department but later can be made up of associates from different departments. This actually improves coordination between departments. Sales departments can also work well in

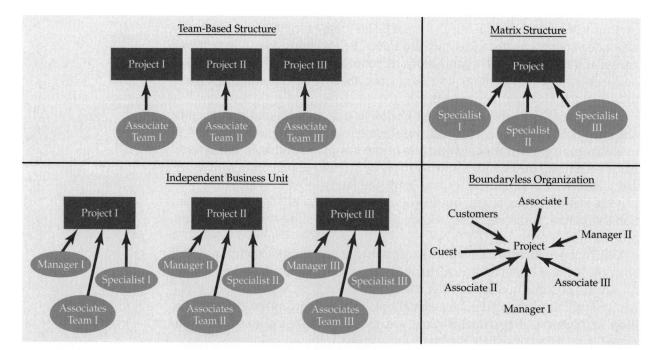

Figure 16–6   *The Four Types of Contemporary Organizational Designs*

teams and so can the banquet kitchen and for that matter most departments in a hospitality operation. However, the team is more likely to consist of associates from one department as opposed to associates from several departments. In any event, teams tend to be more productive. There are two main types of work teams: integrated and self-managed. Integrated work teams are given a number of tasks by the man-

Team based structures can be made up of part or all of the company.

ager, and the team gives specific assignments to members. Self-managed work teams are assigned a goal, and the team plans, organizes, leads, and controls to achieve the goal.[3]

Matrix and Project Structures

The **matrix structure** is an organizational structure that assigns specialists from different departments to work on a project—for example, a new attraction, restaurant, or hotel opening. The specialists come together to pool their knowledge and experience to work on the project. During this time they may have two bosses: their normal department head plus the project manager. To work effectively, project managers and department heads need to communicate on a regular basis. Matrix structures are appealing to organizations that want to speed up the decision-making process or get projects accomplished more quickly.

A matrix organization, however, does not work for everyone. They can be disruptive because the participants must take a leave from their current position, and then, once the project is completed, they need to return to their original position. Additionally, having more than one manager can be frustrating. **Project structures** are those in which employees continuously work on projects. Unlike a matrix structure, members of a project do not return to their departments after project completion. They go on to the next project. An example of a project structure in the hospitality industry would be a preopening team for attractions, hotels, resorts, and restaurants. Teams of employees become part of the project team because they have specific knowledge and expertise. Once the project is complete, the members go on to the next project.

Independent Business Units

Some hospitality companies have adopted the concept of **independent business units (IBUs)** to encourage departments to not only delight the guest but also to watch the money all the way to the bottom line. In other words, the IBU becomes its own independent business and makes decisions accordingly with little or no need to get approval for routine operational decisions. The unit can implement strategies that will improve guest satisfaction or reduce costs by finding a quicker or better way of doing something. Forming IBUs is an excellent

Personal Profile: Isadore Sharp

Chairman, President, and Founder, Four Seasons Regent Hotels

Isadore Sharp, a first-generation Canadian, is the founder and chief executive officer and chairman of the board of Four Seasons Regent Hotels. From one motel on Toronto's Jarvis Street in the early 1960s has grown the world's largest luxury hotel chain—a multimillion-dollar global hotel empire. Four Seasons Regent's success is largely a reflection of the drive, determination, and personal taste and style of Isadore Sharp.

Four Seasons was built slowly, deal by deal. From the first little motel that Sharp literally helped construct to the complex Asian agreement in which Four Seasons acquired Regent Hotels International Inc., the growth of this company is largely the result of one man's vision. Isadore Sharp (called Issy by friends and family) has created a company that friends and foes alike agree is a model for how Canadian companies can compete globally in an increasingly interconnected world economy.

Currently, the Four Seasons Regent manages and owns 65 properties in 29 countries, with 20 more under construction, and continues to move ahead with more hotel plans in different countries. Isadore Sharp's success is all the more remarkable because he did not inherit vast wealth and did not rise through the ranks of a major corporation with ready access to international money markets. He is a self-made man, consistent, who has control of his spirit. He believes in excellent quality for both his hotels and his company. Sharp clearly loves his business and credits the Four Seasons Regent team with the successes of the company. He has been inducted into the Canadian Business Hall of Fame and has received the International Distinguished Entrepreneur Award. Sharp still spends one day in each hotel meeting with employees. Interestingly, none of his three sons is interested in taking over Dad's job.

strategy to get associates to realize the total picture of revenue and expenses for a department. It forces associates to engage in all elements of management to make a profit. IBUs also enable management to seriously look at departments not making sufficient profit contribution, with a view toward making changes and improvements or eliminating the department. Departments that once made a loss are now making a profit as a result of the company installing an IBU system of organizational design.

Boundaryless Organizations

Another contemporary approach to organizational design is the **boundaryless organization,** an organization whose design is not defined by, or limited to, the horizontal, vertical, or external boundaries imposed by a predefined structure.[4] The term was coined by Jack Welch, former chairman of General Electric, who wanted to eliminate vertical and horizontal boundaries within GE and break down external barriers between the company and its customers and suppliers. This idea may sound odd, yet many of today's most successful organizations are finding that they can most effectively operate in today's environment by remaining close to the guest and being flexible and unstructured. The boundaryless organization seeks to eliminate the chain of command, to have appropriate spans of control, and to replace departments with empowered teams. Hospitality organizations are moving in this direction but are not there yet. Some might feel that this is not a concept that will work for hospitality organizations, whereas others might think it's a great idea. Hospitality companies recognize that it is important to stay close to the guest but are challenged to create a boundaryless organization.

Teams and Employee Involvement

Teams are task-oriented work groups; they can either be formally appointed or may evolve informally. We all work with others, to a greater or lesser extent, in order to meet or exceed goals. Both formal and informal teams make important contributions to the company and to associates' need satisfaction. For example, an informal team from one hotel saved the company more than $250,000 a year after the team made a proposal about energy savings. Each team member not only received a sizable bonus, but their employee satisfaction scores were significantly higher than those of associates who did not participate in the team.

Teams are great for doing work that is complex, interrelated, or of a volume larger than one person can handle. Harold Geneen, while chairman of ITT, said, "If I had enough arms and legs, I'd do it all myself." We all know that associates cannot do everything themselves due to limitations of arms and legs, time, expertise, knowledge, and other resources. There is a certain "buzz" in a restaurant on a busy Friday night; when the kitchen is getting "slammed," you know what teamwork is or isn't!

The funny thing about teams, as you have probably experienced by now, is that you don't always get to choose who you work with—just like when you do term papers and projects in teams. And even when you do get to choose classmates, it sometimes doesn't work out. They don't do their fair share or something else doesn't work. Yet, in the hospitality industry we are constantly working in teams to exceed guest expectations. So how can we make teams more effective?

Group Dynamics

Why are some groups more successful than others? Why does a team of mediocre players sometimes beat a team of superior players? You've probably experienced a situation in which, when seemingly against all odds, a team excels. Remember the survival programs on television in the early 2000s? A group of people was dropped off in some remote place, and over a period of time the group members had to survive as teams, *but* they could vote people "off the island." Imagine if we did that in the hospitality industry!

Why and how this happens is called *group dynamics* and includes variables such as the abilities of the group's members, the size of the group, the level of conflict, and the internal pressures on members to conform to the group's norms. Sometimes external influences inhibit the group's performance. Corporate may dictate policies that make it more difficult for the group to succeed,

Principles of Organization for Disaster Operations

Hank Christen and Paul Maniscalco
George Washington University
Unconventional Concepts Inc.

The development of a comprehensive emergency management plan (CEMP) is based on a functional organization, not a hierarchy. The normal top-down flow of orders, instructions, and information through multiple levels of management (a hierarchy) does not translate effectively to disasters. The function, not the title or level of the player(s), is the key.

Disaster management is organic, loose, and flexible. The first principle of this function-based system is decentralization. It is a "flat system" with only three layers: manager/staff, functional directors (operations, logistics, etc.), and sectors. Sectors are established as needed to support the primary functions (example: a food/water sector assigned by the logistics director).

The second key principle is chain/unity of command. Someone is in charge, there are functional directors, and there are sector leaders. Information and direction flows from the manager to the functional directors, to the sector leader, and vice versa. Bottom-up information flow is as relevant in a disaster as top-down information flow. Sector leaders who are physically involved often have more knowledge and insight into specific problems than the boss at the top. Senior managers must empower their subordinates and trust them.

The third key principle of organization is span of control. The span of control in disaster operations is much narrower than in normal business management. A span of control of three to four should be maintained. The environment is stressful, with poor communications, inadequate resources, and short decision times.

An effective organizational tool to keep the span of control within limits is branching: dividing a functional level into two or more segments called branches. For example, the logistics director can divide responsibilities into two areas: service branch, which is responsible for communications and food/water, and support branch, which is responsible for facilities, supplies, and maintenance.

The incident manager needs a staff (called the management staff) for assistance. The three key positions on the management staff are:

- *Liaison*—serves as a point of contact with emergency responders and other involved agencies, companies, or organizations
- *Public information*—coordinates with the local public information officer; drafts and implements public information strategy
- *Safety officer*—coordinates with incident safety officer; responsible for safety monitoring of all employee activities; has authority to suspend unsafe procedures or practices

During emergency activities, the planning director must maintain a disaster organizational chart listing positions and names of employee assignments. Organizational restructuring and personnel assignments must be charted during each briefing period to ensure that all team members fully understand their positions: whom they direct and whom they report to. A preprinted (legal size: 8 1/2″ × 14″) chart showing sector boxes under each functional box needs to be developed. As sectors are established or disbanded, they should be added to or deleted from the chart. A bulletin-board-size (4′ × 6′) chart (use dry-erase material) should be posted in the internal management center. A disaster demands a very flexible and organic structure; sectors are frequently established and dismantled in response to unpredictable event dynamics.

Job descriptions are another organizational tool that helps to ensure effective disaster management. All positions must be defined. The descriptions should be brief and concise. Employees should be assigned to functions and sectors based on their skill sets. For example, a maintenance director is a good choice for the position of logistics director. An individual may shift jobs during emergencies; for example, a marketing manager with previous military planning experience is the logical choice for planning director during an emergency. It is imperative that everyone understand his or her role in the crisis setting, especially if roles change from normal assignments.

Critical Factors

- Focus on functions instead of a hierarchy.
- Maintain a flat organizational structure.
- The ideal span of control is three or four operations.
- Utilize a disaster organizational chart.

or there may be a shortage of resources. One of the fascinating aspects of group dynamics is the members of the group. You may have experienced a group project at college. Sometimes you had to choose whom you worked with, and sometimes your group members were selected randomly. Which worked best?

How Companies Use Teams at Work

Hospitality companies use teams at work in a variety of ways. One way is to structure the organization into teams from the start. Instead of calling them departments, they are called teams. This implies, of course, that employees must be **team players,** which is vital in the fast-paced hospitality industry. Another way management can use teams is through total quality management (TQM) programs that involve associates working in teams to constantly improve the guest experience. Teams are formed from either individual departments or several different departments. They choose an area of the operation that needs improvement, usually one of guest concern, and proceed to make changes that will benefit the guest. TQM teams have made important contributions to the industry and continue to do so.

   Self-managed teams make decisions that were once made by managers. This saves managers time, allowing them to concentrate on more important things. We saw an example in Chapter 4: Hotel housekeepers who score highly on room inspections no longer need to have their rooms checked by a floor housekeeper. These teams of housekeepers actually receive a bonus for superior performance, and the hotel saves the salary of the floor housekeepers. Self-managed teams can and do work successfully in several types of hospitality organizations from theme parks to convention centers.

How to Build Productive Teams

Building productive teams is critical to the success of any organization, especially in the service-oriented hospitality industry. In recent years, the introduction of TQM processes has significantly increased the number of teams in the hospitality industry. At the heart of TQM is process improvement, and associate participation is the heartbeat. **Productive teams** are built by giving associates the authority, responsibility, and encouragement to come together to work on guest-related improvements that will enhance not only the guest experience but also make the associates' jobs easier. Teams need leadership, which is either appointed by management or the team is allowed to choose a leader. As with any other endeavor, goals and objectives need to be set and the team given the resources it needs to accomplish those goals. It is amazing to see the enthusiasm that teams can generate as they work on improving the guest experience. Associates will come up with great ideas that can save money and provide guests with better service. Team building happens when members interact to learn how each member thinks and works. Through close interaction, team members learn to develop increased trust and openness. When a team focuses on goal setting and

Corporate Profile: Six Flags

Six Flags is a world-renowned theme park. The company owns and operates 38 different parks spread out over North America, Latin America, and Europe. Locations include Mexico City, Belgium, France, Spain, Germany, and most major metropolitan areas in the United States. In fact, having a park in 40 of the 50 major metropolitan areas in the United States has earned Six Flags the title of world's largest regional theme park company. Annually, more than 50 million visitors are reported to entertain themselves at Six Flags theme parks worldwide. The company prides itself in claiming that 98 percent of the U.S. population is within an eight-hour drive to any one of the numerous Six Flags theme parks.

Now who is behind this huge success? The founder of the first theme park was a man named Angus Wynne. He was a Texas oil baron with a vision. His vision was to create a family entertainment park that was fun as well as affordable and, most importantly, within reachable distance to where people lived. A simple amusement park was transformed into a theme park by Wynne adding innovative rides with theme presentations. His first park opened in Texas in 1961. The transformation proved to be a huge success with the public; crowds flocked to the newly opened theme park.

The park was named after the six different flags that flew over Texas at one time, representing the six different countries that marked Texas's past history. The theme park was divided into six different regions, each modeled

This ride, called Viper, is located in the Six Flags Magic Mountain theme park in Los Angeles. It is reported to be the world's largest looping roller coaster. It is 188 feet high, with seven loops that turn you upside down at a speed of 70 miles per hour. (Courtesy of Six Flags Magic Mountain.)

after the country it represented. Visitors could marvel at Spanish haciendas or French bistros, all the while in the company of Southern belles and pirates.

Today, Six Flags has a licensing agreement with DC Comics and Warner Bros. This means characters such as Batman, Superman, and Bugs Bunny and the gang can be found wandering around the parks and having their pictures taken with park visitors. With fantastic rides and show-stopping entertainment, the parks have become one of the first-choice amusement parks for entertainment-seeking families and individuals.

Funding for expansion of the company was drawn primarily from the profits made from the first successful parks opened, including the first one in Texas. In 1996 Six Flags went public for the first time, meaning it allowed the public to purchase its stock as opposed to hand-picked private investors. The shares were sold at $18 each, and their purchase totaled nearly $70 million. Only one year later the company had raised $200 million with its public offering. With these kinds of funds, Six Flags continued purchasing land or old amusement parks and turning them into Six Flags theme parks, rapidly expanding their reach. Currently Six Flags employs 42,000 people, representing a 10 percent year-on-year growth rate. The parks have become so successful and have such a high income that large corporations, including AOL, Kodak, Perrier, Pringles, and Univision, signed major sponsorship deals with Six Flags.

who will plan on accomplishing what by when, and so on, the team should be on its way to becoming a high-achieving team.

Job Rotation

Job rotation is an excellent way to relieve the possible boredom and monotony that can be a disadvantage of work specialization because it gives associates a broader range of experiences. Once associates have mastered the jobs they were hired to do, there is a tendency for boredom to set in. Job rotation creates interest and assists in developing associates to take on additional responsibilities. The management training programs of some of the major hospitality corporations are good examples of job rotation; graduates spend a few months in several departments before selecting an area of specialization. Even then, as a front-line manager, you are likely to move through a few departments to build up your knowledge and experience. Job rotation does create some additional costs, mostly in the area of training and reduced productivity, because as associates move into new positions, they need time to become proficient in their new roles. A major benefit of job rotation is that associates become well rounded in the operation of the corporation, and many associates are promoted as a result of gaining the additional knowledge and experience.

Job Enlargement and Job Enrichment

Job enlargement increases the scope of the associates' work. Originally, it was intended as a way of maintaining interest in the work; more recently, it has become an economic necessity. Today, hospitality management professionals have more work and responsibilities than ever before—that's why workplace stress has become an issue. However, no one in the hospitality industry can say that his or her job is uneventful. In our business no two days are alike, and, for many, that's one of the fascinations of the hospitality business, despite the increased workload. **Job enrichment** adds some planning and evaluating responsibilities to a position. It gives associates greater control over their work by allowing them to assume some tasks typically done by their supervisors.

Trends in Organizing

- Computerized scheduling programs save the organizer time and limit the error margin for being over- or understaffed.
- The fact that recipes are just a click away on the Internet helps speed the organizational process tremendously.
- The new dynamic of multitasking has caused a drastic change in the organizational chart. For example, today, front desk workers are responsible for much more than just checking guests in and out. Through multitasking, they simultaneously act as phone operators, customer service agents, tour guides, and occasionally concierges.
- A new trend following the September 11, 2001, tragedy is to decentralize organizations.
- Reduced occupancies at most hotels have led to a reduction in staff and managerial positions. This in turn has led to more decentralized organizations with fewer levels of management.

CASE STUDY

The Organization of Outback Steakhouse

Chris Sullivan, Bob Basham, Trudy Cooper, and Tim Gannon—cofounders of the Outback Steakhouse concept—began their restaurant careers as a busboy, dishwasher, server, and a chef's assistant. So how did they manage to build one of the all-time most successful restaurant concepts? Their careers may have had humble beginnings but they had the money to excel. Chris and Bob met at Bennigan's (part of Steak and Ale). They honed their management skills under the mentorship of industry legend Norman Brinker, who later financed Chris and Bob's franchised chain of Chili's restaurants in Georgia and Florida. They later sold the Chili's restaurants back to Brinker for $3 million. This seed money allowed them to develop a restaurant concept they had been toying with.

The concept was for a casual themed steakhouse and because the partners did not like a western theme (it had already been done by others), they opted for an Australian theme because, at the time, there was a lot of hype about Australia. Australia had just won the America's cup (a major sailboat race held every four years), and the movie *Crocodile Dundee* was popular. Like all new restaurant concepts, they searched for a suitable name. It was Beth Basham who came up with the idea of Outback for the name of the steakhouse—she wrote it on a mirror in lipstick. The Outback themed concept was just what the partners wanted—a casual, fun, family and yes, the highest quality food, which is reflected in their 40 percent food cost (the industry norm for steakhouses is about 36 percent). Chris and Bob asked Tim Gannon, who at the time hardly had enough money to buy the gas to drive to Tampa, to join them. Organizationally, each of the partners "brought something to the table." Chris was the visionary one, Bob the operations person, Tim the chef, and Trudy the trainer. Later they realized they needed a numbers guy and in 1990 Bob Merritt became chief financial officer (CFO).

Instead of fancy marketing research, the partners did lots of talking and observation on what people were eating—remember this was the time when eating red meat was almost taboo. The partners figured that people were not eating as much red meat at home but, when they dined out they were ready for a good steak.

Initially, the partners thought of setting up one restaurant and then few more restaurants, this would allow them to spend more time on the golf course and with their families. So, the success of Outback surprised the partners as well as the Wall Street pundits. The organization grew quickly and by the mid 1990s there were more than 200 stores open; plus they signed a joint venture partnership with Carrabbas Italian Grill giving them access to the high end Italian restaurant segment.

Same store sales increased year after year and the partners looked forward to 500 even 600 units. Financial analysts were amazed at the rise in Outback's stock. So, to what can we attribute Outback's success—a well defined and popular concept, a great organizational manta of "No Rules—Just Right," and the best quality food and service in a casually themed Australian outback decor restaurant. The typical Outback is a little over 6,000 square feet, about 35 tables seating about 160 guests, and a bar area that has eight tables and 32 seats. Outback's target market is "A" demographics and a "B" location which is often a strip mall. Another aspect of Outback's organization is that servers only handle three tables at a time; this increases their guest contact time and allows for more attention to be paid to each table. They also offer an Australian themed menu with a higher flavor profile than comparable steakhouses. The design of the kitchen takes up about 45 percent of the restaurant's floor space—12 percent more than other similar restaurants. This extra space represents a potential loss of revenue but that is the way Outback wanted it done because they realized the kitchen does not run well when its being 'slammed' on a Friday or Saturday night.

There is no organization chart at Outback Steakhouse; everyone at the unpretentious corporate headquarters in Tampa is there to serve the restaurants. There is no corporate human resources department but applicants are interviewed by two managers and must pass a psychological profile test which gives an indication of the applicant's personality. Outback provides ownership opportunities at three levels in the organization: Individual restaurant level, through multi-store joint venture and franchise, and via the employee stock ownership plan. Since there is no middle management, franchisees report directly to the president. Outback's founders had fun setting up the concept and want everyone to have fun too—they will sometimes drop in on a store and ask the manager if they are having fun. Not only are they doing that—they are laughing all the way to the bank!

Discussion Questions

1. From an organizational perspective can Outback continue to grow with so little organizational structure?
2. What kind of organizational structure would you suggest for Outback Steakhouse?

CAREER INFORMATION

The executive chef of the Sheraton Hotel in San Diego, Steve Black, has commented on what he believes tomorrow's managers need in terms of skills, and his thoughts are definitely a dose of common sense. From his job experience, there always seemed to be a lack of common sense as well as basic people skills, both of which are important to managers. Also important is hands-on work, which translates into loads of experience.

Always popular advice on managerial positions relating to organization, is to be trained in multitasking. Instead of being knowledgeable in one job position, try to advance yourself into a position where you are able to perform the job duties of three or four positions, if necessary. Expand on training and, when gaining experience, ask to be put in a new department in order to learn new skills.

SUMMARY

1. The purpose of organizing is to get jobs done efficiently and effectively.
2. Goals are accomplished by organizing the work to be done into specific jobs and departments; assigning tasks and responsibilities associated with individual jobs; coordinating diverse organizational tasks; clustering jobs into units; establishing relationships among individuals, groups, and departments; establishing formal lines of authority; and allocating and deploying organizational resources.
3. Organizational structure is the total framework through which job tasks are divided, grouped, and coordinated.
4. Organizational structure is divided into these parts: work specialization, departmentalization, authority and responsibility, chain of command, delegation, increasing span of control and empowerment, and centralization and decentralization.
5. Organizational designs and decisions consist of mechanistic and organic organizations, coordination, contingency factors, common organizational design, contemporary organizational design, IBUs, and the boundaryless organization.
6. Teams are task-oriented work groups; they can either be formally appointed or may evolve informally.

KEY WORDS AND CONCEPTS

Authority
Boundaryless organization
Centralization
Chain of command
Comping
Contingency factors
Coordination of activities
Decentralization
Departmentalization

Division of labor
Empowerment
Function
Guest
Independent business unit (IBU)
Job enlargement
Job enrichment
Job rotation

Matrix Structure
Mechanistic organization
Organic organization
Organization chart
Organizational structure
Organizing
Product
Productive teams
Project structure

Responsibility
Self-managed teams
Team player
Teams
Territory
Work specialization
Work team structure

REVIEW QUESTIONS

1. Would you rather work in a mechanistic or an organic organization? Why?
2. Looking to the future, which is the best organization structure for a theme park? A 50-room resort? A mid-priced Italian restaurant? An economy 100-room hotel? A 3,000-room casino hotel?
3. Describe a team-based structure.
4. Compare and contrast a matrix structure and a project structure.
5. When might an organization design its structure around independent business units?

INTERNET EXERCISE

1. Organization: Your choice of company
   Web site: Enter the company's URL.
   Summary: Pick a major corporation—like one mentioned in the text and go to its Web site to look for answers to the following questions
   (a) What different types of product offerings do they have?
   (b) In how many countries or regions are they represented?
   (c) What kind of divisions do they have?
   (d) Have different types of guest groups been identified?

APPLY YOUR KNOWLEDGE

Mini Project: This project is based on a real-life experience of the executive chef at the Sheraton Hotel in San Diego. The project is to organize an off-site event, which is an event that is planned and organized by the Sheraton staff but does not take place at the hotel itself.

The Sheraton typically caters the annual San Diego Zoo fund-raiser every year. The attendance for this event is roughly 1,000 people. The caterers organize and cater a reception followed by dinner. Your challenge is to plan this off-site event using planning techniques and organizational skills learned.

ENDNOTES

1. This draws on Gary Dessler, A *Framework for Management*, 3rd ed. Upper Saddle River, NJ: Prentice Hall, 2004, pp. 147–148.
2. Larry J. Gitman and Carl McDaniel, *The Future of Business*, 5th ed. Cincinnati, OH: South-Western College Publishing, 2004, p. 237.
3. Robert N. Lussier, *Management Fundamentals*. Cincinnati, OH: South-Western College Publishing, 2003, p. 198.
4. See, for example, G. G. Dess, A. M. A. Rasheed, K. J. McLaughlin, and R. L. Priem, "The New Corporate Architecture," *Academy of Management Executive*, August 1995, pp. 7–20. As cited in Robins and Coulter, *Management*, p. 271.

WEB RESOURCES

Starbucks
www.starbucks.com

Marriott International
www.marriott.com

Sodexho USA
www.sodexho-usa.com

ARAMARK
www.aramark.com

Communication
and Decision Making

17

After reading and studying this chapter, you should be able to:

- Define communication.
- Improve your interpersonal communication.
- List barriers to effective interpersonal communication and how to overcome them.
- Differentiate between formal and informal communication.
- Explain communication flows and networks.
- Outline the eight steps in the decision-making process.
- Understand why managing is a synonym for decision making.
- Know the difference between rational, bounded rational, and intuitive decisions.
- Identify the situations in which a programmed decision is a better solution than a nonprogrammed decision.
- Differentiate the decision conditions of certainty, risk, and uncertainty.
- Describe the different dimensions of decision-making styles.

Managerial Communication

Communication is the oil that lubricates all of the other management functions of forecasting, planning, organizing, motivating, and controlling. Additionally, because managers spend a high percentage of their time communicating, the communication function becomes doubly important. Managers interact with others throughout the day by the following means:

- Personal face-to-face meetings
- Telephone
- Mail/fax
- Memos, reports, log books, and other internal/external written communication
- E-mail, Internet Web sites

The simplest method of communication involves a sender, a message, and a receiver. However, merely sending a message cannot ensure that the message will be received and understood correctly. Several factors can lead to distortion of the message, such as noise interference or poor listening skills and inappropriate tuning. The middle of a busy lunch service is not the right time to be asking the chef a question about the company's policy on sick-pay benefits. In this chapter we explore these various barriers to effective communication and the importance of good communication to a manager.

What Is Communication?

The definition of *communication* is the exchange of information and meaning. The essence of communication is the exchange of information. Another important aspect of communication is understanding the meaning. The sole transfer of information is not enough to ensure successful communication; the actual meaning must be understood as well. A manager passing along information to an employee in Spanish will find that information of little use if the employee does not understand Spanish. Perfect communication results when a sender communicates a thought or idea and the receiver perceives it exactly as envisioned by the sender. Just because the receiver does not agree with the message does not mean that the communication process has failed. You can disagree with something even though you fully understand it.

Managerial communication includes two different types: **Interpersonal communication** occurs between two or more individuals, and **organizational communication** includes all the different forms, networks, and systems of communication that occur among individuals, groups, or departments within an organization.

Interpersonal Communications Process

Communication between two or more people is described as interpersonal communication. The **interpersonal communications process** is made up of seven elements: the communication source, the message, encoding, the channel, de-

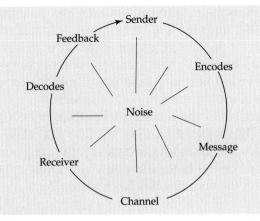

Figure 17–1 *Interpersonal Communications Process (Derived from Stephen P. Robbins and Mary Coulter, Management, 8th ed. Upper Saddle River, NJ: Prentice Hall, 2005, p. 258.)*

coding, the receiver, and feedback (Figure 17–1). Before communication can take place, a *message* must exist and be conveyed. This message is sent from the sender and passed to the receiver. The message will travel in converted form because it has to be *encoded* and then passed by way of a medium, a *channel*, from the sender to the receiver. It is then retranslated by means of *decoding*. When successful communication has taken place, the receiver will give *feedback* to the sender that he or she has correctly understood the message being conveyed.

Noise is often a part of the interpersonal communication process. Noise can consist of various activities going on in the background, sounds of machinery or coworkers, or it can even be as simple as static in the telephone line or illegible print. Therefore, noise is considered a somewhat constant disturbance in the communications process and the cause of distortions of the message. Each element in the process can be influenced and distorted by disturbances. The sender conveys a message by encoding it. During this process, four major things could go wrong and distort the message. The sender can have too little or too much knowledge. He or she can't communicate what he or she does not know.

However, if the proper explanations aren't given, the receiver could falsely interpret the message. Too much knowledge might cause the message not to be understood at all. Preexisting attitudes and the cultural system of the sender can influence the encoding of the message as well. Attitudes and beliefs about subject matters will leave their traces in the message and may be picked up by the receiver.

The message itself, such as a written document, an oral speech, or gestures and facial expressions, can be influenced by disturbances. Noise will influence listening skills during an oral speech. Faulty equipment can lead to disruption of the message if it is conveyed through e-mail or fax. Symbols such as pictures, words, and numbers that are selected by the sender to convey his or her message can be influenced by noise.

The channel used to convey the message is important to the whole communications process. If you choose to use an oral speech to communicate with a person who has a hearing impairment, naturally the message will not be understood as the sender intended it to be. Whether the sender chooses to use an office memorandum, a phone call, e-mail, gestures, or pictures to convey the message will play a large role in how accurately the receiver will understand it. Using two channels can sometimes eliminate distortion—for example, an oral speech followed by a written summary of the speech.

The receiver is limited by the same factors as the sender. If he or she has too little knowledge of the subject, distortions will take place. Likewise, if he or she has too much knowledge, too much can be read into a simple message. The pre-existing attitudes and beliefs of the individual play a role in how distorted the message will be after the decoding has taken place.

Communicating Interpersonally

Managers can communicate in various ways. Examples include face-to-face, telephone, e-mail, fax, group discussions and meetings, memos, formal presentations, bulletin boards, mail, employee publications, and computer-, video-, and teleconferencing. Communication experts generally agree that when two people are engaged in a face-to-face conversation, only a small fraction of the total message they share is contained in the words they use. A large portion of the message is contained in vocal elements such as tone of voice, accent, speed, volume, and inflection. The largest part of the message—and arguably the most important—is conveyed by a combination of gestures, postures, facial expressions and clothing. Although people may listen closely to what is said, nonverbal behavior may constitute two-thirds or more of total communication. And although people have an option not to speak, they can never be uncommunicative nonverbally.[2]

Nonverbal communication is communication without words. Taking examples from everyday life shows how important and frequent nonverbal communication is. Ambulance sirens, a honking horn, the school bell, or the sound of a ringing phone all communicate something to us without using any words. Similarly, gestures, actions, and the type of clothes worn communicate messages to us. A person wearing a police uniform tells us he belongs to the police force. In the same manner, the type of car a person drives or the size of a house conveys to others a message about that person. All of these forms of communication are nonverbal.

Managers may choose to communicate their messages by e-mail.

Facial expressions, a part of body language, convey different meanings.

Body language is facial expressions, gestures, and any other ways of communicating a message with your body. For example, if a person smiles or laughs, a message of joy or friendliness is conveyed. In the same manner, rolling your eyes indicates disbelief or even annoyance. Emotions are typically conveyed purely by body language.

Verbal intonation is using your voice to emphasize certain parts of a phrase or certain words. For example, consider the phrase "What are you doing?" An abrasive, loud intonation of the voice will indicate that the person is upset, angry, and even defensive. However, if the same sentence is said in a calm, soft voice it will be perceived as genuine interest or concern or a friendly inquiry. Verbal intonation is almost more important than the words themselves. A common saying is that it is not what you say but **how** you say it. This is a very important fact that managers should keep in mind.

Check Your Knowledge

1. What is the difference between interpersonal and organizational communication?
2. What are three ways of communicating interpersonally?
3. Describe the interpersonal communications process.

Barriers to Effective Interpersonal Communication

Many elements can influence interpersonal communication.[3] The following are some of the major barriers.

Perception

Everybody perceives things differently. This is due to different backgrounds, upbringing, personal experiences, and major influences in their lives. No two people are alike, and neither is their perception. Whereas one person may be optimistic and perceive a message in a positive light, another may be a pessimist and see only negative aspects of the message. Unwanted news is easily screened out and forgotten about, while things we want to hear are remembered for a longer period of time.

Semantics

The actual meaning of words, or **semantics,** is the cause of many failed communication efforts. The literal meaning of words and the actual meaning can be two different things, but they can be expressed in the same way. For instance, if a restaurant manager tells a server to make the guests feel comfortable, she doesn't necessarily mean that the server will bring pillows, blankets, or even beds into the dining area. The manager may have meant to make the customers feel comfortable in a nonphysical way, by attending to them, making sure they are satisfied with their order, and making sure their water glass is refilled promptly. Using jargon, specialized terminology, or technical language that may be used widely within an organization may be ineffective if used with new employees or people who are not familiar with it.

Nonverbal Communication

Nonverbal communication—communication through body language—is a typical means of communication. However, it can also be considered a barrier to effective communication. The weight of decoding a message lies with the nonverbal communication rather than on the actual encoded message. For example, if a supervisor comes to work in the morning disgruntled about morning traffic, the subordinates might misinterpret the angry facial expression as the supervisor being dissatisfied with their work, although he never actually said so. The next time you have a conversation with someone, be aware of your own nonverbal communication: what you are expressing with gestures and facial expressions.

Misinterpretations of nonverbal communication are especially dominant in cross-cultural communication. Gestures and expressions mean different things in different cultures. For example, in most Asian and African countries, it is considered impolite to make direct eye contact with the person you are speaking to, whereas it is considered courteous to look the speaker in the eye in most Western cultures.

Ambiguity

Ambiguity, vagueness, or uncertainty can occur in a message being conveyed. A message may be ambiguous, meaning the person receiving the message is uncer-

Nonverbal Communication as a Barrier to Effective Communication

tain about the actual meaning. If a manager asks an employee to come to her office as soon as possible, it could mean immediately or next week when the employee has some free time. When the words of a message are clear, but the intentions of the sender aren't, ambiguity occurs. The employee may be unclear as to why the manager wants to see him in the office now. Ambiguity might also be described as the receiver's uncertainty about the consequences of the message. The employee might think or ask, "What will happen if I don't go to her office immediately?"

Defensiveness

When people feel that they are being verbally attacked or criticized, they tend to react defensively. The reaction could be making sarcastic remarks, being overly judgmental, or simply screening out the unpleasant parts of the conversation. This often happens when employees refuse to realize personal flaws. Using defense mechanisms helps them screen out the negative image of themselves, so they can keep their self-esteem. However, acting defensively is a barrier to effective communication.

Overcoming Barriers to Effective Interpersonal Communication

Because the barriers to effective interpersonal communication just discussed do exist, there are ways to improve on the communication to largely overcome them. An essential part of a manager's job is to be an effective communicator. The following suggestions should help make interpersonal communication more effective.

Use Feedback

Right off the bat, offering feedback,[4] the last step in the communications process, will eliminate misunderstandings and inaccuracies regarding the message being conveyed. The feedback can be verbal or nonverbal. After the receiver has decoded the message, the sender should make sure the message has been understood. It can be as simple as asking the employee, "Did you understand what I said?" The ideal response to this question will be more than a yes or no answer. The best form of verbal feedback is a quick restatement and summary of the message that has been conveyed: "You said you switched my shift tomorrow to the night shift." This way the sender can be sure his message has been correctly understood.

The nonverbal form of feedback consists of various reactions to a message. First, the sender can watch for nonverbal cues as to whether the message has been understood or not. Eye contact, facial expression, scratching the head, or shrugging of shoulders all can indicate how accurately the message has been received and understood. Furthermore, the actual actions following the message can be used as feedback. The manager who is explaining a new serving procedure to the staff will know how accurately her message has been understood by observing the staff to see if they follow the new procedure. If some servers do not follow the new procedure, the manager will have to clarify or restate the message.

Active Listening

There is a difference between hearing and actually listening.[5] You might hear what your manager is saying, but did you *really* listen? Hearing is passive, and listening is a deliberate act of understanding and responding to the words being heard. The first step to **active listening** is listening for the total meaning. For example, if a manager tells his employee that the room occupancy is down this quarter, instead of responding, "Don't worry, it'll be fine," the employee recognizes that a problem exists. The second step is to reflect the feelings. This is an important step for the sender of the message because it helps him communicate the emotional part of his message. The receiver would reflect it by saying something like "This situation must be stressful for you." The last step is to note all nonverbal cues and respond to them. These cues might include hand gestures or facial expressions.

Avoid Triggering Defensiveness

Defensiveness is one of the main barriers to effective communication. By avoiding the tendency to criticize, argue, or give advice to a subordinate, defensive behavior can be avoided. Humans don't like being criticized, because that diminishes their self-image. Phrases that convey blame or finger pointing are typically useless. The receiver will respond by arguing or storming off, and the communication has largely failed. A solution to this is to wait for a cooling-off period so that both parties can regain their composure. Generally, managers should avoid overly negative statements.

Interpersonal Dynamics

Leader–managers will get the best results with and through their associates if they adopt these simple suggestions: You must have a great attitude toward your associates, meaning you accept them as colleagues and treat them fairly, with respect, and establish a climate of trust and include your associates in as much decision making as possible. Be sensitive to cultural differences and learn more about the cultures of your associates. Learn the best ways to communicate with your associates. Make sure that your associates know what is expected of them. Actively listen to associates. Involve your associates. Train associates and develop them so they can reach their full potential. Above all, have fun!

Check Your Knowledge

1. Define semantics.
2. Explain ambiguity as it relates to communication barriers.
3. What are three ways of overcoming communication barriers?

Organizational Communication

Organizational communication is necessary in managerial communication. The fundamentals include formal communication versus informal communication, communications flow patterns, and formal and informal communication networks.

Formal and Informal Communication

The two major forms of organizational communication are formal and informal communication. Formal communication is used by managers to communicate job requirements to their employees. It follows the official chain of command. **Formal communication** occurs when, for instance, a manager tells an employee his or her schedule for the following week. The subject matter is always job related and seen as essential to the employment.

Informal communication does not follow a company's chain of command or structural hierarchy. The subject matter may be job related but may not be essential to performing job duties. Examples of informal communication are employees talking at the water fountain, lunchroom, or company gatherings. In every organization employees form relationships with each other, whether as acquaintances or as actual friendships. Employees use informal communication to satisfy their need for social interaction, and it can also improve an organization's performance through better employee relationships and by having a faster, more efficient communications channel.[6] The "grapevine" is a form of informal communication.

Communication Flows and Networks

Communication flows in various directions: upward, downward, laterally, diagonally, and so on, as we will see next.

Upward Communication

Upward communication takes place when managers, or simply superiors, rely on their subordinates for receiving information. It flows upward from employees to managers. This type of communication is important to managers because it helps them determine the satisfaction level of their employees and how they feel about their jobs, the organization in general, or problems with coworkers or even with the manager himself. Some managers even encourage their subordinates to give them ideas about how to make improvements in the organization. Some examples of upward communication include manager performance reports, employee surveys, suggestion boxes, and informal group sessions with other coworkers.

Downward Communication

Communication flowing down from supervisor to employee is considered *downward communication.* Managers use this type of communication for various purposes: to inform employees of company policies, procedures, employee evaluations, or job descriptions and to discuss the future of the employee. Downward communication is often used by their managers to inform, direct, coordinate, and evaluate employees.

Lateral Communication

Communication that takes place between the employees of a company who are on the same hierarchical level in the organization is called *lateral communication.* This type of communication is used by employees to discuss their environment and the organization in general. Lateral communication is also used by cross-functional teams to facilitate communication. The important thing to remember is to always let the supervisor know about decisions made through lateral communication.

Diagonal Communication

Communication that takes place between employees who are on different hierarchical levels and in different departments of the organization is called *diagonal communication.* An example of this type of communication is that of a chef communicating with a front-desk receptionist. The two employees are not on the same level, nor are they in the same department of a hotel. Through e-mail almost every employee is able to communicate efficiently with any other employee in the same organization. However, as with lateral communication, the employees must make a point to update their managers on decisions made during this type of communication.

Two of the forms of communication flow, vertical and lateral, can be combined in various forms. These new forms are called **communication networks**. The most common are chain, wheel, and all-channel (Figure 17–2), as well as the grapevine.

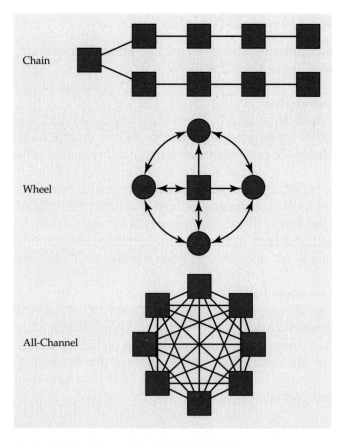

Figure 17–2 *Three Organizational Communication Networks (Derived from Stephen P. Robbins and Mary Coulter, Management, 7th ed. Upper Saddle River, NJ: Prentice Hall, 2002, p. 295.)*

Chain, Wheel, and All-Channel Communication Networks[7]

Communication in a chain network flows according to the existing chain of command of an organization. This includes downward as well as upward communication flow. This type of network is highly accurate, no information can be lost, and the path the message travels is precise. On the downside, the chain network is only moderately fast and moderately popular with employees.

The wheel network is a network in which communication flows between a strong leader and each individual in a group or team. In this network the coworkers do not need to communicate with each other; they communicate solely with their leader. The advantage to this type of communication is that it is relatively fast in speed and accuracy. However, this type of communication is usually not very popular with employees.

The all-channel communication network is differentiated from others by its freely flowing communication between all members of a group or team. This means the leader communicates with her employees, as well as the employees under her, and with their leader. This type of network is very popular with employees, and the speed at which messages travel is almost supersonic. However, the accuracy of the message is not always at 100 percent.

One thing to remember is that every unique situation will require a different communication network. No one network is perfect for every situation.

The Grapevine

This type of communication network may be the most popular and important in an organization. One survey reported that 75 percent of employees hear about matters first through rumors on the grapevine.[8] The definition of the grapevine network is an informal organizational communication network. This network is an important source of communication for the managers of an organization. Through the local informal grapevine, issues that employees consider a reason for stress and anxiety are made known. This network acts as a very effective feedback mechanism and as a filter that sorts out only the issues that employees find important. The negative aspect of this communication network is the occasional rumor that travels through it. This is pretty much unavoidable; however, successful managers can eliminate the negative impact of rumors. This can be done by speaking openly and honestly with employees about any negative feelings or important decisions that are made.

Check Your Knowledge

1. Define informal communication.
2. What is the difference between lateral and diagonal communication?
3. Elaborate on the wheel communication network.

The Decision-Making Process

All individuals in organizations, small or large, are faced with the task of decision making. This can involve decisions as simple as where to have lunch or as
complex as the best place to locate a new franchise. A comprehensive, detailed
decision-making process is utilized when faced with making a complex decision. However, the same model can also be used for simple decisions.

The decision-making process consists of eight major steps (Figure 17–3):

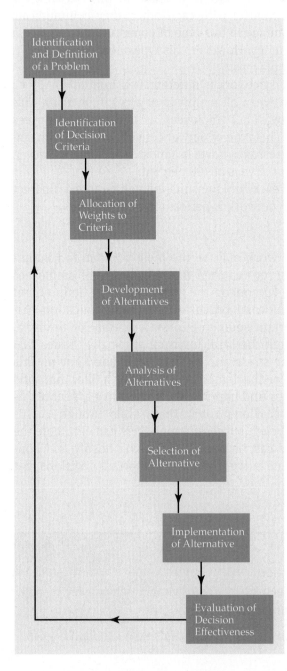

Figure 17–3 *Eight-Step
Decision-Making Process*

1. Identification and definition of problem
2. Identification of decision criteria
3. Allocation of weights to criteria
4. Development of alternatives
5. Analysis of alternatives
6. Selection of alternative
7. Implementation of alternative
8. Evaluation of decision effectiveness

This model can be used for most decisions, from simple ones, such as what to buy for dinner, to complex corporate decisions about new marketing strategies. So let's take a closer look at each step of the decision-making process.

Step 1: Identification and Definition of Problem

Let's say that we are experiencing a discrepancy between current and desired results. In this case, the decision-making process begins with identifying and defining the problem(s). It is not always easy to identify the problem because other issues may muddy the waters. In a hotel setting, problem situations can be identified with respect to, say, guest check-in. In some of the larger city-center, convention-oriented hotels, long lines of guests are frequently waiting to check into the hotel. Defining this problem is best done by writing a problem statement: "The problem is that it takes too long for guests to register." Once the problem has been accurately stated, it becomes easier to move to the next step in the decision-making process.

Another example comes to us from Herb Kelleher, former president of Southwest Airlines, when he made the decision to remove the closets at the front of Southwest planes. This was in response to a problem: It took too long to turn around the planes. To be competitive and successful, it is necessary to reduce the turnaround time in order to squeeze more flights into each day. The situation that caused or contributed to the turnaround problem was that the first people on the plane typically went to the closets first and then grabbed the nearest seats. On landing, the departing passengers were held up while the people in the front rows rummaged through the closets for their bags. The airline now turns around about 85 percent of its flights in 20 minutes or less and is one of the most profitable airlines.

Step 2: Identification of Decision Criteria

Once the problem has been identified and defined, we need to determine the criteria relevant to the decision. Suppose the problem is that we are hungry; then the decision criteria might be the following:

1. What type of food would we prefer?
2. How much time do we have to eat?
3. How much do we want to spend?
4. How convenient is parking?

Personal Profile: Patricia Tam

Vice President of Standards and Corporate Relations Halekulani Corp., Waikiki, Hawaii

Patricia Tam is a role model to everyone who wants to pursue a career in the hospitality industry. It is not hard to see why. Patricia is a woman of great ambition and ability. She has proved herself capable of succeeding at almost anything she attempts to do.[1] Patricia is of Chinese heritage and was brought up in Hawaii. During her childhood years, her ambition was to become an English teacher. Entering the hospitality industry never entered her mind. In fact, she didn't stay in a hotel until she was a young adult: "I was going along with some friends to the mainland for one of the first times I'd been off the island."

When she finished college at age 23, she became proprietor of a bakery. She was then recruited by Amfac Corp. to open a bakeshop at its Royal Lahaina Hotel on Maui in 1975. She says, "When I opened the bakeshop there, I liked the whole aura of resort life, not just because of the guests' experience, but because of the beach and the large infrastructure." She enrolled in the resort's management training program, which would be the start of a long and successful career journey in the lodging industry. Patricia started working at the Halekulani in 1983. Halekulani was first constructed in 1907 as a beachfront home accompanied by five bungalows. In 1983, it reopened as a 466-room low-rise complex. It is Waikiki's premier five-diamond resort.

When Patricia became general manager of Halekulani, the situation was less than desirable. She was promoted in the post–Gulf War period, and the once-glorious Pacific destinations had stagnated. Because most of Hawaii's visitors were Asian, Japan's ongoing recession added to the difficult times. In the 1960s, Hawaii experienced its tourist boom years. But during the early 1990s, Hawaii had to fight for every bit of the global destination market it could capture. Patricia says, "We're sitting in an arena right now where the first one to the finish line is the winner. And I think that it's more exciting to be working in this business now than it would have been in the boom years, when all you had to worry about was how many people you couldn't accommodate tonight."

Patricia realizes that the hotel business can make either a profit or a loss. "I think for a lot of us who get into the business, we see the fun part of it: the bartending, the wait help, the restaurant excitement, the chance to meet really fabulous people from around the world. We see one

side of the vision of what luxury properties are all about," she explains. "But there's the other side of it, which is that it is a business, and what do businesses do? They've got to make money."

Patricia believes that outstanding guest services make a good hotel and maintain guest loyalty. She pays careful attention to detail and perfection and lets nothing pass her by. Even guest complaints are discussed one by one. She says, "You can get so worked up about the attention to detail that unless you're communicating with staff, it can be pretty challenging for them in terms of how to keep this hotel perfect. Not everybody knows how. But everybody tries to keep it that way." Maintaining her great reputation as a general manager as well as the hotel's reputation as a superior destination is her drive for perfection. John Sharpe, president of the Toronto-based Four Seasons hotel, nominated Patricia to be Hotelier of the year. Halekulani, meaning "house benefiting heaven," was voted best hotel in the world by *Gourmet* magazine. It has held its AAA five-diamond rating for years. It was a finalist for Conde Nast Traveler's Reader's Choice "Best Tropical Resorts" award and ranked in the top three hotels in the country in Zagat's U.S. hotel, resort, and spa survey. Its well-known restaurant, La Mer, is Hawaii's only AAA-rated five-diamond restaurant, and it has been known as such for years.

Patricia served as a hotel assistant manager, room's division director, and acting general manager, and also general manager of Halekulani's adjacent sister property, the four-diamond Waikiki Parc hotel. Then, finally, in 1993, she became the general manager of Halekulani. Through it all, she always wanted more. She says, "I could work the operations in a very good management way, but I never had to be the person responsible for the final decision making on a lot of things. The challenge, the intimidation of that process, coming back over as the general manager, was quite overwhelming to me. But that was also my proudest moment because that's when I realized that I really had to buckle down." The readers of *Hotels* magazine have named Patricia "Hotelier of the World."

As for her personality, Patricia is a very genuine person who doesn't credit only herself. She doesn't forget that her success depends on an ongoing and mutually beneficial relationship between Halekulani's owner,

Halekulani Corp., and herself. She says, " I always look at it as a kind of management proposition where you can always learn every day." She adds, "Every day you can learn something new, not only about how to maintain a luxury property, but how to develop it and take it to the next level, because that's what it's all about."

[1] This profile draws on Tony De la Cruz, "Independent Hotelier of the World, Patricia Tam, Reaching for Resort Perfection," **Hotels**, 33, 11, November 1999, p. 64; and www.bizjournals.com/pacific/stories2004/08/02/daily56htm.

Courtesy Patricia Tam

5. What is the restaurant's reputation?
6. How is the food quality?
7. How is the service?
8. How is the atmosphere?

These criteria must have been developed by a group who wants to eat out at a restaurant. Criteria that are not identified are usually treated as unimportant.

Step 3: Allocation of Weights to Criteria

To the decision makers, the decision criteria all have different levels of importance. For instance, is the expected cost of the meal more important than the atmosphere? If so, a higher weight should be attached to that criterion.

One method used to weight the criteria is to give the most important criterion a weight of 10 and then score the others according to their relative importance. In the meal example, the cost of the meal might receive a weight of 10, whereas the atmosphere might be awarded a weight of 6. Figure 17–4 lists a sample of criteria and weights for restaurant selection.

Step 4: Development of Alternatives

In developing alternatives, decision makers list the viable alternatives that could resolve the problem. No attempt is made to evaluate these alternatives—only to list them. Using the restaurant scenario, the alternatives are shown in Figure 17–5.

How much do we want to spend?	10
What type of food would we prefer?	8
How much time do we have?	6
How is the food quality?	9
How is the atmosphere?	6
How is the service?	7
How convenient is parking?	6
How is the restaurant's reputation?	6
How far do we want to go to a restaurant?	7

Figure 17–4   *Criteria and Weights in Restaurant Selection*

KFC

Taco Bell

Pizza Hut

McDonald's

Applebee's

The Olive Garden

Wendy's

Figure 17–5   *Restaurant Alternatives*

Step 5: Analysis of Alternatives

The alternatives are analyzed using the criteria and weights established in steps 2 and 3. Figure 17–6 shows the values placed on each of the alternatives by the group. (It does not show the weighted values.) The weighted values of the group's decision about which restaurant to go to are shown in Figure 17–7.

Once the weighted values are totaled, we can see that Pizza Hut and Wendy's are the restaurants with the highest scores. Notice how these are not the restaurants with the highest scores before the weighted values were included.

Step 6: Selection of Alternative

The sixth step involves the selection of the best alternative. Once the weighted scores for each alternative have been totaled, it will become obvious which is the best alternative.

	KFC	Taco Bell	Pizza Hut	McDonald's	Applebee's	Olive Garden	Wendy's
Price	9	10	10	10	7	7	9
Type of food	7	8	9	8	8	9	9
How much time	9	9	7	10	7	6	10
Quality of food	7	7	8	7	8	8	8
Atmosphere	7	7	8	7	9	9	7
Service	6	6	7	7	8	9	7
Convenient parking	10	10	10	9	10	10	10
Restaurant reputation	8	8	8	7	8	9	8
How far away	8	8	8	10	7	7	8
Total	71	73	75	76	72	74	75

Figure 17–6 *Analysis of Alternatives*

	KFC	Taco Bell	Pizza Hut	McDonald's	Applebee's	Olive Garden	Wendy's
Price	90	100	100	100	70	70	90
Type of food	56	64	72	64	64	72	72
How much time	54	54	42	60	42	36	60
Quality of food	63	63	72	63	72	72	72
Atmosphere	42	42	48	42	54	54	42
Service	42	42	49	49	56	63	49
Convenient parking	60	60	60	56	60	60	60
Restaurant reputation	48	48	48	42	48	54	48
How far away	56	56	56	70	49	49	56
Total	511	529	547	546	515	530	549

Figure 17–7 *Weighted Values Analysis*

Step 7: Implementation of Alternative

We next need to ensure that the alternative is implemented so that the decision is put into action. Sometimes good decisions fail because they are not put into action.

Step 8: Evaluation of Decision Effectiveness

The final step in the decision loop is to evaluate the effectiveness of the decision. As a result of the decision, did we achieve the goals we set? If the decision was not effective, then we must find out why the desired results were not attained. This would mean going back to step 1. If the decision was effective, then no action, other than recording the outcome, needs to be taken.

Check Your Knowledge

1. Define informal communication.
2. What is the difference between lateral and diagonal communication?
3. Elaborate on the wheel communication network.

How Managers Make Decisions

Managers are the main decision makers in any organization. Although all employees are faced daily with decisions, the choices a manager makes impact the future of the organization. Decision making is an integral part of all four primary managerial functions: planning, organizing, leading, and controlling.

Making Decisions: Rationality, Bounded Rationality, and Intuition

The first criterion for making a decision is that it must be rational. Several assumptions are made to define what a rational decision really is. First, the decision itself would have to be value maximizing and consistent within natural constraining limits. This means that the choice made must maximize the organization's profitability. Tying in with this is the natural assumption that the manager making the decision is pursuing the organization's values and profitability, not his or her own interest.

One assumption of **rationality** as it relates to the decision maker is that he or she is fully objective and logical. When making the decision, a clearly stated goal must always be kept in mind. This goes hand in hand with starting with a problem statement.

Bounded rationality means that managers make decisions based on the decision-making process that is bounded, or limited, by an individual's ability to gain information and make decisions. Managers know that their decision-making skills are based on their own competency, intelligence, and, last but not

FOCUS ON: COMMUNICATING DURING DISASTERS

Hank Christen and Paul Maniscalco
George Washington University
Unconventional Concepts, Inc.

Communication during a disaster requires complex interactions. If communications are not effective, myriad problems for the organization result, including irreparable harm to the organization's reputation, significant fiscal harm, and drastically reduced organizational business opportunities after the event.

Many hospitality industry managers fail to grasp the importance of preventing significant damage to their organization's reputation and future business prospects due to disasters. The situation is further complicated by a lack of familiarity with successful crisis communication techniques. The manager must confront events that are emergent and fluid, make quick and effective decisions, and communicate effectively and expeditiously, especially to the media.

Fundamental components of effective disaster communication are (1) defining the disaster/crisis, (2) assembing a communication team, (3) designating and training a spokesperson, and (4) releasing a statement.

1. *Define disaster/crisis for the organization.* A disaster or crisis is any situation that threatens the health, safety, integrity, or reputation of the organization and its employees or patrons. Usually it originates as an unusual event or emergency, such as accident, crime, fire, flood; natural, technological, or manmade disaster. It also is a situation in which the media or the public feels that the organization did not react to a critical situation in a timely or appropriate manner.

2. *Assemble a disaster/crisis communication team.* This team is responsible for writing the organizational communication response delivered during an incident. The team should be composed of key individuals: the chief executive officer or top manager at the facility, the head of public relations, the operations manager, the director of safety and/or security, legal counsel, and the area manager involved in the crisis (an ad hoc assignment in emergent situations).

3. *Designate and train an organizational spokesperson.* Every hospitality management team should have at least one person solely responsible for speaking to the media to represent the organization during a crisis. The organization must speak with a single voice. The speaker needs to be professional, reassuring, and factual, and must have appropriate orientation and education on media relations.

4. *Research the facts, craft a reference sheet, and release a statement.* After researching the events and confirming facts, an event reference sheet should be crafted. It should contain an incident summary, including confirmed particulars, for media release; it should be updated as events or responses change. Collaboration with legal counsel is also necessary to ensure compliance with privacy and organizational security.

Expeditious communication is also critical. Prompt delivery helps to control event interpretation and present the organization's version of the incident. The first statement must identify who, what, where, and when (the four W's). Only confirmed facts received from competent authorities should be given, and the legality of a release should be confirmed before it is issued. The speaker should not speculate.

Providing the four W's and showing compassion and concern for those involved (public and employees) during initial media interactions is the basis of successful communication. Demonstration of genuine compassion and concern secures patron and employee confidence and loyalty. The spokesperson should take the initiative to share information and engender an open and inclusive environment; otherwise, alienated patrons or employees will not be supportive during the company's recovery.

Critical Factor: The Dupont Plaza Hotel fire and TWA Flight 800 exemplify miscue and poor message delivery. Media evaluation of the industries involved was brutal because the managers had failed to release "good and timely" information to the families.

Critical Factor: Release of legal and medical information should be coordinated with the appropriate medical authority. Failure to do so may compromise an investigation or medical privacy protections afforded by law.

least, their rationality. They are also expected to follow the decision-making process model. However, certain aspects of this model are not realistic with respect to true-life managerial decisions, which are made with respect to bounded reality. This comes into play, for example, when decision makers cannot find all of the necessary information to analyze a problem and all of its possible alternatives. Therefore, they find themselves **satisficing,** or accepting, a solution that is just "good enough," rather than maximizing. Consider this example: A chef for a major hotel chain has to prepare a banquet for 50 people. On the menu is half a chicken for every guest, which means that the chef needs 100 whole chickens for this banquet. He purchases the chickens at a market 25 miles away, where he has made the same purchase before for $60. Because he has made purchases from this market before, he knows the quality of the food they sell. What the chef did not know was that there was a free-range chicken farm only ten miles away that would have sold him the 100 chickens for the same price. Instead of researching his alternatives, the chef satisficed himself with the first option that came to mind and settled on it, assuming it was probably not the best but "good enough." This behavior is rationally bounded because the best solution to be found was bounded by the chef's ability to research all alternatives instead of settling on the first acceptable one that came to mind.

Most decisions that managers make are not based on perfect rationality due to various factors, such as time constraints on researching all possible solutions or lack of resources to do the research. Therefore, the decisions are typically based on bounded rationality. In other words, they make decisions based on alternatives that are just satisfactory. At the same time, though, the decision maker will be strongly influenced by an organization's culture, power considerations, internal politics, and an **escalation of commitment.** An escalation of commitment happens when the commitment to a prior decision is increased despite evidence to the contrary. For example, consider the demise of the Planet Hollywood Restaurant chain. At the launch of the chain, the team of marketing professionals deemed it economically sensible to set a high price on their burgers and other food items. The restaurant set out to be a novelty establishment, although the target customers were middle-class citizens. Although it was evident that the decision to have high-priced products in a middle-class establishment was doomed for failure from the beginning, the decision makers stuck with it. The inevitable took place, and Planet Hollywood went belly up and was forced to close its chain with locations all around the world. The negative consumer reaction was predictable, but the decision makers escalated their commitment to the set prices even though it was a bad decision. Rather than search for new alternatives, they did not want to admit to making a bad decision and simply increased their commitment to the original one.[9]

Using rationality and common sense to influence decision making is very important—we must not forget the role of plain and simple human intuition. Intuition is used in everyday life, such as knowing not to grab a hot baking pan with your bare hands. It ranges all the way to the corporate level, where managers often use their own intuition when making corporate decisions. **Intuitive decision making** is a subconscious process of making decisions on the basis of experience and accumulated judgment. Five different identified aspects of intuition

A Day in the Life of Denise Simenstad
National Sales Manager, San Diego Convention Center, San Diego, California

Denise Simenstad is the national sales manager at the San Diego Convention Center. Her work here starts early and usually ends when the timing is good. What she does in those hours, though, is good customer service and remarkable work.

Denise comes into work at about 8 A.M. When she arrives at her office, she checks her voice mail, e-mail, and in-box messages. From then on, the day is not her own. She's working and attending to customer activity.

Her day-to-day activities keep her busy well throughout the day. Denise responds to customer inquiries. These inquiries consist of prospective customers calling her to inquire about date and space availability at the convention center, the cost of renting meeting rooms or exhibit halls, and checking if there are other, similar shows booked in the facility.

She then usually leads a tour or, as it is better known, a "site inspection" of the facility to show customers the available physical space, including the lobby, exhibit halls, ballroom, meeting space, and outdoor space. Then she shows them the ancillary services that the convention center provides, such as the audiovisual facilities, food and beverage, telecommunications, security services, business services center, and so on. All that makes for a complete tour.

Denise then prepares proposals (dates, rates, and space letter) for prospective customers. This ranges from a group of 100 people for one day to a trade show for 15,000 people to 250,000 guests for five days. She has to include a package of information concerning the floor plans, rates, regulations, and other pertinent information.

After all that, Denise answers customers' questions about the facilities available and capabilities. She fields questions on the sizes of rooms, capacities of the facilities, rates, distance between pillars on exhibit floor, floor loads, dimensions of freight doors, number of committable hotel rooms in the downtown area, number of packages available, and more.

Then comes the duty of having to issue and negotiate license agreements (contracts) with outlines, dates, space and rates, insurance requirements, indemnification issues, cancellation classes, guarantees, and so on.

To start wrapping up, Denise attends meetings with other sales managers in the office to discuss business strategy concerning who is considering them for a meeting, how they can close the deal, what other managers are working on, what type of business seems to be prevalent right now, and so on. The meeting sessions continue with yet another meeting with event managers, the people responsible for the operational aspect of an event once it is contracted. In this meeting they all go over any operational concerns and check to ensure that what sales promised is delivered. If a client is in-house, they send a gift to his or her hotel room (just prior to arrival) and then go on the floor to check the show and ensure that clients are satisfied with service received.

The day usually ends at about 5:30 P.M. for Denise. The day can go on even longer if a customer is in town. In this case, she makes sure that her customers are wined and dined and attended to well by entertaining them; providing breakfast, lunch, and/or dinner; and basically showing them what San Diego is all about.

Courtesy Denise Simenstad.

comply with the different types of decisions made. The first is a values- or ethics-based decision. Managers will recall the ethics system they were raised with and base their decisions on personal morals. The second is an experience-based decision. Through trial and error the manager has gained experience and will base a decision on past learning. Affect-initiated decisions are those that are based on a manager's emotions and feelings. The fourth type is a cognitive-based decision. The manager's previous training, learned skills, and gained knowledge influence the decision-making process. Last, the manager utilizes his or her subconscious mind to retain data and process it in such a way that it will influence the type of decision he or she will make.

Intuition and rationality are separate but are often used in combination in most decision making. The two complement each other to offer the manager an ideal solution for the decision-making process. As an example, consider a manager who has to make a decision on a situation that is similar to one he has come across in the past. Instead of using careful analytical rationality, he will make a decision based on a "gut feeling" and act quickly with what appears to be limited information. The decision is ultimately made based on his experience and accumulated judgment.

Check Your Knowledge

1. List criteria for making a rational decision.
2. Give an example of satisficing.
3. What are the five aspects of intuition?

Types of Problems and Decisions

There are several different types of decisions that match different types of problems. They are applied as solutions, depending on the various situations that arise. The managers that are aware of these differences are able to use them to their advantage.

The two major types of decisions are programmed decisions and nonprogrammed decisions. A **programmed decision** involves situations that recur on a regular basis, allowing the response to be a handled with a "programmed" response. In a programmed decision, the response will occur on a repetitive basis; for example, when the number of New York steaks goes below a specified number, an order for more is automatically placed. Programmed decisions generally become a standard operating procedure. Alternatives are not necessary most of the time because the problem statement is familiar and, therefore, the solution is in close reach due to past successful decisions made. The response to a shortage of New York steaks is simply a reorder; the alternatives are truly limited. A programmed decision is made in response to a recurring problem; the approach to dealing with it has become repetitive and therefore does not require a careful analysis.

A **nonprogrammed decision** is nonrecurring and made necessary by unusual circumstances. The type of problem that induces a nonprogrammed decision is a poorly structured problem. These types of problems are usually new or unusual to the decision maker. More often than not, the information on the problem is incomplete or unavailable. This generally increases the difficulty gradient of finding an appropriate solution. Most importantly, though, the problem is unique and nonrecurring, such as which computer hardware and software a restaurant should install or whether to expand by franchising or by

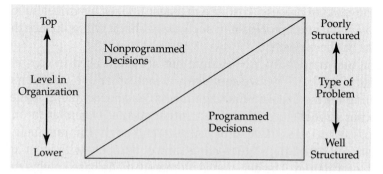

Figure 17–8 *Nonprogrammed and Programmed Decisions (Derived from Stephen P. Robbins and Mary Coulter, Management, 7th ed. Upper Saddle River, NJ: Prentice Hall, 2002, p. 161.)*

company-owned restaurants. These are distinctive decision situations that are not likely to recur for several years and require a custom-made decision.

The more sophisticated a company is, the more programmed decisions are made. Many large corporations have policy and procedure manuals to guide managerial and supervisory decision making. Nonprogrammed decisions call for greater analysis, innovation, and problem-solving skills. Figure 17–8 diagrams programmed and nonprogrammed decisions and the level in the organization.

Decision–Making Conditions

In a perfect world, we would have all the information necessary for making decisions. However, in reality, there are some things that are unknowable. This leads us to decision-making conditions. Decision making includes three major conditions: certainty, risk, and uncertainty. These three conditions all have individual characteristics that define each.

The ideal situation for making a decision is one of **certainty.** A decision of certainty includes having knowledge of all of the alternatives and therefore having no risk involved when making a decision, since the outcome is known. A good example for this condition is illustrated by a hotel investment specialist who is allotted a share of the hotel's profit. The investor's options are clear and defined. He knows exactly how much interest is earned on bonds and how much interest is offered by various banks, the security issues, and how many years it will take for them to mature.

Making a decision that involves **risk** is one of the most common situations. Here the decision maker is not certain of the outcome of the situation. However, through personal experience, or a simple "gut feeling," she is able to estimate the probability of the outcome. Although not all alternatives are properly researched, by using historical data, probabilities can be assigned to various alternatives and the best probable outcome ultimately chosen. This is called a risk condition as it relates to decision making and is characterized by having some knowledge of the outcome of the various alternatives, combined with the element of unpredictability.

For example, a popular hotel is thinking about adding on family apartments to its property. So far the largest room they have is a double; the family rooms would need to have beds for four people along with a kitchenette. Perusing past historical data helps make the decision somewhat clearer. In the past year alone, 40 percent of all customers were families of three or more. Reviewing the customer comments, the demand for a family apartment is relatively large. Although the construction of an apartment building will cut into the revenue, the rental profit made from these more expensive apartments is likely to outweigh costs in less than three years. Also, the hotel is hoping to attract an even larger family crowd to their property once they offer apartments. Although all of the past data is valuable information and can to some extent predict the future, a factor of risk is involved because there is always some level of unpredictability about the future.

Uncertainty situations are characterized by having to make a decision when the outcome is not certain and when reasonable outcome estimates can't be made either. These situations often arise when alternatives to the decision are limited due to lack of adequate information. Although conditions of uncertainty are not as common as situations of risk, managers still find themselves confronted with uncertainty in decision-making situations.

> ### Rational Decision Making
>
> Professional managers at the Sheraton Hotel and Resort in San Diego provided us with a real-life problem that deals with making rational decisions: How much space should we reserve for large parties? For example, if a group of 500 reserves a room, and only 300 show up, the other 200 spaces are basically "dead space," which could have been rented out to another party of 200 people. To protect themselves from this kind of dilemma, the hotel has attached a food and beverage price to each room. If you reserve the room, the food and beverage price is charged automatically, even if the guests don't show up.

Decision-Making Styles

Decision makers differ in their way of thinking; some are rational and logical, while others are intuitive and creative. The rational type of decision maker will look at the information in order. He will organize the information and make sure it is logical and consistent. Only after carefully studying all of the given options will he finally make the decision. An intuitive thinker, on the other hand, can look at information that is not necessarily in order. This person is able to make quick decisions based on her spontaneous creativity and her intuition. Although a careful analysis is still required, these types of people are comfortable looking at all solutions as a whole as opposed to studying each option separately.

The second dimension about which people differ is each individual's **tolerance for ambiguity.** The managers who have a high tolerance for ambiguity are lucky in that they save a lot of time while making a decision. These individuals are

> ### "No ... I mean yes."
>
> A former CEO always said "no" first because he could always change his mind to "yes" later. Today it might be better to say, "Let me get back to you on that request" or "Let's discuss this—can you meet with me on Monday at 10 A.M.?"

Corporate Profile: Starwood Hotels

Starwood is one of the world's largest hotel and leisure companies. Their brand names include St. Regis, the Luxury Collection, Sheraton, Westin, W, and Four Points by Sheraton. Through these brands, Starwood is well represented in most major markets around the world. Operations are grouped into two business segments: hotels and vacation ownership operations. Revenue and earnings are derived primarily from hotel operations, which include the operation of owned hotels, management and other fees earned from hotels managed pursuant to management contracts, and the receipt of franchise and other fees.

Starwood's hotel business emphasizes the global operation of hotels and resorts primarily in the luxury and upscale segment of the lodging industry. They seek to acquire interests in, management or franchise rights with respect to properties in this segment. The hotel portfolio includes owned, leased, managed, and franchised hotels totaling 733 hotels, with approximately 231,000 rooms in 80 countries, and consists of 140 hotels. Starwood has a majority equity interest.

Starwoods revenues and earnings are also derived from the development, ownership, and operation of vacation owner-

ship resorts, marketing and selling VOIs in the resorts, and providing financing to customers who purchase such interests. Generally these resorts are marketed under the preceding brand names. There are 19 vacation ownership resorts in the United States and the Bahamas.

Starwood has assumed a leadership position in markets worldwide based on superior global distribution, coupled with strong brands and brand recognition. The upscale and luxury brands continue to capture market share from competitors by aggressively cultivating new customers while maintaining loyalty among the world's most active travelers. The strength of their brands is evidenced, in part, by the superior ratings received from ho-

tel guests and from industry publications. The November 2004 edition of the *Condé Nast Traveler Magazine* named four Starwood properties in the top 100 "Best in the World," with over 30 properties listed in the Readers' Choice Awards list. In addition, the *Condé Nast Traveler Magazine* January 2005 issue included 51 Starwood properties among its prestigious Gold List and Gold List Reserve—more than any other hotel company. For the third year in a row, we were named the "World's Leading Hotel Group" at the World Travel Awards.

Starwood has distinguished and diversified hotel properties throughout the world, including the St. Regis in New York, New York; the Phoenician in Scottsdale, Arizona; the Hotel Gritti Palace in Venice, Italy; the St. Regis in Beijing, China; and the Westin Palace in Madrid, Spain. These are among the leading hotels in the industry and are at the forefront of providing the highest quality and service.

Starwood's primary business goal is to maximize earnings and cash flow by increasing the profitability of their existing portfolio; selectively acquiring interests in additional assets; increasing the number of hotel management contracts and franchise agreements; acquiring and developing vacation ownership resorts and selling VOIs; and maximizing the value of owned real estate properties, including selectively disposing of noncore hotels and "trophy" assets that may be sold at significant premiums. Starwood plans to meet these goals by leveraging global assets, broad customer base, and other resources, and by taking advantage of their scale to reduce costs. The uncertainty relating to political and economic environments around the world and consequent impact on travel in their respective regions and the rest of the world make financial planning and implementation of Starwood's strategy more challenging.

For more information go to **www.starwood.com**.

able to process many thoughts at the same time. Unfortunately, some managers have a low tolerance for ambiguity. These individuals must have order and consistency in the way they organize and process the information so as to minimize ambiguity.

When reviewing the two dimensions, way of thinking and tolerance for ambiguity, and their subdivisions, four major decision-making styles become evident:

1. The **directive style** entails having a low tolerance for ambiguity as well as being a rational thinker. The individuals that fall into the category of having a directive decision-making style are usually logical and very efficient. They also have a primary focus on the short run and are also relatively quick decision makers. Directive decision makers value speed and efficiency, which can cause them to be remiss in assessing all alternatives, such that decisions are often made with minimal information.

2. Decision makers that fall into the category of having an **analytic style** have a large tolerance for ambiguity. Compared to the directive decision maker, these people require more information before making their decisions and, consequently, they consider more alternatives. Individuals with an analytic style are careful decision makers, which gives them leeway to adapt or cope to unique situations.

3. Decision makers who have a **conceptual style** pertaining to their decision-making skills look at numerous alternatives and are typically very broad in their outlook. Their focus is on the long run of the decision made. These individuals are typically creative and often find creative solutions to the problem with which they are dealing.

4. Decision makers who work well with others are said to have a **behavioral style** of decision making. This entails being very receptive to suggestions and ideas from others as well as being concerned about the achievements of their employees. They commonly communicate with their coworkers through meetings. These individuals try to avoid conflict as often as possible, because their acceptance by others is very important to them.

At least one of these decision-making styles is always utilized by managers. However, it is also quite common for a decision maker to combine two or more styles to make a decision. Most often a manager will have one dominant decision-making style and use one or more other styles as alternates. Flexible individuals will vary their decision-making styles according to each unique situation. If the style is to consider riskier options (analytic style) or if the decision is made based on suggestions from subordinates (behavioral style), each style will eventually bring the decision makers to the optimal solution for the unique problems they are facing.

Check Your Knowledge

1. Name the two dimensions of decision-making styles.
2. Briefly describe the conceptual style of decision making.

Trends in Communication and Decision Making

- Trends such as improving technology to aid with communication are likely to continue. Voice mail, e-mail, and the Internet will increasingly assist hospitality managers and associates with speedier communications. All-way radio connectivity, which allows associates to communicate live, enables them to better serve the needs of discriminating guests.

- An integral part of management's decision-making process is the management support system (MSS). The MSS has two distinctive elements: the management information system (MIS) and the decision support system (DSS). The MIS provides managers with all information needed to routinely run the business, so it is valuable for making routine decisions. Usually included in the information flow are daily or monthly sales data, daily inventory, and employee hours and salaries, to name a few of the pertinent facets of information. The DSS, unlike the MIS, which deals with structured, routine business information, is designed to offer the manager information to assist in solving the nonroutine problems. The DSS processes both internal and external data.

CASE STUDY

Guests at a busy eight-story four-star hotel are constantly complaining about having to wait too long for the elevator. At 8:00 A.M. some of the elevators are in use by the housekeeping department whose associates are going up to begin work on the guest rooms. At the same time, room service has an elevator blocked off to serve in-room breakfasts because the kitchen and the banqueting departments are using the service elevators. Then, at about 10:30 A.M. the housekeepers use the elevators to go down for their morning break. The general manager recognizes your potential and asks you to come up with suggestions to take care of the problem/challenge.

SUMMARY

1. The definition of communication is the transfer and understanding of meaning. Managerial communication is divided into two categories: interpersonal communication and organizational communication. Interpersonal communication takes place between two or more people, and organizational communication consists of all the networks and systems of communication that exist in an organization.

2. The interpersonal communications process can be disrupted or fail based on several factors. To improve on your interpersonal communication skills, you need to eliminate as much noise during the communications

process as possible; that is, close the door to your office or move to a quiet space in the building. Inform yourself about how knowledgeable the receiver is on the subject. Be sure to provide adequate explanations if the knowledge is limited. Last, pick the appropriate channel of communication to ensure successful conveyance of the message.

3. Barriers to effective interpersonal communication include misunderstood perception, misuse of semantics, misguided use of nonverbal communication, ambiguous messages, and defensiveness. Ways to overcome these barriers are through use of feedback, active listening, and avoiding defensiveness.

4. Managers use formal communication to communicate job requirements to their employees. It follows the official chain of command. Informal communication does not follow a company's chain of command or structural hierarchy. The subject matter is typically not job related and is not essential to performing job duties.

5. Communication flows are part of the organizational communication process. Upward communication flows from the employees to the manager. Downward communication flows from manager to employees. Lateral communication takes place among employees who are on the same organizational level. Diagonal communication cuts across organizational levels as well as work areas. The four different types of communicational networks are the chain, the wheel, the all-channel, and the grapevine networks.

6. The decision-making process consists of eight steps: (1) identification and definition of problem, (2) identification of decision criteria, (3) allocation of weights to criteria, (4) development of alternatives, (5) analysis of alternatives, (6) selection of alternative, (7) implementation of alternative, and (8) evaluation of decision effectiveness.

7. Although all employees in a company make decisions on a regular basis, in the end it is the manager's decisions that count. His or her decisions usually represent the final word and are valued as "the right decision." Decision making is a large part of all four primary managerial functions: planning, organizing, leading, and controlling. Hence, word of mouth is that *managing* is a synonym for decision making.

8. A rational decision is based on the following assumptions: The decision is value maximizing and within natural limits, and the manager making the decision is fully objective, logical, and has the organization's economic interest in mind. As a result, the rational decision-making problem is simple and has clearly defined goal limited alternatives, minimal time pressure, low cost for seeking and evaluating alternatives, an organizational culture that supports risk taking and innovation, and measurable and concrete outcomes. Bounded rationality suggests that managers make decisions that are bounded by an individual's ability to process information. Managers often cannot possibly analyze all available information and all alternatives, so they satisfice instead of maximize. Finally, intuitive decision making is a subconscious process of making decisions on the basis of experience and accumulated judgment, including ethics learned.

9. Programmed decisions require a problem situation that is a frequent occurrence, allowing the response to be handled with a routine approach. Programmed decisions generally become standard operating procedures. A nonprogrammed decision is nonrecurring and made necessary by unusual circumstances. These types of problems are usually new or unusual to the decision maker. More often than not, the information on the problem is incomplete or unavailable.

10. The decision condition of certainty includes having knowledge of all of the alternatives and, therefore, having no risk involved when making a decision, since the outcome is pretty much known. Uncertainty situations are characterized by having to make a decision when the outcome is not certain and when at the same time reasonable outcome estimates can't be made either, due to lack of adequate information. In the risk situation the decision maker is not certain of the outcome of the situation. However, through personal experience, historical data, or a simple "gut feeling," he or she is able to estimate the probability of the outcome.

11. Decision-making styles vary depending on a person's way of thinking—rational or intuitive—and a person's tolerance for ambiguity, which can be low or high. Combinations of these differences give us the directive style (low tolerance for ambiguity and rational way of thinking), the analytic style (high tolerance for ambiguity and rational way of thinking), the conceptual style (high tolerance for ambiguity and intuitive way of thinking), and, last, the behavioral style (low tolerance for ambiguity and intuitive way of thinking).

KEY WORDS AND CONCEPTS

Active listening
Allocation of weights to
    criteria
Analysis of alternatives
Bounded rationality
Certainty
Communication
Conceptual style
Decision-making process
Development of alternatives

Directive style
Encoding
Escalation of commitment
Evaluation of decision
    effectiveness
Formal communication
Identification and
    definition of problem
Identification of decision
    criteria

Implementation of
    alternative
Informal communication
Interpersonal
    communication
Interpersonal
    communications process
Intuitive decision making
Nonprogrammed decision

Organizational
    communication
Programmed decision
Rationality
Risk
Satisficing
Selection of alternative
Tolerance for ambiguity
Uncertainty
Upward communication

REVIEW QUESTIONS

1. The most important aspect of a manager's job is typically described as decision making. Do you believe this is so? Explain.
2. When reviewing some important decisions you have made, would you describe them as mostly rational or intuitive decisions? What are the characteristics of each? How does intuition affect the decision-making process?
3. During the communications process, if the receiver disagrees with the sender, does this always mean that the message has not been properly understood? Or could it mean something else? Explain.
4. How can the grapevine network be used to a company's advantage?
5. When communication is not effective, is it always the fault of the receiver? Discuss all options.

INTERNET EXERCISE

1. Organization: You select an organization
   Web site: The site of the organization you find.
   Summary: By searching out sites that can help improve creativity, you will discover what role creativity plays in decision making.

(a) Write two or three paragraphs explaining what role creativity should play in decision making and what you learned from your search about how you can be a more creative decision maker.

APPLY YOUR KNOWLEDGE

Select a hospitality-related problem and write a problem statement. Then, using the decision-making steps, show how you would solve the problem.

ENDNOTES

1. Draws on Stephen P. Robbins and Mary Coulter, *Management,* 8th ed. Upper Saddle River, NJ: Prentice Hall, 2005, p. 282.

2. Paul Preston, "Nonverbal Communication: Do You Really Say What You Mean?" *Journal of Healthcare Management,* March/April 2005, p. 83.

3. Anne E. Beall, "Body Language Speaks," *Communication World,* March/April 2004, p. 18.

4. Draws on Dessler, *A Framework for Management,* 3rd ed. Upper Saddle River, NJ: Prentice Hall, 2004, p. 282.

5. Draws on Robbins and Coulter, *Management,* p. 265.

6. Ibid. pp. 293–6.

7. Ibid. pp. 294–5.

8. "Heard It Through the Grapevine," cited in Forbes, February 10, 1997, p. 22, as cited in Robbins and Coulter, *Management,* p. 293.

9. Personal conversation with John Trombold. July 14, 2005.

Human Resources and Motivation

18

After reading and studying this chapter, you should be able to:

- Explain the importance of job descriptions.
- Give an example of how productivity standards are determined.
- Name and describe the employment-related laws.
- Discuss how to select, recruit, and orient employees.
- Identify methods of employee appraisal and compensation.
- Describe motivation theories and industry practice.

Human Resources Leadership and Management Issues

Human resources are frequently cited as a company's most valuable asset and a competitive advantage, meaning that the employees of one company are better than another. This, as you know, may be true for some companies but not for all. The challenge of finding, retaining, and developing great employees has become more challenging in recent years. Some issues compounding the employment crunch in the hospitality industry are that employees are now looking for a trusting relationship with their employer; this is even truer due to the recent corporate scandals. Previously, the most important thing was benefits. Benefits are still important, but a stable and trusting relationship is more important.[1]

Changing Demographics

In America the birthrate has slowed, and after September 11, 2001, so has immigration and visas such as H1 and J1. Additionally, the American population is aging; millions of baby boomers are about to enter their retirement years. There are now more women and minorities in and entering the hospitality workforce; this brings a fascinating cultural mix to the workplace. The latest figure for the U.S. population is 296,833,747. In 2010 that figure is expected to reach 308 million, with more of the increase coming from Hispanic and African Americans. In the age range from 16 to 64, there are 151 million white, 25 million Hispanic, and 23.6 million African Americans. In California, New Mexico, and Texas, for example, Asian, Hispanic, and African Americans are now the majority.[2] In the United States there are over 10 million employees in the hospitality industry, the majority of which are women and minorities.

The hospitality workforce is increasingly diverse, with many cultures adding to the richness of the work environment.

Turnover

Ask any hospitality leader what the biggest challenge is, and he or she is likely to respond, "Staff—getting them and keeping them!" Not only are there fewer job applicants, but the applicants often lack experience, and when they have experience, they do not stay long, adding to a high turnover, which in many companies is over 100 percent per year. This means that all the employees who are here today will not be here at this time next year. Actually, it doesn't quite work out that way: Some people stay, while others come and go two or three times. The complexity of human resources leadership, management, and development in the hospitality industry is increased by the fact that many unskilled workers are employed for entry-level positions, often with little or no training, which contributes to turnover.

Human resource directors say that they need to earn the trust of their employees. Some companies do this by having an "Employee Promise" to guarantee respect, a safe and hospitable workplace, training, mentoring, fair treatment, equal treatment, employee assistance programs, and advancement opportunities.[3] Employee satisfaction means retention, and employee satisfaction is achieved by creating and maintaining a great working environment. A hospitality company should be the employer of choice, the company that employees prefer to work for, not only when compared to other hospitality companies, but also when compared to other industries, such as retail. Supervisors and managers need to be energetic and participative in leading their employees by showing them what to do and how to do it, because if you wait until they ask you, they are already dissatisfied.

Legal Issues

Legislation and the enforcement of laws relating to the workplace have increased in recent years, mostly to protect workers and the workplace; these laws have increased the human resources workload and complexity. As one manager said to the human resources director, "Your job is to keep me out of court."[4] Later in the chapter we will review some of the laws that affect the hospitality industry.

The Importance of Human Resources

Progressive employers seek to become the employer of choice in their respective industry sector. To become an employer of choice, the employer needs to realize that the leadership and management of human resources are important because the hospitality experience is intangible—meaning that one hotel, restaurant, or tourism enterprise is often much the same as another. What makes the difference is service, service, service, and professionalism. (Remember the quote in Chapter 1 from the general manager of the Oriental Hotel in Bangkok, Thailand? He said, "The reason we are rated one of the best hotels in the world is service, service, and service.") As we already know, the hospitality industry is the largest in the world, employing some 70 million people. No other industry has as much front-line entry-level employee–guest contact as the hospitality industry. Employment ranges from entry-level positions to specialized, supervisory, and managerial–executive positions. Human resources is all about attracting, selecting, orienting, training, coaching, counseling, disciplining and mentoring, developing, evaluating the performance, and supporting and retaining an organization's most important resources: the people.

It is difficult to recruit, hire, train, and retain great employees; the challenge of finding great employees has increased, in part due to the changing demographics of the workplace, one element of which is the aging American population (remember the baby boomers?). Baby boomers are now retiring or about to retire and have the disposable income to travel and are doing so in record numbers. Ironically, this is contributing to the problem of finding enough good employees to serve them and the other guests. In addition to recruiting, hiring, and training, several other functions are a part of human resources: creating job descriptions, developing job specifications, managing payroll and benefits, handling grievances, financial management, community involvement, and ensuring conformance to federal, state, and provincial legislation. Also, there is enormous diversity within the industry. In the next few years, there will be an increasing number of immigrants, minorities, and women entering the hospitality work force. In this chapter we will examine each function of the human resources department. The processes and functions will be explored sequentially from hiring to retirement or termination. Figure 18–1 illustrates the importance of human resources in achieving the corporation's vision and mission.

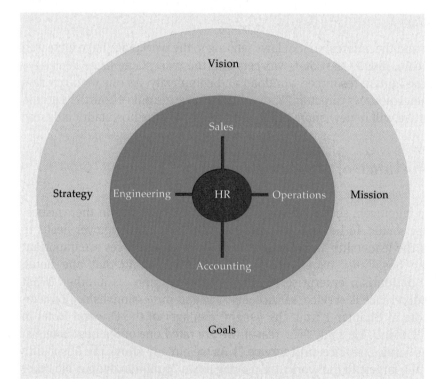

Figure 18–1 *Human resources plays a critical role in achieving the corporation's vision and mission.*

A Human Resources Director and Assistant in Their Office

The Human Resources Department

In a large hospitality operation, the human resources department is headed by the director of human resources. The HR director is an executive position and carries with it the enormous responsibilities of running an efficient and effective HR department. The HR director sets the overall tone of how employee relations will be conducted and establishes the vision for the company's human resources. The director is the advocate for the employees at executive-level decision making. The HR department generally has a co-coordinator, who ensures that all employee and management inquiries are handled with courtesy and given to the appropriate HR manager or director. Most HR departments will have an employment manager, who checks applications and does the employment suitability interviews and reference checks. The benefits manager ensures that all employees apply for and receive their appropriate benefits. Figure 18–2 shows the organization chart of a midsized hospitality company's human resources department.

The Role of the Human Resources Department

The human resources department is responsible for creating and maintaining an environment in which people can flourish, and to do this they do four main things: (1) recruit and select talented associates; (2) maintain outstanding

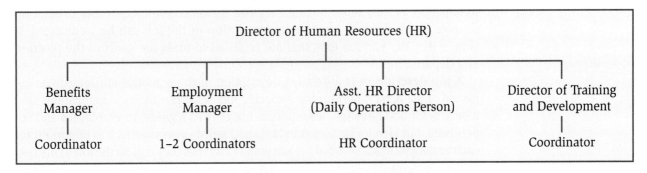

Figure 18–2 *The Human Resources Division of a Midsize Hospitality Company*

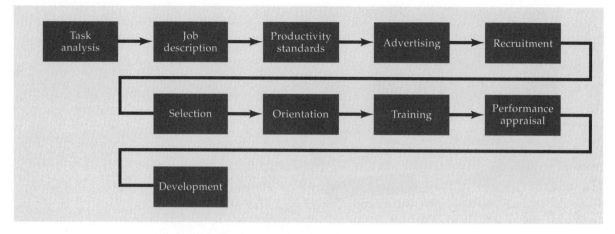

Figure 18–3   *Human Resources Management and Development Process*

employee relations; (3) act as a standard bearer by ensuring that every associate meets or exceeds standards; and (4) ensure legal compliance, training, and development. HR directors spend more time on employee relations than the other functions. This is because HR is the advocate for employees because they need to feel comfortable in coming to you and knowing that conversations will be confidential. Being the advocate for associates also means representing them to management, department heads, and supervisors. In the remainder of this chapter we will examine each of these areas in detail from an industry perspective. Before we can recruit applicants, we must first determine what these applicants will do. We begin with an examination of the job to be performed, which is called *task analysis,* followed by *job description.* Figure 18–3 illustrates the human resources management and development process.

Task Analysis, Job Description, and Job Specification

Because human resources or labor costs are the highest single cost of being in business, it has become necessary, through **task analysis,** to examine every task of each employee to determine the best way of doing the particular task and its potential outcome on the guest experience. For example, think of a housekeeper making up a guest's room; several tasks are involved. What should the housekeeper do and in what order? Hotels seek to find the best way to make up a guest room so that they can maximize efficient use of human resources. From the task analysis, a description of the job can be formulated. It simply lists the various jobs that are required to meet the goals of the position and department.

A **job description** is a detailed description of the activities and outcomes expected of the person performing a specific job. Most hospitality organizations find it very helpful to have job descriptions, not only as a guide for employees and supervisors, but also for quality standards and guest expectations. It is important for each employee to know what the job entails and that they can do the job to the performance standard required. The job description is important because it is a legal document. Some cases have come before the courts, and administrative agencies in which employees who were dismissed have sued the former employer, claiming that they did not know or were not properly informed of the duties required. Surprisingly, a few large multinational hospitality companies still do not use job descriptions because they do not want to have employees tied to specific tasks. Job descriptions are not a contract of employment, and management needs to be able to change them with the changing needs of the corporation. Most job descriptions have the section "and all other duties assigned by management." Today, many companies have employees sign their job descriptions to avoid any confusion or misunderstanding about their job and its responsibilities. The job description specifies the knowledge, qualifications, and skills necessary to do the job successfully. Job descriptions can be used as good performance measurement tools.

Job specifications are sometimes a part of the job description and sometimes a separate document. The job specification does exactly what it says: It specifies the qualities and knowledge the person will need to do the job. For example, a prep cook might have to lift 50-pound bags of potatoes. Or a cook might need to scale a recipe up or down from the manual and make up a recipe in 20 minutes. It would be important to see if the applicant has good knife skills and can understand and follow instructions in making a recipe.

Check Your Knowledge

1. What is task analysis?
2. Why are job descriptions important?

Productivity Standards

With today's high labor costs, increasing employee productivity has become a major issue. Productivity standards may be established for each position within the organization. Measuring or timing how long it takes to do a given task determines the **productivity standards.** Departments are staffed according to forecasted demand, whether for restaurant guests, hotel check-ins, or attendance at a theme park. For example, if there are 200 check-ins at a hotel, they would staff the front desk with three employees to give the level of service the hotel guests expect. Of course, the assistant or front-office manager will assist as necessary.

Employee productivity is measured in dollar terms by dividing sales by labor costs. If sales totaled $46,325 and labor costs were $9,265, productivity would be measured as a factor of five. This means that for every dollar in labor costs, $5 in sales was generated. Another way of expressing employee productivity is to divide the sales by the number of employees to arrive at the sales generated per employee. Other measures of productivity might be the number of tables or guests served by a foodservice employee or the number of rooms serviced by a housekeeping associate.

One good way to set productivity standards is to have a group of the best and quickest employees do the tasks and see how long they take; then average the

Corporate Profile: Marriott International, Inc.

Marriott International is a leading worldwide hospitality company. Its heritage is traced back to a root beer stand opened in Washington, DC, in 1927 by J. Willard and Alice S. Marriott. Today, Marriott International has more than 2,600 lodging properties in the United States and 65 other countries and territories. Marriott International operates and franchises hotels under the following brands:

Marriott Hotels and Resorts: The flagship brand of quality-tier, full-service hotels and resorts with features like fully equipped fitness centers, gift shops, swimming pools, concierge levels, business centers, meeting facilities, and high-speed Internet.

JW Marriott Hotels and Resorts: The most elegant and luxurious Marriott brand offering business and leisure travelers a deluxe level of comfort and personal service.

Renaissance Hotels and Resorts: A quality-tier, full-service brand offering guests the ambiance of a boutique. Brand signatures include business library, swimming pool, fitness centers, and conference and banqueting facilities.

Courtyard by Marriott: A moderately priced lodging brand designed by business travelers for business travelers that has recently increased the number of downtown locations often through conversions of historical buildings. Features include 80 to 150 guest rooms, high-speed Internet access, restaurant, lounge, meeting space, central courtyard, exercise room, swimming pool, and 24-hour access to food.

Residence Inn by Marriott: Designed as a home away from home for travelers staying five or more nights and includes a residential atmosphere with spacious accommodations. Features include complimentary hot breakfast, evening hospitality hour, swimming pool, sport court, personalized grocery shopping, guest suites with separate living and sleeping areas, fully equipped kitchen, and work space with data ports and voice mail.

Fairfield Inn by Marriott: A consistent, quality lodging at an affordable price. Features include spacious guest rooms, daily complimentary breakfast, and swimming pool. Future plans call for exercise rooms.

Marriott Convention Centers: A quality-tier brand specializing in small to midsized meetings. Properties provide the latest audiovisual communications technology, experiential learning facilities, gourmet conference dining, golf, and recreational/fitness facilities.

Towne Place Suites by Marriott: A midpriced, extended-stay brand that provides all the comforts of home in a residential atmosphere.

SpringHill Suites by Marriott: A moderately priced, all-suite lodging brand that offers up to 25 percent larger than standard hotel rooms. Features include complimentary continental breakfast, self-serve business center, indoor pool, whirlpool spa, high-speed Internet access, and exercise room.

Marriott Vacation Club International: A leading developer and operator of vacation ownership resorts with an average weekly interval price of $18,700. Features include spacious living and dining area one- two-, and three-bedroom villas, master bedroom and bath with whirpool spa, private balcony, kitchen, and laundry area.

Horizons by Marriott Vacation Club: A value-oriented vacation ownership resort community with fun amenities and activities for the entire family, the average price of which is $12,000 for a week a year. Features include roomy and functional two-bedroom, two-bath villas, family-friendly living and dining areas, private balcony, "everything but food" kitchen, and washer and dryer.

The Ritz-Carlton Hotel Company, L.L.C: The worldwide symbol for the finest in hotel and resort accommodations, dining, and service. Twice recipient of the Malcolm Baldrige National Quality Award, offering signature service amenities, fine dining, 24-hour room service, twice-daily housekeeping, fitness centers, business centers, and concierge services.

The Ritz-Carlton Club: A collection of private residences in highly desirable resort areas that are exclusive to members and their guests. Three- to five-week ownership fractions range from $136,000 to $510,000.

Marriott ExecuStay: Fully furnished corporate housing for executives and travelers who need temporary accommodations for a month or longer. Features include well-maintained properties in convenient locations, flexible lease terms and options, consistently high level of service, competitive pricing, and rooms attractively furnished and customized to satisfy each individual need.

Marriott Executive Apartments: A corporate housing brand designed to meet the needs of business executives on an overseas assignment for over 30 days or more by offering residential accommodations with hotel-like amenities.

Marriott Grand Residence Club: Fractional property ownership in premier second home destinations offering the services and amenities of a fine hotel. Three- to 13-week ownership fractions range from $83,900 to $550,000.

Marriott has been ranked the number one most admired company in the lodging industry by *Fortune* for the past five years and also one of the "100 Best Companies to Work For" for the past seven years.

time it takes. For example, if it takes a group of housekeepers 2.5 minutes to properly make a bed, then that time becomes the standard and benchmark. An additional benefit will be to come up with the best way of doing the task, which can then be made into a DVD for training purposes. Some companies have color training manuals or Web sites where employees can see how something should look—for example, guest rooms or room service setups.

Employment Law

Employment law has become increasingly more important in recent years due to the number of lawsuits brought against employers and the amount of the settlements and jury awards, often into the millions of dollars. Several laws affect the way hospitality and other corporations conduct themselves with regard to human resource leadership and management. Among the most important legislative acts are the following:

- *The Civil Rights Act of 1964* prohibits discrimination on the basis of race, color, religion, sex, or national origin.
- Equal Employment Opportunity Title VII of the Civil Rights Act established the *Equal Employment Opportunity Commission,* which is charged by law to enforce equal employment opportunity for all persons seeking employment. It is critical that all applicants be treated equally and that all employment decisions be job related.
- *The Equal Pay Act of 1963* requires women and men performing equal jobs to receive equal pay. This act was passed because men and women were being paid different amounts for the same work being performed.
- *The Age Discrimination in Employment Act (ADEA) of 1967* prohibits discrimination in employment for people over 40 years old. With rising productivity expectations and other job-related pressures, older workers were, relative to younger workers, being displaced in greater numbers and then finding it difficult to find alternative employment. The intent of the law is that no employer shall discriminate against an employee because of his or her age when over 40 years. The law applies to both employees and applicants.

- *The Immigration Reform and Control Act of 1986* makes it illegal to hire undocumented employees, and it is the employer's responsibility to verify the documents of the prospective employee. Documentation of proof of employment eligibility (an I-9 form) is required for every employee hired after November 6, 1986, and employers cannot discriminate on the basis of national origin or citizenship.

- *The Americans with Disabilities Act (ADA)* is a far-reaching act forbidding discrimination against people with disabilities in employment and the workplace. Employers need to make "reasonable accommodations" to assist people with disabilities and make the workplace accessible to them if they are qualified for the job they applied for. Similarly, guest accommodations must be accessible to people with disabilities. Under the ADA, a person is considered qualified if they can perform the "essential functions of the job." In practice ADA policies are subjective because there is much debate about what constitutes a disability. Currently, a number of cases are going through the courts relating to ADA and workers' compensation dealing with issues like carpal tunnel syndrome, which employees regard as a debilitating medical condition. However, in the case of carpal tunnel syndrome, the Supreme Court has ruled that it is not a disability. ADA does include and protect those who are HIV-positive or have hepatitis B.

- *The Fair Labor Standards Act of 1938*, as amended, established the minimum wage and the maximum number of workweek hours. Managers are exempt from this standard as long as they are spending the majority of their time in managerial activities. Several multimillion-dollar settlements have recently been made to so-called managers who were supposedly exempt, but when they filed suit, the court found them to be doing the work of hourly paid (nonexempt) employees; therefore, they were awarded millions of dollars in back pay and compensation. The Fair Labor Standards Act is a broad federal statute that covers the following:

  Federal minimum wage law

  Employee meals and meal credit

  Equal pay

  Child labor

  Overtime

  Tips, tip credits, and tip-pooling procedures

  Uniforms and uniform maintenance

  Record keeping

  Exempt versus nonexempt employees

- *The Pregnancy Discrimination Act of 1978* provides various protections for pregnant women. It makes it unlawful to discriminate against women because they might become or are pregnant, giving birth, or other related medical conditions. It is also unlawful not to hire or promote someone because they are pregnant, and employers cannot set the beginning and end of an employee's maternity leave. If in good faith an employer, for example, offers a pregnant employee server an alternative position as a cashier, she must be paid her server salary, including tips.

- *The Family and Medical Leave Act of 1993* allows associates to take up to 12 weeks a year unpaid leave for any of the following reasons: (1) birth or adoption of a child, (2) serious health condition of a child, (3) serious health condition of a spouse or parent, or (4) an employee's own health condition. Another employment-related act is the Drug Free Workplace Act of 1988, which allows drug testing of all applicants.

Recruitment and Selection

Recruitment is finding the most suitable and talented employee for an available position. The process begins with announcing the opportunity; sometimes this is done first within the organization and then outside. Applications are received from a variety of sources: internal promotion, employee referrals, applicant files from people who may have sent in résumés, transfers within the company, advertising, colleges and universities, and government-sponsored employment services.

Application forms and résumés are accepted and screened by the human resources department. Many companies require applicants to come to the property and personally fill out an application form, and some companies use an online application process. Once the application is submitted, the human resources department reviews the application form and résumé for accuracy and checks to ensure that the prospective employee is legally entitled to work in this country. See Figure 18–4 for a description of the recruitment and selection process.

Applicants are invited to attend an interview with the employment manager. This is a general screening interview to determine that the applicant is suitable for employment, which means that they meet the minimum standards required to be employed. Some hospitality companies call this a prescreening interview, where the interviewer looks for eye contact, grooming (hair, nails, clean clothes, and, yes, a *smile*. (One HR manager will not hire people who do not smile as

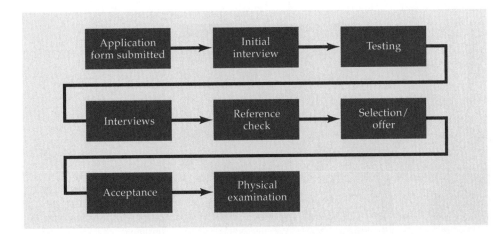

Figure 18–4 *Recruitment and Selection Process*

many times as she does during the interview, and another will not hire people who do not walk as quickly as she does.) One question that might be asked during a prescreening interview is "What motivated you to apply for a position here?" The answer should not be "I need a job" or "I thought it would fit my schedule at school." Some hospitality companies require applicants to do a talent interview. This is to assess their natural talent (caring, positive, energetic, honest, loyal, and natural need for knowing other people). This type of interview also examines the applicant's relationship extension or aggressive hospitality. Is the person likely to speak to the guest first? Can she confront difficult issues (like an unhappy guest at the front desk)? Does he have *persuasion*—meaning can he act graciously when a guest is unhappy because she made a reservation six months ago for interconnecting rooms, and when she arrives, there are no connecting rooms available?

There are three kinds of interviews. In the *structured interview,* the questions are prepared in advance, and the interviewer only asks the questions listed on the interview sheet. The advantage of the structured interview is that all candidates are asked the same questions (this is particularly important when an unsuccessful candidate claims that he was discriminated against in some way); remember how important it is to treat all applicants the same. Of course, there's a downside to the structured interview: It does not allow for responses to the candidate's answers.

With the *unstructured interview,* general questions are prepared before the interview, and interviewers ask additional questions in response to the candidate's answers to questions. An example might be "Why are you applying for this position?" This might be followed with "What qualifications do you have that make you a good candidate for the position?"

The third type of interview is a *semistructured interview.* This is a combination of the structured and unstructured interviews. A preprepared list of questions is asked of all candidates, followed by other questions that arise from the prepared questions.

Employment managers look for dress, mannerisms, attentiveness, attitude, and interest. They also ask questions that encourage the applicant to answer in

Recruiting qualified applicants and selecting the best candidate includes interviewing several people.

some detail. This necessitates asking open-ended questions, such as "What did you like most and least about your last job?" or "Tell me about a time when. . . ." Or "Describe your idea of great guest service." Another popular question asked of college graduates is "What extracurricular activities did you participate in at school?" Questions like this invite the applicant to open up. The two-way exchange of information allows the prospective employee to ask or learn about the job and the corporation. Assuming the applicant makes a favorable impression, she or he will be invited for a second interview with a department manager. The interview within the department will assess the candidate's ability to do the essential functions of the job and his or her interpersonal suitability to join the department team. It is important that skilled interviewers conduct the decision-making interview.

Check Your Knowledge

1. Describe the employment laws.
2. What are the important topics in recruitment and selection?

Selection means to select the best-qualified (not necessarily the most qualified) candidate for the available position. Providing candidates meet the minimum requirements stated in the job specification, the best individual may be selected from the qualified applicants. Part of the selection process might involve tests (personality, intelligence, skill, aptitude, integrity, psychological) to ensure that candidates possess the requisite interpersonal skills or knowledge to do the job. In addition, some companies, as a condition of employment, require new employees to take a drug-screening test. It is advisable to do extensive background checks. Most previous employers will, for legal reasons, generally only give a neutral reference of the beginning and ending dates of employment and the position held and may state if the individual is eligible for reemployment. One high-end hospitality company that does extensive background checks even asked an applicant if he paid for a parking ticket he got five years earlier! Assuming that reference and background checks are positive, a formal offer is sometimes made in writing to the prospective employee. (In many companies, written offers are only made for management positions.) The offer outlines the terms and conditions of employment. The offer should include the title of the position offered, the location, hours of work, and job description. It will be signed by the new employee, showing that he understands the duties and responsibilities, the benefits and orientation schedule, and the performance evaluation methods. The offer may conclude with a date by which the offer must be accepted. The last step in the recruitment and selection process may be a medical examination. The medical examination acts as a precaution for both the employee and the corporation. Proactive companies have a one-day hiring process as a standard for selection.

Personal Profile: Patricia Engfer

Patricia Engfer began her career 25 years ago as a management trainee in Hilton Head, South Carolina. She then worked as an assistant executive housekeeper in Pittsburgh, followed by a long list of Hyatt properties, including a stint as rooms executive at the Hyatt Regency Long Beach during that hotel's opening. She first became a general manager at the Hyatt City of Commerce, California, and held similar positions in Los Angeles, Edgewater, and Newport Beach, California. Patricia took her current position of GM at the Hyatt Regency Orlando International Airport a few years ago. Here are Pat's answers to our questions:

How have your responsibilities changed at Hyatt?
My responsibilities as a GM have not changed. They include three areas of focus: employees, guests, and owners. What has changed are the tools and sophistication needed to succeed. Our guests, employees, and owners have higher expectations than ever. So we have to be open to innovations that help us meet their expectations.

How did you grow into your position as a GM?
Hyatt does a great job of developing careers one position at a time. That gives each of us the opportunity to develop skills while preparing for the next step. Coming up through the rooms division and working in convention, resort, airport, and city-center hotels prepared me to manage hotels in different markets. The common thread is how you interact with people in each location.

What is the biggest challenge of your job?
We all know that the current business climate is challenging and requires focus and dedication from every member of the team to look at opportunities to drive sales and manage costs.

Do women and minorities have equal opportunities at Hyatt?
Yes. But you must have drive and determination and be willing to give 100 percent. Being a woman has never been a disadvantage. To the contrary, Hyatt has provided an environment that makes it possible to have the best of both worlds—a career and a fabulous family.

Do you have a mentor at Hyatt?
Over the years I have looked to several mentors who have helped me develop in several ways. Steve Trent hired me, and we have kept in close contact through the years. Locally, I have developed friendships with women who are true leaders, including Glenda Hood, former mayor of Orlando and now Florida secretary of state. Another is Linda Chaplin, our past county chairperson, who runs an economic think tank at the University of Central Florida. These women started out raising families, began volunteering time, and today are driving the vision of central Florida. That is truly inspirational.

How do you welcome new employees to your property?
I tell employees the only limits they face are the ones they put on themselves. Hyatt offers training to be successful, but only they can bring the personality and commitment. How many other companies offer a great work environment, the opportunity to live almost anywhere, and to grow rapidly, while never having to hop from one company to another? If you put forth the effort, Hyatt provides a platform for success where employees of all races and genders are embraced.

Orientation

The **orientation** is a way to introduce new employees to the company and the specifics of the workplace and associates. When planned and presented properly, an employee orientation is a very useful tool for retention—a large percentage of new employees leave within the first 90 days, citing among other reasons, lack of training or poor training—and when we add the average cost of thousands of dollars to replace an employee, we realize the importance of orientation all the more. New employees need to have someone help them to get acquainted and settle into the new work environment.

Either prior to beginning or during the first few days of employment, new hires are required to attend a new-hire orientation session. At the orientation, new employees learn details about the corporation's history, policies, procedures, and compensation and benefits. Safety and fire prevention are also introduced, as well as the property's service philosophy. Department heads and the general manager usually introduce themselves to the new employees and wish them well in their new positions. Smart companies ask new associates to evaluate the company. This information provides valuable insights for making improvements. The Ritz-Carlton Company has a two-day orientation followed by a review after 21 days. At the review, the HR department can find out how everything went for the new employee and make any necessary adjustments.

Training and Development

Training in many organizations is an ongoing activity conducted by a training department, a training manager, line management, or specially trained individuals within each department. The first step in establishing a training program is to identify the training needs and then set training objectives. Because the training must be geared toward fulfilling guests' expectations, training often focuses on areas where current service falls short of guest expectations, as noted in guest surveys.

There are five main types of employee training: apprentice, simulation, certification, corporate required, and on the job (OJT). Apprentice is training given to people who are new to a particular job. The training is specially designed to teach participants the correct way to do a particular task. This often follows the "tell me, show me, do it" routine. Many chefs are involved in an apprenticeship program, which includes a mixture of classroom and OJT training with seasoned professionals.

Simulation training simulates the actual workplace. For example, there are specially prepared simulation exercises for travel agents on the Sabre and Apollo airline reservation systems. Once the trainee has reached the required level of proficiency, she or he is allowed to do real ticketing. Hotel front-desk employees use simulation software packages for beginner and advanced training.

Certification training enables individuals to gain corporate or professional certification by attaining passing scores on practical or theoretical tests. These tests are generally job specific and are helpful in motivating employees. For example, T.G.I. Friday's has a certification for each station in the

On-the-job training is essential in maintaining standards.

kitchen, and it's a challenge for the line cooks to become certified. Once employees become certified, however, they have a tremendous feeling of accomplishment. ServSafe is a popular certification that is widely used in foodservice operations.

Corporate-required training includes the many workshops and seminars on topics like safety, workplace values, ethics, harassment, supporting service excellence, service essentials, and valuing differences.

On-the-job training helps maintain standards by having managers, supervisors, trainers, or fellow employees coach individuals in the most effective way to do the required work. OJT allows the trainee to quickly learn the best way to do the work based on the experience of trial and error. New hotel housekeepers may work with an experienced employee for a few days to learn the preferred way to do rooms.

Employee Development

Employee development is a natural progression from appraisal. The employee and his or her supervisor make a development plan. The plan will outline the development activity and indicate when the development will take place. In well-run corporations, employee development is ongoing; it may take the form of in-house training or workshops and seminars on specific topics. Development is a way of enhancing existing skills and is used as motivators for midlevel managers. Development is usually used for nontechnical training, such as effective communications, team building, motivation, and leadership. A popular topic is Stephen Covey's *Seven Habits of Highly Effective People.*[5] Other training and development include English classes, which are handled by outside experts. These training methods help individuals to quickly learn the job and to improve their performance in doing the work. Some interesting anonymous industry comments heard in training sessions include the following:

- "People in the organization are a reflection of the leadership."
- "We don't run restaurants, we manage associations."
- "We hire cheerleaders."
- "What! You want my employees to smile? SMILE! I'm lucky if they don't look as if they are in pain!!" (This quote is from a restaurateur, who shall remain anonymous. That reminds me of a student who reported in class one day that she got "bawled out" at work. When asked why, she said that a guest had told her to smile. She had replied to the guest, "Sir, *you* smile." When the guest smiled, she added, Now hold that smile for eight hours! That person is actually now a food and beverage manager with a major hospitality corporation.)
- "We are hiring people today that we wouldn't have let in as customers a few years ago."
- "You can teach nice people, but you can't teach people to be nice."
- "You achieve what you inspect, not what you expect."

Certification is an excellent form of employee development because it validates a person's ability to do an excellent job and become more professional. Certification can be internal and external. Internal certification occurs when a company has identified certain criteria associated with a position (such as knowing the menu, being able to describe each item, and so on). External certification occurs when an employee takes courses toward a professional designation, such as the National Restaurant Association's Foodservice Management Professional (FMP). The American Hotel & Lodging Association also has a number of certification programs in the lodging area. For human resource managers, there is the Professional of Human Resources (PHR) and the Senior Professional of Human Resources (SPHR).

Check Your Knowledge

1. Describe the selection and orientation process.
2. What are a few of the most important legislative acts affecting human resources in the hospitality industry?

Performance Appraisal

The purpose of **performance appraisal** is to compare an employee's actual performance to preestablished standards as described in the job description. Performance appraisal has been viewed by the industry as positive as well as negative. The positive attributes of performance appraisal include giving feedback to employees, building the appraisal into a personal development plan, establishing a rationale for promotion and wage or salary increases, and helping to establish objectives for training programs.

A major difficulty with most performance appraisal systems is that the judgments involved are frequently subjective, relating primarily to personality traits

Performance appraisals allow managers and associates to review past performance and establish goals for the future.

or observations that cannot be verified. Three common distortions in performance appraisals include the following:

1. *Recent behavior influence.* An evaluator's judgment may be overly influenced by the employee's recent behavior (good or bad). Many supervisors wait until the last minute to conduct an appraisal and only look at a short window of employee performance.
2. *The halo effect.* The halo effect occurs when a supervisor is overly concerned with one particular aspect of the overall job, such as punctuality. If an employee is punctual, he or she will likely receive a better evaluation than one who is occasionally late, even if his or her productivity is somewhat better. Of course, the opposite is also true and known as "horns."
3. *Like-me syndrome.* We all tend to like people who are similar to ourselves; naturally, there is a tendency to give a better appraisal to those employees who are most like ourselves. This occurs when managers rate an employee high because they have similar traits.

There is another inherent weakness in all appraisals. Any system by which a superior rates a subordinate is likely to cause resentment in the person being rated or anxiety in the rater. The basic answer to the anxiety problem is to develop a supportive social system aimed at reducing individual anxiety and thus freeing up energies for constructive purposes. The supportive system includes help from peers and supervisors that will make the employee feel more positive toward the experience and offer a real chance for improvement. One main problem with employee evaluations is a lack of management training in doing employee evaluations. That's why companies like Hyatt have a "Walk a mile in my shoes" program so that managers will have a better understanding of how it is to actually do the job.

Performance appraisals make the link between performance standards and organizational goals. Another critical element is the link between the job description, job specification, performance standards, and performance appraisal. Figure 18–5 shows the importance of the linkage among these factors. Performance appraisals need to be fair, consistent, equal, and nondiscriminatory.

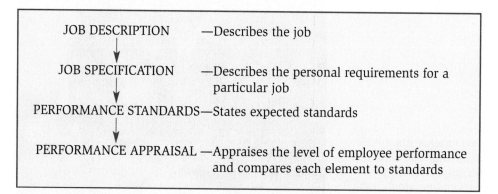

Figure 18–5 *Flow between Job Description, Job Specification, Performance Standards, and Performance Appraisal*

> ## Check Your Knowledge
> 1. Describe the key elements of performance appraisal.
> 2. What is the difference between exempt and nonexempt employees?

Employee Assistance Programs

Employee Assistance Programs (EAPs) have been instituted at many progressive companies. The purpose of an EAP program is to offer confidential and professional counseling and referral services to employees. Employees who have problems may request help (assistance) in confidence, without losing their jobs. The emphasis of most EAPs is on prevention and on intervening before a crisis stage is reached. Typically, EAP programs assist employees with drug- and alcohol-related problems and personal finance, marital, career and job, and legal issues.

Motivation

Motivation is the art or process of initiating and sustaining behavior toward certain goals. Motivating people is all about inspiring them to do something because they want to do it, not because someone tells them to do it. As the American and Canadian hospitality and tourism industries have right-sized the organizational structure by reducing the number of levels of management, the need for motivation has increased. Hotel general managers say that their biggest challenge is how to motivate employees. This chapter should help you understand your own motivation and influence that of those you will lead in the future. A number of theories about motivation have been developed over the years by experts in motivational psychology. Each has made a contribution to where we are today.

McGregor's Theory X and Theory Y

This motivational approach draws on Douglas McGregor's theories. He classified human nature into two categories, based on a set of assumptions: Theory X and Theory Y. [6] **Theory X** describes people in primarily a negative view. The employee that falls under this category is typically a pessimist, has little ambition, generally dislikes work, tries at every cost to avoid responsibility, and needs constant supervision and control to be effectively productive. Unfortunately, some of those employees may be in the hospitality industry! Theory X managers are dictators and behave like tyrants, which is often described as "my way or the highway." **Theory Y,** on the other hand, paints a positive picture of people. Employees that fit the Theory Y profile are primarily optimistic, enjoy working, seek out responsibilities, need little supervision, and typically have a lot of ambition. The typical employee is more likely to have a Theory Y personality. Therefore, McGregor theorized that giving employees more

A Day in the Life of Rob Westfall
Bar Manager, The Speakeasy, Siesta Key, Florida

The Speakeasy has been a staple in Siesta Key's Village for over five years. Known for its exceptional variety of live music, it is also a place where locals feel right at home. Newly remodeled in November 2004, The Speakeasy now features ice-cold air conditioning in a polished, clean environment. Located at the back of the room is our pool table with plenty of space to allow for professional play. Specialty drinks are another draw for patrons at The Speakeasy. Our menu is loaded with innovative cocktails that are tough to find in another establishment. Along with our extensive list of wines by the glass, we also offer many premium single-malt scotches, cognacs, bourbons, and a host of fine liqueurs. The Speakeasy is owned and operated by Café Gardens, which also owns the Daiquiri Deck located directly next door. For more information on The Speakeasy or the Daiquiri Deck, visit our Web site at www.daiquirideck.com.

A typical day for a manager at the Speakeasy goes like this:

9:45 A.M. Arrive for manager meeting at the Daiquiri Deck. All Daiquiri Deck managers, the owners, and I are present at this meeting. The meeting consists of a variety of issues. Typically, the first order of business is reviewing the numbers from the previous week. Numbers like net sales, cost of labor, cost of goods, and promotional costs are discussed. Additionally, budgets are a major concern every week. Budgets are set based on sales projections from the previous year and are very important to the success of the business. Next, we discuss any issues from the previous week. In the bar business, an "issue" could be just about anything from fights to vandalism. We find it extremely important to discuss all of these issues so that the management team is all on the same page. The meeting is adjourned after everyone around the table is given a chance to raise any issues they feel necessary. After everything has been discussed, it's time to go to work.

11:00 A.M. Mondays are very important in the bar business. Inventory must be taken to ensure that costs are in line and that you know what product you need. First, I take an inventory of all beverage products at the Speakeasy. Liquor, beer, wine, cigarettes, cigars, and mixers are all items that must be counted.

12:00 P.M. Upon completion of the inventory, it is time to put your orders together for the week. Knowing your usage is extremely important when placing an order. Buying in bulk is always superior to simply filling holes from week to week. Simply, it allows you more buying power and, essentially, more free goods. Bar supplies also need to be monitored. Straws, olive picks, stir sticks, bar glass cleaner and sanitizer, and bar napkins all need to be kept in stock. The absence of one item can often make or break a busy night at the bar.

1:00 P.M. Confirm band schedule. Booking bands and maintaining an entertainment schedule can sometimes be one of the most frustrating areas of the bar business. However, it can also be the most rewarding. The experience you gain from working with so many different types of entertainment is difficult to replace. The majority of bands show up on time and treat their job professionally, but there are a significant amount of them that do not.

2:00 P.M. Typically there is always some bar maintenance that needs to be addressed. I always take a walk around and check everything out to make sure that everything is working properly. Bathrooms, lightbulbs, and bar cleanliness are all part of this maintenance.

3:00 P.M. Work on any upcoming promotions and ensure their success. Spirit tastings, holidays, Full Moon parties, and private parties are examples of these types of events. Planning is extremely important for the ultimate success of these events.

4:00 P.M. Send memo to corporate office regarding what checks need to be written for entertainment that week. Ensure that each band has proper paperwork filled out for tax purposes.

5:00 P.M. Every day the staff needs to be reminded to step it up. Motivation comes from the top down. The bar business is a stage, and the bartenders are on a stage. The staff will typically need to be reminded of this on a consistent basis. Open lines of communication are very important and allow you to apply constructive criticism or accolades, as they are appropriate.

6:00 P.M. It's time to have a drink.

That's the management side of the bar. The nighttime is another animal entirely.

responsibilities, letting them be part of the decision-making process, and giving them challenges would lead to higher motivation in the workplace.

McGregor's theories cannot be proven, because they are based on assumptions of certain behaviors. There is no guarantee that altering your behavior and treating people according to Theory Y assumptions will improve motivation.

Herzberg's Motivation—Hygiene Theory

A widely accepted and influential theory of motivation is Frederick *Herzberg's motivation and hygiene factors* theory. While studying managers in the work environment, psychologist Frederick Herzberg concluded that two separate and distinct sets of factors influenced individual motivation (see Figure 18–6). Herzberg referred to these groups of factors as satisfiers and dissatisfiers, or motivators and hygiene factors. **Motivators** are the intrinsic factors that increase job satisfaction and, hence, lead to increased motivation in employees. Herzberg identified the motivators as follows:

1. Work itself
2. Recognition
3. Responsibility
4. Achievement
5. Growth
6. Advancement

The *hygiene factors*, on the other hand, were identified as factors that eliminate job dissatisfaction but fail to motivate. Although dissatisfaction is largely eradicated, the employees are not satisfied either. The hygiene factors are as follows:

1. Company policies and administration
2. Salary
3. Working conditions
4. Relationships with supervisors
5. Relationships with peers
6. Relationships with subordinates
7. Security
8. Status

Motivators	Hygienes
Work itself	Company policies and administration
Recognition	Salary
Responsibility	Working conditions
Achievement	Relationships with supervisors
Growth	Relationships with peers
Advancement	Relationships with subordinates
	Security
	Status

Figure 18–6 *Herzberg's Motivation and Hygiene Factors*

The main premise of Herzberg's theory is that if the hygiene factors are not met, it is unlikely that much motivation will occur, no matter how many of the motivators are met. However, once the hygiene factors have been met, significant motivation will occur once the motivator factors are present.

Maslow's Hierarchy of Needs

Maslow's theory of the hierarchy of needs has influenced motivational techniques for many years. The theory suggests that there are five basic needs or motives common to adults:

1. Physiological needs, which are necessities for life, including food, air, and fluids, all of which are essential to our physical existence
2. Safety needs, which provide us with the security and assurance that our physiological needs will be met in the future
3. Love and belonging needs, which are social needs, such as the need for affection and the need for acceptance by others
4. Esteem needs, which are the needs of self-respect and respect from others
5. Self-actualization needs, which are the need for self-fulfillment and the need to reach one's potential

Figure 18–7 shows Maslow's five needs together with examples of how each might be satisfied in an organizational setting. Although Maslow's theory was first proposed years ago, it is still widely and highly regarded as having a significant influence on management and employee motivation.

Now let's relate Maslow's theory to practical hospitality applications. Ask any poor student with unmet physiological and security needs about what mo-

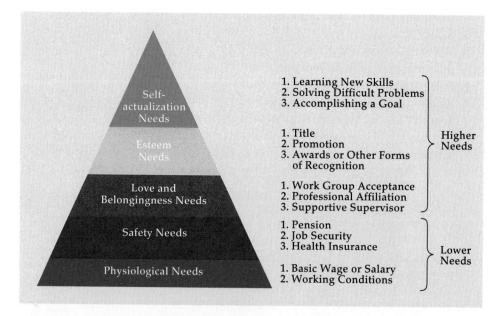

Figure 18–7   *Maslow's Hierarchy of Needs in an Organizational Setting (From Donald D. White, Organizational Behavior: Understanding and Managing People at Work, 2nd ed. Boston: Allyn and Bacon, 1991, p. 149.)*

tivates them. They will most surely say money and security. So wages, benefits, and job security are important and motivating to the lower level needs. But once those needs have been met by a certain level of job performance, they cease to be motivators for greater job-related efforts. Moving up to social and affiliation needs, the hospitality industry has no problem in fulfilling their needs. Hospitality associates work in departments that have built-in groups or teams, allowing for plenty of social interaction. Now, of course, that can be good or bad, depending on the "climate" or culture in the department—but then it's up to management to make it a positive working experience. A win–win situation exists when associates identify with the department and organization and, better yet, when they feel accepted and that they belong. In such a case, they will be motivated to achieve organization and personal goals.

In the social affiliation context, outstanding managers care for their associates and offer praise in public by having award and recognition ceremonies. Additionally, managers who do something unexpected like give tickets to a baseball game to an associate who is a fan increase the associate's feeling of belonging.

Make everyone a winner. As a manager, if you can remove obstacles and make your team winners by providing a good climate, incentives, and rewards, you will have a motivated group. Managers can help motivate associates' natural need for self-esteem by giving them the opportunity to be a winner. Consider this example: One day I was walking through the hotel lobby with a GM of the Westgate Hotel. He bumped into his director of marketing and introduced her as the most professional and best DOM he had ever worked with because she was able to "fill rooms" even in a difficult economy. George went on for a few minutes and was so enthusiastic in his praise that it must have been a perfect self-esteem builder for the director of marketing.

Self-actualization is the need to achieve for its own sake and is expressed in several ways, such as "Developing service excellence" or "We are ladies and gentlemen serving ladies and gentlemen" or "We try harder."

Contemporary Theories of Motivation

Plenty of hypotheses exist about motivation—what drives humans to do something they don't have to do. Contemporary theories include the three-needs theory, the goal-setting theory, reinforcement theory, equity theory, and expectancy theory.

Three-Needs Theory

David McClelland and others proposed a three-needs theory, which says that three needs are a major motivating force in the workplace: [7]

Need for achievement: The drive to excel and to strive to succeed.
Need for Power: The need to make others behave in a way that they would not have behaved otherwise.
Need for affiliation: The desire for friendly and close interpersonal relationships.

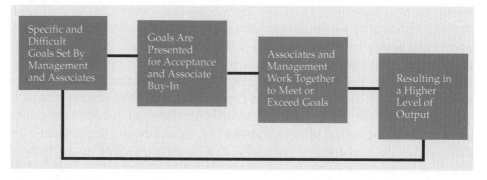

Figure 18–8 *Goal-Setting Theory*

Reflect on your own personal motivation and how each of these theories stimulates your motivation. . . .

Goal-Setting and Reinforcement Theory

Both companies and individuals are better off when they set goals. Even if they are not all reached, the results will be better than if no goals were set. As a result, many companies have included some form of **goal-setting theory** as part of their reward and recognition programs.

Goal setting is a key element in management by objective (MBO) and total quality management (TQM). With MBO, goals are generally set by employees in conjunction with managers. Once the employees have set the individual and group/departmental goals, management approves the goals. Employees are far more likely to achieve and even exceed goals that they have had a hand in setting than they are to achieve goals handed down from above. TQM and empowerment have contributed greatly to employee motivation. Figure 18–8 illustrates the goal-setting theory.

Reinforcement theory suggests that associates behavior is caused by external factors, rather than internal ones, as suggested by the goal-setting theory. Behavior is controlled by **reinforcers** (you may recall the term *positive reinforcement*). In the hospitality industry, the mantra is "catch associates doing something right and praise them because they will likely repeat the performance." Reinforcement is best used in conjunction with other motivators because it alone does not produce the required results.

Equity Theory

If you have ever experienced a situation where you were working for a company and found out that someone in a similar position was making more than you, then you know what equity is—or rather what inequity is. The **equity theory** is about how you felt at that time—most likely demotivated. Associates frequently compare their situations with coworkers; factors of comparison include inputs (expertise, qualifications, experience, and personal qualities like intelligence, drive, and ambition) and outputs (hours worked, rates of pay, flexible working arrangements, power, satisfaction, status, and other benefits). If there are discrepancies, associates want them made equitable.

Associates feel that they are treated fairly if they perceive that their inputs and outputs are equitable with peers. Equity theory significantly influences hospitality associates work performance, yet it is difficult to make expectations between different, but similar, work tasks and the compensation. Two associates with equal experience and qualifications can include personal values and come up with a different perception of "equity." However, equity theory does suggest that associates be rewarded based on performance. So someone who really produces gets the bonus. Associates' responses to inequity include leaving the company, which contributes to turnover, requesting equity (read "pay increase"), or influencing the performance of others via peer pressure.

Expectancy Theory

The most popular and widely accepted motivation theory is the expectancy theory.[8] Developed by Victor Vroom, **expectancy theory** is based on the premise that people will put out effort equivalent to the perceived rewards. If people think they are definitely going to receive rewards, they are more likely to be motivated and give the extra effort required to achieve the goals that lead to those rewards. Bonuses utilize the expectancy theory of motivation. For example, if a foodservice manager meets or exceeds a predetermined level of profitability, she will receive financial and possibly other bonus incentives.

The typical expectancy model is simplified in Figure 18–9. It includes the following steps: personal effort leads to personal achievement, which brings organizational rewards and ultimately leads to individual goals.

The expectancy theory includes three variables or relationships:[9]

1. *Expectancy or effort-performance linkage* is the probability perceived by the associate that exerting a given amount of effort will lead to a certain level of performance.
2. *Instrumentally or performance-reward-related linkage* is the degree to which the associate believes that performing at a particular level is instrumental in attaining the desired outcome.
3. *Valence or attractiveness of reward* is the importance that the associate places on the potential outcome or reward that can be achieved on the job.

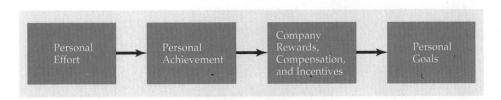

Figure 18–9 *Expectancy Model (Modified from Walker, Introduction to Hospitality, 3rd ed. Upper Saddle River, NJ: Prentice Hall, 2002, p. 569.)*

Check Your Knowledge

1. What are the characteristics of a Theory Y employee?
2. What are reinforcers?
3. Describe the goal-setting theory.
4. Give an example of expectancy theory.

Motivating a Diverse Workforce

With today's diverse workforce, managers must be highly flexible to keep all of their employees motivated. A basic example of the differences in the workforce is what is important for women versus men, older versus younger, and interculturally. The most important thing for managers to remember is that every single one of their employees is an individual with a different background. The goals and needs of an employee who is older working solely for retirement income will be very different from the goals and needs of an employee who may be a single parent, working full time to support a family. Due to employees' varied needs and goals, the motivators will be different as well as the ultimate reward.

How do we motivate this diverse workforce? Several incentive programs can be used, including offering employees flexible working schedules, of which there are many different types. They are primarily designed to accommodate employees who have other duties and/or responsibilities apart from their careers. Such a schedule appeals particularly to single parents, people who need to take care of sick family members, or women who enter the workforce after giving birth.

Let's start with a discussion of the *compressed workweek.* This schedule allows employees to work fewer days a week and make up the hours by working longer on the days they do work. One form of this is to work ten hours a day and only four days a week. Another name for it is the 4–40 program. The con-

When managing a diverse workforce, the need for diversity and teamwork training often arises.

ditions and hours of the compressed workweek vary from organization to organization to fit each individual's needs.

The *flextime* schedule allows for more flexibility than the compressed workweek. It is also known as *flexible work hours*. This system is designed by organizations to allow employees to make their own individual schedule to fit their needs. A required number of hours must be worked during the week, but the individual is free to schedule the hours as they please within limitations. The most common limitation is certain core hours that each employee must work; however, starting times, ending times, and lunch hours are flexible.

Job sharing is the term used to describe a situation in which two or more people share one job. This type of motivation for the workforce is very effective when it comes to parents or retirees who do not want a full-time job, yet want the demands of one.

Last, there is the option of *telecommuting*. This option has been made possible only recently with the advances in high-tech. Employees are able to complete their job duties from home through the use of computers, the Internet, phones, cell phones, and faxes. This form of employment is very convenient because employees have flexible hours; can wear whatever they please, since they often work from home; reduce their commute; and have fewer workplace interruptions. Although this form of work relief is common in many industries, its applicability in hospitality is somewhat restricted in the sense that many positions in hotels and restaurants are labor-intensive, high-customer-contact jobs (front desk, servers, host/hostess, housekeeping, etc.). This, however, does not preclude its use in the back of the house where actual face-to-face guest contact is not necessary. For instance, sales and catering personnel could work from home, providing they have computer access to the property.

"Bowling for Motivation?"

Ken Blanchard, a beloved leader–manager, best-selling author, and marvelous presenter, tells a story about motivation.[1] Dave is a below-average worker—not really motivated. But on Wednesday nights he is the star of the bowling team. If you could only see him then, not only is he very motivated, but he motivates others. Now, just for a moment, suppose he was about to bowl and for some unknown reason he did not get a strike. How do you think he would feel if his manager were to say, "Dave you knocked down only six pins. Why didn't you get them all?" Or worse still, what if the manager were to put a curtain halfway down the lane so Dave could not see what he was aiming at. Yes, you see the analogy. All too often, management spoils any chance of motivating associates by not setting clear goals and objectives. Then they compound the problem by asking why the associate knocked down only so many pins and not all of them. Regrettably, this kind of situation still occurs—maybe you have similar personal experiences.

[1] Ken Blanchard, presentation to the National Restaurant Association. May 18, 2001.

Pay-for-Performance Programs

The *pay-for-performance* program[10] is one of the most popular and widely known methods of motivation. It can be described as any method that relates pay to the quantity or quality of work an employee produces. Examples include a chef meeting the food cost percentage and the engineering department meeting safety goals. Figure 18–10 illustrates pay-for-performance programs.

Piecework Pay Plan

The first type of pay-for-performance plan we are going to look at is the *piecework pay plan*. This plan pays the employee according to an actual

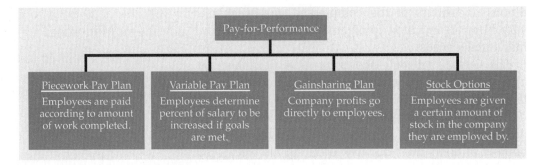

Figure 18–10 *Pay-for-Performance Programs*

amount, or "piece," of work produced. The employee receives a set amount of money for every piece produced. One example of this is to offer servers an extra percent of sales of a specific wine. Thus, the server will be motivated to upsell, and, by doing so, the guests perceive that the server is paying special attention to them. Another method is to determine what the average check is for each station, and for each increase (say, $5 over average) the server receives a bonus or recognition as server of the day, week, or month. The success of this type of motivation can be explained by Vroom's expectancy theory. The theory states that the employee will be motivated and perform well if he knows he will be rewarded. Money is the reward in our example and will motivate the server to recommend wine to customers.

Variable Pay Plan

Another form of pay-for-performance programs is the *variable pay plan,* which is much like gambling. The employee gets to put up a voluntary percentage of her base salary. Let's say 6 percent. If the company's goals for the particular department in which the employee is working are met, she will receive that 6 percent of her salary, and, depending on company policies, it might be doubled or tripled. However, if the goals are not met, the employee loses the 6 percent of her salary. (Maybe this would work in Las Vegas?) This theory can again be explained by looking at Vroom's expectancy theory. The employee not only expects to get a reward if she meets the company's goals, but she also expects to lose a part of her salary if the goals are not met. This would be a negative expectancy.

Gainsharing Plan

When employees are able to directly benefit from a company's profits or gains, the motivational theory is called a *gainsharing plan.* To implement this program, the employer must first of all choose a unit of measure. An example would be cost per unit produced. Next, a funding formula is calculated, such as "47 percent of savings go to employees." Based on individual performance, management then decides how the savings are distributed among employees. If it so happens that an employee is able to achieve cost savings in line with his individual performance goals, the resulting gains are shared with him.

Starbucks, like several other hospitality companies, offers a stock option plan.

A good hospitality example is the *upselling* that is done at the front desk. A guest with a reservation for a standard room that is persuaded by the front-desk employee to upgrade her room to a luxury suit is being upsold. The front-desk employees are promised 50 percent of the profit made from upselling, and this profit is then justly divided among the employees by the department manager. Another example is the energy cost-saving programs that are implemented by hotels. They have certain guidelines that the employees must follow, such as switch off the freezer for certain hours during the day, turn off all lights and electric appliances after cleaning a room, or turn down the heater or air conditioning during peak energy hours. Employees who follow these guidelines are rewarded by a promised 45 percent of the money saved as a result of the electricity cutbacks. Managers are then given the task of justly dividing the 45 percent among the employees.

Stock Options

A pay-for-performance program that almost all companies have implemented in the past 20 years is the **stock option plan.** Employees are given a certain amount of stock in that company either as a reward for good work or as an incentive to get hired. The employee understands that through his hard work, the performance of the entire company will go up, and so will the stock price. The employees are motivated to make the company successful so that they can sell their stock and make some money. Starbucks is an excellent example of a company that uses a stock option plan. The theory of their employment practice is that every single employee is viewed as a partner. When hired, employees receive stock options and are, therefore, considered part owners of the company. Through hard work and performance the stock price will rise—and so will their ultimate reward.

Open-Book Management

As a way of motivating their employees, companies sometimes implement an **open-book management** policy. The book that is open is actually the company's financial records and statements. The theory behind this practice is to let the employees see the direct result of their spending habits and therefore create an interest in each employee to behave as economically and efficiently as possible, thereby saving the company more money and ultimately increasing profit. Naturally employees without a financial background will have to attend courses in how to read and make sense of the financial statements. The idea is to treat them like partners, rather than just employees, and have them see the bottom line of the company's financial assets and pitfalls.

In today's multibillion-dollar-profit, multimillion-employees-type companies, it is hard for employees to see their company's big picture. All they see and know is their own department and how their individual performances affect their direct supervisor as opposed to how it relates to the whole company's performance and profit margin. This is when open-book management makes a huge impact. Employees are able to see the link between their performance, the company's operational results, and ultimately the profit margin and where the company stands in relation to their competitors—all of this just by showing and having them understand the financial statements or "the books."

Check Your Knowledge

1. What are some examples of a flexible work schedule?
2. How do pay-for-performance programs work?
3. Define open-book management.

Motivating the New Workforce

The "new workforce" of today includes a number of employees who have special employment endorsements. They require special attention when it comes to conventional motivation plans. We are going to look at the following groups that make up the "new workforce": professional employees and low-skilled, minimum-wage employees.

Motivating Professionals

The growing group of professional workers includes a typically college-level-educated, specialized, and, most important, well-paid workforce. The challenge is how to motivate these employees because they seem to have a great deal of intrinsic satisfaction in their jobs already. A somewhat stereotypical description of professional employees is that their jobs are pretty much the center of their lives. Their motivation is to improve their job skills and find creative solutions to ever more complex problems. What drives these types of workers is typically not money, since they are paid quite well, but more the acknowledgment of their peers and superiors of their outstanding work. Do you see why it might be a challenge to motivate this workforce?

Instead of monetary rewards, such as bonuses or stock options, this type of employee can be motivated intellectually. Courses, new training programs, and conferences on their particular field of expertise are very important to professionals because they need to keep themselves updated and learn new techniques as soon as they come out in order to stay on top. These training courses and seminars can be used as rewards for good job performance and as incentives to work harder. Additionally, autonomy can be used as a reward and as a sign of trust in the employee for motivation purposes. Let employees schedule their own workweek in ways they find productive, and give them autonomy on new, challenging projects. Recognition in the form of rewards will give them a feeling of importance and also demonstrate sincere interest in their successes.

Motivating Low-Skilled, Minimum-Wage Employees

Some of the workforce is not highly educated, not well trained, and not very professional. In real life, every manager has to deal with employees who have a minimum skill level, little education, and are paid minimum wage. More salary, the typical motivator for employees, is not always a solution because the company may not always be able to afford to raise the salaries of low-level employees. Motivating this workforce is one of the hardest tasks managers have to face. One motivator apart from money that works particularly well with minimum-wage workers is recognition. Employee recognition programs can include certificates, plaques, award ceremonies, celebrations recognizing employees' achievements, or gift certificates. When you walk into Burger King, for example, you will see a designated wall hung with plaques indicating who the employee-of-the-month is. As long as this kind of public praise is sincere and given for legitimate reasons, it works well as a motivator.

In accordance with expectancy theories and job design, there is one other vital way to motivate minimum-wage employees: By empowering front-line workers with more authority in their jobs, they generate feelings of importance and responsibility for the company's success. Empowerment of employees enhances their motivation because they are able to learn new skills, gain experience in autonomy, realize the task significance and identity, and receive feedback. In addition, the employee is able to see the direct success of their performance. They are able to see the link between job performance and the success of the company,

An Employee of the Month

FOCUS ON:

Motivating Individuals in Your Organization for Disaster Preparedness

Hank Christen and Paul Maniscalco
George Washington University
Unconventional Concepts Inc.

Motivation for disaster preparedness begins with convincing staff and employees that they have a problem—namely emergency events. The manager must nurture a culture that assures employees that they are part of the solution to that problem. Employees must understand that their performance in a disaster affects their well-being and may possibly save their life.

When developing a disaster emergency response plans serious consideration should be given to involving representatives from all areas, as it should when implementing any managerial initiative. All departments and a cross-section of employees (managers, supervisors, and line personnel) should be included. Representatives of employee or collective bargaining organizations may also be invited to participate. Such inclusion affords the manager and the organization the opportunity to lay the foundation for a sense of ownership in the process—a useful motivational tool from the very beginning.

A technique that encourages employee representation is involvement of all employees in the threat assessment and vulnerability analysis component of your planning process. Employees should be stimulated to identify threats and vulnerabilities (an ongoing process) and rewarded for good ideas. Rewards should be tangible and immediate for nonmanagement team members; a day off, gift certificates, dinner for two (at another facility), or cash are examples of appropriate rewards. Positive employee contributions should be noted on job evaluations.

Contingency plans should not be dependent on the manager always being on-site or available to get to the property. It is critical that disaster planning team members feel a sense of ownership of the situation in order to ensure that, when crisis strikes, the plan is implemented effectively and appropriately.

The next step in becoming motivated for emergency preparedness is understanding the mission's value. Benefits of an effective emergency preparedness plan include:

- A safer workplace for you, your peers, and your patrons
- Saved lives and a reduction in suffering of your coworkers and customers
- A better chance of resuming business after an event
- Protection of the reputation of your company

Once coworkers and employees understand the value of adopting a sustainable disaster response plan and the plan has been crafted, it must be exercised in order to evaluate projected responses and activities. Exercises provide an opportunity to truly engage team members and heighten their interest and motivation about disaster preparedness. A properly structured exercise evolution creates a highly interactive process that allows the team members to role-play at the highest levels and enables management to identify flaws in the plan. It is an opportunity for disaster planning members to shine and show their skills.

Training is also a motivator. Creativity in using various multimedia formats can eliminate the boredom that employees frequently associate with training. Videos and case studies of real-world events in similar companies or facilities should be employed. The use of as many graphics and visuals as possible will preclude a bland lecture format. Speakers from local agencies and from the hospitality industry who have experienced disasters may be scheduled. Finally, employees should be rewarded for training accomplishments to help ensure their sustained interest in readiness.

Critical Factor: Exercises are a valuable tool for reinforcing orientation to the disaster response plan and for motivating the team to sustain interest in readiness.

Critical Factor: All stakeholders should be involved in the planning process in order to achieve effective emergency response. Employees' ownership of the situation will ensure a sustainable motivation for preparedness.

which translates into their pay. Although motivating low-skill, minimum-wage employees can be a rather difficult task, there are options to achieve motivation.

From Theory to Practice: Additional Suggestions for Motivating Employees

Motivational theories sound good on paper, but how well do they apply in real-life situations? Translating motivational methods from theory into practice is every manager's individual challenge. However, this chapter should help you gain knowledge and an understanding of how to motivate various employees. The following is a summary of suggestions of the essence of motivating employees. [11]

1. *Recognize individual differences.* It is important to realize that each employee is different. That is, each person has different factors that motivate him. Different attitudes, needs, and personality traits account for the individuality of every employee.
2. *Match people to jobs.* Matching the character of each employee with the type of job that best suits his or her needs and wants is a very important factor in employee motivation. An example of this is to match a professional with a high level of education and skill for problem solving with a job that gives her maximum autonomy, room to grow, and challenging goals.
3. *Use goals.* The goal-setting theory plays a large role in motivating employees. Each manager should provide employees with specific goals and feedback on how well they are doing in achieving those goals. The method of setting these goals can vary from person to person. For some workers it is more effective if they are part of the process of goal setting and in some instances are able to set goals for themselves. Other persons work better when their supervisor provides them with clear, determined goals, and they have no say in what those goals will be.
4. *Ensure that goals are perceived as attainable.* The important fact to remember when identifying goals for employees is to make them clearly attainable to the employee. If goals are set at an unrealistic level, it is pointless to the employee to even try to achieve them. This ultimately leads to a lack of motivation. Managers must reinforce that if the employees increase their efforts, they will be able to achieve their goals.
5. *Individualize rewards.* Just as employees all have different characteristics and qualities, they all need different motivator factors for higher performance. For example, money can motivate a minimum-wage worker to achieve higher goals, but it will do little for a worker who is already well compensated and enjoys a challenge. Individualized rewards include more autonomy, promotions, more pay, participation, recognition, and work challenges.
6. *Link rewards to performance.* Sometimes it is not as clear as one would think that the rewards employees receive are a direct result of their performance. It is important to show employees that their rewards are due to their individual achievement, rather than that of others. It is also

important that managers increase the visibility of rewards, to see that they are attainable.

7. *Check the system for equity.* Employees should be aware of the fact that their individual input is rewarded by their individual output. Input must always equal output. This means that if an employee has a higher skill level and experience, he will ultimately be paid higher and given more responsibility than an employee who is below the skill level and has no experience. This ensures that the motivation of the employee will stay high, since he is aware that he cannot compare his reward to that of others who are not on the same level.

8. *Don't ignore money.* Although we said that not all workers are motivated by monetary rewards, it is essential to remember that money is the primary reason most people work. Therefore, performance-based wage increases, piecework bonuses, and other pay incentives are an essential part in motivating most employees. We can state the obvious: If it weren't for the money, no one would show up for work. So what better method to have people show up to work more often than by giving them more of what they want—money?

Check Your Knowledge

1. What is the challenge in motivating professionals?
2. How can a manager successfully motivate minimum-wage employees?

Trends in Human Resources and Motivation

There is increasing diversity among new employees in the hospitality industry. More women and minorities are not only entering the industry, but are also gaining supervisory and managerial positions.

- Understanding the "emotional" aspects of motivation will change the way we manage. Emotional intelligence refers to skills in intra- and interpersonal relations. In the future, managers will view employees from a deeper emotional standpoint rather than on the surface level.

- Increased globalization is making the hospitality workplace even more diverse. Individual differences go past traditional demographics to varying deep-level attitudes and beliefs, particularly with nontraditional cultures that are relatively new to the United States. For example, cruise lines are recruiting extensively from Eastern European countries, forcing managers to change the way they interact with employees.

- Advancing employee skills will help to satisfy needs, particularly in the "new workforce." The "Generation X" group and the younger "Generation Y" group are very concerned with increasing marketability through learning and developing. Managerial efforts to develop skills and knowledge will help in this regard.

- Economic challenges are forcing hospitality organizations to operate "leaner." Hospitality managers will be forced to develop quick, inexpensive methods of maintaining workplace morale. Rather than greater resources to motivate, creativity will be the key.
- The advent of telecommuting will change how we motivate employees. Many teams are now "virtual," meaning that face-to-face interaction between supervisors and employees is decreasing. Managers in the future will need to motivate from afar.
- There is a critical labor-shortage problem.
- There is an increased focus on employee retention.
- There is increased use of flextime.
- Food and beverage management positions are difficult to fill.
- There are fewer people in the labor pool with basic reading, writing, and math skills.
- Legal issues in hospitality employment are of increasing concern to hospitality operators as more lawsuits are brought against them.
- Training has become more important as hospitality corporations strive to gain a competitive advantage by offering outstanding guest service.

CASE STUDY

Michelle Williams recently graduated with a bachelor's degree in hospitality management and has been hired as the front desk manager in a medium-sized hotel located in New York City. The hotel's clientele is truly international, and so is its staff, which originates from more than 20 different nations. Many of the employees speak more than one language, often at work. Michelle is from the midwestern United States and has had little experience in managing and motivating a multicultural work group. Indeed, she knows little or nothing about many of the cultures that surround her.

One challenge put to Michelle when she was hired was to give a "lift" to the staff and try to create more of a team atmosphere. Currently, the employees at the front desk operate as a bunch of individuals, with little sense of teamwork. It seems as though the differences in culture are preventing the group from getting closer. As a result, the atmosphere at the front desk is cool and functional, rather than warm and friendly.

In addition, Michelle must contend with a number of employee problems if the department is going to function properly. For example, Maria, who originally comes from Spain, is excellent with customers but often comes to work late. Even when confronted by past supervisors about her tardiness, Maria failed to see this as a real problem. Bjorn is a Norwegian hospitality student working part time in the hotel. Although Bjorn is always on time and works very efficiently, his demeanor with the customers is lacking. Often, guests and coworkers perceive him as being aloof or standoffish. Bjorn rarely smiles at guests. Finally, Peng from Hong Kong is very diligent about his work and gives 100 percent to any task he is given. Unfortunately, Peng has some difficulty speaking English and has little confidence in his speaking ability. As a result, he tends to rush through interactions with guests and limits his conversations, saying only what he must to complete the task.

Discussion Questions

If you were in Michelle's place as the new front-desk manager, what methods would you use to answer the following?

1. How will you address each of the work-related problems and motivate Maria, Bjorn, and Peng?
2. How will you facilitate a greater understanding of differences in national culture among the team members at the front desk?
3. Decide on how to build a sense of teamwork with this multicultural group.

CAREER INFORMATION

Human resources is a specialized area offering career opportunities and professional growth. A career can lead to becoming a vice-president of human resources. Companies are paying close attention to their investment in employees and are offering a wide variety of incentives to attract and retain talented people. Today, there is a need for HR positions in a variety of hospitality companies. Smaller companies may have someone delegated to take care of human resources and outsource their payrolls. Larger companies and their individual units have human resources departments. College graduates wanting to specialize in HR should gain experience in several departments before becoming an HR coordinator. Part of the allure for HR is the typical five-day workweek, conventional hours, and working in an office setting—albeit in the basement and likely with no windows.

Related Web sites

www.shrm.org/hrmagazine—a human resources magazine
www.hronline.com —Web-based tools for employee and corporate success

Courtesy of Charlie Adams.

SUMMARY

1. The hospitality industry has a large number of entry-level, guest-contact employees, many with little or no training. Human resources is about attracting, selecting, orienting, training, developing, and evaluating the performance of an organization's most important resource—the human ones.

2. Task analysis examines the tasks that comprise a job to determine if they are necessary and to gauge their impact on the guest experience. When approved and listed, the tasks are incorporated into the job description.

3. Productivity standards are established for each position. Productivity is measured in how long it takes an associate to do a particular task or job function. Another way to measure productivity is to divide the sales by labor costs and arrive at a factor.

4. There are several employment-related laws that hospitality human resources managers need to know and abide by.

5. Recruitment is about finding the most suitable candidate for an available position. There are three types of interviews: structured, unstructured, and semistructured.

6. Selection means to select the best candidate, and orientation means to introduce new employees to the company and their job.

7. There are four kinds of training: apprenticeship, simulation, certification, and on-the-job. Employee development is a natural progression from the appraisal; it may be training, attending seminars, or obtaining a certification.

8. The performance appraisal compares an employee's actual performance with preestablished standards, and compensation is the complete reward system. Some benefits are mandated by law: Social Security, workers' compensation, and unemployment compensation. Others are made available if the employer decides to offer them and may include pension plans; medical, dental, optical, and life insurance; tuition reimbursement; and employee stock ownership plans.

9. Motivation is the art or process of initiating and sustaining behavior toward certain goals. Motivating people is basically inspiring them to do something because they want to do it, not because someone tells them to do it. The motivational process begins with a need or a demand that is not met. This creates an uncomfortable situation. The person who experiences this need will search for goals that, if obtained, will satisfy that need or demand, therefore eliminating the uncomfortable situation.

10. Three early motivation theories are McGregor's Theory X and Theory Y, Herzberg's motivation-hygiene theory, and Maslow's hierarchy of needs. McGregor's theory states that there are two kinds of employees. The X person is a pessimist, with a negative attitude toward work, while the Y person is positive and willing to put time and energy into work. Herzberg's theory suggests that hygiene factors actually reduce employee dissatisfaction, while motivators take it a step further and produce job satisfaction. Maslow's hierarchy states the

five needs that humans thrive for in a hierarchical pattern: the most basic first, physiological; then safety; social; esteem; and the highest, self-actualization.

11. Having the employee be an active participant in setting goals actually acts as a motivator to achieve these goals. Employees are far more likely to achieve and even exceed goals that they have had a part in setting than they are to achieve goals prescribed from above. Reinforcers are used in reinforcement theory to motivate employees. They are given to employees as a reward for positive behavior, to make sure it will be repeated in the future. Referents, in the equity theory, are the "others" that people compare themselves to. Employees compare their job's inputs–outcomes ratio to those of their coworkers. Seeing that others work harder or are given more responsibilities acts as a motivator. Expectancies as motivators is based on the premise that people will put out effort equivalent to the perceived rewards. If people think they are definitely going to receive rewards, such as bonuses, they are more likely to be motivated and give the extra effort required to achieve their goals.

12. Managers face a challenge with motivating today's workforce because workers' characteristics are varied; they come from different backgrounds and have different needs and goals. Examples of these employees include immigrants, seniors, young professionals, and minimum-wage employees. Managers must be highly flexible to keep all of their employees motivated.

13. One way to motivate people is to offer a flexible workweek. This can include a compressed workweek, flextime, job sharing, or telecommuting. Another motivational strategy is to have a pay-for-performance program. With a piecework pay plan, variable pay plan, gainsharing, or a stock option plan, employees get paid more or less, depending on their job performance. Finally, open-book management policy, in which a company's financial records and statements are open for any employee to view, is considered a motivational strategy because employees see the direct results of their work in the company's assets and are motivated to work harder.

KEY WORDS AND CONCEPTS

Employee assistance
    program (EAP)
Employee stock ownership
    plan (ESOP)
Equity theory
Expectancy theory

Goal-setting theory
Job description
Job specification
Motivation
Motivators
Open-book management

Orientation
Other (in equity theory)
Performance appraisal
Productivity standards
Recruitment
Reinforcement theory

Reinforcers
Selection
Stock option plan
Task analysis
Three-needs theory
Training

REVIEW QUESTIONS

1. Why are productivity standards important?
2. What are some good questions to ask at an interview?
3. Describe the elements of a performance appraisal and the things to avoid when doing an appraisal.
4. How would you set up a compensation plan for a hospitality corporation?
5. Why is motivation such an important part of everyday work? Managers are always concerned about new ways to motivate their employees. Explain the importance.
6. Use an example from the hospitality industry to illustrate each of the three early motivational theories.

7. Depict the main obstacles that exist when motivating low-level employees, such as the housekeeping staff of a hotel. Give specific examples. What is different from this situation versus motivating professionals such as the head chef?
8. How can the early motivational theories be related to motivating a diverse workforce?
9. What motivational technique would work best for your own individual demands? Which technique would be less effective? Explain your answer.

INTERNET EXERCISE

1. Organization: **Society for Human Resource Management**
   Web site: **www.shrm.org**
   Summary: The Society for Human Resource Management is one of the largest human resource associations. This Web site provides in-depth information to both students and professionals around the world.

   (a) Briefly discuss two of the latest news articles and how they affect the hospitality industry.
   (b) Click on the "Student Program" icon and look at "Getting Started" in HR management. What are some of the current career options being addressed?

APPLY YOUR KNOWLEDGE

1. Develop the criteria for and role-play an employee appraisal.
2. Write a job description and the performance evaluation criteria for a position in the hospitality industry.
3. Plan and role-play an interview for a position in the hospitality industry.
4. Interview three hospitality associates—preferably one manager, one supervisor, and one associate—to find out what motives them.

SUGGESTED ACTIVITY

Ask your librarian for help in finding interesting hospitality trade magazine articles in an area of human resources that interests you. Share your findings with your classmates.

ENDNOTES

1. Personal interview with Charlotte Jordan. April 25, 2005.
2. U.S. Bureau of Labor Statistics, 2005.
3. Personal interview with Charlotte Jordan. May 15, 2005.
4. Personal interview with Roy Jones. April 21, 2005.
5. Stephen Covey, *Seven Habits of Highly Effective People: Powerful Lessons in Personal Change.* New York: Simon and Schuster, 1989.
6. D. McGregor, *The Human Side of Enterprise.* New York: McGraw-Hill, 1960, as cited in Robbins and Coulter, *Management,* 8th ed., p. 394.
7. McClelland, netMBA.com—http://www.netmba.com/mgmt/ob/motivation/mcclelland/.
8. V. H. Vroom, *Work and Motivation.* New York: John Wiley, 1964, as cited in Robbins and Coulter, *Management,* 8th ed., p. 438.
9. Stephen P. Robbins, *Management,* 8th ed. Upper Saddle River, NJ: Prentice Hall, 2005, p. 405.
10. Draws on Gary A. Dessler, *A Framework for Management,* 2nd ed. Upper Saddle River, NJ: Prentice Hall, 2002, pp. 265–267.
11. Draws on Robbins and Coulter, *Management,* p. 415.

WEB RESOURCES

Hospitality careernet.com
www.hospitalitycareernet.com

Hospitality Careers Online
www.hcareers.com

Society for Human Resource Management
www.shrm.org/jobs

HR On-Line
www.hronline.com

U.S. Department of Labor
www.dol.gov

Control

19

After reading and studying this chapter, you should be able to:

- Define control.
- Give reasons why control is important.
- Describe the four-step control process.
- Distinguish among the three types of control.
- Explain the important financial controls.
- Describe the qualities of an effective control system.
- Outline the contemporary issues in control.

Did you ever get to the end of the week or the month and discover that you'd run out of money? Well, at one time or another, we all have, and, yes, it's because we did not exercise proper control. But control is not only about keeping our finances in order—it has a much more broad and important role to play in hospitality management. All hospitality managers need to use a variety of control measures to check and see if the results they achieve are in line with expectations and, if not, to take corrective actions. The control process even sets the parameters for managerial action by setting up control by exception, meaning that managers only take action if the results are outside the acceptable range. Control is often used in conjunction with techniques such as total quality management by allowing associates and management to establish guest service levels.

Control is about keeping score and setting up ways to give us feedback on how we are doing. The feedback leads to corrective action, if necessary. If, for instance, a chef and restaurant manager forecast 250 covers and 320 actually come, then they will have to "prep" more food items in a hurry and guide servers to recommend certain dishes in order to avoid 86'ing too many menu items. These and the many other examples we will read about in this chapter are all control related.

Control has close links to each of the other management functions, especially planning, which, as we know, includes setting the goals and making plans on how to reach the goals.

What Is Control?

What control does is provide a way to check actual results against expected results. Action can then be taken to correct the situation if the results are too far from the expected outcome. If labor costs are 26 percent and they were expected to be 23 percent, the difference is only 3 percent, but that 3 percent could add up to thousands of dollars.

Control is the management function that provides information on the degree to which goals and objectives are being accomplished. Management engages in controlling by monitoring activities and taking corrective actions whenever the goals are not being met. An effective control system ensures that activities are completed that lead to the attainment of the organization's goals.

Control is far broader than you might think. It's not just about checking on outcomes; it is also about providing guidelines and mechanisms to keep things on track by making sure there are "no surprises" when the results are known. Control is also about keeping your eyes and ears open. Every place seems to have someone who steals, so, as a Swiss hotel manager mentor once said to me in his heavy accent, "John, before you can stop someone else stealing the chicken, you must first know how to steal the chicken." The best way to avoid these losses is to have a tight control system.

Why Is Control Important?

Why is control so important? Control is important because it's the final link in the management functions. It's the only way managers know whether organizational goals are being met and, if not, why not. Controlling is involved with planning, organizing, and leading. Figure 19–1 shows the relationship between controlling and the other management functions.

Goals give specific direction to managers. Effective hospitality managers need to constantly follow up to ensure that what others are supposed to do is, in fact, being done and goals are being met. Managers need to develop an effective control system—one that can provide information and feedback on employee performance. An effective control system is important because managers need to delegate duties and empower employees to make decisions. But, because managers are responsible for performance results, they also need a feedback mechanism, which control provides.

Given that management involves leading, planning, organizing, communicating, motivating, and controlling, one might easily get the impression that maintaining control is just something managers do after they are finished planning, organizing, and leading. For example, controlling always requires that some desirable outcomes, such as targets, standards, or goals, be set. Similarly, much of what managers do when they have their leadership hats on involves making sure that employees are doing and will do the things they are supposed

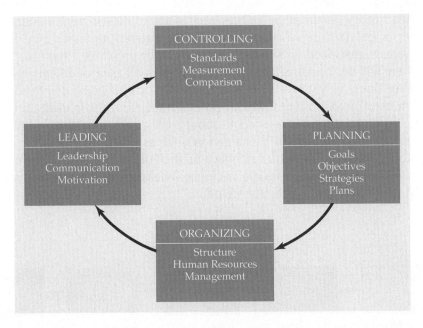

Figure 19–1 *Relationship between Controlling and the Other Management Functions (Modified from Stephen P. Robbins and Mary Coulter, Management, 8th ed. Upper Saddle River, NJ: Prentice Hall, 2005, p. 460.)*

to do. However, as we learned in the chapter on motivation, the sort of self-motivation that derives from empowering teams and putting them in charge is often the better alternative.

Check Your Knowledge

1. Define control.
2. Why is control important?

The Control Process

The **control process** is a four-step process of setting standards, measuring actual performance, comparing actual performance against those standards, and taking managerial action to correct deviations or inadequate performances (Figure 19–2). These standards are the specific goals created during the planning process against which performance progress can be measured.

Setting Standards

In the hospitality industry, setting standards generally means establishing the levels of service, the quality of food and beverages offered, employee performance levels, and return on investment. Standards are normally set in terms of quantity, quality, finances, or time. A caterer has to determine the quantity or number of guests to serve at a function. If the caterer purchases food for too many guests, then food will be left over, but if they prepare for too few guests, then there will not be enough food. When a chef purchases food items, they are controlled upon arrival to ensure that the right quality is being delivered. Budgets are used in controlling financial expenditures and time is used to, for example, control labor costs—a cook should only take a certain number of minutes to prepare a batch of pasta and vegetables.

A word of caution: When developing a method of measurement, one must be absolutely sure first that the goals are indeed measurable. Now, as convoluted as that may sound, let's illustrate the point.

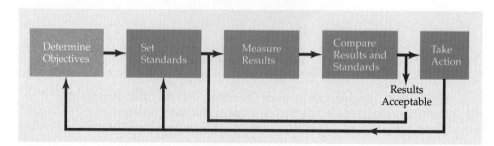

Figure 19–2   *The Control Process*

Information for control purposes can be acquired by a variety of methods, including the telephone.

Suppose after careful planning, with input from staff, all agree that labor costs are too high at 28 percent. So the decision is made to reduce labor costs, and that becomes a stated goal—one that is hard to object to. At the end of the month, the kitchen still has a labor cost of 28 percent, so they have not achieved the goal. During your discussion with the personnel responsible, they claim that their plan to reduce labor costs will not be effective until two months hence. You remind them that the goal was to reduce labor costs, they agree that it was, and you point out that last month's labor cost and this month's are the same. Who is correct here? The answer: Neither. The goal of reducing labor costs is inadequate and it is not measurable or attainable on your part. The kitchen staff has put a plan into effect that they feel will reduce labor costs by the end of the following month; they feel they are doing all that you asked. The dilemma is that the goal lacks specificity. Had the goal been to decrease labor costs to 24 percent by the end of February, it would be measurable and attainable. Then we could say to the kitchen staff that they hadn't met the stated goal, but since we didn't quantify the goal, they are correct.

Measuring

Managers must first know what they are **measuring** and how they are measuring it before they can measure expected performance. Personal observation, by monitoring subordinates to make sure things are done right, is the simplest and most common way of comparing actual performance to standards. So, the chef can see if the cook is cutting, slicing, and dicing correctly and if the right amount is being prepared according to the standardized recipe.

How We Measure

Four common sources of information frequently used by managers to measure actual performance are personal observation, statistical reports, oral reports, and written reports.

Management by walking around (MBWA) is the best way to make personal observations. MBWA

Direct Supervision

The purpose of direct supervision is to detect problems of associate-specific actions as they occur and to make corrections immediately in order to keep associate actions in line with management expectations.

A Day in the Life of Cherry Cerminara
Dietitian and General Manager, Sodexho

I am a registered dietitian and general manager operating a K–12 school foodservice program. I work for the management company Sodexho. Sodexho has been contracted to manage the food and nutrition program for the school I serve. It is a five-building, 4,000-student operation. Sodexho School Services leads the nation in providing food and facilities management solutions that support the educational process. From nutrition education to monitoring air quality, our efforts enable students and faculty to consistently perform at a high level. Every day, Sodexho serves the needs of more than 400 school districts. Our expertise allows school administrators to focus on education leadership activities. Best of all, our partnering approach always saves money. Our programs have been tested, and the results are conclusive: Sodexho's food service and facilities management solutions improve the quality of life for students, faculty, and the communities we serve.

As the general manager for this operation, a day in my life includes hiring, training, and managing of employees, ordering foods, inventory, managing budgets, financial reporting, menu preparation, production, and nutrition.

School meals operations are regulated by the USDA for nutrition according to age-specific needs. Both breakfast and lunch are served. We even provide nutrition education both in the classroom and in the lunchroom.

Other areas of concentration include food safety following HACCP and physical safety for the employees and our customers. We are audited every year by NSF and at least twice per year by the county health department. As a manager, customer service is extremely important in my day-to-day operations. Although the audience is captive, they are still our customers. We look at the student, staff, parents, and administration as our customers. If I cannot train my employees to respect this aspect of their performance, we will lose revenue, and perhaps lose the business to someone perceived to provide a better service. Providing management services to Pine-Richland School District in Gibsonia, Pennsylvania, is really a pleasure. Students are interested in what they eat. They enjoy their meal periods and expect great service. Well-managed, trained, and enthusiastic employees work at Pine-Richland. All of these elements contribute to the company being successful.

is a phrase used to describe when a manager is out in the work area, interacting directly with associates and exchanging information about what is happening. MBWA can pick up factual omissions, facial expressions, and tones of voice that may be missed by other sources. Front office managers will not be aware of how guests are being checked in during the busy early evening check-in period if they are in their offices at that time.

Statistical reports provide information in the form of data that measure results and can be used for comparative purposes. They also use charts, graphs, and other displays that are easy to visualize. Some managers keep charts on the key result areas and plot the department's progress. Others place safety charts on the associate notice board. These charts visually display the importance of safety and the number of accident-free days, which is another type of goal often sought.

Control information can be acquired through oral reports, conferences, meetings, one-on-one conversations, or telephone calls. The advantage of oral control reports is that they can be both quick and allow instant feedback in the form of a two-way conversation. A manager can inquire about the status of a function and get immediate feedback from the banquet captain. In the often fast-paced hospitality industry, oral control communication is often more effective than other forms of communications. Every time a restaurant service team has an "alley rally" they are, in part, using oral control communications to let servers know what to sell, what the specials are—so guests can be encouraged to order them—instead of "slamming" the kitchen with multiple à la carte orders.

Written reports are also used to measure performance. Like statistical reports, these are slower yet more formal than personal observation or oral reports. Written reports generally have more information than oral ones and are usually easy to file and retrieve. General managers usually expect to see the "daily report," which gives details of the performance results from yesterday, on their desks as they walk into their offices. However, they also want a verbal report from any department they may visit on the way to the office, like "Did we sell out last night?"

Given the varied advantages of each of these measurement approaches, comprehensive control efforts by managers should use all four.

What We Measure

We measure the results to see how they compare with expectations. What we measure is more critical than how we measure—what if we are measuring the wrong thing? The results we measure include guest satisfaction, labor costs, food and beverage costs, employee satisfaction, rooms and room rates, bed sheets, energy costs, insurance, labor turnover, and so on.

In simple terms, we measure labor costs because they are the highest of the variable costs. Did we meet our goal of a 24 percent labor cost reduction? Next, did we meet our goal of a 28 percent food cost? To find out if we met our goals, we would need to set up control measuring procedures regarding the daily monitoring of labor costs. Estimates of sales are given to department heads who then plan and organize their labor costs accordingly. In other words, if you know your sales you can then control your labor costs to the 24 percent. For example, for food and beverage cost control we would scrutinize ordering, purchasing, storing, issuing, preparing, and serving of the various food items. We would take inventory, calculate the actual cost of the food, and express the cost as a percentage of sales. Remember, it's the cost over sales times 100.

Whenever performance results can be measured, it is desirable to consider a results-accountability system. Some control criteria are applicable to any management situation. For instance, because all managers, by definition, coordinate the work of others, criteria such as employee satisfaction or turnover and absenteeism rates can be measured.

Most managers have budgets set in dollar costs for their area of responsibility. Keeping costs within budget is, therefore, a fairly common control measure. However, one of the main purposes of control is to influence behavior. As such, a results-accountability control system must be able to detect deviations from desired results quickly enough to allow for timely corrective management action.

Having timely information and acting on that information is crucial in avoiding the following situation: Why is it that at some hospitality operations

Effective Managers

Effective managers first control the "big ticket" items that will be costly if not controlled. Once the more costly items are under control, they can move on to other, less costly items.

each month's income statement results take almost a month to complete? Due to the delay it takes to produce the results, thousands of dollars are lost before any problems can be fixed.

Comparing Results

Comparing results with expectations shows the amount of variation between actual performance and the standard or expected results. Some variation is generally seen between the expected and the actual results—but how big is the variation? The range of variation is the acceptable difference between the actual and expected results.

Managers are concerned with the size and direction of the variance. Let's look at an example: If guest surveys show that one department is not performing up to expectations, then management would make decisions to have the problem fixed. But what if that didn't work? Then more drastic action would be necessary. Meanwhile the survey scores would continue to drop. Management would quickly find out in which direction and how fast the barometer of guest satisfaction was moving.

Taking Managerial Action

The final step in the control process is taking managerial action. **Correcting actual performance** is used by managers if the source of the performance variation is unsatisfactory. For instance, **corrective action** might include changing the way the job tasks are done, changing strategy (doing different tasks), changing structure (changing supervisors/managers' compensation practices), changing training programs, redesigning jobs, or firing employees.

A manager who decides to correct actual performance then has to make another decision: Does she or he use **immediate corrective action,** which corrects problems at once to get performance back on track, or **basic corrective action,** which looks at how and why performance has deviated and then proceeds to correct the source of deviation? Many managers say they don't have time to take corrective action, yet they are the ones perpetually "putting out fires."

Effective managers analyze deviations and, when the benefits justify it, take the time to pinpoint and correct the causes of variance. This kind of control begins with effective associate selection and training. Hiring the right person for the job and ensuring that associates are properly trained increase the chances that they can be trusted to do the right thing.

Good communication is critical to associate control for a number of reasons. The most important reason is that good communication helps associates understand what is expected of them. Employee performance reviews take on added significance when

---

Whom Do We Bill?

A fun lack of control story happened at a five-star hotel restaurant close to Christmas, when a guest signed the check for his table's extravagant business lunch "S. Claus." The server, thinking that the guest had signing privileges, gave the check to the restaurant cashier, who in turn sent it up to the billing office so that it would go out to the client at the end of the month. Three days later, the check came back to the restaurant with the question "Which company is he with?"

viewed from the control perspective. Rather than a method of reviewing past performance, they become a control technique. By rewarding and praising desired behavior, management can use performance reviews to shape future behavior. The opposite will be true of undesirable behavior. Performance reviews are also a good time to consider training, reassignment, raises, and promotion decisions.

Check Your Knowledge

1. What are the elements of the control process?
2. Briefly describe the four common sources of information managers use to measure employee performance.
3. Explain the difference between immediate corrective action and basic corrective action.

It is important to note the motivating influences of raises and promotions and how they act as a form of control. Granting raises and awarding promotions based solely on operating results criteria and desired behavior send an important message to all associates. Those actions say that performance and behavior are being monitored and are the basis for personnel decisions. In this way employee actions are controlled.

Types of Control

Managers can use controls *in advance* of an activity (feedforward control), during the activity (concurrent control), and *after* the activity (feedback control) has been completed. Figure 19–3 shows the three types of control.

Feedforward control focuses on preventing anticipated problems since it takes place in advance of the actual work activity. For example, by carefully explaining the policy on billing for catering functions, a catering manager uses feedforward control to explain to the client that an accurate number of people attending the function must be given in order for the correct space to be allocated for the function. A follow-up number is to be given three months, one month, and two weeks prior to the event, and final guaranteed numbers are required 48 hours prior to a function. This is the number for which food is purchased, prepared, and charged for accordingly. By working closely with the client, the catering manager ensures that there are no surprises.

In the kitchen, recipes are an example of feedforward control; they prescribe the quantity of each ingredient necessary to make a particular dish. Recipes also help with consistency by making each dish look and taste the same. (Now that could be good or bad!) Without recipes we know the result is going to be a disaster.

Another example of feedforward control occurred when McDonald's opened in Moscow. McDonald's sent quality control experts to help Russian farmers

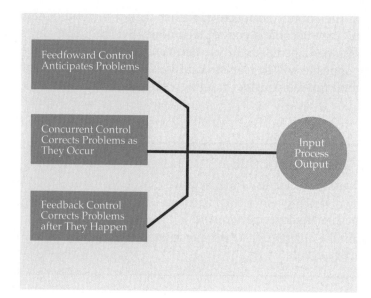

Figure 19–3   *Three Types of Control*

learn techniques for growing high-quality potatoes and bakers to teach processes for baking high-quality breads. Why? Because McDonald's strongly emphasizes product quality no matter the geographic location. They want a McDonald's cheeseburger in Moscow to taste like the one in New York.[1]

Airlines do preventive maintenance on their aircraft; restaurants do the same on their kitchen equipment and dishwashers to prevent any breakdowns during operation. Resorts and hotels also conduct preventive maintenance on the building, the air conditioning system, and so on. These are all examples of feedforward controls.

Feedforward controls are helpful in that they encourage managers to *prevent* problems rather than *react* to them. The challenge is that feedforward controls take more time to organize than the other types of control, yet they save time in the long run.

Concurrent control is a type of control that takes place while a work activity is in progress. When control is enacted while the work is being performed, man-

Chefs Frequently Use Concurrent Control

agement can correct problems before they become too costly. The best form of concurrent control is direct supervision, when a manager can concurrently monitor the actions of associates and correct problems as they occur. Although some delay results between the activity and the manager's corrective response, the delay is minimal. For instance, you may have experienced concurrent control when using a computer program such as word-processing software that alerts you to misspelled words or incorrect grammatical usage. In addition, many organizational quality programs rely on concurrent controls to inform workers if their work output is of sufficient quality to meet standards. Chefs use concurrent control when checking on how a recipe is being prepared; the cook can be guided on the correct consistency of a product.

Feedback control, the most popular type of control, takes place after the activity is done. For example, financial statements are examples of feedback control. If, for instance, the income statement shows that sales revenues are declining, the decline has already occurred. The manager's only option is try to determine why sales decreased and to correct the situation.

Feedback control is helpful in hospitality industry situations where a number of activities repeat themselves: Guests make reservations, are welcomed, checked in, roomed, wined and dined, and so on, so resorts and hotels have developed several controls that help measure and report on these activities. These controls include guest surveys, comment cards, and outside checkers who stay at a property and give a detailed report to management on their findings.

Corporate Control

The catering manager of a large convention and banqueting department received a memo stating that no overtime could be worked unless the F&B director authorized it in advance. Now, for a busy department that did thousands of dollars in business every day and was responsible for most of the F&B Division's profit, that memo from the corporate office was not well received—how could they prevent clients from changing their minds at the last minute—and how dare they impose on our operation in this way? In retrospect, the department was caught up in a blanket policy to reduce labor costs by utilizing feedforward control and it worked because many of the not-so-profitable departments were abusing overtime payments to their associates. The convention and banqueting department services manager planned and scheduled the work more effectively and the catering managers were able to persuade the clients to avoid last minute room changes by explaining that it would involve additional charges at overtime rates. Incentives were also given to clients to select room setups that would involve fewer complete room changes (from a dinner to a classroom setup when a cabaret might be equally as suitable). Substantial companywide savings were made and the conference and banqueting department did react positively to the change (after a brief period of complaining). They also saved several thousand dollars, which, of course, went straight to the bottom line.

Feedback control has two advantages over feedforward and concurrent control. First, feedback provides the managers with meaningful information on how effective their planning efforts were. Feedback that indicates little variance between standard and actual performance is evidence that the planning was generally on target. If the deviation is significant, a manager can use the information when formulating new plans to make them more effective. Second, feedback control can enhance employee motivation. Associates generally want information on how well they have performed.

Remember the profile of T.G.I. Friday's earlier in this book, where the food cost percentage was expected to be 27 percent and the actual was 27.2 percent, meaning the variance was 0.2 of a percentage point. That is feedback control. When a theme park forecasts an attendance of 30,000 on a particular day and the actual comes in at 32,000, that's feedback control.

Other Types of Control

Food and Beverage Controls

Ask any food and beverage operator about controls and you are likely to get a serious look followed by a comment about how important control is to the operation. Lots of money can be made or lost depending on how tight the control is. Most operations will take inventory and calculate the food and beverage costs expressed as a percentage of sales at least once, sometimes twice, a month. A glance at this book's index will indicate several pages where food and beverage controls are discussed in detail, so here we will look at control from a management perspective.

When you become a manager and assume responsibility for controlling food and beverage items, the first thing to do is to get the locks changed because you have no idea who has access to what. The second thing is to review all control procedures. If you really want to exercise tight control, then insist that all orders have your signature or approval—that way, you know what should be received. Next, the stores need to be under the authority and responsibility of one person who is held accountable for all items under their control.

Check Your Knowledge

1. When is feedforward control used?
2. What is the difference between concurrent control and feedback control?

Operational Financial Controls

At the operational level in the hospitality industry, our financial controls mainly consist of **budgets** and **income statements.** Budgets "guestimate" the sales figure for the month/year and allow for up to a specific dollar amount to be spent on any cost of goods sold or controllable costs item. Just preparing the budget has a control-like effect on managers. They are responsible for the financial outcome of their departments and rely heavily on budgets. Instead of just allowing departments to budget the same amount year in and year out, the concept of **zero-based budgeting** has managers begin with a budget of zero dollars and justify all the cost of goods sold, controllable costs, and capital expenditures (things like equipment) they plan on making so that there will be an appropriate amount of profit.

Income statements show the actual sales and expenditures for a month/year. They are used extensively in the hospitality industry as a means of control because they are results driven. Managers use the results for controlling the next period's performance. For example, if the results of the beverage department come in below expectations, then corrective action in the form of increased spot-checks would immediately be instigated along with more frequent inventory checks. Figure 19–4 shows a hotel income statement.

INCOME STATEMENT
APRIL 2006

	CURRENT MONTH						YEAR TO DATE					
	CURRENT	%	BUDGET	%	LAST YR	%	CURRENT	%	BUDGET	%	LAST YR	%
REVENUE												
ROOMS	291,371	61.5%	310,270	66.3%	312,768	66.5%	1,106,897	63.5%	1,150,835	66.1%	1,167,731	64.3%
FOOD	136,868	28.9%	111,503	23.8%	108,176	23.0%	453,192	26.0%	414,868	23.8%	449,848	24.8%
BEVERAGE	22,830	4.8%	23,717	5.1%	26,470	5.6%	90,041	5.2%	84,787	4.9%	100,355	5.5%
TELEPHONE	5,473	1.2%	4,593	1.0%	6,686	1.4%	18,634	1.1%	17,390	1.0%	28,852	1.6%
SUNDRIES	367	0.1%	651	0.1%	798	0.2%	2,020	0.1%	2,368	0.1%	2,868	0.2%
OTHER INCOME	16,605	3.5%	17,270	3.7%	15,109	3.2%	72,914	4.2%	71,108	4.1%	66,559	3.7%
TOTAL REVENUE	473,514	100.0%	468,004	100.0%	470,007	100.0%	1,743,698	100.0%	1,741,356	100.0%	1,816,213	100.0%
DEPT EXPENSES												
ROOMS	68,874	23.6%	68,671	22.1%	63,403	20.3%	272,356	24.6%	273,771	23.8%	246,979	21.2%
FOOD	138,332	101.1%	115,108	103.2%	96,580	89.3%	468,515	103.4%	427,109	103.0%	398,509	88.6%
BEVERAGE	12,809	56.1%	11,080	46.7%	11,464	43.3%	46,567	51.7%	41,676	49.2%	49,675	49.5%
TELEPHONE	4,636	84.7%	4,867	106.0%	5,628	84.2%	20,543	110.2%	19,793	113.8%	21,234	73.6%
SUNDRIES	213	58.0%	418	64.2%	990	124.1%	1,957	96.9%	1,578	66.6%	2,744	95.7%
OTHER INCOME	10,531	63.4%	12,741	73.8%	12,956	85.8%	43,047	59.0%	56,513	79.5%	44,364	66.7%
TOT DEPT EXPENSES	235,395	49.7%	212,885	45.5%	191,021	40.6%	852,985	48.9%	820,440	47.1%	763,505	42.0%
DEPT PROFIT	238,119	50.3%	255,119	54.5%	278,986	59.4%	890,713	51.1%	920,916	52.9%	1,052,708	58.0%
UNDIST EXPENSES												
ADMIN & GENL	47,054	9.9%	38,531	8.2%	43,762	9.3%	206,582	11.8%	168,784	9.7%	184,744	10.2%
MARKETING	26,619	5.6%	30,139	6.4%	15,458	3.3%	91,079	5.2%	88,953	5.1%	57,023	3.1%
REPAIR & MAINT	26,767	5.7%	39,621	8.5%	37,668	8.0%	142,323	8.2%	165,966	9.5%	130,646	7.2%
GROUNDS	22,662	4.8%	26,650	5.7%	29,897	6.4%	108,114	6.2%	107,024	6.1%	95,284	5.2%
UTILITIES	20,494	4.3%	26,785	5.7%	19,010	4.0%	85,988	4.9%	99,652	5.7%	83,380	4.6%
TOT UNDIST EXP	143,596	30.3%	161,726	34.6%	145,795	31.0%	634,086	36.4%	630,379	36.2%	551,077	30.3%
GROSS OPER PROFIT	94,523	20.0%	93,393	20.0%	133,191	28.3%	256,627	14.7%	290,537	16.7%	501,631	27.6%
FIXED EXPENSES												
PROP TAXES	5,734	1.2%	5,734	1.2%	5,099	1.1%	27,015	1.5%	26,983	1.5%	24,443	1.3%
INSURANCE	2,622	0.6%	2,622	0.6%	1,700	0.4%	10,488	0.6%	10,488	0.6%	6,800	0.4%
INTEREST	1,220	0.3%	1,252	0.3%	1,345	0.3%	4,944	0.3%	5,008	0.3%	5,442	0.3%
INCOME TAXES	0	0.0%	0	0.0%	0	0.0%	0	0.0%	0	0.0%	0	0.0%
DEPREC	26,000	5.5%	26,000	5.6%	26,000	5.5%	104,000	6.0%	104,000	6.0%	100,000	5.5%
TOT FIXED EXP	35,576	7.5%	35,608	7.6%	34,144	7.3%	146,447	8.4%	146,479	8.4%	136,685	7.5%
NET INCOME	58,947	12.4%	57,785	12.3%	99,047	21.1%	110,180	6.3%	144,058	8.3%	364,946	20.1%

	CURRENT	BUDGET	LAST YR	CURRENT	BUDGET	LAST YR
ROOMS AVAIL	2,580	2,580	2,670	10,320	10,320	10,680
ROOMS OCCUPIED	1,495	1,670	1,797	5,747	6,078	6,529
OCCUPANCY %	57.9%	64.7%	67.3%	55.7%	58.9%	61.1%
AVG RATE	$151.63	$147.30	$141.56	$147.84	$147.09	$142.50

Figure 19–4 *Hotel Income Statement (Courtesy of Hospitality Concepts, San Diego.)*

Corporate Profile: ARAMARK

In the 1950s, Dave Davidson and Bill Fishman, both in the vending business, realized that they shared the same dreams and hopes of turning vending into a service and combining it with foodservice. The two entrepreneurs joined forces to become the first truly national vending and foodservice company. Automatic Retailers of America (ARA) was born in 1959. Fishman and Davidson had the management skills, the capital, and the expertise to expand. And this they did—ARAMARK is the world's leading provider of quality managed services. It operates in all 50 states and in 11 foreign countries, offering a very diversified and broad range of services to businesses of all sizes, and to thousands of universities, hospitals, and municipal, state, and federal government facilities. Every day, they serve more than 15 million people at more than 500,000 locations worldwide.

ARAMARK's emphasis on the quality of service management was evident from the very beginning of its operations. ARAMARK entered new markets by researching the best-managed local companies, acquiring them, and persuading key managers to stay with the company.

The company's vision, in fact, states that ARAMARK is "a company where the best people want to work." Customers recommend ARAMARK to others because they constantly exceed expectations. In this case, success is measured in the growth of the company, its earnings, and its employees themselves. This is one fundamental constant in ARAMARK's early success: It grew its business by focusing on growing its management. The company's guiding principles reaffirm such a concept:

"Because we succeed through performance, we encourage the entrepreneur in each of us, and work always to improve our service."

"Because we thrive on growth, we seek new markets and new opportunities, and we innovate to get and keep new customers."

With the 1961 acquisition of Slater System, Inc., the largest foodservice business in the country, ARAMARK began the diversification process and has continued since to amplify the portfolio of services it now offers. The focus on management skills at every level, especially the local one, gave ARAMARK an invaluable resource. In fact, with every acquisition, local managers were encouraged and rewarded for becoming multiskilled entrepreneurs. This approach to outsourcing is put more simply, the ability of the company to take the best management skills and apply them to all the lines of business the company uses to diversify.

Among ARAMARK operations are the following:

Food, leisure, and support services: The company provides food, specialized refreshments, dietary services, and operation support to businesses, educational facilities, government, and medical institutions. ARAMARK also manages food, lodging, hospitality, and support services at national parks and other recreational facilities that serve the general public.

Health and education services: ARAMARK provides specialized management services for hospitals and medical services. It also specializes in providing early-childhood and school-age education services.

Uniform services: The company is America's largest provider of uniform services and work apparel for virtually all types of institutions.

Magazine and book services: ARAMARK is the leading wholesale distributor of magazines, newspapers, and books.

ARAMARK successfully manages the diversity of segment concepts under the guideline of one single purpose: to be the world leader in managed services. With annual revenues in excess of $8.8 billion in 2002, the company is among the market leaders in all of its businesses, and it is in an ideal position for further market growth. Joseph Neubauer, chairman and CEO, realizes this: "I am energized by the bright prospects for the journey ahead. . . . I can't wait to get started."

Source: Adapted courtesy of ARAMARK.

As stated earlier, but worth repeating, good managers first control the "big ticket" items that will be most costly if not controlled. Once the most costly items are under control, they can move on to controlling other items. Looking at the labor costs in Figure 19–4, we can see that payroll is the largest of the controllable costs. Labor costs, like any other, need to be controlled in line with sales. Each department will have its own desired labor cost expressed as a percentage of sales. If sales go up, it is easier to control labor costs. However, if sales go down, then the skill of management is to "control" labor costs to avoid losing more than absolutely necessary. Management also needs to be fair with associates. After the September 11, 2001, tragedy, Marriott set an example at many of their hotels and resorts by not laying off any associates—they instead reduced everyone's hours—this did a lot to keep their associates loyal.

In managerial accounting, food and beverage costs are the next largest to be controlled after labor costs. Attractions like Sea World, clubs, resorts, hotels, and restaurants all offer food and beverages to their guests. All food and beverage items need to be costed and priced in advance to yield a certain percentage—let's say 24 percent. We all know that these percentages will vary from one organization to another—the point is that both food and beverage departments need to be "controlled" to produce the expected results, and income statements provide the feedback, written report-type of control.

Things like recipes, portion control, proper purchasing, storage, issuing, and preparation of all food and beverage items will help ensure that the items reach the guest correctly. Next, we need to ensure that all monies reach the bank—no fingers in the cash register! No bags in the kitchen, no internal trades between departments. A proper system must be in place for recording all sales and ensuring that the correct amount is received from guests. Several point-of-sale systems and front- and back-of-the-house systems are available from which hospitality operators can choose. They assist the control process in making the job easier.

Qualities of an Effective Control System

Effective control systems tend to have certain characteristics in common.[2] The importance of these qualities varies with the situation; effective control systems have ten characteristics.

1. *Accuracy.* An effective control system is reliable and produces valid data.
2. *Timeliness.* An effective control system provides timely information.
3. *Economy.* An effective control system must be economical to operate.
4. *Flexibility.* An effective control system is flexible enough to adjust to changes and opportunities.
5. *Understandability.* The users can understand an effective control system.
6. *Reasonable criteria.* Control standards must be reasonable and attainable.
7. *Strategic placement.* Because managers can't control everything, they must choose to control those factors that are strategic to the organization's performance.

8. *Emphasis on exceptions.* Managers can't control all activities; control devices should call attention only to the exceptions.
9. *Multiple criteria.* Measures decrease tendencies toward a narrow focus.
10. *Corrective action.* The control system not only indicates significant deviations, but also suggests appropriate corrective action.

Experienced managers use effective controls by exception, meaning that if the results are outside the acceptable predetermined limits, then they take action; otherwise they concentrate on something else.

Contingency Plans and Control

The most important contingency plan factor that affects the design of an organization's control system is the size of the organization. The control system should vary according to the organization's size. A small organization relies more on informal and personal control approaches. Here, concurrent control (direct supervision) is probably the most cost effective. However, as organizations increase in size, direct supervision is likely to be supplemented by an expanding formal control system of reports, regulations, and rules. Very large organizations will typically have highly formalized and impersonal feedforward and feedback controls. Contingency plans and control cover the "what-if's"—what if our sales dip 8 percent—what will we do? Reduce associate hours, reduce expenditures and attempt to boost sales.

As you move up in the organization's hierarchy, there is a greater need for several different types of control; this reflects increased operational complexities. Additionally, the greater the degree of decentralization, the more managers will need feedback on employees' decisions and performance results. Managers who delegate the authority for making decisions and performing work are still ultimately responsible for the actions of those to whom it was delegated.

The importance of an activity influences whether and how it will be controlled. However, if an error can be highly damaging to the organization, extensive controls are likely to be implemented. It simply makes sense to control the big ticket items.

Adjusting Controls for Cultural Differences

Control is used quite differently in other countries.[3] The differences in organizational control systems of global organizations are seen primarily in the measurement and corrective action steps of the control process. In a global hospitality corporation, managers of foreign operations tend to be controlled less directly by the home office, for no other reason than that distance keeps managers from being able to observe work directly. Because distance creates a tendency to formalize controls, the home office of a global company often relies on extensive formal reports for control. Global companies rely on the power of information technology to provide speedy control reports of results.

Focus on Control and Command in Time of Disaster

Hank Christen and Paul Maniscalco
Unconventional Concepts, Inc.
George Washington University

Before any emergency or disaster occurs, an organization's responsibility for the control of the situation and for the command of each organizational element need to be clearly specified in the emergency/disaster plan. Individual departments and contractors (who provide goods and services) are integral to ensuring the organization's continued operation, reputation, management, and event survivability. One of the most important tasks is defining control of the organizational response to the event in the planning phase. Once this requirement has been identified, the next step is to implement an interim command and control framework that functions as the highest authority responsible for management of the event.

This command configuration places critical departments and subunits under the control of a single authority—the person onsite ultimately in charge of all the organization's resources—the incident commander. This new organizational structure is designed for the sole purpose of resolving the crisis, and it is in effect only in times of emergency. After the crisis has been resolved, the command structure relinquishes its authority to the standard daily managerial configuration. Even though this command structure serves at the direction of the organization and depends upon it for logistical support, its characteristics and qualities are unique to itself and to the mission.

The incident command structure requires an effective command and control design—a system providing for critical department interaction and assuring that all efforts are directed toward achieving a common goal. Without a robust, sustaining support mechanism, the chain of command and communications are fragmented, confusing, and vastly ineffective. By establishing a control mechanism in advance, the organization's command structure is highly adaptable for large and small-scale emergencies and is flexible enough to integrate resources from different corporate and vendor areas. Several critical issues should be considered when designing a command and control system:

✓ Every emergency event demands a structured plan. While more minor emergencies generally do not require a fully scripted response, some guidance is required in all emergency scenarios. Without a response plan, the organization's incident commander is unable to seek the advice and employ the expertise of subordinate commanders.

✓ The command structure must provide a manageable span of control to be effective. Without a manageable span of control, the incident commander quickly becomes overloaded with data and requests. This phenomenon is frequently referred to in the emergency response field as OBE, "overwhelmed by events." OBE must be avoided. Early recognition of span of control issues enables the manager to assign subordinate commanders and avoid OBE.

✓ Comprehensive resource management, distribution, and accountability are also required. Some required resources may have a limited service time, and replacements must be arranged for. Radio batteries must be exchanged and recharged. Repair parts from distant locations may be needed. Personnel must be fed and relieved. These factors demand that the incident manager assign a current status condition to all resources and provide for efficient operation.

✓ Communications systems must be reliable, efficient, and secure. Frequently facility communications are disabled due to the incident. The result is an inability to communicate, control, and prioritize subordinate tasking. In the military, communications is called "the voice of command." Commanders who cannot communicate cannot control. The manager should work with the organization's security department and enhance their radio capacity so that internal resources are in place to sustain crisis communications.

Critical Factors
- Control begins with a structured plan.
- A narrow span of control should be maintained to avoid OBE (overwhelmed by events).
- Operational control is not possible without effective communications.

Technology's impact on control also can be seen when comparing technologically advanced nations with less technologically advanced countries. In countries such as the United States, Japan, Canada, the United Kingdom, France, Germany, and Australia, managers of global companies use indirect control devices, particularly computer-related reports and analyses in addition to standardized rules and direct supervision, to ensure that work activities are going as planned.

In less technologically advanced countries, managers tend to rely more on direct supervision and highly centralized decision making for control. Also, constraints on what corrective actions managers can take may affect managers in foreign countries because laws in some countries do not allow managers the option of choosing the facilities, laying off employees, taking money out of the country, or bringing in a new management team from outside the country.

Contemporary Issues in Control

One issue that can arise as managers begin to design efficient and effective control systems include technological advances in computer hardware and software that have made the process of controlling much easier, but these advances have brought with them difficult questions regarding what managers have the right to know about employee behavior.[4] Another issue is workplace privacy.

Workplace Privacy

If you work, do you think you have a right to privacy at your workplace? What can your employer find out about you and your work? You might be surprised by the answer. Why do managers feel they must monitor what employees are doing? A reason is that employees are hired to work, not to surf the Web checking stock prices, placing bets at online casinos, or shopping for presents for family or friends.

Personal on-the-job Web surfing costs is millions of dollars a year in wasted computer resources and billions of dollars in lost work productivity.

Increased use of computers at the workplace poses risk for privacy issues.

Another reason why managers monitor employee e-mail and computer usage is that they don't want to risk being sued for creating a hostile workplace environment because of offensive messages or an inappropriate image displayed on a coworker's computer screen. Concern about sexual harassment is one of the reasons why the companies might want to monitor or keep the backup copies of all e-mail. This electronic device can help establish what actually happened if an incident arises and can help managers react instantly. Managers also need to be certain that employees are not inadvertently passing information on to others who could use that information to harm the company.

Employee Theft

Would it surprise you to know that a high percentage of all organizational theft and fraud is committed by employees, not outsiders? Any unauthorized taking of company property by employees for their personal use constitutes employee theft, from fraudulent filing of expense reports to removing equipment, software, and office supplies from the

> ### A Prepay Restaurant
>
> There is a great hole-in-the-wall restaurant in New York City where arguably the best front-end control system is in place. Servers have to pay the cooks for the guest's food—so you know that they will get the money from the guests.

company premises. Hospitality businesses have long faced serious losses from employee theft caused by loose financial controls, especially at the start-up of a business.

Why do employees steal? There are several perspectives. The industrial loss prevention professionals suggest that people steal because the opportunity presents itself through lax controls and favorable circumstances. Some people have different social financial problems or pressures such as gambling debts. People steal because they can rationalize whatever they're doing as being correct and appropriate behavior. Hospitality associates also steal because they often feel underpaid, so whether it's a phone call here or a knife, fork, and spoon there, if the opportunity arises, they may take advantage of it. Notice how the concept of feedforward, concurrent, and feedback control to identify measures for deterring or reducing employee theft applies.

Workplace Violence

Factors contributing to workplace violence include employee stress caused by long working hours, information overload, daily interruptions, unrealistic deadlines, and uncaring managers.

This list may not look like the place you work, but some of these factors appear in a good many corporations especially with the pressure of making a profit in the increasingly competitive "24-7-365" environment.

Control is critical in the hospitality industry because we need to know how we are doing all the time. We need to know if goals are being met and standards reached or exceeded. According to the situation, well-managed hospitality businesses use a variety of controls to provide the necessary information to management for decision-making purposes.

Personal Profile: Michael R. Thorpe

The Leader of the Future Will Be a Holistic One

Michael R. Thorpe, who has successfully earned a bachelor of science degree in hotel and restaurant management is an outstanding example of the leadership skills that can be acquired throughout the school and college career.

Mike's leadership abilities developed from an early age, with his involvement in the Boy Scouts of America. Looking back at that memorable time, Mike recognizes how important it is for a leader to be a good role model. He emphasizes the fact that it is necessary to make a sharp distinction between "good" leaders and "bad" leaders, thus establishing a learning process that is based on the identification of both "shoulds" (positive examples, experiences, activities, skills) and "should-nots" (mistakes, negative attitudes). Michael's experience with the Boy Scouts was one that provided him with fundamental values and skills, which were acknowledged when he achieved the rank of Eagle Scout.

In high school as well as in college, Mike's leadership skills were progressively developed and utilized. He believes that the key to learning is involvement. In fact, he always took part in school activities, also emphasizing the importance of maintaining a broad horizon of interests. In particular, Michael chose to actively participate in a variety of extracurricular activities, including academic, service-oriented, and sports organizations. He stressed the belief that there is a strict correlation among such fields that shapes the overall personality of the leader. "The leader of the future will be a holistic one," Mike says.

Michael's involvement in academic organizations, such as the student body government council; in sports, as captain of the football team and vice president of the football club; and in service-oriented enterprises, such as the Hosteur's Society HRTM Club, to which he was elected president, helped him develop the necessary skills for high-quality interaction with people. He learned that a good leader is someone who is able to gather a group of individuals and coordinate each single talent, skill, propensity, and personality into a successful team, joining forces in the pursuit of one common goal. Each member of the team must be fulfilled in his or her need for belonging, personal satisfaction, recognition, and so on. To accomplish this task, Mike understood that a leader must also be extremely respectful of each individ-

ual's personal life, needs, problems, cultural background, and diversity, setting aside personal likes and dislikes. Diversity also provides an opportunity for the leader to learn from the people he or she guides, an opportunity that every leader must have the humility and willingness to pursue.

In Mike's words, the leader must act as a "glue" that unites people, and the organizer who finds the "right place" for each individual, a place in which he or she will be able to excel and perform at his or her full potential.

Work experience throughout his college career has also taught Mike that workers will function at their best in a work environment that is appealing and challenging, and that provides them with the right tools—in terms of knowledge, motivation, rewards, and climate—to produce the optimal outcome.

To achieve such results, Michael excludes, as much as possible, the carrot-on-a-stick approach. He feels that such a method is a superficial remedy that doesn't get to the root of the problem—and thus doesn't solve it—and doesn't consider that a leader deals with human beings intrinsically characterized by a distinct intelligence and personality. Furthermore, when dealing with subordinates' failures or mistakes, Michael prefers to approach the person(s) in question from his or her point of view, trying to understand what the cause of the inefficiency might be and trying to establish whether that person's poor performance is determined by his own possible leadership mistake.

Mike greatly respects a leader who creates a sense of cooperation, community, and teamwork. Just like in a family, the leader should step down from an ivory tower, and be open to each member of the team, to listen and be willing to help with possible personal problems, emphasizing the importance of open communication. And as in a family, the leader must be a caring parent who can also progressively impose discipline and obtain the results expected depending on the members' potential.

Mike understands the role of a father because he has a six-year-old who represents, among other things, the ultimate challenge for leadership. "Workers' livelihoods do depend on the employer/leader."

Check Your Knowledge

1. Briefly explain zero-based budgeting.
2. List the qualities of an effective control system.
3. What are some contributors to workplace violence?

Trends in Control

Increasing use of technology for control helps not only make the job of control easier but also much quicker. Quicker results mean decisions to make necessary changes are made sooner, thus avoiding further losses.

Handheld devices that take inventory are an example of how technology can assist management with inventory taking.

CASE STUDY

The Ritz-Carlton is an outstanding hotel in providing luxury service to its guests. In contrast with the standard goals of ordinary business hotels—to provide a home away from home—The Ritz-Carlton Hotel company decided to take it a step further and provide luxury accommodation to industry executives, meeting and corporate travel planners, and other affluent travelers. The chain is Atlanta based and runs 25 luxury hotels that pursue excellence in each market.

Recently the hotel company was awarded the U.S. government's Malcolm Baldrige National Quality Award. The award praised Ritz-Carlton for its participatory leadership, thorough information gathering, coordinated planning and execution, and trained workforce that was ready "to move heaven and earth" to satisfy their customers. Thinking about control, what types of control mechanisms did Ritz-Carlton need to achieve excellence?

The corporate motto is "Ladies and Gentlemen serving Ladies and Gentlemen." All employees are expected to practice the company's "Gold Standards." These standards are made up of a service credo and the basics of premium service, including processes for solving any problem guests may have.

The difference between this luxury chain and other hotel companies is that their employees are "certified" after the common basic orientation followed by an on-the-job training. This certification to work for Ritz-Carlton is reinforced daily by frequent recognition for achievement, performance appraisal, and daily "lineups." Annual surveys are given to make sure the employees know the quality standards the hotel company expects of them as well as to determine their level of satisfaction with the company. One year 96 percent of the employees surveyed ranked excellence in guest services as their primary duty. Workers are empowered by the company to do whatever it takes to solve any sort of problem a customer might encounter. Employees are required to assist their coworkers in dealing with a guest satisfaction issue leaving no room for any excuse as to why a customer problem was not solved on the spot. In this way, the guest is truly treated as a king; guest satisfaction comes first—always.[5]

Discussion Question

1. In what ways does Ritz-Carlton utilize control to ensure high-quality service?
2. How does the company maintain and foster its employees' high level of commitment?

CAREER INFORMATION

To control the direction that life takes you is to end up where you wanted to be. The control process will help you to set a career path that is definable and predictable. You can then have a clear understanding of what you are doing and how well you are doing it. If you are meeting the standards that you have made for yourself, you will be rewarded in your long-term career.

SUMMARY

1. Control is the management function that provides information on the degree to which goals and objectives are being accomplished.
2. Control is important because it's the final link in the management function. An effective control system is important because managers need to delegate duties and empower employees to make decisions.
3. The control process can be described as setting standards, measuring actual performance, comparing actual performance against those standards, and taking managerial action to correct deviations or inadequate performances.
4. Managers can use controls *in advance* of an activity, which is called feedforward control; *during* the activity, which is concurrent control; and *after* the activity, called feedback control.
5. Budgets and income statements are primarily used for financial control. Budgets "guestimate" the sales figure for the month/year and allow for up to a specific dollar amount to be spent on any cost of goods sold or controllable costs item. Income statements show the actual sales and expenditures for a month/year.
6. Effective control systems have ten characteristics: accuracy, timeliness, economy, flexibility, understandability, reasonable criteria, strategic placement, emphasis on exceptions, multiple criteria, and corrective action.
7. Contemporary issues in control include the increasing use of technological advances, which raise the issue of workplace privacy. Additionally workplace violence and employee theft are issues in the control process.

KEY WORDS AND CONCEPTS

Accuracy
Basic corrective action
Budget
Concurrent control
Control
Control process
Correcting actual performance

Corrective action
Economy
Emphasis on exceptions
Feedback control
Feedforward control
Flexibility

Immediate corrective action
Income statement
Management by walking around (MBWA)
Measuring
Multiple criteria

Reasonable criteria
Strategic placement
Timeliness
Understandability
Zero-based budgeting

REVIEW QUESTIONS

1. Imagine a restaurant that is lacking any kind of control. Describe the negative and positive aspects of this environment and then answer the following question: Why is control necessary?
2. If you were a manager of a Hilton Resort in the Bahamas, what way of measuring actual employee performance would you utilize and why? What are the pros and cons of your chosen method?
3. Explain the three different types of control. Think of a situation where you have been controlled. Which type of control works best for you?
4. Describe how you envision an effective control system. What types of control would you use? How would you measure employee performance? How would you keep employee theft under control? What about workplace violence? Which operational financial control would you implement?

INTERNET EXERCISE

1. Organization: **The ePolicy Institute Web site: http://www.epolicyinstitute.com/disasters/stories.html**
Summary: This site summarizes edisaster stories.

(a) Do you think that it's fair for employers to monitor their employee's e-mails?
(b) What would you do if you caught your boss reading your e-mails?

APPLY YOUR KNOWLEDGE

You are a restaurant manager and the months-end food cost percentage has just arrived on your desk and it shows the actual food cost percentage is 12 percent above budget. What will you do?

ENDNOTES

1. Stephen P. Robbins and Mary Coulter, *Management,* 8th ed. Upper Saddle River, NJ: Prentice Hall, 2005, p. 486.
2. **http://users.rowan.edu/~gianca33/Dell/sld02.htm**.
3. Stephen P. Robbins and Mary Coulter, *Management,* 8th ed. Upper Saddle River, NJ: Prentice Hall, 2005, p. 475.
4. Ibid., p. 475.
5. Adapted from Gary Dessler, *A Framework for Management.* Upper Saddle River, NJ: Prentice Hall, 2002, pp. 376–377.

Glossary

A

Accuracy   A precise and effective control system—one that is reliable and produces valid data.

Active listening   Listening for full meaning without making premature judgments or interpretations.

Actual market share   The market share that a business actually receives; compare with the fair market share, which is an equal share of the market.

ADR   *See* Average daily rate.

Alcoholic beverage   A beverage containing alcohol.

Allied areas   Term used by industry trade associations for suppliers of goods and services.

Allocation of weights to criteria   Allocating different levels of importance to decision criteria according to a weighting method.

Analysis of alternatives   Analyzing alternatives according to the "weights to criteria" method.

Application service provider (ASP)   Delivers a complete booking system tied to the hotel's inventory in real time via the Internet.

Associations   Groups of individuals and corporations who come together for purposes of representing their industry segment to legislators and for the benefit of members in education and other operational benefits.

Authority   The rights inherent in a managerial position to tell people what to do and to expect them to do it.

Average daily rate (ADR)   One of the key operating ratios that indicates the level of a hotel's performance. The ADR is calculated by dividing the dollar sales by the number of rooms rented.

Average guest check   The average amount each group spends; used primarily in a restaurant setting.

B

Baccarat   A traditional table game in which the winning hand totals closest to nine.

Back-of-the-house operations   The support areas behind the scenes in a hotel or motel, including housekeeping, laundry, engineering, and foodservice. Also refers to individuals who operate behind the scenes to make a guest's stay pleasant and safe.

Balance sheet   Itemizes a business's assets and liabilities with regard to the owner's equity at a particular moment in time.

Banquet   A formal dinner.

Banquet event order (BEO)   A document that details the requirements of an event.

Basic corrective action   An action that examines how and why performance deviated and then proceeds to correct the source of deviation.

Batch cooking   The cooking of food in quantities for consumption throughout a meal period. Used in noncommercial foodservice to avoid putting out all the food at 11:30 and having it spoil. Batches are cooked for readiness at 11:30, 12:00, 12:30, and so on.

Beer   A brewed and fermented beverage made from water, barley malt, yeast, and other starchy cereals and flavored with hops.

Behavioral style   A decision-making style characterized by a low tolerance for ambiguity and an intuitive way of thinking.

Benchmarking   Searching for the best practices among competitors or noncompetitors that lead to their superior performance.

Bet   An amount wagered or put into play during a gaming activity.

Beverage cost percentage   Similar to food cost percentage, except that it relates to beverages.

Blackjack   A table game in which the winning hand is determined by whether the dealer or the player gets cards that add up to a number closest to or equal to 21 without going over.

Body language   Gestures, facial expressions, body postures, and other movements of the body that convey meaning, such as the emotional state and attitude of the person.

Boundaryless organizations   Organizations not limited to or bound by vertical or horizontal boundaries.

Brandy   Brandy is distilled from wine and is served as an after-dinner beverage or mixed in cocktails.

Brigade   A team of kitchen personnel organized into stations.

Budget   An itemized listing, usually prepared annually, of anticipated revenue and projected expenses.

Budgeting costs   Allocating and budgeting costs to control an operation's expenses.

Business travel   Travel for business purposes.

C

Call accounting system (CAS)   A system that tracks guest room phone charges.

Capture rate   In hotel food and beverage practice, the number of hotel guests who use the food and beverage outlets.

Career path   Pathway of a career.

Casino   An area in which gaming activities involving table games and slot machines take place.

Casual dining   Relaxed dining; includes restaurants from several classifications.

Catastrophe plan   A plan to maximize guest and property safety in the event of a disaster.

Catering   The part of the food and beverage division of a hotel that is responsible for arranging and planning food and beverage functions for conventions and smaller hotel groups, and local banquets booked by the sales department.

Catering coordinator   The person who coordinates all the activities of the catering department.

Catering services manager (CSM)   Head of the catering services department.

Celebrity-owned restaurant   A restaurant owned, or partially owned, by a celebrity.

Central reservations office (CRO)   The central office of a lodging company where reservations are processed.

Central reservations system (CRS)   A reservation system that is commonly used in large franchises to connect their reservation systems with one another; allows guests to call one phone number to reserve a room at any of the chain properties.

Centralization   The degree to which decision making is concentrated at a single point in the organization.

Certainty   The condition of knowing in advance the outcome of a decision.

Chain of command   The continuous line of authority that extends from upper organizational levels to the lowest levels in the organization and clarifies who reports to whom.

Chain restaurant   Restaurant that is one of a chain of restaurants.

Champagne   Sparkling wine made in the Champagne district of France.

Chef tournant   A chef who rotates the various stations in the kitchen to relieve the station chefs.

Chief steward   The individual in a hotel, club, or foodservice operation who is responsible for the cleanliness of the back of the house and dishwashing areas, and for storage and control of china, glassware, and silverware.

City clubs   Clubs in a city.

City ledger   A client whose company has established credit with a certain hotel. Charges are posted to the city ledger and accounts are sent once or twice monthly.

Clarify   Wine is clarified by adding either eggwhite of bentonite.

Classroom-style seating   A type of meeting setup generally used in instructional meetings, such as workshops.

Club management   The management of clubs.

Cognac   The finest brandy only made in the Cognac region of France.

Commercial foodservice   Operations that compete for customers in the open market.

Commercial recreation   Recreation for profit.

Communication   The exchange of information and the transfer of meaning.

Comping   Offering a complimentary service without charge.

Compressed workweek   A workweek in which employees work longer hours per day but fewer days per week.

Conceptual style   A decision-making style that involves considering numerous alternatives in order to find creative solutions to the problem.

Concurrent control   Control that occurs while the work is being done.

Confirmed reservation   A reservation made by a guest that is confirmed by the hotel for the dates they plan on staying.

Consumer show   A show for consumers.

Contingency factors   Factors contingent upon various circumstances occurring; planning for the what-if's.

Contractor   A company that operates a foodservice for the client on a contractual basis.

Contribution margin   Key operating figure in menu engineering, determined by subtracting food cost from selling price as a measure of profitability.

Control   The provision of information to management for decision-making purposes. The process of monitoring activities to ensure that they are being accomplished as planned and of correcting any significant deviations.

Control process   A three-step process including measuring actual performance, comparing actual performance against a standard, and taking managerial action to correct deviations or inadequate standards.

Controllable expenses Expenses that can be controlled by means of cost-effective purchasing systems, a controlled storage and issuing system, and strict control of food production and sales. These expenses are usually watched over by management.

Convention A generic term referring to any size of business or professional meeting held in one specific location, which usually includes some form of trade show or exposition. Also refers to a group of delegates or members who assemble to accomplish a specific goal.

Convention and visitors bureau 1. An organization responsible for promoting tourism at the regional and local level. 2. A not-for-profit umbrella organization that represents a city or urban area in soliciting and servicing all types of travelers to that city or area, whether for business, pleasure, or both.

Convention center A large meeting place.

Cooking line "The line" is a term used to describe the final cooking and plating area of the kitchen.

Coordination of activities The process of achieving unity of action among interdependent activities.

Corporate culture The overall style or feel of a company. Governs how people relate to one another and their jobs.

Corporate philosophy The core beliefs that drive a company's basic organizational structure.

Correcting actual performance An approach used to correct poor performance; may include redefining job tasks, changing work compensation, offering training programs, or laying off staff.

Corrective action An action that is tending or intended to correct.

Country clubs Clubs that offer golf and sometimes tennis and/or swimming for members' recreation along with restaurants and social activities.

Culinary arts The art of cooking.

Curbside appeal Visual appeal and cleanliness designed to encourage people to dine in a particular restaurant.

D

Daily rate The amount of money required to pay for each person's foodservice a day.

Daily report A report prepared each day to provide essential performance information for a particular property to its management.

Decentralization The degree to which lower level employees provide input or actually make decisions.

Decision making Making choices between alternatives.

Decision-making process The process of developing and analyzing alternatives and choosing from among them.

Departmentalization Organizing resources into departments.

Development The act of developing.

Development of alternatives Listing possible alternatives that could resolve a problem.

Dinner house restaurant A restaurant with a casual, eclectic décor that may promote a particular theme.

Dinner-style room seating Seating all around a table as for a dinner.

Directive style A decision-making style characterized by a rational way of thinking and low tolerance for ambiguity.

Director of catering (DOC) Head of all catering operations.

Director of food and beverage The individual responsible for the successful operation of all restaurant and kitchen duties, including guest satisfaction and profitability.

Diversification A corporate strategy whereby managers try to utilize their organization's resources more effectively by developing new products and new markets.

Diversity An increase in the heterogeneity of an organization through the inclusion of different ethnic groups.

Division of labor Dividing labor and tasks.

DOC *See* Director of catering.

Downward communication Communication flow within the organization from supervisor or manager to employees.

Dram shop legislation Laws and procedures that govern the legal operation of establishments that sell measured alcoholic beverages.

E

Ecotourism Responsible travel to natural areas that conserves the environment and sustains the well-being of the local people.

Effectiveness Completing activities so that organizational goals are attained; also referred to as "doing the right things" or "getting things done."

Efficiency Getting the most output from the smallest amount of inputs; also referred to as "doing things right" or "getting things done well."

Emphasis on exceptions The practice of not questioning a certain routine or way of doing things as long as everything goes well. Only cases of exceptions to routine, such as problems or complaints, have the potential to change the routine.

Employee assistance program (EAP) A program of various kinds of assistance for employees.

Employee recognition Recognizing superior employee performance.

Employee Right to Know Per U.S. Senate Bill 198, information about chemicals must be made available to all employees.

Empowerment The act of giving employees the authority, tools, and information they need to do their jobs with greater autonomy.

Encoding Converting the message into symbolic form.

Entry-level position   First-level position.

Environmental scanning   The screening of large amounts of information to anticipate and interpret changes in the environment.

Equity theory   The theory that an employee compares his or her job's inputs–outcomes ratio with that of relevant others and then corrects any inequity.

Escalation of commitment   Increased commitment to a previous decision despite evidence that it may have been wrong.

Ethics   The study of standards of conduct and moral judgment; also, the standards of correct conduct.

Ethnic restaurant   A restaurant featuring a particular cuisine such as Chinese, Mexican, or Italian.

Etiquette   Appropriate behavior in a business or social setting.

Evaluation of decision effectiveness   Determination of whether specified goals have been achieved.

Executive chef   The head of the kitchen.

Executive committee   A committee of hotel executives from each of the major departments within the hotel generally made up of the general manager, director of rooms division, food and beverage director, marketing and sales director, human resources director, accounting and/or finance director, and engineering director.

Expectancy theory   The theory that an individual tends to act in a certain way based on the expectation that the act will be followed by a given outcome and on the attractiveness of that outcome to the individual.

Exposition   An event held mainly to promote informational exchanges among trade people. A large exhibition in which the presentation is the main attraction, as well as being a source of revenue for an exhibitor.

F

Familiarization (FAM) trip   A free or reduced-price trip given to travel agents, travel writers, or other intermediaries to promote destinations.

Family restaurant   A restaurant that caters to families.

Feedback control   A type of control that takes place after the activity is done and uses the obtained information to remedy the situation.

Feedforward control   A type of control that focuses on preventing anticipated problems because it takes place in advance of the actual work activity.

Fermentation   The chemical process in which yeast acts on sugar or sugar-containing substances, such as grain or fruit, to produce alcohol and carbon dioxide.

FIFO   *See* First-in, first-out.

Fine dining restaurant   Upscale dining, usually with white tablecloths, à la carte menus, and table service.

Fining   The process by which wine that has matured is filtered to help stabilize it and remove any solid particles still in the wine.

First-in, first-out   The supplies that are ordered first are used first.

Flexibility   The ability to undergo change and modification readily.

Flextime/flexible work hours   A scheduling system in which employees are required to work a certain number of hours per week but are free, within limits, to vary the hours of work.

Food cost percentage   A ratio comparing the cost of food sold to food sales, which is calculated by dividing the cost of food sold during a given period by food sales during the same period.

Forecasting   Predicting future outcomes.

Formal communication   Communication that takes place within a prescribed organizational work agreement.

Fortified wine   Wine to which brandy or other spirits have been added to stop further fermentation or to raise its alcoholic content.

Franchising   A concept that allows a company to expand quickly by allowing qualified people to use the systems, marketing, and purchasing power of the franchiser.

Front-line manager/supervisor   A low-level manager who manages the work of line employees and has guest contact.

Front-of-the-house operations   Comprises all areas with which guests come in contact, including the lobby, corridors, elevators, guest rooms, restaurants and bars, meeting rooms, and restrooms. Also refers to employees who staff these areas.

Function   An assigned duty or activity.

G

Gainsharing plan   A group incentive program that shares the gains of the efforts of group members with those group markets.

Gambling   To bet money on the outcome of a game of chance.

Gaming entertainment industry   Businesses that offer games of risk as part of a total package of entertainment and leisure time activities, including resort hotel, various foodservice concepts, retail shopping, theme parks, live entertainment, and recreational pursuits.

Geographic expansion   A strategic growth alternative of aggressively expanding into new domestic and/or overseas markets.

Global distribution system (GDS)   System of global reservations.

Goal   A specific result to be achieved; the end result of a plan.

Goal setting   Traditionally, goals are set at the top level of an organization and then broken down into subgoals for each level of the organization so that all levels work together toward the achievement of the ultimate goals.

Goal-setting theory The proposition that specific goals improve performance and that difficult goals, when accepted, result in a higher level of performance than do easily attainable goals.

Government-sponsored recreation Recreation paid for by government taxes; includes monies sent to cities for museums, libraries, and municipal golf courses.

Gross profit Sales less cost of sales.

Guaranteed reservations If rooms are available on guest demand, the hotel guarantees the guests' rooms on those days.

Guest A person who is the recipient of hospitality in the form of entertainment—at someone's home, as a visiting participant in a program, or as a customer of an establishment such as a hotel or restaurant.

Guest accounting module A system that increases the hotel's control over guest accounts and significantly modifies the night audit routine.

Guest counts (covers) The number of guests dining in a restaurant.

Guest satisfaction The desired outcome of hospitality services.

Guest service department The department that takes care of guests and their needs.

H

Handle The dollars wagered, or bet; often confused with "win." Whenever a customer places a bet, the handle increases by the amount of the bet. The handle is not affected by the outcome of the bet.

Haute cuisine Elaborate or artful cuisine; contemporary cuisine.

Hertzberg's motivation and hygiene factors A theory of Dr. Hertzberg that states that intrinsic factors are related to job satisfaction, and motivation and extrinsic factors are associated with job dissatisfaction.

Hops The dried, conical fruit of a special vine that imparts bitterness to beer.

Horizontal integration The acquisition of ownership or control of competitors that are competing in the same or similar markets with the same or similar products.

Horseshoe-style room seating A meeting room containing tables arranged in the shape of a U.

Hospitality 1. The cordial and generous reception of guests. 2. A wide range of businesses, each of which is dedicated to the service of people away from home.

Host/hostess A greeter and "seater" at the entrance of a restaurant.

Hub-and-spoke system A system by which airline passengers can travel from one small city to another via a hub at a major city.

Hygiene factors Factors that eliminate job dissatisfaction but don't motivate.

I

Identification and definition of a problem Identifying and defining a problem.

Identification of decision criteria Identifying criteria important for making decisions.

Immediate corrective action Corrective action that corrects problems at once to get performance back on track.

Implementation of alternative Implementing the selected alternative.

Incentive market A market for incentive travel.

Income statement A report that lists the amount of money or its equivalent received during a period of time in exchange for labor or services, from the sale of goods or property, or as profit from financial investments.

Independent business unit (IBU) A business that makes decisions with little or no need to obtain approval for routine operational decisions from higher up in the organization.

Independent restaurant A nonfranchise restaurant, privately owned.

Indian Gaming Regulatory Act A federal act that created a statutory basis for the operation of gaming by Indian tribes in order to promote tribal economic development, self-sufficiency, and strong tribal governments.

Informal communication Does not follow a company's chain of command or structural hierarchy, and the subject matter is typically not job related or essential to performing job duties.

Infusion The extraction of flavors from foods.

Inseparability The linkage of hospitality products and services.

Intangible Hospitality service is intangible; it cannot be sampled prior to purchase.

Interdependency of tourism and hospitality Tourism and hospitality are interdependent.

Interpersonal communication Communication between two or more people.

Interpersonal communications process Consists of seven elements: the communication source, the message, encoding, the channel, decoding, the receiver, and feedback.

Intuitive decision making A subconscious process of making decisions on the basis of experience and accumulated judgment.

Inventory control A method for keeping track of all resources required to produce a product.

J

Job description A description of the duties and responsibilities involved in the performance of a particular job.

Job enlargement A horizontal increase in the number of similar tasks assigned to a job.

Job enrichment   A vertical expansion of a job involving the addition of planning and evaluating responsibilities that act as motivators and make the job more challenging.

Job rotation   The systematic movement of workers from job to job to improve job satisfaction, reduce boredom, and enable employees to gain a broad perspective over the work processes within the entire organization.

Job satisfaction   The degree to which a person is satisfied with his or her job.

Job shadowing   A method enabling a person working in a certain field to train for work in another field.

Job sharing   The practice of having two or more people split a full-time job.

Joint venture   An approach to going global that involves a specific type of strategic alliance in which the partners agree to form a separate, independent organization for some business purpose.

K

Key operating areas   The most important functional areas of an organization that work and interact toward the achievement of the organization's goals.

Kitchen manager   The individual who manages the kitchen department.

L

Labor cost percentage   Similar to food cost percentage, except that it relates to labor. The formula is: Labor costs divided by net sales multiplied by 100 equals the labor cost percentage.

Leader–manager   An individual whose duties combine the functions of leadership and management.

Leadership   The influence of one person over another to work willingly toward a predetermined objective.

Leisure   Freedom from activities, especially time free from work or duties.

Liaison personnel   Workers who are responsible for translating corporate philosophy for the contractor and for overseeing the contractor to be sure that he or she abides by the terms of the contract.

M

Malt   Germinated barley.

Managed services   Services that can be leased to professional management companies.

Management   The process of coordinating work activities so that an organization's objectives are achieved efficiently and effectively with and through other people.

Management by objectives (MBO)   A managerial process that determines the goals of the organization and then plans the objectives and the method to be used to reach the goals.

Management by walking around (MBWA)   A management style in which the manager goes into the work area, interacts with associates, and exchanges information about work; enables the manager to pick up information communicated through body language and tone of voice, and shows employees and clients that the manager is available and cares about them.

Management contract   A written agreement between an owner and an operator of a hotel or motor inn by which the owner employs the operator as an agent (employee) to assume full responsibility for operating and managing the property.

Management training program   Programmed training for future managers.

Market penetration   A growth strategy to boost sales of current products by more aggressively permeating the organization's current markets.

Mashing   In the making of beer, the process of grinding the malt and screening out bits of dirt.

Matrix structure   An organizational structure in which specialists from different functional departments are assigned to work on one or more projects.

Measurement   An evaluation or basis of comparison in order to ascertain the dimensions, quantity, or capacity of something.

Mechanistic organization   An organization that is rigid and tightly controlled.

Meeting   A gathering of people for a common purpose.

Meeting planner   An individual who coordinates every detail of meetings and conventions.

Mentor   A person who offers advice and counsel to someone who is new to a job or career track.

Middle manager   A manager between the first-line level and the top level of the organization who manages the work of first-line managers.

Mission statement   A statement of the central purpose, strategies, and values of an organization.

Mother sauce   A foundation sauce in classical French cuisine.

Motivation   The willingness to exert high levels of effort to reach organizational goals, conditioned by the effort's ability to satisfy some individual need.

Motivators   Factors that increase job satisfaction and motivation.

Multiple criteria   An effective control system needs to take into consideration multiple criteria in order to get a more realistic grasp of the situation and narrow down tendencies.

Multiplier effect   A concept that refers to new money that is brought into a community to pay for hotel rooms, restaurant meals, and other aspects of leisure. To some extent, that income then passes into the community when the hotel or restaurant orders supplies and services, pays employees, and so on.

Must A mixture of grape pulp, skins, seeds, and stems.

N

National parks Parks designated by Congress for use and preservation by all Americans.

National Restaurant Association (NRA) The association representing restaurant owners and the restaurant industry.

National School Lunch Program (NSLP) The program that provides free lunches to students from a certain income level.

Net profit Profit after all expenses.

Night auditor The individual who verifies and balances guests' accounts.

Nonalcoholic beverage A beverage without alcohol.

Noncommercial recreation Not-for-profit recreation.

Nonprogrammed decisions A unique decision that requires a custom-made solution.

Nonverbal communication Communication transmitted without words through body posture, gestures, and mimics.

Nouvelle cuisine A mid-twentieth-century movement away from classic cuisine principles. Includes shortened cooking times and innovative combinations. A lighter, healthier cuisine based on more natural flavors, including herbs.

NRA *See* National Restaurant Association.

Nutrition education programs Programs ensuring that food served in school cafeterias follows the nutrition standards set by government programs.

O

Objective A specific result toward which effort is directed.

Occupational Safety and Health Administration (OSHA) Organization whose mission is to ensure the safety and health of America's workers by setting and enforcing standards.

Open-book management A management style in which a company opens its books to the employees, sharing financial data, explaining numbers, and rewarding workers for improvement.

Operating ratios Ratios that indicate an operation's performance.

Operational plans Plans for operation and organization.

Organic organization An organization that is flexible and highly adaptive.

Organization chart A chart that illustrates the organization-wide division of work by charting who is accountable to whom and who is in charge of what department.

Organizational communication All the patterns, networks, and systems of communication within an organization.

Organizational structure Formal arrangement of jobs and tasks in an organization.

Orientation A meeting for new employees in which the operation of the business is explained; usually occurs within the first few days of employment.

Other equity theory Different from that or those implied or specified.

P

Pacific Area Travel Association (PATA) An association for the promotion of excellence in travel within, and to and from, the Pacific region.

Par stock The level of stock that must be kept on hand at all times. If the stock on hand falls below this point, a computerized reorder system automatically reorders a predetermined quantity of the stock.

Pay for performance Any compensation method based on merit or performance rather than across-the-board non-output-based pay.

Performance evaluation or appraisal A meeting between a manager and one of his or her employees to 1. let the employee know how effectively he or she has met company standards, and 2. let the manager know how well he or she is doing in hiring and training employees.

Perishability The limited lifetime of hospitality products; for example, last night's vacant hotel room cannot be sold today.

Perpetual inventory A running inventory that automatically updates itself.

Personal digital assistant (PDA) A computer system that transmits information or orders and retrieves and posts guest payments; often used in restaurants to improve time management and allow faster service.

Philosophy Your personal beliefs.

Piecework pay plan Payment to associates for the amount, or piece, of work produced.

Pilferage Stealing.

Planning The process of defining the organization's goals, establishing an overall strategy for achieving those goals, and developing a comprehensive set of plans to integrate and coordinate organizational work.

Pleasure travel Travel for pleasure, including leisure, recreation, vacations, and visiting friends and family.

PMS *See* Property management system.

Point-of-sale (POS) system A system used in restaurants and outlet stores that records and posts charges; consists of a number of POS terminals that interface with a remote central processing unit.

Poker A card game in which participants play against each other instead of the casino.

Policy A guideline that establishes parameters for making decisions.

Pour-cost percentage   Similar to food cost percentage, except used in beverage control.

Prime cost   The cost of food sold plus payroll cost (including employee benefits). This is the largest segment of a restaurant's costs.

Procedure   A series of interrelated sequential steps that can be used to respond to a well-structured problem.

Product   A tangible good or intangible service produced by human or mechanical effort or by a natural process.

Product development   The strategy of improving products for current markets to maintain or boost growth.

Product specification   The establishment of standards for each product, determined by the purchaser. For example, when ordering meat, the product specification includes the cut, weight, size, percentage of fat content, and so forth.

Production control sheet   A checklist/sheet itemizing the production.

Productive teams   Workplace teams built by giving associates the authority, responsibility, and encouragement to come together to work on guest-related improvements that will enhance the guest experience and make the associates' jobs easier.

Productivity standards   Standards of measurement established to gauge employee productivity.

Program   An organized list of procedures, events, or other pertinent information; a schedule.

Programmed decisions   A repetitive decision that can be handled by a routine approach.

Prohibition   The period from 1919 to 1933 when alcohol was banned in the United States.

Project management   The process of completing a project's activities on time, within budget, and according to specifications.

Project structure   An organizational structure in which employees work continuously on projects.

Proof   A figure representing liquor's alcohol content.

Property management system (PMS)   A computerized system that integrates all systems used by a lodging property, such as reservations, front desk, housekeeping, food and beverage control, and accounting.

Purchase order   An order to purchase.

Purée   A blended item.

Q

Quick-service restaurant   A restaurant that offers quick service.

R

Rationality   Consistent with or based on reason; logical. A rational decision needs to be value maximizing and consistent within natural restraining limits.

Real Estate Investment Trust (REIT)   A method that enables small investors to combine their funds and protects them from the double taxation levied against an ordinary corporation or trust; designed to facilitate investment in real estate in much the same way a mutual fund facilitates investment in securities.

Reasonable criteria   Control standards in an effective control system must be attainable and realistic.

Receiving   The back-of-the-house area devoted to receiving goods.

Recreation   Refreshment of strength and spirits after work; a means of diversion.

Recreation for special populations   Recreation designed to accommodate persons with disabilities, for example the Special Olympics.

Recruitment   The process by which an organization attracts prospective employees.

Referral associations   Associations—members—usually hotels and resorts that refer guests to one another.

Reinforcement theory   The theory that behavior is a function of its consequences—that is, a reward is a consequence that triggers a desired response or performance.

Reinforcer   Any consequence immediately following a response that increases the probability that the behavior will be repeated.

Responsibility   The obligation to perform any assigned duties.

Responsible alcoholic beverage service   Serving alcoholic beverages responsibly.

Restaurant forecasting   The process of estimating future events in the restaurant.

Restaurant manager   The head of operations in a restaurant.

Rev par   *See* Revenue per available room.

Revenue management   Revenue management strives to maximize revenue for the property by increasing rates when demand increases and when the date of rooms required gets closer.

Revenue per available room (Rev par)   Total Rooms Revenue for Period divided by Total Rooms Available During a Period.

Risk   The conditions under which the decision maker is able to estimate the likelihood of certain outcomes.

Room management module   A system that tracks the status of rooms; it assists the housekeeping department and the front desk with their duties.

Room occupancy percentage (ROP)   The number of rooms occupied divided by rooms available; a key operating ratio for hotels.

Room rates   The various rates charged for hotel rooms.

Room service   The cleaning of rooms and resupplying of materials (towels, soap, etc.) by the housekeeping staff.

Rooms division   The rooms division is made up of the following departments: front office, communications, reservations, guest services, concierge, and housekeeping.

Roulette A traditional table game in which a dealer spins a wheel and players wager on which number a small ball will fall.

Roux A paste for thickening sauces, made from equal quantities of fat and flour.

Rule A very specific action guide that associates must follow.

S

Satisficing Acceptance of solutions that are good enough.

Scheduling Detailing what activities have to be done, the order in which they are to be completed, who is to do each, and when they are to be completed.

Selection The process of determining the eligibility and suitability of a prospective employee.

Selection of alternative Choosing the alternative with the highest weighted score.

Self-managed team A type of work team that operates without a manager and is responsible for a complete work process or a segment of it.

Self-operator A company that manages its own foodservice operations.

Semantics The study of the actual meaning of words.

Service-oriented A service orientation.

Shoppers People who are paid to use a bar as regular guests would, except that they observe the operation closely.

Slot machine An electronic gaming device.

SMERF Social, military, education, religious, and fraternal.

Social responsibility A business firm's obligation, beyond that required by law and economics, to pursue long-term goals that are beneficial to society.

Sous chef (soo shef) A cook who supervises food production and who reports to the executive chef; he or she is second in command of a kitchen.

Sparkling wine Wine containing carbon dioxide, which provides effervescence when the wine is poured.

Special event An event of importance.

Spirits Distilled drinks.

Standing plans Plans that are ongoing and that give guidance for repeated situations or activities.

Station chef Chef in charge of a station in the kitchen.

Stock option plan A plan by which employees are offered options to buy stocks in the company.

Strategic alliance An approach to the expansion of a business's activities (entering new markets) that involves a partnership with another organization(s) in which both share resources, guests, and knowledge in serving existing clients and in the development of new products and services.

Strategic management The process of identifying and pursuing the organization's strategic plan by aligning internal capabilities with the external demands of its environment, and then ensuring that the plan is being executed properly.

Strategic placement In an effective control system, the emphasis that managers place on certain factors that are vital to the system's performance.

Strategic planning Identifying the current business of a firm, the business it wants for the future, and the course of action it will pursue.

Strategy Action taken to achieve goals.

Suggestive selling Servers in a restaurant increase sales by suggesting appropriate additional items to customers. For example, a server may suggest a Mondavi fumée blanc to complement a fish dish.

Sustainable tourism Tourism that has minimal impact on the environment and culture of the host community.

SWOT analysis A strategic planning tool for analyzing a company's strengths, weaknesses, opportunities, and threats.

T

Task analysis Analysis of the tasks required to complete a particular job.

Team A task-oriented work group that either evolves informally or is appointed formally.

Team player An employee who is committed to the team's objectives, members, and goals.

Telecommuting A job approach in which employees work at home and are linked to the workplace by computer and modem.

Territory The area for which a person is responsible as a representative or agent; a sphere of action or interest.

Theater-style room seating A meeting setup usually intended for a large audience that is not likely to need to take notes or refer to documents. It generally consists of a raised platform and a lectern from which the presenter addresses the audience.

Theme park A recreational park based on a particular setting or artistic interpretation; may operate with hundreds or thousands of acres of parkland and hundreds or thousands of employees.

Theme restaurant A restaurant distinguished by its combination of decor, atmosphere, and menu.

Theory X The assumption that employees dislike work, are lazy, avoid responsibility, and must be coerced to perform.

Theory Y The assumption that employees are creative, enjoy work, seek responsibility, and can exercise self-direction.

Three-needs theory A theory proposed by McClelland and others that says there are three acquired needs that are major motivators: need for achievement, power, and affiliation.

Timeliness Occurring at a suitable time; well timed; opportune.

Tolerance for ambiguity Individuals with a high tolerance for ambiguity are very time efficient in making decisions because they are able to process many thoughts at the same time. Those with a low tolerance for ambiguity need more time to make a decision because they process information in a consistent and ordered way in order to minimize ambiguity.

Top manager A manager at or near the top level of the organization who is responsible for making organization-wide decisions and establishing the goals and plans that affect the entire organization.

Total quality management (TQM) A managerial approach that integrates all of the functions and related processes of a business such that they are all aimed at maximizing guest satisfaction through ongoing improvement.

Tourism Travel for recreation or the promotion and arrangement of such travel.

TQM *See* Total quality management.

Trade show An event that promotes informational exchanges among trade people. Also called *exposition.*

Training An activity conducted by a training department, a training manager, line management, or specially selected individuals within each department to orient and teach new employees how to perform their jobs.

Transactional leadership A type of leadership that focuses on accomplishing the tasks at hand and on maintaining good working relationships by exchanging promises of rewards for performance.

Transformational leadership A type of leadership that involves influencing major changes in the attitudes and assumptions of organization members and building commitment for the organization's mission, objectives, and strategies.

Transient occupancy taxes (TOT) Tax paid by people staying in a city's hotels.

Tray line The lineup of trays on which all the food for hospital patients is placed.

U

Uncertainty A situation in which a decision maker has neither certainty nor reasonable probability estimates available.

Understandability To have understanding, knowledge, or comprehension; being easy to understand.

Uniform system of accounts A system of accounts used in the hospitality industry whereby all accounts have the same type of coding and all accounting procedures are done the same way.

Upward communication Upward information flow within the organization from employees to supervisors or managers.

V

Vacation ownership Offers consumers the opportunity to purchase fully furnished vacation accommodations in a variety of forms, such as weekly intervals or points in point-based systems, for a percentage of the cost of full ownership.

Vacation package A packaged vacation that includes a combination of travel- and tourism-related products and services such as air, ground transportation, and hotel.

Variable cost A cost that varies according to the volume of business.

Variable pay plan A compensation plan that may reduce or increase some portion of an individual employee's pay, depending on whether the company meets its financial goals.

Vertical integration The ownership of or linkage with suppliers of raw materials or airlines owning hotels.

Vintage The year in which a wine's grapes were harvested.

Voluntary organization A nongovernmental, nonprofit agency serving the public.

W

Wager The amount of a bet.

White spirits Gin, rum, vodka, and tequila.

Win Dollars won by the gaming operation from its customers. The net spending of customers on gaming is called the win, also known as *gross gaming revenue (GGR).*

Wine Fermented juice of grapes or other fruits.

Wine and food pairing The pairing of wine and food so that they complement one another.

Wine tasting Tasting wine for an appreciation of its qualities.

Work group information system Data and information shared within a department.

Work specialization The degree to which tasks in an organization are divided into individual jobs; also called *division of labor.*

Work team structure Work structured into teams of employees to delight the guest.

World Tourism Organization A specialized agency of the United Nations made up of 146 countries that aim to play a decisive role in tourism promotion, sustainability, and socioeconomic development.

Wort In the making of beer, the liquid obtained after the mashing process.

Y–Z

Yeast Yeast converts sugar to ethyl alcohol.

Zero-based budgeting Managers begin with a budget of zero dollars and justify all the costs of goods sold, controllable costs, and planned capital expenditures in order to ensure an appropriate amount of profit after the deduction of all expenses.

Photo Credits

Part 1 (p. 1): Volvox/Index Stock Imagery, Inc.

Chapter 1
p. 2: ImagState Royalty Free
p. 4: Getty Images—Digital Vision
p. 6, top: © Dorling Kindersley, Courtesy of The Venetian, Las Vegas
p. 6, bottom: Genovese, Catrina Omni-Photo Communications, Inc., Genovese, Catrina photographer
p. 9: John R. Walker
p. 10: Courtesy Marriott International
p. 13: Courtesy Luis Barrios
p. 14: Courtesy William B. Martin
p. 19: Courtesy Ryan Lashway
p. 21: Nik Wheeler/Corbis/Bittmann
p. 24: AGE Fotostock America, Inc., Jerry Edmanson photographer

Chapter 2
p. 30: Stewart Cohen/Taxi/Getty Images
p. 32: Dana Edmunds/PacificStock.com
p. 35: © Dorling Kindersley
p. 37: William Fisher
p. 38: Getty Images, Inc.—Photodisc
p. 40: Christine Jaszay
p. 42: Index Stock Imagery, Inc., Stewart Cohen photographer
p. 44: James Schnepf Photography, Inc.
p. 46: Josh Shear
p. 47: Sodexho
p. 51: © Syracuse Newspapers/C.W. McKeen/The Image Works
p. 52: William Waterfall/PacificStock.com
p. 54: John M. Slemp/Creative Eye/MIRA.com
p. 55: PhotoEdit, Bonnie Kamin photographer
p. 56: Beth Lukens
p. 58: © Dorling Kindersley, Courtesy of the Bellagio Resort Hotel, Las Vegas
p. 60, left: Bokelberg.US, Inc.
p. 60, right: Novastock/The Stock Connection
p. 62: PhotoEdit, Cindy Charles photographer
p. 64: Ap. 64: Animals Animals/Earth Scenes, photo by Jerry Cooke

p. 66: MasterFile Corp., Sherman Hines, photographer
p. 68: Alan Keohane © Dorling Kindersley

Chapter 3
p. 80: Michael Fiala/Corbis Zefa Collection
p. 83: The Stock Connection, Dallas and John Heaton photographer
p. 86, left: AP Wide World Photos
p. 86, right: Agence France Presse/Getty Images
p. 88: Princess Cruise Lines
p. 91: Carlson Corporation
p. 89: Royal Caribbean International
p. 92: Carnival Cruise Lines
p. 94: AGE FotoStock America, Inc., Walter Bibikow photographer
p. 99: Robert Harding World Imagery, Philip Craven photographer
p. 102: Patti Roscoe
p. 103: John Miller/Robert Harding World Imagery
p. 106: Getty Images Inc.—Stone Allstock, Robert Everts photographer
p. 109: Marriott International
p. 108: Lynne Christen
p. 110: ROBERT ARMSTRONG/Photolibrary.com
p. 111: Stock Boston, Michele Burgess photographer
p. 112: Jean Pragen/Getty Images—Stone Allstock
p. 113: Animals Animals/Earth Scenes

Chapter 4
Part 2 (p. 119): Getty Images—Medio Images
p. 120: Wynn Las Vegas
p. 123: Omni-Photo Communications, Inc., Jeff Greenberg photographer
p. 126: Cendant
p. 127: Quality International
p. 129: William Waterfall/PacificStock.com
p. 131, top: Courtesy of the Hospitality Industry Archives, University of Houston
p. 131, bottom: Michael Moran © Dorling Kindersley
p. 135: Andrew Layerle, © Dorling Kindersley

p. 338: © Dorling Kindersley
p. 339: Ian O'Leary, © Dorling Kindersley
p. 340: Clive Streeter, © Dorling Kindersley
p. 341: Linda Whitwam © Dorling Kindersley
p. 342 left: Ian O'Leary, © Dorling Kindersley
p. 342, right: Ian O'Leary, © Dorling Kindersley
p. 344: Jay Shrock
p. 345: Getty Images Inc.—Photodisc, Steve Mason photographer
p. 347: The Robert Mondavi Family of Wineries
p. 348: Getty Images Inc.—Image Bank, Michael Melford, Inc.
p. 349, top: Trevor Hill, © Dorling Kindersley
p. 349, bottom: Trevor Hill, © Dorling Kindersley
p. 350, bottom: Jules Selmes and Debi Treloar, © Dorling Kindersley
p. 350, top: Shane Dudley
p. 351: Peter Arnold, Inc., Markus Dlouhy/Das Fotoarchiv
p. 353, top: Jules Selmes and Debi Treloar, © Dorling Kindersley
p. 353, bottom: Getty Images, Inc.—Photodisc, EyeWire Collection
p. 355, top: Animals Animals/Earth Scenes, Betram G. Murry, Jr., photographer
p. 355, bottom: Dave King © Dorling Kindersley, Courtesy of the Big Cup, New York
p. 356, top: Getty Images, Inc.—Photodisc, Eye-Wire Collection
p. 356, bottom: David Murray, © Dorling Kindersley
p. 359: Starbucks
p. 360: PhotoEdit, Amy C. Etra photographer
p. 362: Magnus Rew © Dorling Kindersley
p. 364: Rob Reichenfeld, © Dorling Kindersley
p. 365: Photo by Norbert von der Groeben, The Image Works
p. 368: AP Wide World Photos
Part 4 (p. 379): Picturequest—Royalty Free

Chapter 11

p. 380: © Look/eStock Photo
p. 382: Fotopic, Omni-Photo Communications, Inc.
p. 383, top: Erik Aeder/PacificStock.com
p. 383, bottom: The Stock Connection, James Kay photographer
p. 385: Getty Images Inc.—Stone Allstock, Sylvain Grandadam photographer
p. 386: Corbis/Bettmann, © Phil Schermeister
p. 387, left: Getty Images, Inc.—Photodusc, Eye-Wire Collection
p. 387, right: Al Bello/Getty Images, Inc.—Allsport Photography
p. 389, top: Omni-Photo Communicatons, Jeff Greenberg photographer
p. 388: Animals Animals/Earth Scenes, E. R. Degginger photographer
p. 389, bottom: Max Alexander © Dorling Kindersley
p. 390: Stock Boston, Jim Pickerell photographer
p. 391: SuperStock, Inc.
p. 394: LEA/Omni-Photo Communications, Inc.
p. 395: SuperStock, Inc., © Ron Dahlquist
p. 398: Edward Shaughnessy
p. 397: Getty Images—Photodisc, EyeWire Collection
p. 401: AP Wide World Photos

p. 405: Bart Bartlett
p. 407: Luis Azucena

Chapter 12

p. 414: © IT Free/eStock Photo
p. 417: New York New York Hotel & Casino
p. 418: Alan Keohane © Dorling Kindersley
p. 419: Kathryn Hashimoto
p. 421: Nature Picture Library, Gavin Hellier photographer
p. 423: Las Vegas Hilton
p. 425: Alan Keohane © Dorling Kindersley
p. 427, left: Cwener Photography, Index Stock Imagery, Inc.
p. 427, right: © Dorling Kindersley, Courtesy of the Mirage, Las Vegas
p. 428, left: Jochen Tack/Das Fotoarchiv, Peter Arnold, Inc.
p. 428, right: Index Stock Imagery, Inc., James Lemass photographer
p. 429, both photos: Wynn Las Vegas
p. 431: Index Stock Imagery, Inc., Barry Winiker photographer
p. 432: Alan Keohane © Dorling Kindersley
p. 433: Joe Sohm/Chromosohm, The Stock Connection
p. 436: Index Stock Imagery, Inc., James Lemass photographer

Chapter 13

p. 442: Andrew Yates Productions/Image Bank/Getty Images
p. 444: PhotoEdit Inc., David Young-Wolff photographer
p. 447 both: National Restaurant Association
p. 451: Henry T. & Lynn Christen
p. 452: Triangle Images, Getty Images/Digital Vision
p. 453: David McNew/Liaon/Getty Images
p. 456: The Ritz-Carlton Hotel Company, L.L.C.
p. 457: Courtesy of Carol Wallace
p. 460: PhotoEdit, Mark Richards photographer
p. 463: Kathleen Doeller
p. 464: Dave King © Dorling Kindersley
p. 465: Providence R.I. Convention Center
p. 470: Las Vegas Convention and Visitors Auth.
Part 5 (p. 477): Richard Drury/Image Bank/Getty Images

Chapter 14

p. 478: © J. Westrich/CORBIS All Rights Reserved
p. 481: Courtesy of Southwest Airlines
p. 483: UPI/Bettmann
p. 484: William Fisher
p. 487: Calrlson Companies
p. 489: Steve Pinneti
p. 492: PhotoEdit Inc., Michael Newman photographer

Chapter 15

p. 500: Corbis Digital Stock
p. 502: G & M David de Lossy, Getty Images Inc.—Image Bank
p. 506: Jessica Leibovich
p. 511: Courtesy Evans Hotels
p. 513: Courtesy of Tim Mulligan
p. 516, top: Hank Christen

p. 516, bottom: Paul Maniscalco
p. 517: Quality International

Chapter 16

p. 526: Photodisc/Getty Images
p. 528: Photo by Koji Sasahara, AP Wide World Photos
p. 531: Tim Hall/Photodisc/Getty Images
p. 534: PhotoEdit Inc., Michael Newman photographer
p. 535: Andrea Kazanjian
p. 539: John R. Walker
p. 541: Sodexho
p. 542: Courtesy of Four Seasons Hotels and resorts
p. 546: Courtesy of Six Flags

Chapter 17

p. 552: Picturequest—Royalty Free
p. 556: Photo by SEAN JUSTICE, Getty Images, Inc.—Taxi
p. 557: Getty Images/Digital Vision
p. 558: Triangle Images, Getty Images/Digital Vision
p. 566: Courtesy of Patricia Tam
p. 572: Denise Simenstad
p. 576: Courtesy of Starwood Hotels and Resorts

Chapter 18

p. 582: Getty Images, Inc—Stockbyte
p. 584: Corbis Digital Stock
p. 587: Churchhill & Klehr Photgraphy
p. 590: Dana Edmunds/PacificStock.com
p. 594: PhotoEdit, Michael Newman photographer
p. 596: Patricia Engfer
p. 597: PhotoEdit Inc., Billy E. Barnes photographer
p. 599: Stock Boston, Richard Pasley photographer
p. 602: Rob Westfall
p. 608: Sodexho
p. 611: AP Wide World Photos
p. 613: Getty Images Inc.—Stone Allstock, Stewart Cohen photographer

Chapter 19

p. 622: © IT/eStock Photo
p. 627: PhotoEdit Inc., David Young-Wolff photographer
p. 628: Cherry Cerminara
p. 632: Courtesy of Sodexho
p. 636: ARAMARK
p. 640: Getty Images, Inc.—Photodisc, Ryan McVay photographer
p. 642: Courtesy of Michael Thorpe

Index